P9-DVE-498

DATE DUE

DEMCO 38-296

THE MARK TWAIN PAPERS

Mark Twain's Letters
Volume 4: 1870–1871

THE MARK TWAIN PAPERS AND WORKS OF MARK TWAIN
is a comprehensive edition for scholars of the private papers
and published works of Mark Twain (Samuel L. Clemens).

THE MARK TWAIN LIBRARY
is a selected edition reprinted from the Papers and Works for
students and the general reader. Both series of books are published
by the University of California Press and edited by members of the

MARK TWAIN PROJECT
with headquarters in The Bancroft Library,
University of California, Berkeley.

Editorial work for all volumes is jointly supported by grants from the

NATIONAL ENDOWMENT FOR THE HUMANITIES,
an independent federal agency,
and by public and private donations,
matched equally by the Endowment, to

THE FRIENDS OF THE BANCROFT LIBRARY

MARK TWAIN PROJECT

EDITORS

Frederick Anderson

Dahlia Armon

Paul Baender

Howard G. Baetzhold

Walter Blair

Edgar Marquess Branch

Robert Pack Browning

Richard Bucci

Louis J. Budd

Gregg Camfield

Hennig Cohen

Leon T. Dickinson

Terry Firkins

Victor Fischer

Michael B. Frank

John C. Gerber

William M. Gibson

Hamlin Hill

Robert H. Hirst

Mary Jane Jones

Lewis Leary

Paul Machlis

Francis V. Madigan

Hershel Parker

Robert Regan

Franklin R. Rogers

Lin Salamo

Kenneth M. Sanderson

Harriet Elinor Smith

Henry Nash Smith

Bernard L. Stein

Albert E. Stone

John S. Tuckey

BOARD OF DIRECTORS

Jo Ann Boydston

Don L. Cook

Frederick Crews

Peter E. Hanff

Peter Lyman

William J. McClung

Michael Millgate

George A. Starr

G. Thomas Tanselle

Elizabeth Witherell

Early Tales & Sketches, Volume 1 (1851–1864)
Edited by Edgar Marquess Branch and Robert H. Hirst,
with the assistance of Harriet Elinor Smith
1979

The Adventures of Tom Sawyer · *Tom Sawyer Abroad*
Tom Sawyer, Detective
Edited by John C. Gerber, Paul Baender, and Terry Firkins
1980

Early Tales & Sketches, Volume 2 (1864–1865)
Edited by Edgar Marquess Branch and Robert H. Hirst,
with the assistance of Harriet Elinor Smith
1981

Adventures of Huckleberry Finn
Edited by Walter Blair and Victor Fischer,
with the assistance of Dahlia Armon and Harriet Elinor Smith
1988

Roughing It
Editors: Harriet Elinor Smith and Edgar Marquess Branch
Associate Editors: Lin Salamo and Robert Pack Browning
1993

THE MARK TWAIN LIBRARY

No. 44, The Mysterious Stranger
Edited by John S. Tuckey and William M. Gibson
1982

The Adventures of Tom Sawyer
Edited by John C. Gerber and Paul Baender
1982

Tom Sawyer Abroad · *Tom Sawyer, Detective*
Edited by John C. Gerber and Terry Firkins
1982

The Prince and the Pauper
Edited by Victor Fischer and Michael B. Frank
1983

A Connecticut Yankee in King Arthur's Court
Edited by Bernard L. Stein
1983

Adventures of Huckleberry Finn
Edited by Walter Blair and Victor Fischer
1985

Huck Finn and Tom Sawyer among the Indians, and Other Unfinished Stories
Foreword and Notes by Dahlia Armon and Walter Blair
Texts established by Dahlia Armon, Paul Baender, Walter Blair, William M.
Gibson, and Franklin R. Rogers
1989

OTHER MARK TWAIN PROJECT
PUBLICATIONS

The Devil's Race-Track: Mark Twain's Great Dark Writings
The Best from Which Was the Dream? *and* Fables of Man
Edited by John S. Tuckey
1980

Union Catalog of Clemens Letters
Edited by Paul Machlis
1986

Union Catalog of Letters to Clemens
Edited by Paul Machlis,
with the assistance of Deborah Ann Turner
1992

Samuel L. Clemens, 1870.
Photographed 8 July by Mathew Brady.
Mark Twain House, Hartford, Connecticut
(CtHMTH).

THE MARK TWAIN PAPERS

General Editor, ROBERT H. HIRST

Contributing Editors for this Volume
DAHLIA ARMON
ROBERT PACK BROWNING
RICHARD BUCCI
KENNETH M. SANDERSON
HARRIET ELINOR SMITH

A Publication of the Mark Twain Project
of The Bancroft Library

MARK TWAIN'S
LETTERS

VOLUME 4 ❧ 1870–1871

Editors
VICTOR FISCHER
MICHAEL B. FRANK

Associate Editor
LIN SALAMO

Mark Twain

UNIVERSITY OF CALIFORNIA PRESS
Berkeley · Los Angeles · London
1995

Riverside Community College
Library
4800 Magnolia Avenue
Riverside, California 92506

PS 1331 .A4 1988 v.4

Twain, Mark, 1835-1910.

Mark Twain's letters

FOR
SCHOLARLY EDITIONS
·AN APPROVED EDITION
MODERN LANGUAGE
ASSOCIATION OF AMERICA

The texts of Mark Twain's letters, now established from the original
documents, © 1995 by Chemical Bank as Trustee
of the Mark Twain Foundation, which reserves all
reproduction or dramatization rights in every medium.
Editorial introductions, notes, and apparatus
© 1995 by the Regents of the University of California.

University of California Press
Berkeley and Los Angeles, California

University of California Press, Ltd.
London, England

Manufactured in the United States of America

Library of Congress Cataloging-in-Publication Data

(Revised for vol. 4)

Twain, Mark, 1835–1910.
Mark Twain's letters.

(The Mark Twain papers)
Vol. 3: editors, Victor Fischer, Michael B. Frank; associate editor, Dahlia Armon;
v. 4: editors, Victor Fischer, Michael B. Frank; associate editor, Lin Salamo.
Includes bibliographical references and indexes.
Contents: — v. 1. 1853–1866 — v. 2. 1867–1868 — [etc.] — v. 4. 1870–1871.
1. Twain, Mark, 1835–1910—Correspondence.
2. Authors, American—19th century—Correspondence.
3. Humorists, American—19th century—Correspondence.
I. Branch, Edgar Marquess, 1913–   II. Frank, Michael B.
III. Sanderson, Kenneth M.
IV. Roy J. Friedman Mark Twain Collection (Library of Congress).
V. Title.   VI. Title: Letters.   VII. Series.
VIII. Series: Twain, Mark, 1835–1910.   Mark Twain papers.
PS1331.A4   1987   818′.409 [B]   87-5963
ISBN 0-520-03669-7 (v. 2 : alk. paper)   ISBN 0-520-03670-0 (v. 3 : alk. paper)
ISBN 0-520-20360-7 (v. 4 : alk. paper)

In memory of

ROBERT N. MINER

whose generous gift to
The Friends of The Bancroft Library,
together with grants from the
NATIONAL ENDOWMENT FOR THE HUMANITIES,
has made possible the publication of this volume.

Contents

Acknowledgments

Editorial work on this volume in the Mark Twain Papers was again made possible by the continuing generosity of the American taxpayer, and by the support of reviewers, panelists, Council, and staff members of the National Endowment for the Humanities, an independent federal agency, which has funded the Mark Twain Project by outright and matching grants since 1966. We are grateful for that intellectual and material support, part of which the Endowment provided for the present volume by matching a major gift from the late Robert N. Miner, whose great generosity to the Project is acknowledged on a separate page in this volume.

The Endowment's recent grants were also made possible by an outpouring of private support for the Mark Twain Project. We are grateful for the generosity of the following major donors: William H. Alsup; Jonathan Arac; Mr. and Mrs. John P. Austin; The Behring-Hofmann Educational Institute; The House of Bernstein, Inc.; J. Dennis Bonney; Edmund G. and Bernice Brown; Class of 1938, University of California, Berkeley; Chevron Corporation; Chronicle Books; Don L. Cook; the late Alice C. Gaddis; Launce E. Gamble; John C. Gerber; Dr. and Mrs. Orville J. Golub; Marion S. Goodin; Constance Crowley Hart; the late James D. Hart; William Randolph Hearst Foundation; Hedco Foundation; Heller Charitable & Educational Fund; Janet S. and William D. Hermann; Mr. and Mrs. Stephen G. Herrick; Kenneth E. Hill; Hal Holbrook; Holger Kersten; Koret Foundation; Horst and Ursula Kruse; Irene and Jervis Langdon, Jr.; Mark Twain Foundation; Bobby to Donny for the Mississippi; Jane Newhall; Jeanne G. O'Brien and the late James E. O'Brien; Hiroshi Okubo; David Packard; The Pareto Fund; Mr. and Mrs. Noel Perry; Connie J. and David H. Pyle; Catherine D. Rau; Verla K. Regnery Foundation; John W. and Barbara Rosston; L. J. Skaggs and Mary C. Skaggs Foundation; Marion B. and Willis S. Slusser; Thomas More Storke Fund; Koji Tabei; Mrs. Joseph Z. Todd; Gretchen Trupiano; the late John Russell Wagner; and Mrs. Paul L. Wattis.

We also want to thank the following recent donors for their timely gifts to the Project: Paul Alpers; Mr. and Mrs. Ward Anderson; Harold Aspiz; Roger Asselineau; John Edward Back; Julia Bader; Nancy and Howard Baetzhold; Brenda J. Bailey; David Barrow; Trenton Don Bass; H. H. Behrens; Dr. Leslie L. Bennett; Carol C. Bense; Mary K. Bercaw; Lawrence I. Berkove; Alice R. Berkowitz; Paul Berkowitz; Roger Berry; Marilyn R. Bewley; David V. Bianculli; Diane B. Bickers; Diane Birchell; John Bird; W. Edward Blain; William Makely in memory of Walter Blair; Kevin J. and Margaret A. Bochynski; Dennis A. Bohn; Dr. Richard J. Borg; Harold I. and Beulah Blair Boucher; Mr. and Mrs. Philip E. Bowles; Boone Brackett, M.D.; Philip and Katherine Bradley; The Brick Row Book Shop; Earl F. Briden; Richard Bridgman; Professor Stanley Brodwin; Timothy Buchanan; Louis J. and Isabelle Budd; Linda E. Burg; Richard Byrd; Gerald K. Cahill; Mr. and Mrs. Grant W. Canfield; Clayton C. Carmichael; Professor James E. Caron; Paul Carrara; June A. Cheit; Jean R. and Sherman Chickering Fund; Patricia Christensen; Fred Clagett; Mrs. Wanda Clark; William A. and the late Mildred Clayton; Edwina B. Coffing; Dana T. Coggin; Hennig Cohen; Marvin M. Cole; James L. Colwell; Bob Comeau; Mrs. Shirley Larson Cook; Nancy Cook; Wayne and Germaine Cooper; Cornell University Library; Ruth Mary Cordon-Cradler; Joan and Pascal Covici, Jr.; James M. Cox; Frederick Crews; Harry W. Crosby; Charles L. Crow; Sherwood Cummings; Sally J. Letchworth in memory of Susan Letchworth Dann; Beverly (Penny) David; Carlo M. De Ferrari; Edgar and Elinor De Jean; Mrs. Wilma Cox DeMotte; Joseph E. Doctor; Carl Dolmetsch; William G. Donald, Jr., M.D.; Edgar L. Dow; Dow Chemical Corporation Foundation; Victor A. Doyno; Jon A. Dubin; William J. Duhigg, Jr.; Dennis Eddings; Sanford S. Elberg; Everett Emerson; Allison R. Ensor; William W. Escherich; Mrs. Eric Eweson; Joel M. Fisher; Shelley Fisher Fishkin; Gerald L. and Norma J. Flanery; George R. Flannery; Margaret Anne Fraher; Peter L. Friedman, M.D., Ph.D.; Friends of Caxton; Robert E. Futrell; Louis G. Gambill; Joe Gannon; Guy G. Gilchrist; Jerry S. Gilmer, Ph.D.; Jay E. Gillette; Dorothy Goldberg; Gloria R. Goldblatt; Stephen L. Golder; Shoji Goto; Mr. William J. Graver; C. Gordon Greene; Ralph J. Gregory; Kenneth L. Greif; Jean

F. Guyer; Frank W. Hammelbacher; Peter E. Hanff; Robert N. and Arlene R. Hansen; John Mitchell Hardaway; Mrs. Mercedes Haroldson; Paul C. Harris, Jr.; Susan K. Harris; William N. Harrison; Peter D. Hart; Mr. and Mrs. David P. Hawkins; Miss Quail Hawkins; Juan C. Hayes; E. Dixon Heise; Katherine Heller; Katherine Heller and Rolf Lygren Fund; Betty and Carl Helmholz; H. S. Henderson; Judith B. Herman; Aurora and Jim Hill; Charles J. Hitch; Sandra Hjorth; Patricia A. Holland; Professor and Mrs. Richard H. Holton; Walter Hoops; James M. Hotchkiss, Jr.; George J. Houle; Professor Kay S. House; Goldena Howard; Lawrence Howe; George Lowman Howell; W. Robert Howell; David S. Hubbell, M.D.; Justine Hume; Hiroyoshi Ichikawa; Masago Igawa; Dr. M. Thomas Inge; Jane A. Iverson; Iwao Iwamoto; Dr. Janice Beaty Janssen; Robert Jenkins, M.D., Ph.D.; Alastair Johnston; Fred Kaplan; Nick Karanovich; Lawrence Kearney; Dennis and Hene Kelly; Lynn Kelly; Dr. Charles C. Kelsey; Dr. Derek Kerr; Howard Kerr; Harlan Kessel; Dr. David B. Kesterson; Mr. and Mrs. Dudley J. Kierulff; Dr. J. C. B. Kinch; John K. King Books; Michael J. Kiskis; Paul and Elisa Kleven; Robert E. and Margarete Knudsen; Larry Kramer; Mr. and Mrs. S. L. Laidig; Lucius Lampton, M.D.; Baldwin G. and Ormond S. Lamson; Mr. and Mrs. H. Jack Lang; J. William and Jeanne Larkin; Jennifer S. Larson; Roger K. Larson, M.D.; Richard W. LaRue; Jacklyn Lauchland-Shaw; Mary-Warren Leary; Philip W. Leon; Joan V. Lindquist; William S. Linn; Robert Livermore; Joseph H. Towson for Debbie L. Lopez; Frederic B. Lovett; George J. Houle in memory of Matthias (Matt) P. Lowman; Lolita L. Lowry; Karen A. Lystra; Peter McBean; Senior United States District Judge Thomas J. MacBride, Eastern District of California; William J. McClung; Joseph B. McCullough; Coleman W. McMahon; Hugh D. McNiven; Laura McVay; Wilson C. McWilliams; James H. Maguire; George F. Mahl; Thomas A. Maik; Steven Mailloux; David C. Mandeville; Mila Mangold; Mark Twain Society, Inc.; Miss Jean E. Matthew; Ronald R. Melen; Dr. Jeffrey A. Melton; Thomas M. Menzies; Eileen N. Meredith; Elsa Meyer Miller in memory of Elsa Springer Meyer; Jay and Elise Miller; Victoria Thorpe Miller; Michael Millgate; R. E. Mitchell, M.D.; Tokuhiro Miura; F. Van Dorn Moller; James M. Moore; Rayburn S. Moore; Frank and Gabrielle Morris; Ron Morrison; Steven G. Morton; Ann Elizabeth and Robert Murtha; Alan Nadritch; Makoto Nagawara; Koichi Nakamura; Suzanne Naiburg; Frances M. Neel; Fred M.

Nelsen; Ralph G. Newman, Inc.; Robert S. Newton; Emily V. Nichols; Cameron C. Nickels; Sandy Niemann; Charles A. Norton; L. Terry Oggel; Koji Oi; Peter K. Oppenheim; Chris Orvin; David C. Owens; Hershel Parker; Mary Jane Perna; Frederick D. Petrie; Thelma Schoonmaker Powell; Linda Propert; Randall House Rare Books; R. Kent Rasmussen; Allen Walker Read; Reader's Digest Foundation; Robert Regan; Miss Elizabeth Reid; Maryanne and Thomas Reigstad; Richard W. Reinhardt; Arno W. Reinhold; Elinor Reiss; Louise Burnham Rettick; Mrs. Barbara H. Riggins; The Riverdale Press; Taylor Roberts; Dr. Verne L. Roberts; Mrs. Kip Robinson; Mr. and Mrs. S. R. Rose; Bernard M. Rosenthal; Brandt Rowles; Sharon L. Ruff; Linda Haverty Rugg; Lynne M. Rusinko; E. Penny Salanave; Kenneth M. Sanderson; Gary D. Saretsky; Evelyn H. Savage; Katherine Schmidt; Timothy and Sue Schulfer; Lucy W. Sells; Caroline Service; Carol Sharon; Irene W. and Thomas J. Shephard, Sr.; Laura Beth Sherman; John R. Shuman; Oscar Alan Sipes; Ward B. Skinner, D. D. S.; Richard Skues; Mr. and Mrs. Robert Thomas Slotta in memory of Caroline Harnsberger; Elinor Lucas Smith; Gene Snook; David N. Socholitzky; Betty Jean and Jim Spitze; Marjorie H. Sproul; Verne A. Stadtman; J. D. Stahl; George Starr; Horace D. Stearman; Richard T. Stearns; Dwight C. Steele; Jeffrey Steinbrink; Carol Steinhagen; Jody Steren; Janet P. Stone; Albert E. Stone; Edward W. Swenson; Eleanor H. Swent; G. Thomas Tanselle; Barbara W. Taylor; Harry Tennyson; Jeffrey and Evelyne Thomas; Eloyde J. Tovey; Col. Robert T. Townsend; Dorothy Tregea; Frederic B. Tankel in memory of Donald G. Tronstein; Masao Tsunematsu; Charles S. Underhill; Marlene Boyd Vallin; Patrick J. Vaz; Robert W. Vivian; Sally Walker; Willard D. Washburn; Jeanne H. Watson; Abby H. P. Werlock; Mr. and Mrs. F. A. West; John and Kim Wheaton; John Wiesemes; T. H. Wildenradt; Christine Williams; Ilse B. Williams; Frederick B. Wilmar; James D. Wilson; Merilynn Laskey Wilson; Edward O. Wolcott; Harold A. Wollenberg; Tom and Amy Worth; Laurel A. and Jeffrey S. Wruble; Jin-Hee Yim; Mary A. Young; Alvin Ziegler; Jim Zwick; and Kate Zwirko.

Our thanks go also to the members of the Council of The Friends of The Bancroft Library for their efforts on our behalf: Thomas B. Worth, chair; William H. Alsup, Cindy Arnot Barber, Kirsten Bickford, A. T. Brugger, June A. Cheit, John C. Craig, Carol Hart Field, Rita Fink, Edwin V. Glaser, Oakley Hall, Peter E. Hanff, E. Dixon Heise, Janet S. Hermann, Thomas High, Charles Hobson, Andrew Hoyem, Lawrence W. Jordan, Jr., Lawrence Kramer, Robert Livermore, Rollin Post, Connie J. Pyle, David Robertson, George Sears, and Katharine Wallace. Special thanks go also to Kelly Penhall-Wilson, development assistant to the Council.

We are indebted to the generations of scholars who pioneered in finding, copying, collecting, and publishing Mark Twain's letters, particularly to Albert Bigelow Paine and his successors as Editor of the Mark Twain Papers: Bernard DeVoto, Dixon Wecter, Henry Nash Smith, and Frederick Anderson. Paine's *Mark Twain: A Biography* (1912) and *Mark Twain's Letters* (1917) are still indispensable books, and are sometimes the only source now known for letters collected here. Wecter's *Mark Twain to Mrs. Fairbanks* (1949) and *The Love Letters of Mark Twain* (1949) were the first editions to publish Mark Twain's letters in accord with modern scholarly standards, both in annotation and transcription of the manuscripts. Henry Nash Smith and William M. Gibson's *Mark Twain–Howells Letters* (1960) established a new and higher standard for publishing letters. Frederick Anderson assisted Smith and Gibson in that work and, until his death in 1979, was the Series Editor for the Mark Twain Papers, which included among its first volumes Hamlin Hill's *Mark Twain's Letters to His Publishers, 1867–1894* and Lewis Leary's *Mark Twain's Correspondence with Henry Huttleston Rogers, 1893–1909.* We have profited from all of these pioneering efforts in ways too numerous to bear mention in the notes.

Research for the documentation of Mark Twain's letters has continued to require assistance of many kinds. For valuable aid over many years we are grateful to the staff of The Bancroft Library, especially Acting Director Peter E. Hanff, Alyson K. Belcher, Anthony S. Bliss, Audrey Cree, Franz Enciso, David Kessler, Bonnie Hardwick, Cynthia Hoffman, and William M. Roberts. Special thanks go to Jo Lynn Milardovich and the cheerful and efficient staff of the Interlibrary Borrowing Service in the Main Library. Their efforts found many rare and valuable resources that have notably enriched the annotation. We are also indebted to Daniel L. Johnston of the Photographic Service in the Main Library for his extraordinary care in producing many of the photographs published here, and to Marnie Jacobsen, also of the Photographic Service, for expediting our many requests. We are also indebted to Wendy Mitchell, formerly of the Graduate School of Education of the University of California, for invaluable advice about fundraising.

The Mark Twain Papers in The Bancroft Library is the resident archive for nearly one third of the original letters published in this volume. This collection of Mark Twain's own private papers was brought to the University of California in 1949 through the persuasive powers of Dixon Wecter and the generosity of Clara Clemens Samossoud. Subsequent gifts and purchases over the years have added substantially to the original papers. For gifts of letters and other documents used in this volume we are grateful to the late Violet Appert, Mrs. Dorothy Clark, Robert Daley, Marie Snow Doyle, Mr. and Mrs. Robert M. Gunn, the late Mrs. Eugene Lada-Mocarski, Jervis Langdon, Jr., Mrs. Robert S. Pennock, and Mrs. Bayard Schieffelin. One letter in the volume was purchased through The Bancroft Library's Joseph Z. and Hatherly B. Todd Fund.

Other repositories of letters published here are: the Boston Athenaeum; the Boston Public Library and Eastern Massachusetts Regional Public Library System; the Cape Ann Historical Association in Gloucester, Massachusetts; the University of Chicago Library; the Chicago Public Library; the Public Library of Cincinnati and Hamilton County; the Ella Strong Denison Library of the Claremont Colleges in Claremont, California; the Robert Hutchings Goddard Library of Clark University in Worcester, Massachusetts; the James S. Copley Library in La Jolla, California; the Dartmouth College Library in Hanover, New Hampshire; the Roesch Library at the University of Dayton in Dayton, Ohio; the Detroit Public Library; the Houghton Library of Harvard University; the Henry E. Huntington Library in San Marino, California; the Rare Book Room of the University of Illinois at Urbana-Champaign; the Library of Iwaki Meisei University in Iwaki City, Japan; the Linderman Library of Lehigh University in Bethlehem, Pennsylvania; the Library of Congress; the Mark Twain House in Hartford, Connecticut; the Montana Historical Society in Helena; the Nevada State Historical Society in Reno; the New York Historical Society in New York City; the Henry W. and Albert A. Berg Collection of the New York Public Library, Astor, Lenox and Tilden Foundations, in New York City; the University Library of the University of Southern California, Los Angeles; the Green Library of Stanford University; the Harriet Beecher Stowe Center in Hartford, Connecticut; the Harry Ransom Humanities Research Center of the University of Texas at Austin; the United States National Archives and Records Service of the National Archives Library in Washington, D.C.; the Vassar College Library in Poughkeepsie, New York; the Clifton Waller Barrett Library of the University of Virginia in Charlottesville, Virginia; Washington University in St. Louis, Missouri; the Memorial Library of the University of Wisconsin in Madison; and the Beinecke Rare Book and Manuscript Library of Yale University. We are grateful for the unfailing cooperation of these libraries, who have given permission to publish their holdings, and have provided photocopies and answered questions about the provenance of their collections. We are likewise grateful to the following for permission to examine, photocopy, and publish letters and documents in their collections: Barbara Gunnison Anderson; Todd M. Axelrod; Fred D. Bentley; Royden Burwell Bowen, Jr.; William G. Bowen; Mrs. Robin Craven; Robert Daley; Chester L. Davis, Jr.; Alan C. Fox; Mrs. Paul W. Franke; Mr. and Mrs. Roy J. Friedman; Hallmark Cards; Mrs. T. V. Hedgpeth; Victor and Irene Murr Jacobs; Wayne M. Joseph; Nick Karanovich; the Rowfant Club of Cleveland, Ohio; Robert T. Slotta; Alberta Gunnison Stock; and Marion Gunnison Weygers. We also thank Chris Coover of the Books and Manuscripts department at Christie's, New York, and Jay Dillon, formerly of Sotheby's, New York, as well as Selby Kiffer and other members of the staff of the Books and Manuscripts department at Sotheby's, for their generosity and helpfulness in permitting us to examine and proofread letters temporarily in their care.

In the course of transcribing, annotating, and tracing the provenance of the letters we have been assisted by a great many individuals. We have benefitted from the unfailing generosity of Carlo M. De Ferrari, Tuolumne County historian; Jervis Langdon, Jr., of Elmira, New York; Gretchen Sharlow, Herbert A. Wisbey, Jr., Mark Woodhouse, and Jan Kather of the Center for Mark Twain Studies at Quarry Farm and the Mark Twain Archives, Elmira College, Elmira, New York; Professor Douglas H. Shepard in Fredonia, New York; and Beverly J. Zell at the Mark Twain House in Hartford. We received further invaluable help from: John Ahouse at the University Library of the University of Southern California; Lisa Backman and Catharina Slautterback of the Boston Athenaeum; William P. Barlow, Jr.; Professor David Barrow at Northern Illinois University in DeKalb; JoAnne E. Barry of the Philadelphia Academy of Music Archives; Fred Bauman and Jennifer Brathovde at the Library of Congress; Carol Beales, Ron Vanderhye, and Marian Holleman at the James S. Copley Library; Mary F. Bell of the Buffalo and Erie County Historical Society in Buffalo; Professor Lawrence I. Berkove at the University of Michigan in Dearborn; Professor Edgar M. Branch; Kelli Ann Bronson, Christine Fagan, Sara S. Hodson, Frances Rouse, Elsa Lee Sink, and Jennifer A. Watts of the Huntington Library; Linda Brown of the Paterson (New Jersey) Public Library; Jerry Bruce of the Lancaster County Library in Lancaster, Pennsylvania; Nancy A. Buckland of the Jackson (Michigan) Public Library; Linda Cary of the Edgar County Genealogy Library in Paris, Illinois; Eleanore R. Clise of the Geneva (New York) Historical Society and Museum; Philip N. Cronenwett and Kathleen E. O'Neill of the Dartmouth College Library; Professor Leon T. Dickinson; Judith Dobzynski of the Sciappa Branch Library in Steubenville, Ohio; Cathy Henderson and other members of the staff at the Humanities Research Center of the University of Texas at Austin; Fred W. Jenkins of the Roesch Library at the University of Dayton; Amanda C. Jones of the Ulster County Historical Society in Kingston, New York; Christine M. Leety of the Scranton (Pennsylvania) Public Library; Linda J. Long and Sara Timby at the Green Library of Stanford University; William H. Loos of the Buffalo and Erie County Public Library in Buffalo, New York; William Luck of the Lancaster County Historical Society in Lancaster, Pennsylvania; Danielle C. McClellan and Patricia C. Willis of the Beinecke Rare Book and Manuscript Library of Yale University; Professor Joseph B. McCullough of the University of Nevada, Las Vegas; Nancy S. MacKechnie of the Vassar College Library; Cairie Marsh and Judy Harvey Sahak of the Ella Strong Denison Library of the Claremont Colleges; Judith A. Meier of the Historical Society of Montgomery County in Norristown, Pennsylvania; Eric N. Moody of the Nevada State Historical Society; Eva S. Moseley at the Schlesinger Library on the History of Women in America of Radcliffe College; Marta G. O'Neill of the Special Collections Division at the Chicago Public Library; Patricia A. Parker of the Jamestown (New York) *Post-Journal;* Michelle L. Rainey of the University of Virginia Library in Charlottesville; Diana Royce of the Harriet Beecher Stowe Center in Hartford; Mary Russell of the Monroe C. Gutman Library of the Graduate School of Education, Harvard University; the Reverend John Ledyard Fletcher (Jack) Slee; Linnita Sommer of the Museum Association of Douglas County in Tuscola, Illinois; Charles S. Underhill; Janet

Whitson of the Rare Book Room at the Detroit Public Library; and the Wyoming Historical and Geological Society of Wilkes-Barre, Pennsylvania.

Throughout the process of design and typesetting for this volume we have had expert assistance from the University of California Press. We would especially like to thank Sam Rosenthal, who guided the book safely and surely through the production process; Doris Kretschmer, Fran Mitchell, and Marilyn Schwartz, who helped speed the book in various ways; and Sandy Drooker, who created the dust jacket. Our typesetters, Wilsted & Taylor Publishing Services, Oakland, California, have again provided expert and essential help with the typographical transcription of Mark Twain's letters. In addition to LeRoy Wilsted and Christine Taylor, we are indebted to Jennifer Brown, Kimberly Cline, Melissa Ehn, Nancy Evans, Stephen Fraser, Craig Friedman, Melody Lacina, Bronwen Morgan, Rosemary Northcraft, Janet Stephens, and Kim Zetter. Allen McKinney of Graphic Impressions, Emeryville, California, has again provided excellent halftones for all the photographic facsimiles in this volume, with the assistance of Tom Beidler.

We thank Professor Noel Polk at the University of Southern Mississippi in Hattiesburg for his thoughtful and thorough inspection of this volume for the Modern Language Association's Committee on Scholarly Editions, which granted its seal of approval in 1995.

Finally, we wish to thank our present and former associates in the Mark Twain Project for their many indispensable contributions, not only in their areas of special expertise about Mark Twain, but also in all of the painstaking efforts of checking, collating, and proofreading. Former colleague Dahlia Armon prepared transcriptions of nearly half the letters in the volume and did research into the 1869–70 lecture tour. Robert Pack Browning read transcriptions against manuscript letters at a number of collections, both public and private. Former colleague Richard Bucci read transcriptions of manuscript letters at several sites across the country and shared his research into the provenance of Mark Twain's letters. Kenneth M. Sanderson brought his expertise to bear on the establishment and checking of letter texts. Harriet Elinor Smith contributed informed help, as always, particularly on the history of composition for *Roughing It*. The *Union Catalog of Clemens Letters* (1986) and the *Union Catalog of Letters to Clemens* (1992), edited by our former colleague Paul Machlis—the latter with the assistance of Deborah Ann

Turner—were each vital to the orderly preparation of this volume. Graduate intern David Glenn Briggs performed the editorial work of proofreading and checking with care and enthusiasm. Simon J. Hernandez was indefatigable in tracking down sources for obscure publications. Several other students—Kandi Arndt, Beth Bernstein, Courtney Clark, Ashley D'Cruz, Deborah Goldberg, Julia Pastor, Severine Tymon, and Sandra Yue—assisted with a variety of clerical and editorial tasks, greatly facilitating our work. Brenda J. Bailey, our administrative assistant, juggled office business and essential proofreading with energy and enthusiasm. For the contributions of all of these colleagues and friends, we are indeed grateful.

V. F.   M. B. F.   L. S.

Introduction

THIS VOLUME opens on 6 January 1870, with Clemens on the final leg of the lecture tour he had begun in November 1869. Having fourteen lectures to deliver by 21 January, he was impatient to finish "the long agony" (p. 10) and prepare for his marriage on 2 February to Olivia Langdon. "I wouldn't do another lecture season unless I were in absolute *want*, almost," he wrote Olivia on 10 January (p. 15). Flush now with the continuing critical and commercial success of *The Innocents Abroad*, which was producing income averaging about $1,300 per month, and established as co-owner and co-editor of the Buffalo *Express*, Clemens looked forward to a settled life in Buffalo, in which he and Olivia—"a life companion who is *part of me*—part of my heart, & flesh & spirit"— would be together, "never more to part again in life" (pp. 18, 31). Nevertheless, before the end of 1871, when the volume closes, both Buffalo and the *Express* had been discarded and Clemens was once again far from Olivia and enduring the "*eternity* a lecture-season is" (p. 15). The 338 letters published here, the majority for the first time, document a tumultuous two years for Samuel and Olivia Clemens, a period in which the satisfactions of Clemens's career and the gratifications of married life were nearly overwhelmed with "beetling Alps of trouble" (p. 363), frustration, and grief.

These letters capture Clemens's irrepressibly restless and multi-faceted mind at work devising literary projects, lectures, business schemes, and his first patented invention ("Mark Twain's Elastic Strap"). As his confidence in the profitability of the Buffalo *Express* and his creative commitment to it waned, he sought and found a broader readership by writing a well-received monthly "Memoranda" department for the *Galaxy* magazine, published two versions of his wildly popular burlesque war map, the "Fortifications of Paris," and tried to capitalize further on his popularity by issuing a hastily prepared "pamphlet," *Mark Twain's (Burlesque) Autobiography and First Romance,* which proved a failure. Most importantly, inspired by the "booming" sales of *Innocents,* in late August 1870 he began writing a new book, *Roughing It.* And he found time to entertain a variety of other works that he abandoned or postponed, among them a proposed book about Washington, D.C. (possibly a precursor to *The Gilded Age*); a volume of sketches for the American Publishing Company (finally published in 1875 as *Mark Twain's Sketches, New and Old*); a "Noah's Ark book" that he returned to periodically thoughout his life without finishing; a pamphlet version of "The Celebrated Jumping Frog of Calaveras County"; a "humorous picture-book" for which he was to merely provide captions; and a book on the South African diamond mines, researched by proxy (his friend John Henry Riley), but never begun.

This professional ferment was more than matched in the personal sphere. A series of catastrophes and near catastrophes that commenced within six months of the Clemenses' marriage profoundly altered both of their lives. In late June they were called to Elmira, New York, for the beginning of the death watch at the bedside of Jervis Langdon, that most generous father and father-in-law, which finally ended when he died of stomach cancer on 6 August. Before Olivia, then five months pregnant, could recover from that loss and the strain that preceded it, her visiting friend, Emma Nye, fell ill with typhoid fever, dying on 29 September in the Clemenses' Buffalo bedroom. Following a near miscarriage in October, Olivia gave birth on 7 November to Langdon Clemens. This happy event was complicated by the baby's prematurity and recurrent illnesses, and the Clemens house in Buffalo consequently was filled with doctors and a succession of day nurses, night nurses, and wet nurses. The baby's persistent debility and Olivia's progressive exhaustion, as she tried to care for him while managing the household, culminated in her succumbing to typhoid fever herself in early February 1871 and remaining near death for more than a month. Clemens, fearing for her life and "in a state of absolute frenzy" (p. 365), was unable to make needed progress on *Roughing It.* After ending his commitment to the *Galaxy,* he was forced to contend, furiously, with a new distraction, the demands of his brother, Orion, whom he had recommended as editor of his publisher's house paper, the *American Publisher,* for regular contributions.

Associating Buffalo with the "infernal damnable chaos" of his life, by March 1871 Clemens had come to loathe the city "so bitterly (always hated it) that yesterday I advertised our dwelling house for sale, & the man that comes forward & pays us what it cost a year ago, ($25,000,) can take it" (pp. 337–38, 366). The next month, leaving Buffalo without selling the house, Jervis Langdon's surprise wedding gift, the Clemenses settled in at the Langdon family home in Elmira, where they contemplated a permanent move to Hartford, Connecticut. In Elmira, Olivia's health slowly improved and Clemens managed to establish a literary routine that enabled him to forge ahead on *Roughing It.* Before mid-June, determined to support his family with his own income, not with Olivia's inheritance, and clearly impelled by past medical expenses, by the cost of living in Elmira while still maintaining the Buffalo house, and by the impending costs of the move to Hartford, Clemens began actively planning a lecture tour for the season of 1871–72, writing a series of possible lectures. In August he went to Hartford himself, to read proof of *Roughing It,* and then, in mid-October, having settled Olivia, now pregnant again, and Langdon in a rented house there, he took to the railways and the lecture platform once more. This tour was perhaps the most difficult of his career, chiefly because of his inability to write a lecture acceptable to a public that regarded him as the foremost humorist on the circuit. It was not until December, after nearly two months of frequently indifferent, and sometimes hostile, audiences and critics, that he discovered his best subject—"Roughing It," drawn from his forthcoming book. But if his listeners warmed to him then, that was insufficient consolation to Olivia. On 3 December she wrote: "I *can not* and I WILL NOT think about your being away from me this way every year, it is not half living—if in order to sustain our present mode of living you are obliged to do that, then we will change our mode of living—" (p. 511, n. 2). And on 31 December, in the final letter in this volume, Clemens, responding to her longing with his own, advised her: "Be bright & happy—accept the inevitable with a brave heart, since grieving cannot mend it but only makes it the harder to bear, for both of us. All in good time we shall be together again—& *then*—!" (p. 530).

V. F.   M. B. F.

Editorial Signs

THE EDITORIAL conventions used to transcribe Mark Twain's letters were designed, in part, to enable anyone to read the letters without having to memorize a list. The following is therefore offered less as a necessary preliminary than as a convenient way to look up the meaning of any convention which, in spite of this design, turns out to be less than self-explanatory. Only the editorial conventions used in this volume are given here, since each new volume will require a slightly different list. Not included are the typographical equivalents used to transcribe Mark Twain's own signs and symbols in manuscript. For those equivalents, and for a more discursive explanation of editorial principles, see the Guide to Editorial Practice in *L3*, 551–78.

EDITORIAL HEADING

From . . .	Clemens is named in the heading only when he wrote jointly with someone else.
. . . with a note to . . .	Used when two persons are addressed in the same letter, but Clemens intended the second to read *only* the briefer part, or "note."
per . . .	Precedes the name or identity of the amanuensis or agent who inscribed the document sent or received.
2? May	On this day—give or take a day.
1–3 May	On any day (or days) within this span.
1 and 2 May	On both days.
(MS)	The source document is the original letter, almost invariably Clemens's holograph manuscript.

(*damage emended*)   The source document has sustained significant damage, and the transcription therefore includes, without brackets, emendation to restore the affected text.

(MS facsimile)   The source document is a photographic facsimile of the MS, not the MS itself.

(Paraphrase)   The source document preserves some of the *words* of the original letter, but is manifestly not a deliberate transcription of it.

(Transcript)   The source document is a printed, handwritten, or typed (TS) transcription of the letter, not necessarily made at first hand.

LETTER TEXT

NEW-YORK   Extra-small small capitals with no initial capitals signify printed text *not* originated by Clemens, such as letterhead or the postmark.

ⓒ   *Italicized* extra-small small capitals within an oval border transcribe monograms or initials printed or embossed on personal stationery.

Feb. 13,   Text above a dotted underscore was inscribed in a printed blank in the original document.

. . . .   Editorial ellipsis points (always centered in an otherwise blank line) signify that an unknown amount of the original letter is judged to be missing.

Ruled borders are an editorial device to represent the edge of a document, usually printed or partly printed, such as a telegram blank or newspaper clipping.

A two cance-
deletions,   Cancellation is signified by slashes for single characters (and underscores), rules for two or more characters.

Well, *I* pass.   A hairline rule signifies a mock, or pretended, cancellation: words lightly and distinctively crossed out, easily read, and often still necessary to the sense.

marking it ˏupˏ   Insertion is signified by a single caret for single charac-
                  ters, two carets for two or more characters.

shaded words   Gray background identifies parts of a letter originated
                  and inscribed by someone other than Clemens.

[ ]   Author's square brackets are transcribed this way to
                  avoid any confusion with editorial brackets.

[ ]   Editorial square brackets enclose [*editorial description*];
                  words or characters omitted by the writer an[d] now in-
                  terpolated by [the] editors; and text modified by de-
                  scription, such as [*in margin:* All well].

◊iamond   The diamond stands for a character, numeral, or punc-
                  tuation mark the editors cannot read because it is phys-
                  ically obscured or obliterated. It *never* stands for the
                  space between words.

double=   The hyphen is to be retained. Single hyphens at the ends
hyphen   of lines therefore signify division only.

Sam*ˡ*   Superscript ell is always italicized to prevent confusion
                  between one (^{1}) and ell (^{1}). The sign ___ transcribes
                  the author's paraph.

✉━━━━━━   The envelope and full-measure rule signal that every-
                  thing transcribed below them was written, stamped, or
                  printed on the envelope or on the letter itself at the time
                  of transmission or receipt.

| Signifies the end of a line in the source document.

Dan Slote's—
Thursday, 9 A.M.

Good luck, sweetheart!

The Amenia train has been changed to 3.30 instead of 4, PM., & so it is just right. I can arrive there at 7.21, whoop my lecture & clear out again.[1]

I was so tired last night that I slept soundly in the cars & really feel refreshed this morning—a rare experience in Railway travel. I read 3 pages of Robinson Crusoe, lost & found the book some twelve or fifteen times, & finally lost it for good a couple of hours ago. It is just like me. I *must* have a nurse.

Dan has just come in, & says he has already selected a Doré for me (for you) & ordered it ~~expr~~ to be expressed to Elmira to-day.[2] Tell Mrs. Susie that I leave my Don Quixote in her keeping till I come, & I hold her strictly responsible for it. And she might as well abuse Livy as abuse that book. Which she is not likely to abuse Livy, & so she will take care of the Don.[3]

Livy dear, suppose you take a Philadelphia Bulletin notice & part of a Boston Advertiser notice (cutting out & destroying the paragraph of synopsis in the latter,) & mail them to the *O*swego man—you need not write anything, but just put them in an envelop & mail them to him. Will she?—she's a good girl.[4]

I feel right well this morning.

I can't write worth a cent, now, because a friend[5] whom I do not like particularly well is standing around talking to me, & I am getting irritated with his gabble.

Give my warm love to all the loved ones at home, & be you at peace & happy, my own little darling.

Sam

Miss Olivia L. Langdon | Elmira | N. Y. [*return address:*] SLOTE, WOODMAN & CO. BLANK BOOK MANUFACTURERS, 119 & 121 WILLIAM ST., BEE. FULTON AND

JOHN, NEW YORK. [*postmarked:*] NEW YORK JAN 6   2 P.M. [*docketed by OLL:*]
168th

[1] Clemens had just reached New York City after traveling overnight from Elmira (about 165 miles) on his way to Amenia, New York, 70 miles to the north.

[2] At least four editions of *Paradise Lost* illustrated by Gustave Doré had been
published since 1866. Clemens paid fifty-seven dollars for the one Slote chose,
which has not been further identified (SLC's account statement from Slote,
Woodman and Company for 1 Jan 70, CU-MARK; *NUC*, 385:309).

[3] Clemens presumably entrusted *Don Quixote* to Susan Crane instead of Olivia
because he regarded it as unfit "for virgins to read" until culled of its "grossness"
(*L3*, 132–33).

[4] For the Boston *Advertiser*'s review of "Our Fellow Savages of the Sandwich
Islands," see *L3*, 392. Olivia evidently had multiple copies of it, and of the following review in the Philadelphia *Evening Bulletin:*

> Mark Twain, the celebrated humorist, was honored last night with one of the largest
> audiences ever assembled in the Academy of Music. He lectured upon "The Sandwich
> Islands," and mingled with much very interesting information a vast amount of hu-
> morous anecdote, witty allusion, and of that odd, incongruous, surprising divergence
> from his theme, which is his charming characteristic. Mr. Clemens deserved the com-
> pliment bestowed upon him. We regard him as the very best of the humorists of his
> class. He is more extravagant and preposterous than John Phoenix; he is superior to
> Artemus Ward, not only in the delicate quality of his humor, but because he has a decent
> regard for the English language, and does not depend for his effects upon barbarous
> orthography. Josh Billings is not to be compared with him. Billings is merely a prover-
> bial philosopher who has some wit, plenty of hard common sense, a shrewd knowledge
> of human nature, but not one particle of genuine, irrepressible fun. He has said some
> good things, but they are all marred by the wretched spelling which the author consid-
> ers necessary to his success. Mark Twain indulges in humor because it is his nature to
> do so. It is impossible to read his productions or to hear him speak without being im-
> pressed with the conviction that his cleverest utterances are spontaneous, natural, un-
> premeditated. Like all men of his temperament he has a hearty hatred of sham, hypoc-
> risy and cant, whether in religion, social life or politics. Some of his sturdiest blows
> have been aimed at the follies of the times; and we believe that he may, if he chooses,
> exercise a very considerable influence as a reformer. Ridicule, cleverly used, is one of
> the most powerful weapons against pretension and humbug; for it not only robs them
> of their false dignity, but it appeals strongly to the popular reader, and finds ready ac-
> ceptance where serious discussion would not be permitted. We do not suppose that Mr.
> Clemens has any notion of starting out upon a mission of reformation; but uncon-
> sciously he may do a good work in this direction, while at the same time he furnishes
> the nation with the purest and best entertainment in his lectures and his screeds. There
> may be some who will regard his calling as of smaller dignity than that of other men.
> Perhaps this is the class with which he is at war. The mass of intelligent people will agree
> with us that genuine humor is as rare and excellent a quality as any other, and that it is
> as respectable to amuse mankind as to stupefy them. The number of persons engaged
> in the former work is small; those who attempt the latter abound in quantities. ("Mark
> Twain," 8 Dec 69, 4, clippings in Scrapbook 8: 61, 63, CU-MARK)

Clemens emphasized "*O*swego" to distinguish it from *O*wego, New York. For
Olivia's response, see 10 Jan 70 to OLL (2nd), n. 8.

[5] Unidentified.

To Mary Mason Fairbanks
7 January 1870 • Amenia, N.Y.
(MS: CSmH)

Amenia, N. Y., 6th ⎫
Jan., Midnight.[1] ⎭

Well, Mother Dear—

You ought to see Livy & me, now-a-days—you never saw such a
serenely satisfied couple of doves in all your life. I spent Jan 1, 2, 3 & 5
there, & left at 8 last night.[2] With my vile temper & variable moods, it
seems an incomprehensible miracle that we two have been right together
in the same house half the time for a year & [a] half, & yet have never
had a cross word, or a lover's "tiff," or a pouting spell, or a misunderstanding, or the faintest shadow of a jealous suspicion. Now isn't that
absolutely wonderful? *Could* I have had such an experience with any
other girl on earth? I am perfectly certain I could not. And yet she has
attacked my tenderest peculiarities & routed them. She has stopped my
drinking, entirely. She has cut down my smoking considerably.[3] She has
reduced my slang & my boisterousness a good deal. She has extermi-
nated my habit of carrying my hands in my pantaloons pockets, & has
otherwise civilized me & well nigh taught me to behave in company.
These reforms were calculated to make a man fractious & irritable, but
bless you she has a way of instituting them that swindles one into the
belief that she is doing him a *favor* instead of curtailing his freedom &
doing him a fatal damage. She is the best girl that ever lived—& you
spoke truly a year & four months ago when you said that I was not worthy
of her—nor any other man.[4] Now that the frenzy, the lunacy of love, has
gone by, & I can contemplate her critically as a human being instead of
an angel, I see more clearly than ever, & more surely, how excellent she
is. I used to say she was faultless (& said it with a suspicion that she had
her proper share of faults, only I was too blind to see them,) but I am
thoroughly in my right mind, now, & I do maintain in all seriousness,
that I can find no fault in her.[5] When you come to know her as I do,
Mother, you will hold exactly this opinion yourself.

We are to be married on Feb. 2^d, instead of the 4th—the latter date

was too near the end of the week for Mrs. Langdon's housekeeping convenience. We shall take the train for Buffalo after the marriage, & that
will constitute our bridal trip. We shall not be likely to stir from that
town for several months, for neither of us are fond of traveling. I doubt
if we *ever* stir again, except to visit home & you. I lecture no more after
this ~~sa~~ season, unless dire necessity shall compel me. My book is waltz-
ing me out of debt so fast that I shan't owe any man a cent by this time
next year. By the 1ˢᵗ of February I will have paid $15,000 out of my own
pocket on two or three indebtednesses, ~~& shall still have~~ since the first
of last August, & shall still have three or four thousand left in bank—for
a rainy day. It has been quite a money-making year to me—most of it
came from the book—I have not drawn a penny from the Express.[6] I have
been able to ~~give my mother~~ pay my mother & sister a thousand dollars
during the last two months. And I got my life insured for $10,000 for my
mother's benefit.[7]

I mean to write another book during the summer. This one has
proven such a surprising success that I feel encouraged. We keep six
steam presses & a paper mill going *night & day* on it, & still we can't
catch up on the orders. The gross sales of the book, ~~reached~~ for 27 days
during December, amounted to $50,000. (That is 12,000 copies,) (Var-
ious styles of binding—we sell about as many at $5 apiece as at $3.50.)[8]

Greer *is* Blucher. The oyster-brained ass, couldn't he tell that? Now
what the mischief did any banker, or any banker's daughter, want with
that innocent?[9]

You *must* come to the wedding—so, that ends *that* question. I want
to see you—& *we* want to see you. I love you & honor you, & you shan't
be burned up on a funeral pyre at all, for we are *not* done with you, &
never shall be. Bring our Severances along, too—I want to see Solon &
I want to see Mrs. Solon, too, & right badly. Tell Solon I am not "trem-
bling in my boots," & I feel entirely able to "bear it like a man," & glad
of the chance.[10]

(Yes, I think of getting one more satchel, for my trousseau is pretty
voluminous—I have bought more high-toned store-clothes than any
other man has got. But you ought to see Livy's harness—Oh my! And
wasn't it a lively bill the Governor had to ~~fot~~ foot? But you never saw
such a good father as Mr. L. He insisted on going around day after day,
shopping with Livy in New York, & night he would go through the list
& check off the purchases & straighten everything up—& when dresses

arrived even at 11 at night he would not go to bed till he had opened all the packages & seen that everything was right—took a living interest in the whole trousseau business from beginning to end, & so touched Livy with this loving unbending to her little womanly affairs that she could not tell me of it without moistened eyes.[11]

I saw Charley in Philadelphia & played some billiards & had some talk with him, but some strange instinct kept arresting my tongue, & I actually was with him two hours & yet never asked him one question about any of you—never even mentioned any of you—& yet you were all in my mind from the first to the last. I am glad, now, that I was silent. Long ago you told me enough to lead me to fear that the matter had gone as far as it ever would. If it were me I could not live. It is awful.[12]

I send a world of love to Mollie my darling, & to all of you.[13] Tell Mollie I shall come & see her yet, & bring her new sister along—a young woman whom Mollie will delight to love.

Good-bye. Always your loving cub— Sam.

P. S.—I always write to Livy in this way—in my note-book, after I go to bed.[14]

(over.)

P. S.—My widowed sister & her young daughter Annie Moffett, are coming to the exhibi coming to the execu to the wedding, & I have written her to be sure to stop over a whole 24 hours at Chicago & rest, & another 24 at Cleveland. Told her to stop at the Kennard[15] & send her card to the Herald & the Cleveland Mother she has heard so much about will call on her, & maybe come along with her. My sister should reach Elmira about Jan. 25. But I didn't know about your going to Norwich (*what* Norwich?—there's a 1,000 of them) after Allie.[16] So I guess you will not be in Cleveland when she comes cavorting through there.

[1] The early hours of 7 January.

[2] On 4 January Clemens traveled with Olivia thirty miles east of Elmira to Owego, where he lectured. They returned together that night (10 Jan 70 to OLL [1st]).

[3] See *L2*, 284, 354; *L3*, 436; and 13 Jan 70 to OLL.

[4] That is, in early September 1868, just after Olivia rejected Clemens's first proposal (*L2*, 249 n. 1).

[5] Compare *L2*, 316, 330, and *L3*, 70.

[6] These "two or three indebtednesses" included $12,500 owed to Jervis Langdon and $10,000 owed to Thomas A. Kennett for the purchase of Kennett's share in the Buffalo *Express* in mid-August 1869. They probably also included $1,000 owed to Elisha Bliss for an 1868 advance against royalties on *The Innocents*

Abroad. In November 1869 Clemens's plan for the larger debts was to pay them off "within two years" (*L3*, 387), so by his current reckoning he was ten months ahead of schedule. But his known assets and income between August 1869 and February 1870 were not quite adequate to this accelerated rate ($15,000 in six months' time). In August, he had about $3,000 in two cash accounts (one with Charles Langdon, one with Slote, Woodman and Company). Between August and February *Innocents* royalties were about $7,400; the *Express* paid him about $2,500; the lecture tour brought another $2,500 in profit (estimated at half the fees on fifty lectures at $100 each), for a total of $15,400. The advance against royalties doubtless claimed $1,000 of that, but Clemens did not finally pay down these debts as rapidly as anticipated here. He did, in fact, draw $567.09 in cash from his *Express* earnings in 1869, and his income from royalties proved somewhat less than he was counting on (*L2*, 176–77; *L3*, 43, 261 n. 2, 294 n. 2, 384 n. 9, 385–86, 483–86; 2 and 3 Mar 70 to Langdon, n. 4; SLC's account statements from the Express Printing Company for 9 Aug 69–1 Jan 70 and 1 Jan–19 May 70, from Charles J. Langdon dated 9 Aug 69, and from Slote, Woodman and Company for 1 Jan 70, all in CU-MARK; Hirst 1975, 314–16; 28 Jan 70 to Bliss).

⁷Jane Clemens recorded payments from her son of $25 on 24 November, 1 or 2 December, and 18 December 1869, as well as $500 on 6 January 1870. Clemens also sent $100 to pay Pamela and Annie Moffett's rail fares to Elmira (for his wedding), for a total of $675. In November 1869 he had paid $200 to have his life insured (JLC, 4; 15 Jan 70 to PAM; *L3*, 387).

⁸Bliss gave these figures to Clemens as he passed through Hartford on 27 December (*L3*, 439–40). Mrs. Fairbanks used one of them in the Cleveland *Herald* of 10 January: "The sale of Mark Twain's new book, 'The New Pilgrim's Progress,' amounted to $5[0],000 in December. Mark is making some progress toward a fortune" ("Personal Intelligence," 4).

⁹In March 1869 Clemens told Mrs. Fairbanks that Frederick H. Greer, from Boston, was the prototype of the "Interrogation Point," described in *Innocents* as "young and green, and not bright, not learned and not wise. He will be, though, some day, if he recollects the answers to all his questions." But the engraving of this character resembled Charles Langdon (chapter 7; *L2*, 386; *L3*, 169). Mr. Blucher was characterized as "confiding, good-natured, unsophisticated, companionable; but he was not a man to set the river on fire" (chapter 2). Evidently both descriptions were apt, except to Greer himself. Mrs. Fairbanks told Pamela and Annie Moffett that

> when *The Innocents Abroad* came out she was delighted with it, but she did feel badly over the transparent caricature of one of the passengers. Later, when this man came to see her, she could hardly bear to go downstairs, and when he began talking about Mark's book her heart was in her mouth. But he went on: "The only thing I didn't like was ——" and he mentioned the character that was clearly himself. But he went on: "That was so obviously meant for ——" and he mentioned a fellow passenger. Mrs. Fairbanks told Annie: "The next time I saw Mark I said, 'Mark, if I'm in that book I want to know it!'" (*MTBus*, 108)

Greer's connection with "any banker, or any banker's daughter" has not been documented.

¹⁰See 8 Jan 70 to OLL (1st), n. 4.

¹¹See *L3*, 406 n. 1.

¹²Twenty-two-year-old Alice Holmes Fairbanks (Mrs. Fairbanks's stepdaughter) and Charles B. Stilwell had broken their engagement. Clemens prob-

ably saw Stilwell while in Philadelphia to lecture on 7 December, or while passing through the city at the end of the month (*L2*, 132 n. 10; *L3*, 485).

[13] That is, in addition to Alice and Mrs. Fairbanks, to: Frank Fairbanks, twenty-four, Mrs. Fairbanks's stepson; Abel Fairbanks, her husband; and Charles Mason and Mary Paine (Mollie) Fairbanks, their children, fourteen and thirteen, respectively (Lorenzo Sayles Fairbanks, 552).

[14] Clemens wrote eight such letters to Olivia in late 1869, and two to members of his family (*L3*, 381–82 n. 1, 542–47). In 1870 he used notebook pages for his letters to Olivia on 8 January (1st), 10 January (both), 13 January, and 14 January.

[15] Cleveland's Kennard House had opened in 1866 and was patronized by "statesmen, theatrical artists, and prominent businessmen" (Rose, 335).

[16] Norwich, New York, where Mrs. Fairbanks's cousin William N. Mason lived. Clemens had stayed with Mason in December 1868 (*L2*, 326). See 15 Jan 70 to PAM, n. 2.

To Olivia L. Langdon
8 January 1870 • (1st of 2) • Troy, N.Y.
(MS: CU-MARK)

Troy, Jan. 7.

Darling, I have had no chance to-day to write till now—midnight. I talked in Cohoes tonight (got your little letter, pet,) & then came here to find a good hotel.[1]

Last night was delightful. Pleasant audience, & then spent the night with the very pleasantest kind of people—an old bachelor named Payne, & his 3 nieces, dainty, childlike, beautiful girls of 16, 17, & 20, & each looking & seeming 3 years younger than she really was. [*in margin:* I *love* you old sweetheart.] They soon got to regarding me as a sort of elder brother, & they got me up a delightful supper after the lecture, & made me stupefy them with smoke in the parlor, & let me smoke in my bedroom, & then let me sleep till I got ready to get up (10 AM,) & got me a hot breakfast, & 2 hours later sent me off comfortably with a stirrup cup of fresh hot coffee.[2]

Olive Logan had left them her autograph, with this boshy clap-trap legend of humbuggery attached:

"Yours ever, for God & Woman."

I followed it with my signature, & this travesty:

"Yours always, without regard to parties & without specifying individuals."

You think that is wicked, you little rascal—but it isn't as wicked as Logan's.[3]

Mr. Payne has remained a bachelor to devote his life to the rearing of those sweet little girls, & it is beautiful to see them all together, they love each other so fondly. [*in margin:* ~~Sunday~~ ‚Saturday‚ morning—It is snowing, & I am lying here smoking & thinking of our "old times" of a year & more ago₁, Livy dear.]

Little sweetheart, I enclose Mrs. F.'s letter.[4] Allie & Charley have broken it off. Well, it was to be expected. Lovers who write twice a week to each other & sit a whole evening the width of a room apart, are too awfully proper to love *very* much. It cost me very few pangs to hear of it.

I have answered Mrs. F at good length. Good-night, & God bless & protect my precious Livy.

Sam.

✉—————————————————————————————

[*in ink:*] Miss Olivia L. Langdon | Elmira | N. Y. [*postmarked:*] TROY N.Y. JAN 8   3 PM. [*docketed by OLL:*] 169ᵗʰ

[1]Clemens was at the Troy House, writing in the early hours of Saturday, 8 January. He had lectured in Cohoes, New York, about four miles north of Troy, on Friday evening. "Our Fellow Savages of the Sandwich Islands," like the other lectures sponsored by the Sons of Temperance and the Grand Army of the Republic, was poorly attended. It was a critical success, however. The Cohoes *Cataract* called it "altogether a novel production, so different, in fact, from what people usually hear from the platform, that the audience was somewhat disappointed; but quite agreeably so, however, for all complained that the lecture was too short, notwithstanding the speaker occupied a full hour in the delivery of his queer, quaint and quizzical remarks" ("Mark Twain's Lecture," 15 Jan 70, no page; "City Notes," Troy *Times*, 10 Jan 70, 3).

[2]Nothing further is known about Payne, Clemens's host in Amenia on 6 January. The poet Joel Benton (1832–1911), manager of the Amenia lecture course and former editor of the Amenia *Times* (1851–56), was supposed to introduce Clemens. But in 1898, Benton recalled that before he and the speaker

left the anteroom he particularly requested me not to introduce him to the audience, and I told him (for he called it "a whim of his") that his little whim should be respected. When we reached the stage I began, after a while, to feel not a little nervous for fear that he would never introduce himself. But he at last arose, and taking a semicircular sweep to the left, and then proceeding to the front, opened something like this:

"Ladies and Gentlemen: I—have—lectured—many—years,—and—in—many —towns,—large—and—small. I have travelled—north—south—east—and—west. I —have—met—many—great—men: *very*—great—men. But—I—have—never—yet —in—all—my—travels—met—the—president—of—a   *country*—lyceum—who— could—introduce—me—to—an—audience—with—that—*distinguished*—consideration—which—my *merits* deserve."

After this deliverance the house, which had stared at me for several minutes with vexed impatience for not "pressing the button," was convulsed at my expense, and gave him unremitting attention to the end. (Benton, 610–11)

[3] Olive Logan (1839–1909) had retired in 1868 after fourteen years as an actress, but was now a writer of stories, books, and plays, as well as a lecturer. She had just published *Before the Footlights and Behind the Scenes: A Book about "the Show Business" in All Its Branches* (1870). Her play *Surf, or Summer Scenes at Long Branch*, opened at the Fifth Avenue Theatre in New York on 12 January, closing just five weeks later. The subject of women's rights was prominent among her various lectures; her current topic was "Girls," a survey of female stereotypes, of which the "strong-minded girl" was her favorite. "She believes in the power of the ballot in woman's hands to set all things right" ("Olive Logan 'On Girls,' " Elmira *Saturday Evening Review*, 4 Dec 69, 3). Clemens's contempt for Logan is explained by what he wrote in 1898:

Olive Logan's notoriety grew out of—only the in[it]iated knew what. Apparently it was a manufactured notoriety, not an earned one. She *did* write & publish little things in newspapers & obscure periodicals, but there was no talent in them, & nothing resembling it. In a century they would not have made her known. Her name was really built up out of newspaper paragraphs set afloat by her husband, who was a small-salaried minor journalist. During a year or two this kind of paragraphing was persistent; one could seldom pick up a newspaper without encountering it.

"It is said that Olive Logan has taken a cottage at Nahant, & will spend the summer there."

"Olive Logan has set her face decidedly against the adoption of the short skirt for afternoon wear."

"The report that Olive Logan will spend the coming winter in Paris is premature. She has not yet made up her mind." . . .

On the strength of this oddly created notoriety Olive Logan went on the platform, & for at least two seasons the United States flocked to the lecture halls to look [at] her. She was merely a name & some ˌrich & costlyˌ clothes, & neither ˌof these propertiesˌ had any lasting quality, though for a while they were able to command a fee of a hundred dollars a night. She dropped out of the memories of men a quarter of a century ago. (SLC 1898a, 10–11, 13–14)

Like Clemens, Logan was represented by James Redpath's Boston Lyceum Bureau, but only in the seasons of 1869–70 and 1870–71. Her publicist (second) husband was William Wirt Sikes (1836–83), a journalist and also a lecturer for Redpath in 1869–71. They were married on 19 December 1871 ("Olive Logan's New Book," Elmira *Saturday Evening Review*, 1 Jan 70, 4; *Lyceum:* 1869, 3; 1870, 3; *NAW*, 2:422–24; "Olive Logan was married . . . ," Cleveland *Plain Dealer*, 20 Dec 71, 2).

[4] Mrs. Fairbanks's letter has not been recovered. Olivia wrote her on 9 January (CtHMTH):

My dear Mrs Fairbanks

We have been very desirous of hearing from you, Mother wrote you and Mrs Severance some weeks ago and as she has not heard from you she feared that you did not receive ꞁt ˌthe letter,ˌ—she directed to the Herald Office and thought perhaps Mr Fairbanks, like many [a] gentleman was carrying it in his pocket—

I *do* want you *very much* to come to our wedding— Do not disapoint us— Mr Clemens' own Mother cannot be here and I am sure that he should have his foster Mother here—

We shall have a quiet wedding, only particular friends will be invited, and of course we are *very* anxious to have such friends with us— I hope that you and Mr Fairbanks, Allie and Mr Stillwell, Mr and Mrs Severance will come— If you are in the least undecided I am sure that if I could see you for about ten minutes I could persuade you to come, because I do want you so very much, that I should grow eloquent on the subject— But I hope that you *are* NOT undecided.

Mother's letter to Mrs Severance was enclosed in the one to you as she did not know her address—

With love to Allie and kind regards to the other members of your household, I am lovingly

your friend
Livy L. Langdon

P. S. Mr Clemens lectures in Albany tomorrow night, then about in that vicinity until the seventeenth— We have had letters from Charlie ‚from‚ Yokohama, he reached there in safety after a pleasant trip—

For a record of those attending the wedding, see pp. 42–44.

To James Redpath
8 January 1870 • Albany, N.Y.
(MS: ViU)

Albany,[1] Jan. 8.

Friend Redpath—

Cohoes was another infernal no-season-ticket concern—paid me in 7,000 ten-cent shin-plasters, so that my freight cost more back to Albany than my passage did.[2] I hate these one-horse concerns. I have no regular season courses lately. They *call* them regular courses, but are not respectable, & have no season tickets.[3] We have had good houses, but would have had better if their system had been the right one.

But I am wandering from the object of this letter—which is *not* to kick up, now, when the long agony is nearly over, but to ask Mr. Fall to send my bill to Elmira so that it will reach there about Jan. 25th or 27th— & then I can dispute the items & raise Cain with him before the wedding—couldn't get mad enough *after* it, unless you allow time on it when people are peculiarly situated. I do not think you are men who would take advantage of a man's situation & send in a bill at a time when he couldn't naturally have presence of mind enough to dispute it.[4] And what is the use of *having* a bill unless you can dispute it? [I sent you $125 the other day—did you get it?][5]

Yrs,
Clemens.

✉——————————————————————————————————————

[letter docketed:] S. L. Clemens | Albany N.Y. Jan. 8 '70

[1] Clemens's business in Albany, about eight miles south of Troy, probably concerned his lecture there on Monday, 10 January. He returned to Troy later in the day, remaining there through part of 10 January ("City Notes," Troy *Times,* 10 Jan 70, 3).

[2] Clemens's actual fee in Cohoes is not known. His usual fee at this time varied between $75 and $100, with a high of $120 in Pittsburgh, where he opened the Mercantile Library Association's lecture course (*L3,* 382 n. 2, 384 n. 9).

[3] The previous December Clemens had canceled one such engagement in Brooklyn (*L3,* 417–21). By July 1870 the Boston Lyceum Bureau had published twelve "Hints to Lyceums," two of which urged applicants to "state whether you represent an organization or propose to act independently," and "whether you shall have one or more lectures: if more than one, how many, and whether you intend to sell season tickets" (*Lyceum* 1870, 1).

[4] George L. Fall (1837–75) was Redpath's partner in the Boston Lyceum Bureau from 1868 until 1873, when poor health compelled his retirement. In 1875 he was about to return to the bureau when, on 5 May, he died suddenly from "hemorrhage of the lungs" ("Deaths," Boston *Evening Transcript,* 6 May 75, 4). In memorializing Fall, Redpath lauded his integrity, courage, and "perfect purity of character":

> As a business man, he was trustworthy, exact, methodical, clear-headed, punctual, and truthful; and all in the highest degree. His system was so admirable that he was a synonyme among those who knew him for clerical infallibility. During his last business year in the Bureau, although he answered thousands of letters, each involving railroad rides, dates, and distances,—the year work of a hundred lecturers, as well as of concerts,—he did not make a single mistake. His judgment was so rarely at fault that he was constantly consulted as to their own business by scores of persons with whom he was brought into official relations.

Fall, he concluded, was "a man not of genius, but character, which is less shining, but of a purer light" (Redpath 1875).

[5] Redpath had billed Clemens for the Boston Lyceum Bureau's ten percent commission on his recent lecture fees (Pond, 541; Eubank, 128–32).

To Olivia L. Langdon
8 January 1870 • (2nd of 2) • Troy, N.Y.
(MS: CU-MARK)

Troy, Saturday, Jan. 8.

Sweetheart, this is the anniversary of the battle of New Orleans, which was fought & bloodily won by Gen. Jackson, at a time when England & America were at peace.[1]

It is also the anniversary of other events, but I do not know what they were, now.

I have been reading some new arguments to prove that the world is very old, & that the six days of creation were six immensely long periods. For instance, according to Genesis, the *stars* were made when the world was, yet this writer mentions the significant fact that there are stars within reach of our telescopes whose light requires 50,000 years to traverse the wastes of space & come to our earth.[2] And so, if we made a tour through space ourselves, might we not, in some remote era of the future, meet & ~~shake han~~ greet the ~~lag~~ first lagging rays of stars that started on their weary visit to us a million years ago?—rays that are outcast & homeless, now, their parent stars crumbled to nothingness & swept from the firmament five hundred thousand years after these journeying rays departed—stars whose peoples lived their little lives, & laughed & wept, hoped & feared, sinned & perished, bewildering ages since these vagrant twinklings went wandering through the solemn solitudes of space?

How insignificant we are, with our pigmy little world!—an atom glinting with uncounted myriads of other atom worlds in a broad shaft of light streaming from God's countenance—& yet prating complacently ~~about~~ of our speck as the Great World, & regarding the other specks as pretty trifles made to steer our schooners by & inspire the reveries of ",puppy", lovers. Did Christ live 33 years in each of the millions & millions of worlds that hold their majestic courses above our heads? ~~Ou~~ Or was *our* small ~~glov~~ globe the favored one of all? Does one apple in a vast orchard think as much of itself as we do?—or one leaf in the forest,—or one grain of sand upon the sea shore? Do the pismires argue upon vexed questions of ~~theology~~ pismire theology,—& do they climb a molehill & look abroad over the grand universe of an acre of ground & say "Great is God, who created all things for Us?"[3]

I do not see how astronomers can help feeling exquisitely insignificant, for every new page of the Book of the Heavens they open reveals to them more & more that the world we are so proud of is to the universe of careering globes ~~is~~ as ˄is˄ one mosquito to the winged & hoofed flocks & ~~hea~~ herds that darken the air & populate the plains & forests of all the earth. ~~Verily, What is Man, that he should be considered of God?~~ If you killed the mosquito, would it be missed? Verily, What is ⱨMan, that he should be considered of God?[4]

One of these astronomers has been taking photographs of tongues of flame 17,000 miles high that ~~shot~~ shoot aloft from the surface of the sun, & waver, & sink, & rise again—all in two or three minutes,—& sometimes in *one* minute swinging a banner of flame from left to right a distance of 5,000 miles—an inconceivable velocity! Think of the hurricanes that sweep the sun, to do such miracles as this! And other tongues of flame stream upward, ~~arch &~~ bend & hang down again, forming a crimson arch 28,000 miles in height, through which our poor globe might be bowled as one bowls ~~an apple~~ ˏa football˳ between a boy's legs.[5]

But I must stop. I have concluded to stay here to-day & tomorrow, as this hotel suits me first-rate. I had the sagacity to enter my *nom de plume* on the register, & so they have made me very comfortable. (For I find that the landlord[6] is a frantic admirer of mine.) He is a good fellow, too (naturally.)

Go to bed, sweetheart. Go to bed, & sleep peacefully, & awake refreshed & happy, my darling.

Sam

Add to list of after-cards for San Francisco:

Mr. & Mrs. Dr. Bruner.

Mrs. Joseph Woodworth, care of Dr. Bruner.[7]

Miss Olivia L. Langdon | Elmira | N. Y. [*return address:*] TROY HOUSE TROY, N.Y. CHAS. H. JONES. PROPRIETOR. [*postmarked:*] TROY N.Y. JAN 10 [*docketed by OLL:*][8] 170th

[1] Fought on this date in 1815, the Battle of New Orleans came two weeks after the treaty ending the War of 1812 was signed, but five weeks before its ratification on 17 February. American troops under Andrew Jackson decisively defeated an invading British force. Clemens also mentioned the anniversary in an 1868 letter to Emeline Beach (*L2*, 147).

[2] Clemens was reading "The Early History of Man" in the *Eclectic Magazine* for January 1870 (n.s., 11:1–16, reprinting the *North British Review*, n.s., 11 [July 69]: 516–49; cited in Cummings, 11). The anonymous writer rejected the "popular chronology" that put the earth's age at less than 20,000 years:

> It is familiar that the defenders of this chronology—which is as purely a *human* invention as is the bicycle velocipede—have been obliged to stretch the days of creation, as given in Genesis, into periods of time of indefinite duration—millions of years, if necessary. . . . Our next remark is that astronomy sets the existence *of the world* more than 20,000 years ago beyond doubt, by showing that there are stars now visible to us whose light takes at least 50,000 years to cross the space that separates us from them. (6–7)

That Clemens read the *Eclectic* was first deduced from his use of pages torn from a copy of it (*L3*, 394 n. 3, 400 n. 1 *top*).

³Revelation 4:11: "Thou art worthy, O Lord, to receive glory and honour and power: for thou hast created all things, and for thy pleasure they are and were created."

⁴Psalms 8:4: "What is man, that thou art mindful of him? and the son of man, that thou visitest him?"

⁵Clemens's source here was "Solar Wonders," also in the January 1870 *Eclectic Magazine* (n.s., 11:112–14, reprinting the London *Spectator* 42 [13 Nov 69]: 1328–29; cited in Cummings, 12). Its unidentified author reported:

> We have before us as we write a series of colored prominence-pictures taken by Dr. [Johann Karl Friedrich] Zöllner, the eminent photometrician. It is impossible to contemplate these strange figures without a sense of the magnificence of the problem which the sun presents to astronomers. . . . First, there is a vast flame, some 18,000 miles high, bowed towards the right, as though some fierce wind were blowing upon it. It extends in this direction some four or five thousand miles. The next picture represents the same object ten minutes later. The figure of the prominence has wholly changed. It is now a globe-shaped mass, standing on a narrow stalk of light above a row of flame-hillocks. It is bowed towards the left, so that in those short minutes the whole mass of the flame has swept thousands of miles away from its former position. Only two minutes later, and again a complete change of appearance. The stalk and the flame-hillocks have vanished, and the globe-shaped mass has become elongated. Three minutes later, the shape of the prominence has altered so completely that one can hardly recognize it for the same. The stalk is again visible, but the upper mass is bowed down on the right so that the whole figure resembles a gigantic A, without the cross-bar, and with the down-stroke abnormally thick. This great A is some twenty thousand miles in height, and the whole mass of our earth might be bowled between its legs without touching them! (112–13)

⁶See the return address.

⁷Clemens had known physician William H. Bruner and his wife, the former Jane Woodworth, since the mid-1860s. The Bruners had a son and two daughters before they divorced in 1874. After the divorce, Jane Bruner contributed to newspapers and wrote a novel, *Free Prisoners: A Story of California Life* (1877), and a play, *A Mad World*, which had a brief run in San Francisco and which, in 1882, Clemens tried to help her have produced in the East. Mrs. Joseph Woodworth was either her sister-in-law or, more likely, her mother. Clemens probably knew Joseph Woodworth, a San Francisco dealer in mining stock from 1863 to 1866. He lived in San Francisco only sporadically between 1867 and 1871, but city directories list him at the same address with Bruner in 1864 and again in 1871, so Mrs. Woodworth may have been there when Clemens wrote this letter (Jane W. Bruner to SLC, 29 Mar 82 and 7 Apr 82, CU-MARK; Langley: 1863, 82, 380, 405; 1864, 86, 419; 1865, 98, 464; 1871, 127, 685).

⁸Clemens's next letter to Olivia (docket number 171), presumably written from Troy on 9 January, is missing (*L3*, 479).

To Olivia L. Langdon
10 January 1870 • (1st of 2) • Albany, N.Y.
(MS: CU-MARK)

Noon.

Albany, Jan. 10.

It is snowing like fury, Sweetheart—but no matter: we have already got the biggest audience of the whole season, so they say—& if my darling were here, now, I would throw into this lecture all the frills I know—& she shouldn't feel deserted, & unwelcome & abused, either. Poor child, it cuts me to the heart to think I could not conceal my down-heartedness at Owego, & so save you from distress, (for you felt more than you showed, my darling.) But Livy, I knew perfectly well that I would have no confidence in that little audience, & consequently would simply utter lifeless *words*—words with no animating soul in them—& such a speech is just as well read from a newspaper as heard from a stage. I felt & *knew* that you would judge harshly of the lecture, hearing it under such or circumstances, but that you would not if you heard it before a great metropolitan audience. *I was a dead body that night,* & so I never succeeded in infusing life into that torpid Owego house—& I knew how it would be beforehand—at least I thought I did.[1] But I only hate myself for not siezing *with pleasure* upon that or *any* opportunity to do your desire, instead of thinking of nothing but *myself* in the matter. You never would have thought of *your*self in such a case. And until I learn to hold you & your wishes above myself & mine, I shall go on groping in the dark & grovelinging in the dirt & making us both unhappy. But I WILL learn it.

It still snows—& the wind drives it in pal almost horizontal sheets. What an *eternity* a lecture-season is! It seems a full week since I went over to Troy ˬCohoes, from here. Sometimes I chafe so at the dragging days that I almost resolve to break my appointments & go home. I wouldn't do another lecture season unless I were in absolute *want*, almost.

I am reading Ivanhoe. Ivanhoe was a knight in Sir Walter Scott's time. He is dead, now. He married Cedric the Saxon, & the fruit of this union was a daughter by the name of Reginald Front-de-Boeuf. The whole six fell in battle at Ashby de la Zouche. Not one of the family survived this melancholy slaughter but a casual acquaintance ~~that~~ ˌcalled by the name of˷ Rachel the son of Beowulf. All the characters are well sustained, especially that of the Atlantic Ocean. You know all that it is necessary to know about this romance, now, Livy darling, & so if you have not read it subsequently you needn't.

I telegraphed these people that I would remain in Troy until this evening, & so they are patiently waiting till I come. Hence I have not yet got my letters.[2]

Pleasant dreams, sweetheart, & blessings on your dear old head.

Sam

✉—————————————————————————————————

[*in ink:*] Miss Olivia L. Langdon | Elmira | N. Y. [*return address:*] DELAVAN HOUSE, ALBANY, CHAS. E. LELAND. CLARENDON HOTEL, SARATOGA SPRINGS, CHAS. E. LELAND. LELAND HOTEL, SPRINGFIELD, ILL. H.S. LELAND & CO. METROPOLITAN HOTEL, NEW-YORK. S. LELAND & CO.[3] [*postmarked:*] ALBANY N.Y. JAN 10 [*docketed by OLL:*] 172nd

[1] Olivia accompanied Clemens to Owego on 4 January and attended his lecture there that evening. He was anxious to perform well because he felt he failed to do so on the only other occasion she had heard him lecture, in November 1868 (*L2*, 285–86 n. 1, 288; *L3*, 30). Despite Clemens's misgivings, his Owego lecture (sponsored by the local Y.M.C.A.) seems to have been a success. The Owego *Gazette* noted that there was "a full house . . . and all went away satisfied, after a full hour of side-splitting laughter" ("Mark Twain had . . . ," 6 Jan 70, 3). The Owego *Times* reported that the audience was

> unusually large and refined. His introduction of himself was novel and happy. The awkward Yankee manners assumed by the lecturer were none the less pleasing in that they failed to mask the characteristics of a finished gentleman. His voice was singularly beautiful, and his enunciation very clear and distinct. . . . The lecture was not particularly instructive, but superbly entertaining. Yet many new ideas respecting the Sandwich Islands were more indelibly impressed, perhaps, than would have been by a long dry lecture exclusively descriptive. The fault most seriously complained of was seeming brevity. . . . The house, as an exception in Owego, must have been a paying one. ("The Twain Lecture," 6 Jan 70, 3)

[2] Clemens's telegram to his Albany sponsors, the Grand Army of the Republic, has not been found. Olivia had a copy of his itinerary and therefore wrote to him in care of his contact on the local lecture committee, in this case Robert W. C. Mitchell, a bookkeeper for the firm of James Mix, Jr., manufacturing jeweler ("Lectures," "Amusement Notes," Albany *Evening Journal,* 10 Jan 70, 3; *L3*, 416; *Albany Directory:* 1868, 125, 223, 264; 1869, 132, 231, 264; 1870, 132, 232, 249).

[3] "How many thousand Lelands there are in the hotel business is more than any ordinary mortal can say, but one would think there were enough to run every establishment of that kind in the country," according to the New York corre-

spondent of the Buffalo *Courier* (Rapidan). Clemens had stayed at the Delavan House—"at the junction of all the railroads"—in December 1868, when he may have met Charles E. Leland, who was either the brother or the cousin of his San Francisco friend, Lewis Leland (*Albany Directory:* 1868, 350; 1870, 350). The Leland Hotel in Springfield was built in 1866. H. S. Leland has not been further identified. The Metropolitan Hotel was well known to Clemens. It was still owned and operated by Simeon Leland and Company, although in December 1870 both Lewis and George S. Leland were referred to as "graduates from the Metropolitan" (Rapidan), indicating they had served a managerial apprenticeship there. That is almost certainly what Clemens referred to in late 1868 when he wrote that Lewis Leland was about to become the "proprietor of the Metropolitan Hotel in New York" (*L2*, 358, 331 n. 3, 2; Krohe, 201, 262; Wilson 1869, 646, 761).

To Olivia L. Langdon
10 January 1870 • (2nd of 2) • Albany, N.Y.
(MS: CU-MARK)

In Bed—⎱
Albany, Jan. 10. ⎰

Had an immense house, tonight, little sweetheart, & turned away several hundred—no seats for them. It is hard to make al Albany Dutchmean laugh & applaud, but the subscriber did it.[1] One day less to worry through before my rascally pilgrimage is finished & we resign ourselves to rest & refreshment in the tranquil privacy of our own home, my darling.

Bless your little heart, you did no "impertinent thing" in opening a letter addressed to me, Livy dear. You can open *any* letter addressed to me—whatever is mine is Livy's. The letter was from John McComb & I will enclose it to you. I have a secret to tell you about him when I see you again, if I do not forget it. I will write him to-night to hunt up that Blind Tom letter. I am glad & proud that my little wife takes such an interest in my scribblings.[2] I plainly see, now, why Joe Goodman gradually lost all interest in his poetry (he was a born poet) & finally lost all ambition in that direction & ceased to write. The one whose applause would have been dearer to him & more potent than that of all the world beside, could not help him, or encourage him or spur him, because she was far below his intellectual level & could not appe appreciate the work

of his brain or feel an interest in it. When I told him you took care of my
sketches for me & listened with a lively interest to any manuscript of
mine before it was printed, he dropped an unconscious remark that was
so full of pathos—so fraught with "It might have been"—that my heart
ached for him.[3] He *could* have been so honored of men, & so loved by all
~~who~~ for whom poetry has a charm, but for the dead weight ∅ & clog ~~of a~~
~~wife~~ upon his winged genius, of a wife whose soul could have no com-
panionship save with the things of the dull earth.[4]

But I am blessed above my kind, with ~~a~~ *another self*—a life companion ∅ who is *part of me*—part of my heart, & flesh & spirit—& not a
fellow-pilgrim who lags far behind or flies ahead, or soars above me. Side
by side, my darling, we walk the ways of life; & the ray of light that falls
upon the one, illumines the face of the other; the cloud that darkens the
hope of one casts its sable shadow upon the other; & the storms that come
will beat upon no single head, but both will feel ~~its~~ ˏtheirˏ might & brave
~~its~~ ˏtheirˏ desolation.

Oh, think of Mrs. Fairbanks—a ~~Pa~~ Pegasus harnessed with a dull
brute of the field. Mated, but not matched, must be the direst grief that
can befall any poor human creature—& when I think how I have escaped it when so many that are worthier than I have suffered it, I am
filled with a thankfulness to God which I can *feel*—that rare thankfulness
that such as I feel all too seldom. It is at such times that one's *heart* lifts
up its unspoken gratitude, & no choicely worded eloquence of lip &
brain is like unto itˏ, or half so puissant.

I shall love the silk quilt, not only because our mother gave it you,
but because it will always preserve that old dress that was so dear to me.[5]
And we never can sleep under it, darling, & forget the old pleasant days
that were ours when it was ˚still "in the flesh," if I may so speak. We will
cherish the quilt well, & help it hoard its memory-treasures. It must be
sacred to our bed—guests cannot have it.[6] And I am very glad, too, that
it has in it something ~~to~~ that knew you when you were a little girl—for I
always feel a sense of loss, when I reflect that *I* never knew you when you
were little. [*in margin:* You darling little rascal, you must spell "suffice"
as I spell it now. That's all that's wrong, sweetheart.]

My child! I thought you had a full list.[7] Here it is:

> Jan. 11 (tomorrow) West Troy
> 12—Rondout—H. M. Crane

13—Cambridge (N. Y.) A. H. Comstock
14.—Utica—W. P. Carpenter.
15—Oswego—Joseph Owen
16—*Sunday.*
17—Baldwinsville (N. Y.) W. F. Morris.

ᴀ——

——ᴀ

20—Hornellsville
21—Jamestown, (N. Y.) C. E. Bishop.

That is the end of the list, now, & I hope no additions will be made to it.

If you hurry, honey, I guess you can get the newspaper notices to the Oswego man in time.[8]

I have received the bookseller's receipt for the money paid for the Doré book, & so I suppose the book has reached you by this time—it was to be sent right away.[9]

Sleep in peace, my own darling, & all good angels guard your dreams & give them happy omens.

Sam.

⋈————————————————————————

[*in ink:*] Miss Olivia L. Langdon | Elmira | N. Y. [*return address:*] DELAVAN HOUSE, ALBANY, CHAS. E. LELAND. CLARENDON HOTEL, SARATOGA SPRINGS, CHAS. E. LELAND. LELAND HOTEL, SPRINGFIELD, ILL. H. S. LELAND & CO. METROPOLITAN HOTEL, NEW-YORK. S. LELAND & CO. [*postmarked:*] ALBANY N.Y. JAN 11 [*docketed by OLL:*][10] 173rd

[1] The Albany *Evening Journal* reported that Clemens

delighted an immense audience last night. Tweddle Hall was packed in every part. The Sandwich Island Savages were described in a peculiarly droll and interesting manner, which kept the audience in a broad grin from commencement to close. Mark is decidedly the best of our humorists, and what is more to his credit, he never descends to the trick of bad spelling in his writings. ("'Our Fellow Savages,'" 11 Jan 70, 3)

The Albany *Argus* agreed, calling Clemens "the best humorist now before the public" and a success "from first to last" ("'Mark Twain' at Tweddle Hall," 11 Jan 70, 2).

[2] McComb was one of the editors and owners of the San Francisco *Alta California*. The secret about him remains a secret. Clemens had described the blind, black piano prodigy Thomas Greene Bethune (1849–1908) in an *Alta* letter published on 1 August 1869. Olivia must have reminded him of his earlier promise to get a copy of it for her (*L2*, 12 n. 1; SLC 1869b; Southern, 251–54; *L3*, 431).

[3] This exchange took place in late December or early January, either in New York City or Elmira, before Goodman went on to Europe (*L3*, 431). Goodman's first wife, Ellen, was a native of Ireland. They remained married until her death in 1893 (Caleb Goodman, 5).

[4] According to journalist Samuel P. Davis (1850–1918), Goodman's poetry, which regularly appeared in his Virginia City *Territorial Enterprise*, earned him the title "Boss Poet of the Comstock." Goodman was often called upon for ceremonial verse: "year after year he furnished the odes for Decoration Day, Fourth of July and Pioneer anniversaries. . . . Whenever Joe had to shut himself up and write a poem for the public, Mark Twain, who was on the paper, would describe his employer as being chained in a cell on a fish-and-water diet, wrestling with the muses" (Samuel Post Davis). Most of Goodman's poetry perished with the files of the *Enterprise*, but some characteristic poems can be found in *Poetry of the Pacific*, published in 1867 (Newman).

[5] Probably "the particular blue silk dress" that Clemens associated with the early days of his courtship (*L3*, 78). The gift of a bridal quilt from mother to daughter had been an American tradition since colonial times (Holstein, 27).

[6] "Entertainment of a welcome visitor not immediate 'kin' demanded that the spare bed be formally decked in all the glory of the *pièce de résistance* of the housewife's quilts; not so to dress a guest's bed was a social slight" (Finley, 128).

[7] Olivia had been using the lecture itinerary that Clemens sent her on 29 November 1869, which did not include his lectures in Oswego, Hornellsville, and Jamestown, nor two others he did not yet know about: Ogdensburg and Fredonia, New York, on 18 and 19 January, respectively. Clemens's contacts at West Troy (George R. Meneely, a bell manufacturer), Rondout (Henry M. Crane, a bookkeeper), and Utica (William P. Carpenter, a bookkeeper) have been previously identified (*L3*, 315 n. 1 *bottom*, 357 n. 1 *top*, 415–16, 486). For his Oswego contact see note 8. For his Cambridge, Fredonia, and Jamestown contacts, see 14 Jan 70 to OLL, nn. 1 and 5, and 20 Feb 70 to Langdon, n. 2. His contact at Baldwinsville is identified only by the present list. The names of his Ogdensburg and Hornellsville contacts are not known.

[8] Olivia had not sent the reviews Clemens requested on 6 January because she did not know who "the Oswego man" was. She may now have sent them to Joseph Owen, a real estate broker and a member of the local Y.M.C.A. lecture committee. In publicizing the lecture, the Oswego *Commercial Advertiser and Times* excerpted reviews from the Boston *Advertiser* and the Boston *Evening Transcript* (misidentified as the "*Journal*"), both of 11 November 1869, the Hartford *Courant* of 25 November 1869, and the Troy *Times* of 12 January 1870, but not the Philadelphia *Evening Bulletin* (6 Jan 70 to OLL, n. 4). Afterward, the Oswego paper pronounced the performance a success, remarking that following some "heavy lectures . . . Twain's was thrown in just at the right nick of time to make the course rest a little easier on our stomachs, so to speak—like the wine after dinner" (Oswego *Commercial Advertiser and Times*: "Real Estate Office," 13 Jan 70, 3; "'Mark Twain,' . . . ," "Mark Twain—Notices of the Press," "Y.M.C.A. Lecture Course," 14 Jan 70, 3; "Twain's Lecture," 17 Jan 70, 3).

[9] See 6 Jan 70 to OLL, n. 2.

[10] Clemens's next two letters to Olivia (docket numbers 174 and 175), probably written on 11 and 12 January after his lectures in West Troy and Rondout, are missing (*L3*, 479).

To Olivia L. Langdon
13 January 1870 • Cambridge, N.Y.
(MS: CU-MARK)

Cambridge, Jan. 13.

No, Livy dear, I shall treat smoking just exactly as I would treat the fore-finger of my left hand: If you asked me in all seriousness to cut that finger off, & I saw that you really meant it, & believed that the finger marred my well-being in some mysterious way, & *I* it was plain to me that you could not be entirely satisfied & happy while it remained, I give you my word that I would cut it off. I might think what I pleased about it, & the world might *say* what it pleased—it should come off. There would be nothing foolish in the act—& all wordy *arguments* against it would sink to their proper insignificance in presence of the one *unanswerable* argument that *you desired it,* & our married life could not be completely in unison while that bar remained.

Now there are *no* arguments that can convince me that *moderate* smoking is deleterious to me. I cannot ac attach any weight to either the arguments or the evidence of those who know nothing about the matter personally & so must simply theorize. Theorizing has no effect on me. I have smoked habitually for 26 of my 34 years, & I am on the only healthy member our family has. (What do mere theories amount to in the face of a *fact* like that.) My health is wholly faultless—& has been ever since I was 8 years old. My physical structure—lungs, kidneys, heart, brain—is without blemish.[1] The do life insurance doctor pronounced me free from all disease & *remarkably* sound.[2] Yet I am the victim of this fearfully destructive habit of smoking. My brother's health has gradually run *down* instead of *up*—yet he is a model of propriety, & has *no* bad habits. My mother smoked for 30 years, & yet has lived to the age of 67.

Livy dear, make no argument of the fact that you have seen me "nervous, irritable," &c., &c., for it happens to *be* no argument. You can see your father nervous, worn, restless—you can see *any* anti-smoker affected just as you have seen me. It is not a stat condition confined to smokers—as you ps possibly know in your own experience.

There *is* no argument that can have even a feather's weight with me against smoking (in my case, at least,) for I *know,* & others merely *suppose.*

But there is one thing that will make me quit smoking, & only one. I will lay down this habit which is so filled with harmless pleasure, just as soon as you write me or say to me that *you desire it*. It shall be a sacrifice—just the same as if I simply asked you to give up going to church, knowing that no *arguments* I offered could convince you that I was right. It will not be hard for me to do it. I stopped chewing tobacco because it was a mean habit, partly, & partly because my mother desired it.[3] I ceased from profanity because Mrs. Fairbanks desired it. I stopped drinking strong liquors because you desired it. I stopped drinking all other liquors because it seemed plain that you desired it.[4] I did what I could to learn to leave my hands out of my pantaloons pockets & quit lolling at full length in easy chairs, because you desired it. There was no sacrifice about any of these things. Discarding these habits curtailed none of my liberties—on the contrary the doing it released me from various forms of slavery. With smoking it is different. No argument is against it is valid—& so to quit it I must do without other reason that that *you* desire it. The desires of all others have weight with me, but are not strong *enough* quite.

But even if you never *said* the words, if I saw that my smoking was a bar to our *perfect* wedded unity and happiness, it should go by the board—& pitilessly.[5]

You seem to think it will be a Herculean task for me to suddenly cast out a loved habit of 26 years, Livy dear. Either you do not know me, or I do not know myself. I think differently about it. Speak the words, Livy dear—unaccompanied by any of the hated arguments or theories—& you shall see that I love you well enough to follow your desires, even in *this* matter. Nothing shall stand in the way of our perfect accord, if I can help it.

If you had ever harried me, or persecuted me about this thing, I could not speak as I do—for persecution only hardens one in evil courses. But it is you, darling, that have suffered the persecution (& yet, being you, it has *seemed* to be me, & so I have resisted all along.) You have had to listen to it all, & it grieves my heart to think of it. It has had its necessary effect in making me more loth to yield up this habit than I would have been otherwise. We do hate to be driven.

Ah, Livy, if the whole matter had been left solely in *your* hands, I would have been quit of the habit of smoking, long ago, & without a pang or a struggle. It was bad judgment to attack so strong a vice saf save through you. There could be little prospect that other means would succeed if your gentle ministrations failed.

It is about supper time, & some new friends are to come in after supper & sit with me till lecture time. Just as usual, I am in splendid trim for this little country town—& just as usual I must get up at 6 in the morning & be in a lifeless lethargy for the next large city—Utica, & so make a botch of it.

I am so sorry I have been the prime cause of blasting a happy Sunday for my darling—sorry & dejected—& resolved to make up for it in some way. Poor child, nobody shall harass you when my roof covers you. I won't even let Mr. Langdon do it, dear good father though he is to both of us.[6] I kiss you good night, darling.

Sam.

✉——————————————————————————————

[*in ink:*] Miss Olivia L. Langdon | Elmira | N. Y. [*return address:*] IF NOT DELIVERED WITHIN 10 DAYS, TO BE DELIVERED TO [*postmarked:*] CAMBRIDGE N.Y. JAN 14 [*docketed by OLL:*] 176th

[1] Clemens was consistent in his accounts of when he began smoking, and of the habit's effects on him, but did not always claim moderation. In 1882 he wrote:

> I am forty-six years old, and I have smoked immoderately during thirty-eight years. . . . During the first seven years of my life I had no health—I may almost say that I lived on allopathic medicine, but since that period I have hardly known what sickness is. My health has been excellent, and remains so. As I have already said, I began to smoke immoderately when I was eight years old; that is, I began with one hundred cigars a month, and by the time I was twenty I had increased my allowance to two hundred a month. Before I was thirty, I had increased it to three hundred a month. (14 Mar 82 to Alfred Arthur Reade, in Reade, 120–21)

[2] In November 1869 (*L3*, 387).

[3] In early 1859 (*L3*, 76 n. 3).

[4] By November 1867 (swearing) and November 1868 (alcohol) (*L2*, 122, 166, 284, 354).

[5] Clemens had long anticipated such gentle persuasion (*L2*, 354). He did stop smoking not long after his marriage—possibly as soon as 6 February—although complete abstinence was only temporary (see the next note).

[6] Nothing has been learned of the pretext for Jervis Langdon's most recent remarks to Olivia about Clemens's smoking. Possibly she shared Clemens's facetious report of stupefying his Amenia hosts "with smoke in the parlor" (8 Jan 70 to OLL [1st]). Since their discussion spoiled a Sunday and, according to the next letter, Olivia returned "from church all worn & unhappy," her father may have enlisted the family's pastor, Thomas K. Beecher, at Congregational (later Park) Church, on 9 January. Jervis Langdon soon made a direct appeal to Clemens, some details of which are preserved in the diary of Annie Adams Fields, wife of Boston publisher James T. Fields. Describing an occasion in March 1876 when

Clemens told her husband "the whole story of his life," she made special note of an incident that demonstrated Clemens's "strength of character and rightness of vision":

> He said he had not been married many months when his wife's father came to him one evening and said, "My son, would n't you like to go to Europe with your wife?" "Why yes, sir," he said, "if I could afford it." "Well then," said he, "if you will leave off smoking and drinking ale you shall have ten thousand dollars this next year and go to Europe beside." "Thank you, sir," said Mark, "this is very good of you, and I appreciate it, but I can't sell myself. I will do anything I can for you or any of your family, but I can't sell myself." The result was, said Mark, "I never smoked a cigar all that year nor drank a glass of ale; but when the next year came I found I must write a book, and when I sat down to write I found it was n't worth anything. I must have a cigar to steady my nerves. I began to smoke, and I wrote my book; but then I could n't sleep and I had to drink ale to go to sleep. Now if I had sold myself, I could n't have written my book, or I could n't have gone to sleep, but now everything works perfectly well." (Diary entry of 6 Apr 76, in Howe, 244–46)

In 1882 Clemens recalled that his abstinence lasted "a year and a half," but he probably exaggerated its length (14 Mar 82 to Alfred Arthur Reade, in *RI 1993*, 819). No documents have survived to show that he did not quit smoking as soon as he was married, but the remembered interview with Jervis Langdon could not have occurred before 1 May. By mid-December he was smoking only on Sundays, and his work on *Roughing It*, begun in late August, had stalled. He may not have fully resumed smoking until March or April 1871, when he also resumed work on the book in company with Joseph T. Goodman (2 Sept 70 to OC, n. 1; 19 Dec 70 to Twichell; 18 Apr 71 and 30 Apr 71, both to OC; *RI 1993*, 819–42).

To Olivia L. Langdon
14 January 1870 • Troy, N.Y.
(MS: CU-MARK)

Troy, Jan. 14.

Livy darling, I have been worrying sorely over the letter I wrote you yesterday about smoking—& wondering what I said in it—for as usual, none of the language is left in my memory. I only remember having in my mind a picture of you returning from church all worn & unhappy, & a consciousness in my mind that you had been wrongfullyed & treated, & were blameless & should not have been made to suffer for the sin of another. And I had upon me a rasping, chafing sense of

There, there, there—let us bother with the hateful subject no more. I am sure it has caused us both more real suffering that than would accrue from smoking a million cigars.

And this is a bad time for me to write about exciting matters, for my nerves, & my ~~whoo~~ whole physical economy, are ~~kno~~ shattered with the wear & tear of travel, lecturing, ten thousand ~~puny~~ petty annoyances & vexations, & an unusual loss of sleep. When things get to going wrong, they keep it up. Yesterday afternoon I arrived at Cambridge & drove to the hotel through a driving storm of sleet—it was dreary & cold. ~~The~~ My spirits began to ebb. Then the Committee (with customary brilliancy of judgment,) informed me that the Troy *Times* had published my entire lecture, praising it highly, & using numberless dashes & hyphens to imitate my drawling manner of speaking——& further informed me that ~~ever~~ the *Times* had a large circulation in Cambridge. My spirits fell lower—my anger began to rise. I abused my informant in no minced language, for knowing no better than to *tell* me I was to talk to an audience to whom my speech would be no news. Then he left (to return after supper) & I was alone in my fury.[1] I opened your letter, & lo, even the darling of my heart could not be spared! You had received another shot upon that old, old subject whose bare mention by any lips but yours is getting to be sufficient to make my hair rise. For I am a full grown man, & with gray hairs in my head, & have all a man's repugnance to ~~bee~~ being ~~per~~

There I go again. Well, I had but little time to spare, & so I must have written as I felt—I must have copied my condition. And it was not a happy condition. In due time the Chairman returned, & at 7 the fire-bells rang, & he sprang to his feet & exclaimed, "My God, there is the lecture-hall in flames!"

Mentally I uttered a thanksgiving so fervent that if ever prayer of mine pierced the vault of Heaven that one did. I did not move from my chair, & so my wildly excited chairman halted in his mad flight to the door. I said: "You can see by the blinding glare from the windows that nothing can save your hall—why need you rush there for nothing?"

He cooled a little & sat down—& as the fires glowed through those tall windows my spirits came up till I felt that all I needed to be entirely happy was to see the Troy Times editors & this chairman locked up in that burning building.

But my rising spirits were crushed to earth, & exasperation came again. The house was saved. It was burned a little, & flooded with water. But within the hour they scrubbed & the floors, let out the smoke & warmed the place up again—& I lectured.[2]

Of course, after the lecture, a lot of committeemen invited them-selves to my room—although they knew I must rise at 7 in the morn-ing—& presently I grew cheerful & kept them there till 12 o'clock.

This morning the porter failed to call me. I woke, surprised to see it so light, looked at my watch—14 minutes to 8—train leaves at 8.05—depot 4 or 5 blocks distant—no vehicle in sight. Inside of 4 minutes I was not only fully dressed, but down stairs making trouble. The landlord[3] was crazy as a loon in 3 seconds—darted this way & that—yelled for a coach—tore his hair—swore at his porter, & was in despair—said the jig was up, & the best he could do was to take a buggy & drive me to Troy—30 miles—thermometer already below zero & growing steadily colder.

I said, "Collect your senses & don't go wild—~~show me~~ we have still 6 minutes—show me to the depot—run!" And he *did* run—ran a tol-erably good gate, but I beat him to the depot & jumped on the train—he arrived the next second with my hand-sachel & I was safe for Utica![4] Hurrah!

Don't grieve over anything I said ~~or a~~ about smoking, my poor child, but remember that in *all* moods I love you & honor you—no storm can ~~ruffle that~~ move the depths of that sea—& remember, also, that whenever, unbiased by any influence but your own ʃ calm, just & char-itable judgment, or your own dear, resistless desire, I am called upon to give up smoking, or any other habit of mine, I stand ready to do it—not reluctantly or churlishly, but cheerfully & with a loving whole=heartedness & devotion to your happiness, my Livy.

Peace be with you my precious wife.

                                          Sam.

P. S.—I talk in Fredonia, N. Y., Jan. 19.—(L. McKinstry.)[5]

[*in ink:*] Miss Olivia L. Langdon | Elmira | N. Y. [*return address:*] IF NOT DELIVERED WITHIN 10 DAYS, TO BE DELIVERED TO [*postmarked:*] TROY N.Y. JAN 14 3 PM. [*docketed by OLL:*] 177th

---

[1]Clemens indicated in the next paragraph that his informant was the com-mittee chairman (not further identified) of the Cambridge, New York, "Regular Lecture Course of 1869–70." Clemens's local contact, A. H. Comstock, was its corresponding secretary. Cambridge was only thirty miles northeast of Troy, where the synopsis of his 11 January lecture was published the next day ("Reg-ular Lecture Course of 1869–70," Cambridge *Washington County Post,* 7 Jan 70, 3; 10 Jan 70 to OLL [2nd]; "Mark Twain," Troy *Times,* 12 Jan 70, 3). Clemens

repeatedly complained of and tried to prevent such synopses (*L2*, 209; *L3*, 379–80, 392).

[2] The Cambridge *Washington County Post* reported that the janitor "had lit the chandelier which lights the hall, it being lowered by means of a rope and pulley to within about three feet of the floor for the purpose, and went into one of the dressing rooms to hoist it up. He took hold of the rope and began to pull when the chandelier fell to the floor. In an instant it was all ablaze" ("Narrow Escape from Conflagration of Ackley Concert Hall," 14 Jan 70, 3). The paper's report of the lecture gave Clemens's self-introduction verbatim and was replete with paraphrase and quotation, approximating the Troy *Times* synopsis. It noted that the "hall was well filled, notwithstanding the fire the fore part of the evening and the severe weather" ("Mark Twain's Lecture," 14 Jan 70, 3).

[3] Unidentified.

[4] That is, Clemens knew he would reach Troy in time to make connection to Utica, eighty-five miles northwest.

[5] Louis McKinstry (b. 1844) was secretary of the Fredonia Library Association, which sponsored Clemens's lecture. Since 1867 he had been co-publisher, with his father, Willard, of the Fredonia *Censor* ("Lecture Course of the Fredonia Library Association, '69–70," Fredonia *Censor*, 26 Jan 70, 4; *Chautauqua County*, 2:109–11; 28 Jan 71 to McKinstry, n. 1).

To Olivia L. Langdon
15 January 1870 • Utica, N.Y.
(MS: CU-MARK)

BAGG'S HOTEL.   T. R. PROCTOR & CO., PROPRIETORS.

UTICA, N. Y., Jan. 15, 1870.

You dear little rascal, why didn't you open & read Mrs. Hooker's letter? Can't I ever teach you to open & read any letter of mine that you happen to want to read? Especially if it be from a woman. Sometimes men write things to me that would offend my darling's eyes, & I would be sorry to have her read such—still, I want her to read *any* letter she chooses. That it is directed to *me*, gives my Other Self full authority to read it.[1]

Sweetheart, I am drawing the first thoroughly happy breaths I have enjoyed for some days—for I have been dreadfully harassed, annoyed, chafed & angered—but *now*, I do wish I could throw my arms about you & revel in the joy of your loved presence! *Now* I could listen to *any* proposed curtailment of my vicious pleasures you might broach, & without any rebellious chafings. Though darling, I never have chafed at *you*—I have only sorrowed that sins of mine should be visited upon *your* innocent head. It is so wrong, so uncharitable, so *unjust,* that you should be made to suffer for [what] *I* have done—you who never gave any one cause to hurt you.

Even now my pleasure is marred by the thought I have almost surely said things that caused you tears, in my last two feverish letters. But if so, hold no hard feeling against me, Livy dear, for I was not myself,—I could not, in cold blood, say anything to hurt you, in whose love I live, whose love is all that gives life a real zest to me, you who are the world itself, who are all in all to me—w̶ & who would take with you the sunshine, & all the glory & beauty of earth & life, if I lost you.

We had a noble house to-night (Oh, it is bitter, bitter cold & blustery!)—the largest of the season, they believe, though they cannot tell till they count the tickets to-morrow.[2] And I saw at a glance that it was a house wholly friendly & in sympathy with me; & so, as in Portland, I stood patient & silent, minute after minute, apparently, till my roused good-nature passed from my heart ˄& countenance˄ to theirs along a thousand invisible electrical currents &̶ ̶s̶w̶e̶p̶t̶ & conquered their reserve, swept their self-possession to the winds, & the h̶o̶u̶s̶e̶ great house "came down" like an avalanche! No man knows better than I, the enormous value of a whole-hearted welcome achieved without a spoken word—and no man will t̶a̶k̶e̶ d̶o̶ dare more than I to get it. An audience captured in that way, *belongs* to the speaker, body & soul, for the rest of the evening. Therefore, isn't it worth the taking some perilous chances on? I enjoyed myself prodigiously for an hour & ten minutes & then dismissed a stormy house. I think I may say it was b̶u̶l̶l̶y̶ jolly.[3]

I saw Taylor[4] & his wife. Taylor is to call on me in the morning.

All right, honey—I will be there at the reception—will write my sister to hurry up & get there by the 24th or 25[th.]

God bless & preserve you, darling.

Sam.

I am so glad the Milton[5] pleases my idol—I am delighted. Oh, we'll read, & look at pictures when we are married!

Shall send you Mrs. Hooker's letter as soon as I have answered it. Give my l̶o̶v̶e̶ warm love to mother & father of ours, & sister Crane.

✉——————————————————————————

Miss Olivia L. Langdon | Elmira | N. Y. [*return address:*] IF NOT DELIVERED WITHIN 10 DAYS, TO BE DELIVERED TO [*postmarked:*] UTICA N.Y. JAN 15 [*docketed by OLL:*] 178th

[1] Isabella Beecher Hooker's letter has not been found. A good friend of the Langdons', she had a somewhat strained acquaintance with Clemens. He had previously urged Olivia to freely read his letters and even proofs (10 Jan 70 to OLL [2nd]; *L3*, 135 n. 3, 136, 140–41, 161–64, 172–73).

[2] Clemens was writing after his 14 January Utica lecture, and probably after the usual visit from the lecture committee, so it is likely that the time was after midnight, making the date 15 January, as inscribed.

[3] In Utica Clemens lectured for the Mechanics' Association. The Utica *Observer* of 15 January remarked that "from the first appearance of the lecturer upon the stage, to the close of the lecture, the audience were kept in as good humor as they are while reading one of his inimitable sketches," but it did not comment on Clemens's "patient & silent" opening ("Mark Twain," 14 and 15 Jan 70, 3). He must have described a similar opening to his December lecture in Portland, Maine, in a letter to Olivia that is now lost (*L3*, 479, 485). The Portland reviewers were complimentary, but also said nothing about the opening ("M. L. A.": Portland *Advertiser*, 23 Dec 69, 4; Portland *Eastern Argus*, 23 Dec 69, 3; Portland *Press*, 23 Dec 69, 3; "The Lecturer," Portland *Transcript*, 1 Jan 70, 317).

[4] Ezekiel D. Taylor, Jr., city editor of the Utica *Morning Herald*, Olivia's first cousin ("Obituary," Elmira *Advertiser*, 17 Feb 72, 4).

[5] See 6 Jan 70 to OLL, n. 2.

To Pamela A. Moffett
15 January 1870 • Utica, N.Y.
(MS: NPV)

BAGG'S HOTEL.   T. R. PROCTOR & CO., PROPRIETORS.

UTICA, N. Y., Jan. 15 1870.

My Dear Sister—

Am in a great hurry. Forwarded a check for $500 to Ma the other day,[1] & also took the liberty to send you $100 to pay your Railway fares with. I believe I wrote Mrs. Fairbanks that you would send your card to her from the Kennard House, Cleveland—but unhappily, she will no doubt be in Connecticut, then, with her husband & eldest daughter. However, you might send up to the Herald office & find out. His name is A. W. Fairbanks.[2]

Hurry up, Pamela, you & Annie, & get to Elmira by the 24th or 25th if you can. Telegraph me or Mr. Langdon ~~what~~ from Cleveland or Salamanca, or somewhere, what hour you will reach Elmira.[3] I shall be there by the 22d, to remain. I take no more lecture engagements after 21st.

We had an enormous house here to-night. And we had a splendid time. I guess I could get engagements enough to last the rest of the year if I wanted them or could stand the fatigue.

I enclose a note from Tom Fitch by which Orion will see that Tom is moving in the matter. Let Orion drop him simply a line, thanking him.[4]

Love to all of you, every one. Livy & the rest instruct me to remember them warmly to all of you.

Affectionately
Sam.

[1] Jane Clemens received this check on 6 January (JLC, 4).

[2] The Fairbankses either did not go on, or had already returned from, their trip when Pamela and Annie reached Cleveland (see 7 Jan 70 to Fairbanks). Years later Annie's son, Samuel C. Webster, recalled:

> Annie and Pamela stopped off at Cleveland and stayed with Mrs. Fairbanks for three days. This was Annie's first trip East, and she always thought of Mrs. Fairbanks as her first Eastern acquaintance. She was charmed with her good sense and informality, just as Uncle Sam had been. (*MTBus*, 107)

[3] In a ledger entry for 24 January, Jane Clemens noted: "M. &. A started Y N Y" (JLC, 11). ("M." stood for "Mela," a family nickname for Pamela.) If they reached Chicago that same day, remained "a whole 24 hours" as Clemens advised (7 Jan 70 to Fairbanks), then went to Cleveland on 26 January and visited "for three days" (27, 28, and 29 January), they would not have arrived in Elmira until 30 January. Salamanca, New York, was about 160 miles east of Cleveland and 100 miles west of Elmira.

[4] The "matter" was Orion Clemens's alleged overpayment in 1863–64, as secretary of Nevada Territory, for the printing of the laws and documents of the territorial legislature. In June 1869, R. W. Taylor, comptroller of the United States Treasury Department, had begun pressing Orion for repayment of $1,330.08 (*L3*, 388 n. 1). The enclosure from Thomas Fitch, a Nevada acquaintance of the Clemens brothers' and now the Republican congressman from Nevada, has not been found. But Fitch must have reported his recent attempt to intervene on Orion's behalf, evidently at Clemens's request. On 5 January, in his official capacity, Fitch had written to Taylor:

> I have the honor to enclose a communication from Mr Orion Clemens formerly Secretary of Nevada Territory, and to say that I have no doubt of the truth of the statements made by Mr Clemens. I was editor of the Virginia City Union in 1863 and a portion of 1864 and can vouch for the accuracy of his representations with regard to the price of printers labor and materials. I hope that you will afford to Mr Clemens any relief in your power not inconsistent with the interests of the department.

Orion's "communication," dated 3 January 1870, was also addressed to Taylor. In it he again explained the "embarrassing peculiarities of my position in Nevada Territory," which had kept him from obeying "to the letter" the Treasury Department's guidelines for payment to printers, its prohibition of advance payments, its insistence that printing be done within the territory even if it could be done more cheaply elsewhere, and its requirement that work be paid for in "greenbacks" rather than gold. "I hope you will see the dilemma I was placed in," Orion concluded, "and appreciate the fact that human nature, with the best intentions, was liable to make some mistakes; and equally liable to have motives misconstrued and actions misunderstood" (Fitch and Orion Clemens letters in "Territorial Letters Received," transcriptions in CU-MARK, courtesy of Robert D. Armstrong). The available records do not indicate if Taylor granted relief to Orion (Armstrong, 47 n. 52).

To Olivia L. Langdon
20 January 1870 • Hornellsville, N.Y.
(MS: CU-MARK)

Hornellsville, 20th.

My child, I am within sixty miles of you, & so I *do* feel that your unseen presen/ce is stronger about me than when you are away at the other side of a State—but further than this, your proximity does not benefit me, little one, but on the contrary is rather a matter to growl at, Because it only makes me want the more to see you, without giving me the opportunity. I cannot right truly say I haven't the opportunity, either, for I *could* be with you at this moment, & remain with you half a day, & then run up here in time. But I am not going to have my Jubilee of joy at having *finished* the lectures for good & all, ta & my other Jubilee of joy in the reflection that I am with you never more to part again in life, marred & diluted by a little unsatisfying taste of the holiday & glimpse of you, my darling. No, sir—I want the enfranchisement from worry & work to be *complete*, & the joining company with you, to my child, to be just as complete,, perfect & lasting.

I left Buffalo at 4 PM yesterday, & went to Dunkirk, & thence out to Fredonia by horse-car, ,(3 miles), rattled my lecture through, took horse-car again & just caught 9.45 ʄ P.M. train bound east—sat up & smoked to Salamanca (midn (12.30,) stripped & went to bed in a sleeping car till two hours & a half, & then got up & came ashore here at 3 o'clock this morning,—& had a strong temptation to lie still an hour or two longer & go to Elmira. But I resisted it. By coming through in the night, I saved myself 2 hours extra travel.[1]

Sweetheart, tomorrow you must go into the wardrobe in my room

& burrow into those pasteboard boxes & get out a new shirt, & an un-
dershirt & drawers, & put them on the bed I am to sleep in when I get
home—*provided* I am to stay in Charley's room or the front chamber. But
if I am to occupy the room these clothes are now in, of course you need
not bother with them. And before you go to bed tomorrow night you
must write a note, telling me how to get into the house & what bed to
take—& you must put that note in the newspaper box at the side gate,
so that I can get it when I arrive. Those are your orders, Livy darling, &
you will be court-martialed if you don't obey them.

We did have a most delightful audience at Fredonia, & I was just as
happy as a lord from the first word of the lecture to the last. I thought it
was about as good a lecture as I ever listened to—but some of the serious
passages were impromptu—never been written.[2]

This, my precious Livy, is the last letter of a correspondence that
has lasted seventeen months—the pleasantest correspondence I ever
had a share in. For over two months of the time, we wrote every other
day. During the succeeding twelve months we have written *every* day
that we have been parted from each other. And no man ever did have a
dearer, more faithful little correspondent than you have been to me, my
heart's darling. Your letters have made one ray of sunlight & created a
thrill of pleasure in every one of these long-drawn days, howsoever
dreary the day was otherwise. And so I thank you & bless you now, once
more, as I have thanked you & blessed you all these days. And I pray for
you, even as I have done with the closing in of each night, ever since you
moved my spirit to prayer seventeen months ago. This is the last long
correspondence we ever shall have, my Livy—& now ~~it~~ on this day it
~~ceases~~ passes forever from its honored place among our daily occupations, & becomes a *memory.* A memory to be laid reverently away in the
~~re~~ holy of holies of our hearts & cherished as a sacred thing. A memory
whose mementoes will be ~~sacred~~ precious while we live, & sacred when
either one shall die.[3]

They[4] have come for me, my sweet Livy.

                                        Good-bye & God bless you,
                                                              Sam.

————————————————————————————————

Miss Olivia L. Langdon | Elmira | N. Y. [*return address:*] OSBORNE HOUSE,
H. HUNT, PROPRIETOR, HORNELLSVILLE, N. Y. FIRST-CLASS HOTEL. OPPOSITE DEPOT.
[*postmarked:*] HORNELLSVILLE N.Y. JAN 20 [*docketed by OLL:*] 184th

[1] Five letters that Clemens wrote to Olivia between 15 and 19 January (docket numbers 179–83) are lost. During that interval he lectured in Oswego (15 January), Baldwinsville (17 January), Ogdensburg (18 January), and Fredonia (19 January). Early on the morning of 19 January, he departed Ogdensburg for Buffalo, where he tried in vain to meet with John D. F. Slee, Jervis Langdon's business associate, who had agreed to find a suitable boarding house for him and Olivia (see p. 45). He may also have looked in at the offices of the Buffalo *Express* before continuing on to Dunkirk, New York, on Lake Erie, and from there to Fredonia. By the time he reached Hornellsville at 3 A.M. on 20 January, he had lectured twice (at Ogdensburg and Fredonia) and traveled more than 350 miles, all within thirty-one hours. After lecturing in Hornellsville on 20 January, he had to travel 80 miles west to Jamestown, where he concluded his tour the following evening, then immediately made the 125-mile trip east to Elmira (*L3*, 480, 486).

[2] The Fredonia *Censor* praised the lecture and described the effect of its "serious passages": "Mr. Clemens incorporated enough good sense and interesting information with the fun in his lecture on the Sandwich Islands to prevent any regrets over an evening spent merely for nonsense, and the jokes were consequently the more enjoyed." Clemens again employed the "patient & silent" opening he had used on 14 January in Utica, for the *Censor* remarked: "Imagine a lean, cadaverous looking speaker, standing upon the platform for five minutes like a school boy who has forgotten his 'piece,' and then drawling out with ministerial gravity his own introduction, because the Chairmen of Lecture Committees never introduced him 'strong enough' " ("Mark Twain's lecture . . . ," 26 Jan 70, 3).

[3] For a calendar of Clemens's courtship letters, and the only letter from Olivia known to survive from that period, see *L3*, 393–94 n. 1 and 473–80.

[4] The Hornellsville lecture committee. Clemens's performance was judged "a fizzle" ("Mark Twain's lecture . . . ," Hornellsville *Tribune*, 28 Jan 70, 3).

To Elisha Bliss, Jr.
22 January 1870 • Elmira, N.Y.
(MS: CU-MARK)

Elmira, Jan. 22ₜ, 1870.

Friend Bliss—

Our boys in Buffalo wrote you something about a ratio of prices for clubs & books, &c., & they are anxious to get an answer—been waiting 2 or 3 weeks. Tell them about it. They are much pleased with your sending their bills & circulars to your agents.[1]

I don't copyright the "Round the World" letters because it don't hurt anything to be well advertised—& these are getting pretty well advertised—but you see out of 50 letters not more than 6 ˌor 10ˌ will be copied into any *one* newspaper—& *that* don't hurt.²

I mean to take plenty of time & pains with the Noah's Ark book— maybe it will be several years before it is *all* written—but it will be a perfect lightning-striker when it *is* done.³ ~~I wish~~ You can have the *first say** on that or *any other* book I may prepare for the press. As long as you deal in a fair, open & honorable way with *me*, I do not think you will ever find me doing otherwise with *you*.

I wish Fairbanks would keep still about that Noah's Ark book— somebody will steal the idea from me. I had no business ever mentioning it to a man of his limitless gab.⁴

I am prosecuting Webb in the N. Y. Courts—think the result will be that he will yield up the copyright & plates of the Jumping Frog, if I let him off from paying me money. Then I shall break up those plates, & prepare a new vol. of Sketches, but on a different & more "taking" model.⁵

I can get a book ready for you any time you want it—but you *can't* want one before this time next year—& so I have plenty of time.

I wish you could have the quarterly statement here *by Feb. 1*—be-cause we are to be married *Feb. 2*, & would like to know what we are doing it on, & whether we can afford it or not. But no matter—if it isn't ready then, forward it to Buffalo. We leave for Buffalo at noon, Feb. 3. You may *telegraph the amount* to us here, Feb. 1ˢᵗ or 2ᵈ—that is what I chiefly want to know. I have been keeping fine large stories afloat about our sales.⁶

Miss Nellie did no harm, in opening the letter.⁷

Yrs Truly

Sam*ˡ*. L. Clemens.

*That is plain enough.

[*letter docketed:*] √ auth [*and*] Mark Twain | Jan 22/70

¹Bliss soon asked Clemens for another copy of this proposal from the Buffalo *Express* "boys" (28 Jan 70 to Bliss). The earliest evidence of his reply to it was an 18 February advertisement for the Buffalo *Weekly Express* that offered terms to clubs (groups of subscribers), ranging from a single extra copy of the paper, up to reduced rates for fifty subscribers and a free copy of *The Innocents Abroad* "to each person who raises a club of 20 or more new subscribers." The same advertisement also called for agents to sell *Innocents* "in every town and district of the United States and Canada" ("The Press," Buffalo *Express*, 18 Feb 70, 3).

²Clemens's "Around the World" letters began appearing in the Buffalo *Ex-*

press on Saturdays in late 1869. Seven letters had appeared to date; one final letter by Clemens appeared on 29 January, followed by two from Darius R. Ford, on 12 February and 5 March. Most of Clemens's letters were devoted to western memories and were soon absorbed into the manuscript of *Roughing It* (*L3*, 360–61 n. 5; SLC 1869k, m–n, q–r, 1870i, k–*l;* Ford 1870a–b; *RI 1993*, 805–6).

³Clemens first planned a "Deluge" or "Noah's Ark" book in 1866, produced "70 or 80 pages of it" by late June 1869, and returned to it fitfully throughout his life without managing to complete it (*L3*, 312, 313 n. 3, 313–14 n. 7).

⁴Clemens had last seen Abel Fairbanks in Cleveland in mid-July 1869, when he might have told him about the "Noah's Ark book" (*L3*, 281 n. 4). Fairbanks's "limitless gab" could allude to a report in the *Herald*, but none has been found.

⁵*The Celebrated Jumping Frog of Calaveras County, And other Sketches* (New York: C. H. Webb, 1867) had been a disappointment on several counts, especially its lack of royalties (*L2*, 39–40, 48–49 n. 1, 58 n. 1, 369–70). Since Webb had copyrighted the book in his own name, Clemens wished to secure his rights to its contents, and to prevent Webb from reissuing it, before proceeding with his own plans. Probably late in 1869, he hired a lawyer, but no evidence of court proceedings has been found (26 Nov 70 to Webb; Feinstein, 12–14). For an account of the *Jumping Frog* book, see *ET&S1*, 503–46.

⁶Royalty payments for *The Innocents Abroad* were due Clemens at the end of October, January, April, and July. Mary Mason Fairbanks had printed one "fine large" story about sales (7 Jan 70 to Fairbanks, n. 8). Whitelaw Reid's New York *Tribune* printed another on 15 January: "The American Publishing Company of Hartford inform us that they have sold 45,000 copies of Mark Twain's 'Innocents Abroad,' and are now running six presses to keep up with the demand for the book" ("New Publications," 8). That report was reprinted in the Hartford *Times* on 17 January ("Literary Announcements," 2) and in the Jamestown *Journal* on 28 January, a week after Clemens's lecture there ("Literary Items," 4). By the end of January, total sales were 6,000 short of the reported figure (28 Jan 70 to Bliss, n. 5).

⁷Miss Nellie (last name unknown) was evidently a clerk for Bliss at this time. She became a typesetter on *Sketches, New and Old* (1875) and *The Adventures of Tom Sawyer* (1876) (5 Nov 70 to OC; *ET&S1*, 642; *TS*, 512).

To James N. Gillis
26 January 1870 • Elmira, N.Y.
(MS facsimile: CU-MARK)

Elmira, N. Y., Jan. 26,/70.

Dear Jim—¹

I remember that old night just as well! And somewhere among my relics I have your remembrancer stored away.² It makes my heart ache yet to call to mind some of those days. Still, it shouldn't—for right in the depths of their poverty & their pocket-hunting vagabondage lay the germ of my coming good-fortune. You remember the one gleam of jollity that shot across our dismal sojourn in the rain & mud of Angel's Camp— I mean that day we sat around the tavern stove & heard that chap tell about the frog & how they filled him with shot. And you remember how we quoted from the yarn & laughed over it, out there on the hillside while you & dear old Stoker panned & washed. I jotted the story down in my note-book that day, & would have been glad to get ten or fifteen dollars for it—I was just that blind. But then we were *so* hard up. I published that story, & it became widely known in America, India, China, England,—& the reputation it made for me has paid me thousands & thousands of dollars since.[3] Four or five months ago I bought into that Express (have ordered it sent to you as long as you live—& if the bookkeeper ~~bill~~ sends you any bills, you let me hear of it) & went heavily in debt[4]—never could have dared to do that, Jim, if we hadn't heard the Jumping Frog story that day.

And wouldn't I love to take old Stoker by the hand, & wouldn't I love to see him in his great specialty, his wonderful rendition of "Rinaldo" in the "Burning Shame!" Where *is* Dick, & what is he doing? Give him my fervent love & warm old remembrances.[5]

A week from to-day I shall be married—to a girl even better than Mahala,[6] & lovelier than the peerless "Chapparal Quails."[7] You can't come so far, Jim, but still I cordially *invite* you to come, anyhow—& I invite Dick, too. And if you two boys *were* to land here on that pleasant occasion, we would make you right royally welcome.

The young lady is Miss Olivia L. Langdon—(for you would naturally like to know her name.)

Remember me to the boys—& recollect, Jim, that whenever you or Dick shall chance to stumble into Buffalo, we shall always have a knife & fork for you, & an honest welcome.

Truly Your Friend
Sam*ˡ*. L. Clemens.

P. S. California plums *are* good, Jim—particularly when they are stewed.[8]

Do they continue to name all the young Injuns after me—when you pay them for the compliment?

<hr>

[1] James Norman Gillis (1830–1907) was a native of Georgia. In 1848 he received a diploma from the Botanico-Medical College in Memphis, Tennessee,

which trained practitioners of herbal medicine. The following year he arrived in San Francisco and set off for the gold mines of Calaveras County. After two years of mining, he began ranching near Sacramento, continuing at that for most of the succeeding eleven years. In 1862 he moved to Tuolumne County, where he settled in a cabin on Jackass Hill, near Tuttletown, and resumed mining. He spent the rest of his life in the area, except for occasional visits to San Francisco, where his parents lived and in the mid-1860s were acquainted with Clemens. According to Dan De Quille (William Wright), Jim Gillis was the "Thoreau of the Sierras," a devoted naturalist who was "not only a thorough English scholar, but also well versed in Greek and Latin." He was, in addition,

> acknowledged to be the most expert and successful pocket miner in California—indeed he is the father of all the pocket mines. He was the first to discover the laws that govern that kind of mining and reduce the business to a science. He now has eight mines running in California and every one paying. (William Wright 1891)

It was while visiting San Francisco late in 1864 that Gillis met Clemens, who already knew his younger brother Steve (1838–1918). In financial straits, Clemens was anxious to avoid having to honor a $500 bail bond he had posted for Steve, who had been arrested for injuring a bartender in a fight and had fled to Nevada to avoid prosecution. He therefore accompanied Jim Gillis to his cabin on Jackass Hill. Joined also by Gillis's partner, Dick Stoker, and the youngest Gillis brother, William (1840–1929), he spent much of the next three months there and in nearby Angel's Camp ("James N. Gillis—His Life and Death," Sonora [Calif.] *Sierra Times*, 14 Apr 1907, clipping in CU-MARK; Fulton, 54–55; Gillis, 53–58; De Ferrari 1964, 107–8; Evans et al.; Norwood, 416–19; *L1*, 313–14 n. 3). Clemens described his visit to the region in chapters 60 and 61 of *Roughing It*, making one character, a miner "who had had a university education," a loose amalgam of Gillis and Stoker, and recreating Gillis's tall tale about Dick Baker and his cat, Tom Quartz (*RI 1993*, 412–20, 703–5).

[2]Clemens probably recalled the following occasion, described in his notebook for 1865: "New Years night 1865, at Vallecito, magnificent lunar rainbow, first appearing at 8PM—moon at first quarter—very light drizzling rain" (*N&J1*, 69). The same notebook may identify the "remembrancer": "(New Year 1865 (watch-ȳkey to be returned to James N. Gillis, care Major A Gillis, 12 m apres date" (*N&J1*, 68).

[3]For Clemens's Jumping Frog note, see *N&J1*, 80. For an account of the writing and reception of the story, see *ET&S2*, 262–72.

[4]See *L3*, 294 n. 2.

[5]Jacob Richard Stoker (1820–98), Gillis's partner and cabinmate, was originally from Kentucky. In 1849, after fighting in the Mexican War, he joined the gold rush, settling on Jackass Hill, where he spent the rest of his life as a pocket miner (*RI 1993*, 704–5). Stoker was Clemens's prototype for Dick Baker, owner of the cat Tom Quartz, in chapter 61 of *Roughing It*. He was also a willing foil for Gillis, whom Clemens later called "a born humorist and a very competent one":

> Every now and then Jim would have an inspiration, and he would stand up before the great log fire, with his back to it and his hands crossed behind him, and deliver himself of an elaborate impromptu lie—a fairy-tale, an extravagant romance,—with Dick Stoker as the hero of it, as a general thing. Jim always soberly, pretended that what he was relating was strictly history—veracious history, not romance. Dick Stoker, gray-headed and good-natured, would sit smoking his pipe and listen with a sweet gentle, serenity to these monstrous fabrications and never utter a protest. In one of my books—"Huck-

leberry Finn," I think—I have used one of Jim's impromptu tales, which Jim ˌheˌ called "The Tragedy of the Burning Shame." I had to modify it considerably to make it proper for print, and this was a great damage. As Jim told it—inventing it as he went along—I think it was one of the most outrageously funny things I have ever listened to. How mild it is in the book, and how pale; how extravagant and how gorgeous in its unprintable form! I used another of Jim's impromptus in a book of mine called "The Tramp Abroad," a tale of how the poor innocent and ignorant woodpeckers tried to fill up a house with acorns. . . . I used another of Jim's inventions in one of my books—the story of Jim [i.e., Dick] Baker's cat, the remarkable Tom Quartz. Jim Baker was Dick Stoker, of course; Tom Quartz had never existed; there was no such cat—at least outside of Jim Gillis's imagination. (AD, 26 May 1907, in *MTE*, 360–62)

See chapters 22 and 23 of *Huckleberry Finn* and chapter 3 of *A Tramp Abroad*.

  [6]Unidentified. Possibly a nickname, *mahala,* meaning "squaw," deriving from the Yokut word for "women." The Yokuts lived in the San Joaquin Valley and the adjacent Sierra Nevada, near Gillis's haunts.

  [7]Phenila (or Phenelia; Nellie) and Mary (Mollie) Griswold were eighteen and fifteen, respectively, when Clemens knew them. They lived with their mother, Margaret Griswold, and her second husband, Nehemiah John Daniels, on a ranch near Mormon Creek, close to Jackass Hill, and so were commonly called "the Daniels girls," although they never formally adopted that surname (Hood, 23; Carlo M. De Ferrari, personal communication; De Ferrari 1984a). Because their home was adjacent to a dense growth of chaparral and because, as William R. Gillis explained in 1924, they were "so pretty and plump," the sisters were known as the "Chaparral Quails." Gillis recalled an occasion when Clemens accompanied him on a visit to them:

> When we got there Sam suggested that we take a walk, and so we started out. We knew of some late clingstone peaches growing on Black Creek, two miles away, so we walked over and got some. When he started back Mol[lie] said, "I know a trail through the chemisal that will cut off half the distance." So we took it, and went a long way before we discovered that we were lost. We had to get down on our hands and knees and crawl through the chaparral. Then we decided to give up and go back and around the long way.
>
> It was nearly midnight when we got home, and Mrs. Daniels was furious. She gave us a good tongue lashing, and she directed most of it at Sam. He said: "Mrs. Daniels, it wasn't my fault, it was Billie's fault[.]" She said:
>
> "Mr. Clemens, Mr. Gillis has been walking with the girls a hundred times, and this never happened before. Besides, you are older and ought to have better sense."
>
> "I'm very sorry," Sam said, "and I promise you it won't happen again. But now we are tired and hungry. We are almost starved."
>
> "Well, you'll get nothing to eat in this house tonight!" said Mrs. Daniels.
>
> Just then Sam saw Miss Nellie's guitar in a corner of the room. He picked it up and began playing, and presently he sang "Fly Away Moth" and then "Araby's Daughter." He sang very softly. Mrs. Daniels listened, and presently her face softened. When he was through she left the room and went out in the kitchen. In a few minutes we heard a chicken squawk, and a little later we fell to on hot biscuit and fried chicken and coffee.
>
> As we were walking home Sam said to me: "Billie, you've read the old saying, 'music hath charms to soothe the savage breast.' You've seen how it soothed that savage old lady. If you have any talent for music, cultivate it." (West, 18)

Clemens himself remembered the sisters in "The Innocents Adrift," written in 1891:

> . . . "Chapparal Quails." That was their pet name in the mountains where they lived. They were sisters, seventeen & eighteen years old, respectively; beautiful creatures,

clean-minded, good-hearted, well meaning, favorites with old & young; yet they could outswear Satan. It was the common speech of that remote & thinly settled region, they had come by it naturally, & if there was any harm in it they were not aware of it. (SLC 1891, 106–7†)

For an example of their swearing, see *N&J1*, 69.

[8] In 1907 Clemens described an instance when Gillis's "energetic imagination got him into trouble." A squaw offered to sell him "some wild fruit that looked like large green gages." Dick Stoker, who "knew that that product was worthless and inedible," nevertheless "heedlessly, and without purpose" remarked that "he had never heard of it before":

> That was enough for Jim. He launched out with fervent praises of that devilish fruit, and the more he talked about it the warmer and stronger his admiration of it grew. He said that he had eaten it a thousand times; that all one needed to do was to boil it with a little sugar and there was nothing on the American continent that could compare with it for deliciousness. He was only talking to hear himself talk; and so he was brought up standing, and for just one moment, or maybe two moments, smitten, dumb, when Dick interrupted him with the remark that ~~what he was saying was all a lie, and that~~ if the fruit was so delicious why didn't he invest in it on the spot?

Trapped, Gillis bought the fruit and proceeded to boil it for two hours, adding "handful after handful of sugar" while Clemens and Stoker stood by

> laughing at him, ridiculing him, deriding him, blackguarding him all the while, and he retaining his serenity unruffled. At last he said the manufacture had reached the right stage, the stage of perfection. He dipped his spoon, tasted, smacked his lips, and broke into enthusiasms of ~~contentment~~; grateful joy; then he gave us a taste apiece. From all that we could discover, those tons of sugar had not affected that fruit's malignant sharpness in the least degree. Acid? It was all acid, vindictive acid, uncompromising acid. . . . We stopped with that one taste, but that great-hearted Jim, that dauntless martyr, went on sipping and sipping, and sipping, and praising and praising, and praising, and praising, until his teeth and tongue were raw, and Stoker and I nearly dead with gratitude and delight. During the next two days neither food nor drink passed Jim's teeth; so sore were they that, they could not endure the touch of anything; even his breath passing over them made him wince; nevertheless he went steadily on voicing his adulations of that brutal, mess and praising God. It was an astonishing exhibition of grit, but Jim was like all the other Gillises, he was made of grit. (AD, 26 May 1907, in *MTE*, 362–64)

To James Redpath
26 January 1870 • Elmira, N.Y.
(Paraphrase: AAA 1924, lot 530)

530. CLEMENS (SAMUEL L.) Autograph Letter Signed: "*Clemens.*" 3pp. 8vo, Elmira, Jan. 26, 1870. To James Redpath.

A FINE LETTER, in which Clemens mentions that he is to be married in a week, and must therefore economise.

To Elisha Bliss, Jr.
28 January 1870 • Elmira, N.Y.
(MS: CU-MARK)

Elmira, Jan. 28.

Friend Bliss—

I want you to do just as á you please with that Evans. I wash my hands of him. I guess he is just as likely to be a "beat" as anything else— though fools are so cheap & so plenty that I had placed him in that catalogue, for charity's sake.[1]

I re-enclose the Express letter, as you desire. I only meant you to correspond with our people about it. I never bother or meddle with the concern's *business* matters—& ought to have told *them* to write you, & not shove it off on to *my* shoulders. I don't care two cents about the concern's business. And what I want *you* there for, is because I want a man who can *run* the business department without boring anybody else with it.[2] I hate business.

Yes, I *am* satisfied with the way you are running the book. You are running it in staving, tip-top, first-class style. I never wander into ý any corner of the country but I find that aný agent has been there before me, & many of that community have read the book. And on an average about ten people a day come & hunt me up to thank me & tell me I'm a benefactor!! I guess that is a part of the programme we didn't expect, in the first place.

Indeed *I* don't want to bother with booksellers or anybody else. That chap in Buffalo wanted me to speak a word to you for him, & I said I was too lazy—& if he would make Larned[3] write the letter, I would endorse, w it, whether it were true or false. And I did. But when I saw a great stack of "Innocents" in his bookstore, next d an hour or so afterward, I was rather sorry I did.[4]

January & Dec. have November didn't pan out as well as December—for you remember you had sold 12,000 copies in December when Twichell & I were there on the 27ᵗʰ or 28ᵗʰ. But $4,000 is pretty gorgeous. One don't pick that up often, with a book. It is the next best thing to lecturing.[5]

I think you are rushing this book in a manner to be proud of; & you will make the finest success of it that has ever been made with a subscription book, I believe. What with advertising, establishing agencies, &c., you have got an enormous lot of machinery ~~to~~ under way & hard at work in a wonderfully short ~~p~~ space of time. It is easy to see, when one travels around, that one must be endowed with a deal of genuine generalship in order to maneuvre a ~~volume~~ publication whose line of battle stretches from end to end of a great continent, & whose foragers & ~~sh~~ skirmishers invest every hamlet & ~~bel~~ besiege every village hidden away in all the vast space between.

    I'll back you against any publisher in America, Bliss—or elsewhere.

Yrs as Ever

Clemens.

[*letter docketed:*] √ [*and*] Mark Twain | Jany 28/70 [*and*] Mark Twain | Jany 28/70

  [1] Albert S. Evans (1831–72), originally from New Hampshire, was the city editor and local reporter of the San Francisco *Alta California* and also a correspondent for the Chicago *Tribune* and the New York *Tribune*. Between 1864 and 1866, corresponding for the Gold Hill *Evening News* under the name "Amigo," Evans engaged with Clemens, the local reporter for the San Francisco *Morning Call* and then the San Francisco correspondent for the Virginia City *Territorial Enterprise*, in a war of published insults and personal attacks informed by genuine bad feeling on both sides. Throughout their running feud Clemens referred to Evans contemptuously as "Stiggers" or as "Fitz Smythe," borrowing the names of the comic foils Evans created in his columns. Presumably the well-publicized commercial success of *The Innocents Abroad* had led Evans to approach the American Publishing Company with a book proposal, and Bliss had in turn asked Clemens for comment. Later in 1870, Bliss did publish Evans's *Our Sister Republic: A Gala Trip Through Tropical Mexico in 1869–70*. Evans died aboard the steamer *Missouri*, which burned at sea en route from New York to Havana on 22 October 1872 (*ET&S2*, 39–40, 329, 336; Smith and Anderson, 17–47; Evans 1866a–c; 29 Oct 70 to Bliss, n. 2; "Col. Albert S. Evans," San Francisco *Illustrated Press* 1 [Jan 73]: 6; "Horrors of Travel," New York *Tribune*, 31 Oct 72, 1).

  [2] See 22 Jan 70 to Bliss, n. 1. Clemens's notion that Bliss should help manage the *Express* resulted from dissatisfaction with its profitability. He remained uneasy about the paper's financial condition for at least a month (23 Feb 70 to Bliss; 2 and 3 Mar 70 to Langdon; 13 May 70 to Langdon).

  [3] Josephus N. Larned.

  [4] Sale of *Innocents* by a bookstore for less than the standard price threatened the income of Bliss's subscription agents. The Buffalo bookseller has not been identified.

[5]Bliss had sent at least a preliminary reply to Clemens's 22 January request for the second quarter (1 Nov 69–31 Jan 70) royalties on *Innocents*. Bliss's royalty check for $4,309.42, dated three days after this letter (NN-B), represented sales of some 23,500 copies. Total sales since publication were about 39,000; total royalties about $7,404 (Hirst 1975, 314, 316).

To Joseph H. Twichell
per Telegraph Operator
28–31 January 1870 • Elmira, N.Y.
(MTBus, 108)

I *have* invited the Blisses.[1]

[1]According to Samuel C. Webster, Annie Moffett's son:

> One of the incidents of the pre-wedding days that my mother remembers is that Uncle Sam received a telegram from Hartford from Mr. Twichell: "You haven't invited the Blisses." It was through Mr. Bliss, his publisher, that Mark Twain had met Mr. Twichell, who became a lifelong friend. He immediately sent a telegram to the Blisses with the invitation, and another to Mr. Twichell, which read: "I *have* invited the Blisses." (*MTBus,* 108)

The exchange of telegrams (none of the originals is known to survive) has not been precisely dated, but Annie probably could not have been on hand to witness it before 28 January. Elisha and Amelia Bliss did not attend the wedding (15 Jan 70 to PAM, n. 3; 23 Feb 70 to Bliss, n. 1). For Clemens's introduction to Twichell by Amelia, see *L2,* 269 n. 4.

NO LETTERS are known to survive for about a week—from the end of January until 6 February, four days after Clemens and Olivia Langdon were married. The wedding took place on the evening of Wednesday, 2 February, at the Langdon home at 21 Main Street, Elmira. The presiding clergymen were Thomas K. Beecher of Congregational Church, and Joseph H. Twichell of the Asylum Hill Congregational Church in Hartford. According to Albert Bigelow Paine, "the guests were not numerous, not more than a hundred at most" (*MTB,* 1:394). One of the guests, Almira Hutchinson Munson, a childhood friend of Jervis Langdon's and now an Elmira neighbor, noted in her diary: "I think there were about 75 present" (Jerome and Wisbey 1990, 4; Munson's figure might actually read "95," however). The family contingent included, in addition to Olivia's parents: Susan L. Crane, Olivia's foster sister, and her husband, Theodore; Anna M. Crane (1838–1916), Theodore's unmarried half-sister; probably Eunice Ford, Olivia's eighty-seven-year-old paternal grandmother; Olivia's first cousins Edward L. Marsh and Anna Marsh Brown, children of Olivia Lewis Langdon's twin sister, Louisa Lewis (Mrs. Sheppard) Marsh; Anna Marsh Brown's husband Talmage, a Des Moines lawyer, paving contractor, and business associate of Jervis Langdon's whom Clemens later characterized as "a blatherskite . . . a smart man, but unscrupulous, ₓ& intemperately religious," and blamed for mismanaging Langdon's Memphis paving contract (AD, 23 Feb 1906, 26 Mar 1906, CU-MARK, in *MTA*, 2:135–39, 243–56, with omissions; 6 July 70 to OLC, n. 1; p. 326); possibly first cousin Harriet Lewis, daughter of a brother or half-brother of Olivia Lewis Langdon, and confidante to both Clemens and Olivia during their courtship; and Pamela and Annie E. Moffett, the only members of the Clemens family. Olivia's brother, Charles, did not attend, having departed on a world tour in October 1869 (*L3*, 21–24, 349–50, 359, 369 nn. 2, 5).

Among the other guests were: the Reverend Edward Payson Adams, of Syracuse, and his wife, the former Charlotte A. (Lottie) Stanley, a good friend of Olivia's (the Adamses' wedding reception took place at the Langdon home on 1 July 1868); Mrs. Fidelia E. Stanley (d. 1891), Lottie's mother, the matron of Elmira Female College, where in 1859 and 1860 Lottie and Olivia were students in the Preparatory Department; Julia Jones Beecher, wife of Thomas; Hiram Bartlett Berry, a telegrapher for the Elmira *Advertiser,* his wife, the former Leonora Wisner, and, evidently, their daughter, Leonora; David T. Billings (1819–90), an Elmira farmer who was an old friend of the Langdons' and possibly a former employee of Jervis Langdon's, and his wife, Lucy (1820–1911), also a long-time family friend and the sister of Almira Hutchinson Munson; Henry J. and Fidele A. Brooks, Langdon family friends from New York City, and their young son, Remsen; Julia McDowell Clark (wife of Jefferson B. Clark, who may have attended), of Elmira, her daughter Ida, who was engaged to Charles J. Langdon, and one or possibly both of her other daughters, Josephine and Fanny; probably Olivia's Hartford friend Alice Hooker Day, her husband, John, and her parents John and Isabella Beecher Hooker, friends of Jervis and Olivia Langdon's; General Alexander S. Diven, a distinguished Civil War veteran and prominent Elmira attorney, railroad contractor, and former Republican congressman (1861–63), who in 1855 had inspired Jervis Langdon to enter the coal business, and his wife, Amanda; Abel and Mary Mason Fairbanks, and their daughter Alice; Rachel Brooks Gleason, co-founder of the Elmira Water Cure and physician to the Langdons and later the Clemenses, and her sister, Lucy Zipporah Brooks; Josephus N. Larned, political editor of the Buffalo *Express* and one of Clemens's partners; Elmira physician Henry Sayles, his wife, the former Emma Halsey, their daughter, Emma (Olivia's friend since childhood), and son, Henry; possibly Solon and Emily Severance, of Cleveland, Clemens's friends from the *Quaker City* excursion; Henry C. Spaulding, an Elmira lumber, building supplies, and coal dealer, his wife, the former Clara Wisner, and their daughters Alice and Clara, the latter Olivia's closest friend; and Harmony Cushman Twichell, wife of Joseph. Delos Holden, an Elmira wholesale grocer and tea jobber, and his sister, Mrs. L. Holden Dent, also attended and probably were the guests described in 1946 by Samuel C. Webster:

> A certain woman in town had not been invited to the wedding because there was no particular reason why she should be invited. The Langdons had ignored hints on the subject from her relatives, who had been invited. But when the wedding hour came the invited man arrived minus his wife, who was ill, and with his relative in tow. When the bride and groom had received congratulations and were still standing together she barged up and asked Uncle Sam to promenade around the room with her. Uncle Sam was rather stumped, but in his dazed condition he complied. Later on he came to, and had a lot to say on the subject in private. My mother remembers Aunt Livy standing alone. Even her sweet disposition was in danger of disintegration. (*MTBus*, 108–9)

(Holden's wife, Anna, had been another of Olivia's 1859–60 classmates at the Elmira Female College.) The Langdons, Cranes, Adamses, Browns, Fidele A. Brooks, and Mary Mason Fairbanks signed the marriage certificate as witnesses (Slotta; reproduced in Appendix F).

According to Annie Moffett, after the reception (actually the next day, 3 February):

A small company of guests accompanied the bride and groom to Buffalo where Uncle Sam was to join the staff of the *Buffalo Express,* in which he had bought an interest. A private car was furnished to Mr. Langdon by the railroad. Uncle Sam was singing a great deal of the time:—

> There was an old woman in our town,
> In our town did dwell,
> She loved her husband dearily
> But another man twicet as well,
> Another man twicet as well . . .

which does not seem particularly appropriate for a wedding trip.

Uncle Sam had already given Mr. Thomas K. Beecher a liberal fee, but on the train he went around the car and borrowed small change until he collected $1.00. This he took to Mr. Beecher and handed it to him as the wedding fee. Mr. Beecher accepted it. He said "Thank you, Mr. Clemens, if you feel that that is all it is worth I am satisfied." Then Mr. Beecher went to Mrs. Beecher. He said: "Mrs. Beecher, until January 1st you received the salary and I had the wedding fees, but since January 1st you have had the fees and I have had the salary. Here, Mrs. Beecher, this is yours."

There was a great secret known to everyone except Uncle Sam, my mother, and myself: Mr. Langdon had bought a house on Delaware Avenue. It was completely furnished, Aunt Livy having selected everything. It had required great caution and watchfulness to keep this from Uncle Sam. They did not let us into the secret because they felt that we might unwittingly disclose it. Then, too, Mrs. Langdon said it was so hard for them to sympathize with him in his trouble in finding a suitable boarding house that they felt it a great relief to have us there ready to condole with him. He poured out his grievances and we felt that he was very badly used. A Mr. S[l]ee of Buffalo who was supposed to make all the arrangements had mysteriously "left town" when Uncle Sam had gone to Buffalo a few days earlier to see that all was in order.

When we reached Buffalo Mr. and Mrs. Langdon, my mother and I were hurried to a carriage and rushed, as we supposed, to the Tif[f]t House, where the rest of the party was gathering. Although there was no longer any point in keeping the secret, they forgot to tell us, and we were so much surprised to be taken to this beautiful house that it was a long time before we could understand it.

In the meantime, to give us plenty of time, the rest of the party were placed in carriages and sent to the Hotel. Uncle Sam could not restrain his indignation. He said he never knew anything so badly managed in his life. The idea of keeping the Bride and Groom to the very last! When the Bride and Groom arrived the four of us were in the hall ready to greet them. Uncle Sam was so overwhelmed that it seemed impossible for him to understand; he kept asking for "Mrs. Howells," a fictitious name given him as the keeper of the boarding house. The next morning the rest of the party came. They ran all over exclaiming at the beauty of the drawing-room, all in a lovely shade of blue, the coziness of dining room and library, and so on. Mr. Beecher lay down on the floor and rolled over and over. Mrs. Beecher exclaimed "What are you doing, Mr. Beecher?" He said, "I am trying to take the feather edge off." At last all gathered in the drawing-room. Mrs. Beecher insisted we must all sing together "Heaven is my Home." She said they would never remember it, in that charming house, unless we sang this. (*MTBus*, 109–10)

The wedding received widespread coverage in the press. The fullest such account, by Mary Mason Fairbanks, appeared in the Cleveland *Herald* of 7 February 1870 (2):

The Wedding of "Mark Twain."

Samuel L. Clemens, more widely known as "Mark Twain," was married on the evening of the 2d inst. to Miss Olivia L. Langdon, daughter of Jervis Langdon, Esq., of Elmira, N.Y. The ceremony was performed by the Rev. Thos. K. Beecher, of that city, assisted by the Rev. Joseph E. Twichell, of Hartford, Ct. There was no "Jenkins" [Winifred Jenkins, the gossipy maid in Smollett's *Humphry Clinker*] among the guests to give publicity to all the pretty detail of the occasion. Suffice it that the sweet-faced girl who that evening hid her blushes in the folds of her bridal veil, has been reared in a household whose very atmosphere is love and refinement, and the humorous author, with all his rapidly increasing popularity, has received no endorsement which can compare with the cordial surrender of this treasure to his keeping.

The quiet, impressive ceremony with all its beautiful appointments is sacred to the few who witnessed it, but "Mark Twain" belongs to the public which has a right to know that he filled the role of bridegroom with charming grace and dignity.

Through the politeness of the President of the Pennsylvania Northern Central road [unidentified], a Director's car was sent on from Baltimore and placed at Mr. Langdon's disposal, while the Superintendent of the N. Y. Central [James Tillinghast] supplemented the complimentary arrangement, by orders for its conveyance to Buffalo. The wedding party, including a number of invited guests[,] proceeded to Buffalo on Thursday, Mark arrogating to himself a considerable amount of artificial dignity in consequence of his new position, and the magnificence of his "trousseau" to which he attached much importance.

Here comes in a delicious bit of romance, which as a reporter we have no right to give, but which, holding it too good to keep, we venture to share with the friends of Mark Twain in this city.

It had been arranged that Mr. and Mrs. Clemens should proceed at once to their boarding house, on arriving in the city, while the rest of the party were to be domiciled at the "Tif[f]t House." The securing of a desirable, genteel home in a private family, had been delegated to an intimate friend and resident of Buffalo, who understanding the tastes and requirements of the young couple would of course be the best person to make for them judicious arrangements. Mr. Clemens, having been absent on his lecturing tour for the past few months, accepted the assurance that everything had been attended to. At the depot hearty "good nights" were exchanged, the larger party driving to the hotel, the bride and groom taking carriage for more quiet quarters. Stopping in front of a modest but very attractive brick house in the upper part of Delaware street, Mr. Clemens was somewhat surprised to be met in the hall by the father and mother of the bride and his own sister, whom he supposed already quartered at the hotel. The landlady of the house suddenly disappeared from the scene, and as leaf by leaf of the charming little drama unfolded, Mark Twain found himself the victim of what he termed "a first class swindle," the proprietors and abettors of which were the delighted father and mother, who stood there silent spectators of the happiness they had prepared for their children in the gift of this beautiful home. For once the fun-loving Mark failed in rapartee, and moistened eyes spoke deeper thanks than words.

Nothing that love or wealth could suggest or supply was wanting to make the scene the fulfillment of the poet's dream, from the delicate blue satin drawing room to the little sanctum quite apart, with its scarlet upholstery, amid the pretty adornments of which inspiration must often come to its happy occupant.

Long life and happy days to our young friends, whose morning sky gives such rosy promise.

This article was much reprinted: in her commonplace book, Olivia Clemens preserved a clipping of the Boston *Advertiser*'s extract of the final three paragraphs ("Mark Twain's wedding-day . . . ," 14 Feb 70, 1; CU-MARK).

A secondhand, but circumstantial and seemingly authoritative, version of the "romance" appeared in the Elmira *Saturday Evening Review* on 19 February (5), under the rubric of columnist "Christopher Croquill":

Mark Twain, for once, according to all accounts, was nonplussed, when he reached Buffalo, the other day, to enter upon his newly wedded life. Rev. Mr. Ball [evidently A. M. Ball, a former minister at Congregational Church in Elmira] had been delegated to act as master of ceremonies and receive the wedding party on their arrival in that city. He managed his part well. The friends and relatives who made up the escort of the bridal train from this city, upon arriving at the Buffalo depot, and not finding Mr. Ball present, at once took carriages, it was supposed, for the Tif[f]t House. After they had gone some time on their way, belated Mr. Ball (a little justifiable ruse practised to carry out the illusion more apparently,) suddenly appeared on the scene, and with many profuse apologies explained his delay to Mark, who, not yet seeing the point, did not quite relish stopping so long in a depot, when elegant quarters were waiting his immediate possession elsewhere. His feelings were quieted, and the carriage soon drove the party to an elegant mansion—Mark's conjectured boarding house—on Delaware Avenue. He remarked that there was a general illumination about the premises, as if the inmates were glad to see their guests, rang the front door-bell, and was met by his father-in-law and sister, who, with the rest of the party, who had not gone to the Tif[f]t House, stood ready to welcome the new owners to a completely furnished and beautiful new home. Mark was more abashed than ever, could say nothing, but to pronounce the whole affair a "first class swindle." The gift house was found complete in all its appointments—tasteful boudoirs, a perfect little gem of a study, pretty bed chambers, green, blue and crimson apartments.

Clemens himself described Jervis Langdon's "first class swindle" in his letters of 6 February 1870 to William Bowen and 6? February 1870 to John McComb. Nearly fifteen years later, on 10 December 1884, he recreated the episode for a Buffalo audience that had come to hear him and George Washington Cable read from their works:

> I remember one circumstance of bygone times with great vividness. I arrived here after dark on a February evening in 1870 with my wife and a large company of friends, when I had been a husband twenty-four hours, and they put us two in a covered sleigh, and drove us up and down and every which way, through all the back streets in Buffalo[,] until at last I got ashamed, and said, 'I asked Mr[.] Slee to get me a cheap boarding house, but I didn't mean that he should stretch economy to the going outside the state to find it.' The fact was there was a practical joke to the fore which I didn't know anything about, and all this fooling around was to give it time to mature. My father-in-law, the late Jervis Langdon, whom many of you will remember, had been clandestinely spending a fair fortune upon a house and furniture in Delaware avenue for us, and had kept his secret so well that I was the only person this side of Niagara Falls that hadn't found it out. We reached the house at last, about 10 o'clock, and were introduced to a Mrs. Johnson, the ostensible landlady. I took a glance around and then my opinion of Mr. Slee's judgment as a provider of cheap boarding houses for men who had to work for their living dropped to zero. I told Mrs. Johnson there had been an unfortunate mistake. Mr. Slee had evidently supposed I had money, whereas I only had talent; and so, by her leave, we would abide with her a week, and then she could keep my trunk and we would hunt another place. Then the battalion of ambushed friends and relatives burst in on us, out of closets and from behind curtains[,] the property was delivered over to us and the joke revealed, accompanied with much hilarity. Such jokes as these are all too scarce in a person's life. That was a really admirable joke, for that house was so completely equipped in every detail—even to house servants and coachman—that there was nothing to do but just sit down and live in it. ("Twain and Cable," Buffalo *Courier,* 11 Dec 84, 4)

In her diary, Almira Hutchinson Munson reported that the group accompanying Clemens and Olivia to Buffalo numbered "about 20" (Jerome and Wisbey 1990, 4). It must have included, in addition to those recalled by Annie Moffett, most of the other family members who had attended the wedding and also the three Fairbankses. Theodore Crane did not make the trip, and Eunice Ford probably remained behind as well. The Twichells came to Buffalo, but not until 7 February, after Clemens summoned them by telegram (9 Feb 70 to the Langdons). John D. F. Slee, who managed the subterfuge concerning the Buffalo house, evidently did not attend the ceremony in Elmira. Reportedly, Slee, abetted by Charles M. Underhill and John J. McWilliams, employees of Jervis Langdon's, met the wedding party in Buffalo and conveyed the Clemenses to their "boarding house." He seems not to have accompanied them inside, for on 5 February they called at his Buffalo home, where he was bedridden with a throat condition, and apparently only then did he learn of the effect produced by Langdon's gift (6 Feb 70 to Bowen, n. 5; Reigstad 1989, 1). The Langdons and other celebrants returned to Elmira on the evening of 4 February ("Personal," Buffalo *Express*, 3 Feb 70, 4; "Mark Twain Married," Virginia City *Territorial Enterprise*, 5 Feb 70, 3; "Miss Anna M. Crane," Elmira *Advertiser*, 10 Feb 1916, no page; *Des Moines Directory:* 1869, 15; 1871, 66; 1873, 49; 1874–75, 46; Langdon family guest book, 2, 3, CtHMTH; "Hymeneal," Elmira *Advertiser*, 2 July 68, 4; "Former Matron of the College Dead," Elmira *Gazette and Free Press*, 14 Dec 91, 5; OLL to Alice B. Hooker, 7 June 67, 17 June 67, 4 Oct 67, 28 Nov 67, 11 Feb 68, 24 May 69, 1 Nov 69, CtHSD; OLL to Mary Mason Fairbanks, 9 Jan 70, CtHMTH; *MTB*, 1:395; Towner, 128, 314, 596–601; "In Memoriam," Elmira *Saturday Evening Review*, 13 Aug 70, 5; Boyd and Boyd, 2, 68, 74; "D. L. Holden & Co.," Elmira *Advertiser*, 2 Feb 70, 1; *L3*, 76 n. 4, 119 n. 4, 182–83 n. 6; Jerome and Wisbey: 1983, 1, 3; 1990, 4, 5; 1991a, 4–5; 1991b, 6; Wisbey: 1979, 7–8; 1990, 4; 1993, 1–2; Palmer, 105–6; *NCAB*, 8:296; Twichell to Albert Bigelow Paine, 19 Jan 1911, in Chester L. Davis 1970, 4).

To William Bowen
6 February 1870 • Buffalo, N.Y.
(MS and transcript: TxU and CU-MARK)

$\boxed{c}$

Sunday Afternoon,
At Home, 472 Delaware Avenue,
Buffalo Feb. 6, 1870.

My First, & Oldest & Dearest Friend,

My heart goes out to you just the same as ever! Your letter has stirred me to the bottom.[1] The fountains of my great deep are broken up & I have rained reminiscences for four & twenty hours.[2] The old life has swept before me like a panorama; the old days have trooped by in their old glory, again; the old faces have looked out of the mists of the past; old footsteps have sounded in my listening ears; old hands have clasped mine, old voices have greeted me, & the songs I loved ages & ages ago have come wailing down the centuries! Heavens what eternities have swung their hoary cycles about us since those days were new!—~~What~~ Since we tore down Dick Hardy's stable; since you had the measles & I went to your house purposely to catch them; since Henry Beebe kept that envied slaughter-house, & Joe Craig sold him cats to kill in it; since old General Gaines used to say, "Whoop! Bow your neck & spread!;" since Jimmy Finn was town drunkard & we stole his dinner while he slept in the vat & fed it to the hogs in order to keep them still till we could mount them & have a ride; since Clint Levering was drowned; since we taught that one-legged nigger, Higgins, to offend Bill League's dignity by hailing him in public with his exasperating "Hello, League!"—since we used to undress & play Robin Hood ~~wi~~ in our shirt⸗ tails, with lath swords, in the woods on Holliday's Hill on those long summer days; since we used to go in swimming above the still-house branch—& at mighty intervals wandered on vagrant ¢ fishing excursions clear up to "the Bay," & wondered what was curtained away in the great world beyond that remote point;[3] since I jumped overboard from the ferry boat in the middle of the river that stormy day to get my hat, & swam two or three miles after it (& *got* it,) while all the town collected on the wharf & for an hour or so looked out across the angry waste of "white⸗

caps" toward where people said Sam. Clemens was last seen before he went down; since we got up a ~~mutiny~~ rebellion against Miss Newcomb, under Ed. Stevens' leadership, (to force her to let us all go over to Miss Torry's side of the schoolroom,) & gallantly "sassed" Laura Hawkins when she came out the third time to call us in, & then afterward marched in ,in, threatening & bloodthirsty array,—& meekly yielded, & took each his little thrashing, & resumed his old seat entirely "reconstructed;" since we used to indulge in that very peculiar performance on that old bench outside the school-house to drive good old Bill Brown crazy while he was eating his dinner; since we used to remain at school at noon & go hungry, in order to persecute Bill Brown in all possible ways—poor old Bill, who *could* be driven to such extremity of vindictiveness as to call us "You *infernal* fools!" & chase us round & round the school-house—& yet who never had the heart to hurt us when he caught us, & who always loved us & always took our part when the big boys wanted to thrash us; since we used to lay in wait for Bill Pitts at the pump & whale him; (I saw him two or three years ago, & *I* was awful polite to his six feet two, & mentioned no reminiscences); since we used to be in Dave Garth's class in Sunday school & on week-days stole his leaf tobacco to run our miniature tobacco presses with; since Owsley shot Smar; since Ben Hawkins shot off his finger; since we accidentally burned up that poor fellow in the calaboose; since we used to shoot spool cannons¡, & cannons made of keys, while that envied & hated Henry Beebe drowned out our poor little pop-guns with his booming brazen little artillery on wheels; since Laura Hawkins was my sweetheart————————[4]

Hold! *That* rouses me out of my dream, & brings me violently back unto this day & this generation. For behold I have at this moment the only sweetheart I ever *loved*, & bless her old heart she is lying asleep upstairs in a bed that I sleep in every night, & for four whole days she has been *Mrs. Samuel L. Clemens!*[5]

I am 34 & she is 24; I am young & very handsome (I make the statement with the fullest confidence, for I got it from her,) & she is much the most beautiful girl I ever saw (I said that before she was anything to me, & so it is worthy of all belief) & she is the *best* girl, & the sweetest, & the gentlest, & the daintiest, & the most modest & unpretentious, & the wisest in all things she should be wise in & the most ignorant in all matters it would not grace her to know, & she is sensible & quick, & loving & faithful, forgiving, full of charity—& her beautiful life is ordered by

a religion that is all kindliness & unselfishness. Before the gentle majesty
of her purity all evil things & evil ways & evil deeds stand abashed,—
then surrender. Wherefore without effort, or struggle, or spoken exor-
cism, all the old vices & shameful habits that have possessed me these
many many years, are falling away, one by one, & departing into the
darkness.

Bill, I know whereof I speak. I am too old & have moved about too
much, & rubbed against too many people not to know human beings as
well as we used to know "boils" from "breaks."[6]

She is the very most perfect gem of womankind that ever I saw in
my life—& I will stand by that remark till I die.

William, old boy, her father surprised us a little, the other night.
We all arrived here in a night train (my little wife & I were going to
board,) & under pretense of taking us to the private boarding house that
had been selected for me while I was absent lecturing in New England,
my new father-in-law & some old friends drove us in sleighs to the daintiest, darlingest, loveliest little palace in America—& when I said "Oh,
this won't do—people who can afford to live in this sort of style won't
take boarders," that same blessed father-in-law let out the secret that this
was all *our* property—a present from himself. House & furniture cost
$40,000 in cash, (including stable, horse & carriage), & is a most exqui-
site little palace (I saw no apartment in Europe so lovely as our ~~little~~
drawing-room.)

Come along, you & Mollie,[7] just whenever you can, & pay us a visit,
(giving us a little notice beforehand,) & if we don't make you comfortable
nobody in the world can.

[And now ₐmyₐ princess has come down for dinner (bless me, isn't
it cosy, nobody but just us two, & three servants to wait on us & respectfully call us "Mr." and "Mrs. Clemens" instead of "Sam." & "Livy!") It
took me many a year to work up to where I can put on style, but now I'll
do it. My book gives me an income like a small lord, & my paper is ~~not~~
a good ~~po~~ profitable concern.[8]

Dinner's ready. Good bye & ~~g~~ God bless you, old friend, & keep
your heart fresh & your memory green for the old days that will never
come again.

                                            Yrs always
                                            Sam. Clemens.

[1] A year younger than Clemens, Bowen was his closest boyhood friend and partner in mischief. The two were Mississippi riverboat pilots together between 1859 and 1861, then were estranged for five years after a misunderstanding about Bowen's repayment of a two-hundred-dollar loan, and a clash over his pro-secession views at the onset of the Civil War. Clemens made his peace with Bowen, who eventually became a pilot for the North during the war, in letters of 7 May and 25 August 1866 (*L1*, 338–41, 357–60). After leaving the river in September 1868, Bowen joined the Hannibal insurance firm of his brother-in-law, Moses P. Green. By March 1870 he had moved to St. Louis, where he was employed by the Phoenix Insurance Company. Subsequently he established his own agency there before relocating to Austin, Texas, around 1880 (Hornberger, 7; Bowen to SLC, 31 Mar 70, CU-MARK). Clemens based Tom Sawyer partly on Bowen and also used him as the model for Joe Harper in *Tom Sawyer* and *Huckleberry Finn* (for more details of Clemens's friendship with Bowen and his family see *L1*, passim, and *Inds*, 303–6).

[2] Genesis 7:11: "the same day were all the fountains of the great deep broken up, and the windows of heaven were opened."

[3] Holliday's Hill, which became Cardiff Hill in *The Adventures of Tom Sawyer*, overlooked the Mississippi River, just north of Hannibal, and was probably named for the family that owned it; the "still-house branch" was a stream that emptied into the Mississippi near Holliday's Hill, furnishing water for a Hannibal distillery; the Bay de Charles was a large inlet on the Mississippi some two miles above Hannibal (*Inds*, 269, 325).

[4] The Hannibal acquaintances mentioned in this passage were: Richard Hardy, an artist and sign painter; Henry Beebe, a schoolboy bully; Joe Craig, son of a tanyard owner; "General" Gaines, a town drunkard; James Finn (d. 1845), another town drunkard and the prototype for Huck Finn's father; Clint Levering (1837?–47); Higgins, a slave owned by the family of Clemens's Sunday School teacher, David J. Garth (1822–1912), a prosperous tobacconist in Hannibal in the 1850s and later nationally; William T. League (1832–70), Clemens's fellow apprentice printer at the Hannibal *Missouri Courier*, who in 1851 helped found the Hannibal *Whig Messenger* and in 1853 purchased Orion Clemens's Hannibal *Journal;* Mary Ann Newcomb (1809–94), whose Select School Clemens attended; Edmund C. Stevens (b. 1834?), a classmate and then, in 1861, a member of the Marion Rangers, the feckless band of would-be Confederate volunteers Clemens joined briefly before decamping for Nevada Territory; Miss Torrey (or Torry), a teacher at Mary Ann Newcomb's school; Anna Laura Hawkins, Clemens's first sweetheart, and her older brother Benjamin (see 6? Feb 70 to Frazer); William Lee Brown (1831?–1903), whom Clemens later remembered as having drawn attention by being much larger, and also older, than his classmates; William R. Pitts (b. 1832?), who became a prosperous harness maker and saddler and in 1870 helped found a Hannibal bank; William Perry Owsley (b. 1813) and Sam Smarr (1788?–1845), a merchant and a farmer, respectively, who in 1845 figured in a Hannibal street murder that became the basis of the Sherburn-Boggs incident in chapter 21 of *Huckleberry Finn;* and Dennis McDermid, who died in 1853 in a fire he accidentally started in the Hannibal "calaboose," where he was imprisoned, using matches Clemens had given to him. For further biographical detail

about these individuals and Clemens's literary uses of them, see *Inds*, 299–351.

⁵Olivia's sense of those first four days is preserved in the following letter to her parents (CtHMTH):

472 Delaware Ave.
Buffalo Feb. 6ᵗʰ

Darling Father and Mother
      It is a bright day— Mr Clemens has gone to church and I sit in our beautiful Library with the doors into the drawing room, into the dining room and into the hall all open because this room is prettie warm and I want to make it cooler—
      Ellen and Patrick have gone to church, ~~Harriate~~ Harriete is at home, as I write I hear her stepping about over head getting the work done— I talked with the two girls last night about their church and made arrangements so that they should both be able to go, and yet not go at the same time, they were both very good and willing about it— So far I have had no unpleasant words or looks from any of them, nothing but cheerful willingness to do any thing that I suggest, of course I cannot but expect that the clouds will come some time, but I pray that when they do I may be woman enough to meet them—
      Ellen asked me last night if I was not homesick, I said "no, that I was as happy as a queen"— It seems almost naughty not to feel homesick after the dear old home—but that I am not you are responsible—perhaps if I had hourly to meet strangers about me I should have a homesick longing for the old ~~home~~ ‚faces‚, but with only Mr Clemens with me there is no danger of my growing to feel strange—
      I wish that you could have seen us this morning before our beautiful blue clock, Mr Clemens took off the shade and wound it, the more closely we examined it the more enthusiastic we grew, concerning its beauties—
      Father it is charming, I thought several that I saw in New York were as exqu[i]site as they could be but this exceeds any of them—the enameling is *perfect*—
      Samuel said yesterday that it was well that there was no one with us now, because they might be almost surprized at our constant exclamations of delight— When he looked in at our bed room the other morning, he said that he fairly *started* at seeing the beauty of it— The first tarnish that we have got on our new home is three spots ‚of‚ ink on our bright scarlet table cover, we did not know which did it, but we both mourned that it was done—but I immediately ceased the mourning saying that the house was to be a home, so those spots were the first evidence that the house was *used*, so we put our ink ~~with~~ stand ~~th~~ over them and comforted ourselves—but yesterday when we went down town to do two or three errands Mr Clemens bought two large sheets of blotting paper to put down on the table under the ink stand, one here, and one in his study—
      We went out yesterday morning and did two or three errands and called at Mr Slee's, Mr. Slee's throat had broken the night before and he was much better, and wanted to see us, so we went up to his room, and had a *delightful* visit, staying from half an hour to an hour, I should think— Mr Clemens told Mr Slee that never in his life did he have such an intoxicating rush of pleasure as when I told him that this was *our home*— Even when I said *"yes"*, to him the pleasure was not so great because of course there was little or no surprize in it—
      If I could write you a reem of paper I could not begin to tell you half that I want to tell you— I wish that I could remember some of the funny things that Mr Clemens says and does—and besides these ~~pl~~ funny things, he is so tender and considerate in every way—
      Mr Slee said that he should come here the first time that he rode out, I asked them to come and take dinner with us tomorrow if he felt ~~able and~~ that the change would be a rest to him—
      Mother we want the porcelain pictures ‚of you & father—‚so that we can have

them in our room on the mantle, where we can see them every morning—to y You can judge about the shade of blue by Emma Sayles brackets—

My dresses have not come yet I presume that they will tomorrow, but I had here a dress that I should have worn if it had seemed best for me to go—+ to church today—

We *love*, LOVE, LOVE you,—

Don't fail to make mention of us in your prayers—you are not forgotten in ours— I feel some times that we need the prayers of friends more now in our great joy, than we shall when days of darkness and trial come to us—

Remember me to all about the house, Laura, Mary Crossey, Mary Green, Mrs Barnes, *all*— Love to Grandma, Theodore, Susie, and the dear friends that are with you— I would rather have Theodore and Susie come to us by themselves when they come—even than to have them here with dear cousin Anna— Thank Theodore for his "ģ Good bye"— I am glad he sent it because I realized when we were really started that he had not bidden us good bye— I approved of the way that his letter was directed it did not make it seem quite so unnat unnatural—"Mrs Olivia Langdon Clemens"——

Mother can you send me one or two old worn table cloths to wrap bread and the like in— Don't if it is any trouble— Now and always lovingly Livy

[*new page:*]

P. S.

One more item of interest—Mr Clemens told Mr Slee that if he ever wanted to go to a Theater *very much,* and any thing should hinder him, and fill him with disapointmint, he would go into the drawing room and take off the covers and look at the room, then he should be *perfectly* satisfied—

About the first words that he uttered on waking the other morning were, oh that drawing room! is a perf It is a perfect *vision* of loveliness

The time of not eating and not sleeping has gone by for both of us—we eat and sleep now—again Lovingly Livy—

Clemens was at the Lafayette Street Presbyterian Church, which he and Olivia attended regularly during their first few months in Buffalo (13 Feb 70 to Fairbanks; 19 June 70 to the Langdons; Reigstad 1990, 1–2). Mentioned by Olivia: domestics Ellen White and Harriet, the former a Langdon family servant who, according to Olivia's cousin Hattie Lewis, was "installed as housekeeper" (Paff, 7), but also seems to have been the cook; coachman Patrick McAleer (1846– 1906), who served the Clemenses almost without interruption until 1891; four of the remaining Langdon household staff (Laura, Mary Crossey, Mary Green, Mrs. Barnes); Emma Sayles; John D. F. Slee; Eunice Ford; Susan and Theodore Crane; and, possibly, Anna Marsh Brown (16 Apr 70 to Crane; 11 June 70 to White; *MTB*, 1:396; 15 May 72 and 10 June 74, both to OC and MEC, CU-MARK; 26–27? July 72 to MEC, CU-MARK; "Coachman Many Years for Mark Twain," Hartford *Courant*, 26 Feb 1906, 6).

[6]A boil is a turbulent swirl or eddy in a river. A break, which looks like a streak on the water's surface, is an ominous sign of a snag or other submerged obstacle (*Inds*, 269).

[7]Mary Cunningham Bowen (d. 1873), Bowen's first wife. They had been married since 1857 (*Inds*, 305).

[8]See 28 Jan 70 to Bliss, n. 2.

To George E. Barnes
6? February 1870 • Buffalo, N.Y.
(Transcript: CtHMTH)

[enclosures:]

Olivia L. Langdon.

Mr. & Mrs. S. L. Clemens.

472 Delaware Ave.
Buffalo.

[*on the inside envelope:*]

Goodbye, Barnes[1]

[*on the flap:*] (LC)

[1] Barnes was editor and co-owner of the San Francisco *Morning Call*. He had fired Clemens from the paper in October 1864, after four months of his "indifferent" local reporting, but the two men had remained on good terms (*L1*, 302, 317–18 n. 3; *L3*, 354–55). On 15 February, he published the following:

> "Mark Twain" is married. The confirmed bachelor has become the Benedict. He has followed the prophetic law, and is in one sense no longer "Twain," but one flesh with the other "Twain." We have received the wedding cards, pink-tinted, monogrammed envelop, motto and all, and so are forced to yield him up to Hymen as well as to Cupid. He has long been a worshipper of Momus, and holds a high place in his Cabinet. And so the missionary to the Sandwich Islands has at last made a convert, the "Innocent Abroad" has become a wise man at home. The modern "Pilgrim" henceforth will have an extra staff in his travels through life, and may he never want for scrip or staff on his journey. To our old confrere we send our congratulations. ("Marriage of Mark Twain [Sam. L. Clemens]," 2)

In 1956, Barnes's grandniece, Elizabeth D. Theobald, who presumably inherited the wedding cards, reported that the

> wedding announcement is quite different than those of the modern day in that the envelope is embossed on the back flap with the intertwined initials CL, and enclosed are two cards, one engraved Olivia L. Langdon and the other Mr. and Mrs. S.L. Clemens, 472 Delaware Ave, Buffalo. (Theobald to Cyril Clemens, 8 Dec 1956, CtHMTH).

The Langdons were following the fashion, reported early in 1869 by the New York *Home Journal*, of embellishing wedding invitations, and doubtless announcements as well, "with a large monogram in relief, entwining the combined initials of the bride and groom" (Rochester [N.Y.] *Democrat*, 1 Mar 69, reprinting the *Home Journal*). Probably accompanying the cards was "a note announcing the marriage on the 3d [i.e., 2d] of February, in New York" (6? Feb 70 to McComb). The cards reproduced here at actual size are in the Mark Twain Papers. They are off-white, however, and perhaps were proofs or have faded from pink. The date assigned would have allowed Barnes's cards to reach the West Coast by overland mail in time for his 15 February notice in the *Call*. Clemens probably addressed cards to his special friends at a single sitting, and so the same date has been assigned to each of the next five letters. Except for the one to John McComb, however, any of these might have been mailed somewhat later, judging by a request Olivia made on 12 February in a letter to her family in Elmira: "If you will send us about 50 after cards we will address them to people that Mr C. forgot to mention" (CtHMTH). In Elmira, Annie Moffett also mailed wedding cards for Clemens (9 Feb 70 to the Langdons).

To Horace E. Bixby
6? February 1870 • Buffalo, N.Y.
(Paraphrase: New Orleans *Times-Democrat*, 7 May 82)

Thirty tons of paper have been used in publishing my book Innocents Abroad. It has met with a greater sale than any book ever published except Uncle Tom's Cabin.[1] The volumes sell from $3 to $5, according to finish, & I get one-half the profit. Not so bad for a scrub pilot, is it? How do you run Plum Point—a son-of-a-gun of a place?[2] I would rather be a pilot than anything I ever tried.[3]

[*enclosures of wedding cards*][4]

————————————————————————————————

[*on the flap of the inside envelope:*] (LC)

[1] Harriet Beecher Stowe's novel was a benchmark for Clemens in gauging sales of *Innocents* (*L3,* 440). But *Uncle Tom's Cabin* (1852) sold in excess of 100,000 copies during its first six months, whereas *Innocents* sold 39,000 (Hart 1950, 110–12; Hirst 1975, 314, 316).

[2] According to an 1857 river guide, Plum Point, near Osceola, Arkansas, was "one of the most difficult places to pass on the Mississippi. . . . Quite a number of boats have been lost here" (James, 33, 34). In 1875, in the second installment of "Old Times on the Mississippi," Clemens had a group of pilots answer the same question he here asked Bixby, his piloting instructor in 1857–59 (SLC 1875b, 221–22).

[3] An assertion that Clemens made repeatedly (see *L1,* 327, 358). In 1875 he expanded on it in his sixth installment of "Old Times on the Mississippi":

> I loved the profession far better than any I have followed since, and I took a measureless pride in it. The reason is plain: a pilot, in those days, was the only unfettered and entirely independent human being that lived in the earth. Kings are but the hampered servants of parliament and people; parliaments sit in chains forged by their constituency; the editor of a newspaper cannot be independent, but must work with one hand tied behind him by party and patrons, and be content to utter only half or two thirds of his mind; no clergyman is a free man and may speak the whole truth, regardless of his parish's opinions; writers of all kinds are manacled servants of the public. We write frankly and fearlessly, but then we "modify" before we print. In truth, every man and woman and child has a master, and worries and frets in servitude; but in the day I write of, the Mississippi pilot had *none.* (SLC 1875b, 721)

See also chapter 14 of *Life on the Mississippi* and the Autobiographical Dictation of 7 July 1908 (CU-MARK, in *MTE,* 304, and *AMT,* 291).

[4] The text of this letter is based on Bixby's report of it in an 1882 interview in which, asked if he ever heard from Clemens, he said, somewhat inaccurately: "Yes, he used to write, and let me know of his whereabouts. On his return from the Holy Land, he sent me a letter which contained his wedding card" ("Mark

Twain. How the Boy Became a Pilot and the Pilot a Humorist," New Orleans *Times-Democrat*, 7 May 82, 3, reprinted in part in Turner, 15–17). The cards and envelope are not known to survive: see 6? Feb 70 to Barnes.

To Laura H. Frazer
via Elijah or Benjamin Hawkins
6? February 1870 • Buffalo, N.Y.
(Fielder, 11)

[*enclosures of wedding cards*]

✉——————————————————————————

[*on the inside envelope:*][1]

Mrs. ——— (married name unknown to me).

(Formerly Miss Laura Hawkins, first sweetheart of one of the within named parties 29 years ago.[2] Pardon the suggestive figures.)
[*on the flap:*] ⟨LC⟩

[1] The cards and envelope are not known to survive: see 6? Feb 70 to Barnes.
[2] Clemens immortalized Anna Laura Hawkins (1837–1928) as Becky Thatcher in *Tom Sawyer* and *Huckleberry Finn*. In 1858 she had married James W. Frazer (1833–75), a physician in Madisonville and then in Rensselaer, Missouri, with whom she had two sons. This brief note—written on "the inner cover" of wedding cards enclosed to one of Laura Frazer's brothers (Fielder, 11)—marks Clemens's last known contact with her until 30 May 1902, when they met in Hannibal. On 13 October 1908 Frazer visited Clemens at Stormfield, his home in Redding, Connecticut ("Mark Twain's Childhood Sweetheart Recalls Their Romance," *Literary Digest* 56 [23 March 1918]: 75; Love, 2; "Stormfield Guest-Book," CU-MARK). Frazer's brother Benjamin (b. 1822?) had been Hannibal city marshal in the early 1850s. He was the prototype for Captain Haskins, the militia captain and sheriff in "Tom Sawyer's Conspiracy," an unfinished story Clemens worked on from 1897 to about 1902 (*Inds*, 134–213, 289–93). Another brother, Elijah (b. 1828?), was a Hannibal dry goods merchant. He, and perhaps Benjamin, were still living in Hannibal in 1870. For further details of Clemens's acquaintance with the Hawkins family, see *Inds*, 95, 322–24.

To John McComb
6? February 1870 • Buffalo, N.Y.
(Paraphrase and transcript: San Francisco
Alta California, 14 Feb 70)

"MARK TWAIN" MARRIED AND SETTLED.

By the last mail we received a delicate pink envelope containing still more delicate cards of a still more delicate pink, one bearing the words, "Mr. and Mrs. S. L. Clemens, Delaware Avenue," and the other, "Olivia L. Langdon,"[1] and a note announcing the marriage on the 3d of February, in New York. So Mark and Miss Langdon have been made "Twain" according to the statute in such cases made and provided, and his host of friends will wish him joy at his good fortune, for the lady is spoken of as being beautiful, accomplished and amiable. And Mark has prospered financially, for his book yields him a handsome income, and his lecturing receipts should make happy any ordinary mortal.

It seems Mark's father-in-law played an elaborate practical joke on him on the night of the wedding. The bridegroom, being busy with his lectures, and not readily finding a house for sale that suited his purse and taste, instructed Mr. Langdon's agent in Buffalo to secure him rooms and board in some nice family, where there would be but few other boarders; and though the commission was executed, Mark could not learn the name of the family or the street where they lived; and he privately determined to caution his father-in-law, as soon as admitted into the family, against continuing such a stupid agent in the management of his business. Finally, a dozen particular friends escorted the bridal party from Elmira to Buffalo, in a palace car, and on arriving proposed to call on the newly-married pair in the morning. By some more stupidity on the part of the agent the bride and groom were the last to leave the car, on account of the carriages being blocked in, and when Mark reached his "boarding house," he found all his friends waiting for him in a magnificent mansion, ($40,000) elegantly furnished, stable, coach, horses, liveries for servants, check on the bank for a handsome amount—and all a present from the father-in-law.[2] He said it only needed a drop curtain and a prompter to place the characters in position to make it like a scene in a sensation drama. In his letter he says: "I have *read* those absurd fairy tales in my time, but I never, never, never, expected to be the hero of a romance in real life as unlooked-for & unexpected as the wildest of them." In the postscript to his letter he says: "In the good old-fashioned fairy tale, the hero would infallibly happen to notice an opal hued mother-of-pearl box on the centre-table, & would heedlessly open it & find in it a deed for all the newly acquired property. But, bless you, I never have had any experience in playing hero in a tale, & so no matter who shoved that box toward me, or hinted darkly at its contents, my calm, unruffled stupidity was victorious every time, & at last they had to shove the box under my nose in the most unromantic way, & open it & display the deed & insurance papers. All hands laughed at & abused me, but I told them it was all so new to me—tackle me again with another house, & see how I would sail through my part. The check on the bank, accompanying the gift, was not necessary, for my book & lecturing keep me equal to minor emergencies!"[3]

✉️———————————————————————————————

[on the flap of the inside envelope:] (LC)

[1] The wedding cards and envelope are not known to survive: see 6? Feb 70 to Barnes.

[2] Joseph H. Twichell, after visiting the newlyweds on 7 February, reported that "the house and furniture was worth not less than $40,000" (Charles Dudley Warner to George H. and Lilly G. Warner, 14 Feb 70, CtHSD). On 6 February Clemens also specified $40,000, but on 9 February he put their cost at $42,000. About a year later he valued the house at $25,000 and the furniture at "$10,000 or $12,000" (6 Feb 70 to Bowen; 9 Feb 70 to Church; 3 Mar 71 to Riley; 4 Mar 71 to OC). The amount of Langdon's "handsome" check is not known.

[3] McComb, Clemens's close friend, as well as his employer, at the San Francisco *Alta California* was clearly the recipient of these confidences and the author of this notice.

To Charles Warren Stoddard
6? February 1870 • Buffalo, N.Y.
(MS: ViU)

[enclosures of wedding cards][1]

✉️———————————————————————————————

[on the inside envelope:]

Chas Warren Stoddard

Tell me—what is the matter with Bret ~~Hare~~ Harte?—why all these airs?[2]

Mark.

[*on the flap:*] (LC)

[1] The cards are not known to survive: see 6? Feb 70 to Barnes.

[2] Specific evidence of Harte's "airs" has not been found. Clemens's irritation with his old friend stemmed at least in part from the "*most daintily contemptuous & insulting letter*" Harte had sent him in September 1869, resenting his difficulty in getting a review copy of *The Innocents Abroad* (*L3*, 355–56; 26 Nov 70 to Webb).

To William Wright (Dan De Quille)
6? February 1870 • Buffalo, N.Y.
(MS: CU-BANC)

[*enclosures of wedding cards*][1]

[*on the inside envelope:*]

Old Dan, my abused roommate—[but who stole old Mrs. Fitch's pies, nevertheless—& Daggett's wood.][2]

[*on the flap:*] (LC)

[1] The cards are not known to survive: see 6? Feb 70 to Barnes.

[2] On 19 May 1874, writing from Virginia City, Nevada, Wright enclosed this envelope and its contents in a letter to his sister in Cedar Falls, Iowa, Lou Wright Benjamin, who had asked for some specimens of Mark Twain's handwriting. Wright explained:

> In looking through my desk and trunk I found an *I* invitation to Mark's wedding. I send you the cards and envelope just as it came, minus the outside envelope. You will observe that I carried it in my pocket till it became dirty and worn. What he refers to on the back of the envelope is a trick he played on me with an old lady, the mother-in-law of *$* Hon. Tom Fitch, Congressman from Nevada. Just across the hall from the rooms occupied by Mark and I lived Hon. Tom Fitch, wife, sister-in-law and mother-in-law. They were kind enough very frequently to place a pie and pitcher of milk in our room as a lunch for us when we came home at one or two [o'cl]ock in the morning. Mark found out where the pies were kept and stole a few during the day when he got a chance then when something was hinted about pies being lost by the Fitches he told them that he had sometimes seen me coming from the room where the pies were, but he had not the least idea that I touched them. All this I found out long afterwards and I raised a storm about it. Mrs Fitch ~~had~~ never said a word to me about the theft, till I mentioned it, when she said she "knew it was Sam from the way he drawled and stammered." The wood stealing i[s] of a piece with the above. He would go to the end of the hall and get

an armful of Daggett's wood (by the way Daggett is now editor in chief of this paper) then as soon as he opened the door backing ~~out~~ into our room he would call out: "Damn it, Dan, you hav[e]n't been at Daggett's wood again, have you? It's too bad to take so much of his wood." Then he would throw the wood on the floor and make a great racket, at the same time crying out: "Damn it, Dan, don't make such a noise! Everybody in the house hears you!" All this when I was not in the house at all. It turned out that the greater part of the wood he nipped was the property of poor Tom Fitch—Tom *was* poor then. To this day Mark takes pride in the trick he played me about the pies and wood; but I got even and more than even. (William Wright Papers, CU-BANC)

These highjinks took place between 28 October 1863 and 29 May 1864, while Clemens and Wright were roommates in Virginia City. Their lodgings and those of Thomas and Anna M. Fitch and the latter's mother and sister were in a building owned by stockbroker Warren F. Myers and his partner Rollin M. Daggett, who became editor-in-chief of the Virginia City *Territorial Enterprise* in 1874, after a decade on the editorial staff (*L1*, 310–11 nn. 1, 3). Wright first published a version of the wood theft episode in the San Francisco *Golden Era* in 1863, without naming Daggett and Fitch as the victims. Thirty years later he told about the wood and the pies in the San Francisco *Examiner*, virtually reproducing the account he gave to his sister in 1874 (William Wright: 1863, 5; 1893, 13). Although he described his enclosures to his sister as "an invitation to Mark's wedding," it is clear they were the same cards and announcement that Clemens sent to his other old friends after the wedding. No evidence has been found that Clemens personalized the wedding invitations. The invitations received by Pamela and Annie Moffett (CU-MARK) and by John and Alice Day (CtHSD), the only ones known to survive, were probably typical: sent by the Langdons, they were handwritten on their personal stationery. Like the preceding note to Stoddard, Clemens's note to Wright appeared on the front (not the back) of the inside envelope.

To John H. Bancroft
7? February–30? April 1870 • Buffalo, N.Y.
(AAA 1914, lot 72)

Buffalo, 1870.

Master Jno. H. Bancroft—Yes Sir, if so small a matter can confer a favor upon "a schoolboy" I am the very man to do it.[1]

Samuel L. Clemens

Mark Twain

[1] This letter is assigned arbitrarily to the earliest likely period in 1870 when Clemens was in Buffalo, but he might have written it there in any of five later periods: 10 or 11 May–6 June; 12–22 June; 12? August–1? October; 9? October–9? December; or 17–31 December. The request for an autograph may have come

from John H. Bancroft (1856?–1936) who later became controller of the American Sugar Refining Company ("Aged Jersey Couple Die 3 Hours Apart," New York *Times*, 12 June 1936, 23).

To John Fuller
8 February 1870 • Buffalo, N.Y.
(MS: CtY-BR)

OFFICE "EXPRESS" PRINTING CO.

BUFFALO, Feb 8 1870.[1]

DEAR SIR:

IN ANSWER I AM OBLIGED TO SAY THAT IT WILL NOT BE POSSIBLE FOR ME TO ACCEPT YOUR KIND INVITATION. I SHALL NOT BE ABLE TO LECTURE AGAIN DURING THE PRESENT SEASON. THANKING YOU KINDLY FOR THE COMPLIMENT OF YOUR INVITATION, I AM

YOURS TRULY,

SAM'L L. CLEMENS.

["MARK TWAIN."]

AGENTS:

BOSTON LYCEUM BUREAU,

20 BROMFIELD STREET,

BOSTON.

P. S. You must write the "Express" folks about the change of the Weekly—I never go near the office.[2]

Don't know what No. of the Broadway that article was in.[3]

Am just married, & don't take an interest in *any*thing out of doors.

Give my love to Frank first time you see him or write him.

Yrs

Mark.

[1] Four additional examples of this printed form letter have been found. One that Clemens dated "March 1" but did not personalize, even with the name of its recipient, is not collected here (see Will M. Clemens 1900, 27). For the others, see 16 Mar 70 and 13 Feb 71 to Unidentified, and 26 Apr 70 to Fuller.

[2] John Fuller, of Boston—the brother of Frank Fuller, Clemens's business and lecture agent in 1867—was probably a cashier at the Merchants National Bank

at this time. It is not known under what auspices he invited Clemens to lecture. His second request concerned a change in his subscription to the weekly edition of the Buffalo *Express*, a gift from Clemens (26 Apr 70 to Fuller; *Boston Directory 1869*, 251; "The Express," Buffalo *Express*, 8 Feb 70, 2; *L2*, 5–6, 40–42, 53, 60).

[3] "Cannibalism in the Cars," a macabre sketch about passengers snowbound on a train, apparently written in January 1868, appeared in *The Broadway: A London Magazine* in November of that year (SLC 1868e; *ET&S1*, 551). For a detailed discussion of "Cannibalism in the Cars," see Branch, 585–91.

To Francis P. Church
9 February 1870 • Buffalo, N.Y.
(Transcript and paraphrase: Mott 1957, 3:364)

Feb. 9.[1]

. . . .

[*paraphrase: Mark Twain . . . had married and settled down at Buffalo in a house which, as he boyishly wrote Colonel Church,*] a generous father-in-law has built & furnished at the comely figure of $42,000 [*paraphrase: and he had bought an interest in the Buffalo Express, which, he says,*] pays me an ample livelihood, & does it without my having to go near it. I write sketches for it, & occasional squibs & editorials—that is all. I don't go to the office.

. . . .

[1] Frank Luther Mott, who saw the original of this letter, reported that it was "dated February 9 [1870]" and addressed to William Conant Church (1836–1917), co-founder and editor of the *Galaxy* magazine, and a brevet lieutenant colonel during the Civil War. Mott believed that William was also the "Friend Church" whom Clemens addressed in letters of 22 February 1868, and 11 March, 18 October, and 23 December 1870 (Mott 1957, 364, 366–68). Although Mott may have been right about the 1868 letter (*L2*, 200–201), no replies from William are known to survive. His younger brother, and his co-founder and co-editor, Francis Pharcellus Church (1839–1906), signed all of the extant letters to Clemens about his *Galaxy* work (26 Apr 70 to 13 June 71, CU-MARK). The evidence, therefore, is that Clemens wrote exclusively to him during that period. In the present letter Clemens seems to have replied to an inquiry about his willingness to write for the *Galaxy*, perhaps on an extended or exclusive basis. Within a few weeks he had virtually agreed to do so: see 11 Mar 70 to Church.

From Samuel L. and Olivia L. Clemens
to Jervis and Olivia Lewis Langdon
9 February 1870 • Buffalo, N.Y.
(MS: CtHMTH)

Noon.
At Home, Feb. 9. 1870.

My Dear Father & Mother—

Livy has gone shopping, & to visit the Slees, & I remained at home to write a newspaper letter, but find after pacing the floor for an hour that I have no special interest in the subjects that present themselves. A man cannot do a thing well which his heart is not in, & so I have dropped the newspaper scribbling for to-day.

We have called upon the Slees once—*I* have called upon them once—*they* have called upon *us* once—& now *She* has gone to call upon *them*——so the lines of communication between these two households are unbroken, thus far, & are likely to remain so.[1]

We telegraphed the Twichells to come, & they did—& remained twenty-four hours by the watch, & were happy, & so were we. They took full account of the house & all its belongings, partly because they vastly enjoyed doing it, & partly because they expect to have to tell, & retell, & iterate & reiterate the details of our grandeur to all them that be in Hartford, & & ₍& who₎ somehow of late appear to take an interest in us.)[2]

I went after them with the carriage at 3.40 PM day before yesterday, & from that till dinner time (at 5,) we showed them elaborately over the house, & made Twichell wipe his feet & blow his nose before entering each apartment (so as to keep his respect up to an impressive altitude,)— & we listened to their raptures & enjoyed the same—ẅ & I told them the story of what happened to ₍L₎ittle Sammy in Fairy Land when he was hunting for a B̶a̶ Boarding House, & they enjoyed *that*. But I never let them go near that drawing room t̶h̶e̶y̶ till they thought they had seen all the glories of the palace—till after dinner, in fact, for I wanted to have the gas ablaze & the furniture-covers removed. It looked magnificent! I think they will give a good account. Mrs. T. says Alice Day's house is vulgarly showy & out of taste.[3] I am awful glad of it. (So is Livy, but she don't say so—at least she don't want it mentioned outside.) ˌ(Its no such thing and Mrs T. did not say so—ahem! naughty Youth)ˌ

Livy makes a most excellent little housekeeper, & I always knew she would. Everything goes on as smoothly as if it were worked by hidden machinery. The servants are willing & entirely respectful toward her (which they had *better* be.)

Livy has a dreadful time making her cash account balance; & she has a dreadful time economising a turkey in such a way as to make him last a week; & she has a dreadful time making the servants comprehend that they must buy nothing whatever on credit & that whatever they ~~mu~~ buy they must make the butcher or the grocer set down in the pass-book to be critically scanned by her eagle eye. These are all the dreadful times she has *on the surface*. She naturally has her little ~~down~~ sad moments within, & she confesses it—but you may take an honest man's word for it that I think she secretly reproaches herself for not being sad *oftener,* so as to show a proper grief ~~for~~ ˌatˌ leaving so lovely & so dear a home. The plain fact of the matter is that she has undergone the most astounding change—for verily she is become so boisterous, so noisy, & so lawless in her cheery happiness that I, even I, am forced ~~int~~ to put on an irksome gravity & decorum in order to uphold the dignity of the house. She pulls & hauls me around, & claws my hair, & bites my fingers, & laughs so that you might hear her across the street; & it does appear to me that I never saw anybody so happy as she is in all my life—except myself.

We entirely enjoy these glad days. We sit alone in the loveliest of libraries, in the evening, & ~~she~~ I read poetry—& every now & then I come to a passage that brings the tears to my eyes, & I look up to her for loving sympathy, & she inquires whether they sell sirloin steaks by the pound or by the yard. Ah, the child's heart is in her housekeeping, not in the romance of life.[4]

We are very regular in our habits. We get up at 6 o'clock every morning, & we go to bed at 10 every evening. We have three meals a day—breakfast at 10 oclock, lunch at 1 PM & dinner at 5. The reason we get ~~us~~ up at 6 in the morning is because we want to see what time it is. ~~We then go back to be~~ Partly this, & partly because we have heard that early rising is beneficial. We then go back to bed, & get up finally at half past 9.

Lovingly *Your Son*
Sam¹. L. Clemens.

I have returned from my shopping expedition and now Mr Clemens has gone down town— I purchased a clothes bar, a bread box a flat iron stand, a flower stand &c &c—

The names enclosed Mr C. wants after cards sent to— Annie will probably know if he has duplicated any—[5] I would like it if Sue could find from Zippie Hattie Marsh Tylers address and send after cards to her also to Lucy Gage Cursons—[6]

We are as ⌀ happy as two mortals can well be—

Lovingly Livy—

[1] John D. F. Slee and his wife, the former Emma Virginia Underhill, returned Olivia's call on 11 February. "Mr and Mrs Slee spent the evening with us last evening," Olivia wrote her family on 12 February, "we had a good social chat, then Mrs Slee and Mr Clemens, Annie and I played High, Low, Jack—Mr Slee & Mrs Moffett visiting meanwhile—" (CtHMTH; *L3*, 119 n. 4). Pamela and Annie Moffett came to Buffalo from Elmira, probably on 11 February (see note 5).

[2] Clemens resented those Hartford residents who had hesitated to support his effort in 1869 to become a partner in the Hartford *Courant* (*L3*, 440). Upon his return to Hartford, Twichell reported on the Clemenses' "grandeur" (6? Feb 70 to McComb, n. 2; 23 Feb 70 to Bliss, n. 1).

[3] Alice Hooker had married John C. Day on 17 June 1869 (*L3*, 265 n. 1, 276). The Days' house was at 32 Garden Street in Hartford (Geer: 1869, 99; 1870, 106).

[4] Around the time he wrote this letter Clemens made two starts on a sketch (never finished) about his and Olivia's inexperience at housekeeping (SLC 1870m–n). He returned to the theme of his own incompetence at it in "Political Economy," part of his "Memoranda" in the *Galaxy* for September 1870 (SLC 1870vv, 424–26).

[5] The list of wedding card recipients enclosed for Annie Moffett does not survive. Her son, Samuel C. Webster, reported that she remembered

> sitting at a table with Clara Spaulding, Livy's girlhood friend, helping to address wedding announcements from a list of his friends that Uncle Sam had made out—with unconventional annotations on the character of the people involved. (*MTBus*, 112)

Webster also reported that after Clemens's wedding, Annie and her mother "went to Fredonia, about forty miles away, and rented a house. . . . Then they returned to Elmira and spent a week with the Langdons" (*MTBus*, 112). But in a 16 February letter to her mother, Olivia said that "Mrs Moffett and Annie went yesterday to Fredonia to see if they could find any inducements there that would lead them to move ~~East~~ ‸there‸— . . . We are having a very pleasant visit from them— We expect them back some time today—" (CtHMTH). So the house-hunting trip to Fredonia came during their visit to Buffalo, which followed their week-long stay with the Langdons.

[6] Mentioned here were Susan L. Crane; Lucy Zipporah Brooks (d. 1912), Rachel Brooks Gleason's sister and, by 1873, also an Elmira physician; Hattie Marsh Tyler, possibly a daughter of Louisa Lewis (Mrs. Sheppard) Marsh, and therefore Olivia's first cousin, who seems to have lived in or near Buffalo (see 26 Feb 70 to Jervis Langdon); and the former Lucy A. Gage, of Crittenden, New York, who in 1861–62 had been a student at Elmira Female College (Wisbey:

1990, 4; 1993, 2; "Dr. Zippie Brooks Wales Passes Away," Elmira *Advertiser,* 5
July 1912, 5; "Capt. E. L. Marsh," obituary from unidentified Elmira newspaper inserted in AD, 26 Mar 1906, CU-MARK, in *MTA,* 2:250–51; *Elmira Female College,* 11).

To Charles Cole Hine
10 February 1870 • Buffalo, N.Y.
(MS: CU-MARK)

ⓒ

472 Delaware Ave. ⎫
Buffalo, Feb. 10. ⎭

My Dear Mr. Hine—
    You make out a very strong case—there can be no question about
that; & if you had made it out a single month earlier it would have been
potent. I would have succumbed. But now I am *married*—I renounce my
former life & all its belongings. I have begun a new life & a new system,
a new dispensation. And the bottom rule of this latter is,
    To Work No More than is Absolutely Necessary.
I've got plenty of money & plenty of credit—& so I won't write about
your wicked & dreadful insurance business[1] till my gas bills go to protest
& the milk-man ceases to toot his matutinal horn before the gates of

Yours Truly & Defiantly,
Sam*l*. L. Clemens
"Mark Twain"

✉———————————————————————————

Personal. | C.C. Hine Esq | P.O. BOX *3688* | New York [*on the flap:*] ⓒ
[*postmarked:*] BUFFALO N.Y. FEB 11 [*and*] 7 00 PM MAIL

[1] Since 1868 Hine (1825–97) had been editor of the monthly *Insurance Monitor,* which was established in 1853 and was "*the oldest insurance journal in the
United States, and the largest in the world,*" with a circulation of 24,000. He remained its editor until his death (Rowell, 706; Mott 1938, 94 n. 214). Hine was
also the author of *Eighteen Years in the Office of the Insurance Monitor: A History
of Life Insurance in the United States* (New York: Insurance Monitor, 1870). His
"very strong case" for an article by Clemens probably consisted, at least in part,
of recalling Clemens's "How, For Instance?" which mocked the advertised cov-

erages of an accident insurance company. First published in the New York *Weekly Review* on 29 September 1866, that sketch was reprinted the following year as "An Inquiry About Insurances" in the *Jumping Frog* book (SLC 1866g, 1867a).

From Samuel L. and Olivia L. Clemens
to Mary Mason Fairbanks
13 February 1870 • Buffalo, N.Y.
(MS: CSmH)

Boarding-House ⎫
Buffalo, Feb. 13. ⎭

Dear Mother—

Thank you for your letter (which my sister has sent to St Louis. She & Annie are making a visit with us. They ask me to tell you that they very much desire to stop & visit with you again,[1] according to your invitation, & they hope to be able to do it, but they cannot tell as yet, whether they shall have the time. However, for my part I strongly wish that they may tarry with you again, & learn to know you truly as you *are*, & love [you] as do all who know you well.

[This is execrable paper, but Livy don't allow me to use the nice paper. Well I guess she would let me use it to write to *you*, but every time I write a grocery order under her imposing monogram, I tell you there is trouble in the camp.]

We are glad you printed that graceful account of our wedding & our Surprise—we were glad enough to have *you* do it, because you know how such things should be done—but I made a special request (for Livy's sake) of all the other writers present, ~~that~~ at the wedding, that they put all they had to say into one stickfull, & leave out the adjectives.[2]

We are settled down & comfortable, & the days swing by with a whir & a flash, & are gone, we know not where & scarcely care. To me, passing time is a dream, in that it drifts so smoothly—but it is strong & stalwart & convincing reality, in the substantial comfort, & satisfaction & contentment it comes freighted with. ~~There~~ Every day I nerve myself, & sieze my pen, & dispose my paper, & prepare to buckle on the harness & *work!* And then I pace the floor—back & forth, back & forth, with vacuous mind—& finally I lay down the pen & confess that my time is not come—that I am utterly empty. But I must work, & I *will* work. I will go straight at it & *force* it. I used to do it every day of my life between Gibraltar & the Bermudas, & of course it can be done again. And it was so hard then! Will it be so now? Worse, maybe.[3]

But there is no romance in this existence for Livy ,*(False)*,. She embodies the Practical. The Hard, the Practical, the Unsentimental. She is lord of all she surveys.[4] She goes around with her bunch of housekeeper's ~~kee~~ keys (which she don't know how to unlock anything with them because they are mixed,) & is ~~ob~~ overbearing & perfectly happy. When things don't go right she breaks the furniture & knocks everything endways. You ought to see her charge around! When I hear her war-whoop I know it is time to climb out on the roof. But law me, *you* know *her.*

But Livy keeps the cash account straight. She keeps three sets of books & she can tell you just what goes with every fragment of a five= dollar bill, as deftly as if she had been born & bred to housekeeping.

But what worries *us* is our coachman. I went & tricked him out in a livery coat (w̶ pale blue with a deep cape,) & with enormous brass buttons with a ^G on them (they had none with a C.) But I couldn't stand those buttons, & had them taken off. And I got him a stove-pipe hat with a broad velvet band & a brass buckle. But I couldn't stand the buckle. And after all, when we were getting ready for church this morning I felt that I was ,not, equal to the cape,—nor yet to the velvet band. And so I had them both stripped—& it was like stripping a h an exultant peacock of his tail. Afterward I relented, as to the cape, & so we bowled off to church with a coachman who, if liveries ~~desi~~ designated politics, would have been a neutral. But wait a little—wait. I can't take a whole box of pills at one dose, but I can/ take a barrel of them give me time. I'll get along further & further ~~till~~ with this livery business, till by & bye Patrick[5] shall be so gorgeous that the street boys shall follow us hoping thereby to curry favor ~~th~~ with the circus we are probably connected with.

We got off to church at last, the ladies ~~no la,~~ ,(no ladies went but the wife of the writer), within & I outside with Patrick,—Patrick with his fearfully tall & fearfully shiny hat. Do you know, that coat of Patrick's cost me more than did any that ever *I* wore?—& it is so handsome. It did not seem to me that a man's coachman ought to wear a finer coat than himself, & so, under way, I swapped coats with Patrick, and—

Dr Heacock is an exceedingly pleasant & hearty man. ~~He~~ After church he trotted us out before his Sunday School & gave us a chance to show our trousseaux. I can never forget him. I never can forget his kindness to the stranger within his gates.[6] Some ministers—most ministers, perhaps—would have allowed us to come, & go, with chilly unrecognition, & with no thought as to whether we wished to show our clothes— with no—[7]

I feel that we shall get along well here in Buffalo, & with its people, & that we shall be happy & content. I know that in your heart you hope this for us. And we two will get along well together,—I feel it, I *know* it. We have been married eleven days, & not thirty-five ₐ(not one)ₐ cross words have passed between us. It is a blessed union—a union of hearts as well as hands. I never saw such a couple as *we* are in all *my* life.

Your blessing Mother!

Always Lovingly
The Elder Cub.[8]

Dear Mother (?) Fairbanks

Mr Clemens wanted me to go through this letter and tell the truth of the facts that he has been romancing about, but it seems to me a hopeless undertaking, so with the few corrections that you will find in it I shall let it go—

We are having a pleasant visit with Mrs Moffett ~~and~~ and Annie, I hope it will not be very long before you will make us a visit in our new home— I am sure that we could make you happy, and I know it will make us happy to have you with us—

We will make Mr Clemens read aloud to us in Mrs Browning—Felicity to us—but what to him?[9]

With love to Allie[10]—~~and a large amount to yourself~~ ₐ(taking to some of Mr C's habits, you see)ₐ

I am with ever increasing love for yourself your

Livy—

P. S. The parenthesis refers to the manner of erasing words—not to Allie. S.

How thankful I am that you have some one to interpret my letters for you   L.

It is a sort of grammar that renders interpretation very necessary. S.

I don't think so—BECAUSE—

L.

And I *do* think so, for the same reason. S.

No—L.

Go to bed, Woman! S.

I am not sleepy—L.

This it is to be married. S.

Yes indeed—Woe is me! this it *is* to be married L.

Go on—jaw—jaw—jaw. S.

I don't *think* so—L.

Well, *take* the last word. S.

[1] See 15 Jan 70 to PAM, nn. 2, 3.

[2] See pp. 46–47.

[3] Clemens recalled the period of 24 October to 11 November 1867 when the *Quaker City* steamed from Gibraltar to Bermuda, en route to New York. He used that time to catch up on his newspaper correspondence (*L2*, 108, 110 n. 4, 113, 114 n. 1, 397).

[4] "I am monarch of all I survey" (William Cowper, "Verses Supposed to Be Written by Alexander Selkirk," stanza 1).

[5] McAleer.

[6] "Remember that thou keep holy the Sabbath-day. . . . In it thou shalt do no manner of work; thou, and thy son . . . and the stranger that is within thy gates" (4th Commandment, "The Order for the Administration of the Lord's Supper, or Holy Communion," *Book of Common Prayer*, 283).

[7] Grosvenor Williams Heacock (1822–77) had been pastor of Buffalo's Lafayette Street Presbyterian Church for more than twenty-four years (Reigstad 1990, 1). On the day before this letter Olivia wrote to her family in Elmira: "This morning we had a very pleasant call from Dr Heacock—he spoke approvingly of Mr Clemens book—" (CtHMTH), presumably *The Innocents Abroad*.

[8] The younger "cubs" were Charles J. Langdon and Julius Moulton (*L2*, 64–65, 130, 243–44).

[9] Compare *L3*, 26, 27–28 n. 5, 95, 241.

[10] Alice Holmes Fairbanks.

To Joel Benton
20 February 1870 • Buffalo, N.Y.
(MS: NPV)

Buffalo, 20[th.]

Friend Benton—

No, I write European Letters occasionally for the Express, & they are all we need.[1]

I will do my best to remember to put the "Times" on the X list,[2] but as I don't go to the office once a week it will simply be a marvel if I don't forget it. ~~But if you had dropped a line to the "Publishers" it would have been all right—savez?~~ I'll tie a string round my finger, though, & I'll *determine* to recollect—& so I think I can safely say that I *will* remember to fix that thing, sure.

We are about as happy in our Aladdin's Palace (*I* think it is a little more tasteful & exquisite in all its appointments than most palaces are,) as if we were roosting in the closing chapter of a popular novel.[3]

Pray remember me kindly to our delightful friends the Payne's,[4] & we shall be glad at any time to see you & them at 472 Delaware Avenue, Buffalo.

Yrs Sincerely
Saml. L. Clemens.

[1] If Clemens did in fact write "European Letters" for the *Express*, they have not been identified. His series of "Around the World" letters did not describe European travel (22 Jan 70 to Bliss, n. 2). Benton seems to have offered to sell the *Express* some European travel letters, possibly his own, not further identified.

[2] That is, the exchange list of the Buffalo *Express*. The Amenia *Times* was Benton's former newspaper (8 Jan 70 to OLL [1st], n. 2).

[3] Clemens's comments about his absence from the *Express* offices and about his domestic happiness show that he wrote shortly after the wedding, hence 20 February.

[4] See 8 Jan 70 to OLL (1st).

From Samuel L. and Olivia L. Clemens
to Olivia Lewis Langdon
20 February 1870 • Buffalo, N.Y.
(MS: CtHMTH)

At Home, Sunday 4 P.M.

Our Dear Mother—

I thank you ever, ever so much, mother dear, for the pretty fork & the charming napkin-ring (for it *is* just as charming as it can be,) & I will try to deserve your loving kindness to me. The fork & the ring are in keeping with everything else about our home—which is the daintiest, & the most exquisite & enchanting that can be found in all America—& the longer we know it the more fascinating it grows & the firmer the hold it fastens upon each fettered sense. It is perfect. Perfect in all its dimensions, proportions & appointments. It is filled with that nameless grace which faultless harmony gives. The colors are all rich, & all beautiful, & all blended ~~with~~ & interchanged & interwoven without a single marring discord. Our home is a ˏceaseless, unsurfeiting˗ feast for the eye ~~& for~~ & the soul, & the whole being. It is a constant delight. It is a poem, it is music—~~&~~ & it speaks & it sings, ˏto us,ˏ all the day long. I think we are thankful to our loved father, our precious father.

Livy gets along better & better with her housekeeping, & indeed she astonishes me sometimes by the insight she shows into things one wouldn't suppose she knew anything about. But while she surprises me with her ability to follow the old beaten paths of housekwifery, her ~~achev~~ achievements when she branches out of those beaten paths surprise me still more. Now this morning she had a mackerel fricaseed with pork & oysters ˏ(*False*),ˏ & I tell you it was a dish to stir the very depths of one's benevolence. We saved every single bit of it for the poor.

I never saw anybody look ~~as~~ so unearthly wise as Livy does when she is ordering dinner; & I never saw anybody look so relieved as she does when she has completed her order, poor child —(This is false too, mother dear, prettie nearly). {So you see she has come down from her roost for the afternoon & is prepared to look after me.}

You can't think what a carver I have become. I hardly ever have to take hold of a chicken by the leg, now. And I look mighty imposing, too, at the head of my table, with my big fork, & my carving-knife & my glove-stretcher about me. {I use the glove-stretcher to hold the chicken open while I get out the stuffing—Livy is keeping her eyes shut till I tell her she may look & see what I am to do with the glove-stretcher.}

Isn't he a funny Youth?

The other day I went into the drawing room with Mr Clemens to see Mr Lock (Nasby)[1] and a Mr Bishop who entertained Mr Clemens in Jamestown,[2] and what should I see on entering ~~on~~ the room, but the covers to two of the chairs turned up to show the satin covers underneath— he is as delighted with that room as a boy with a top or his first pair of boots— Mr C. said something the other day about having the covers off, but finally did not want it done because he had had an experience with one friend[3] that he uncovered it for that taught him a lesson, the gentleman sat on the sofa, and ~~long~~ lounged about in the chairs till Mr Clemens was as nervous as he could well be and was very much relieved when he got him out of there up into his study— He has grown wonderfully care taking, the other evening the bell rang, and he told Harriet to bring who ever came into the Library, I could not think why, but that night when we went to bed, he said he thought while this snow lasted we better bring people into the Library, so that they would not carry the snow ~~into~~ in onto that carpet,—he made Mr Lock go out after he had entered the room and wipe the snow off his feet— It does amuse me who would have ever *dreamed* of seeing Mr Clemens so carefull— Livy—

[Thank you, Livy darling.]

With all duty & affection, Mother,
Your loving son
Samuel.

✉—————————————————————————————————

Mrs. J. Langdon | Elmira | N. Y. [*postmarked:*] BUFFALO N.Y. FEB 21

[1]Clemens had met Petroleum V. Nasby (David Ross Locke) in March 1869 (*L3*, 158–60). Olivia was meeting him for the first time, but she was familiar with his writing, known as much for its bizarre spelling as for its political satire. In a letter of 1 November 1869 to Alice Hooker Day, she reported telling Clemens that "if Naseby had my talent for misspelling he would not have to make any effort in that direction" (CtHSD). Nasby was in Buffalo on 18 February to lecture for the Woman's Suffrage Association on "The Struggles of a Conservative with the Woman Question" ("Amusements," Buffalo *Express*, 15 Feb 70, 4). Clemens wrote the review of the lecture that appeared in the Buffalo *Express* the following day (SLC 1870o).

[2]Coleman E. Bishop (1838–96) was the contentious editor of the Jamestown (N.Y.) *Journal*. If Clemens was not yet aware of that paper's treatment of his 21 January lecture there, he probably learned something about it during this visit from Nasby and Bishop. Bishop's review on 22 January was part of an ongoing attack on the local Y.M.C.A.'s lecture course. It was sarcastic about the lecture committee and about those in the audience who were disappointed by, or unappreciative of, a humorous lecture. Bishop himself professed to be satisfied and appreciative, but his praise was backhanded and condescending, particularly in his characterization of the lecture as "*nothing* and intended as such."

> Our advice to Mr. Clemens is to settle down on the conviction that his *forte* is not that of a missionary, a preacher, a philosopher, a reformer, a teacher nor any of these solemn callings. Every time he tries to do these things he will be out of his element. (Coleman E. Bishop 1870b)

Two days later the *Journal* published a letter to the editor, signed "MANY CITIZENS," denouncing both Clemens and his lecture. It was possibly tongue in cheek, although Clemens was not amused. In 1886, his rancor at the "Many Citizens" letter found vent in an "Unmailed Answer" addressed to its author, whom he knew but did not name: "You wrote that thing about my lecture, sixteen years ago, in the Jamestown, N.Y., *Journal*—property of that ostentatiously pious half-human polecat, Bishop! Nasby told me it was you, at the time; & he got it from Bishop himself" (SLC 1886; "Editorial Small Talk," Elmira *Advertiser*, 25 Jan 70, 1; *Chautauqua County*, 2:114–15; Rowell, 696; Coleman E. Bishop 1870a; Many Citizens; Lorch 1953, 1954; Jones).

³ Unidentified.

To Elisha Bliss, Jr.
23 February 1870 • Buffalo, N.Y.
(MS: CU-MARK)

At Home Feb. 23.

Friend Bliss—

Why bless your soul, I never have time to write letters these days—takes all my time to carry on the honey-moon.¹ I would like to talk to Mrs Bliss² two or three or four hours about my wife now, if she could stand it——she *used* to stand it very well when I was at your house.

Express gets along well. I have a strong notion to write a——

Well, never mind, I'll ₩ tell you about it another time.³

I am glad Mrs. Barstow has retrieved her credit—I was about to write you to charge her $150″ to me, when your second letter came. I am very glad, ~~more f~~ simply for her own sake, that she has kept up her credit.⁴

6,000 & upwards, in 16 days, is splendid—*Splendid*, isn't it?⁵

I don't go near the Express office more than twice a week—& then only for an hour. I am just as good [as] other men—& other men take honey-moons I reckon.

Hello!—there's the bell—my wife is taking a nap & I am receiving calls.

Yrs Ever,
Mark

✉—————————————————————————

[*letter docketed:*] √ auth Mark Twain | Feb 23/70

¹Clemens was replying to two recent letters from Bliss, only the first of which survives (CU-MARK):

HARTFORD CONN. Feby. 15 18 70

Samˡ L Clements

Buffalo

Dear Clemens,

Have not heard from you for some time— Trust you "still live"   Why dont you drop me a line occasionally, & let me know how you are— Did our Check arrive safely & *in time*— Trust you had a "merry wedding"   Have seen Twitchell once since he came back. He was at my house to a little "*bender*" we had there this week. He told me about your Buffalo "surprise"— Dont think such things are hard to take—

How goes the Express? & does it gain ground any? The Book moves. Have sold about *5,000* so far this month   We are outst[r]ipping all the rest. We have 5 presses still running on it—printing now the 50 to 55ᵗʰ000. We of course keep some way ahead of shipments— We are proposing to *boost it this spring*— And now about a matter I want help in— Mrs *Kate D. Barstow* suddenly disappeared from our sky, owing $157.40. We hear nothing from her. Can you ascertain her whereabouts— Think she should be looked after— She always seemed to be prompt, till she stept out. We wrote to Washington & elsewhere but no, answer. Enquiry by you at Washington may disclose her residence— Please let me hear from you. Respects & kind regards to Mrs. C—

Truly yrs &c

E Bliss Jʳ⋅

Four days after this letter, the Hartford *Courant* reported: "The American Publishing company are now printing the sixtieth thousand of Mark Twain's new book. They have already sold over fifty-five thousand, and have orders ahead faster than they can supply them" ("Brief Mention," 19 Feb 70, 2).

²Amelia Bliss (*L3*, 15 n. 4).

³Clemens's "strong notion" was probably to write for the *Galaxy,* an undertaking he suspected Bliss might not approve (see 11 Mar 70 to Bliss).

⁴In September 1869 Clemens had persuaded Bliss to award the Virginia agency for *Innocents* to Kate D. Barstow, a Nevada friend in financial straits. Ultimately she was not able to pay for all of the books she received, and Clemens had to reimburse Bliss (*L3*, 339–41, 345). Barstow was so chagrined by her failure that she did not write to Clemens for ten years. On 16 October 1881 she apologized, and asked Clemens to finance her study of medicine at Howard University, in Washington, D.C., promising to "repay you the total indebtedness when I get into practice!" (CU-MARK). Clemens agreed and Barstow received her medical degree in 1884. It is not known if she repaid him (Barstow to SLC, various letters 1881–84, CU-MARK).

⁵Bliss evidently updated the sales report on *Innocents* to 16 February, indicating that he wrote his now missing second letter only a day or two after his first. This "splendid" showing brought the total number of books sold (as distinct from printed) to about 45,000.

From Olivia L. and Samuel L. Clemens
to Jervis Langdon
26 February 1870 • Buffalo, N.Y.
(MS: CtHMTH)

(LC)

Buffalo Feb. 26th 1870
Our Home, 242. Del.

My darling Father
    Your note came to late in all respects, I had already written Mr
and Mrs Barnard,[1] such a note as it was it went home unsealed so that
Mother could read it if she chose, it was truthful, and yet I think would
be satisfactory—
    The laundry tubs were already changed when your letter came, and
I cannot really regret it, because that ~~selar~~ cellar was very damp— I did
wish at the time that I had you here to counsel with ~~at first ,when your~~
~~letter came,~~ ,When your letter came, I felt like mourning that I had done
it, but I reflected that as I had done to the best of my ability, I would not
worry, that is your phylosophy, Father—
    The cost of moving the tubs, ʄ carpenter and plumbers work is to
be 28.00—they are all moved now— You may readily believe that we
shall be slow to make alterations—
    I am as happy in housekeeping as you can immagine— I have been
all about the house this morning, all through the cellar, told Patrick[2]
about looking over a barrell of apples that are decaying— I wish that you
and Mother would run up and see us next week   Can't you do it,? we
will rest you like every thing—
    I had two disagreeable things to speak with Ellen and Harriet about
this morning, and I did dread it, but I went right at it, and being assiled
in ~~that~~ that way the mountain became an anthill and amounted to nothing at all—
    I have, as yet had none ,of, the trouble that ladies groan over, but I
suppose a three weeks experience is hardly enough to crow over, Hattie
Marsh Tyler was here yesterday and was telling me about how much
trouble the Buffalo ladies have with their girls, I hope it will not come to

me and some way believe it will not— No more this time *dear*, DARLING
Father, we do love you with all our hearts   I use *we* advisedly—

—Love to Grandma, Mother[,] Sue,[3] and all, I shall write again today
or tomorrow—

Lovingly Livy—

Dear Father—It was to please me that Livy moved the wash-tubs,
~~I~~ maybe—because I said "Let them be moved, Mrs. Clemens—I have
hunted high & low & cannot find anything about the house to alter
or improve, & it is entirely too bad—it is not showing proper respect
to a father who pulls *his* house to pieces all the time—Move the wash=
tubs, ~~madam,~~ into the woodhouse, Madam, pile the wood in the stable
& put the horse in the laundry—I tell you something *must* be altered
quick, or your father won't like it."

Lovingly Your Son
Samuel.

[*OLC:*] Mr J. Langdon | Elmira | N. Y. [*on the flap:*] (LC) [*postmarked:*]
BUFFALO N.Y. FEB 26

[1] Unidentified.
[2] McAleer.
[3] Crane. "Grandma" was Eunice Ford.

From Olivia L. and Samuel L. Clemens
to Susan L. Crane
26 or 27 February 1870 • Buffalo, N.Y.
(*MTB*, 1:409)

·   ·   ·   ·

Sue, we are two as happy people as you ever saw. Our days seem to be
made up of only bright sunlight, with no shadow in them.

·   ·   ·   ·

Livy pines & pines every day for you, & I pine & pine every day for you,
& when we both of us are pining at once you would think it was a whole
pine forest let loose.[1]

·   ·   ·   ·

[1] These fragments cannot be precisely dated, but may belong to the letter Olivia promised her father on 26 February.

From Samuel L. and Olivia L. Clemens to Jervis Langdon
2 and 3 March 1870 • Buffalo, N.Y.
(MS: CtHMTH)

Polishing Irons.
———

March. 2.

Dear Father—

Got your dispatch, & shall talk no business with my partners[1] till Mr. Slee gets back.

The "Peace" has arrived, but Livy don't know it, for she has got some eternal company in the drawing-room & it is considerably after dinner-time. But I have spread the fringed red dinner-table spread over the big rocking-chair & set up the beautiful thing on it, & in a prominent place, & it will be the first thing Livy sees when she comes in.

Later—She went into convulsions of delight when she entered. And I don't wonder, for we both so mourned the loss of the first Peace that it did not seem possible we could do without it—& for you to send another in this delightful & unexpected way was intensely gratifying. You have our most sincere gratitude—Livy's for the present itself, & mine because I shall ⸝ enj so much enjoy looking at it.[2]

March 3.

Your two letters came this morning, father, & your dispatch yesterday afternoon. [Mem.—En Ellen's in the stable & the horse in the attic looking at the scenery.][3]

We think it cannot be worth while to enter into an explanation of the Express figures, for the reason that Mr. Slee must have arrived in Elmira after your letter was written, & he would explain them to you much more clearly & understandingly than I could.

I thank you ever so much for your offer to take my money & pay me interest on it until we decide whether to add it to the Kennett purchase or not. I was going to avail myself of it at once, but waited to see if Mr.

Slee & MacWilliams couldn't make Selkirk's figures show a little more
favorably. As I hoped, so it has resulted. And now, upon thorough conviction that the Express is not a swindle, I will pay some more on the
Kennett indebtedness.[4]

I am very glad to begin to see my way through this business, for
figures confuse & craze me in a little while.[5] I haven't Livy's tranquil
nerve in the presence of a financial complexity—when her cash account
don't balance (which ~~do is about~~ does not happen oftener than once a
day) ‚*false*‚ she just increases the item of "Butter 78 cents" to "Butter 97
cents"—or reduces the item of "Gas, $6.45" to "Gas, $2.35" & *makes*
that account balance. She keeps books with the most inexorable accuracy
that ever mortal man beheld.

Father it is not true— Samuel slanders me—

I wrote "Polishing Irons" at the head of this letter the other night to
remind either Livy or me to write about them—didn't put it there for a
~~tet~~ text to preach from.[6]

The report of my intending to leave Buffalo ~~w~~ Livy & I have concluded emanates from Hartford, for the reason that it really started in
the newspapers only a very little while after my last visit & your last letter
to Hartford, & has been afloat ever since.[7]

Yr son
Samuel.

[1] Josephus N. Larned and George H. Selkirk (*L3*, 300 n. 2, 401–2 n. 2).

[2] In a 16 February letter to her mother, Olivia reported (CtHMTH):

> I have had a grief this morning! The beautiful statuett of ~~Piece~~ Peace is all
> broken to pieces—the head and arm are both severed from the body, I do not want to
> believe my own eyes— I had put the ~~Piece~~ ‚Peace‚ in about half a doz. different places
> in the house, and now that its exquisite beauty should be destroyed‚— That it was a gift
> from Mr and Mrs Diven made it especially dear to me, and that Mr Diven should have
> taken the care of it himself—
>> It seemed well packed—every thing has seemed well packed, and we have as yet
> found nothing else broken—
>> I feel almost like having a good hard cry now, and wishing that all the rest of my
> things had been broken and that saved—

After receiving the replacement she wrote (CtHMTH):

> Buffalo March 2nd
>> Dear Father or Mother which ever of you did it, I *do* thank you for the "Peace", the
> beautiful ~~Peach~~ Peace, it came this afternoon— How could you do it, how good you
> were to do it, *every thing*— I don't know what to say—
>> I came out from the drawing room this afternoon from a caller and found the
> scarlet table spread fixed on a chair and the "Peace" standing on it, the effect was charm-

ing, and of course I cried out with delight, at first I thought that my old statuette was made whole, but looked immediately to the top of the clock where the head of my poor broken Peace had been put, and there the head still was—of course the truth all dawned upon me ~~then~~ then— I ~~wakened~~ wakened this morning thinking that you could not have rec'd the letter telling about the disaster as you had none of you refered to it in any way— The Peace is as exquisite as it can be and I do thank you with all my heart— If you were here I think that I could tell you about it a little better than I can write—
      As I write Samuel is playing and singing—
      Tell me about everything when you write— We love you all at Elmira
      Mr Clemens is very anxious to have the polishing irons come I should get some here but they do not seem to keep them, I could not get any— I do not know whether there is any way to hurry them, but the Youth does not like to wear his shirts done up without them—
      Mr and Mrs Selkirk are coming in this evening, I believe I must not write more this time—
      Thank you, *thank you*, THANK YOU, for your last loving token that you would have no mar on the perfection of everything in my life if you could order it—
                                                            Lovingly Livy—

The statuette has not been identified; for the Divens, see p. 44.
   [3] Only one of these communications is known to survive (PH in CU-MARK):

                                                       Elmira March 2^{d}/70
Dear Samuel,
      You should have the privilege of following in the footsteps of your illustrious mother, so you should. You can make changes. You may put the Carriage in the Cellar, the horse in the drawing room, & Ellen in the stable. Please your own tastes my boy, some have peculiar tastes & ought to be gratified
      I am for liberty—
                                                 Your affectionate father
                                                       J Langdon

The anecdote about Jane Clemens that Langdon referred to has not been identified.
   [4] Although the first payment on the $10,000 Clemens owed to Thomas A. Kennett was not due until August, he planned here to use at least part of his second quarter *Innocents* royalties to pay "some more on the Kennett indebtedness." Within a few days, however, he changed his mind. Apparently he did pay Kennett $2,500 in August, with subsequent payments in 1871 and 1872. John James McWilliams, a bookkeeper in the Buffalo office of Langdon's coal firm, was one of Clemens's first Buffalo friends. He had assisted Slee in the "boarding house" ruse after the wedding (28 Jan 70 to Bliss, n. 5; 3 Mar 71 to Riley, n. 3; *L3*, 316–17, 333, 334 n. 4).
   [5] The *Express* figures were not the only ones to agitate Clemens. On 16 February Olivia wrote her mother: "Mr Clemens says that I had presents and a good time when I was married, and when I reached here people came to see ~~me~~ me, but his first salutation was a paper enquiring about his income tax— That income tax has been a matter of most intense anxiety to him, he could not *possibly* comprehend it—" (CtHMTH). Clemens turned his anxiety into a sketch, "A Mysterious Visit," published on 19 March in the *Express*. In it he told how an unfortunate boast to the tax assessor—"Two hundred and fourteen thousand, cash, is my income for this year if *I* know how to cipher"—threatened financial calamity until he learned to manipulate the "eleven saving clauses under the head of 'Deductions'" (SLC 1870w). The sketch was reprinted in "the *Revenue*

Record, the official organ of the Internal Revenue Department," at the suggestion of

> an Assistant Assessor of Internal Revenue, who writes that it is the unanimous opinion
> of the Assistant Assessors of the Thirtieth District that it ought to be published in the
> *Record.* It is suggestive, he adds, "of some fun, and any amount of truth in reference to
> the assessment of incomes, and we think it would be interesting to revenue officers
> generally." ("The last number . . . ," Buffalo *Express,* 12 Apr 70, 2)

[6] Olivia's 2 March letter was her second reminder about these irons—used for
polishing starched shirtfronts, collars, and cuffs. She had first written to her
mother about them on 20 February: "This Youth of mine does not want his shirts
ironed till the polishing irons come— We ordered them from ~~Roes~~ Charlies
store, if it will not trouble Sue [Crane] to enquire about them some time when
she is down town I should like to get her to do so—" (CtHMTH). With his father's backing, Charles Langdon became a partner in Ayrault, Rose and Company, an Elmira hardware store, in 1868 (Whitney and Smith, 4:4594; *L2,* 341–
42 n. 3).

[7] Clemens was last in Hartford on 27 December 1869, at which time he informed Olivia that Isabella Beecher Hooker had been writing to "Mr. Langdon
to make us sell out in Buffalo & come here" (*L3,* 440). No report of Clemens
leaving Buffalo has been found in a Hartford paper. On 13 January 1870, however, the Buffalo *Commercial Advertiser* announced: "Mark Twain (SAMUEL L.
CLEMONS,) formerly of this city, lectures in Fredonia on Wednesday evening of
next week" ("Brevities," 3). On 21 January the Cleveland *Herald* made the point
explicit: "The Buffalo *Commercial* intimates that Mark Twain has left that city"
("Personal Intelligence," 4). Clemens evidently saw even more decided versions
of the rumor among the Buffalo *Express*'s exchanges, leading him to publish a
disclaimer (7 Mar 70 to the Public).

To Elisha Bliss, Jr.
3 March 1870 • Buffalo, N.Y.
(MS: CU-MARK)

Buf, Mch 3.

Friend Bliss—

Won't you send a free copy to an old preacher-friend of my boyhood: ˌRev.ˌ *L. F. Walden,*[1] *Rolla, Mo.?* [He hasn't got a cent.]

And one also to *George Routledge & Sons, 416 Broome street, N. Y.*

I wrote them to know if it would pay me to go ~~in~~ over the Niagara
river & get a British copyright, & you see what he says.[2]

Say—When any of your family come to Buffalo, we want you to put up at 472 Delaware street if you like the accommodations—will you? We have the honor to refer to Rev. J. H. Twichell & wife, J. Langdon & wife, Mrs. A W. Fairbanks, & others. This house has been recently refitted & furnished entirely new, & supplied with all the modern improvements, & is kept wholly on the European plan. [That is to say, we get up & take breakfast when we *want* to,—not when we *have* to.] We hope to merit a share of the public patronage—that is, such share of it as we officially invite. ~~Oh, but don't we put on airs? I reckon not!~~

Yrs Truly
Mark.

✉ ──

[*letter docketed:*] ✓ author [*and*] Mark Twain | March 3/70

[1] Lewis Frank Walden: see the next letter.
[2] The enclosure does not survive, but must have been a reply from Joseph L. Blamire, or some other New York representative of George Routledge and Sons, of London. He doubtless informed Clemens that no British copyright on *Innocents* could now be had, in Canada or elsewhere, because Clemens had not published it *first* in England. He might have added that temporary residence in Canada, even when a book *was* first published in England, would not necessarily prevent unauthorized Canadian publication, since not all Canadian publishers regarded such books as protected. The Routledges had, by May 1871, agreed to publish *Roughing It* in England before Bliss published it in the United States, thereby securing its British copyright ("Personal," Buffalo *Express*, 12 May 70, 2; Roper, 31–35, 82; *RI 1993*, 855). For an account of Clemens's developing relations with the Routledges and their rivalry with John Camden Hotten, see *ET&S1*, 546–55, 570–71, 586–608.

To Lewis Frank Walden
4 March 1870 • Buffalo, N.Y.
(Hannibal *Evening Courier-Post*, 6 Mar 1935)

Buffalo, March 4.

Friend Frank:—

It was a little surprising to get a letter from you for when one has been out of one's range of vision for 20 years, one is apt to forget him.[1]

I am glad you are in the ministry, & hope your career may be long & useful. It is the highest dignity to which a man may aspire in this life, &, when its duties are faithfully performed, the satisfaction felt must be greater than that customarily felt by men in the ordinary walks of life.[2]

I have quit lecturing for the present & settled down to doing nothing—at least it nearly amounts to that. I do write some. I am a third owner of an old established daily paper here. I shall not travel any more—at least until obliged to—if that day ever comes. I was married a month ago & so have cast away the blue goggles of bachelordom & now look at the world through the crystal lenses of my new estate.

I have ordered my publisher to send you a copy of my book, & it will reach you in time, but not right away, because the supply of books still remains considerably behind the demand.

Good bye & good luck to you.

> Your friend,
> Saml. L. Clemens.

[1] In 1935 the Hannibal *Evening Courier-Post* gave this account of Clemens's boyhood friendship with Walden (d. 1924):

> Clemens lived in the family home on Hill street while Frank Walden lived on what, years ago was known as Palmyra avenue but which is now Mark Twain avenue, at the very foot of Cardiff hill, and there was a well defined pathway from the top of the hill, where the two boys, with other friends, played soldier and "hunted Indians," to the back door of the Walden home.
>
> Sam and Frank went swimming in the Mississippi and in the old "swimming hole" on Bear creek, hunted rabbits and fished together, and played boyish pranks. As youths they set type together in the same printing office, here, the old Hannibal Courier, which several years later was purchased by Walden. ("Frank Walden and Mark Twain Kept Alive Boyhood Friendship; Family Has Letters," 6 Mar 1935, 9C)

Clemens had been an apprentice printer to Joseph P. Ament, publisher of the Hannibal *Missouri Courier,* from May 1848 until January 1851. Walden's ownership of the *Courier* has not been confirmed, but it seems likely he was the Lewis F. Walden who, from 19 May to 21 June 1856, published a short-lived daily edition of the weekly Hannibal *True American,* a Know-Nothing paper (*L1,* 1–2, 113–14 n. 5; Holcombe, 988; Gregory, 358).

[2] Walden had become a Methodist preacher. Clemens had similarly praised the ministry in 1865 (*L1,* 322–24).

To Robert M. and Louise M. Howland
with a note to James W. Nye
6 March 1870 • Buffalo, N.Y.
(MS: CU-MARK)

Buffalo, Mch. 6.

T Dear Bob & Lady—[1]

I have had so much to do of late (had so much "setting around" to do, being now in the fourth week of the honeymoon,) that I have had no comfortable opportunity to answer your welcome letter.

I wish you had told me—you experienced people—if it is always as pleasant as it is now. If all of one's married days are as happy as these new ones have been to me, I have ~~fooled~~ deliberately fooled away 30 years of my life. ~~One or~~ If it were to do over again I would marry in early infancy instead of wasting time cutting teeth & breaking crockery. ~~Hey Bob?~~

"It's a great country—Hey Bob?"[2]

I had a long letter from Jonny Kinney a week or two ago, & want to answer it but things interfere—but I will, shortly. He is a partner in his father's bank—E. Kinney & Co., Cincinnati,[3]

I wonder how the late Miss Lou likes married life. Better than trotting up & down between Miss Clapp's school & Mr. Meyer's ranch, I suspect.[4]

But this letter ~~will probably~~ ₍may₎ never reach you—so why prolong it? I wish you both all the happiness that you *deserve*—& if you get all that, you will not even ask for any more yourselves.

Contentedly
Yr friend
Sam*ˡ*. L. Clemens.

Mr. Robert M. Howland | Care Hon. James Nye | U. S. Senate | Washington [*postmarked:*] BUFFALO N.Y. MAR 7 [*across envelope end:*]

~~IF NOT DELIVERED WITHIN 10 DAYS, TO BE RETURNED TO~~
Please forward it, Governor, & oblige[5]

Yrs Ever
~~Sam*ˡ*.~~ Mark Twain.

[1] Robert Muir Howland met Clemens in Nevada in August 1861 and soon became one of his mining partners. Howland had married Louise Althea Meier on 10 November 1867. The Howlands made a wedding journey to New York, the groom's home state, and then went to Washington, D.C., where Clemens probably saw them in late December 1867 or early January 1868. Howland appeared as one of the stranded passengers in "Cannibalism in the Cars," written in January 1868 (*L1*, 142 n. 2, 156, 161 n. 2; SLC 1868a; "Married," "Gone to the Land of Honeymoon," Virginia City *Territorial Enterprise*, 12 Nov 67, 3; Howland, 4–5; 8 Feb 70 to Fuller, n. 3).

[2] Evidently a Nevada catch phrase. Clemens repeated it in a 3? September 1877 letter to Howland (CU-MARK).

[3] No correspondence is known to survive between Clemens and John D. Kinney, another of his first Nevada friends. The two men were involved in several timber and mining speculations between September 1861, when Kinney arrived in the territory, and March 1862, when he returned to Cincinnati. One venture formed the basis for chapters 22 and 23 of *Roughing It*, where Kinney appeared as "Johnny K——." The other members of the banking firm were Eli Kinney (John's father) and F. M. Hulburd (*L1*, passim; *RI 1993*, 147–57; *Cincinnati Directory* 1870, 351).

[4] Emanuel Meier (variously spelled) and his family, including his daughter Louise (b. 1848?), were natives of Ohio. From 1854 to 1859 they lived in Downieville, California, where Meier kept a general store. In the early 1860s he had a "milk ranch" near Carson City. Louise Meier was attending Hannah K. Clapp's Sierra Seminary in Carson City when Robert Howland and Clemens first met her. Clemens described the school in a letter of 14 January 1864 to the Virginia City *Territorial Enterprise* (Berlin, 24–79 passim, 154, 187–89, 447; Kelly: 1862, 69, 85; 1863, 97, 107; "Local Matters," Virginia City *Territorial Enterprise*, 20 May 66, 3; Angel, 220, 228; *MTEnt*, 134, 226; SLC 1864a).

[5] Nye, formerly governor of Nevada Territory (1861–64), was elected a Republican senator in 1864 when Nevada became a state. Clemens had last seen him in Washington in early 1868 (SLC 1868a; *L2*, 177 n. 3).

To George Griswold
7 March 1870 • Buffalo, N.Y.
(Transcript and paraphrase: AAA 1916, lot 157)

Buffalo, March 7.

. . . .

[*paraphrase: A hurried answer to a request for his autograph,*] some friends have just arrived . . . we have been waiting supper for them & they are now waiting supper for me.[1]

. . . .

[1] Neither Griswold nor Clemens's friends have been identified.

To the Public
7 March 1870 • Buffalo, N.Y.
(Buffalo *Express*, 8 Mar 70)

PERSONAL.

The paragraph now going the rounds of the press to the effect that I am going to withdraw from Buffalo & the Buffalo EXPRESS is entirely foundationless. I am a permanency here. I am prospering well enough to please my friends & distress my enemies, & consequently am in a state of tranquil satisfaction. I will regard it as a favor if those journals that printed the item referred to will also mention this correction.[1]

SAMUEL L. CLEMENS.
"Mark Twain."

Buffalo, March 7.

[1] The *Express* published this "correction" at the head of its editorial columns on 8, 9, 10, and 11 March. Presumably Clemens's request that it be copied was widely granted. The Buffalo *Commercial Advertiser,* which seems to have started the offending rumor in January (2 and 3 Mar 70 to Langdon, n. 7), printed the correction, appending these remarks:

> We give the above very cheerfully. "Mark" is so original a genius that his shortest items are worth copying, and he always tells us something new. In the above, for example, he gives us not only a new word, but a new idea. We never heard a man styled a "permanency" before. And for the first time, also, we learn that "Mark" has "enemies." We supposed he was everybody's friend and *vice versa.* ("Personal," 8 Mar 70, 3)

The Cleveland *Herald* also amended its January item with a paraphrase of Clemens's letter ("Notes and Comments," 10 Mar 70, 2).

To Francis P. Church
11 March 1870 • Buffalo, N.Y.
(Mott 1957, 364)

March 11.

. . . .

If I can have entire ownership & disposal of what I write for the *Galaxy,* after it has appeared in the magazine, I will edit your humorous department for two thousand ($2,000) a year[1]—& I give you my word that I can start out tomorrow or any day that I choose & make that money in two weeks, lecturing.[2]

.   .   .   .

[1] As the next letter indicates, Church and his brother, William, the *Galaxy*'s editors, had offered $2,400—contingent upon their retaining copyright to Clemens's "humorous department." Under the terms Clemens proposed here, his "Memoranda" appeared monthly in the *Galaxy* from May through December 1870 and in January, February, and April 1871 (SLC 1870dd, kk, pp, ss, vv, yy, hhh, nnn, 1871b, f, h).
[2] Since Clemens did not lecture on Sundays, he could have made $2,000 in two weeks, not counting expenses, if his fee had averaged about $167. But even by the season of 1871–72 it had risen only to $125 or $150 from the $75 or $100 he received in 1869–70 (10 June 71 to Redpath and Fall, n. 6; 19 July 71 to Redpath; 23 July 71 to Bowen; *L3*, 214–15, 384 n. 9).

To Elisha Bliss, Jr.
11 March 1870 • Buffalo, N.Y.
(MS: NN-B)

ₐ*Confidential*—for the present.ₐ

Buffalo, Mch. 11.

Friend Bliss—

I turned the check for $4,309.45 over to Mr. Langdon yesterday—I shall not use the money for a month yet, & he will pay me *f* interest. I expected to want it peremptorily in February, but didn't.[1]

A first-class New York magazine wants me to edit a humorous department in it. They want ten pages a month. They offer twenty-four hundred dollars a year for the service, & then they want a publishing house there to ₐhave the privilege of,ₐ issuₑinġ the matter in book form at the end of the year in a $1.50 book (250 pp. 12mo,) & pay me a royalty of 20 ~~per~~ cents̜ on each copy sold. I have just written them that you would have to have a bid in the matter.[2] I also wrote that I would do the ~~editing for $2,000 a year~~ ~~editing for a little trifle~~ editing only on condition that

I *own* the matter after use in the magazine & have the privilege of doing just what I please with it. All this had better be kept still for the present.

No—shan't go east for a long time.

I have a sort of vague half-notion of spending the summer in England. I could write a telling book. But ~~who~~ we don't like to leave our delightful nest even for a day. ~~When~~ Have you heard yet what the possibilities are in the matter of selling our book there?³

Yrs

Clemens

P. S.—I ~~take~~ ˏconsiderˏ the magazine because it will give an opening for higher-class writing—stuff which I hate to shovel into a daily newspaper.

[*letter docketed:*] √ auth [*and*] Mark Twain | March 11/70 | Author

¹See 28 Jan 70 to Bliss, n. 5, and 2 and 3 Mar 70 to Langdon, n. 4.

²The admonition about Bliss's "bid" was probably in the missing portion of the previous letter. The publisher of the *Galaxy* was Sheldon and Company in New York.

³Bliss's reply does not survive, but could hardly have been encouraging (3 Mar 70 to Bliss, n. 2). Clemens's thoughts of England may have been prompted by an offer from Jervis Langdon to underwrite a European trip (13 Jan 70 to OLL, n. 6).

To Unidentified
16 March 1870 • Buffalo, N.Y.
(MS: Joseph)

OFFICE "EXPRESS" PRINTING CO.

BUFFALO, Mch. 16 1870.

DEAR SIR:

IN ANSWER I AM OBLIGED TO SAY THAT IT WILL NOT BE POSSIBLE
FOR ME TO ACCEPT YOUR KIND INVITATION. I SHALL NOT BE ABLE TO LEC-
TURE AGAIN DURING THE PRESENT SEASON. THANKING YOU KINDLY FOR
THE COMPLIMENT OF YOUR INVITATION, I AM

YOURS TRULY,

SAM'L L. CLEMENS.

["MARK TWAIN."]

AGENTS:

BOSTON LYCEUM BUREAU,

20 BROMFIELD STREET,

BOSTON.

P.S.—I replied this morning ṃ by telegraph. I have not accepted an invitation (except one last night to help Mr. Nicholls *read* for the G.A.R.) since the 21st of Jan. I would like well to talk in Rochester, but must stick to present policy & decline. I am far behindhand with literary contracts that must be fulfilled.[1]

Yrs Truly
Sam*l*. L. Clemens.

[1] Clemens had no pressing "contracts." For Nichols, see p. 456 n. 2.

To Hattie Booth
18 March 1870 • Buffalo, N.Y.
(MS: CtHSD)

Buffalo, Mch. 18.

Miss Hattie Booth—

I do it cheerfully, ~~Mi~~ for I am glad enough to ~~k~~ find that I can still "bring tears to eyes unused to weep."[1] I had thought it was one of my Lost Arts. I *used* to do that thing right handy, with boys under my size.

Yrs Truly
ₐMark Twain andₐ Saml. L. Clemens.

[1] The request from Booth (who remains unidentified) was presumably for an autograph and probably included this phrase. No other source for it has been found. The monogram on this letter signified "Livy L. Clemens."

To James T. Fields
21 March 1870 • Buffalo, N.Y.
(MS: ViU)

MORNING EXPRESS $10 PER ANNUM.
EVENING EXPRESS $8 PER ANNUM.
WEEKLY EXPRESS $1.50 PER ANNUM.

OFFICE OF THE EXPRESS PRINTING COMPANY,
NO. 14 EAST SWAN STREET.

BUFFALO, Mch. 21 18 70 .

James T. Fields Esq[1]

Dear Sir:

Fields Osgood & Co. do not appear to send us any more books to notice. We haven't got one lately. ~~We~~ Will you be so kind as to kill the person who is to blame, & appoint a more reliable officer in the murdered man's place? We do not like to intrude, but really it is utterly impossible to ~~git~~ get along without books.[2]

With many apologies—

Yrs Truly
Mark Twain

[1] Until his retirement in late December 1870, Fields (1817–81) was the senior partner in Fields, Osgood and Company, the Boston publishing firm whose list

included Browning, Emerson, Longfellow, Lowell, Tennyson, Thackeray, and Whittier, among many others. For ten years he was also editor of the *Atlantic Monthly,* a post he relinquished to William Dean Howells in July 1871. Clemens had known him at least since December 1869 (Weber, 109, 111–12, 115–17; Mott 1938, 493 n. 1; *L3,* 382–83 n. 6).

[2] This mock complaint may have had a real effect. Among the books briefly reviewed in the Buffalo *Express* of 26 March was one recently published by Fields, Osgood and Company: *Hedged In,* a novel by Elizabeth Stuart Phelps ("Literary," 2). There is no indication that Clemens himself wrote the review.

To James Redpath
22 March 1870 • Buffalo, N.Y.
(*MTL,* 1:172)

Buffalo, March 22.

Dear Red:

I am not going to lecture any more forever. I have got things ciphered down to a fraction now. I know just about what it will cost us to live & I can make the money without lecturing. Therefore old man, count me out.[1]

Your friend,
S. L. Clemens.

[1] The Boston Lyceum Bureau's promotional magazine for the 1870–71 lecture season, which appeared in July 1870, included the following notice (*Lyceum* 1870, 16):

Mark Twain.

"Mark Twain" (Mr. Clemens), we fear, must be numbered for a season among the Lost Stars of the Lyceum firmament.

The fate of Midas has overtaken this brilliant but unfortunate lecturer. He lectured—and made money; he edited—and made money; he wrote a book—and made money: and when a relative, under the guise of friendship, perpetrated "a first-class swindle" on him, he made a great deal of money by that. Even the income-tax collector has failed to soften the rigor of his fate. Under these disheartening circumstances, he cannot be made to see the necessity of lecturing:—

"Just for a vault full of silver he left us!"

R. & F.

For the "first-class swindle," see pp. 45–49; for Clemens's encounter with the tax collector, see 2 and 3 Mar 70 to Langdon, n. 5. Redpath and Fall's closing quotation was a play on a line from Robert Browning's "The Lost Leader": "Just for a handful of silver he left us."

From Samuel L. and Olivia L. Clemens
to Mary Mason Fairbanks
22 and 24 March 1870 • Buffalo, N.Y.
(MS: CSmH)

Buf. 22ᵈ Mch.

Silence, Woman!

(That is to Livy—not you, Mother dear—she is carrying on here, at a dreadful rate, & saying "Oh, I *do* think they are so lovely!—& Oh, the EXQUISITE head-work!" Already, though, I have got her trained so that she tones down & ~~almost~~ stops talking ~~when~~ at the word of command.) ‸[I deny it, I am woman's rights   Livy]‸ The things *are* beautiful—however, we bridegrooms don't get anything. I think it is disgraceful to be a bridegroom.

Mother dear, I am glad you liked the Revenue article.[1] And now I will disclose to you that I am going to edit a department in the "Galaxy." They are not to advertise that it will be a *Humorous* department, but simply *a* department. The humor shall be relieved all along by serious paragraphs, dainty bits subtracted from your letters, poetry, pathos, statistics—*every*thing that an artistic taste may suggest for effect.[2] They pay me a good salary & let me have my trash ~~en~~ again after they have used it in the magazine. I just came to the conclusion that I would quit turning my attention to making money especially, & go to writing for enjoyment as well as profit. I needed a ~~m~~Magazine wherein to shovel any fine-spun stuff that might accumulate in my head, & which isn't entirely suited to ~~the~~ either a daily, Weekly, or *any* kind of newspaper. You see I often feel like writing something, & before I set down the first word I think, "No, it isn't worth while to write it—might do for a magazine, but not a newspaper." Do you see? I can make a *living* without any trouble, & still write *to suit myself*—& therefore wouldn't *you* do as I am doing, if you were me? I shall still write for the Express, of course, but not every week, perhaps. People who write every week *write themselves out*, and tire the public, too, before ʄ very long.

However, I have to go to work now, & write an appreciative & complimentary obituary on Geo. Wakeman, journalist, who I never heard of

till to-day,—& so I will let Livy finish this. [P. S.—I forgot to state that
Mr Wakeman is dead.] That is one reason why I have to write an obituary
about him. He would not be so particular about it if he were not
departed.[3]

Yrs Son
Sam

Dear Mother Fairbanks
    I have detained the letters for Cleveland for a day because I
wanted to send a word to you with the rest— I wish that you could see
how prettie the bureau cover looks on the bureau, how dainty and delicate ₓallₓ the things are in their proper places— I do thank you all so
much, I think nothing is quite so dear to me as the work of friends, to
think that their ingenuity their time and their strength should have been
ₓputₓ in something for me, always touches me——
    Three or four days ago I felt somewhat like a stranger in a strange
land,[4] and I thought now if we lived in Cleveland I should have Mrs Fairbanks to Mother me— When I had made stupid blunders in trying to
find the houses of callers, I could go to her and laugh it off, Mr Clemens
is splendid to laugh it off with, but then when it comes to his giving me
any practical advice in these matters I find him a little incompetant. He
can't quite understand this call making, he wants to send word to people
that we are coming such an evening and we want them to be at home &c.
&c. It is funny but ₓandₓ we enjoy it ₓ— I called about two weeks since
on a lady,[5] did not find her in, so & left my card. I discovered yesterday
that I had not been to her house at all. I had been to some ones house
that I did not know and had never heard of— I think I shall get the name
of leaving my cards at strange houses in rather a peculiar way, if I am not
careful—
    We do love you in this house hold, and shall be so glad when we can
welcome you here— Let us hear from you just as often as you can we are
always so happy to get a letter from you—

Lovingly your daughter
Livy—

March 24ᵗʰ 1870

[*cross-written over signature and dateline:*]
    P. S. Livy left this letter open & told me to direct the wedding-card
envelop[6] & put it in here. I was writing newspaper stuff & heard, but

never *comprehended* a word she said—so I put that thing (*without* directing it,) in *another* envelop, & by a great effort succeeded in addressing it to you instead of to Livy herself.

Your loving whelp,
Sam

It is a *slander* a *perfect* SLANDER, he was reading a newspaper not writing

[1] "A Mysterious Visit" (2 and 3 Mar 70 to Langdon, n. 5).

[2] Clemens's own advertisement of his *Galaxy* department left no doubt that it was to be humorous (SLC 1870y). But his "Introductory," itself largely tongue in cheek, stated explicitly: "These MEMORANDA are not a 'humorous' department. I would not conduct an exclusively and professedly humorous department for any one" (SLC 1870dd, 717).

[3] Wakeman (b. 1841) died of pneumonia on 19 March. After beginning his career on the New York *Ledger* in 1858, he had moved to the New York *World* when it was founded in 1860, working as a reporter (known for his facility at shorthand) and an editor. In 1868 he became stenographer of the New York state senate. He also was a regular contributor to New York periodicals:

> Soon after his first connection with the *World* he began to write sketches of a more or less humorous or literary character, and three years ago he commenced a series of similar papers, contributed to the *Galaxy*, which were received with considerable favor. In these he displayed great skill in finding out literary oddities, and showed some degree of quaint humor in his manner of dealing with them. He had been advised to appear as a public lecturer on subjects of the same nature as those which he had treated in his magazine articles, and had begun the preparation of a course of popular addresses. ("George Wakeman," New York *Times*, 20 Mar 70, 5)

Clemens's obituary, which he called an "earnest tribute," appeared as part of his first *Galaxy* "Memoranda," in May 1870 (SLC 1870dd, 721; Allibone, 3:2536; Mott 1950, 350). For Wakeman's *Galaxy* contributions, see References (Wakeman 1866a–1870c).

[4] Exodus 2:22: "And she bare him a son, and he called his name Gershom: for he said, I have been a stranger in a strange land."

[5] Evidently Mrs. Charles F. Wadsworth (27 Mar 70 to the Langdons, n. 8).

[6] See 6? Feb 70 to Barnes.

To Jane Lampton Clemens and Family
26 March 1870 • Buffalo, N.Y.
(MS: NPV)

Buf, Mch. 26.

Dear Folks—

The coffin of "Enterprise" files has come—$ expressage $9.50.[1] Nothing unright about that, but I had had a sort of a general idea that it would come ~~W~~ as slow freight along with Annie's piana. However, it would not ~~a~~ have been as safe.

Livy got Annie's letter yesterday, & both of us were pleased with it,—I, chiefly with the just remarks made about Livy's comeliness & other attractions. I thought it showed a profound judgment & a mature appreciation, & thus was remarkable coming from one so young. [I will endeavor not to let Livy meddle with that sentence.]

I am going to edit a ten-page department in the "Galaxy" Magazine. The berth is exceedingly easy & the salary liberal. I am to ~~own~~ ₐrentₐ the matter to them, not sell it—& so I can use it in book form afterward without ~~divi~~ sharing the proceeds ₐwithₐ them.

But I am in a hurry—so I will say good-bye & love to all—

Sam

---

[1] For an account of these "files" of western clippings, see *RI 1993*, 801–4.

From Samuel L. and Olivia L. Clemens to Jervis and Olivia Lewis Langdon
27 March 1870 • Buffalo, N.Y.
(MS: CtHMTH)

ₐ*Afternoon.*ₐ
At Home, Sunday 26th

Dear Father & Mother—

It is snowing furiously, & has been, the most of ~~the part~~ the day & part of the night. We are glad that you are safe beyond its jurisdiction—for albeit snow is very beautiful when falling, its loveliness passes away very shortly afterward. The grand unpoetical result is merely chilblains & slush.[1] ~~Anoth~~

Cousin Anna is here—came last night.[2] She enjoys the beautiful home, naturally. Livy has just gone to roost. Theodore's dispatch ₐtoₐ ~~informing~~ us that Anna would arrive at 8.30 *P.M.* made a mistake & said *8 A.M.* The consequence was that we were up at such a vile, inhuman hour in the morning that we shall be torpid & worthless for a day or two. Livy & I are delicate creatures & cannot stand dissipation.

Anna brought flowers from Sue; & Livy ~~has~~ made some handsome bouquets, & immediately grew riotous & disorderly because, she said, "Nobody ever comes to call when we have fresh flowers." Well, somebody had *better* come—else I will take a club & go & invite half a dozen or so. Our flowers are not to go to waste *this* time, f merely for want of a little energetic affability.

The roof of the house on the corner right opposite Mr. Howells' (diagonally opposite Mr Lyon's), caught fire this morning & blazed pretty lively for a while—& but for the snow on the roof there would have been a conflagration—for when I discovered it from our bedroom window & went over there to stir up the family, there was ∅ but one man in sight anywhere, & he came to *help*, instead of going for the firemen. It burned so slowly that Patrick, who followed me, climbed out on the roof & put it ~~almost out~~ half out with snow before we succeeded in getting buckets of water to him. After he had got it under complete control ~~the~~ a couple of steam engines came, but the occupant of the house persuaded them to go away without damaging anything.[3]

There, now—perhaps we need not go to explaining, now, why we have not written you before (still, if any letters have miscarried & you haven't received them, we ~~wit~~ wish to be understood as having written those letters,)—we need not, now, explain, perhaps, since it is so late in the day. I know it isn't Livy's fault. (Now if she stands by me faithfully & says as much for me, we are surely proven blameless.) Which I think she'll do it.

Yes, mother, whenever you issue your call, we stand ready to voyage over the ocean with you, right cheerfully.

Thank you for Charley's journals. I have given up Prof. Ford, & shall discontinue the "Round the World" letters—*have* done it. The Prof. has now been 6 months writing 2 little letters, & I ten—making 12 in all. If they continue their trip 18 months, as they propose, the Prof. will succeed in grinding out a grand total of 6 letters, if he keeps up his present vigor. So I shall quietly drop the "Round the World" business & simply ~~take~~ write ‚(from Charley's journal,)‚ what shall seem to be simply a vagrant correspondence from some George M. Wagner or other person who writes letters when he happens to feel like it, & travels for the comfort of it.[4] ~~I am~~

I have taken the editorship of a department in the "Galaxy" magazine, New York, & am to furnish ten pages of matter every months (made up of my own ∤ writing & contributions together,) for $2,000 a year, I ∮ to absolutely *own* the matter & print it in book form after they have used it, if I want to. I shall write ~~once~~ ₐone, or two sketches a month for the Express, & I have an idea that for a good while I shall do nothing else on the paper.[5] Thus the Galaxy & the Express together ~~with~~ will give me fully six days' work every month, & I positively need the rest of the time to admire the house in. Need it, too, to write a book in. The "Innocents" sells just as handsomely as ever. ~~9 to 10,000 copies a month.~~ It is still netting me $1,400 a month.[6]

But I most stop, & leave room for a line from Livy. And so, with all love & duty, I am

Yr ~~Som~~ Son
Saml.

Mother dear

Cousin Anna, Mr Clemens and I are sitting about the Library table, we have been having a pleasant visit— Now Samuel is speaking of Olive Logan—[7]

Our house is just as prettie and pleasant as ever, perhaps a little more so, we want to see you & father here in it— I am sure you will think it a restful place—

I was out on∉ two calling expeditions last week— I have rec'd about seventy calls— I had a very pleasant call at Mrs Wadsworths last week— I thought that I called there two ~~or thr~~ ⚬⚬ weeks ago, but discov[er]ed that I went to the ~~wrg~~ wrong house & left my card—, Mrs George Wadsworth has called too—she is also very attractive—[8] Mr & Mrs Gray (he is editor of the Courier) are attractive people, seem as if they might be friends—[9]

Good night

Lovingly Livy—

[1] Clemens alluded to "Beautiful Snow," the popular poem by John Whittaker Watson, first published in 1869. On 18 March 1870 the Langdons, accompanied by their friend and physician Henry Sayles and his wife, Emma, had departed snowbound Elmira on a six-week trip through Virginia, South Carolina, and Georgia. The Clemenses had their itinerary, however, and could reach them by mail at specified points along the way. It was hoped that the milder climate and the respite from business would be a tonic for Jervis Langdon, who had been suffering since 1868 from what proved to be terminal stomach cancer (Jerome and Wisbey 1991a, 4; Elmira *Advertiser:* " 'Beautiful Snow,' " 18 Mar 70, 4; "Our

Snow," 19 Mar 70, 4; Elmira *Saturday Evening Review:* "Local Jottings," 26 Mar, 23 Apr 70, 8; 16 Apr 70 to Crane, n. 1).

[2] Possibly Anna Marsh Brown.

[3] According to the next day's Buffalo *Express:* "The alarm sounded from signal box No. 62, yesterday noon, was occasioned by the roof of the residence of J. M. Gwinn, No. 455 Delaware street, taking fire from a defective chimney. The flames were extinguished by citizens before the arrival of the Fire Department. The damage was trifling" ("City Notes," 28 Mar 70, 4). J. Morris Gwinn was a teller at Buffalo's Marine Bank. James Howells, a stone dealer and contractor, lived opposite him at 452 Delaware, on the corner of Virginia Street. James S. Lyon, a real estate and insurance agent, lived diagonally opposite Gwinn, across Virginia, at 468 Delaware, near the Clemenses at 472 Delaware. The Clemenses' coachman, Patrick McAleer, put out the fire. In 1924, Albert Bigelow Paine relayed this account of the incident, presumably from Clemens himself:

> One Sunday morning Clemens noticed smoke pouring from the upper window of the house across the street. The owner and his wife, comparatively newcomers, were seated upon the veranda, evidently not aware of impending danger. The Clemens household thus far had delayed calling on them, but Clemens himself now stepped briskly across the street. Bowing with leisurely politeness, he said:
> "My name is Clemens; we ought to have called on you before, and I beg your pardon for intruding now in this informal way, but your house is on fire." (*MTB*, 1:413)

Gwinn had lived in his Delaware Avenue house for at least five years (*Buffalo Directory:* 1866, 220; 1870, 17, 376, 397, 429).

[4] On 26 March the Elmira *Saturday Evening Review* reported that Ford and Charles Langdon had

> reached Cairo, Egypt. Thence they are to visit the Holy Land, pass through Turkey, Russia, and Prussia, spend several months in Germany, France, and Great Britain, and reach home about Christmas. ("Local Jottings," 8)

Clemens did not make use of Langdon's journals, which are not known to survive. For the "Around the World" letters, see 22 Jan 70 to Bliss, n. 2.

[5] In April 1870 Clemens contributed four "sketches" to the *Express*, but in the nine subsequent months, ending with January 1871, the number of original sketches he published there each month dropped off precipitously. Forty-one items by him, both signed and unsigned, have been identified in the *Express* for this period, but these include occasional editorials, obituaries, anonymous letters to the editor, as well as sketches simply reprinted from the *Galaxy* (see References: SLC 1870x–1871e, most entries). Of these forty-one only about ten qualify as original sketches, and more than half of those sketches appeared in April and May. (Not included in the forty-one are eight items signed "Carl Byng" that were sometimes mistakenly attributed to Clemens: see 22 Jan 71 to Aldrich, n. 3.) Additional contributions by Clemens, especially unsigned editorials, doubtless remain to be identified (*L3*, 710–11; McCullough 1972).

[6] During the first six months *Innocents* was on the market, sales had averaged about 6,500 copies per month, producing average royalties of about $1,200 per month. During the third quarter (1 Feb–30 Apr 70) monthly sales averaged about 7,125 copies and monthly royalties about $1,300 (22 Jan 70 to Bliss, n. 6; 28 Jan 70 to Bliss, n. 5; 7 May 70 to Bliss, n. 2).

[7] The occasion for Clemens's remarks to Olivia and her cousin is not known;

Logan did not lecture in Buffalo at this time. For his opinion of her, see 8 Jan 70 to OLL (1st), n. 3.

[8] George Wadsworth was a Buffalo attorney. He and his wife lived at 370 Franklin Street, about two-and-a-half blocks from the Clemenses. The other Mrs. Wadsworth probably was the wife of Charles F. Wadsworth, president of the Wadsworth Iron Works. They lived on Ferry Street, about seven blocks from the Clemenses (*Buffalo Directory* 1870, map, 18, 527).

[9] David and Martha Gray did indeed become longtime friends. Clemens had probably met David Gray on 14 August 1869, just after acquiring an interest in the Buffalo *Express*, at a dinner for the city's press corps (*L3*, 295). Gray (1836–88) was born in Edinburgh, Scotland, and had come to the United States in 1849, settling with his family on a farm in Wisconsin. In 1856, at the invitation of relatives, he moved to Buffalo, where he worked as secretary and librarian to the Young Men's Christian Union and as bookkeeper for his uncle's milling firm, until, in 1859, he joined the Buffalo *Courier* as commercial reporter, becoming associate editor late that same year. In 1860 he purchased a one-fourth interest in the paper; in 1868 he assumed the responsibilities of managing editor. A poet and, like Clemens, a former travel correspondent (who had considered writing a book about his own 1867 journey to the Holy Land), Gray was a newlywed, having married Martha Guthrie on 2 June 1869. In Autobiographical Dictations of 16 and 22 February 1906, Clemens recalled that friendship with the Grays was "all the solace" he and Olivia had during their "sorrowful and pathetic brief sojourn in Buffalo" (CU-MARK, in *MTA*, 2:118, 132; Larned 1888, 1:1, 11–16, 30–31, 60–61, 67–68, 70, 75–76, 78–83, 100–101, 112–15, 129–30, 192–95).

To Charles F. Wingate
31 March 1870 • Buffalo, N.Y.
(MS: NN)

Buffalo, Mch. 31.

Dear Sir:[1]

I am grateful always for sincere & voluntary~~eer~~ expressions of satisfaction with the book, & therefore I am grateful for the ~~pr~~ knowledge that you & yours have derived pleasure from reading it. Mrs. Browning knew right well that one such note of private & voluntary commendation ~~g~~ is able to give an author more comfort than the patronizing ~~crit speeches toleration, imbecile criticism~~ toleration and awkward English of forty *Nation* critiques can take away.[2]

In return for the *Nation* notice (which I had not seen,) I enclose a notice written by the traveled & scholarly David Gray, of the Buffalo *Courier.* It is at least good English—a merit which the Nation notice lacks.[3]

Yrs Truly

Sam[l]. L. Clemens.

Chas F. Wingate Esq   ⎫
~~200~~ 210 E. ~~31~~ 30th N. Y.[4] ⎬
                              ⎭

[1]Charles Frederick Wingate (1848–1909) was a New York correspondent ("Carlfried") of the Springfield (Mass.) *Republican.*

[2]The *Nation's* 2 September 1869 review of *The Innocents Abroad* was indeed patronizing. The unidentified critic said, in part:

> It might better have been a thinner book, for there is some dead wood in it, as there has to be in all books which are sold by book-agents and are not to be bought in stores. The rural-district reader likes to see that he has got his money's worth even more than he likes wood-engravings. At least, such is the faith in Hartford; and no man ever saw a book-agent with a small volume in his hand. (*Nation* 9:194–95; reprinted in Anderson and Sanderson, 21–22)

Elizabeth Barrett Browning's observations on "private & voluntary commendation" have not been identified.

[3]Gray had spent most of 1865–68 traveling in Britain, Europe, and the Holy Land, recording his observations in a series of fifty-eight letters to the Buffalo *Courier* (reprinted in Larned 1888, volume 2; see also Larned 1888, 1:100–128). His long review of *Innocents* appeared in the *Courier* on 19 March 1870, nearly eight months after the book's publication. A clipping of the review survives in the Mark Twain Papers, and the full text is reprinted in Appendix B.

[4]Wingate lived at this address with his parents (Wilson 1869, 1193).

To Jane L. Stanford
April 1870 • Buffalo, N.Y.
(MS: CSt)

E pluribus Unum.

This sentiment has been attributed to others, but it originated with

Ys Truly

Saml L. Clemens.

Mark Twain.

Hartford, Apl '70.

Mrs Stanford.
    Sacramento.[1]

[1] Jane Eliza Lathrop Stanford (1828–1905), originally from Albany, New York, had been married since 1850 to Leland Stanford, governor of California from 1861 to 1863 and one of the builders (as well as president and director) of the Central Pacific Railroad (*NAW*, 3:340–42). Clemens was not in Hartford in April 1870: his dateline is therefore a fiction, intended to seem appropriate once this "sentiment" was inserted in a gift copy of *The Innocents Abroad*. In customary fashion, he sent this page to the American Publishing Company in Hartford, to be forwarded with a book (compare 23 Apr 70 to Bliss).

From Samuel L. and Olivia L. Clemens
to Jervis and Olivia Lewis Langdon
1 April 1870 • Buffalo, N.Y.
(Transcripts: CU-MARK)

                                        Buf. ~~Mch~~ Apl. 1.

Dear Father & Mother:[1]

I can use this heading just as well as Samuel and why shouldn't I do it while he is folding a letter to go to some one else. I am sitting on his lap and so helping him along, oh I am of unbounded help to him in this way. If I had a couple more such helps I wouldn't have to do anything at all. I don't know whether that last is complimentary or not but I am afraid it is not—he is a witch, but then I have to get along with him—

Come and see us quick, we are all ready to go to England— I have run out making dreadful calls again today, but the youth rode in the carriage with me so that made it bearable— Lovingly Livy

We are to have the Twins, Monday evening, to stay a week or so— I mean the Spaldingzes.[2] And the advance guard of *my* tribe will make their exodus from St. Louis about the 10th of April—the same consisting of my mother & the German girl.[3] They will visit relatives & friends before coming finally hither, but they don't know whether to visit up the Mississippi ~~in~~ or in Kentucky, & the chances are that at the last moment they will try to go both ways & damage themselves. My sister & Young Sam will follow them after a brief interval, & Annie will straggle along after her school is finished.[4]

They seem to be using my editorial in Pennsylvania—I received the enclosed today from Pottstown or Pottsville, Pa., simply directed to Mark Twain, & with no comments.[5]

Yes, I guess we are about ready to start for England. My Galaxy work gives me a chance to travel if I want to—but if I hadn't taken it I would have been tied hand & foot here & forever & ever. It also gives me a chance to write what I please, not what I *must*. Thus far I am very glad I undertook it.[6]

Mr. Larned needs $2,000 to pay a payment on his stock to Clapp, & I believe I will lend it to him on the security of his stock, at usual interest, instead of paying it over to Kennett.[7]

Bliss is *very* anxious that I should go abroad during the summer & get a book written for next spring, but I shan't unless you find that you will have to go.

Love to you both, & large amounts of it.

In haste,
Saml.

P. S. Livy is abusing me about using this fine paper, when she *knows* that I always go to all the expense I can when I write *you*, so as to show that I love you & that there ain't anything mean about *me*. He fabricates. I only desire that he be duly economical and use up his half sheets clean—you see ˏhe usesˏ two stamped pages[8] and the others are left, that is the way he uses paper leaving half of it unused. I fix common paper for him ˏso—ˏbut it is very wrong for him to used *stamped* paper in this way—still he does it, and although he is *so* bad, "I care for um"

Again lovingly Livy—

Talk about economy! If I hadn't just happened to come along in the nick of time, she would have had this into an envelop & there would have been a clean waste of a page & a half of good paper, & of the stamped kind at that. It is the ~~subscriber that~~ undersigned that looks after the real economies of this establishment.

~~And this evening she had *shad* for dinner—~~ [*word illegible*] ~~she has~~

~~shad four times a day (She [*word illegible*] thinks they are shad, but privately between ourselves, they are mackerel— Still it is a comfort to her to talk~~

But nonsense enough for one time—Good-bye

Saml.

[1] The Langdons were still traveling (27 Mar 70 to the Langdons, n. 1).

[2] Alice and Clara Spaulding were sisters, but not twins (*L3*, 182–83 n. 6).

[3] The Moffett family maid, thirty-one-year-old Margaret Theil (Douglas H. Shepard to Michael B. Frank, 8 May 1994, CU-MARK).

[4] These travel plans were revised somewhat (21 Apr 70 to OC).

[5] The original enclosure has not been found, but it was apparently a newspaper reprinting of "'More Wisdom,'" an unsigned editorial that Clemens published in the Buffalo *Express* on 9 March (SLC 1870s). The clipping sent to Clemens (showing that he and perhaps his personal allegiances were recognized in spite of the anonymous format) was probably from one of two English-language newspapers in Pottsville, Pennsylvania: either the *Miner's Journal* or the *Standard* (Rowell, 738). Potts*town*, in Montgomery County, was an agricultural, as well as iron- and steel-producing center. Potts*ville*, in Schuylkill County, was in the anthracite-producing region to which Shamokin, some thirty-five miles away in Northumberland County, also belonged. In Shamokin, recent violence may have threatened some of Jervis Langdon's mining personnel—violence that Clemens's editorial blamed on the miners' union. Reminiscent of "The 'Monopoly' Speaks," an editorial published on 20 August 1869 in the *Express*, "'More Wisdom'" spoke up for the miners' employer, who "has a soul to save, too," while denouncing "those persecuted lambs, the miners." Clemens clearly wrote both editorials to please his father-in-law. The full text of the enclosure is given in Appendix B where, in the absence of the Pottsville reprinting, the original printing in the *Express* is transcribed.

[6] Clemens was preparing his first "Memoranda," for the May 1870 *Galaxy* magazine (SLC 1870dd).

[7] Almon M. Clapp, founder of the Buffalo *Express*, and his son, Harry, had formerly shared ownership of the Express Printing Company (publishers of the paper) with Josephus N. Larned, George H. Selkirk, and Thomas A. Kennett. In April 1869, when Almon Clapp was appointed congressional printer, he and his son sold their interests in the company to the other partners. Four months later, Clemens purchased Kennett's share, incurring the indebtedness he alludes to here. By mid-April 1870 he agreed to lend Larned $3,000 (2 and 3 Mar 70 to Langdon, n. 4; 16 and 17 Apr 70 to the Langdons; *L3*, 294 n. 3, 297 n. 2).

[8] It is not known which of their monogram-embossed stationeries the Clemenses used in this letter.

From Olivia L. and Samuel L. Clemens
to Susan L. Crane
16 April 1870 • Buffalo, N.Y.
(MS: CtHMTH)

⟨*c*⟩

Buffalo April 16th
1870

My darling Little Woman

It seems as if it was a month since I had heard from you or Father and Mother— We had a letter from Father about ten days ago, that is the last that we have heard,[1] we do love you and we do desire to hear from you— We had a delightful visit with the girls,[2] it was quiet and was not the least of a tax— It seems strange that no ones going leaves loneliness— We are so happy that nothing seems able to mar our joy— Our little home is just as pleasant as ever and we do love it— There is only one thing that I would like to add to the pleasures that we have, that is the hills about our valey, as the Spring days come, it makes me sorry that we cannot go into the woods— I love you little woman—

Yesterday morning I had a talk with Harriet, and told her that as she could not agree with Ellen, I thought it was better for both of us that we make a change, I got on very easily with it after I had really taken hold of it, she thought it was best and said that she wanted a rest this Spring— I had a bad dream last night— I am on track of an other girl, I went yesterday and left word to have her come and see me— Ellen told me yesterday that she had written Mary Crossey that she wished that she would come on here, I told Ellen that she ought not to have written that because I did not want to take Mary away from Mother— She said that Mary Crossey's Mother would not let ⟨h⟩ her come any way.

I dreamed last night that after the German girl had been hired and commenced her work, that Mary came, and there was a great stir and I had a deal of trouble—

The girl that I am going to have comes well recommended, she has lived three years with the family that she is now with, and only leaves them because the work is too hard—

The Ivy in my hanging basket does well, but the other things do not seem to flourish as well— Susie dear, when some one is coming here, will you send, if you have them and it is *no inconvenience* to you, two slips of ivy, I want to train them about my dining room window—you know if it is not entirely convenient we can get some here, I can find out where to get Iv them— and Susie dear, will you send us a couple of cats by the next minister or other party that is coming this way. We have not a cat on the place, & the mice will not patronize the little trap because it is cheap & small & uncomfortable, & not in keeping with the other furniture of the house. If you could send us a kitten or two like "Livy," it would suit Mr. Clemens,'s idea of what a house-cat should be.

What a witch it is, I left my letter for two or three minutes, and lo when I return, the page is filled— Ellen wants to know every little while if I have written Mr Crane to know about the price of tea & coffee by the chest, if Theodore knows let him tell me, but he need not take any thought or step about it— Susie dear, you will think this letter is filled with requests, but one more thing, will you see if mother can spare one pair of pillow cases like that would fit my large pillows, I have only one pair, so the pillows have to go without[3]

[1] Olivia referred to the following letter from her father:

Richmond April 2[d] 1870

Dear Children

The weather has been unpleasant most of the time since I came here, but it has given me a good time to rest which I much needed   I live on simple diet exercise what I am able, which has been very little, but my stomach has finally consented to digest the food, & I look now for rapid improvement

We shall moove on from here tomorrow, for Charlston & Savannah. We want to hear from you very much and I hope you will write immediately on recpt of this at Savannah Gi., at Screven House—

I have thrown off all care. 1st Seamless Kegg

2 M[c]Intyre Coal Co.

3 Shamokin Coal

4 General business in Elmira—

5th Every thing—

so you see how good I am to follow the counsel of my children—

Doct Sayles has been a great comfort to me, I could not have got along without him, all my organs seemed to have susbended their functions, I would eat food moderately for two days and then throw it up. My bowells would not moove untill mooved by medicine   I have been some times 4 days but now for 4 days I have not thrown up my food & my liver seems to have assumed its function, but very slugishly

I think I shall return entirely restored. I do not intend to return untill I am well—

Since writing this much your mother has ret[d] from Breakfast with a letter from Susie from which we learn there is a letter from you awating us at Charlston, which makes us in a hurry to get there   It will however take us untill Tuesday evening we shall only go to Weldon Monday, we shall probably stay in Charlston untill next week

Monday. However that will depend upon Circumstances, we do not hold ourselves to
any rules but moove with the spirit—
      Samuel, I love your wife and she loves me, I think it only fair that you should
know it but you need not flare up, I loved her before you did and she loved me before
she did you & has not ceased since   I see no way but for you to "make the most of it"—
my wife sends much love

Your father
J. Langdon

For Langdon's Shamokin cares, see 1 Apr 70 to the Langdons, n. 5. The Mc-
Intyre Coal Company, evidently troublesome as well, was a new enterprise of his
to mine bituminous coal in Pennsylvania: see 30 Aug 71 to Smith, n. 1. Nothing
has been learned of his "Seamless Kegg" concerns.
    [2] Alice and Clara Spaulding.
    [3] Despite the abrupt ending, the letter appears to be complete. Clemens filled
the last page, so Olivia squeezed her final sentences into the margins of the first
page and was left without room for a complimentary close or signature.

From Samuel L. and Olivia L. Clemens
to Jervis and Olivia Lewis Langdon
16 and 17 April 1870 • Buffalo, N.Y.
(MS: CtHMTH)

Buf Apl. ~~16~~ 17.[1]

Dear Father & Mother—
      Day before yesterday I loaned Mr. Larned $3,000, ~~on~~ taking as se-
curity one-half of his ownership in the ¢ Express—the loan is for one
year. Bowen & Rogers drew the papers at Mr. Slee's instance. Took Mr
Slee's advice in everything. I have concluded to keep him here, for I cannot well do without him, but will get you a good man in his place. My
wife will still need Mrs. Slee for some time yet, also, & so ~~there~~ it seems
absolutely necessary that we retain the family here for the present.[2]
      Yesterday received a letter from Kennett asking if it would be con-
venient for me to pay something now as he has a couple of the Clapp
notes to meet. I told him we might spend the summer in Europe, & in
that case I would need the money myself. If he makes it an object to me
I will let him have two or three thousand dollars, but not ~~otherwise, I
think., unless he is content to wait a fortnight or so~~ otherwise, I think.[3]
      We have had the twins here for ten days—Allie & Clara Spaulding—
& we all enjoyed it exceedingly. They went home day before yesterday—

partly because Miss Clara had some trees to plant, & partly because we were beginning to look for my tribe from St. Louis. In which case we should want both the spare rooms.

Livy discharged Harriet yesterday, after a week of solemn & imposing preparation, & I tell you I am glad the thing is done, for it hung over us like a pall & shadowed all our sunshine. Toward the last the mere mention of it was sufficient to make me shudder, & I came to regard it as an awful ordeal which we had got to pass through & which might let go in the midst & blow ~~up~~ us to Jericho. But it is all over, now, & we still live. But I had rather discharge ~~the~~ a perilous & unsound cannon than the soundest servant girl that ever was.

Livy overhauled her books yesterday & demonstrated that our living expenses average exactly fifty dollars a week. Other expenses will not ~~rh~~ amount to more than fifty more, & so we are safe, beyond all peradventure. Every cent of the returns from the book can go to the liquidation of the "Express" debt if necessary. [*in margin:* (That includes servants & all—Livy)][4]

Mr. Beecher came Saturday & preached morning & evening. The evening ~~sem~~ sermon, to a crowded house, was received with prodigious favor & he went away from here ~~with~~ leaving a great fame behind him. From Elmira we learn that ~~M~~ D[r] Heacock created a similar furore in the Opera House Sunday night. It does these people good to change off & shin around a little. [I was going to put that "move around," but Livy said "shin around" was pleasanter. ~~it is~~ (is it is a fabrication)][5]

We think of you oftener than we write you, & a good deal oftener, too. There is no spot & no article in our lovely home but remind us of your love & loving care for us. And we will *write* you oftener, too, in future—my word on that. I will now leave the other page to Livy.

Lovingly Yr Son
Sam[l].

Dear Father and Mother

I feel as if it was a little too bad to have had visits from so many of our friends before you have been here— I think that I shall be very proud when I can entertain you ~~here~~— I am sure that you would luxuriate in the quiet of our dear little nest— We expect Mr Clemens friends now every day—after their visit I want Ida to come—[6] Then some time I want Emma Sayles and Sue[7] to come together— ~~We f~~

We find that we are located in a very delightful neighborhood, there are four young married people that live on in the block below them, the four ladies are very pleasant, we have met only two of the gentlemen— another young married lady who has called here is going to move into the block this Spring— I liked what I saw of her *very much*—

Lovingly Livy—

I neglected to bring my hand glass with me—did you send it in one of the boxes— It is too bad to trouble you with these things but I do not see any way to help it— *I* I know that it would be well for me to open the boxes before I write of these things, but I have not the time now to take care of the things—

Mrs Moffett says "give my love to your Mother"—[8]

Mr Clemens and I went to church to day, Mr Dr Heacock gave us a very good sermon, at first I was afraid that it was to be treatise like, the sentences were perfect, the language felicitous, but at the end he gave us reflections on the subject (Our Father which *who art in Heaven*) which brought it home to our hearts—

Dr Heacock has and exceedingly fine face, when he was preaching, there would sometimes come into his face an expression that reminded me of Anna Dickinson—[9] I came about as near having a touch of homesickness this morning in church as I have at any time— I thought of you in church, with the Spauldings[10] sitting in front of you, all listening to *our* teacher—and I thought that I should like to be there with you—

Lovingly Livy—

---

[1] It is likely that Clemens in fact wrote his portion of this letter on 16 April: as the preceding letter makes clear, the firing of Harriet, the maid, reported in the fourth paragraph here as happening "yesterday," came on 15 April. He may have changed the date simply to reconcile it with Olivia's portion of the letter, clearly written on 17 April, Easter Sunday.

[2] Dennis Bowen and Sherman S. Rogers were the Buffalo lawyers who had managed the legal details of Clemens's purchase of Thomas A. Kennett's share of the Buffalo *Express*. Kennett and Larned were still in debt to Almon M. Clapp, their former partner in the paper (1 Apr 70 to the Langdons, n. 7). Jervis Langdon, who was increasingly unable to work and was currently traveling for his health, wanted Slee to relocate to Elmira, which he did soon after the formation of the new J. Langdon and Company partnership (9 Feb 70 to the Langdons; 2 and 3 Mar 70 to Langdon; 22 May to Langdon, n. 2; 25 June 70 to Fairbanks; *L3*, 294 n. 2; Reigstad 1989, 5).

[3] Clemens's first payment to Kennett was not due until August (2 and 3 Mar 70 to Langdon, n. 4).

[4] In addition to the $10,000 he owed to Kennett, Clemens owed $12,500 to Jervis Langdon. Although in August 1869 Langdon was uninterested in dis-

cussing repayment, Clemens planned to sign a note and pay the interest "as it falls due" (*L3*, 311). By 9 November 1869, when he put his total *Express* indebtedness at $22,000 and vowed to clear it "within two years," he had apparently paid $500 to Langdon (*L3*, 387, 389 n. 5). He evidently paid another $5,000 before Langdon's death on 6 August 1870 (11 Nov 70 to OC, n. 3). If *Innocents* royalties were now averaging about $1,400 a month (27 Mar 70 to the Langdons), applying that much toward the *Express* debt could liquidate it by August, rather than November, 1871. But it is less clear how he then would have provided the $5,200 per year ($100 per week) he and Olivia required for living expenses. He could count on $2,000 from his contract with the *Galaxy* and perhaps another $2,500 from the *Express* if it paid him the same amount it did in 1869 (7 Jan 70 to Fairbanks, n. 6). The remaining $700 might have been made up, at least in part, from interest on investments or savings, which presumably had been bolstered by Jervis Langdon's "handsome" wedding check and were about to be bolstered again by a further check for $1,000 (6? Feb 70 to McComb; 13 May 70 to Langdon). Finally, Olivia had a continuing interest in the Langdon coal firm, although Clemens prided himself on not using her money (26 Oct 70 to Bliss). In any event, he did not apply as much as $1,400 per month to his *Express* indebtedness. By the end of December 1871 he was able to declare the Langdon portion of it "all paid up," but he still owed $5,000 to Kennett (28 Dec 71 to OLC; 3 Mar 71 to Riley, n. 3).

[5] The Buffalo *Express* of Saturday, 9 April, had announced this pulpit exchange:

> To-morrow the Rev. Thomas K. Beecher, of Elmira, will preach in Rev. Dr. Heacock's place, in the Lafayette Street Church. Mr. Beecher is one of the ablest divines of the day, and will give the members of Dr. Heacock's church a discourse worth listening to. ("The Churches," 4)

Beecher gave complete satisfaction in both morning and evening sermons, although the *Express* singled out the first of these as "very able and eloquent," printing a long synopsis ("The Pulpit," 11 Apr 70, 4). Heacock's performances in Elmira, in the morning at Congregational Church, and later at the Elmira Opera House, Beecher's controversial Sunday evening stand (*L3*, 57 n. 9, 183 n. 7), demonstrated that he was "justly entitled to the reputation which he enjoys, of being one of the ablest and most eloquent Divines in the State." The Langdons, who were still traveling in the South, missed the excitement ("City and Neighborhood," Elmira *Advertiser*, 11 Apr 70, 4; 27 Mar 70 to the Langdons, n. 2; Buffalo *Commercial Advertiser:* "Religious," 9 Apr 70, 3; "Church Services Yesterday," 11 Apr 70, 3).

[6] Ida B. Clark was Charles Langdon's fiancée. By "Mr Clemens friends" Olivia evidently meant the same thing her husband meant when he mentioned "my tribe from St. Louis" (third paragraph).

[7] That is, the younger Emma Sayles, not her mother (see p. 44), and Susan Crane.

[8] Pamela Moffett's greetings arrived by letter; she had not yet reached Buffalo (21 Apr 70 to OC).

[9] The resemblance was more than skin-deep. Heacock shared the progressive social views espoused by Dickinson, the prominent lecturer on abolition and women's rights, and by the Langdons, who were her close friends and regular

Elmira hosts (she had most recently called at their house while passing through Elmira on 26 March, although the Langdons were away). On 17 April, for example, he delivered a second, evening sermon—on the "moral and religious lessons of the XVth Amendment," which had become law on 30 March 1870 ("Easter," Buffalo *Express*, 18 Apr 70, 4; *L2*, 337–38 n. 6; *L3*, 192 n. 2, 414 n. 1; "Local Jottings," Elmira *Saturday Evening Review*, 2 Apr 70, 8).

[10]Alice and Clara Spaulding, their parents, Henry and Clara, and possibly their brother, Charles, who was a partner in the family lumber, building supplies, and coal business in Elmira (Boyd and Boyd, 2, 22, 197; Towner, 128; advertisement, Elmira *Saturday Evening Review*, 10 Dec 70, 5; *L3*, 182 n. 6).

To Orion Clemens
19? April 1870 • Buffalo, N.Y.
(MS: CU-MARK)

Orion, if this needs a stamp, put it on.[1]

As for the land, sell it at once & forever, if that Pittsburgh man sticks to his word. ˏ$50,000 is *all it is worth*ₗ, maybe.ˏ[2]

Yrs
Sam.

Orion Clemens Esq | 1114 Locust st | St. Louis | Mo. [*postmarked:*] BUF-FALO N.Y. ◊◊◊ ◊◊[3]

[1]Clemens wrote this note on a scrap of paper, the bottom third of a full sheet. Its approximate date is suggested by the third paragraph of the next letter. As *that* letter indicates, the present enclosure was probably a letter of introduction for Orion to either mail or deliver by hand.

[2]The land was the large tract in undeveloped Tennessee that Clemens's father had acquired in about 1830 and that his sons had been trying to dispose of profitably at least since the late 1850s. Clemens had renounced his interest in it in November 1869 (*L1*, 77, 326, 341, 343; *L2*, 11 n. 1, 59 n. 5, 219; *L3*, 270–72, 279–80, 386–87). The "Pittsburgh man" may have been the "Capt. White" whose proposals for a sale or trade Orion was still considering in June (PAM to OC and MEC, 14 June 70, and JLC to OC and MEC, 25 June 70, both in CU-MARK).

[3]Despite the partly illegible postmark, this envelope almost certainly belongs

to this letter. The Moffett family's move to Fredonia (see the next letter) had caused Orion and Mollie Clemens to relocate from 1511 Pine Street, in St. Louis, where they had lived with the Moffetts for seven months. This new address was a boarding house belonging to Elizabeth M. Kennedy, a widow. By 28 June Orion and Mollie had moved again—to "comfortable quarters" at 1112 Locust Street, the home of a "Mrs. H.," not otherwise identified (PAM to OC and MEC, 28 June 70, CU-MARK; *L3*, 280 n. 2; Edwards 1870, 494, 966).

To Orion Clemens
21 April 1870 • Buffalo, N.Y.
(MS: CU-MARK)

Buffalo, Apl. 21

My Dear Bro—

I enclose (*I* if I do not forget it, after writing it,) a letter of introduction to Col. Knapp. I do not know Mr. Garrett,, & so of course I cannot introduce you to him. It isn't ~~never~~ good ~~judgment~~ to deal with understrappers anyhow. A word from the chief is worth ~~a pa~~ a chapter from *them*.[1]

Ma arrived this afternoon & is with us now. ~~s~~She seems to have come through without extraordinary fatigue. She has a cold which she says has been upon her for a month, & is not worse than usual. Pamela, ~~Mollie~~ Margaret & Sammy got off at Dunkirk at noon, as they came along, & are in Fredonia, now. I am going to write them, presently, to come up & stay over Sunday with us. They will find it unsettled & forlorn in Fredonia just yet.[2]

I wrote you a ~~le~~ little note the other day in which I said $50,000 was ~~w~~ more than our land is worth, & I guess it *is* a *deal* more. If the man's title to his property is good, I think I would take it at once, if I were Mellen. I wouldn't fool away any time about it. Providence will not deliver another lunatic into our hands if we slight this present evidence of his beneficent care for us.[3]

Ma is wool-gathering fearfully, if I may be so bold. When we were riding up from the cars she said Pamela & Sammy & Margaret got off the cars at Dunkirk today. Afterward, at dinner, about 5 or 6 o'clock, she said they *didn't* come on with her & *didn't* get off at Dunkirk. *Now*, an hour later, she says they are coming *here*, tonight, & says she hasn't mentioned them previously, to-day. She is laughing, & so are we—but what does Pamela think of the joke if she is waiting for an escort now, down yonder at the depot?

We all send love to you & Mollie.

Affectionately
Sam

˪It ~~would~~ was simply heedlessness, my not mentioning Mollie—it was never intentional.˼

✉—————————————————————————————————————

Orion Clemens Esq | 1114 Locust st | St Louis | Mo. [*across envelope end:*] If not ~~taken~~ received please return to "Mark Twain," Buffalo. | [*rule*] [*postmarked:*] BUFFALO N.Y. APR 21

[1] In January 1870 Orion had described himself as "penniless, and working for my daily bread on a daily morning newspaper (the [St. Louis] Democrat) reading proof at $25 a week" (OC to R. W. Taylor, 3 Jan 70, in "Territorial Letters Received," transcription in CU-MARK, courtesy of Robert D. Armstrong). Evidently he had now asked his brother for help in finding a better job. Clemens's letter of introduction (now lost) was addressed either to George Knapp (1814–83), a proprietor since 1837, and the senior proprietor since 1854, of the St. Louis *Missouri Republican*, or to his brother, John (1816–88), a proprietor as well as business manager of the paper since 1855. George Knapp had served in the Mexican War, rising to the rank of lieutenant-colonel, and later helped organize the Missouri Republican Guards for service with the Union forces during the Civil War. John Knapp was a colonel in the Missouri militia, and had served in the Mexican and Civil Wars. Thomas E. Garrett was an assistant editor and the drama critic of the *Missouri Republican* (Edwards 1870, 65, 223, 348; Scharf, 1:914–15; Stevens, 1:172).

[2] Dunkirk was a busy commercial port and railroad terminus on Lake Erie, about forty miles southwest of Buffalo and three miles north of Fredonia. Transportation between Dunkirk and Fredonia was by horsecar. Jane Clemens remained in Buffalo until 23 May, noting in her ledger for that date a train fare of $1.25 "from Buffalo to Dunkirk" (JLC, 12). It is not known if Pamela, her son, and the family maid came to Buffalo to stay through Sunday, 24 April. Pamela's daughter, Annie, was not with the family, having remained in St. Louis with friends while she finished the school year. She arrived in Fredonia in July (John Homer French, 214; 20 Jan 70 to OLL; 1 Apr 70 to the Langdons; 22 May 70 to Langdon; and, in CU-MARK: PAM to OC and MEC, 14 June 70, 23 June 70; PAM to Annie E. Moffett, 28 June 70).

[3] John S. Mellon worked for J. E. Merriman and Company of St. Louis, the real estate agency Orion had commissioned in 1869 to sell the Clemenses' Tennessee land. The firm's exclusive option on the property had been due to expire at the beginning of April 1870. Orion must have renewed it, however, for Mellon was still acting on his behalf in the summer of 1870 (*L3*, 272 n. 4, 279–80 n. 1; Edwards 1870, 607, 609, 1069; PAM to OC and MEC, 14 June 70, CU-MARK; JLC to OC and MEC, 25 June 70, CU-MARK; 1 Aug 70 to OC).

From Samuel L. and Olivia L. Clemens
to Theodore W. Crane
22 April 1870 • Buffalo, N.Y.
(MS: CtHMTH)

472, 22^d, 6 PM
1870.

Brother Theodore—

I enclose you an official letter acknowledging rec'pt of check.[1]

All right—I will come down & break one of the horses ~~alon~~ while you break the other. But are you sure your plan is good? It *looks* feasible, but at the same time I cannot feel certain that it is the safest way. My custom heretofore, when I wanted to break a horse, was to do it with a rail. You cannot get hurt then—unless of course the horse bites you.

Start Mrs. Brown along just as soon as you please—we are ready to welcome her & make her entirely comfortable. (But don't you suppose "Bell" will prefer to have his visit out with you, first, before *he* comes?— ɢGlad to have him, but don't wish to ~~infe~~ interfere with *you*.][2]

[~~Bett~~ Between you & I,—for Livy would not like it to be known —she remarked awhile ago that she would "comb" those dressmakers if they sent any more messages to me. I don't know what "combing" is, but that was the remark she made. ₐIt is entirely *false*, I hate to say so]—ₐ]

I hear that Mr. Bailey has been elected superintendent of the Industrial School. Can that be true?[3]

We send our love to our Susie.

All well—& all happy.

Yrs

Saml.

[1] The enclosure has not been found. The check probably was for all or part of the $4,309.42 that Clemens had allowed Jervis Langdon to hold for him on 10 March. He may now have wanted the funds because of his recent loan to Larned, or for a payment on his debt to Kennett, or for the expenses he alludes to in the next letter. With Langdon still traveling and John D. F. Slee in Buffalo, Crane— like Slee, Langdon's business associate and soon-to-be partner—was responsible for sending the check to Clemens (11 Mar 70 to Bliss; 16 and 17 Apr 70 to the Langdons).

[2] Neither Mrs. Brown nor "Bell" has been identified. They probably were *not* Anna Marsh Brown, and her husband, Talmage. Anna Brown may already have visited the Clemenses (27 Mar 70 to the Langdons).

[3] Isaac H. Bailey (1821–95), a tin cutter manufacturer, was a fellow parishioner of the Langdons' and Cranes' at Congregational Church. Clemens may have been surprised at Bailey's reported election because, since its founding in June 1869, the Elmira Industrial School, which the Langdons and Cranes helped support, had been managed by a group of women volunteers. Among them was Anna M. Crane, Theodore Crane's half sister, who was one of the teachers, and Mrs. J. D. Steele, the superintendent (possibly outgoing). At the school's two-hour sessions, currently held on Saturday afternoons at the First Methodist Church, about fifty girls "from homes of poverty and vice" were encouraged in habits of "punctuality, improvement and cleanliness" while being taught to sew. The goal was for pupils to learn "*how to earn bread*, . . . quite as important to the poor as a knowledge of Geography and Grammar" ("Industrial School," El-mira *Advertiser,* 1 Mar 70, 4; "Death of Isaac Bailey," Elmira *Gazette and Free Press,* 31 May 95, 8; Boyd and Boyd, 62; "Annual Report of the Industrial School," Elmira *Saturday Evening Review,* 9 July 70, 8; Gretchen Sharlow and Herbert A. Wisbey, Jr., personal communications).

To Elisha Bliss, Jr.
23 April 1870 • Buffalo, N.Y.
(MS: CU-MARK)

Buf., Apl. 23.

Friend Bliss—

All right—the ~~tri-~~ quarterly statement will arrive in a good time.[1] For I shall pay a debt or two then, & I shall be paying a thousand dollars & some other money toward buying a beautiful home for my mother in a ~~neighboring town~~ ˄village˄ near here—my sister paying the other five or six thousand.[2]

When you come we'll talk books & business. I wish my wife wanted
to spend the summer in England, but I'm afraid she don't. But we shall
soon know, now, whether Mr. Langdon will try Europe or not.[3] ~~I shall
watch this~~

I shall watch this Galaxy business pretty closely, & whenever I seem
to be "letting down," I shall withdraw from literature & recuperate. But
this month's "Memoranda" hasn't hurt my reputation, & next month's
won't—I want to bet something ~~in~~ on that.[4]

Will you let some neat-handed & artistic person, like Miss Nellie,[5]
for instance, paste the enclosed in the ~~title-page~~ fly-leaf of the nicest copy
of the Innocents you have got, & send it *express paid* (& charged to me,)
to

Mrs. Bart. Bowen,[6]

Columbia,

Mo.

& oblige yrs

Clemens.

✉——————————————————————————————————

[*letter docketed:*] √ auth Mark Twain [*and*] /70

[1] The third quarter for *Innocents* ended on 30 April. Bliss's letter, to which
Clemens replied here, has not been found.

[2] In Fredonia, about forty miles from Buffalo, the Moffetts and Jane Clemens
rented a brick house on Day Street (across from the village common), the former
rectory of Trinity Episcopal Church. Pamela may have hoped to buy this house,
which the church designated for sale on 24 March, setting the price at $5,000 on
17 May. It sold, however, to Sarah Greene on 18 March 1871. Probably in late
November 1871 the Moffetts and Jane Clemens moved to the frame house on
Temple Street where they were living by 1875. Local records indicate that Pamela did not purchase the Temple Street house either. In 1912, Paine reported that
in recommending Fredonia, Clemens had advised Pamela to "Try to select a
place where a good many funerals pass. Ma likes funerals. If you can pick a good
funeral corner she will be happy" (*MTB*, 1:424). According to Douglas H. Shepard of Fredonia, "both the Day St. and the Temple St. homes were on the direct
route for almost all funerals in Fredonia" (Shepard to Michael B. Frank, 14 Nov
1993, 26 Jan 1994, 4 Feb 1994, 30 Apr 1994, 8 May 1994, CU-MARK; *MTBus*,
112, 129, 170).

[3] Clemens was anticipating the Langdons' return. On the day of this letter the
Elmira *Saturday Evening Review* reported that they "are now in Savannah, and

are not expected home for two weeks" ("Local Jottings," 8). See 4 May 70 to Janney, n. 1.

[4] Clemens's first "Memoranda" appeared in the *Galaxy* for May, published by mid-April (SLC 1870dd). The New York *Tribune* called "Memoranda" a "pleasant admixture of sense and nonsense" ("New Publications," 15 Apr 70, 6). The Elmira *Advertiser* observed:

> MARK TWAIN's Department is especially noticeable, and will be a feature of the Magazine much sought after. This gentleman forms another example of the truth of the saying that the person who possesses qualities of the richest humor, has also command of the tenderest pathos. His Memoranda is composed of matter, part of which will move one to mirth, and another part induce sadness and sympathy. ("Editorial Small Talk," 18 Apr 70, 1)

On 26 April, Francis Church wrote Clemens, enclosing a "check for the 12th part of $2000 for the May Memoranda" and an unidentified review or reviews, indicating that "it has made a hit" (CU-MARK). He also reminded Clemens that copy for the June issue was due by 3 May. The June "Memoranda" (SLC 1870kk) was also well received. The New York *Tribune* pronounced it one of the *Galaxy's* best elements; the Elmira *Advertiser* called it "overwhelmingly funny"; and the Elmira *Saturday Evening Review* said that "Mark Twain's contributions now constitute a steady and very valuable feature—they are super excellent" ("New Publications," New York *Tribune,* 19 May 70, 6; "Editorial Small Talk," Elmira *Advertiser,* 23 May 70, 1; "Dramatic Notes," Elmira *Saturday Evening Review,* 28 May 70, 5). Clemens's own confidence in both the May and June "Memoranda" remained strong: he eventually reprinted six of their eleven sketches, both in 1872 with George Routledge and Sons (*Mark Twain's Sketches*) and in 1875 with Bliss (*Sketches, New and Old*).

[5] See 22 Jan 70 to Bliss, n. 7.

[6] Sarah Robards Bowen (1836–1918), a former Hannibal schoolmate, was the recent widow of Clemens's good friend and fellow pilot, later captain, Barton W. Stone Bowen, who had died at Hannibal on 21 May 1868 (*L1,* 340–41 n. 4; *Inds,* 94, 97, 304, 345; "Death of Captain Bart Bowen," St. Louis *Dispatch,* 2 June 68, 1; "Death of a Steamboat Captain," San Francisco *Times,* 23 June 68, 1).

To Frank Fuller
26 April 1870 • Buffalo, N.Y.
(Transcripts: WU and AAA 1924c, lot 64)

Buf. Apl. 26

Dear Frank:—

I was powerful glad to hear from you & sorry that I can't insure with you—am insured for $10,000 in the old Continental, Hartford, & I reckon it is about all this frail tenement is worth. But after I collect *that*, count me in for the Hope.[1]

I sent that Newark gentleman a paper with a joke in it.[2]

Yes, we print a Weekly, but not to outrage our friends with—its legitimate prey are the public. I don't write for it much. Its price is only a dollar & a half & so the swindle isn't heavy. I send it to your brother John free of charge—confound him, it keeps him still a little, once a week, & gives some of the Bostonians a chance to edge in a word.[3] I'll not send it to you, because you don't talk enough anyhow. You never talked enough to satisfy *me*, my boy, & I would like to be listening to you this very moment.

Now *say*—between you & me, you have got a literary sneak thief in Philadelphia who signs himself "John Quill" & I want you to keep a sharp lookout on him after the June Galaxy comes out. He sent me a newspaper article the other day signed with his name & purporting to be the original of the blowing up of the boy with nitro-glycerine (a catastrophe which I credited to some "unknown but exceedingly ingenious author") in the May Galaxy. Without mentioning his name, I have salted him down in my MSS. for June as "A Literary Old Offender in Court with Suspicious Property in his Possession"—& declining to accept of his testimony. Send me his reply a month hence or perish. May 13 or 14 or along there.[4]

Frank, if you think there is any likelihood of your remaining in Philadelphia several months longer, before you sell out & start something fresh, I shall be glad to send you our Weekly & not even charge you what any calm, dispassionate rag-man will tell you it is worth.[5] What do you say? For notwithstanding I am so willing to do this, I do not want to do it to you unless *you* are willing.

See other side. I'm out of the lecture field permanently, I hope. It is a dismal sort of business, even to a lazy man like me—it would kill a nervous thunderbolt like you.

IN HASTE

Yrs Ever

Mark.

Frank, don't you ever dare to stop at any hotel in Buffalo except this one of mine, 472 Delaware Street.

[*on the back:*]

OFFICE "EXPRESS" PRINTING CO.

BUFFALO, ... 1870.

DEAR SIR:

IN ANSWER I AM OBLIGED TO SAY THAT IT WILL NOT BE POSSIBLE
FOR ME TO ACCEPT YOUR KIND INVITATION. I SHALL NOT BE ABLE TO LEC-
TURE AGAIN DURING THE PRESENT SEASON. THANKING YOU KINDLY FOR
THE COMPLIMENT OF YOUR INVITATION, I AM

YOURS TRULY,

SAM'L L. CLEMENS.

["MARK TWAIN."]

AGENTS:

BOSTON LYCEUM BUREAU,

20 BROMFIELD STREET,

BOSTON.

---

[1] Fuller, who was now living in Philadelphia, apparently represented the Hope Insurance Company, of Providence, Rhode Island, purveyors of life, fire, and marine insurance ("Insurance," Buffalo *Express*, 26 Apr 70, 4; Wilson 1869, 526). For Clemens's insurance, see *L3*, 387.

[2] Unidentified.

[3] See 8 Feb 70 to John Fuller.

[4] In a footnote to "The Story of the Good Little Boy Who Did Not Prosper," Clemens acknowledged that he borrowed its climax "(without the unknown but most ingenious owner's permission) from a stray newspaper item" (SLC 1870dd, 726). He was now completing his manuscript (due on 3 May) for the June "Memoranda." In the "Literary 'Old Offender'" segment of it he explained that he found that climax "drifting about the sea of journalism, in the shape of a simple statement of the catastrophe in a single sentence, and attributed to a California paper." He added that a "Philadelphia person" had since sent him

a half-column newspaper article, dated December 22, signed with his name, and being what he says is the original draft of the nitro-glycerine catastrophe.

The impulse to make pleasant mention of this person's name and give him the credit he claims, is crippled by the fact that I, or any one else acquainted with his literary history, would feel obliged to decline to accept any evidence coming from him, upon any matter, and especially upon a question of authorship. His simple word is worthless; and to embellish it with his oath would merely make it picturesque, not valuable. This person several of us know of our own personal knowledge to be a poor little purloiner of other men's ideas and handicraft. . . . Anybody capturing the subject of these remarks and overhauling the catalogue of what he calls his "writings," will find in it two very good articles of mine, and if the rest were advertised as "strayed or stolen," they would doubtless be called for by journalists residing in all the different States of the Union. (SLC 1870kk, 863)

Although Clemens therefore knew that the original had appeared in the Philadelphia *Evening Bulletin,* no evidence has been found that he was also aware that the "purloiner's" claim had already been published there too. On 22 April, in reviewing the May *Galaxy,* the *Bulletin* had remarked:

> Mr. Twain's efforts begin this week; he is not in his very freshest vein. . . . By the by, as he terminates his wildest story with a catastrophe confessedly borrowed, we may properly help him to the authorship of the fancy he appropriates. The citizens of Philadelphia remember well enough, what Mr. Twain, in his journey to the sanctum in New York, has dropped the knowledge of, that his boy exploded with nitro-glycerine was an invention of "John Quill," of the PHILADELPHIA BULLETIN. ("New Periodicals," 2)

Clemens may even have been unaware that John Quill was a pseudonym for Charles Heber Clark (1841–1915), a *Bulletin* editor who became better known as Max Adeler (Dussere, 44, 93–130, 357). Clark had published his exploding boy story, "The Fate of Joe M'Ginnis: A Warning to Mothers," in the *Bulletin* of 22 December 1869 (Clark 1869c). As in Clemens's story, the title character sits in spilled nitroglycerine and then is inadvertently dispatched by a spanking. Clark's version had been reprinted in the weekly San Francisco *Golden City* for 23 January 1870, possibly the "California paper" that Clemens's source (presumably one of the Buffalo *Express*'s numerous exchanges) had summarized. The "two very good articles" that Clark may have borrowed were "Aurelia's Unfortunate Young Man" and "The Steed 'Oahu,'" which he could have found in the 1867 *Jumping Frog* book. Clark's similar sketches were "How Wm. McGinley Suffered" and "That Horse of Mine," in the Philadelphia *Evening Bulletin* of 26 November and 4 December 1869, respectively (SLC 1864b, 1866a; Clark 1869a–b). The *Bulletin* did not respond to Clemens's June "Memoranda": in its condescending review of that month's *Galaxy* the "Memoranda" were never mentioned ("New Periodicals," 21 May 70, 6). In 1889, however, Clark renewed hostilities by accusing Clemens of having appropriated much of *A Connecticut Yankee in King Arthur's Court* from a short story that, as Max Adeler, he had twice published—in 1881 as "Professor Baffin's Adventures" and in 1882 as "The Fortunate Island" (Clark 1881, 1882). For interpretation of the entire Clemens-Clark embroglio, see: Ketterer; Kruse 1990, 1991.

⁵Fuller, whose locations and occupations had been varied, did not remain long in Philadelphia. There is no listing for him in city directories for 1871–72, and by 1874 he was in the health food business in New York City (*L2,* 5–6, 241 n. 7; "Frank Fuller Dead; Utah War Governor," New York *Times,* 20 Feb 1915, 5).

To Charles C. Converse
30? April 1870 • Buffalo, N.Y.
(Paraphrase: Buffalo *Express*, 9 May 70)

In reply, I wrote this pleasant-spoken gentleman that I had just telegraphed to New York for the *Independent* article, so that I could set Dr.
T. right, before as many of the public as I could reach, (for it seemed
perfectly plain that I had been wronging him,) and I said I wished to
make this reparation "intelligently & immediately," without waiting a
month for the *Galaxy* to issue again.[1]

[1]Clemens's "About Smells" in the May "Memoranda" had attacked Thomas
De Witt Talmage (1832–1902), popular pastor of the Central Presbyterian
Church in Brooklyn, for bigoted remarks Talmage made in "How!" in the New
York *Independent* on 9 December 1869 (2). Clemens had seen the offensive pas-
sage as reprinted in the 6 January 1870 Chicago *Advance,* a Congregational
weekly (*WIM*, 535; Mott 1957, 76–77), which he quoted in the *Galaxy:*

> I have a good Christian friend who, if he sat in the front pew in church, and a working
> man should enter the door at the other end, would smell him instantly. My friend is not
> to blame for the sensitiveness of his nose, any more than you would flog a pointer for
> being keener on the scent than a stupid watch dog. The fact is, if you had all the
> churches free, by reason of the mixing up of the common people with the uncommon,
> you would keep one-half of Christendom sick at their stomach. If you are going to kill
> the church thus with bad smells, I will have nothing to do with this work of evangeli-
> zation. (SLC 1870dd, 721)

Probably on 30 April, Clemens received the following letter, subsequently published in "Personal," his long follow-up to "About Smells" in the Buffalo *Express*
of 9 May (SLC 1870gg):

> BROOKLYN, April 28.
> MARK TWAIN, *Galaxy Office, New York:*
> DEAR SIR:
> Rev[.] T. de Witt Talmage is a representative democratic preacher, whom to see in
> a "spike-tailed coat and kids" would astonish his friends quite as much as does your
> apparent misconception of his real character and views touching the free-church ques-
> tion. Will you please read his entire article in the *Independent* from which you quote in
> the *Galaxy* for May and favor your readers with such a memorandum as it may suggest,
> and greatly oblige,
>
> Yours truly,
> C——— C———,
> Of Mr. Talmage's Church.

The writer was Charles Crozat Converse (1832–1918), a lawyer and composer,
whose father, Maxey Manning Converse, had been a prominent Elmira music
teacher (Towner, 284). Clemens's reply was probably immediate, but is known
to survive only in his own paraphrase of it, also published in "Personal." There
he further explained that a second letter from Converse reached him in Elmira

(about 4 May) and "the next day I dropped everything else and wrote a full explanation of how the *Advance* had defrauded me into wronging Dr. Talmage." But when he "was just about to mail this for publication in the *Independent*, (and had even enveloped and directed it,)" an "Eastern mail brought me Dr. Talmage's original *Independent* article in full, and I waited to read it." That was probably on 6 May at the latest. On reading Talmage's article, Clemens decided not to send his drafted "reparation" because:

> I was sorrowfully disappointed—for alas! the most analytical mind in the world could not tell which was the Doctor's sarcasm and which was his "real earnest!" It was plain that the *Advance* had right fair reason for regarding as a serious utterance a paragraph which Dr. T. stated to be "irony." I am not questioning Dr. T.'s honesty, now. On the contrary I am satisfied that he really looks upon his little paragraph as irony, and very fair irony at that, but it is certainly the opaquest sarcasm that ever got into print. Any unprejudiced man who will read Dr. T.'s *Independent* article and then get its author or a parishioner to explain it to him, will say that the Rev. Dr. Talmage has no business meddling with a pen. Writing is not his specialty. . . .
>
> Rev. Dr. Talmage is not a bad man. I have credible evidence that he is a very excellent man and that his heart is really in the freeing of the churches. . . . I, for one, am sorry I criticised him harshly—no, not that. But I am sincerely sorry that he ever hurled that execrable column of decomposed grammar, irreverence and incipient lunacy into print and so betrayed me into unchivalrously attacking a literary cripple. (SLC 1870gg)

Clemens instead wrote and immediately mailed "Personal" to Buffalo, where it was presumably received on Saturday, 7 May, typeset on Sunday, and published on Monday, 9 May.

To Mary Janney
4 May 1870? • Elmira, N.Y.
(MS: CtHMTH)

Elmira, N. Y. May 4.[1]

Miss Mary Janney—[2]

It took me a good ~~while to make out what~~ while to make out what those two slanting lines meant, (\\ ), but a burst of inspiration finally revealed to me that two Marks necessarily stand for Twain, & then the rest was easy—as, no doubt, it was to you. I think it is a good rebus.[3]

Thanking you very kindly indeed for your pleasant note, I am

Very Truly & Resp'ly Yrs
Sam*l*. L. Clemens.

✉——————————————————————————

[unidentified hand on back of letter as folded:] For Mary

[1] On Monday, 2 May, the Elmira *Advertiser* reported that the Clemenses were "in the city. They will spend the next week or two with friends here." They prob-

ably arrived on Sunday (1 May), for the *Advertiser* also noted that "Mr. JERVIS LANGDON and wife and Dr. SAYLES and wife, returned from their southern trip on Friday evening. The health of the party was not much benefitted by the journey. Particularly was this the case with Mr. LANGDON, who lost some thirty pounds in weight during his absence" ("City and Neighborhood," 4). Langdon's illness now must have seemed ominous indeed, although there was lingering hope that it would still prove to be merely "dyspepsia" (13 May 70 to Langdon). Langdon himself seems to have begun preparing for the worst by seeing that his business affairs were in good order. On 1 May he officially reorganized his firm as J. Langdon and Company, taking as partners his son, Charles, his son-in-law, Theodore Crane, and his trusted associate John D. F. Slee (22 May 70 to Langdon, n. 2; 25 June 70 to Fairbanks, n. 1).

²Mary Janney is unidentified. Clemens himself may never have met her, for on the back of this letter, someone wrote "For Mary," indicating that it was hand delivered or enclosed by an intermediary. The paper, ink, and handwriting are similar to those in 23 Apr 70 to Bliss, but with Janney unidentified, the assigned year remains doubtful: 1869 and 1871 are each somewhat less likely but still possible.

³Clemens had used a similar rebus in January 1869 (*L3*, 14).

To Elisha Bliss, Jr.
5 May 1870 • Elmira, N.Y.
(Transcript: WU)

Elmira May 5

Friend Bliss—

We return home a week hence. We shall go to the Adirondacks with the Twichells. I would have published that bookseller in that New York town if I had remained in Buffalo—but here I only "loaf."[1]

What went with the *Sun* paragraph you spoke of? (Your letter was not sealed & it was gone.) Was it complimentary, or the reverse? Was it about me? I will bet I will make some of those people sick, yet.[2]

I telegraphed you to send statement & check here—did you get it? I have a bid for a book from a Philada subscription house[3] offering unlimitedly.

Tell me what the *Sun* paragraph was, sure. Tell me right away.

Love to you & yours
Saml L Clemens

✉—————————————————

[*letter docketed:*] —70

[1] The unidentified bookseller was probably selling copies of *The Innocents Abroad* purchased, contrary to company policy, from a subscription agent.

[2] Bliss's letter is not known to survive. The clipping it enclosed and referred to was probably the following:

> A dog, the property of Mr. M—— T——, a well-known writer, afforded on one occasion a remarkable instance of the sagacity of his race. His master was in the habit of giving him two pennies every morning at breakfast time, and sending him to buy a SUN of a newsboy. One morning the boy, having sold all his SUNS, offered the dog a Daily *Times*. But the sagacious animal, knowing his master's politics, wagged his tail, put out his tongue, and went to a news-shop to buy the needful journal. ("A Knowing Dog," New York *Sun*, 30 Apr 70, 2, reprinting the *Comic Monthly* of unknown date)

The New York *Sun*, edited by Charles A. Dana, was a lively, somewhat sensational paper with increasingly conservative sympathies. The more staid New York *Times*, edited by Louis J. Jennings, was, like the Buffalo *Express*, a reformist Republican paper (Rowell, 692, 699; Mott 1950, 374–78, 382–84).

[3] Unidentified.

To Elisha Bliss, Jr.
7 May 1870 • Elmira, N.Y.
(MS: CU-MARK)

J. LANGDON, MINER & DEALER IN ANTHRACITE &
BITUMINOUS COAL   OFFICE NO. 6 BALDWIN STREET

Private.

ELMIRA, N.Y. May 7 186 70

Friend Bliss—

I have just been stricken with an idea, in the shape of a scheme to secure a wide-spread advertisement. Whenever our sales reach 100,000,—no matter when that may be—you ~~have tho~~ or the Directors call me to Hartford to an oyster supper in celebration of the event—the ~~city~~ Hartford editors to be present[1]—& I will either come there & make a speech that will travel well in the papers, or I will send one to be read there that will travel. ~~Of course, if you speak of this,~~ If you can think of something simpler & just as effectual, let's have it—for suppers are sometimes a nuisance, & besides, the object of this one might be too glaringly apparent. Set your invention to work.

~~I calcu~~

I sent you dispatch yesterday to acknowledge rec'pt of your check for $3,914.62, & also to express my eminent satisfaction at the way the book is selling.[2]

Mr. Langdon has been dangerously ill for some days, & it is plain that he cannot travel a mile this year. So we shall not move out of reach of sudden call. That closes out all notion of crossing the ocean—though we expect to go th to the Adirondacks with the Twichells.

Yrs Ever

Mark.

[*letter docketed:*] Mark Twain | May 7/70 [*and in pencil:*] July 20/69 393 copies rec'd from bindery[3]

[1] At this time the directors of the American Publishing Company, all Hartford residents, were: E. G. Hastings, also the firm's president, a dealer in shirts; Thomas Belknap, an independent publisher; Sidney Drake, the former president, a bookbinder; George S. Gilman, an attorney; George F. Hills, cashier at the State Bank; Henry J. Johnson, a provisions merchant; and James S. Tryon, cashier at the First National Bank. Elisha Bliss, presently the secretary of the firm and by July 1870 its president, was at all times its chief executive officer. His twenty-six-year-old son Francis (Frank) was the treasurer. The principal Hartford newspaper editors were: Joseph R. Hawley and Charles Dudley Warner, of the *Courant;* L. R. Riggs and H. H. Barbour, of the *News;* Isaac H. Bromley and Joseph L. Barbour, of the *Post;* and Warren H. and Willie O. Burr, of the *Times* (Geer: 1869, 50, 62, 69, 107, 129, 144, 150, 162, 198, 264, 423, 495; 1870, 46, 64, 72, 507; Elisha Bliss to SLC, 2 May 70, CU-MARK; "Hartford Residents," Bliss Family, 1; *L3*, 97 n. 5; Rowell, 624).

[2] On 2 May Bliss had written to Clemens at Elmira, as instructed (CU-MARK):

Friend Clemens.

Enclosed please find Statement of sales, & Check for 3914.65 amount of copyright, which we trust will come safely to hand, & be satisfactory to you, & show you "we still live"   We will at the end of the year give you a statement of *every Book bound* with report of what has been done with all. *Every vol* that we do not pay copyright on (*i e Editors &c*) so as to make it all plain & square with you. *This is our style—* Dont think your *Galaxy articles* hurt your reputation at all. it was good, *capital capital*   I sent your Book to Mrs *Bowen* Col. as you directed. Please acknowledge recpt of Check, & state how you feel as regards sales &c. Respects to Mrs. C

Ever yours

Bliss

Bliss enclosed a statement, dated 1 May, of third quarter (1 Feb–30 Apr) sales of *The Innocents Abroad.* Clemens's royalty on 21,378 copies came to $3,925.90, from which Bliss deducted $11.25 for "7 books shipped to parties by order ,& express chgs,." *Innocents* had sold a total of 60,378 copies, with total royalties amounting to about $11,300 (22 Jan 70 to Bliss, n. 6; 28 Jan 70 to Bliss, n. 5). Once Clemens realized that sales would not "reach 100,000" for some time, he modified his "oyster supper" scheme (30 May 70, 18 July 70, 21? Sept 70, all to Bliss).

[3] According to American Publishing Company records, the first 403 copies of

The Innocents Abroad were received from the bindery on 20 July 1869, about ten days before the book was officially issued (APC, 45; *L3*, 287 n. 1). This penciled notation indicates that ten of those copies were not counted in sales, possibly because they were defective, or set aside for promotional use. The appearance of the notation here suggests that Bliss had risen to Clemens's challenge to "set your invention to work" and, with some new promotional scheme in mind, had instructed an employee to document the receipt of first copies. By June he had devised a "tip-top" advertising circular (27 June 70 to Bliss).

To James Redpath
10 May 1870 • Elmira, N.Y.
(Will M. Clemens 1900, 27, and four others)

Elmira, N. Y., May 10, 1870.

Friend Redpath,—

I guess I am out of the field permanently. I am sending off these circulars to all lecture applicants now.[1] If you want some more of them I can send them to you—for they are very convenient for you to mail to people & save penmanship.

Have got a lovely wife, a lovely house, bewitchingly furnished, a lovely carriage, & a coachman whose style & dignity are simply awe-inspiring—nothing less;[2] & I am making more money than necessary, by considerable, & therefore why crucify myself nightly on the platform. The subscriber will have to be excused from the present season at least.

Remember me to Nasby, Billings & Fall. Luck to you! I am going to print your menagerie, Parton and all, and make comments.[3]

In next Galaxy I give Nasby's friend and mine from Philadelphia (John Quill, a literary thief) a "hyste." I don't consider that the Rev. Talmage has the weather gage of me yet.[4]

Yours always & after,

Mark.

[1] Doubtless copies of Clemens's printed form letter for declining lecture invitations: see 8 Feb 70 to Fuller.

[2] Patrick McAleer.

[3] Petroleum V. Nasby (David Ross Locke), Josh Billings (Henry Wheeler Shaw), and James Parton (1822–91), the well-known biographer and contributor to the *Atlantic Monthly,* were among the lecturers managed by Redpath and Fall (*Lyceum* 1870, 2–3). Clemens had compared experiences with Locke and Shaw

in November 1869 and Locke called on the Clemenses in February 1870 (*L3*, 387, 397 n. 3, 405, 406, 409, 411; 20 Feb 70 to Langdon). Clemens sent Shaw his wedding cards, in reply to which Shaw returned congratulations on 14 February, reporting that he had "agreed to let Redpath mould me for next season, if I am able to shout, and have gave him entire control of my *"Milk"* (CU-MARK). Clemens may also have written to Shaw shortly after the present letter, on or about 16 May, but all that survives of his draft is that date and a salutation on a page later used by Olivia for a household shopping list (CU-MARK). Clemens did not publish anything about Redpath's "menagerie," at least not in the Buffalo *Express*. The subject continued to tempt him, however, and in 1898 he wrote about Nasby and others for his autobiography (SLC 1898a–b).

[4]See 26 Apr 70 to Fuller, n. 4, and 30? Apr 70 to Converse, n. 1.

From Olivia L. and Samuel L. Clemens
to Jervis Langdon
13 May 1870 • Buffalo, N.Y.
(MS: CtHMTH)

Buffalo May 13th 1870

Dear Father

There is no end to surprizes to this young woman, when I opened the check I expected to see five hundred dollars at the most, when I saw the *one*, I thought it was one hundred, and could scarcely believe my eyes when I saw that it was *one thousand* dollars— I felt as if I had suddenly discovered a fathomless mine—as if I had all the money that I could *ever* need— I thought Father that you were going to economize this year, you have not shown much economy in your dealings with me.

Well all I can say is that I thank you *very* much and feel as if I ~~have all the money that I could can possibly want to spend~~ was *immensely* rich—

I was glad to learn by Theodores letter that you were ₐmoreₐ comfortable yesterday morning— I *do* hope that you will improve and I do wish that it might be rapidly— We do want to see you and Mother here—

We found Mrs Moffett here when we arrived.₍~~we~~ We came through very comfortably—[1]

I bought today a beautiful plated syrup cup, I had none, and once

when we had syrup on the table it was put on in my ~~japanes~~ Japanese
pitcher and Mr C. did not think that was in keeping—

I wish we could know just how you are feeling tonight— I enclose
a cure for dyspepsia which Mrs Moffett was very anxious to have me
send—

Samuel will finish this letter are not you glad? he is splendid.

Lovingly Livy

(No, that isn't so.) Livy is delighted with her check, & I am as delighted as she is, to see her enjoy it so, and besides it is a real pleasure to
see father give, because he does it so ungrudgingly. (There, I have written that as if I were talking it to Livy instead of writing it to you, father—
for I am so dreamy tonight, & so seemingly dazed, that I think & talk &
write in reverie. Have been awake since 5.30 AM.) But we did enjoy the
check father, just exactly as much as if we had found the money buried
in a pot in the backyard, because a present from you never frets, or hu-
miliates or loads ~~wi~~ one with a sense of having contracted a debt & given
an invisible note for it secured by a lien on the ~~rece~~ recipient's pride &
peace of mind, ~~till~~

C. C. Converse has written to ~~$~~ Selkirk to ˄send˄ him a lot of those
Expresses with the Talmage article in it (I happened to see the package
& inquired about it.) The congregation probably find it interesting.[2]

We'~~ll~~ shall not send for my brother. We have editorial help enough
already, & we are going to discontinue the Evening paper & let the job
office to two printers on a per centage. Moreover, ~~Joe is going~~ we have a
chance to sell the Evening telegraphic franchise, *if we find upon examination that when one buys that sort of property he owns it.* The Evening
paper & the job office were *leaks* from the start, & these boys did not
know it. That is the sort of business man Selkirk is. Now we'll have a
little better income.[3]

I am beginning to yearn to furnish the billiard-room & make it
lovely—& just as soon as I break down Livy's sensible prejudices about
one's spending money while one is still in debt you will hear of the up-
holsterers & carpenters being at work in the sky parlor.

Were those flowers to be planted with the roots up—or just in the
old way? It is Livy's question. I think their peculiarity, if they have any,
is probably in their fragrance, & not in the fanciful fashion of planting
them, but Livy says she knows different.

Love & warm good wishes to all of you.

With strong affection,

Yr Son

Sam*l*.

---

[1] The Clemenses returned to Buffalo by 10 or 11 May—earlier than planned, perhaps to greet Pamela, who nevertheless preceded them (5 May 70 to Bliss; 13 May 70 to Langdon).

[2] See 30? Apr 70 to Converse.

[3] Clemens had previously tried to help Orion find work elsewhere than on the shrinking Buffalo *Express* (21 Apr 70 to OC, n. 1). On 16 May the *Express* announced that

> Messrs Louis Hansman and William McK. Gatchell have become associates with the Express Printing Company in the Job Department of the Express printing establishment, the business of which will hereafter be conducted by them. Both these gentlemen have been connected with this establishment for several years, Mr. Hansman, as the foreman of the Job Department, and Mr. Gatchell, in a like capacity in the Newspaper Department. Both are thorough printers of the first class, and possessed of all the qualifications which ensure success in such a business. ("The Express Job Printing Office," 4)

An evening edition called the Buffalo *Bee and Evening Express,* begun in January, ceased on 30 May (Buffalo *Express:* "The Bee and Evening Express," 4 Jan 70, 4; "The Express," 28 May, 30 May 70, 2). It is not known how the telegraphic franchise was disposed of. "These boys" were Clemens's partners, Larned and Selkirk.

To Elisha Bliss, Jr.
20 May 1870 • Buffalo, N.Y.
(MS: Daley)

Confidential.

Buf—A May 20.

Friend Bliss—

Appleton wants me to furnish a few lines of letter ff press for a humorous picture-book—that is, two lines of remarks under each picture. I have intimated that if the pictures & the pay are both good, I will do it. What do you think of it? I thought that inasmuch as half the public would think I made the engravings as well as did the letter-press, it would be a unique & splendid advertisement wherewith to boost the "Innocents." ‸I am to see proofs of the pictures before I contract.‸[1]

Yrs

Mark.

[*letter docketed:*] Mark Twain | May 20/70 | Author

[1]Bliss objected to this proposal from D. Appleton and Company, of New York, eventually leading Clemens to end the "picture-book" negotiations (23–26 June 70 to Appleton; 4 July 70 to Bliss).

To Edward H. Paige
20? May 1870 • Buffalo, N.Y.
(MS: MiD)

[*on the back:*]

E. H. PAIGE,

NO. 446 MAIN STREET,

BUFFALO, N. Y.

Thank you & Mrs. Randall very kindly & sincerely.
I think this is by far the best picture I ever had.[1]

S. L. C.

[1] Mrs. J. C. Randall kept the boarding house at 39 Swan Street where Clemens lived in 1869. She may have introduced him to photographer Edward H. Paige, who lived nearby at 23 West Swan, not far from the Buffalo *Express* offices at 14 East Swan (*L3*, 318 n. 3; *Buffalo Directory* 1870, 460, 471). On 5 May, the *Express* reported that an "admirable" photograph of Mark Twain "was taken some time since by Mr. Paige, and is now on exhibition, together with many other specimens of his fine workmanship, at his gallery over 446 Main street" ("Paige's Photographic Gallery," 4). When Clemens sat for Paige is not known, but the photograph on exhibit was probably also used for this *carte de visite*, a supply of which Clemens had only just received when he sent one to James Redpath on 21 May.

To Frank Fuller
21 May 1870 • Buffalo, N.Y.
(MS, *damage emended:* Axelrod and ODaU)

Buf. May 21.

Dear Frank:

You are the infernallest pleasantest scribbler that lives. I want to say that & clinch it, before I proceed to business.

No *sir*—I won't lecture for a level year from this day & date.[1] The very best lecture manager in America without any exception will pay me five thousand dollars a month, *one half in advance,* ~~to talk for him.~~ & the other payments daily or weekly, as I chose, ₐ(just note the grammatical flourishes, as you go along),—& I had the nerve to *refuse!*[2] Therefore, seal thy lips upon the good old lecturing business, for there is hardly enough money in America to coax the subscriber on to the platform. Avaunt & quit me sight!

Now look here—why did n't you know enough to send me *name &*

address of the hound who announces "Mark Twain's New Papers"[3]—or did you want to go there & eat him yourself? Go straight & get his name & number—& show him this letter n & notify the son of a prostitute to take in that sign.

Watch "John Quill,," & just haze him once He will probably know enough to not let on that he is the party I am refer to.[4]

No—I don't write for *anything* but Express & Galaxy—& publish books nowhere outside of *Hartford.* Oh, I'll make him ,that "New Papers" man, famous! Hurry & send me his name & address so that I can publish him.

Have ordered our Weekly sent regularly to—

"Gov. Frank Fuller,
Girard House, Phil^a."

You can stand it, I know, for I shan't write for it very often.

Well I *would* like to see you, you stately old fool!

Yrs always

Mark

If she miscarries, please return to "Mark Twain," Buffalo.

,[Extra stamps on the other side may be sent to the Conscience Fund, to pay for all these outside remarks.],
Personal,
Private &
Confidential

Gov. Frank Fuller
Girard House
Philadelphia.

[*cross-written:*] Send me a copy of that thief's advertisement, Frank, so that I shall have documentary evidence against him. [*postmarked:*] BUF-FALO N.Y. MAY 21

[1]Clemens's resolve wavered in October, but he did not return to the lecture circuit until October 1871 (9 Oct 70 to Redpath; 10 June 71 to Redpath and Fall; 16 Oct 71 to OLC).

[2]These terms greatly exceed Clemens's usual fee of $75 or $100 per lecture. The offer may have come from Thomas B. Pugh, manager of the Star Course of

Lectures and Concerts in Philadelphia, for on 5 July the Washington correspondent of the Sacramento *Union* interviewed Clemens and reported that he had

> given up lecturing for the present, although overrun with offers. I suppose you [have] known that $50 per night are the usual terms of ordinary lecturers. Those of the "upper crust" get $100 a night. But Philadelphia recently offered our California humorist $225 a night for any reasonable number of nights! ("Letter from Washington," Sacramento *Union*, 19 July 70, 1)

In 1871 Pugh paid Clemens $250 for a single lecture in Philadelphia (11 Mar 70 to Church, n. 2; 14 Nov 70 to Pugh, n. 1; 10 June 71 to Redpath and Fall, n. 4).

[3] Unidentified.

[4] See 26 Apr 70 to Fuller, n. 4.

To James Redpath
21 May 1870 • Buffalo, N.Y.
(Will M. Clemens 1900, 27; AAA/Anderson
1935c, lot 39)

Buffalo, May 21.

Dear Redpath:

I mislaid the letter inquiring about Cambridge, N. Y., till this moment. It got mixed with my loose papers.

They told me that the society I talked for was the leading & favorite. They half burned down the hall at 7 P.M. & yet at 8 had a full house, though a mighty wet & smoky one. It was a bad night, too.[1]

Now this picture is "Something like"—it flatters me & that is what I have been trying to get, these many years. I have ordered 1500 copies.[2]

Yours,
Mark.

[1] See 14 Jan 70 to OLL.

[2] Although the enclosed *carte de visite* has not been found, it was identical (except for any inscription) with those sent to Paige on 20? May, to Bowen on 21? May, and to an unidentified person on 4 July.

To William Bowen
21? May 1870 • Buffalo, N.Y.
(MS: Bowen)

[*on the back:*]

E. H. PAIGE,

NO. 446 MAIN STREET,

BUFFALO, N. Y.

Been too busy & too frightfully lazy to write, Bill—do you pity me?

Mark.[1]

[1] Clemens probably sent this *carte de visite* at about the same time he enclosed one in the previous letter. Possibly he was replying belatedly to Bowen's most recent known letter to him (CU-MARK):

A. F. SHAPLEIGH. PRESIDENT. D. P. ROWLAND. VICE PRESIDENT. A. KEMPLAND. SECRETARY.
PHŒNIX INSURANCE COMPANY OF ST. LOUIS   CHARTERED 1849.
CAPITAL STOCK $250,000. OFFICE 304 N. MAIN ST.

ST. LOUIS March 31st 18 70

Sam'l Lang*don* Clemens
    Buffalo New York
      D[r] Sam
          On arrival of Keokuk Packet I went on board (this morning) to meet Sallie Bowen and who do you suppose I met?
          No less distinguished visitors, than "Kitty Hawkins" (Lauras Sister) and "Old Lucy Davis" for a more particular description of them, reference is hereby made to latter portion of Shakespears Seven Ages. Old *Luce'* asked for you instanter! Said you were the worst Boy, "and **I declare in my heart** he's the funniest man in my acquaintance"   Wants to know if you still climb out on the roof of the house and jump from 3[d] story windows

                           Yours Ever
                             Bill

Sallie was Sarah Robards Bowen. Catherine (Kitty) Hawkins was the older sister of Annie Laura Hawkins Frazer. Lucy Davis was a Hannibal schoolteacher (23 Apr 70 to Bliss, n. 6; 6? Feb 70 to Frazer; *Inds*, 95, 322). Bowen's allusion was to *As You Like It*, act 2, scene 7, perhaps especially to these lines: ". . . The sixth age shifts / Into the lean and slipper'd pantaloon, / With spectacles on nose and pouch on side."

To Jervis Langdon
22 May 1870 • Buffalo, N.Y.
(MS: CtHMTH)

                                 At Home, May 22.

Dear Father—

     For several days the news from you has grown better & better, till at last I believe we hardly seem to feel that you are an invalid any longer. We are just as grateful ~~for~~ as ever two people were in the world. Your case was looking very ominous when we came away, & if we had been called back within a day or two we could not have been surprised. Now we hope to see you up here with mother, just as soon as you can come. Everything is lovely, here, & ~~we~~ our home ~~as~~ is as quiet & peaceful as a monastery, & yet as bright & cheerful as sunshine without & sunshine within can make it. We are burdened & bent with happiness, almost, & we do need to share it with somebody & so save the surplus. Come & partake freely.

I do not think we shall be easily able to go home when Anna Dickinson visits you, & so it has not been right seriously in our minds, perhaps,, as yet. We expect to spend a full month in the Adirondacks (August or Sept.), & I shall have to do all that amount of Galaxy & Express writing in advance, in order to secure the time. So I shall make myself right busy for a while now—shall write faithfully every day.[1]

I want Theodore to send $150 to Charley for me, & I *never* shall think ~~to fix it~~ of ,it, when down town. Can Theodore send the money & just charge it up against me with interest till I see Elmira again? I have asked Charley to get a fine microscope for me, & I guess he would like me to trot the money along.[2]

We are offered $15,000 cash for the Tennessee Land,—Orion is in favor of taking it provided we can reserve 800 acres which he thinks contain an iron mine, & 200 acres of cannel coal. But inasmuch as the country is soon to be threaded with railways, the parties who ~~desire~~ are trying to buy (they are Chicago men,) may very much prefer to have the iron & coal themselves. So I advise Orion to ~~take $~~ offer them the entire tract of 30 or 40,000 acres of land at $30,000 without reserving anything; *or,* all except that 1,000 acres of coal & iron for $15,000. Our own agents have for two or three years been holding the tract complete, at $60,000, & have uniformly hooted at any smaller price.[3]

My sister writes that the plants have not yet arrived from Elmira.

She also writes that she & Margaret have finished making & putting down the most of the carpets, though the one for the parlor has not transpired yet. [Transpired is no slouch of a word—it means that the ¢ parlor carpet has not *arrived* yet.] And ~~she writes that~~ ,she writes that, the kitten slept all the way from Buffalo to Dunkirk & then ,stretched &, yawned, ~~& stretched,~~ issuing much fishy breath in the operation, & said the Erie road was an *infernal* road to ride over. [The joke lies in the fact that the kitten did not go over the Erie at all—it was the Lake-Shore.][4]

Livy is sound asleep, I suppose, for she went to our room an hour ago & I have heard nothing from her since.

Ma will go to Fredonia tomorrow to advise about the Tennessee land, but she may return, as ~my~ my sister's house must be pretty well tumbled yet.[5]

Mr. & Mrs. Slee are well. We saw them Friday evening.

We took dinner & spent yesterday evening most pleasantly with the Grays⟩ (editor Courier,)—they are going to Addir⟩awndix with us.

Must write the Twichells.

With very great love to all of you, including Mother, Sue, Theodore & Grandma[6]—& in very great haste—

Yr Son

Sam*l*.

[1] The exact date of this visit had not been fixed when Susan Crane wrote Anna Dickinson (DLC):

Elmira N.Y.

Tues June 14. 70

Dear Miss Dickinson

We had hoped that June would bring your cheering presence to our home again, but June has come & is half gone, while no message has gone to you— This delay has not been of thoughtlessness, but I have waited, and hoped for Father's decided improvement, that I might say to you, come.

Then too, he has been most unwilling to have the pleasure of a visit from your Mother & yourself denied him. And until this morning has felt that in a few days he should be able to write you that he was able, and ready to enjoy your visit.

Now, however he consents to have me write, that as his progress toward health is so slow, and uncertain[,] the anticipated visit must be delayed for a time

Father and Mother regret this more than you can, and send to you messages of loving remembrance.

They returned from the South Ap 29 having gained nothing, unless it be that Father learned more fully the importance of taking care of himself, which he now tries to do, although his active working head compels his worn, weary body, far beyond his remaining strength

The nature of his difficulty[,] nervous dyspepsia, is such, that we are constantly vacillating between hope and fear— We are hopeful when for several days he retains his food, (beef tea, milk &c) Then we are cast down and fearful, when for three successive days he retains nothing. He is about the house and yard much of the time, but suffers constantly from pain and weariness.

Mother is worn with nursing and anxiety, still is wonderfully sustained and hopeful most of the time. Of course you can realize somewhat of the darkness which would overcast this household on Fathers illness. June, with its usually cheerful influences, has not power to lift, or brighten the cloud.

Livy and Mr Clemens were at home for a few days last week. They were well and very happy.

Sat night I dreamed so pleasantly of you, that since then I have seemed to carry with me your dear personal presence. You are a guest in my heart and know it not. I know it, and am thankful. Is it any comfort to know that all over the land, wherever you go, there are great hearts—and little hearts thus carrying you with them, in loving thought? I know it for you. Hoping that you may have a pleasant restful Summer I am Yours sincer[e]ly

Susan L. Crane.

The Clemenses visited Elmira briefly in early June, returning to Buffalo on 11 June (9 June 70 to Bliss).

[2] After spending February, March, and April in the Holy Land, Charles Langdon and Darius Ford were now in Paris, their base for the European leg of the world tour they had begun in October 1869. On 27 April Langdon had written home for permission to extend his stay in Europe, and to invite his parents to join him, perhaps because Ford had to return to Elmira College in August, several months ahead of schedule (12 June 70 to PAM). The Langdons replied:

Elmira May 30 1870—

My dear Son

Your letter of 27[th] April „from Beirut„ to your Father & Mother only is this morning rec[d]— I have written you one letter upon the subject when in the South, which you have not rec[d]—& my opinion is you had better calculate to reach home as nearly as you can consistent[l]y one year from the time you left. We do not feel that we can do without you longer, and think it may be as well for you to visit Europe further some day, when perhaps Clemens, Livia & Ida can go with you. My health is not good & the Doctor thinks a sea voyage at present would be hazardous as my difficulty is altogether or nearly so in the stomach, I am doing very well now & believe home is the best place for me to secure my health

I wrote you in my other letter, that I had made arrangements for you in business that I had no doubt would be satisfactory to you   I did not mention what it was for the reason that I do not want any thing to divert you from the object of your going viz health & mental improvement, but I will state: I organized a firm J. Langdon & Co. May 1st

J. D. Slee	10 pr ct of profits
T. W Crane	10 " " " "
C. J. Langdon	10 " " "

Slee to receive a salary from the firm of $4000 per annum.
Crane   3.000
C J Langdon $1.500 for the 1st 2 years
            2.000 "   " 2[d] 2 do
            3.000. "   " the balance of the time, which is 8 years——

I intend when you return to give you the notes I hold for your investment in the Hardware business—

With industry & prudence this will enable you to support Ida comfortably—— I expect to lean much upon you & to have great comfort in both Ida & you— She has been here this morning, helping Susie prepare flowers for the Decoration of Soldier graves

She seems in good health— About your wedding we are making no calculations, or arrangements, I propose to leave that to Ida & you as far as I am concerned——

Your Mother will finish, if there are further questions to be answered in your letter. I cannot write more. Give my love to Prof Ford & say I should write him if I was in my usual health. Am very glad to receive letters from him

Your aff. father
J. Langdon

My very dear one.—We were very very glad to get your letter this morning.—Your father has answered it, and I will not detain it to add anything more now but will try & write you by the Saturday's steamer June 4th. Good bye my son Your Mother

Love to Prof. Ford—

(PH in CU-MARK, courtesy of Jervis Langdon, Jr.)

Ida B. Clark, Charles's fiancée, was helping Susan Crane prepare for Elmira's Memorial Day observance. For the "Hardware business" see 2 and 3 Mar 70 to Langdon, n. 6.

[3] In April Orion had been considering an offer of $50,000 from a "Pittsburgh man" (19? Apr 70 and 21 Apr 70, both to OC).

[4] The Lake Shore and Michigan Southern Railway Line had four daily trains which made the forty-mile trip from Buffalo to Dunkirk in at most two hours. The Erie Railway connected Elmira and Buffalo. Pamela's most recent visit to Buffalo seems to have lasted about a week ("Travelers' Guide," Buffalo *Express*, 23 May 70, 2; "Railways," Elmira *Saturday Evening Review*, 21 May 70, 5; 13 May 70 to Langdon).

[5] Jane Clemens had been in Buffalo for a month (21 Apr 70 to OC).

[6] Eunice Ford was eighty-eight on 11 March (Jerome and Wisbey 1991a, 4).

To the Buffalo Street Commissioner
26 May 1870 • Buffalo, N.Y.
(Buffalo *Express*, 27 May 70)

STREET SPRINKLING.

The manner in which Delaware street is sprinkled above Virginia is simply ridiculous. A crippled infant with a garden-squirt could do it better. The work is done by the city government & paid for by the property owners along the street—& the pay is amply secured & the work contracted for for three years. Now one thing or the other is absolutely true, viz: Either the contractor is not paid enough to justify him in doing his work well, or else he shamefully shirks his duty. Which is it?

472 DELAWARE.[1]

[1] The Buffalo *Express* published this reply on Memorial Day, 30 May:

> STREET SPRINKLING.—In answer to the communication published on Friday, under "Notes From the People," with regard to the sprinkling of Delaware street, we are requested to state that the contract for sprinkling the public streets does not commence until the 1st of June. (4)

The same day the *Express* also reported:

> Street Commissioner [George W.] Gillespie has with commendable forethought and energy secured a sufficient number of street sprinklers to thoroughly sprinkle Delaware street and the roads in the cemetery, previous to the moving of the procession today. ("City Notes," 4)

The Memorial Day procession included civic officials, clergy, and numerous groups of Sunday School students and twice passed the Clemenses' house at 472 Delaware ("Memorial Day," Buffalo *Express*, 30 May 70, 4; *Buffalo Directory* 1870, 62).

To Unidentified
28 May 1870 • Buffalo, N.Y.
(Newark Galleries 1930, lot 40)

Buffalo, May 28.

.   .   .   .

Hapsburgh's Minister acknowledges, &c., &c., & cheerfully complies.

.   .   .   .

Samuel L. Clemens
Mark Twain

To Benjamin P. Shillaber
28 May 1870 • Buffalo, N.Y.
(MS: IU-R)

Buffalo, May 28.

My Dear Shillaber—

Yourself & daughter *must* spare a moment to read my thanks for your hearty words & good wishes—& with mine go my wife's with all her heart.[1]

I believe I *am* out of the lecture field & I tell you it is imperial luxury to believe it, too.

We are arranging to spend August & part of Sept in the Adirondacks—& I do hope we shall get a chance to see you all for a moment in Boston while we *are* wandering away from home. For I can kiss the book & hold up my hand & depose, with Nasby, that "I would rather be a lamp-post in Boston than Mayor of another town."[2]

Yrs Sincerely
Sam'. L. Clemens.

[1] Benjamin Penhallow Shillaber (1814–90), printer, journalist at the Boston *Post* and other papers, humorist, and lecturer, was the creator of the loquacious

Mrs. Partington, whose comical sayings and doings filled a series of popular books. He had founded a Boston weekly, the *Carpet-Bag* (1851–53), where Clemens published "The Dandy Frightening the Squatter," in 1852 (*ET&S1*, 63–65). Probably in response to Clemens's wedding cards, Shillaber had sent the following poem, which Clemens published in the Buffalo *Express* on 12 February 1870 (2):

Congratulatory.

[B. P. Shillaber (Mrs. Partington) discourses pleasantly and kindly concerning a late occurrence as follows:]

> Dear brother of the happy pen,
> Your card is just beneath my ken
> Announcing that 'mongst married men
>   You've taken place:
> Well, Heaven bless you, "but and ben,"
>   With fortune's grace.
>
> There's none deserving more the prize
> Of good that 'long life's pathway lies,
> Lit by sweet smiles and sunny eyes,
>   Than you, my friend,
> And o'er you may benignant skies
>   Forever bend.
>
> The world to you a tribute brings,
> And on your bridal altar flings,
> Grateful and glad for myriad things
>   Your muse has lent,
> And one grand epithalamium sings
>   O'er *the* event.
>
> We've gloried in the race you've run,
> We've gloried in the fame you've won
> Ere yet your life's meridian sun
>   Has gained its height,
> Illuming by his rays of fun
>   A pathway bright.
>
> And better far than all, dear Mark,
> Thou'st found the matrimonial ark
> In which the true who there embark
>   Find many a charm,
> That prudence whispers those who hark
>   To save from harm.
>
> And I, your latest friend, am fain
> To pour my tributary strain,
> In unpretending rhyming vein,
>   And thus appear,
> Invoking blessing on the *Twain*,
>   With heart sincere.
>   *Benny* dicite,

Boston, February 7.   B. P. S.

(The Buffalo *Commercial Advertiser* printed the poem the same day ["A Recent Wedding," 3].) Shillaber's "hearty words & good wishes" may have come in a recent letter or were possibly delivered by John W. Ryan, assistant editor of the Boston *Gazette*. On 1 May Shillaber wrote a letter of introduction for Ryan, asking Clemens to "Please receive him graciously for his sake, your sake and my sake" (CU-MARK; *Boston Directory* 1869, 535).

²Clemens had been in Boston twice with Nasby in 1869 (*L3*, 164, 169, 405–8). It is not known where or even whether Nasby published this remark about Boston.

From Samuel L. and Olivia L. Clemens
to Mary Mason Fairbanks
29 May 1870 • Buffalo, N.Y.
(MS: CSmH)

Buf ~~Ma~~ May 29.

Dear Mother:

Our plans for the Adirondacks are pretty definitely fixed—start with the Twichellses 1ˢᵗ of Aug. & return middle of Sept.

I *do* wish we could trot out & see you, but it does seem impossible to do it soon. I have to get all literary work done up for a month or two ahead, so that ~~I~~ our proposed holiday will *be* a holiday with no compulsory labor in it. Not that I mean to lead a stupid, useless life in the woods—by no means. I shall exert myself in every way that promises to harden my muscles & toughen & strengthen my frame. ~~E~~ I shall use method in my exercises, too. I shall ~~chang lie under a tree——~~change & change about—not lying under one tree until ~~suffering~~ injury from over=ex[er]tion sets in, but changing to another now & then. And I shall not "sit around" till overheated, but will keep watch of my pulse & go to bed ~~in time~~—as soon as I find I am crowding my powers. Some people ruin their health by pure injudiciousness—but you never catch me ripping & tearing around. I go along careful. That is the reason why I never break myself down.

Well, I guess we *shall* have to go with you to California in the Spring, for the publishers are getting right impatient to see another book on the stocks, & I doubt if I could do better than rub up old Pacific memories & put them between covers along with some eloquent pictures. When we get to Cleveland—or when you come here—(*please* come, in June or July—it is no distance at all coming east'ard)—we'll talk the Cal. trip all over.¹

We would pack up & clear for Cleveland tomorrow, as true as ever I sit here, if it were not for Mr Langdon's ill health. We want to go, badly, & *would* go but for that,—but for the fact that *when* we leave our nest, it is plainly understood that the destination must be Elmira. I can't get time to trot around *much*, & so when we *do* move we are sure to be in arrears for a visit home, & thither we have to go. We were to have gone on yesterday, but being dissatisfied with next Galaxy (July,) I begged a delay of Livy till I could make some changes in the MSS. before mailing them to N. Y.[2] Do you know, Madam, that I would rather write for a Magazine for $2 a page than for a newspaper at $10? I *would*. One takes more pains, the "truck" looks nicer in print, & one has a pleasanter audience. It is the difference between lecturing in "the States" & doing the same thing in delectable Nevada.

We *shall* hie to Cleveland (hie is a pretty good word, considering that it was just hurled in without any study or deliberation)—Yes, we shall hie to Cleveland the very first chance we get—honest injun. Now you think I am lying under under a hallucination (how is hallucination "for high?") but I am not. To my mind a visit to Cleveland is comprehensive, corelative, comp combustible & in every way subsequent & invidious, & for one *I* am right anxious to make it. [*in top margin:* —Samuel is a pretty boy] All that Mrs Clemens desires, on this earth, is to sun herself in the light of my countenance & eat. Consequently *she* is ready to start whenever I am.

I like um

—He is good too—

I have to write up side down of the table so of course I am at the other side

Give our love to all the tribe.[3] After drawing so much shrubbery & interlining so much, Livy would like to write another word or two maybe—so she may close this.

We both love you and want to see you. I wish that as it does not seem possible for us to go to you that you could come to us next month—one reason that we cannot go far from home, is that we want to reach father quickly in case he should want us— Of course we shall not go to the Adirondacs unless he is much better— Love to Allie, bring her and Molly ˯the family˯ with you—

Lovingly Livy—

[1] Clemens's recent interest in his old clippings (26 Mar 70 to JLC and family) may indicate that he was even then contemplating a book about his western experiences. Apparently, however, he felt the need for immediate experience in writing such a book, and so was inclined to postpone work on it until the spring of 1871 (see *RI 1993*, 802–4).

[2] The manuscript for the July installment of "Memoranda" was due early in June. For its final contents, see References (SLC 1870pp).

[3] See 7 Jan 70 to Fairbanks, nn. 12, 13.

To Elisha Bliss, Jr.
per Olivia L. Clemens
with revisions by Samuel L. Clemens
30 May 1870 • Buffalo, N.Y.
(MS: CtY-BR)

Buffalo May 30th 1870

Mr E. Bliss
    Dear Sir
        Will you send a copy of the book to *Mr A. D. Munson 187 Broadway N. Y.* I will enclose an autograph to be put in it— He has been reading from the book and has been the means of selling 30 coppies of it, and his ~~copp~~ copy has become so soiled by parties handling it to find out how to ~~get~~ ˏsend forˏ a copy that he wants a new one—[1]

The scrap which I enclose about the Russian minister is ˏentirelyˏ reliable—

About the dinner—I cannot go on to Hartford very well for the dinner and I have a plan which seems to me a good one, ˏ*Write a dinner invitation* to me and,ˏ Let me write a speach ~~for the dinner and publish it, as a speach made at a dinner in honor of our having reached 70000 copies of the book—~~ ˏIN ANSWER ~~to an~~ˏa dinner,ˏ ~~invitation from you, and you,~~ˏand you publish it.ˏ That will answer the same purpose as if we had a dinner, and I should have to send the speach to the dinner any way instead of going myself— What do you think of that plan?[2]

                                                        Yours Truly
                                                        Samˡ L. Clemens
                                                        Per O. L.

[enclosure:][3]

> THE Russian Minister is so pleased with
> Mark Twain's account of the reception of
> the passengers of the "Quaker City" by
> the Emperor and his household that he is
> making a translation of the interview from
> "The Innocents Abroad," which he intends
> sending to Russia.

✉—————————————————————————————————

[letter docketed:] √ *[and]* Mark Twain | May 30/70 | Author

[1] Munson edited and published *The Minnesota Messenger, Containing Sketches
of the Rise and Progress of Minnesota* (St. Paul: 1855). Nothing is known of his
readings from *The Innocents Abroad*.

[2] See 7 May 70 to Bliss.

[3] The original enclosure has not been found: it is simulated here, from the
Buffalo *Express* of 23 May 1870 (2), reset line for line. Clemens described Tsar
Aleksandr's reception in chapter 37 of *Innocents*, and, in 1867, in his notebook
and in letters to his family and to the New York *Tribune* and the San Francisco
Alta California (*N&J1*, 404–11; *L2*, 81–83; SLC 1867d–f). In July he arranged
to have copies of the book sent to the tsar and to Konstantin Gavrilovich Kata-
kazi (1830–90), Russian minister to the United States from 1869 to 1872 (*Russkii
Biograficheskii Slovar*, 8:546): see 18 July 70 to Bliss.

To Robert M. Howland
1–6 or 12–21 June 1870 • Buffalo, N.Y.
(MS: CU-MARK)

In memory of old times in ~~El~~ Esmeralda & Carson—times ₐ(in the
former case, at least,)ₐ when it was above ordinary to have dried apple
pies on Sunday, & absolutely aristocratic to have canned peaches.[1]

Sam*l*. L. Clemens.

(Mark Twain.)

Buffalo June, 1870.[2]

[1] Clemens's most difficult period in Nevada was the summer and early fall of
1862, which he spent prospecting near Aurora, in Esmeralda County, while des-

perately short of funds. Howland was among his partners then (*L1*, 214–41). In 1876 the Virginia City *Territorial Enterprise* recalled that "Bob and Mark were not flush" as cabin mates:

> They lived principally on hardtack and beans. On Sundays, however, they managed to get hold of some few extras in the grub line. When Sunday came they feasted on canned oysters, canned turkey, chicken and the like, with something in the fruit and jelly line. When the cans had been emptied of these luxuries the "boys" ostentatiously threw them out in front of the door of their cabin.
>
> In the course of a few weeks the accumulation of cans that had contained oysters, turkey, jellies and other good things began to attract attention. Miners passing their cabin used to gaze upon the many cans and say: "By Jove, those fellows live like fighting cocks!"
>
> It was finally noised about the camp that Clemens and Howland lived like two princes—fared sumptuously every day. It was thought they never ate anything but oysters and turkey and they were looked upon as "Big Injuns" by the whole camp.

Anxious to preserve their reputation under the scrutiny of some suspicious miners, Clemens and Howland reportedly resorted to nocturnal foraging in garbage dumps to maintain their facade of empty cans ("How They Played It," 28 Apr 76, 3).

[2] Clemens wrote this note in Robert and Louise Howland's autograph album. Since the Clemenses spent 7–11 and 22–30 June in Elmira, the Howlands must have visited them in Buffalo sometime between 1 and 6 or 12 and 21 June.

To Elisha Bliss, Jr.
9 June 1870 • Elmira, N.Y.
(MS: CtHMTH)

J. LANGDON, MINER & DEALER IN ANTHRACITE & BITUMINOUS COAL   OFFICE NO. 6 BALDWIN STREET

ELMIRA, N.Y. June 9 186 70.[1]

Friend Bliss—

Please have the enclosed pasted in a nice copy of the book, & express the same *right away*, to *Edward H. House, Occidental Hotel, San Francisco.* Don't trust that California agency to attend to it. They have broken up a friendship ~~between~~ of years, between Bret Harte & me.[2]

Mr. House has just left us & gone for a sojourn in Japan. ~~You~~ He has long been one of the Tribune's ablest editorial writers, & correspondents, & will of course write Japan letters to that paper. It was House & Dion Boucicault ~~who~~ that wrote Arrah-na-Pogue in partnership. House is a nephew of Charles Reade the novelist & comes of a fine literary breed. I guess his Japan letters will attract attention. Be sure & send him the book, for I am under large obligations to him for favors done me three or four years ago in the Tribune.[3]

~~Say—~~

We shall return home ~~in~~ on Saturday.

I like your idea for a book, but the *inspiration* don't come. Wait till I get rested up & rejuvenated in the Adirondacks, & then something will develop itself *sure*.[4]

In a hurry—

Yrs

Clemens.

[letter docketed:] √ auth *[and]* Mark Twain | June 9/70

[1]Clemens later recalled: "Mrs. Clemens and I went down to Elmira about the 1st of June to help in the nursing of Mr. Langdon" (AD, 15 Feb 1906, CU-MARK, in *MTA*, 2:113). In fact, however, they did not go until 7 June (OLC to Alice Hooker Day, 6 June 70 from Buffalo, CtHSD; 12 June 70 to PAM, n. 1).

[2]See 26 Nov 70 to Webb.

[3]House (1836–1901) met Clemens in New York in January 1867 and published an important flattering review, in the New York *Tribune* of 11 May 1867, of his first New York lecture (*L2*, 6–7, 43–44, 291, 417–19). A would-be composer, House had become the *Tribune*'s music and drama critic in 1858 after four years with the Boston *Courier* at the same posts. He was also a *Tribune* editorial writer and special correspondent, reporting from Harpers Ferry and Charleston, Virginia, on John Brown's activities and afterward accompanying Union forces during the first year of the Civil War. It was while he was in London in 1865–67, working as a theatrical manager, that he met Dion Boucicault (1820–90), the prolific Irish-born dramatist, whose *Arrah-na-Pogue* [Arrah of the Kiss], or, *The Wicklow Wedding*, opened in Dublin in 1864 and in London the following year. In 1890 Clemens recalled that House

> told me more than once that he wrote ~~a great part of~~ ˄the bulk of˄ "Arrah na Pogue." . . . I have been laughed at for believing Mr. House's statement, but I did believe it, all the same. He told me that his share of the proceeds was $25,000. ~~I judged from that that he wrote nine-tenths of it; & I had a right to judge so~~ A theatre manager assures me that Mr. House merely wrote a few lines in "Arrah na Pogue" to protect Mr. Boucicault's rights here against pirates. (SLC 1890, 19–20†)

Still later Clemens claimed that Boucicault declared House's claim "a straight lie, with not a vestige of truth in it" (AD, 28 Aug 1907, CU-MARK†). The exact extent of House's contribution to *Arrah-na-Pogue* is not known, although he is credited with having made some revisions and with co-writing the version of "The Wearing of the Green," condemning British tyranny, that was sung in the play. Boucicault ultimately assigned him all United States rights in the play and in 1891 House secured American copyright on it. In going to Japan in 1870, to gather material for a book, he relinquished his position as music and drama critic of the New York *Times*, which he had held since 1869. He remained in Japan for a decade, teaching English language and literature, writing, sending dispatches to the New York *Herald*, and editing the Tokyo *Times*, an English-language weekly. He also published historical and fictional works about the country (House 1875a–c, 1881, 1888). Probably around the mid-1890s he returned to Japan, remaining until his death. The suggestion here that he had recently visited Buffalo ("Mr. House has just left us") is confirmed by one of Clemens's marginal prompts in his 1890 account of their acquaintance: "~~Buffalo in '70?~~" (SLC 1890, 10†; Fawkes, 157–58; Krause, 33–34; *NUC*, 69:114, 124; *N&J3*, 545–46 n. 188; "Journalistic Jottings," New York *Evening Telegram*, 12 May 69, 2; Boston *Advertiser:* "In General," 7 Mar, 10 Mar 70, 1).

⁴The letter Clemens answered does not survive, and nothing is known of Bliss's idea. Albert Bigelow Paine asserted that he had "proposed a book which should relate the author's travels and experiences in the Far West" (*MTB*, 1:420). Although such a suggestion might have reinforced Clemens's recent interest in a western book, he of course had long been planning it (see *RI 1993*, 801–4).

To Ellen White
11 June 1870 • Elmira, N.Y.
(City Book Auction, lot 130)

Elmira, June 11.

Send for us half past eleven tonight—Erie Depot.[1]

Sam*l*. L. Clemens.

✉————————————————————————

Mrs. Ellen White | 472 Delaware Ave. | Buffalo.

[1]Clemens and Olivia must have taken the Erie Railway's "Day Express," which departed Elmira at 7:07 P.M. Since even a passenger train required only about four-and-a-half hours to reach Buffalo, and Buffalo's "free delivery system" provided for several mail deliveries each day, Clemens knew that this directive to White, the family housekeeper, doubtless sent on the 9:35 A.M. "Mail Train," would arrive in ample time for her to have the family carriage waiting at the depot ("Railways," Elmira *Saturday Evening Review*, 11 June 70, 7; "The Letter Carrier System," Buffalo *Express*, 4 June 70, 4).

From Samuel L. and Olivia L. Clemens
to Pamela A. Moffett
12 June 1870 • Buffalo, N.Y.
(MS: NPV)

Buffalo, June 12.

My Dear Sister:

We were snatched away suddenly by an urgent call to come to Elmira & help nurse Mr Langdon for a couple of weeks at some Pennsylvania springs he was going to visit. But he decided not to go, & so we simply rested a moment & then hurried back here.[1] I have thus lost valuable time, & must make it up by steady work. I shall not have a chance to stir out again till we leave for the woods or sail for France—for the latter is urged upon us by Mr Langdon, who wants us to stay with Charley 3 or 4 months in Paris & keep him out of bad company & hold his nose steadily to the grindstone of study until he acquires some knowledge of the French L̶ language. (The Professor has to come home in August & resume his c̶h̶a̶r̶g̶e̶ chair in the College.) We may not leave home at all—but still, in view of the possibilities, ̶i̶s̶ ̶i̶t̶ is wisest for me to rush my work along & get ready for emergencies.[2]

The Galaxy ought to go to you. I so ordered it. Will try to think to speak of it to the publishers. I ordered it addressed to Mrs. *William* A. Moffett.

Good-bye. I will leave Livy room to write a line. I am *exceedingly* glad to hear that Orion's l̶i̶t̶t̶l̶e̶ machine is so favorably thought of by Munn & Co.[3] An inventor is a poet—a true poet—and nothing in any degree less than a high order of poet—̶&̶ ̶c̶ ˛wherefore˛ his noblest pleasure dies with the stroke that completes the creature of his genius, just as the painter's & the sculptor's & other poets' highest pleasure ceases with the touch that finishes their work—& so only he can understand or appreciate the *legitimate* "success" of his achievement, littler minds being able to get no higher than a comprehension of a vulgar moneyed success. We would all rejoice to see Orion achieve a moneyed success with his inventions, of course—but if he can d̶o̶ ˛eventually do˛ some-

thing great, something imperial, it were better to do that & starve than
not to do it ~~al~~ at all. To be Governor of Nevada is to be a poor little creep-
ing thing ~~than~~ that a *man* may create—a very pitiful little office-holding
accident, with some better man's brass collar on[4]—but to invent even
this modest little drilling machine shows the presence of the patrician
blood of intellect—that "round & top of sovereignty"[5] ~~in whose presence whose source~~ which separates its possessor from the common mul-
titude & marks him as one not beholden to the caprices of politics but
endowed with greatness in his own right.[6]

Dear Sister—

Unless Mr Clemens' ˌwork˲ presses him up to the *very last minute*,
we shall go to Fredonia there is no doubt about that—[7] I think that he
will be able to go at the last, and I do not mean to be disapointed of my
visit there—

How is Ma? I hope well— When does Annie come?[8] I think that
our going to Paris is very improbable—but, of course we cannot tell how
things may shape themselves.

You know that I do not like travelling particularly, and dislike to
leave home—

Father is gaining a little but very slowly, he and Mother are coming
here just as soon as he can bear it—

Mother keeps up remarkably— The rest at home are in usual
health. With love to all, I am lovingly your sister

Livy Langdon Clemens

[1] Almira H. Munson, the Langdons' friend and neighbor, noted in her diary
on 7 June: "Mr & Mrs Langdon are going to Minequa Spring tomorrow." And
the following day she wrote: ". . . saw Mrs Langdon & Mrs Clemens. . . . Mrs
Langdon thinks her husband is improving but they are not going to Miniqua"
(Jerome and Wisbey, 1991a, 4–5). Minnequa Springs was a summer resort in
Canton, Pennsylvania, known for its mineral waters.

[2] The four- or five-day trip to Elmira had put Clemens behind with his *Galaxy*
"Memoranda." He presumably mailed the copy for the July number in early
June, but with the Adirondacks trip or a trip to France proposed for August, he
was intent on preparing *Galaxy* copy for the August number (due in less than a
month) as well as anything that he intended to publish in the Buffalo *Express*.
Darius Ford's impending return to Elmira College must have been an unantici-
pated development. Previous plans were for him to continue on his world tour
with Charles Langdon until as late as the spring of 1871 (22 May 70 to Langdon,
n. 2; *L3*, 369 n. 5).

[3] Publishers of the *Scientific American* since 1846, Munn and Company (Orson
D. Munn, Alfred E. Beach, and Salem H. Wales), of New York, was also a lead-

ing firm of patent solicitors, having processed over 30,000 applications by 1870 (Wilson 1870, 77, 878, 1249).

⁴In the 1860s Orion Clemens, then secretary of Nevada Territory, had served as acting territorial governor whenever Governor James W. Nye was away (*L1*, 146 n. 2, 249–50 n. 5, 281).

⁵*Macbeth*, act 4, scene 1.

⁶On 14 June Pamela Moffett sent this letter to Orion and Mary (Mollie) Clemens in St. Louis, hoping that it would "raise Orion's spirits, and Mary's too" (PAM to OC and MEC, 14 June 70, CU-MARK). Orion never patented his drilling machine or any of the other inventions he conceived, including a wood-sawing machine, a wheel and chain device intended to power a boat, a knife, and an "Anti-Sun-Stroke hat." Samuel Clemens received his own first patent, for a garment strap, in December 1871 (7 June 71 to OC and MEC; 8 Sept 71 to OLC; 16 Sept 71 to OC; 6 Oct 71 to Leggett; *L2*, 198 n. 2).

⁷The Fredonia trip was postponed until October (4 Oct 70 to Redpath, n. 1).

⁸See 21 Apr 70 to OC, n. 2.

From Samuel L. and Olivia L. Clemens
to Jervis and Olivia Lewis Langdon
19 June 1870 • Buffalo, N.Y.
(MS: CU-MARK)

Buf. M June 19.

Dear Father & Mother:

We are all set & ready for you. Livy has been down town & bought a spring-lounge & a spring-mattrass to put on it & has set apart for its occupancy the place now occupied by the "awful short" lounge in the library. Father can lie there & talk ~~think~~ & be comfortable & never discommode ~~either~~ *me*, because I can lie just as comfortably standing up—all I want is a *chance*. Mother & Livy & I will endeavor to make the time glide along pleasantly—they all day, & I after 3 or 4 P.M. We are waiting & hoping for the telegram announcing your ~~immediate dep~~ departure for Buffalo.

We are rather too full for utterance, just now, either by pen or word of mouth—for Livy's neighbor, Mrs. White sent us an ample dish of enormous strawberries of her own raising while we were at dinner a moment ago, & we are in a surfeit, now, from an overdose of them. This is the pleasantest neighbor we have.¹

D[r.] Heacock leaves here, about next Wednesday or Thursday, to be gone a month—is going to swap pulpits with a Chelsea minister named Plum[2]—so I shall get a chance to go to Westminster church for a while, Livy & other circumstances permitting. I am suffering for some good music. Our "congregational" singing grows steadily more & more atrocious—until I have got afraid to go ~~there~~ ˏto our churchˏ when it storms, for ~~fear our caterwauling will exasperate~~ fear the lightning will strike it. Such music as we have is just tempting Providence & inviting calamity all the time.

Our shrubbery is coming along finely & attracting a good deal of attention. We have got one panzy in bloom, ˏ(Indeed we had *thirty two* in bloom day before yesterday—Livy)ˏ & one rosebud straining itself awfully. But you can tell Mr. Slee that we are beginning to look upon our Irish Juniper as a failure. It looks like a fox-squirrel's tail. The man told me it was an evergreen—I *thought* he f said that, but I guess maybe he really said it was a nevergreen.

Lovingly yr son

Sam[l].

~~Sue~~

We have a rose bush that has *ever so many* buds on it, it is a moss rose too— *Be sure to come to us, don't fail us*— We have all our strawberries & pine apples canned. 11 ˏcansˏ of the former. 6 of the latter— We *do* want to see you.

Livy

Mr C. says 11 strawberries canned but it aint 11 berries it is eleven *cans*—

---

[1] The wife of either Henry G. White, a "House, Boat and Fresco Painter" who lived at 523 Delaware Avenue, on the same block as the Clemenses, or Erskine N. White, pastor of Westminster Presbyterian Church (mentioned in the next paragraph), who lived at 726 Delaware, adjacent to the church and about three blocks from the Clemenses (*Buffalo Directory* 1870, map, 17, 89, 114, 536).

[2] Albert H. Plumb, of Chelsea, Massachusetts, was one of several clergymen, all former parishioners of Heacock's, who were in Buffalo on 12 June to commemorate the twenty-fifth anniversary of the Lafayette Street Presbyterian Church and Heacock's ministry there (Buffalo *Express:* "Religious," 11 June 70, 4; "Quarter Centennial," 13 June 70, 5; Buffalo *Commercial Advertiser:* "Religious," 11 June 70, 3).

To John Munroe and Company
23 June 1870 • Elmira, N.Y.
(Paraphrase: Dawson)

The other day he did some "tall telegraphing," as he rightly terms it. His brother-in-law traveling, nobody knew where, in Europe, was wanted home immediately. Mark telegraphed to Monroe & Co., the American bankers in Paris, to telegraph all over Europe and ascertain his whereabouts. In eight hours after sending the dispatch to Monroe & Co. a reply was received here that the brother-in-law was in Bavaria.[1]

[1] The Clemenses had returned to Elmira on 22 June. On 25 June Clemens wrote Mary Mason Fairbanks that "Charley was telegraphed for, day before yesterday." Clemens sent his telegram to John Munroe and Company, the Wall Street bankers, whose Paris office was at 7 Rue Scribe. The telegram itself has not been found. This paraphrase of it was based on Clemens's own recollection, on 5 July, in an interview with the Washington correspondent of the Sacramento *Union*, George F. Dawson (25 June 70 to JLC and family; Wilson 1870, 878; Dawson; Poore 1870, 121).

To D. Appleton and Company
23–26 June 1870 • Elmira, N.Y.
(Anderson Auction Company 1914, lot 51)

Elmira

. . . .

The terms of existing contracts would render the undertaking a breach of faith on my part—else it would delight me to do it.[1]

. . . .

[1] The undertaking was the "humorous picture-book" that Appleton and Company had proposed to Clemens around mid-May (20 May 70 to Bliss). This fragment probably belonged to the second of two responses to Appleton that Clemens summarized in his 4 July letter to Bliss, where he wrote that Appleton had had "~~two or~~ ample time to have written me half a dozen times since." Two or three weeks before 4 July would imply a date of 20 or 13 June, when Clemens

was still in Buffalo. If he wrote from Elmira on 23 June, the earliest likely date, Appleton would have had eleven days for "half a dozen" letters. But he might have written as late as 26 June and still allowed them "ample time" of about a week. Although Clemens and Bliss had been discussing a new book for the American Publishing Company, no contracts had yet been signed (29 May 70 to Fairbanks; 9 June 70 to Bliss).

To Jane Lampton Clemens and Pamela A. Moffett
25 June 1870 • Elmira, N.Y.
(MS: NPV)

J. LANGDON, MINER & DEALER IN ANTHRACITE &
BITUMINOUS COAL   OFFICE NO. 6 BALDWIN STREET

ELMIRA, N.Y. June 25 18$ 70

My Dear Mother & Sister:

ₐWeₐ Were called here suddenly by telegram 3 days ago. Mr Langdon is very low. We have well nigh lost hope—all of us except Livy. Mr. Langdon, whose hope is large is one of his most prominent characteristics, says himself, this morning, that his recovery is only a *possibility*, not a *probability*. He made his will this morning—that is, appointed executors[1]—nothing else was necessary. The household is sad enough. Charley is in Bavaria. We telegraphed Munroe & Co., Paris, to notify Charley to come home—they sent the message to Munich. Our message left here at 8 in the morning & Charley's answer arrived less than eight hours afterward.[2] He sails immediately. He will reach home 2 weeks from now. The whole city is troubled.[3]

As I write (at the office,) at dispatch arrives from Charley, who hassn reached London, & will sail thence on 28th. He wants news. We cannot send him any.

Affectionately

Sam.

P. S.—I sent $300 to Fredonia Bank for Ma.—It is in her name.

[1] Langdon's executors were his widow, his son Charles, John D. F. Slee, Theodore W. Crane, and Clemens (Jervis Langdon).

[2] According to the Elmira *Saturday Evening Review*, the telegram was sent "at 8 A. M., and a reply received back at 3 P.M." ("To illustrate . . . ," 25 June 70, 5).

³During the spring and summer of 1870 both the Elmira *Advertiser* and the Elmira *Saturday Evening Review* reported on Jervis Langdon's condition, with the *Review* issuing bulletins on a nearly weekly basis (Elmira *Advertiser:* "City and Neighborhood," 2 May, 15 June, 8 Aug 70, 4; Elmira *Saturday Evening Review:* "Local Jottings," 26 Mar, 23 Apr, 18 June, 25 June, 9 July, 23 July, 30 July, 6 Aug 70, 8).

To Mary Mason Fairbanks
25 June 1870 • Elmira, N.Y.
(MS: CSmH)

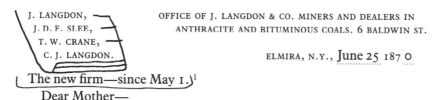

J. LANGDON,
J. D. F. SLEE,
T. W. CRANE,
C. J. LANGDON.

OFFICE OF J. LANGDON & CO. MINERS AND DEALERS IN ANTHRACITE AND BITUMINOUS COALS. 6 BALDWIN ST.

ELMIRA, N.Y., June 25 187 0

The new firm—since May 1.)¹

Dear Mother—

We are summoned here by telegram, & you ~~may expect~~ imagine why. It does appear that Mr Langdon's five-month sieze of illness ~~mul~~ must presently culminate in death. All of us are in deep grief, this morning, for death seems nearer at hand than at any time before. Mr. L. made his will this morning—that is, appointed executors. It is the saddest, saddest time. There is no sound in the house—"the mourners go about" like spirits.² Blinds are down & the gloom in the hearts of the household finds its type in the sombreness of hall & chamber. Charley was telegraphed for, day before yesterday. His answer came from Bavaria in less than 8 hours. He is now in London, but telegraphs to-day for further news, & says he cannot sail till 28ᵗʰ·

~~The~~ You understand what trouble we are in, & how the sunshine is gone out. The town ~~mourns~~ is distressed—the solicitude is general.

Lovingly Your Son
Samuel.

¹See 22 May 70 to Langdon, n. 2. In 1906 Clemens recalled that Slee, Crane, and Charles J. Langdon became

partners in the business, by gift. But they were unknown. The business world knew J. Langdon, a name that was a power, but these three young men were ciphers without a unit. Slee turned out afterward to be a very able man, and a most capable and persuasive negotiator, but at the time that I speak of his qualities were quite unknown. Mr. Langdon had trained him, and he was well equipped for his headship of the little firm. Theodore Crane was competent in his line—that of head clerk and Superintendent of the subordinate clerks. No better man could have been found for that place; but his capacities were limited to that position. He was good and upright and indestructibly honest and honorable, but he had neither desire nor ambition to be anything above chief clerk. He was much too timid for larger work or larger responsibilities. Young Charley was twenty-one, and not any older than his age—that is to say, he was a boy. His mother had indulged him from the cradle up, and had stood between him and such discomforts as duties, studies, work, responsibility, and so on. He had gone to school only when he wanted to, as a rule, and he didn't want to often enough for his desire to be mistaken for a passion. He was not obliged to study at home when he had the headache, and he usually had the headache—the thing that was to be expected. He was allowed to play when his health and his predilections required it, and they required it with a good deal of frequency, because *he* was the judge in the matter. He was not required to read books, and he never read them. The results of this kind of bringing up can be imagined. But he was not to blame for them. His mother was his worst enemy, and she became this merely through her love for him, which was an intense and steadily burning passion. It was a most pathetic case. He had an unusually bright mind; a fertile mind; a mind that should have been fruitful. But because of his mother's calamitous indulgence, it got no cultivation and was a desert. Outside of business, it is a desert yet.

Charley's deadly training had made him conceited, arrogant, and overbearing. Slee and Theodore had a heavier burden to carry than had been the case with Mr. Langdon. Mr. Langdon had had nothing to do but manage the business, whereas Slee and Crane had to manage the business and Charley besides. Charley was the most difficult part of the enterprise. He was a good deal given to reorganizing and upsetting Mr. Slee's most promising arrangements and negotiations. Then the work had to be all done over again. (AD, 23 Feb 1906, CU-MARK†, partly published in *MTA*, 2:135–36)

[2] Ecclesiastes 12:5: "Also when they shall be afraid of that which is high, and fears shall be in the way, and the almond tree shall flourish, and the grasshopper shall be a burden, and desire shall fail: because man goeth to his long home, and the mourners go about the streets."

To Charles Scribner and Company
25 June 1870 • Elmira, N.Y.
(MS facsimile: CU-MARK)

Elmira, N. Y. June 25

SATURDAY   Dr Sirs:

Please send me Dr. Bushnell's volume entitled "Christian Nurture,"[1] to above address, & charge to

Yrs Truly
S. L. Clemens

[1] A book on child rearing and family life by Horace Bushnell (1802–76), the eminent Hartford Congregational clergyman. The Clemenses wanted it because Olivia was now about three months pregnant. It is likely that Clemens wrote to Scribner and Company, at 654 Broadway in New York, who had issued several printings of it since 1861 (Wilson 1870, 1092).

To Elisha Bliss, Jr.
27 June 1870 • Elmira, N.Y.
(Transcripts: WU; Anderson Galleries 1921
and 1922, lots 151 and 52A; Chicago, lot 113)

J. LANGDON,	OFFICE OF J. LANGDON & CO. MINERS AND DEALERS IN
J. D. F. SLEE,	ANTHRACITE AND BITUMINOUS COALS. 6 BALDWIN ST.
T. W. CRANE,	
C. J. LANGDON.	ELMIRA, N.Y., June 27 187 0

Friend Bliss—

Yes, the "Reading the Innocents" is good—tip-top.[1] We came here in a great hurry a week ago. Mr. Langdon is very ill. Sometimes we feel sure he is going to get well, but then again hope well nigh passes away. This morning the case looks so well that all are pretty cheery again.

Yrs
Mark.

[1] See the next page. The circular's sales boast was a gross exaggeration. Total sales of *The Innocents Abroad* through the first three quarters (ending 30 April) were approximately 60,378 copies. By the end of the fourth quarter (30 July) sales totaled some 69,500 copies (Hirst 1975, 314, 316, 317).

150,000 Already Sold.

AS MANY QUARRELS

Have arisen lately in families, on account of each member wishing the first reading of

Twain's "Innocents Abroad,"

we have had engraved, from a photograph, an evening scene in a family where a compromise of the difficulty was made between the parties by one of them

Reading "THE INNOCENTS" Aloud.

The cut tells its own story. It proves that Twain is entitled to the title of

The People's Author,

as no writer has ever been able so fully to interest all classes and ages.
Buy the book and read it at home aloud. Your whole family will thank you. Your boys and girls will stay at home to hear you. The old folks will laugh till they cry, and in its pages you will find ample material for cheerfulness, mirth and gladness, to supply the whole family a month Mark's drollery and bright sayings are enough to make even "the cat laugh." Furnished by publisher's agents or by addressing

AMERICAN PUBLISHING COMPANY, Hartford, Ct.

Circular advertising *The Innocents Abroad.* Yale University Library (CtY). Courtesy of Leon T. Dickinson. See 27 June 1870 to Elisha Bliss, Jr.

To Daniel Slote
27 June 1870 • Elmira, N.Y.
(MS: CtHMTH)

                                                    Elmira, June 27.
Dear Dan—

Charley has been telegraphed to come home, & leaves London tomorrow in the Abyssinnia—recollect it. I do not know what to write you
in the premises, further than that he will probably go to you for news
when her a he arrives. His father is very ill—dangerously so. The
chances are greatly against his recovery. You must look out for Charley
and whatever the news may be by June 8 you will have to communicate
it.[1] I will write you again.

                                                    Yrs always
                                                    Sam Clemens.

[1] The *Abyssinia* departed Liverpool on 28 June and arrived in Boston on 8 July.
Clemens and the Langdons evidently believed that its destination was New
York, and therefore wanted Slote, who lived there, to meet Charles ("Passen-
gers," "Transcript Marine Journal," Boston *Evening Transcript*, 9 July 70, 3).

To Elisha Bliss, Jr.
4 July 1870 • Elmira, N.Y.
(MS: Daley)

                                                    Elmira, July 4.
Friend Bliss:

Mr Langdon is ever so much better, & we have every reason to believe that he is going to get well, & that speedily.

I fancy the book you speak of must be the Appleton book.[1] I cannot
think of any other, & have no knowledge of any other. But I shall probably never have to do the Appleton book. They asked me to name a price.
I named a pretty stiff one. And at the same time, I said that *if it were a*

subscription book I could afford easier terms. They misunderstood me and thought that I was *suggesting* that it be made a subscription work— & so they *accepted* ~~the idea~~ my suggestion and offered *higher* pay than I spoke, of. But I wrote them immediately that they had misconstrued me, & that I could not do a *subscription* book for them *at any price whatever.* And moreover, that I could n̸ do *nothing* more than the original proposition called for. And that I could not even do that unless I could do it either before or immediately after my Adirondack trip. They have had ~~two or~~ ample ~~to~~ time to have written me half a dozen times since, & haven't done it. Therefore it is *far* from likely that any "humorous book" ~~is~~ will issue from my pen shortly.

If Mr L. gets thoroughly well, in time, my wife & I will go straight from Buffalo to Vergennes, Vt., ~~the~~ at the end of July, & be joined there by the Twichells. It is our shortest & straightest route to the woods.

We shall be here 10 days or 2 weeks yet. Come—come either here or to Buf.[2]

Yrs

Mark.

[letter docketed:] √ *[and]* Mark Twain | July 4/70 *[and]* Elmira—N.Y.

[1] Bliss's letter is not known to survive. Clemens never published a book with Appleton and Company (20 May 70 to Bliss; 23–26 June 70 to Appleton and Company).

[2] For more than two months Clemens had been expecting Bliss to come "talk books & business" (23 Apr 70 to Bliss).

To Unidentified
4 July 1870 • Elmira, N.Y.
(MS: JIm)

[*on the back:*]

E. H. PAIGE,

NO. 446 MAIN STREET,

BUFFALO, N. Y.

Excuse delay—which sounds strangely, yours being dated June 15, &
this being July 4—but st nevertheless "Excuse delay" is proper, inasmuch as your note has been to hand 6 or 7 days.

Yrs Truly
Clemens.

To Olivia L. Clemens
6 July 1870 • Washington, D.C.
(MS: CU-MARK)

ₐP. S. Got your letter, sweetheart—thank you.ₐ

11.15 PM, July 6.[1]

Livy my darling, I have put in a tremendous day's work. Got up at 6—
shaved & breakfasted & cleared out on business. Went to several places.
Finally, at 9, got a carriage & took Mr. Stewart to the Senate. Then
hunted up Smith of Tennessee & told him to get Brownlow to address a
note to Colfax asking him to take the bill out of its order. Smith was full
of the idea. Then I called on Colfax. He said it was so late in the session
that nothing on earth could save the bill but ~~an~~ a *favorable* report from
the Judiciary Committee. Then I ₐ"went for" the members of that Committee once more—did all I could in that direction.[2] Then I got afraid
that Mr. Smith was sleepy & slow—~~& so, concluding~~ & just then I heard
that parson Brownlow's son was here taking care of his ~~dying~~ invalid
father.

I knew *him* personally away out in the Mountains—~~"w~~ called on
him—he was out; went & got the Postmaster of the Senate to call on the
senior—the senior was too sick to be seen. I then laid a proper train for
fixing the thing subsequently, & left. I went all through the Gov't printing office with old Clapp & then went to meet one of ~~ƶ ƶ~~ five invitations
to dine—throwing off & atrociously discarding old friends in order to
dine with *your* old friend, Sunset Cox.[3]

And presently Mr. Stewart came in & said his Committee (the Judiciary) had reported *favorably* on our bill!!!

My stars, yesterday our Tennesseeans hadn't any idea such a thing
~~(thing (they~~ could be accomplished (they been working for it for
weeks—even months, maybe.) Stewart said I was the only man he knew
of who could have got that ~~stubbo~~ committee to change its ancient policy
& report that bill favorably.

Well I felt so comfortable over this big success that I had half a notion to clear out home & ~~lef~~ leave the passage of the bill to Lewis,[4] Smith
& the others—but when I came to think how ~~worse~~ inefficient they have

been so far, I guessed it would be safest to stay here a day or two & try to get the thing on its final passage.

Livy darling, it is almost foolishness to hope to get it through both houses before the adjournment[5]—it *is* foolish to hope it—but then I do so hate to give a thing up after starting in. It seems like my courting days over again, & I feel as if I want to go & tackle that whole Congress & mak & hang to them till they say *yes*. Just as *you,* did, little sweetheart.

I have the advantage of obscure lobbyists, because I can get any man's ear for a few moments, & also his polite attention & respectful hearing. The most of them—all of them, in fact—tacitly acknowledge an indebtedness to me for wisdom supplied to them by my pen, & it is a very influential point in one's favor, don't you see?

Dined from 6 to 8.30. Called on the Fitch's from 8.30 to 9.30.[6] Then went to see Mr. & Mrs. Bennett & played euchre till 11.[7]

I am tired, my own darling. Good night precious sweetheart.

Sam

✉—————————————————————————

Mrs. Sam*[l]*. L. Clemens | Elmira | N. Y. [*return address:*] RETURN TO J. LANG-
DON, ELMIRA, N. Y. IF NOT DELIVERED WITHIN 10 DAYS. [*postmarked:*] WASHING-
TON D.C. JUL 7

[1]Clemens departed Elmira for Washington on the night of 4 July, sharing a sleeping car with, among others: William Henry Kelsey (1812–79), Whig and Republican congressman from New York (1855–59, 1867–71); Hamilton Ward (1829–98), Republican congressman from New York (1865–71); and Cornelius Cole (1822–1924), Republican senator from California (1867–73). On 5 July he began lobbying for passage of Senate Bill 1025, which had been introduced, then referred to the Committee on the Judiciary, on 29 June. The bill stipulated a reorganization of the Tennessee judicial system, which was of crucial importance to the Langdon family, particularly in light of Jervis Langdon's deteriorating health. Langdon was involved in a lawsuit, begun in 1869, against Memphis. The city owed him five hundred thousand dollars for the paving of its streets by a firm in which he had invested, Brown and Company of Des Moines, Iowa, headed by his nephew by marriage, Talmage Brown. The suit was stalled in Tennessee's overburdened judiciary, which consisted of a single judge riding circuit between three districts. The bill would establish two districts with a judge for each and was expected to expedite pending cases (Cornelius Cole to Olive Cole 5 July 70, CLU-S/C; Keyes; *BDUSC,* 189, 806, 1297, 2006; Dawson; *Congressional Globe:* 1870, 6:4976; 1871, 2:909; U.S. Congress, Senate; *L3,* 264–65 271, 278–79; see pp. 43, 325–26).

[2]The second session of the Forty-first Congress was scheduled to end on 1

July 1870. The members of the Senate Judiciary Committee were: Lyman Trumbull (1813–96), Republican from Illinois (1855–73), who was chair; William Morris Stewart (1827–1909), Republican from Nevada (1864–75, 1887–1905), who had employed Clemens as private secretary in Washington in November and December 1867; George Franklin Edmunds (1828–1919), Republican from Vermont (1866–91); Roscoe Conkling (1829–88), Republican from New York (1867–81); Benjamin Franklin Rice (1828–1905), Republican from Arkansas (1868–73); Matthew Hale Carpenter (1824–81), Republican from Wisconsin (1869–75, 1879–81); and Allen Granberry Thurman (1813–95), Democrat from Ohio (1869–81) (Poore 1870, 11, 56; *L2*, 78, 109–10 n. 2, 139 n. 4; *L3*, 458 n. 3; *BDUSC*, 187, 746, 816, 951, 1711, 1877, 1938–39, 1957).

[3] In addition to the members of the Senate Judiciary Committee, the individuals mentioned in the first two paragraphs of this letter were: William Jay Smith (1823–1913), Republican congressman from Tennessee (1869–71); William Gannaway Brownlow (1805–77), formerly a Methodist minister and now the Republican senator from Tennessee (1869–75), who had sponsored Senate Bill 1025; Brownlow's son James (1841?–79), a distinguished Civil War veteran, whom Clemens had met in San Francisco in June 1868; Vice-President Schuyler Colfax (1823–85); Charles S. Taft, postmaster of the Senate; Almon M. Clapp, founder and a former proprietor of the Buffalo *Express*, congressional printer since April 1869; and Samuel Sullivan (Sunset) Cox (1824–89), former journalist, author of several successful books, and Democratic congressman, first from Ohio (1857–65) and now from New York (1869–73, 1873–85, 1886–89), known for his controversial support of the South during Reconstruction. Cox's acquaintance with Olivia Clemens has not been explained (*BDUSC*, 187, 688, 836–37, 1840; Boyd 1870, 504; Cox 1852, 1865, 1869; *L2*, 219–20; *L3*, 296–97 n. 2, 368–69).

[4] Either John Francis Lewis (1818–95), Republican senator from Virginia (1870–75), or Joseph Horace Lewis (1824–1904), Democratic congressman from Kentucky (1870–73) (*BDUSC*, 188, 1369, 1370).

[5] House Bill 1573, proposing the division of Tennessee into two judicial districts, had been introduced by William J. Smith on 21 March 1870 and was immediately referred to the House Judiciary Committee (*Congressional Globe:* 1870, 3:LXXIX, 2094; 1871, 2:909).

[6] Thomas and Anna Fitch. Among the subjects discussed were Thomas's potential as a lecturer and, probably, his intercession in Orion Clemens's dispute with the Treasury Department (15 Jan 70 to PAM, n. 4; 10? July 70 to Redpath; 10? July 70 to Fitch).

[7] David Smith Bennett (1811–94), Republican congressman from Buffalo (1869–71), had been in the produce business before his election (*BDUSC*, 608; *Buffalo Directory* 1869, 72, 226).

To Olivia L. Clemens
8 July 1870 • Washington, D.C.
(MS: CU-MARK)

Wash. July 8.

Livy my Darling, the bill having been reported in the Senate last night, & ~~th~~ not yet being printed—& the House proposing to take it up ~~&~~ in its original form & come snap judgment on the Senate, to-day, ~~there was naturally (whic~~ (but never got to it,) there was naturally nothing for me to do but *wait*—which I did.[1] Borrowed $100 from Bennett (having come off with only $50 or thereabouts, & I had ordered a suit of clothes for my friend Riley,~~)~~ this morning,)[2] & spent half the day ~~(after an~~ in the House gallery (after first giving an hour to Brady to take my picture in.)[3]

This evening dined with Ex-Vice President Hamlin, Senator Pomeroy, Mr. Gardiner G. Hubbard & Mr. Richard B. Irwin, & had a good time. Hubbard wants to be remembered cordially to father, & Irwin spoke with great ~~satisfact~~ appreciation of how Charley wrote back from Japan to thank him for the pains he had taken to make him & the Prof. comfortable in the ship—a courtesy which Irwin said most people forgot after enjoying his hospitable services & reaching dry land where they no longer needed his attentions. I was glad to hear him compliment Charley so.[4]

Drove up to the Senate & staid till now (10.30 PM) & came back to hotel. Oh, I have gathered material enough for a whole book! This is a perfect gold mine.

Called on the President in a quiet way this morning. I thought it would be the neat thing to show a little embarrassment when introduced, but something occurred to make me change my deportment to calm & dignified self-possession. It was this: *The General was fearfully embarrassed himself!*[5]

I have promised to come down some time & go off with Gen. Dent on a "tear" for a whole day.[6]

I was sorry to hear that father was feebler, but very glad to know that it was nothing serious.

My precious child, I shall stop now, write a note to Twichell killing our trip,[7] & then go to bed. God bless & angels keep my darling.

Sam

✉ ——————————————————————————————————

Mrs. Sam*ˡ*. L. Clemens | Elmira | N. Y. [*return address:*] RETURN TO J. LANG-
DON, ELMIRA, N. Y., IF NOT DELIVERED WITHIN 10 DAYS. [*postmarked:*] WASHING-
TON D.C. JUL 9

[1]Although Senate Bill 1025 was reported out of committee on 7 July, no further action was taken on it. House Bill 1573 was not reported out of committee
until 2 February 1871, during the third session of the Forty-first Congress
(*Congressional Globe:* 1870, 6:5344; 1871, 2:909; *BDUSC*, 187). Clemens made
another, ultimately futile, attempt to secure passage of the legislation at that time
(see pp. 325–26).

[2]John Henry Riley (1830?–72), a Philadelphian, had emigrated to California
in 1849, eventually becoming a newspaper reporter in San Francisco, where he
met Clemens. In November 1865 he departed for Washington, D.C., where he
corresponded for the San Francisco *Alta California* and other papers and served
as a clerk to the House Committee on Mines and Mining. Clemens described
him in "Riley—Newspaper Correspondent," in the *Galaxy* for November 1870,
and based the "mendicant Blucher," in chapter 59 of *Roughing It*, on him (*RI
1993*, 407–11, 701–3; *L2*, 196 n. 1; Boyd 1870, 506; "South African Diamonds,"
Chicago *Times*, 21 Dec 71, 1; SLC 1870hhh, 726–27).

[3]Clemens visited the House of Representatives press gallery, as he had also
done on 7 July, when he was "made much of by his brethren of the quill" ("Washington News and Gossip," Washington *Evening Star*, 7 July 70, 1). Mathew B.
Brady (1823–96) photographed Clemens at his National Photographic Art Galleries on Pennsylvania Avenue (Boyd 1870, facing p. 9, 42). The photograph that
he took on 8 July is reproduced here. For the photograph of Clemens taken at
Brady's galleries in 1871, see Appendix F.

[4]Clemens's dinner companions were: Hannibal Hamlin (1809–91), Lincoln's
first vice-president and currently Republican senator from Maine (1869–81);
Samuel Clarke Pomeroy (1816–91), Republican senator from Kansas (1861–73),
who became the model for the corrupt Senator Dilworthy in *The Gilded Age;*
Gardiner Greene Hubbard (1822–97), lawyer, pioneer in education of the deaf,
and, beginning in the mid-1870s, leader in the commercial development of the
telephone invented by his son-in-law, Alexander Graham Bell; and Richard B.
Irwin, of the Pacific Mail Steamship Company in San Francisco, who had assisted Charles J. Langdon and Darius R. Ford (Bryant Morey French, 87–95;
L3, 369 nn. 3, 5).

[5]In a reminiscence of Grant dictated in 1885, Clemens recalled this occasion:

> Senator Bill Stewart, of Nevada, proposed to take me in and see the President. We
> found him in his working costume, with an old, short, linen duster on, and it was well
> spattered with ink. I had acquired some trifle of notoriety through some letters which
> I had written, in the New York Tribune, during my trip round about the world in the
> Quaker City expedition. I shook hands and then there was a pause and silence. I could
> n't think of anything to say. So I merely looked into the General's grim, immovable
> countenance a moment or two, in silence, and then I said: "Mr. President, I am em-
> bar[r]assed—are you?" He smiled a smile which would have done no discredit to a cast
> iron image, and I got away under the smoke of my volley.

In the same sketch, Clemens recalled his next meeting with Grant, in 1879, when
the mayor of Chicago, Carter H. Harrison

said would n't I like to be introduced to the General? I said, I should. So he walked over with me and said, "General let me introduce Mr[.] Clemens." We shook hands. There was the usual momentary pause and then the General said: "I am not embar[r]assed— are you?"

It showed that he had a good memory for trifles as well as for serious things. (SLC 1885, 1–3)

[6] Frederick Tracy Dent (1821–92), Grant's military secretary, was also his brother-in-law and his former classmate at West Point. During the Civil War he had served as Grant's aide-de-camp, as the military governor of Richmond, and as commander of the garrison of Washington, attaining the rank of brigadier-general in the United States Volunteers.

[7] Jervis Langdon's condition may not have been the only reason for cancellation of the Adirondacks trip. Olivia Clemens was now over four months pregnant, possibly making the excursion seem impractical.

Samuel L. Clemens. Photographed by Mathew Brady in Washington, D.C., 8 July 1870. Mark Twain House, Hartford, Connecticut (CtHMTH). See 8 July 1870 to Olivia L. Clemens.

To James Redpath
10? July 1870 • Elmira, N.Y.
(*Lyceum* 1871, 27)

Buffalo, N. Y., July, 1870.[1]

Friend Redpath,—I find in your list of lecturers the name of Hon. Thomas Fitch, Member of Congress from Nevada. My attention was more particularly called to this matter by your inquiry as to what I might chance to know about him. I know him well, as lawyer, newspaper-editor, silver-miner, & Congressman.[2] I know him to be an orator by birth, education, & instinct. He is a fascinating speaker. I pledge my word that he will hold any audience willing prisoners for two hours that can be gathered together before him, in any city of America, from Boston to New Orleans, & from Baltimore to San Francisco. And no matter what subject he chooses, whether it be worn or fresh, old or new, he will make his audience think they never listened to any thing so delightful before. I have heard Mr. Fitch pretty often; & so I am not afraid to make these strong statements.[3]

Yours truly,
Mark Twain.

[1]Clemens probably returned to Elmira from Washington on Saturday, 9 July, or the day following. He and Olivia presumably did not return to Buffalo until, at the earliest, 22 August, a day after the memorial service for Jervis Langdon (7 Aug 70 to Larned, n. 1). But since he was associated with Buffalo in the public mind, Clemens headed this letter accordingly.

[2]See *RI 1993*, 678–79, and *ET&S1*, 262–66.

[3]Clemens may have promised a "puff" when he saw Fitch in Washington on 6 July and encouraged him to lecture. The present letter was too late for inclusion in the Boston Lyceum Bureau's promotional magazine for the 1870–71 season, published shortly before 13 July. Redpath used most of it ("I know him . . . statements."), however, in newspaper advertisements for Fitch's 29 November lecture in Boston (see the textual commentary). He surely also used it to advertise the other lectures Fitch delivered during a two-week tour that concluded before the third session of the Forty-first Congress convened on 5 December (3 Dec 70 to Redpath, n. 2). The entire letter appeared in the bureau's promotional magazines for 1871–72, 1872–73, and 1873–74, when Fitch, having been defeated for re-election to Congress, lectured more extensively. Redpath's successor, George H. Hathaway, reprised it in 1883–84 for Fitch's return to the platform ("New Publications," Boston *Advertiser*, 13 July 70, 2; *BDUSC*, 187, 1000; Redpath 1876; Pond, xxv; *Lyceum:* 1871, 27; 1872, 37; 1873, xii; 1883, 21).

To Thomas Fitch
10? July 1870 • Elmira, N.Y.
(Fitch 1903)

·   ·   ·   ·

Now try & not put the audience to sleep, & don't be the heedless cause
of my first lie.[1]

·   ·   ·   ·

[1] Clemens probably enclosed an excerpt from, or copy of, the preceding letter
to Redpath. Fitch's 1870 lecture was a success (3 Dec 70 to Redpath, n. 2).

To Orion Clemens
15 July 1870 • Elmira, N.Y.
(MS: CU-MARK)

Elmira, July 15.

Ɖ My Dear Bro:

Per contract I must have another 600-page book ready for my publisher Jan. 1, & I only began it to-day.[1] The subject of it is a secret, because I may possibly change it. But as it stands, I propose to do up Nevada & Cal., beginning with the trip across the country, in the stage.
Have you a memorandum of the route we took—or the ɸ names of any
of the Stations we stopped at? Do you remember any of the scenes,
names, incidents or adventures of the coach trip?—for I remember next
to *nothing* about the matter. Jot down a foolscap page of items for me.[2] I
wish I could have two days' talk with you.

I suppose I am to get the biggest copyright, ~~ever~~ this time, ever paid
on a subscription book in this country.[3]

Give our love to Mollie. Mr. Langdon is very low.

Yr Bro

Sam.

◧

Orion Clemens Esq | Night Editor "Democrat"[4] | St Louis | Mo. [*return
address:*] RETURN TO J. LANGDON, ELMIRA, N. Y., IF NOT DELIVERED WITHIN 10
DAYS. [*postmarked:*] ELMIRA N.Y. JUL 16

[1] Bliss had gone to Elmira to draft this contract, dated 15 July 1870, which was
fulfilled with *Roughing It* (see Appendix E). Clemens did not actually begin writing the book until late August (2 Sept 70 to OC, n. 1).

[2] See 27 July 70 to JLC and family, 2 Sept 70 to OC, and 11 Nov 70 to OC.

[3] Clemens had requested "half profits," but Bliss persuaded him that the seven
and a half percent copyright (royalty) specified by the 15 July contract was the
equivalent: see *RI 1993*, 806–8. Clemens's royalty on *The Innocents Abroad* was
five percent (*L2*, 421).

[4] Orion was apparently promoted to this position from proofreader sometime
after mid-April, at which time he had been seeking a better job. His pay increased by two dollars—to twenty-seven dollars per week (21 Apr 70 to OC, n.
1; 11 Nov 70 to OC).

To Elisha Bliss, Jr.
18 July 1870 • Elmira, N.Y.
(MS: NN-B)

Elmira, 18[th.]

Friend Bliss—

Mr. Langdon is perceptibly better. The doctor has some hope of his
recovery.

As I am now unquestionably notorious, it will be justifiable to have
a steel portrait of the author in the new book—if not in late editions of
the Innocents.[1]

Upon second thoughts I have concluded to simply put the Czar &
his Minister on cards, to be slipped loosely within the fly-leaves of the
books—not fastened in any way. Send the Minister's to him by some
personal friend of his, ‸(Gen. Hawley I think you said,)‸ & send the
Czar's through our Minister at St Petersburgh.[2]

Whenever you are ready for a "blow" on the 75th thousand, send me
a brief note to INQUIRE if I could attend a dinner to celebrate it—& I

will answer No as afflably & felicitously as possible, & thus we'll save the dinner & yet compass the advertisement.[3]

My love to your folks & hearty congratulations to Frank.[4]

Yrs ever

Mark.

[1] In 1869 Clemens had rejected the "effrontery" of having such a frontispiece in *Innocents* (*L3*, 168). He may now have favored a portrait as a corrective to one he disliked, by Gaston Fay, that was appearing as the frontispiece in the *Galaxy* magazine for August 1870, particularly since he now had in hand the "best picture I ever had" (20? May 70 to Paige; 27 June 71 to Redpath). No portrait was used in *Roughing It* or in later printings of *Innocents*. The first of Clemens's books to include his portrait was *A Tramp Abroad* (1880).

[2] The United States envoy extraordinary and minister plenipotentiary in St. Petersburg was Andrew G. Curtin (1815?–94), former governor of Pennsylvania (U.S. Department of State, 10). Joseph R. Hawley, editor of the Hartford *Courant* and a Civil War veteran and former governor of Connecticut, had been an acquaintance of Clemens's at least since 1869 (*L3*, 97 n. 5). The present letter must have enclosed the autographed cards (which have not been recovered) to go into gift copies of *Innocents*. For the inspiration for these gifts, see 30 May 70 to Bliss.

[3] See 7 May 70 and 30 May 70, both to Bliss.

[4] Bliss's folks were his wife Amelia, his four children, and his father Elisha Bliss, Sr. (1787–1881), a widower, who lived with the family. The oldest son, Francis, had become engaged (*L3*, 15 nn. 1, 4; Geer 1870, 57; "Hartford Resi dents," Bliss Family, 1; 15 Sept 70 to Bliss and French, n. 1).

To Josephus N. Larned
18 July 1870 • Elmira, N.Y.
(Paraphrase: Larned 1870a)

PERSONAL.—We rejoice to learn from our colleague, Mr. Clemens, who has been in attendance for several weeks at the sickbed of Mr. Jervis Langdon, of Elmira, that a change for the better has taken place in the condition of that gentleman, and that the physicians now entertain hopes of his recovery, which for some time they had about abandoned.[1]

[1] Clemens probably sent this news on the same day as the preceding letter, in a letter or telegram to Larned, his closest associate on the Buffalo *Express*, who doubtless wrote this item.

To C. A. King
22 July 1870 • Elmira, N.Y.
(MS: MWC)

J. LANGDON, MINER & DEALER IN ANTHRACITE &
BITUMINOUS COAL   OFFICE NO. 6 BALDWIN STREET

ELMIRA, N.Y. July 22 18~~6~~ 70

C. A. King, Esq[1]
    Dear Sir:
        I can't possibly do it. Nothing would give me greater plea-
sure if I were still in the field, but I trust & believe I have permanently
~~quiet~~ quit all manner of lecturing & public speaking. With many thanks
& many regrets—

                                Yrs Truly
                                Sam[l]. L. Clemens.

[1] Possibly Charles Artemas King (1851–1917), who lived in Binghamton, New
York, as a young man and later worked in the New York City Customs Department. It is somewhat more certain that Clemens's correspondent was at least the
C. A. King who compiled "Mark Twain: Excerpts from Magazines," a collection
of photographs of Mark Twain and clippings of articles by and about him, now
in the Alderman Library at the University of Virginia ("Charles A. King,"
"Died," New York *Times*, 25 July 1917, 11; *NUC*, 296:290).

To Josephus N. Larned
per Telegraph Operator
25 July 1870 • Elmira, N.Y.
(Paraphrase: Larned 1870b)

PERSONAL.—A dispatch yesterday from our colleague, Mr. Clemens, informs us that Mr. Langdon continues to improve, and that his
recovery is now fully expected.

To Jane Lampton Clemens and Family
27 July 1870 • Elmira, N.Y.
(MS: NPV)

Elmira, July 27.

Dear Folks—

Mr Langdon is getting along very well, & slowly progressing toward recovery*,*, we think. But we still sit up with him night & day.[1]

We are glad you are all so well satisfied in Fredonia.

But why is Margaret going?—what is the matter? You seem to take it for granted that we know all about it. If Margaret needs a nice new trunk, I want you to get her one, & a common dress & also a fine one for Sunday, & send the bill to me, ₐ(and do not be stingy in the prices.)ₐ I am very sorry she is going away. I had hoped she would spend all her days with you.[2]

I am going to write a 600-page 8vo. book (like the last) for my publishers (it is a secret for a few days yet.) It will be about Nevada & California & must be finished Jan 1. I shall begin it about a month from now. By request, Orion has sent me his note-book of the Plains trip. Now I always thought that we used $600 of my money (& so we did), but I see no mention of it here. I wonder if we ever had any settlement of that account. I suppose of course we had—else I would pay my indebtedness to Mollie with that sum & interest to date.[3]

Affection'ly

Sam.

P. S. The "Innocents Abroad" paid me 12 to $1500 a month—the next book will pay considerably more.[4]

---

[1] In 1906 Clemens recalled:

Mrs. Clemens, her sister, (Susy Crane,) and I did all the nursing both day and night, during two months until the end. Two months of scorching, stifling heat. How much of the nursing did I do? My main watch was from midnight till four in the morning—nearly four hours. My other watch was a midday watch, and I think it was only three hours. The two sisters divided the remaining seventeen hours of the twenty-four between them, and each of them tried generously and persistently to swindle the other out of a part of her watch. The "on" watch could not be depended upon to call the "off" watch—excepting when I was the "on" watch.

I went to bed early every night, and tried to get sleep enough by midnight to fit me for my work, but it was always a failure. I went on watch sleepy and remained miserably sleepy and wretched straight along through the four hours. I can still see myself sitting by that bed in the melancholy stillness of the sweltering night, mechanically waving a palm-leaf over the drawn white face of the patient; I can still recall my noddings, my fleeting unconsciousnesses, when the fan would come to a standstill in my hand, and I would wake up with a start and a hideous shock. I can recall all the torture of my efforts to keep awake; I can recall the sense of the indolent march of time, and how the hands of the tall clock seemed not to move at all, but to stand still. Through the long vigil there was nothing to do but softly wave the fan—and the gentleness and monotony of the movement itself helped to make me sleepy. The malady was cancer of the stomach, and not curable. There were no medicines to give. It was a case of slow and steady perishing. At long intervals, the foam of champagne was administered to the patient, but no other nourishment, so far as I can remember. . . .

I was well and strong, but I was a man and afflicted with a man's infirmity—lack of endurance. But neither of those young women was well nor strong, yet ‚still‚ I never found either of them sleepy or unalert when I came on watch; yet, as I have said, they divided seventeen hours of watching between them in every twenty-four. It is a marvelous thing. It filled me with wonder and admiration; also with shame, for my dull incompetency. Of course the physicians begged those daughters to permit the employment of professional nurses, but they would not consent. The mere mention of such a thing grieved them so that the matter was soon dropped, and not again referred to. (AD, 15 Feb 1906, CU-MARK, in *MTA*, 2:113–15)

[2] Margaret Theil, the family's maid, reportedly "missed her St. Louis friends and finally decided to go back" (*MTBus*, 116).

[3] In fact, in the summer of 1861 Clemens had enough money saved from his piloting wages to advance Orion $400 for both of their stagecoach fares from St. Joseph, Missouri, to Carson City, Nevada Territory, and also to provide about another $800 for expenses (*L1*, 122; *RI 1993*, 574–75, 576). His indebtedness to Mollie Clemens has not been explained.

[4] Clemens was about to receive a fourth quarter statement of sales on *The Innocents Abroad*, as well as a summary statement of the entire first year's sales, amounting to about 69,500 copies (5 Aug 70, 4 Sept 70, both to Bliss). Neither document has survived, but his five percent royalty, applied to existing bindery and sales records and using an average price of $4.00 per book, yields a total first year return of about $14,000, or about $1,167 per month. This is substantially consistent with Clemens's 1906 recollection that he received "about twenty-two cents per volume," which generates a royalty of $15,290, or about $1,274 per month (AD, 23 May 1906, CU-MARK, in *MTE*, 151–52; Hirst 1975, 315–17).

To Orion Clemens
1 August 1870 • Elmira, N.Y.
(MS: CU-MARK)

Elmira, Aug. 1.

My Dr Bro.—

Pamela has at last sent your various letters to me. You must have known that would be the final result, for you knew she could not spare the $200 from her living.

I have tried for 24 hours to write, but I am too infernally angry & out of patience to write civilly.

You can draw on me for two or three hundred dollars, but only on one condition, viz: that you consider yourself under oath to either sell ~~or~~ at some price or other, or **give away,** one full half of the Tennessee land within 4 months from date—but it must be honestly parted with, & *forever.*

The family ~~has~~ have been bled for 40 years to keep that cursed land on their hands & perpetuate our father's well intended folly in buying it. I washed my hands of it 5 years ago, & I never will have anything more to do with its care or its sale.[1] I have always contended that the family were too poor to keep a luxury like that worthless land, but I never expected to convince them of it. If any stupid fool will give 2,000 for it, do let him have it—shift the curse to his shoulders.

I want you to consider yourself under oath to offer Mellon[2] as follows:

25 per cent. if he sells
half or all the land in 60 days.
20 per cent. if in 90   ″
15 ″   ″   ″ ″ 120   ″
~~10 ″   ″~~

And Mr. Mellon to be hampered by no set price, but get what he can,, ,& to sell the land out-&-out, without mineral reservations.,

On these terms a man can be hired to sell the land, & on no other.

My idea is ~~to to~~ that *all* the land be sold (& that you bind yourself so,) within 4 months *if possible*—every effort to be made to do it—& in any case one-half of it to be sold or given away in that time.

Mr Swope is acting just as he ought to. I see no reason to find fault with him.[3]

If, in order to sell this land in four months, it be absolutely necessary, you can increase the draft upon me (at sight) f to $500.

I prefer that you telegraph the amount of money you want, so that you need ~~not write me~~ never mention that land again to me by letter. I will never read another letter, from *any*body, that mentions it. You cannot form even a faint idea of how *I* malignantly I hate that vile subject.

Now if you draw any portion of this money from me, it is with the understanding that you are under oath to the whole programme laid down in this letter, in all its details. Otherwise the trade is "off." If you are not prepared to subscribe to these requirements, I would much rather put the money in the fire than in Tenn. land. I particularly call your attention to the programme of commissions ,(& the fact that no mineral reservations are to be ~~insisted~~ made.), to be paid to Mellon (or other agent, tho' I think Mellon ought to have it),. No man can afford to sell this wildcat at lower commissions. [*in bottom margin:* (OVER.)]

I am sorry, if these conditions seem hard, for this is the last time I will ever have anything to do with the care, protection, or sale of ~~the~~ that doubly & trebly hated & accursed land.

Yrs affly

Sam

[1] Clemens had been helping his family pay the taxes on their Tennessee property, despite washing his hands of it in 1866 and renouncing his share of it in 1869 (*L1*, 326, 341, 343; *L3*, 272, 387, 425).

[2] See 21 Apr 70 to OC, n. 3.

[3] Possibly Isaac, Joel, or Meyer Swope, St. Louis boot and shoe dealers until 1869, when Isaac left the firm for the paper collar manufacturing business (Edwards: 1868, 707; 1869, 755; 1870, 852; 1871, 640). What action Swope took remains undetermined.

To Elisha Bliss, Jr.
2 August 1870 • Elmira, N.Y.
(MS: OCi)

J. LANGDON, OFFICE OF J. LANGDON & CO. MINERS AND DEALERS IN
J. D. F. SLEE, ANTHRACITE AND BITUMINOUS COALS. 6 BALDWIN ST.
T. W. CRANE,
C. J. LANGDON. ELMIRA, N.Y., Aug 2, 187 0

Friend Bliss—

You know I already had an offer ¢ of *ten* per cent from those same parties in my pockct when I stipulated for 7½ with you. I simply promised to *give them a chance to bid,;* I never said I would publish with them if theirs was the best bid. If their *first* offer had been 12½ I would merely have asked you to climb along up *as near that figure as you could & make money,* but I wouldn't have asked anything more. Whenever you said that you had got up to what was a fair divide between us (there being no *risk,* now, in publishing for me, while there WAS, before,) I should have closed with you on those terms. I never have had the slightest idea of publishing with anybody but you. (I was careful to make no promises to those folks about their bid.)[1]

You see you can't get it out of your head that I am a sort of a rascal, ₫ but I ain't. I can stick to you just as long as you can stick to me, & give you odds. I made that contract with all my senses about me, & it suits me & I am satisfied with it.[2] If I get only half a chance I will write a book that will sell like fury provided you put pictures enough in it.

Yes, we'll put the portrait in the new book.[3]

Say—when does Franks wedding come off?[4]

Ask Frank ~~when~~ if he is going to get up the *annual* account of sales for me which you spoke of?[5]

We still sit up with Mr. L. He is somewhat worse again.

Yrs
Mark.

[*letter docketed:*] √ [*and*] Mark Twain | Aug 2/70

[1] Bliss's erstwhile competitor may have been Appleton and Company, although their proposal to Clemens in May was for a much slighter book than he had promised Bliss on 15 July (20 May 70 to Bliss; 15 July 70 to OC).

[2] Clemens's dissatisfaction with the contract, especially with the royalty it stipulated, emerged just months after *Roughing It* was published in 1872 (see *RI 1993*, 877–80).

[3] See 18 July 70 to Bliss, n. 1.

[4] See 15 Sept 70 to Bliss and French, n. 2.

[5] See 7 May 70 to Bliss, n. 2.

To Elisha Bliss, Jr.
5 August 1870 • Elmira, N.Y.
(MS: CLjC)

J. LANGDON, OFFICE OF J. LANGDON & CO. MINERS AND DEALERS IN
J. D. F. SLEE, ANTHRACITE AND BITUMINOUS COALS. 6 BALDWIN ST.
T. W. CRANE,
C. J. LANGDON. ELMIRA, N.Y., Aug. 5 187 0

Friend Bliss—

Let Frank send the quarterly statement here, if it will be ready within a week.[1]

The physicians pronounce Mr Langdon's case utterly hopeless. The family are shrouded in gloom, awaiting the end.

Yrs

Clemens.

[*letter docketed:*] √ [*and*] Mark Twain | Aug 5/70

[1] The fourth quarter (1 May–30 July 70) statement for *The Innocents Abroad* does not survive, but must have reported the sale of about 9,122 volumes. This was a significant falling off from the 15,500, 23,500, and 21,378 sold in the first three quarters, respectively. Elisha Bliss's check, dated 5 August 1870, was for $2,000 (PH in CU-MARK, courtesy of Hamlin Hill; *L3*, 441 n. 2; 28 Jan 70 to Bliss, n. 5; 7 May 70 to Bliss, n. 2).

To Pamela A. Moffett
per Telegraph Operator
6 August 1870 • Elmira, N.Y.
(MS, copy received: NPV)

THE WESTERN UNION TELEGRAPH COMPANY.

DATED   Elmira   Aug 6   186 70

RECEIVED AT   Fredonia   " 6   "

TO   Mrs. P. A. Moffett

Father died this afternoon[1]

S. L. Clemens.

---

[1] Jervis Langdon died at around 5 P.M.

To Josephus N. Larned
7 August 1870 • Elmira, N.Y.
(Larned 1870c)

.   .   .   .

Mr. Langdon was a great & noble man, in the best & truest acceptation of those terms. He stood always ready to help whoever needed
help—wisely with advice, healthfully with cheer & encouragement, &
lavishly with money. He spent more than one fortune in aiding
struggling unfortunates in various ways, & chiefly to get a business
foothold in the world. He had so charitable a nature that he could always
find some justification for any one who injured him; & then his
forgiveness freely followed. Instead of sending to prison a man whom he
had pecuniarily befriended in time of need, & who, being persuaded by
an ill-adviser, defrauded his benefactor out of a great sum, he forgave

him & helped his family when straightened circumstances fell to their lot again.[1] All the impulses of Mr. Langdon's heart were good & generous. He could not comprehend the base or the little. His nature was cast in a majestic mould.

Whatever he did, he did with his whole heart. He never was hesitating or lukewarm in anything. In business he worked with all his might; & as fast as his great gains accumulated he toiled to sow them broadcast for the good of the city, the church & the poor.[2] In politics he showed the same decision & energy; he was an Abolitionist from the cradle, & worked openly & valiantly in that cause all through the days when to do such a thing was to ensure to a man disgrace, insult, hatred & bodily peril.[3]

Throughout his long illness all grades of the community, from the highest to the lowest, came daily to inquire about his state; & the cheer that lit their faces when the news was good, or the sadness that fell upon them when it was ill, was touching testimony to the truth of what is here set down concerning him & to the whole community's respect & strong love for him.[4] He was a very pure, & good, & noble Christian gentleman. All that knew him will grieve for his loss. The friendless & the forsaken will miss him.[5]

.   .   .   .

[1] On the evening of Sunday, 21 August, Thomas K. Beecher delivered a memorial tribute to Langdon before "one of the largest audiences that ever assembled in the Opera House" ("The Late Jervis Langdon," Elmira *Advertiser,* 22 Aug 70, 4). Beecher remarked that:

> tenderness of heart and weakness of resistance, when his sympathies were once enlisted, was Mr. Langdon's principal fault or blemish. . . .
>
> I can not remember a time in the sixteen years of my acquaintance with him in which he was not embarrassed by pecuniary obligations, incurred for friends, and generally incurred against his better judgment, being led by his heart rather than guided by his head. The administrators of his estate will find, among the hardest problems they have to solve, the liquidation of debts and settlement of accounts which have come upon his books against his will, and contrary to his judgment, but because he could not say No to them whom he loved or pitied. (Thomas Kinnicut Beecher, 31)

[2] Langdon's "great gains" resulted in an estate of about one million dollars, which was to be divided among his wife and their two children, Olivia and Charles. Susan Crane, his adopted daughter, received title to Quarry Farm (Jervis Langdon; "In Memoriam," Elmira *Saturday Evening Review,* 13 Aug 70, 5).

[3] Beecher recalled:

> At a time when opposition to slavery was costly, when it ruled a man not only out of his political party but out of his church and out of good society, and caused his children to be pointed at with a sneer; at a time when his business prospects must needs suffer,

and even his personal property be endangered, Mr. Langdon was a pronounced and determined anti-slavery man.

Very few fugitives from slavery have passed through this region without receiving a benefit from him. . . . And when at last, by the costly compulsions of civil war, the system of slavery was abolished, Mr. Langdon's redoubled exertions in behalf of the now freed men were sufficient testimony that his previous zeal had not been a cheap destructiveness, rejoicing in judgments and denunciations, but a true and tender-hearted philanthropy. He has given, I can not tell you how many thousand dollars, toward the education of whites and blacks in our southern states, and, without murmuring, has paid other thousands annually, in the shape of taxes, which he scorned to swear off or dodge in any way, even though he might feel that he was paying more than his share. (Thomas Kinnicut Beecher, 27–28)

Among those Langdon assisted was Frederick Douglass (*L3*, 428 n. 2).

[4] On 8 August, by request of Elmira Mayor John Arnot, local businesses closed for two hours during Langdon's funeral (Elmira *Advertiser:* "Notice to Citizens," 8 Aug 70, 1; "City and Neighborhood," 8 Aug 70, 4; "Funeral of Mr. Langdon," 9 Aug 70, 4).

[5] The cover letter that presumably accompanied this tribute, which Clemens probably wrote early on 7 August, has not been found. The Buffalo *Express's* obituary of Langdon appeared on 8 August and incorporated Clemens's eulogy, described as "a brief communication that we received from him yesterday" (Larned 1870c). The following day the Elmira *Advertiser*, which had published its own tribute on 8 August, reprinted the *Express*, and on 13 August the Elmira *Saturday Evening Review* published still another obituary (Elmira *Advertiser:* "Death of Jervis Langdon," 8 Aug 70, 1; "Death of Jervis Langdon, of Elmira," 9 Aug 70, 1; Elmira *Saturday Evening Review:* "In Memoriam," 13 Aug 70, 5).

To Elisha Bliss, Jr.
11 August 1870 • Elmira, N.Y.
(MS: OCi)

Elmira, Aug. 11.

Friend Bliss—

I meant to telegraph Mr Langdon's death to you, but was kept too busy.

This is a house of mourning, now. My wife is nearly broken down with grief & watching.[1]

However, I believe I did⸝ telegraph you.

I wrote that publisher that your bid was lower than his, but not enough lower to justify me in deserting you. He wrote back a hot answer, saying "he was surprised to hear me confess that his bid was the highest, & in the same letter say that I had awarded the book to you." I sent him

back a warm one in which I said *I* was surprised at his infernal imper-
tinence—& then I ~~showed~~ talked sassy to him for a page or so & wound
up by saying I judged he would be able from the foregoing to form a sort
of ~~vagu~~ shadow of an idea of my private opinion of him & his kind. If he
don't go mighty ~~sh~~ slow I will print something personal about him.[2]

Say—I learn from Constantinople that the celebrated guide, "Far=
Away Moses" goes to the American Consulate & borrows my book to
read the chapter about himself to English & Americans, & he sends me
a beseeching request that I will forward *that* a copy of *that chapter* to
him—he don't want the whole book, but only just that to use as an advertisement. Can't you take the loose sheets of that form & send them
to him with my compliments (you ,or Frank, can write the autograph,)
care of the American Consulate?[3]

Ys

Mark.

[1] See 27 July 70 to JLC and family, n. 1.
[2] See 2 Aug 70 to Bliss.
[3] The "celebrated Turkish guide, 'Far-away Moses'" is described in the
opening paragraph only of chapter 35 of *The Innocents Abroad*.

To Pamela A. Moffett
17 or 24 August 1870? • Elmira or Buffalo, N.Y.
(MS: NPV)

Wednesday.[1]

My Dear Sister—
    I will come as soon as I can leave Livy—& will give you notice
beforehand. My coming at this time would stop Livy's progress; for
whilst she sleeps but poorly now, she may be said to not sleep *at all* when
I am away—even when she is well. If she went without sleep now that
she is weak & suffering, it would be very bad for her, of course. I do hope
Ma will get better fast, & get *well*—& I hope I may see her so when I
come.
    Livy & I send abundance of love to Ma & you, & all.

Sam.

over.

I wish you would get all the gossip you can out of Mollie about Cousin James Lampton & family, *without her knowing it is I that want it.* I want every little trifling detail, about how they look & dress, & what they say, & how the house is furnished—& the various ages & characters of the tribe. Mollie does up gossip mighty well. I have preserved the other letter she wrote you about that gang. I wish to write the whole thing up—but not publish it for a great many years. That is, if the story I write from it could be recognized by Jim or the family.[2]

SLC

[1] The Clemenses probably remained in Elmira at least through 21 August, for the public tribute to Jervis Langdon. Clemens might have written this letter either on 17 or 24 August, *if* it enclosed a letter from his cousin Fred Quarles (see 31 Aug 70 to PAM). If it did not enclose Quarles's letter, then even the year is somewhat doubtful. Clearly he wrote it before early January 1873, however, by which time he and Charles Dudley Warner were at work on *The Gilded Age* (7 Aug 70 to Larned, n. 1; 20 Apr 73 to Whitelaw Reid, DLC). See note 2.

[2] Mollie Clemens's letter to Pamela about James J. Lampton (1817–87), his wife, Elizabeth (1820–95), and their five children has not been found. Lampton, Jane Clemens's first cousin, was a St. Louis bill collector, traveling salesman, cotton and tobacco merchant, and, by the early 1870s, an attorney. He became the model for Colonel Sellers in *The Gilded Age* (*Inds*, 397; Lampton: 1989, 7–8; 1990, 136–41). Clemens may already have had such a political satire in mind, for in Washington in early July he had "gathered material enough for a whole book!" (8 July 70 to OLC).

To Pamela A. Moffett
31 August 1870 • Buffalo, N.Y.
(MS: NPV)

Buffalo, Aug. 31.

My Dr Sister:

I know I ought to be thrashed for not writing you, but I have kept putting it off. We get heaps of el letters every day, & it is a comfort to have somebody like you that will let us shirk & be patient over it.

We got the book[1] & I *did* think I wrote a line thanking you for it— but I suppose I neglected it.

But I *know* I sent you a letter from Fred Quarles th a week or two ago—a *second* letter, I mean.[2]

We are getting along tolerably well. Mother is here, & Miss Emma Nye.[3] Livy cannot sleep, since her father's death—but I give her a narcotic every night & *make* her.

I am just as busy as I can be—am still writing for the Galaxy & also writing a book like the "Innocents" in size & style. Otherwise I would have gone run down to see Margaret before she leaves for Ł St. Louis. I have got my work ciphered down to *days,* & I haven't a single day to spare between this & the date which, by written contract I am to deliver the MSS. of the book to the publisher.[4]

In a hurry

Affectionately
Sam.

P. S. We all send love—Mother included, who says she is much obliged for your & Ma's letters.

[1] Unidentified.

[2] William Frederick S. Quarles (1833–98) was the son of Jane Lampton Clemens's sister, Martha Ann (Patsy) Lampton (1807–50), and her husband, John Adams Quarles (1802–76). As a boy Clemens had spent summers on the Quarles farm near Florida, Missouri (*Inds*, 342; Lampton 1990, 57).

[3] Nye (1846–70), Olivia Clemens's former Elmira schoolmate, had arrived for a visit from Aiken, South Carolina, where she had been living with her parents and siblings since late 1869 (Wisbey 1991, 1–3; *L2*, 324 n. 7; *L3*, 506).

[4] The contract called for delivery of the manuscript "as soon as practicable, but as early as 1st of January next, if said Company shall desire it" (Appendix E).

To Orion Clemens
2 September 1870 • Buffalo, N.Y.
(Transcript and MS: *MTL*, 1:175, and CU-MARK)

Buf., 1870.

Dear Bro:

I find that your little memorandum book is going to be ever so much use to me, & will enable me to make quite a coherent narrative of the Plains journey instead of slurring it over & jumping 2,000 miles at a stride. The book I am writing will sell.[1] In return for the use of the little memorandum book I shall take the greatest pleasure in forwarding to you the third $1,000 which the publisher of the forthcoming work sends me—or the *first* $1,000, I am not particular—they will both be in the first quarterly statement of account from the publisher.[2]

In great haste,

Yr Obliged Bro.

Sam.

Love to Mollie. We are all getting along tolerably well.

Orion Clemens Esq | 1227 Chesnut st. | St. Louis, Mo. [*across envelope end:*] Leave it in Mellon's hands but *give him 25 per cent*—can you never get that necessity before your face?[3] [*postmarked:*] BUFFALO N.Y. SEP 3

[1] Clemens had received the memorandum book by 27 July, at which time he expected to begin writing what became *Roughing It* in "about a month" (27 July 70 to JLC and PAM). His letters of 2 September to Fairbanks and 4 September to Bliss indicate that he began as planned and completed drafts of the first four chapters, which were clearly dependent on the memorandum book, between 28 August and 2 September. It is therefore apparent that he wrote the present letter on 2 September and sent it in the envelope postmarked 3 September. The letter itself survives, however, only in Albert Bigelow Paine's transcription, which lacks a clear date. The memorandum book itself has not survived (see *RI 1993*, 769–77).

[2] Clemens's gratitude helped inspire Orion to send additional material for the western book (11 Nov 70 to OC).

[3] See 1 Aug 70 to OC.

From Samuel L. and Olivia L. Clemens
to Mary Mason Fairbanks
2 September 1870 • Buffalo, N.Y.
(MS: CSmH)

Buffalo, Sept 2.

Dear Mother:

Up to where Shargar & Robert overtake the vessel, on Lord

Rothie's horses, the book is just *splendid*—but from that to the end it ~~is~~
is pretty flat.[1] My! but the first half of it is superb! We just kept our pen-
cils going, marking brilliant & beautiful things—but there was nothing
to mark, after the middle. Up to the middle of the book we did so admire
& like Robert—& after that we began to dislike & finally ended by de-
spising him for a self-righteous humbug, devoured with egotism.

I guess we hated his grandmother from the first. ‚I did not. I liked
her all the time, her heart was all right and what was wrong came of her
education— Livy‚ The author was always *telling* us her goodness, but
seldom letting us see any of it.

Shargar was the only character in the book ~~worthy to live & worthy~~
~~of~~ who was *always* welcome, & ~~him~~ of him the author gave us just as little
as possible, & filled ~~him~~ his empty pages with the added emptiness of
that tiresome Ericson & his dismal "poetry"—hogwash, *I* call it.

Oh, yes, & there was Dooble Sanny, an imperial character—but *of
course* he had to die in order to give Robert a chance to air some of his
piety‚, & talk like a blessed Sunday-school book with a marbled cover
to it. ‚~~thats not correct—~~ thats not correct—‚

But what on earth the author lugged in that inanЄity‚ Miss Lindsay,
for, goes clear beyond my comprehension. Page after page, & page after
page about that ineffable doughnut, & not even the poor satisfaction of
reflecting that Lord Rothie ruined her, after all. ‚how dreadful‚ Hang
such ~~an author!~~ a character!

And Miss St. John—well there ~~w~~ never was any interest about *her*,
from the first. And when she concluded that the man she first loved was
small potatoes & that ‚that‚ big booby of an Ericson was the man͢ that
completely filled her idea of masculine perfection I just wanted to send
her a dose of salts with my compliments.

Mind you, we are not through ~~yo~~ yet—two or three chapters still to
read—& that idiot is still hunting for his father. I hoped that as he grew
to years of discretion he would eventually appreciate the efforts of a wise
~~p~~ Providence to get the old man out of the way (seeing that he wasn't ~~eli~~
very eligible property, take him how you would,)—but no, nothing
would do him, clear from ~~in~~ juvenile stupidity ~~to~~ up to mature imbecility
but tag around after that old bummer. ‚*scandalous*‚ I do just wonder what
he is going to make of him now that he is about to find him. A missionary,
likely, along with Rev. De ~~Fleaur~~ Fleuri, & trot him around peddling

sentiment to London guttersnipes while *he* continues his special mission upon earth of reclaiming venerable strumpets and ~~trotting out~~ ˌexhibitingˌ his little wonders at midnight for the astonishment & admiration of chance strangers like the applauding Gordon.

I would make erasures in this letter but it is a hopeless undertaking, I should have to erase the last three pages of ~~the book letter~~ ˌitˌ—— However I know that he is rather ashamed of it because he said that he had left plenty of room for me to say something pleasant—

The last part of the book we have not enjoyed as much as the first part, but the first we did enjoy intensely—

Lovingly yours
Livy—

P. S. Livy is getting along tolerably well, now—takes a ǹ sleeping potion every night & sleeps refreshingly.

Miss Emma Nye is here & is right sick—she cannot go on to Detroit yet awhile, where she is to teach.[2]

Mrs. Langdon is with us & is reasonably well contented.

I have written four chapters of my new book during the past few days, & I tell you it is going to be a mighty starchy book—will sell, too. But then, considering how I have talked about Robt ~~Faulkener,~~ Falconer, I mean to let you abuse it as much as you want to.

Come & see us whenever you can, & we will run out & see you whenever *we* can, for we all love you ever so much. Love to all your household—including Mollie[3] always.

Yrs Eldest.
Sam'.

[1] Mrs. Fairbanks had recommended *Robert Falconer,* by British author George MacDonald, first published in 1868.

[2] Nye planned to teach at the girls' academy run by John Mahelm Berry Sill (1831–1901), Detroit's first superintendent of public schools (1863–65) and a leading Michigan educator. Presumably she was also teaching there in December 1868, when Clemens, in Detroit to lecture, called on her at the Sill home, where she was living (*L2,* 340; Wisbey 1991, 3).

[3] Mary Paine Fairbanks.

To Elisha Bliss, Jr.
4 September 1870 • Buffalo, N.Y.
(MS: CU-MARK)

Buf. Sept. 4.

Friend Bliss—

During past week have written first four chapters of the book, & I tell you the "Innocents A̶ B̶ Abroad["] will have to get up early to beat it. It will be a book that will jump right strait into a continental celebrity the first month it is issued. Now I want it illustrated lavishly, & if We shall sell 90,000 copies the first 12 months. if it I haven't even a shadow of a doubt of that.[1] I see the capabilities of my subject.

Got Franks ac/.[2] All right.

Yrs
Clemens.

✉————————————————————————

[*letter docketed:*] √ [*and*] Mark Twain | Sep 4/70

[1] That is, nearly a third more than *The Innocents Abroad* had sold in its first year (69,500). *Roughing It* actually sold about 75,000 copies in its first year (*RI 1993*, 890–91).
[2] Frank Bliss's statement of the first year's sale of *Innocents*, which Clemens had been expecting for a month. It does not survive (27 July 70 to JLC and family, n. 4; 2 Aug 70 to Bliss).

To Ella Wolcott
7 September 1870 • Buffalo, N.Y.
(MS: CU-MARK)

ⓒ

472 Delaware st. ⎫
Buffalo, Sep. 7. ⎭

Dear Miss Wolcott—

It always hurts me to the heart to say no to an application from a writer struggling upward.[1] Every few days such applications come, &

then I have to sit down & write the same old, old, hard sentences—not *always*, for once or twice I have succeeded in lo finding a place for a candidate. But now I have no resources. My own paper has all the expense of a literary kind that it can bear—so one of my partners tells me, (in whose hands rests the *entire* power to hire literary assistance[)].[2] I say "no resources." It amounts to that, for I shall forward the poems to the "Galaxy," & in with a request that they buy open negotiations with you for such for publication—in and in due time will come polite thanks & excuses, but *no trade*. Possibly not—& let us hope not—but such is my usual experience, & it is by the lamp of experience that we customarily walk.[3]

Do not speak to me of "boring"—for when one applies to me in behalf of one possessing real & *manifest* talent, then I am complimented, not bored. And even an application from a plain & painfully talentless source creates more of sorrow than anger in the recipient, more of pity than of ridicule—for there is something so pathetic in the simplicity of it all, & the author's cheery readin eagerness to step out upon the wide desert that in whose far centre sits the shining Damascus of success.

Poor little Emma Nye lies in our bed-chamber fighting wordy battles with the phantoms of delirium. Livy & a hired nurse watch her without ceasing, night & day. It is not necessary to tell you that Livy sleeps as little as nurse or patient, & sees little but that bed & its occupant. The disease is a consuming fever—of a typhoid tu type—& also the lungs seem stricken with disease. The poor girl is dangerously ill. W Ours is an excellent physician, & we have full confidence in him.[4]

With great respect I am

Very Truly Yrs,

Sam[l]. L. Clemens.

Miss Ella Wolcott | **Care H. B. Hooker, Esq** | Rochester, N. Y.[5] [*postmarked:*] BUFFALO N.Y. SEP 8 [*and*] CARRIER SEP 8

[1] Ella Louisa Wolcott (b. 1828) was a friend of the Langdons' and like them a member of Congregational Church (Wolcott, 390; *Park Church*, 6–9). On 5 September she had written Clemens (CU-MARK):

> I am greatly interested in a young man whom I do not know, but whose friends think him a "right good fellow"—& these friends are "right good fellows" to me. Frank Huntington is traveling and studying in Germany on slender resources, and would be glad to prolong his stay by writing for the press. I have copied these verses from his

letters home, and beg to know if you can find place for any of them, either in The Galaxy or your own paper, also whether any letters might be available now, when all the world is talking of Germany. If rejected please return me the manuscripts.

The following verses were among those Wolcott sent (the ellipses are hers):

> This land of ours, this America here,
> It wouldn't be such a very poor land,
> If its equal rights gabbling citisens
> Would only come to understand
> — — — — — —
> That lately the world has been found to be round

[2] George H. Selkirk, Buffalo *Express* business manager.

[3] The *Galaxy* did not publish any poetry by Huntington (1848–1928), who later became a writer and editor and from 1874 to 1902 was on the staff of *Appletons' Annual Cyclopædia*, contributing articles on international political, military, and commercial history.

[4] Possibly Andrew R. Wright (11 Nov 70 to Ford, n. 5).

[5] Horace B. Hooker, a nurseryman, had his home and business at 255 North St. Paul Street in Rochester (*Rochester Directory*, 108, 261).

To Pamela A. Moffett and Family
per Telegraph Operator
8?–29 September 1870 • Buffalo, N.Y.
(Paraphrase: *MTBus*, 49–50)

When we moved to Fredonia about ten years after this and my grandmother was rather lonely at first, we consoled her by saying, "At any rate, Mrs. Holliday will never visit us here." But the first thing we knew we had a telegram from Uncle Sam, who had recently married and was living in Buffalo, saying to expect her. She had turned up at his house but as someone was very ill there he had not permitted her to get out of the cab but had given her fifty dollars and sent her on to us.[1]

[1] Melicent S. Holliday (b. 1800?) had lived in a mansion on Holliday's Hill (Cardiff Hill in Clemens's fiction) near Hannibal. After the Civil War she was reduced to "visiting" with friends, among them Jane Clemens and the Moffetts, whom she sometimes stayed with in St. Louis, without invitation (*Inds*, 325). Clemens's telegram is known to survive only in this paraphrase by Annie Moffett Webster. He could have sent it soon after he realized the seriousness of Emma

Nye's illness—that is, at about the same time he wrote the previous letter to Ella Wolcott and the next one to Orion Clemens—or at any point before Nye died on 29 September.

To Orion Clemens
9 September 1870 • Buffalo, N.Y.
(MS: NPV)

Buf. 9th.

My Dear Bro—

O here! I don't want to be consulted at all about Tenn. I don't want it even mentioned to me. When I make a suggestion it is for you to act upon it or throw it aside, but I beseech you never to ask my advice, opinion or consent about that hated property. ~~My~~ If it was because *I* felt the slightest personal interest in the infernal land that I ever made a suggestion, the suggestion would never be made.

Do exactly as you please with the land—always remembering this: that so trivial a percentage as ten per cent will never sell it. It is only a bid for a somnambulist.

I have no time to turn round. A young lady visitor (schoolmate of Livy's) is dying in the house of typhoid fever (parents are in South Carolina) & the premises are full of nurses & doctors & we are all fagged out.[1]

Yrs ~~E~~
<u>Sam</u>

[1] Among the nurses were one, and possibly two, of Emma Nye's Elmira friends. On 8 September 1870, Thomas K. Beecher wrote Ella Wolcott: "Allie Spaulding has gone to take care of her, and if the illness continues Julia [his wife, Julia Jones Beecher] will go to relieve her when she gets tired" (CtHSD). Alice Spaulding, Olivia Langdon, and Emma Nye had been among the pupils in Mrs. Beecher's Sunday School class in the late 1850s and early 1860s (*L3*, 506). As the monogram indicates, Clemens used a sheet of Nye's stationery for this letter.

From Samuel L. and Olivia L. Clemens
to Francis E. Bliss and Frances T. French
15 September 1870 • Buffalo, N.Y.
(MS: CtHMTH)

Buf. Sept. 15.

Dear Frank—

We are obliged to send regrets, as we have a young lady friend permanently & seriously ill in the house (typhoid fever,) & the doctor gives us no encouragement that we & the hired nurses can cease to watch her for a month or two to come. We are obliged to send regrets to Charley Langdon also, (my wife's brother), whose wedding comes off at the homestead in Elmira the middle of October.[1]

But we just wish you & the pro[s]pective bride[2] the same amount of peace, & restful comfort, & absolute & unalloyed happiness as *our* new married life is filled with, fully aware that in wishing you this we are wishing you the sum of all earthly good.

Sincerely Yours,
Sam*l*. L. Clemens
and *Mrs*. Sam*l*. L. Clemens.

~~Mrs~~ Mr. and eventually *Mrs* Frank Bliss, Hartford.

---

[1] See 13 Oct 70 to Fairbanks.
[2] Bliss and French were married at the bride's home in Mount Holyoke, Massachusetts, on 28 September ("Married," Hartford *Times*, 30 Sept 70, 2; "Hartford Residents," Bliss Family, 1).

To the Postmaster of Virginia City, Mont. Terr.
(Hezekiah L. Hosmer)
15 September 1870 • Buffalo, N.Y.
(MS: MtHi)

Buffalo, Sept. 15.

Dear Sir:[1]

Four or five years ago a V̶ righteous Vigilance Committee ₄in your city₄ hanged a casual acquaintance of mine named Slade, along with twelve other prominent citizens whom I only ⌀ knew by reputation. Slade was a "section-agent" at Rocky Ridge station in the Rocky Mountains when I crossed the plains in the Overland stage ten years ago, & I took breakfast with him & survived.[2]

Now I am writing a book (MS. to be delivered to publisher Jan. 1,) & as the Overland journey has made six chapters of it thus far & promises to make six or eight more, I thought I would just rescue my late friend Slade from oblivion & set a sympathetic public to weeping for him.[3]

I̶N̶ Such a humanized fragment of the original I̶ Devil could not & *did* not go out of the world without considerable newspaper eclat, in the shape of biographical notices, particulars of his execution, etc., & the object of this letter is to beg of you to ask some one connected with your city papers to send me a Virginia City newspaper of that day if it can be done without mutilating a file.

⎰⎰⎰ *[If found, please enclose in* LETTER *form,* ⎱
⎱⎱⎱ *else it will go to the office of Buffalo "Express"* ⎰
  & be lost among the exchanges.] ⎱

I beg your pardon for writing you so freely & putting you, or trying to put you, to trouble, without having the warrant of an introduction to you, but I did not know any one in Virginia City & so I ventured to ask this favor at your hands. Hoping you will be able to help me[4]

I am, Sir,

Your Obt. Serv't

Mark Twain.

---

[1]Hosmer (1814–93) had been the first chief justice of the supreme court of Montana Territory, serving from 1864 to 1868. Then from 1869 to 1872 he served

as postmaster of Virginia City, the territorial capital. Clemens may not have
known Hosmer, or even his name, but assumed that the postmaster could redi-
rect this request appropriately.

[2] On the morning of 3 August 1861, the ninth day of his overland journey to
Nevada Territory, Clemens had breakfasted with Joseph A. (Jack) Slade (1829?–
64), an Overland stage agent and a notorious desperado and murderer, who was
hanged on 10 March 1864 in Virginia City, then part of Idaho Territory. He had
already recalled their encounter in his seventh "Around the World" letter, in the
Buffalo *Express* of 22 January 1870 (*RI 1993*, 584–88, 810–11; SLC 1870k).

[3] Clemens devoted chapters 10 and 11 of *Roughing It*, both of which he completed in March 1871, to Slade's nefarious career (*RI 1993*, 60–75, 811, 819,
835–36).

[4] Hosmer's reply is not known to survive, but it seems likely that he sent Clemens, or referred him to, Thomas J. Dimsdale's *The Vigilantes of Montana* (1866).
The book, based on articles Dimsdale had published in the Virginia City *Montana Post* in 1865–66, was a primary source for Clemens's account of Slade in
Roughing It (*RI 1993*, 584–86, 811).

To Elisha Bliss, Jr.
21? September 1870 • Buffalo, N.Y.
(MS: CCC)

[on back of letter as folded:]
I turn this over to you.

Am going to write you soon. Yes, *will furnish article for paper.*[1] Have written Frank. Finished 7th or 8th chap. of book to-day, forget which—am
up to page 180,—only about ~~1,500~~ ₗ1500ₗ more to write.[2] *[in margin:*
~~maybe~~]

 Our patient the young lady will hardly recover.[3]

 Write me supper invitation—cannot leave home before spring.[4]

       Yrs

        Clemens.

OLDEST PAPER IN THE COUNTY. TWO DOLLARS A YEAR. ESTABLISHED 1855.
CIRCULATION 1,000.

JOB WORK PROMPTLY AND ARTISTICALLY DONE AT REASONABLE RATES. THE CITY OF LANSING IS BEAUTIFULLY SITUATED ON THE MISSISSIPPI RIVER, IN ALLA-MAKEE COUNTY, ONE OF THE BEST POR-TIONS OF THE STATE.	ADVERTISING RATES, STRICTLY PAYABLE EVERY QUARTER: 1 SQUARE, 1 WEEK, – $ 1 50 EACH SUBSEQUENT INSERTION, 75 1 COLUMN, 1 YEAR, – 80 (LESS SPACE 25 PER CENT. ADDITIONAL.)

THE LANSING WEEKLY MIRROR, METCALF & CO., JOHN T. METCALF,
JAMES T. METCALF, PUBLISHERS AND PROPRIETORS.

LANSING, IOWA, Sept. 19th, 1870.[5]

My Dear Sir:

I want to read your admirable book ("The Innocents Abroad") but us poor d——s of country newspaper men can't afford to buy one. We don't know your publishers. Can't we notice or advertise, and thus come into possession of something good for the mind, of a standard heaps of newspaper men want to reach, but you hold so successfully at your service?

Yrs. Truly

J. T. Metcalf[6]

Ed.

S. F Clemens
Esqr.

[*letter docketed:*]

‸Please send this back to me on a/c of back of it.‸ Please attend to this it was sent to Clements & from him to me. Think you had better send copy & let him adv.[7]

Bliss

[*and, in another hand:*] √ [*and*] Mark Twain | Sept 19/70[8]

[1]Bliss's paper, which advertised American Publishing Company books, is-sued once, in late October 1870, as the *Author's Sketch Book.* Retitled the *American Publisher,* it reappeared in early March 1871 (29 Oct 70 to Bliss, n. 1; 4 Mar 71 to OC, n. 3).

[2]The draft of chapters 7 and 8 differed significantly from the final version of those chapters in *Roughing It.* For an account of the differences, and an expla-nation of Clemens's estimate of remaining work—which was affected by his use of clippings of a number of his Buffalo *Express* articles (with each page of clip-

pings counted as the equivalent of four manuscript pages)—see *RI 1993*, 812–18.

[3] Emma Nye died on the morning of 29 September. That night her body was taken to the Elmira home of Clara and Alice Spaulding. She was buried the following day. With Olivia now seven months pregnant, and worn down by four months of deathbed attendance on her father and Nye, the Clemenses did not make the trip to Elmira for her funeral ("Sad News to Friends," Elmira *Advertiser*, 30 Sept 70, 4).

[4] See 7 May 70 to Bliss.

[5] If mailed on 19 September, this letter probably reached Clemens by 21 September, and he could have sent it on to Bliss that same day or shortly thereafter.

[6] It is not known whether John T. or James T. Metcalf wrote this letter.

[7] Bliss lined through Clemens's letter to indicate that it had been answered and that a copy of *Innocents* had been sent. No review has been found in the available file of the weekly Lansing *Mirror*, which, however, lacked several issues between September and December 1870.

[8] Since Clemens did not date his note, the American Publishing Company's clerk adopted Metcalf's date to file it.

To Elisha Bliss, Jr.
22 September 1870 • Buffalo, N.Y.
(MS: CU-MARK)

Buf. 22^d.

Friend Bliss—

My map is attracting a deal of attention.[1] We get letters requesting copies from everywhere. Now what you need is something to make the postmasters & the public *preserve* your posters about "Innocents" & stick them up & if you would put that map & accompanying testimonials[2] right in the centre of the poster & the thing is accomplished, *sure*.

If you want to do this, write or telegraph me at once, & I will have a stereotype made & send to you.[3]

Ys

Clemens.

✉

[*letter docketed:*] √ [*and*] Mark Twain | Sept 22/70

[1]In the Buffalo *Express* of Saturday, 17 September, Clemens published his burlesque war map, "Fortifications of Paris" (see 10? Oct 70 to Spofford for a facsimile). It parodied newspaper maps of the Franco-Prussian War (19 July 1870–21 May 1871), probably including the New York *World*'s "The Fortifications of Paris" (11 Aug 70, 1; 10 Sept 70, 1) and the New York *Tribune*'s "The Defences and Environs of Paris" (13 Sept 70, 1). On 19 September the *Express* published the following notice:

> TO BE CONTINUED.—As we have been unable to supply the demand for Saturday's issue of the EXPRESS, we hereby give notice that the "Map of the Fortifications of Paris," will be published in the WEEKLY EXPRESS which will be issued Wednesday morning. ("City and Vicinity," 4)

Publication of the weekly on Wednesday (21 September), rather than on Thursday as customary, was perhaps intended to meet the feverish demand for the map, which was a broadside supplement to the paper (*BAL*, 3320). Clemens also reprinted it, as "Mark Twain's Map of Paris," in the *Galaxy* for November, explaining there that he did so "to satisfy the extraordinary demand for it which has arisen in military circles throughout the country" (SLC 1870ggg, 724). In February 1871, Donn Piatt, Washington correspondent of the Cincinnati *Commercial*, reported a conversation in which Clemens described the circumstances of the map's creation:

> "Only think," said he, "I knew that confounded thing had to be done, and, with a dear friend lying dead before me, and my wife half distracted over the loss, I had to get off my articles so as not to disappoint my publishers, and when I sat down with a board and penknife, to engrave that map of Paris, I did so with a heavy heart, and in a house of lamentation." (Piatt 1871b)

The dear friend was surely Emma Nye, not Jervis Langdon, as has been suggested (Steinbrink, 205–6 n. 8). Langdon died on 6 August in Elmira. Nye "lingered a month" in Buffalo, mortally ill, and finally expired on 29 September, twelve days after the map was first published (13 Oct 70 to Fairbanks). Nevertheless, Clemens persisted in believing that he created the map after, or very shortly before, Nye died. In his notebook for 1900, he specifically linked the map with her death:

> Map of Paris. Emma Nye lying dead.
> Reversing the map was not intentional—it was heedlessness. (Notebook 43, TS page 3, CU-MARK†)

And in 1906, he connected the map with the "last two or three days" of her illness:

> Those two or three days are among the blackest, the gloomiest, the most wretched of my long life.
> The resulting periodical and sudden changes of mood in me, from deep melancholy to half insane tempests and cyclones of humor, are among the curiosities of my life. During one of those spasms of humorous possession I sent down to my newspaper office for a huge wooden capital *M* and turned it upside-down and carved a crude and absurd map of Paris upon it, and published it, along with a sufficiently absurd description of it, with guarded and imaginary compliments of it bearing the signatures of General Grant and other experts. (AD, 15 Feb 1906, CU-MARK, in *MTE*, 251)

After Clemens's own death in 1910, Josephus N. Larned recalled that Clemens also worked on the map at the *Express* offices:

I doubt if he ever enjoyed anything more than the jackknife engraving that he did on a piece of board for a military Map of the Siege of Paris, which was printed in The Express from his original "plate," with accompanying explanations and comments. His half day of whittling and the laughter that went with it are something that I find pleasant to remember. (Larned 1910)

[2] Bogus "Official Commendations" from: Ulysses S. Grant; Prussian Premier Otto von Bismarck; Brigham Young; French Emperor Napoleon III; J. Smith, otherwise unidentified; Achille François Bazaine, supreme commander of French forces; Louis Jules Trochu, the military governor of Paris; Lieutenant-General William T. Sherman; and William I, king of Prussia (called William III by Clemens).

[3] Bliss may have incorporated the "Fortifications of Paris" into an advertising poster for *The Innocents Abroad* (see 29 Oct 70 to Bliss), but no examples of it are known to survive.

To Franklin D. Locke
24 September 1870 • Buffalo, N.Y.
(MS: CtHMTH)

42 472 Del.—9. 24th.

Dear Mr. Locke—[1]

By authority of this document I introduce you to my wife, & beg that you will administer the accompanying oath & otherwise complete & make valid the accompanying power of attorney.[2]

It will be a very great ~~fe~~ favor if you can save her the necessity of getting out of the carriage, ~~for is not strong~~ & ~~face~~ facing the terrors of the law in your awe-inspiring den.

Very Truly Yrs

Sam*l*. L. Clemens.

[1] Locke was an attorney at the Buffalo law firm of Dennis Bowen and Sherman S. Rogers, which regularly handled legal matters for Clemens. By 1871 the firm had become Bowen, Rogers and Locke (16 and 17 Apr 70 to the Langdons; *Buffalo Directory:* 1870, 304, 426, 550; 1871, 276, 422, 576).

[2] Doubtless authorizing Clemens to act on his wife's behalf in financial matters. He already was one of the executors of Jervis Langdon's estate.

To Joseph T. Goodman
28? September 1870 • Buffalo, N.Y.
(Paraphrase: Virginia City *Territorial Enterprise*, 7 Oct 70)

MARK TWAIN'S new book is to be all about his experience in California and Nevada and coming to this coast by the Overland stages. It will be a volume of 600 pages octavo. He has started in on it, but at last accounts was two days' journey the other side of Salt Lake with it;[1] so we need not get excited here about the "chief amang us" for some time to come. His book will be out in April next.[2]

[1] That is, Clemens had written as far as the ninth day of his overland journey (3 August 1861), on which he crossed the Continental Divide, east of Salt Lake City. This became part of the matter of chapter 12 of *Roughing It*. He had not yet completed what became chapters 10 and 11, however (15 Sept 70 to the postmaster of Virginia City, n. 3; *RI 1993*, 791, 818–19).

[2] Allowing sufficient time both for Clemens to have written about four chapters of his new book since his 21? September letter to Bliss, and for mail to reach Virginia City, Nevada, by 6 October, it is likely that this progress report, doubtless to Goodman, was written around 28 September. In a portion of the letter not paraphrased Clemens may have asked Goodman, and other former colleagues on the *Territorial Enterprise*, for assistance of the sort he had already requested from Orion Clemens and Hezekiah Hosmer (15 July 70 to OC; 15 Sept 70 to the postmaster of Virginia City).

~~To George M. Smith~~
To James Redpath
4 October 1870 • Fredonia, N.Y.
(MS: MH-H)

ˌ*Private.*ˌ

Fredonia, Oct. 4.[1]

~~Geo. M. Smith Esq~~[2]
         ~~Dear Sir:~~
ˌDear Redpath:ˌ 𝒯 If Mr. Prang is the shrewd manager I take him to be I can insure money to him & to myself too, ~~if he~~ (and to you likewise,

for I will give you one-fifth of any terms you can get him to pay me, either in the way of per centage or purchase of copyright.) The idea is this: Let this Map boom along & advertise itself all it possibly can, by appearing in the Galaxy, the World, the Boston Sun, & the &c., & some of Bliss's Am. Pub. Co. posters,[3] & thus advertise itself till it is a great celebrity & everybody anxious to get & *keep* a copy (for papers are always lost or destroyed bev before a person can cut a thing out,) and then, on top of this great tide of popularity,[4] come out with a nice, picturesque Chromo, *revised, corrected,* certain startling *essentials* added, ⟨—certain portraits of sovereigns & generals, maybe—& some more letter-press description & remarks——and if it don't sell an awful swathe of copies I miss my guess. This improved edition I would draft & *copyright.* If Prang *should* issue the present one, & co (which I do not object to, but do tender to him my appreciation of his honorable conduct in first consulting me,) & is it *should* strike a successful current, any other lithographer or all the lithographers ₐ& chromo menₐ could come in & cripple the speculation if they chose, for there is no copyright on the Map.

If you will get up a bargain with Prang for this thing, & send me a written contract to sign with him, ₐfor Iₓ I will improve this Map in such a way that people shall say "Oh that Map that was in the *papers* isn't the best—what you want is the *Chromo.*" And I will give you one-fifth of whatever terms Prang will make with me,ₐ—for it is not your business to work for me for nothing, nor mine to ask you to do it.ₐ[5]

Never mind that photograph—I its cost was the merest trifle—I never dre thought of such a thing as your paying for it.[6]   ₓOVERₓ

Yrs. Truly

Sam*ˡ*. L. Clemens.

P. S. Send your answer to BUFFALO, as usual. I return there day after to-morrow. Letters & telegrams easily reach me—& besides I may return there any moment.

OVER.

Do not you see, yourself, that all this gratuitous advertising makes it per the new edition ₐ(provided we issue one),ₐ far more profitable & easy of circulation than if we could have made ₐthe case with,ₐ an original unadvertised chromo of this the Map? It is perfectly plain to me.

S. L. C.

Friend Redpath—You see I wrote all that to Geo. M. Smith (129 Washington st. Boston), but I have changed my mind & write it to you, because I have no mind to be bribing Prang's agents to ~~be~~ influence him in a business matter. I do not write Prang himself because it would make delay, & this advertising ought to be taken advantage of. You are a good talker & a good bargainer, & besides I know you & have confidence in your fidelity. ⟨

I think there is a deal of money in this thing ⟨for the ~~may~~ map is celebrated all over the continent, & yet even in Boston where it has been published just ask~~, for cu~~ every man you meet for one day & you will find that he has heard of but not *seen* ~~it,⟩~~ it. Now do you go to Prang & talk it up & make a bargain with him & draw a contract & send it along—& without the least trouble in the world we shall take in some money. And can't you get out a *German* edition?

I will now write Mr. Smith & say: "Mr. Prang has my permission to print the present Map₍,₎ of course, but I have written to Mr. Redpath ₍my lecture & business agent₎, suggesting that he see you & Mr. Prang and propose the drafting of a new & improved edition of the work ~~&~~, to be *copyrighted* & thus made ~~p~~ available for profit to both himself & me."

~~Can~~ Will you put this thing right through, Redpath? Write or telegraph me a word.

Yrs

Mark.

✉

[*letter docketed:*] BOSTON LYCEUM BUREAU. REDPATH & FALL. OCT 8 1870 [*and*] Sam L. Clemens | Oct. 4 '70

¹Clemens and Olivia spent most, if not all, of the first week of October in Fredonia, visiting his family. The visit had been planned since mid-June, but was delayed by the fatal illnesses of Jervis Langdon and Emma Nye ("Local and Miscellaneous," Fredonia *Censor*, 5 Oct 70, 3; 12 June 70 to PAM; 13 Oct 70 to Bliss; JLC to SLC and OLC, 28 July 70, CU-MARK).

²George M. Smith and Company was a Boston bookseller and publisher, as well as the American Publishing Company's general agent for New England. Smith was also an agent of some kind for Louis Prang (see note 5) (*Boston Directory* 1870, 611, 742; "Advertisements," *Author's Sketch Book* 1 [Nov 70]: 3–4; advertisement, Portland [Maine] *Transcript*, 19 Mar 70, 407).

³Clemens's "Fortifications of Paris" was reprinted in the supplement of the Boston *Sun* on 25 September, on the first page of the New York *World* on 2 Oc-

tober, and by Clemens himself in the November *Galaxy,* where it was tipped in as a folded insert. It may also have been used in one of the advertising posters Bliss published for *The Innocents Abroad,* but no copy of such a poster has been found (Howard, item 5; 22 Sept 70 to Bliss, nn. 1, 3; 29 Oct 70 to Bliss, n. 1).

[4]The Boston *Evening Transcript* of 8 November 1870 (4) reported striking evidence of the popularity of Clemens's burlesque:

> THE GALAXY has printed and sold of the November number four editions. The first edition was as large as has ever been called for before during an entire month; but this time the entire edition was sold within five days of its publication [in mid-October], and three times since then the publishers have been obliged to stop all other work to get out fresh editions. This looks like success.

[5]Louis Prang (1824–1909), the Prussian-born lithographer, had started in business in Boston in 1856. In 1867 he had added a large printing establishment in nearby Roxbury to satisfy the great demand for his colored lithographs of famous paintings—"chromos" as he was the first to call them. Prang's interest in producing a chromolithograph of Clemens's "Fortifications of Paris" grew out of his publication of genuine war maps. In 1861 he produced the first such map marketed in the United States, a lithograph of Charleston harbor, placed on sale within a few days of the attack on Fort Sumter, the opening engagement of the Civil War. Subsequently he published and sold large numbers of other Civil War maps and battle plans. In 1870 he published maps of the Franco-Prussian War showing the actual fortifications of Paris (Prang 1870a–b). Prang was evidently "consulting" Clemens through his agent George M. Smith.

[6]Clemens had doubtless sent a copy of one of his most recent photographs to Smith upon request (20? May 70 to Paige; 8 July 70 to OLC, n. 3).

To Elisha Bliss, Jr.
8–13? October 1870 • Buffalo, N.Y.
(MS: CU-MARK)

.   .   .   .

[*cross-written on envelope of enclosure:*]
I have no comments to make—this deadbeat that coolly refused to honor my *written request* that he would give Bret Harte a book & look to you for restitution, suits me for an agent if he suits you; I have not a word to say for or against him. I simply won't answer his letters or pay any attention to him. If he is the best ~~g~~ agent for the coast, it is "business" to employ him. ~~But if otherwise, & you employ somebody else, I wish you would~~

He did well with the book—& would have done A GOOD DEAL better if he had any sense about handling newspaper people. Think of an agent refusing to give copies to the chief papers! He is an infernal fool.[1]

Clemens.

If you keep him you better send books to the papers *yourself*.

> Mr S. C. Clemens
> Editor "Express"
> Buffalo
> N. Y.
>
> [*return address:*] BOOK & STATIONERY HOUSE OF H. H. BANCROFT & COMPANY, SAN FRANCISCO, CAL. OFFICE IN NEW YORK, 113 WILLIAM ST. OFFICE IN LONDON, 10 WARWICK SQUARE, E.C. OFFICE IN PARIS, 5 RUE NEUVE ST. AUGUSTIN. [*postmarked:*] SAN FRANCISCO CAL. SEP 29

[1] Only the envelope of the letter from Hubert H. Bancroft (West Coast agent for *The Innocents Abroad*) to Clemens is known to survive. Clemens wrote this note on that envelope and presumably enclosed it (with Bancroft's letter inside) in a letter to Bliss—possibly his letter of 13 October, or some earlier letter (now lost). Bancroft's letter was postmarked in San Francisco on 29 September. Assuming a transit of nine days, Clemens probably received it in Buffalo by 8 October, about the time he returned from Fredonia. For his fuller account of Bancroft's refusal, see 26 Nov 70 to Webb.

To James Redpath
9 October 1870 • Buffalo, N.Y.
(MS: Axelrod)

Buf. Sunday.

Dear Redpath—

Have had a death in my house, & am hurried with literary work beside[1]—& so I give up the additions to the Map. Let Prang go ahead with the Map just as it is. One of these days, if the opportunity offers I will try to get up something which can be copyrighted & thus enure to mutual benefit. I wish I had the time to fix up the additions to this Map, for ~~this~~ there might be a success made of it—but circumstances have put a veto on it. I hope Prang will make some money out of this work of art for I haven't—& can't, now because of my neglect to copyright it.[2]

I *would* like to lecture next year, but don't know.

I have a notion to get up a hideous panorama & a bully accompanying lecture & put some fellow into your lecture field to go through the lyceums with it.

Ys

Mark.

[*letter docketed:*] BOSTON LYCEUM BUREAU. REDPATH & FALL. OCT 11 1870 [*and*]
S. L. Clemens | 10/11 | '70 [*on attached slip:*]

Dear Mr Prang:—

The enclosed speaks for itself.

Please return it

Yours

James Redpath

[1] Since Emma Nye's death on 29 September, Clemens had made little progress on *Roughing It* and, as this and the letter of 4 October show, was beginning to distract himself with other projects. See *RI 1993*, 819–25.

[2] The next letter indicates that Clemens may nevertheless have tried to copyright "Fortifications of Paris" long after it had been published and reprinted by others. He may also have changed his mind about Prang's reprinting it, for Prang evidently did not do so. And although Clemens never revised his map, he did reprint it in 1872 in *Mark Twain's Sketches*, in 1874 in *Mark Twain's Sketches. Number One*, and in 1878 in *Punch, Brothers, Punch! and Other Sketches*.

To Ainsworth R. Spofford
10? October 1870 • Buffalo, N.Y.
(MS: DLC)

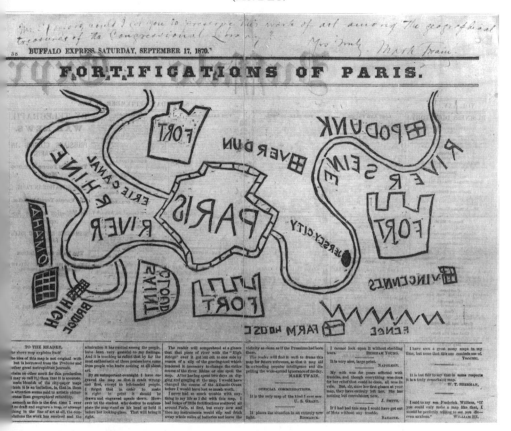

BUFFALO EXPRESS. SATURDAY, SEPTEMBER 17, 1870.

[1] Clemens's inscription reads:

Mr. Spofford, could I get you to preserve this work of art among the geographical treasures of the Congressional Library?

Yrs Truly
Mark Twain.

Ainsworth Rand Spofford (1825–1908) had been associate editor of the Cincinnati *Commercial* from 1859 until 1861, when he left the paper to become chief assistant to the librarian of Congress. He became librarian himself in 1864, holding the post until 1897, at which time he resumed, for the remainder of his life, the position of chief assistant. The informality of Clemens's request, his first known letter to Spofford, suggests that the two men were already acquainted, probably since late 1867 and early 1868, when Clemens lived in Washington (*L2*,

108–59, 170–202). Spofford evidently did not treat this letter as a copyright application: the records of the Copyright Office do not include a registration of the "Fortifications of Paris," reproduced here at 37 percent of actual size (Lehr).

To Mary Mason Fairbanks
13 October 1870 • Buffalo, N.Y.
(MS: CSmH)

Buffalo, Oct ~~12~~ 13.

Dear Mother:

Your news is superb—about All̦ie, I mean. I never was satisfied with that old match, but we both (Livy & I,) take ever so kindly to the new one. We send reams of good wishes & congratulations—& now & henceforth the chiefest of them is that Allie ~~& her~~ in her new relations may be as entirely ~~ha~~ and perfectly happy & contented as Livy & I are. If I wished all night & started fresh in the morning & kept it up a century I could not wish her better than that.[1]

We were fully expecting a visit from you & yours this very day, but your letter blighted all that, & we are so disappointed. But you *must* stop on your way east & stay as long as you can—& if you can't on your way east, then you must tarry on your return. We'll not have any shirking on *that* matter.[2]

We have a telegram from home saying that Charley's wedding passed off all right, yesterday, & that the two happy children left for the east at noon. I was entirely too busy to leave here, & Livy couldn't go.[3]

My book is not named yet. Have to write it first—you wouldn't make a garment for an animal till you had seen the animal, would you? I am getting along ever so slowly—so many things have hindered me.[4]

Miss Emma Nye lingered a month with typhoid fever, & died here in our ~~blue~~ own bedroom on the 29th Sept. She was buried in Elmira. Her family are still in S.C.

I kissed Livy several times for you, according to order. Will do it again.

The reason I haven't written before is because I am in such a terrible whirl with Galaxy & book work that I am so jubilant whenever ~~my~~ each day's task is done that I have to dart right off & play—nothing can stop me. I never want to see a pen again till the task-hour strikes next day.

Now you'll stop here, you understand.

Lovingly

Sam[.]

---

[1] Alice Holmes Fairbanks had become engaged again, this time to William Henry Gaylord (b. 1842), a Cleveland lawyer (7 Jan 70 to Fairbanks, n. 12; 8 Jan 70 to OLL [1st]; Lorenzo Sayles Fairbanks, 552; *Cleveland Census*, 91; *Cleveland Directory* 1870, 123, 139).

[2] Within the week Mrs. Fairbanks evidently did stop in Buffalo (5 Nov 70 to OC, n. 5).

[3] Charles J. Langdon and Ida B. Clark were married at the Elmira home of her parents, Jefferson Burr Clark and Julia McDowell Clark, the latter a member of "one of the oldest and in their times most conspicuous families" of Chemung County, New York (Towner, 615). George H. McKnight, pastor of Elmira's Trinity Episcopal Church, and Thomas K. Beecher, the Langdons' pastor, officiated. Olivia Clemens, beginning her eighth month of pregnancy, was confined to Buffalo. Clemens was kept there by the literary commitments he goes on to describe (Hebb, 1; "Local Jottings," Elmira *Saturday Evening Review*, 15 Oct 70, 8; Boyd and Boyd, 43).

[4] Clemens did not settle on "Roughing It" as the title for his book until October 1871, just three months before the first bound volumes were ready (*RI 1993*, 869, 871, 873, 876).

To Elisha Bliss, Jr.
13 October 1870 • Buffalo, N.Y.
(MS: MB)

Buf. Oct. 13.[1]

Friend Bliss:

I have a notion to let the Galaxy publishers[2] have a volume of old sketches for a "Mark Twain's Annual—1871"—provided they will pay me about 25 per cent. That is what they offered once, I believe. ~~My idea is to use in this, among other things, some few sketches which will not "keep."~~ I believe a Christmas volume will out-pay Josh Billings' Allminax.[3] What do you think? Write me at once—& don't discourage me.[4]

Did that scalawag of a boy of yours trot through here the other day? We found a card of the firm, with his name underscored, & guessed he

had stopped at the office. However, ~~he~~ we were at Fredonia, N. Y., all
the week & so if he *was* here we couldn't have seen him. I never once
thought of Frank's being absurd enough to take upon himself one of
those ghastly tortures called a "bridal trip," else we would have grieved
to think we couldn't entertain the couple a few days[5]—for the young lady
was very low then & we couldn't have made room—(she died on the 29th
in our bedroom—perhaps I wrote you.)

I am driveling along tolerably fairly on the book—getting off from
12 to 20 M pages (MS.) a day. I am writing it so carefully that I'll never
have to alter a sentence, I guess, but it is *very* slow work. I like it well,
as far as I have got. The ~~pep~~ people will read it.

Yrs in haste.

Mark.

✉

[*letter docketed:*] √ [*and*] Mark Twain | Oct 13/70. | Author

[1]Clemens again used a sheet of Emma Nye's stationery, as he had done on 9
September in writing to Orion Clemens.

[2]Isaac E. Sheldon and Company, of New York.

[3]Henry Wheeler Shaw (Josh Billings) published *Josh Billings' Farmer's Allminax for the Year 1870* (New York: George W. Carleton), the first of ten comic
annuals, in October 1869. On 14 February 1870 Shaw wrote Clemens: "The 'All-
manax' has about given up its ghost, but sold 80 thousand. = For such a trifling
affair, it[s] success came near ravishing me. = " (CU-MARK). Other reports indicated that it sold 90,000 copies within three months, one-third of them in the
first week after publication (*L3*, 397 n. 3). On 11 October 1870 the Buffalo *Courier* reported on advance sales for the second year's version: "Of Josh Billing's
Farmers Alminax for 1871, Carleton, the publisher, has received *a single order*
for 100,000 copies—the largest number ever sold, at one time, of any work in
this country" ("Literary," 1).

[4]See 26 Oct 70 to Bliss.

[5]See 15 Sept 70 to Bliss and French, n. 2.

To Francis P. Church
18 October 1870 • Buffalo, N.Y.
(MS facsimile: Mott 1957, facing 255)

Oct. 18th

Friend Church,

The matter referred to in the last paragraph of this "Memoranda"
is a quiet satire on your infernal Galaxy portraits & is accompanied by a

ghastly likeness of King William which I have ~~work~~ worried over till it is bad enough to suit me[.] It must be engraved *exactly* as I have drawn it or it will ~~not be~~ suffer damage. It *can not* be improved on, by making it either better or worse.[1]

The whole thing is good, but if you do not want it, just drop off the paragraph which refers to it & I will understand, & will publish it as a lithograph, through Prang.[2]

Sometimes I ~~am~~ get ready to give you notice that I'll quit at the end of my year because the Galaxy work crowds book work so much, but I am very fond of doing the Memoranda, & take a live interest in it always—& so I hang on & hang on & give no notice—still the chances are that I shall be frightfully crowded for time eventually; & so it is better that I make some mention of it while yet it is far off, so that if I have to give notice at last it won't seem like taking "snap-judgment" you know.[3]

Yrs faithfully
Clemens.

[*enclosure:*][4]

WILLIAM III,
King of Prussia.

[1] In addition to his drawing of King William, Clemens presumably enclosed his manuscript for the December "Memoranda," whose final paragraph read:

> ALL my soul is in Art lately, since I have been taking lessons in drawing and painting. I have drawn, and am now engraving, an elegant portrait of King William of Prussia, as a companion to the customary GALAXY portraits, and to complete the set. This work of Art, with accompanying remarks, will appear in the January number of this magazine. (SLC 1870nnn, 885)

The *Galaxy* usually printed a full-page engraving of one of its contributors, or of some public figure in the news, as a frontispiece. The August 1870 number had used an unflattering likeness of Mark Twain (see 27 June 71 to Redpath). The burlesque "portrait" of King William occupied almost a full page of the "Memoranda" in the January 1871 *Galaxy* and was accompanied by "commendations" from famous artists and other prominent individuals, including the king (SLC 1871b, 150–52).

[2] See 4 Oct 70 and 9 Oct 70, both to Redpath.

[3] For Church's reply, see the enclosure with the next letter.

[4] The original drawing that Clemens enclosed has not been found, but is reproduced here (at 56 percent of actual size) from the engraving made from it. The printer's copy for the December "Memoranda" is also lost; for its contents, see References (SLC 1870nnn).

To Elisha Bliss, Jr.
26 October 1870 • Buffalo, N.Y.
(MS: Axelrod and CU-MARK)

Buf. Oct. ~~25~~ 26.

Friend Bliss:

My man took my telegram down town asking for answer to my letter, & then brought your letter up from my office.[1]

It is all right. It is too late now to get out the annual. If I believed that writing for the Galaxy hurt the sale of ~~th~~ my books ~~without~~ anybody who didn't make that excuse simply because they wanted an excuse of *some* kind, I would retire from the magazine to-morrow. But I cannot believe it. It is a good advertisement for me—as you show when you desire me to quit the Galaxy & go on your paper.[2] But if I *am* hurting myself through the Galaxy, I want to know it—& then I will draw out of that & write for *no* periodical—for ~~certainly~~ I have chewed & drank & sworn, habitually, & have discarded them all, & am well aware that a bad thing should be killed entirely—*tapering off* is a foolish & dangerous business.[3]

A week or ten days ago I notified the Galaxy that my year would end with the April number, & although I hated to quit I might find it necessary, because the magazine interfered so much with other work & I half expected to lecture a little next year. I enclose the answer,, just received.

Tell Frank to be prompt with his ac/[4]—my expenses have been as high as $600 & $700 a month, latterly, because of sickness & funerals, & I don't allow my wife to help pay my bills.

Yrs

Clemens

[*enclosure:*]

OFFICE OF THE ARMY AND NAVY JOURNAL,[5]
39 PARK ROW, NEW YORK.

22[d]

Dear Twain:

The portrait is all right. I will give it to the engraver immediately.

We wont talk about your giving up at the end of the year. It is something not to be even thought of for a moment.[6]

Truly Yours

F. P. Church.

[*letter docketed:*] √ [*and*] Mark Twain | Oct 26/70

[1] That is, Bliss's reply to Clemens's letter of 13 October. Neither it nor Clemens's telegram, probably sent for him by his coachman, Patrick McAleer, is known to survive.

[2] Bliss's current house paper was the *Author's Sketch Book*, which he replaced in 1871 with the *American Publisher* (21? Sept 70 to Bliss, n. 1). In addition to objecting to "Mark Twain's Annual—1871," proposed in Clemens's letter of 13 October, on the grounds that it would cut into sales of *The Innocents Abroad*, Bliss must have reminded Clemens of his 15 July book contract with the American Publishing Company. It stipulated that he was "not to write or furnish manuscript for any other book unless for said company during the preparation & sale of said manuscript & book" (Appendix E). Clemens was disinclined to be entirely restricted by that provision, however. Although he abandoned the annual, in December 1870 he contracted with its would-be publishers, Sheldon and Company of New York, for *Mark Twain's (Burlesque) Autobiography and First Romance*. And on 29 December, still wishing to republish the old articles that would

have been included in the annual, he contracted with the American Publishing Company for a sketches volume (see *ET&S1*, 435).

³Clemens had discarded these habits to please three women: Jane Lampton Clemens, Olivia Langdon, and Mary Mason Fairbanks (13 Jan 70 to OLL; *L2*, 122, 134, 166, 222, 234, 284, 295, 353, 354; *L3*, 76 n. 3, 90, 178, 436).

⁴The statement of fifth quarter sales of *The Innocents Abroad*, due at the end of October. Clemens acknowledged receipt of it in his letter of 7 November to Bliss.

⁵This "great weekly unofficial spokesman of the military establishment of the United States" was published by Francis P. Church and his brother, William, who had founded the magazine in 1863 and remained its editor until 1917 (Mott 1938, 547).

⁶Nevertheless, Clemens's last "Memoranda" appeared in the April 1871 *Galaxy*, just a year after his debut.

To Iretus G. Cardner
26 October 1870 • Buffalo, N.Y.
(MS: ODaU)

Buf. Oct. 26.

How men do lose their tempers without any absolute necessity for it! Why, I sent for that bill from St Louis Mo., more than 3 years ago, & there never was a bill in the world that I would have paid with more alacrity or felt more as if I had got my money's worth. I am very careless, heedless, forgetful, & all that, but never had any desire to defraud you for affording me intelligent & efficient relief on that needful occasion. So you were all wrong when you got angry about it—it was fooling away good vigorous indignation that could have been used on some fellow that felt guilty, & then it would have had a deal more effect. However, if you enjoy getting out of temper, level it all at me—I don't mind it. Newspaper abuse has made me callous, & so if I can be useful to you as a target, in further payment of a bill that has run so disgracefully ~~long, I suppose I had as well~~ long, my moral alligator-skin is at your service.

~~Bet~~ But seriously I am a good deal more annoyed at this bill ~~have~~ having run all these years than I am at your remarks. I should hate to give a man my time & services in good faith & then have to wait 3½ years for my pay. I can comprehend the situation.

Saml. L. Clemens.

Dr. Cardner.[1]

[1] Clemens must have consulted Cardner, a New York City physician, shortly before departing New York on 3 March 1867 for a visit of nearly six weeks with Jane Lampton Clemens and Pamela A. Moffett in St. Louis. The unidentified ailment Cardner treated possibly was the same one Clemens had first complained of in late 1866 (*L1*, 363, 371; *N&J1*, 244 n. 3, 245, 268, 270, 275; Wilson: 1866, 163; 1870, 186; *L2*, 1, 18 n. 1, 21).

To Elisha Bliss, Jr.
28 October 1870 • Buffalo, N.Y.
(MS: NN-B)

Buf. Oct. 28.

Friend Bliss:

Please forward a copy of "Innocents" to my friend Mortimoreer Thomson, "better known," (as they have the thrice-infernal fashion of saying of me,) as "Q. K. Philander Doesticks, P.B.,"[1]

He has gone to his reward——I mean he has been promoted from literature to politics, & is now storekeeper of a U. S. Bonded Warehouse[2]—& may be President of the United States, yet, for all *we* know, for there is no telling how these things will end.

Anyway, you send the book to him. The book will not obstruct his political advancement,—unless it makes him too virtuous. Of course you can use your pleasure about sending it yourself or ordering it through your N. Y. agency—but send it.[3] His ͵Thomson's͵ address is:

42 ͵45͵ WATER STREET, NEW YORK.

Yrs
Clemens.

[*letter docketed:*] √ [*and*] Mark Twain | Oct 28/70 | Author

¹On 21 October, journalist, satirist, and humorous lecturer Mortimer Neal Thomson (1831–75) had sent Clemens a lengthy appeal, which read in part:

> When we met here in 186 whatever it was, 68 I believe, you told me you were going to go off in the Quaking City—you stated that if there was any book-matter in the journey, the ship, the people, or the heathen lands and the inhabitants thereof, you proposed to extract the same and build a book— You said also that I, even *I* should be favored with a copy of the said volume without money and without price and with the autograph of the Author put in in the appropriate places . . .
> Very well—the book is built—the architecture is complete but nary a copy have I—not a cop-
> Now Marcus, this is not fair—that book I want—that book I must have—and, do you think I am so wild, so insane as to go and pay money for a funny book, when I have made funny (?) books my own self! Not very much— (CU-MARK, in Lorch 1949, 447–48)

²Part of the "UNITED STATES INTERNAL REVENUE, COLLECTOR'S OFFICE, 32D DISTRICT, N. Y." (envelope return address, Thomson to SLC, 21 Oct 70, CU-MARK).

³Bliss apparently sent Thomson an order on his New York agent—B. Schenck, otherwise unidentified, at 114 Broadway. After using it to redeem the book, Thomson thanked Clemens in a letter of 5 November, complaining facetiously that he had had to pay thirty cents shipping charges. He enclosed the "chirographic outrage your Publisher attempted to inflict on me as your genuine autograph," pointing out that "they've put a 't' in your name—just as many folks, including Sam'l Clemens, put a 'p' in *my* name." The autograph was in Bliss's hand (CU-MARK, in Lorch 1949, 449; "Advertisements," *Author's Sketch Book* 1 [Nov 70]: 3).

⁴Thomson's warehouse address. He lived at 119 Dekalb Avenue, in Brooklyn (Wilson 1871, 1143).

To Elisha Bliss, Jr.
29 October 1870 • Buffalo, N.Y.
(MS: Daley)

Buf. Oct. 29.

Friend Bliss—

I got the poster & Sketch-Book. They are fine.¹

Colonel Albert S. Evans's trip through Mexico! Who made him a *Colonel?* ~~A regular dead beat of the first water—or rather a literary fraud—an excessively~~ A one-horse newspaper reporter, who has been trying all his life to make a joke & never has & never *will* succeedss. A

Colonel! He would run from a sheep. *I* know him like a book. You publishers are pretty hard up for books, Bliss, I am dreadfully afraid, when our friend the "Col." must be called in to help. And don't he hate *me?* I should *think* so. I used to trot him out in the papers lang syne.[2]

SLC

Say, now, Bliss, if *I* were a publisher, I would send *you* a book occasionally, but here I am suffering for the "Col's" book, & for "Beyond the Missippi" & *f* for the "Indian Races," & *especially* for the "Uncivilized Races," & [you] never say "boo" about sending them. You must give me the "Uncivilized Races["] & the "Col's," anyhow.[3]

Yrs

Mark.   (over)

My wife has been sick abed for a week, but is much better now.[4]

Ys

Mark.

[*letter docketed:*] √ [*and*] Mark Twain | Oct 29/70

[1] The poster may have been along the lines Clemens suggested on 22 September or a version of the circular Bliss had prepared in June (27 June 70, 22 Sept 70, both to Bliss). The November 1870 *Author's Sketch Book*—the only number of this American Publishing Company paper issued—included extracts from chapters 19 and 39 of *The Innocents Abroad* ("New Books," 1:3).

[2] See 28 Jan 70 to Bliss, n. 1. Evans's *Our Sister Republic: A Gala Trip Through Tropical Mexico in 1869–70* had been published by the Columbian Book Company of Hartford, a subsidiary of the American Publishing Company established on 2 March 1870 and managed by Richard Woolworth Bliss (b. 1826), Elisha's younger brother, who was its secretary and treasurer. The *Author's Sketch Book* prominently advertised Evans's volume ("Our Sister Republic," "Advertisements," "A New and Timely Book," 1:2, 3, 4; Geer 1870, 57, 91, 435, 508; "Hartford Residents," Bliss Family, 2).

[3] Albert Deane Richardson's *Beyond the Mississippi* (1867; expanded edition 1869), Charles De Wolf Brownell's *The Indian Races of North and South America* (1865), and John George Wood's *The Uncivilized Races, or Natural History of Man* (1870) were all published by the American Publishing Company. For discussion of Clemens's use of Wood's and Richardson's books in the writing of *Roughing It*, see *RI 1993*, 575–76, 579, 597, 600, 605–6, 610–11, 635, 683–84, 695, 705–6, 820–21.

[4] Olivia Clemens had almost given birth prematurely, probably on the night of 19 October (5 Nov 70 to OC, n. 5).

To Elisha Bliss, Jr.
31 October 1870 • Buffalo, N.Y.
(MS facsimile: CU-MARK)

Buf. 31[st.]

Friend Bliss—

Oh, I didn't mean to attribute selfish motives to you. I *did* ask you for an honest opinion, & got it, & was perfectly satisfied with it & cheerfully *acted* upon it. Since which the subject hasn't entered my mind once, but was dropped, & permanently. All I wanted to know was, whether to do or *not* do the thing I had in mind[1]—it didn't cost a pang to give it up.

Say, for instance—I have a brother about 45—an old & able writer & editor. He is night editor of the Daily St Louis Democrat, & is gradually putting his eyes out at it. He has served four years as Secretary of State of Nevada, having been appointed to the place by Mr. Lincoln— he had all the financial affairs of the Territory in his hands during that time & came out with the name of an able, honest & every way competent officer. He is well read in law, & I think understands book-keeping. He is a very valuable man for any sort of *office* work, but not worth a cent *outside* as a business man. Now I would like to get him out of night-work but haven't any other sort to offer him myself. Have *you* got a place for him at $100 or $150 a month, in your ~~em~~ office? Or has your brother?[2] Let me hear from you shortly, & do try & see if you can't give him such a place.

I am very sorry to hear of your sickness, indeed, but am always expecting it, you work & drive & hurry so.

When is your paper coming out? Did you ever receive the article I sent you for it from Fredonia? Tell me.[3]

Yrs

Clemens.

[*letter docketed:*] Mark Twain | Oct 31/70 | Author

[1] Clemens's proposed comic annual (13 Oct 70, 26 Oct 70, both to Bliss).
[2] See 29 Oct 70 to Bliss, n. 2, and 3 May 71 to Bliss, n. 1.

³For Bliss's reply, see the enclosure with 5 Nov 70 to OC. Apparently Bliss was already planning the *American Publisher,* his replacement for the just-issued *Author's Sketch Book.*

To Iretus G. Cardner
2 November 1870 • Buffalo, N.Y.
(MS: Fox)

Buffalo, Nov. 2.

Dᴿ J. G. Cardner
    Dear Sir:
        Yours of 29ᵗʰ is to hand & all is right & pleasant except that the latter portion of it speaks as if you had not received the money I sent, viz., $31.50—consisting of a $20, a $10, a $1, & a 50ᶜ bill. How is ~~the~~ that? Was not the money & your bill in my letter?¹ ~~And if not was~~
    Please answer with all convenient dispatch.
                        Yrs Truly
                        ₐS. L.ₐ Clemens

¹See 26 Oct 70 to Cardner.

To Orion Clemens
5 November 1870 • Buffalo, N.Y.
(MS: NPV and CU-MARK)

Buf. 5ᵗʰ·

My Dear Bro:
    Pamela said the other day that if you only had *easy work* at $100 a month, no night work, ~~plent~~ liberty after supper to rest & work at your machine, it was about what was required.¹ I could give you an editor's berth on the paper, but it would be night work—so I wrote my publisher to look around & see if he had any work indoors that you could do for $100 a month,—for I knew he had no high-priced employments—one girl is all he needs in the office.²

But he is going to issue a *monthly gratuitous paper,* say about 100,000 copies, to advertise his books in, & will get all his authors to contribute occasional articles. He believes he can eventually put a *price* on it & make it a lucrative literary sheet. Well, you see he offers you the editorship of it at $100 a month till he can do better by you. It gives you a chance to *make* him do better by you,—I mean by proving yourself indispensable—,& that is the only ~~way~~ terms on which ~~an ambitious man~~ a man ought to want preferment. You will probably have precious little work to do on a monthly sheet, but ~~it~~ the work can be done all the better for that,—& besides, it gives the *machine* a chance. I desire that you throw up that cursed night work & take this editorship & conduct it so well that editorships will *assail* you at the end of a year. It is an easy thing to do. Bliss offered me in effect $4,000 a year to ~~edit~~ take this berth he offers you—& so he has confidence in his little undertaking.[3] He ~~sh~~ is shrewdly counting on two things, now—one is, by creating a position for you, he will keep me from "whoring after strange gods,"[4] which is Scripture for deserting to other publishers; &, 2[d], get an occasional article out of me for the paper, a thing which would be *exceedingly* occasional otherwise. He is wise. He is one of the smartest business men in America, & I am only a dullard when I try to ~~pierce~~ conceive *all* the advantages ₐhe₍ expects to derive from having you in the employ of the Am. Pub. Co. But all right—I am willing. Only I know this—that if you take this place, with an air of *perfect confidence* in yourself, never once letting anything show in your bearing but a quiet, modest, entire & perfect confidence in your ability to do *pretty much anything in the world,* Bliss will think you are the very man he needs—but *don't* show any shadow of timidity or unsoldierly diffidence, for that sort of thing is fatal to advancement. I warn you ~~this~~ thus because you are naturally given to knocking your pot over in this way when a little judicious conduct would make it boil. And I am writing all this about a ~~matter~~ situation of apparently precious little consequence~~fidence~~ because I am looking at the *possibilities* of the place, not the place itself & its meagre salary.

———⁓———

Whenever you are ready to come, write me & I will send $100 to pay your passages to Fredonia—for *we* probably cannot receive anybody for a month or two—I am trying to keep Livy's mother away, & *have* telegraphed her brother not to come—(he meant to stay over Sunday.) Livy narrowly escaped miscarriage a fortnight ago. I have moved her—

bed & all—down stairs into the library, & there I mean she shall stay till her confinement in December.[5] Annie will be here tomorrow to stay a day or two, for her mother has been here so long I could not ~~dem~~ deny her—& besides Annie & Livy know each other well & so it won't excite or fatigue Livy to see her.

I should think that if Pamela remains here you might leave Mollie at Fredonia till you go to Hartford & get things ready & then write for her to follow.

I have told Bliss *positively* that you are *an able editor* & I don't want you by word or gesture to show any lack of confidence or any diffidence about assuming responsibility. This will seal *his* confidence, *sure.*

Yr Bro.
Sam.

[*enclosure:*]

Htf. Nov. 2. 70

Dear Twain

Yours recd   Yes I got your article. *"It is accepted"* (a. la. N.Y. Ledger)[6] Thanks for same—

Paper will be out last of the month—[7]

How would your Bro. do for an editor of it—?

Would he be satisfied with $100. per month for present, until we could do better by him—?—

You see we have no real place just now for him, but would like for *your sake* to *create a position* for him, if possible—would this do? perhaps if here by & by we could see some opening which would pay good— ,[I guess ~~he has an~~ " it is safe to trust him to find "openings" if ~~enoug~~ if you & he get along well together.],

Say! Is he anything like his younger brother—?

When does he want to leave St Louis,?

Tell me what you want, &, what you think about it &c &c—

Truly
Bliss

P. S. Maybe Bliss isn't ready for you immediately—shall hear from him again in 2 or 3 days.

Sam.

Bliss is the ,very, livest kind of a Yankee business man. Don't reveal anything to him about your main, big machine, but at the proper time if there is any money or any success in it you can just rely on him every time to *get it out of it,*—a thing which you inventors *never* are worth a cent at attempting.,

Sam.

You don't want a European patent—it isn't worth fifteen cents.

[1] Probably Orion's drilling machine, but possibly one of his other inventions (12 June 70 to PAM, n. 6).

[2] "Miss Nellie" (22 Jan 70 to Bliss, n. 7).

[3] The offer cannot be confirmed, even "in effect," in any of Bliss's few surviving 1870 letters to Clemens. Later, however, Bliss offered Clemens substantially more for contributions to this new "*monthly gratuitous paper,*" the *American Publisher* (27 Jan 71 to Bliss, n. 1).

[4] A paraphrase of a recurrent biblical locution, for example: Exodus 34:15 and 16, Deuteronomy 31:16, Judges 2:17, and 1 Chronicles 5:25.

[5] According to Clemens's 12 November letter to the Twichells, it was Olivia's "hurried drive to the depot one day" that nearly caused her to give birth prematurely. In 1906 he recalled that:

> We had a visitor in the house and when she was leaving she wanted Mrs. Clemens to go to the station with her. I objected. But this was a visitor whose desire Mrs. Clemens regarded as law. The visitor wasted so much precious time in taking her leave that Patrick had to drive in a gallop to get to the station in time. In those days the streets of Buffalo were not the model streets which they afterward became. They were paved with large cobblestones, and had not been repaired since Columbus's time. Therefore the journey to the station was like the Channel passage in a storm. The result to Mrs. Clemens was a premature confinement, followed by a dangerous illness. (AD, 15 Feb 1906, CU-MARK, in *MTE*, 249–50)

The departing guest almost certainly was Mary Mason Fairbanks. Clemens's letters to her of 13 October and 5 November indicate that she visited Buffalo sometime between those dates. Moreover, the "gallop" to the depot—with Langdon Clemens's arrival nearly coming, as Clemens told the Twichells, "that night"— must have occurred no later than 19 October, since the baby was "staved off" and "missed the earthquake" that struck the following morning.

[6] This Saturday paper, founded in 1844, serialized popular fiction and had a large circulation—making it a model for Bliss's planned paper (Mott 1950, 299–300, 319; Rowell, 702; Hudson, 646–55).

[7] In fact the first number of the *American Publisher* was for April 1871 and issued in March. The article Bliss acknowledged here doubtless was the unidentified piece that Clemens had sent from Fredonia at the beginning of October. It may have been among the sketches that he soon asked to have returned (31 Oct 70 to Bliss; 22 Feb 71 to OC). For the sketch by him that appeared in the first *American Publisher,* see 4 Mar 71 to OC, n. 3.

To Elisha Bliss, Jr.
5 November 1870 • Buffalo, N.Y.
(MS: NN-B)

Buf. Nov. 5.

Friend Bliss:

It is a splendid idea! He will ~~mad~~ make a tip-top editor—a better than I, because he is full of talent & besides is perfectly faithful, honest, straightforward & reliable. There isn't money enough in America to get him to do a dishonest act—whereas I am different. You just take him in hand & laugh with him & talk with him & keep him jolly, & I will answer for his editorial ability. I don't fancy that you will have much trouble keeping him jolly, either, though he is not quite so sprightly & idiotic as I am. I find he is getting $1,300 a year where he is, but if you can't stand the extra hundred, I'll pay it. He gets $25 a week = $1,300 a year.

I have written him to let me know how soon he can come on, & have advised him to leave his wife here or at Fredonia with my sister till he goes to Hartford & arranges for board or house-rent.

I guess that after you have had him a year you will find that he is really worth a deal of money to you—I am well enough satisfied of it to bet money on it.

Well I thank you very much, Bliss, ~~I'd~~ & I hope that results will in every way justify your kindness & leave you nothing to regret in the matter.

~~Ys~~ Yrs
Clemens.

[*letter docketed:*] Mark Twain | Nov 5/70 | Author

To Mary Mason Fairbanks
5 November 1870 • Buffalo, N.Y.
(MS: CSmH)

Buf. Nov. 5.

Dear Mother:

Livy is doing pretty well—doctor says ⨍ she may drive a hundred yards every day, but I am a little afraid of it.

I want you back ⨦ here just as quick as you can get through there at home. Susie will wait till then. Theodore appears to have mysteriously decided not to spend Sunday here—for which I am duly thankful. But he will die if he has to go ten days without seeing Sue. Charley writes me privately that Theodore remarked, when Sue came here, that "every time any of them in Buffalo had the stomach ache his wife had to go up there"—& intimated that he was tired of it. So you see we naturally want to send Sue home to the calf as soon as possible.[1]

Come along here, now, as soon as possible, & prune my manuscript. Don't delay.

Love to all of you from both [of] us, & hearty congratulations likewise for Allie, & full sympathy with her in her fair dreams of a fair future.[2]

Lovingly Yr Son
Saml.

P. S. I am *real* sorry I wrote that letter.[3]

---

[1] Susan Crane had arrived in Buffalo at the earliest on 29 October; she remained until 12 November (12 Nov 70 to the Twichells).
[2] See 13 Oct 70 to Fairbanks, n. 1.
[3] Unidentified.

To Olivia Lewis Langdon
per Telegraph Operator
7 November 1870 • Buffalo, N.Y.
(MS, copy received: CtHMTH)

THE WESTERN UNION TELEGRAPH COMPANY.

DATED[1]   Buffalo 7th ˏNov^rˏ   187 0

RECEIVED AT   2-50 PM 7—

TO   Mrs J Langdon

Elmira

Langdon Clemens was born at eleven this morning mother & child doing well.[2] Mr Fairbanks[3] is coming.

Saml L Clemens

17 DH Paid—

J/n

[*telegram docketed:*] Theodore | Please preserve this | O. L.[4]

[1] "Nov^r" was added in pencil by an unidentified hand.

[2] The baby had not been expected until around the first week in December. Mrs. Langdon replied to Clemens's telegram with a telegram of her own, later the same afternoon: "The Mothers and Grandmas blessing on mother and child"—referring to herself and to her mother-in-law, Eunice Ford. Olivia Clemens preserved her mother's telegram in her commonplace book (CU-MARK).

[3] The telegrapher's error: Clemens had summoned *Mrs.* Fairbanks. On 8 November, clearly replying to a 7 November cable from him, she sent a telegram that Olivia preserved in her commonplace book (CU-MARK): " 'Heres to you & your **family** may they live long & prosper' hope to Dine with you saturday next at six Pm will arrive on five oclock train." Then—presumably responding to a letter, now lost, that Clemens wrote in Langdon's voice (see 11 Nov 70 to Eunice Ford and 12 Nov 70 to the Twichells)—Mrs. Fairbanks sent the following letter, which Olivia also preserved in her commonplace book:

(F)

Cleveland Nov. 11th

My Dear Langdon

I am delighted to learn of your safe arrival, and gratified that you should have so promptly reported yourself to me, your venerable relative—on your father's side.

Evidently however, you are a stranger in these parts, and are not familiar with my *idiosyncrasies*, else your ~~would~~ first greeting would not have been so *familiar* or so *slangey.* Your father ought to have told you, that I am opposed to every thing of the kind. He has had good reason to know. It may seem a little severe that I should caution you so soon, but my rigid ideas of propriety must be considered.

I fully intended to be among the first to welcome you to this planet, but you have been somewhat irregular in your movements,—another marked resemblance to the head of the house. I flatter myself, that your very early acquaintance with *me,* will serve as a healthful and counteracting influence against the besetments of your daily association with your literary parent. I propose to make myself to you, "a bright and shining light," and to assume the p[r]erogative of all grandmothers, (when they first are introduced to their new responsibilities,) of annihilating in your nature all tendencies that ~~point~~ remind me of your father's short-comings.

Without doubt, you and I have a mission! *Mine* to advocate certain principles—*Yours* to illustrate said principles.

I infer from your *over-coat,* that you are not pompous or foppish in your style, and have at once adopted a simplicity of costume which is commendable.

I have resolved to present myself to you to-morrow, for a brief interview. Possibly you will not drive to the depot for me, but on this occasion, I will waive the ceremony. I am already arranging for you to spend your college vacations with us. I have spoken only of your *father,* because in my introduction to his son, I have felt impressed with the importance of at once *revising* and *correcting* this *pocket edition.*

Of your sweet mother, I have only now to add, the **more** you have of her nature, the *less* I shall have to do. Put your tiny hand up to her neck, and tell her as she kisses & fondles it to remember, that I am sharing her joy with her.

Your very loving Grandmother

The allusion to Langdon's *"over-coat"* suggests that Clemens's lost letter included a drawing, probably like the ones sent to Susan Crane on 19–20? November. Mrs. Fairbanks arrived on Saturday, 12 November, and returned to Cleveland before 19 November (12 Nov 70 to the Twichells; 19 Nov 70 to Fairbanks).

[4]Langdon Clemens was Olivia Lewis Langdon's first grandchild. Susan (her foster daughter) and Theodore Crane, married since 1858, were, and remained, childless.

To Elisha Bliss, Jr.
7 November 1870 • Buffalo, N.Y.
(MS: CU-MARK)

Buf. Nov. 7. 1870.

Friend Bliss:

This is to acknowledge recpt of your draft for ~~$~~ $835 & odd cents. for which I thank you. Statement all O. K.[1]

Born to us this day, a *boy.* Mother & child doing only tolerably well but we hope for the best. *Tell the Twichells.*

Yrs in haste
Clemens.

✉

[*letter docketed:*] ✓ [*and in ink:*] Mark Twain | Nov 7/70 | Author

[1] The check and statement were for fifth quarter (1 Aug–31 Oct 70) sales of *The Innocents Abroad*, amounting to about 5,000 copies (Hirst 1975, 317). Since the corresponding royalty would have been about $1,000, Bliss may have made some deductions, including the cost of books Clemens had recently requested (21? Sept 70, 28 Oct 70, and 29 Oct 70, all to Bliss).

To James Redpath
8 November 1870 • Buffalo, N.Y.
(Boston *Morning Journal,* 9 Nov 70)

A son was born to me yesterday, & with the true family instinct he has gone to lecturing already. His subject is the same as Josh Billings's— "*Milk.*"[1] You are hereby constituted his agent, & instructed to make arrangements with Lyceums.[2]

S. L. Clemens.

[1] This popular lecture, sometimes called "Milk and Natral Histry," was a rambling discourse in which Billings made only teasing reference to his nominal subject (*L3*, 397 n. 3; Kesterson, 109–12, 117–18).

[2] The Boston *Morning Journal* published the telegram with the following preface:

> THE RULING PASSION STRONG IN—BIRTH. The Boston Lyceum Bureau has just received the following telegram, dated Buffalo, Nov. 8, from the famous humorist and lecturer, Mark Twain: ("Boston and Vicinity," 9 Nov 70, 2)

For details of the telegram's reprinting, see the textual commentary.

To Whitelaw Reid
per Telegraph Operator
8 November 1870 • (1st of 2) • Buffalo, N.Y.
(Paraphrase: New York *Tribune,* 9 Nov 70)

Mark Twain telegraphed last night from Buffalo, in answer to a frantic demand from THE TRIBUNE for election returns, that he had a son just born to him and had to play nurse, a vocation which he seemed to think preferable to that of reporter. We congratulate Mark, and know

that nothing short of so momentous an event could have interfered with
his devotion to our interests, or lured him away from the exciting study
of election returns.[1]

[1] On 6 November Reid had written Clemens:

> I don't credit you with as profound a knowledge of election returns as would be nec-
> essary to constitute you editor of *The Tribune* Almanac, but you must have some person
> who can send us good dispatches on election night. I append a copy of a letter which
> we are sending out to friends in every district in the State. If you can't do this for us
> yourself won't you please put it into the hands of some trusty person . . . (Reid's copy
> of letter, without enclosure, DLC)

The *Tribune* report of Clemens's telegram was widely reprinted: for details see
the textual commentary.

To Whitelaw Reid
8 November 1870 • (2nd of 2) • Buffalo, N.Y.
(MS: DLC)

                                                   Buffalo, Nov. 8.
Friend Reid:

As per my telegram to you, I am confined at home, to-day, giving
the weight of my experience to the care of our new baby, (mother & child
doing well,) but I have instructed our political man to send you the election returns.[1]

By this mail I send a photograph & autograph to you, & a large one
& a small one to ˌforˌ your friend,[2] in the same package.

With all good wishes

                                                   Yr friend
                                                   Sam⁽. L. Clemens.

[1] On 9 November, the day after the elections, Josephus N. Larned, the Buffalo
Express's political editor, assessed the outcome. His editorial indicates why the
New York *Tribune*, like the *Express* a reformist Republican paper, was anxious
to have the earliest Buffalo returns:

> The corrupt money power of Tammany has again overcome us in the State, notwith-
> standing a material reduction made in the former frauds of the metropolis. This time
> the "rural districts," as they term the outside State in New York city, appears to be

wholly responsible for our defeat. General Apathy, in fact, has had too extensively the command of the Republican forces.

In this county we have lost our Congressman without a doubt, . . . The whole county ticket, in fact, is gone, and we save nothing from the wreck. (Larned 1870d)

And on 11 November he informed *Express* readers: "It is in the State of New York, alone, that the Republican party retreats from a disastrous field, with broken and disordered columns" (Larned 1870e).

[2]Unidentified. The photographs presumably were prints of one or both of those Clemens had recently taken (20? May 70 to Paige; 8 July 70 to OLC, n. 3).

To Orion Clemens
11 November 1870 • Buffalo, N.Y.
(MS: CU-MARK)

Buffalo, Nov. 11.

My Dear Bro:

You have got the same curious ideas that all novices have—you must stipulate *before*hand whic what shall be done *in case* you prove a literary treasure. Hang it, man, ten thousand such stipulations would be worthless. It is simply absurd for one man to try to *bargain* such a thing out with another—your work must not only show you to be worth more money, but must is itself *compel* its price. If you would rather be slave all night in St Louis for $8 more a month than do easy & gentlemanly work in Hartford in daylight, I applaud your wisdom & say nothing against it. I will only remark that Bliss offers you, as I as exactly three times as much as the work is worth. I would take the job myself at less money if I were living in Hartford & my name did not appear as editor.

I have never intended to intimate that *this* work was worth $100 a month, but meant to intimate that it could be made a stepping stone & opportunity to make you known & valuable. My *name* to it is what Bliss was willing to [pay] $4,000 for.

But I will remark that when I discovered, before Pamela went away, that your present pay was $108 a month instead of $100, I wrote ⫫ Bliss that if you went there he could pay you $108 a month & charge the ⫫ $8 to me. But *I* would rather live on $100 a month & live like a human being, than have ⫫ $8 more & live like an owl.[1]

I do *resent* that idea of stipulating for advance of wages IN CASE a man is worth, it. I haven't had anything incense me so in six months. Might as well stipulate that one should have *two* ⱨ golden harps hereafter before know under certain conditions, before finding out whether he is going to be able to play acceptably on *one* first.

I have thought that the proper way ẃ to get you east will be for the "Democrat" people to get ˏfreeˎ passes for both of you over the roads clear to Hartford.[2] They can do it easily & thought to do it. I say all this because I find my expenses in one way or another are stretching up in the neighborhood of a thousand dollars a month, & I have foolishly cripp[l]ed myself by paying one man $5,000 who was not in a hurry & by lending another man $4,000 who pays me nothing more than legal interest.[3] But ˏAndˎ I am looking for ∕ heavy bills to come in during the next few weeks—a four or five hundred-dollar doctor's bill, a sixty-dollar nurse bill, a hundred & seventy-dollar∕ sleigh-bill, a two-hundred dollar life-insurance bill,[4] a three-hundred dollar carpenter's bill, & a dozen or two of twenty-five dollar debts, & we owe the servants seven hundred dollars which they can call for at any time—*& I am sitting still with idle hands*—for Livy is very sick & I do not believe the baby will live five days.[5]

Under which circumstances get those ˏfreeˎ passes if you can, but if you can't, then let me know & I will provide the money. I didn't expect quite such an avalanche of bills at a time when my household expenses are so greatly augmented. I will not allow me myself to be caught in such a close place again. Of course I can *borrow* all the money I want, but I will saw wood before I will borrow.

Do just as you please about the Tenn. land—always.

I am glad you have sent such full Nevada notes[6]—though as they have just come & I am stealing a few minutes from the sick room to answer a pile of business letters, I haven't read a sentence of them yet

Yr Bro

ˏin haste   Sam

P. S. Wait till I hear again from Bliss.

---

[1] See 5 Nov 70 to OC and 5 Nov 70 to Bliss.

[2] The St. Louis *Missouri Democrat* employed Orion as night editor.

[3] In April 1870 Clemens had made a loan, of only $3,000, however, to Josephus N. Larned. He had probably paid $5,000 to Jervis Langdon before Langdon's

death on 6 August. By the end of 1871 Clemens had repaid the entire $12,500 Langdon had advanced in 1869 for his Buffalo *Express* purchase (16 and 17 Apr 70 to the Langdons; 28 Dec 71 to OLC, n. 4).

[4]In fact Clemens paid the annual premium of $187.60 on his $10,000 life insurance policy on 7 November. In 1871 he allowed the policy to lapse (*L3*, 387, 389–90 n. 6).

[5]Langdon Clemens's condition had become critical on 9 November, but evidently improved very shortly after Clemens wrote this letter (11 Nov 70 to Brooks; 12 Nov 70 to Redpath).

[6]Complements to the memorandum book Orion had sent in July. Clemens misplaced the notes, perhaps before he had a chance to use them in writing *Roughing It* (15 July 70 to OC; 27 July 70 to JLC and family; 2 Sept 70 to OC; 4 Apr 71 to OC; *RI 1993*, 822).

To Fidele A. Brooks
11 November 1870 • Buffalo, N.Y.
(Buffalo *Courier*, 26 Dec 70)

.   .   .   .

He, fancyfying that people down here dress the same as they do up there, has come without his bandbox; & I wish you would buy him a cloak & cap, & order the groceryman that you buy them of to send them express to me.[1]

.   .   .   .

[1]The Buffalo *Courier* reported that Mark Twain made these remarks about his baby "in a letter to a friend." The recipient may have been Fidele A. Brooks, a New York acquaintance he had made through the Langdons. On 12 November she wrote to him, celebrating Langdon Clemens's recovery and remarking: "We all cry hurrah for cap and cloak. It sounds like coming down to see *Aunt Fidele*. Tell Livy I will buy out Stewarts for her. Anything, everything that she may desire she shall have. The dear little mother" (preserved in Olivia Clemens's commonplace book, CU-MARK). The *Courier*'s source, probably one of its newspaper exchanges, has not been identified. And since Clemens sometimes repeated himself in announcing an event, it is possible that his letter was to someone other than Mrs. Brooks. Alexander T. Stewart's dry-goods emporium, built in 1862, occupied an entire block between Ninth and Tenth streets and Broadway and Fourth Avenue.

To Eunice Ford
11 November 1870 • Buffalo, N.Y.
(MS: CtHMTH)

_^*NOTICE.*—Do not tell grandma who the letter is from. Let her find
out as she goes along.

—⌇⌇—

(*c*)

Buffalo, Nov. 11.

Dear Grandma:

I have waited with some impatience to hear from you or from
some other member of the family, but up to this _^time_^ no letter has arrived for me. I have received enthusiastic notice in telegrams from Cleveland & in congratulations from Mr. Brooks in New York—& the telegrams from Elmira have been gladly received & carefully ~~prefer~~
preserved.[1] But from you personally, ~~ha~~ I have not heard, at least in the
shape of a letter, & I am obliged to say that I am hurt at it. Every now &
then I think it all over & then I comprehend that you cannot write in
these latter years without great difficulty.[2] Of course that makes me feel
better about it, but it does not last long. I soon get to worrying again &
saying to myself that you might have written me *one* line at least. But
never mind, I know it is all just as it should be, & that you have neglected
me not because you *desired* to do it, but because you could not well *help*
it. For I will not believe but that you love me. I am four days old to-day
at eleven o'clock. Do you recollect when *you* were only 4 days old? I'
guess you don't. I am looking for Granny Fairbanks tomorrow, & will
be glad to see her, too, but I shall be outrageously sorry to part with Aunt
Susie Crane, for she was here when I first came, & ~~ha~~ I have come to like
her society very much, & she knows my disposition better than anybody
except Auntie Smith.[3]

I am boarding with a strange young woman by the name of Brown,
& *her* baby is boarding with my mother. I expect Mrs. Brown could take
several more boarders like me, for I am not a very hearty eater. I don't
understand this little game, but I guess it is all right. It is some little neat
trick of my father's to save expense, I fancy.

I have a ridiculous time of it with clothes. Except a shirt which aunt

Hattie[4] made for me I haven't a rag in the world that fits me. Everything is too large. You ought to see the things they call "slips." ⱥ I am only ₁8 ₐ13ₐ inches long, & these things are an as much as 3 feet. Think of it. I trip & break my neck every time I make a step, for I can't think to gather up the surplus when I am in a hurry.

I tell ₐyouₐ I am tired being bundled up head & ears nine-tenths of my time. And I don't like this thing of being stripped naked & washed. I *like* to be stripped & warmed at the stove—that is real bully—but I do despise this washing business. I never I believe it to be a gratuitous & unnecessary piece of meanness. I never see them wash the cat.

And I tell you it is dull, roosting around on pillows & rocking chairs & everybody else spinning around town having a good time. Sometimes they let that borr other baby lie on the kitchen table & wink at the sun, but bless you *I* never get a show. Sometimes I get so mad that I can*not* keep my temper or my opinion. But it only makes things worse. They call it *colic*, & give me some execrable medicine. *Colic*. Everything ⱥ is *colic*. A baby can't open its mouth about the simplest matter but up comes some wise body & says it is *wind in its bowels*. When I saw the dog ₐtheₐ first time, I made a noise which was partly fright & partly admiration—but it cost me a double dose of medicine for wind in the bowels. Does these people take me for a balloon?

I am not entirely satisfied with my complexion. I am as red as a lobster. I am ₐreallyₐ ashamed to see company. But I am perfectly satisfied with my personal appearance, for I think I look just like aunt Susie. They keep me on the shortest kind of rations, & that is one thing that don't suit the subscriber. My mother has mashed potatoes, & gruel, & tea, & toast, & all sorts of sumptuous fare, but she never gives *me* a bite— & you can risk your last dollar on it that I don't ASK for it. It would only be another case of "wind in the bowels." You'll have to excuse *me*. I am learning to keep my remarks to myself. [But between you & I, Grandma, I get the ev advantage of them occasionly—now last night I keep kept aunt Smith getting up every hour to feed me— but and between you & me ₐandₐ I wasn't hungry once.]

That doctor has just been here again. Come to ɡ play some fresh swindle on *me*, I suppose. He is the meanest looking white man I ever saw. Mind, now, this is not a̖ splenetic & prejudiced outburst, but a ȡ calm & deliberate opinion formed & founded upon careful observation. Won't I "lay" for him when I get my teeth?[5]

Good-bye Grandma, good-bye. Great love to you & grandma[6] & all the whole household.

Your loving great-grandson,
Langdon Clemens.

[1] Only one telegram from Cleveland and one from Elmira have survived (7 Nov 70 to Langdon, nn. 2–3). The congratulations from Henry J. Brooks, husband of Fidele, are now lost, but probably also came by telegram on 7 or 8 November.

[2] Eunice Ford, Langdon Clemens's eighty-eight-year-old great-grandmother, had been in a state of "almost helplessness" for the past few years, but her sense of humor reportedly remained intact (*L3*, 164–65 n. 5).

[3] The baby's regular nursemaid at this time. The title was honorary, not familial (19 Nov 70 to Langdon).

[4] Harriet (Hattie) Lewis, Olivia Clemens's maternal first cousin, had been the Clemenses' confidante during their courtship (*L3*, passim, especially 23 n. 2). She maintained a close relationship with them, recalling in 1897: "I had the pleasure of visiting them several times while they remained in Buffalo. More often after the baby came" (Paff, 8).

[5] Andrew R. Wright (1825–1900) began his medical studies in Buffalo, served as a ship's surgeon for two years, and completed his education in Paris and at the Cleveland Homeopathic College before returning to Buffalo in 1859. He practiced out of his home at 162 Pearl Street and seems to have delivered Langdon and then attended him at least until mid-March 1871 (14 Mar 71 to Crane; "Dr. A. R. Wright Dead," Buffalo *Express*, 25 Feb 1900, 13; *Buffalo Directory:* 1870, 582; 1871, 285, 613).

[6] Olivia Lewis Langdon.

To Olivia Lewis Langdon
11? November 1870 • Buffalo, N.Y.
(MS: CtHMTH)

.   .   .   .

~~mother dear, & tell Charley~~ ,& tell Charley, we reiterate our desire to pay him a liberal salary & expenses for every time he will give us a visit; with proportionate increase of pay whenever he will bring any of the rest of the home household with him.[1]

Lovingly,
Sam[1].

[1] In the missing portion of this letter Clemens may have specifically invited Mrs. Langdon and his new sister-in-law, Ida Langdon, as replacements for Susan Crane, who returned to Elmira on 12 November. See 14 Nov 70 to Langdon.

To Edwin D. White
per Telegraph Operator
11 or 12 November 1870 • Buffalo, N.Y.
(Paraphrase: Boston *Morning Journal*, 14 Nov 70)

Mark Twain sent a telegraphic dispatch, saying that he was busily engaged in singing "Rock Me to Sleep, Father," and could not possibly attend.[1]

[1]Clemens responded to the following telegram from White—a reporter for the Boston *Morning Journal* and secretary of the Boston Press Club—which reached Buffalo on the evening of 11 November and was preserved in Olivia Clemens's commonplace book: " 'The press club' Sups tomorrow Eve. Come and bring the Baby" (CU-MARK). The occasion was the club's annual dinner, at Young's Hotel, known for "its choice table" (*L3*, 395 n. 4; *Boston Directory* 1870, 692). The *Morning Journal* of 14 November may have paraphrased the actual telegram received by White. The paraphrase printed the same day in both the Boston *Advertiser* and the *Evening Transcript* almost certainly derived from a reporter's transcription of the telegram as it was read aloud:

> Mark Twain begged to be excused on account of an engagement to perform to the tune of "Rock Me to Sleep." ("The Boston Press Club Dinner": Boston *Advertiser*, 1; Boston *Evening Transcript*, 4)

"Rock Me to Sleep, Mother," first published in 1860, had words by Elizabeth Anne Chase Akers Allen (pseudonym Florence Percy; 1832–1911) and music by Obadiah Bruen Brown (pseudonym Ernest Leslie; 1829–1901) (*NAW*, 1:36–38; *NUC*, 79:275–76, 328:239; *NCAB*, 12:256).

To James Redpath
12 November 1870 • Buffalo, N.Y.
(MS: MH-H)

Buf. 12.

Dear Redpath:

That was all right. I knew you'd print the dispatch—but next morning the little stranger's health was so precarious that I thought I would try to stop the publication, ~~merely~~ on his mother's account, for it he was taken away, all printed jokes about him would grate upon her feelings of course. But he seems to be doing pretty well, & so it was perfectly proper to print the message.[1]

I wish I could be at the Press Club dinner tonight. I have sent the boys a dispatch.[2] If I happen over to the telegraph office I will answer your letter by telegraph.

Love to you.

Yrs
Mark.

[*letter docketed:*] BOSTON LYCEUM BUREAU. REDPATH & FALL. NOV 3 1870[3] [*and*] N. Y. | Buffalo | Mark Twain | Nov. 12 '70

[1] Apparently Clemens had telegraphed on 9 November, trying to forestall publication of his previous day's telegram. Neither the 9 November telegram, nor Redpath's reply, nor the further telegram Clemens promises in the next paragraph is known to survive.
[2] The previous letter.
[3] The bureau's receipt stamp had not been properly set.

To Joseph H. and Harmony C. Twichell
12 November 1870 • Buffalo, N.Y.
(MS: CtY-BR)

Buffalo, Nov. 12.

Dear Uncle & Aunt =

I came into the world on the 7th inst., and consequently am about 5 days old, now. I have had wretched health ever since I ~~have~~ made my appearance. First one thing & then another has kept me under the weather. One hour it would be wind—next, indigestion—next, colic—& as a general thing I ~~am~~ have been chilly & uncomfortable.

I am not corpulent, nor am I robust in any way. At birth I only weighed 4½ pounds ~~wh~~ with my clothes on—& the clothes were the chief feature of the weight, too, I am obliged to confess. But I am doing finely, all things considered. I was at a standstill for 3 days & a half, but during the last 24 hours I have gained nearly an ounce, avo[i]rdupois.

They all say I look very old & venerable—& I am aware, myself, that I never smile. Life seems a serious thing, what I have seen of it—& ~~as~~ my observation teaches me that it is made up mainly of hiccups, ~~disagreeable~~ unnecessary washings, & wind in the bowels. But no doubt you, who are old, have long since grown ~~acu~~ accustomed & reconciled to what seems to me such a disagreeable novelty.

My father said, this morning, when my face was in repose & thoughtful, that I looked precisely as young Edward Twichell[1] of Hartford ~~y~~ used to look some ~~18~~ 12 months ago,—chin, mouth, forehead, expression—everything.

My little mother is very bright & cheery, & I guess she is pretty happy, but I don't know what about. She laughs a great deal, notwithstanding she is sick abed. And she eats a great deal, though she says that is because the nurse desires it. And when she has had all the nurse desires her to have, she asks for more. She is getting along very well indeed.

My aunt Susie Crane has been here some ten days or two weeks, but goes home today & ~~Mrs.~~ Granny Fairbanks of Cleveland arrives to take her place.

I was not due here ~~h~~ on this planet until ~~some~~ about ₐtheₐ first week in December, but my mother took a hurried drive to the depot one day & the consequence was that it was all the doctors & nurses could do to keep me from looking in on the family that night. But by faithful exertions they got me staved off ~~till~~ two weeks, & by jings I missed the earthquake.[2]

But we appear to be all right now, uncle, & some day we'll come & see you & my young cousins.[3]

Very lovingly,

Langdon Clemens.

P. S. Father said I had better writ/e, because you would be more interested in me, just now than in the rest of the family.

✉—————————————————————————————

[letter docketed by Joseph Twichell:] (Langdon natus)

[1] Born on 10 August 1867 ("Hartford Residents," Twichell Family, 1).

[2] The drive to the depot apparently was with Mary Mason Fairbanks on 19 October (5 Nov 70 to Orion, n. 5). The earthquake struck at about 11:15 A.M. on 20 October, jolting the northeastern and north central portion of the continent as far north as Quebec and as far west as Cincinnati. In Buffalo the tremors reportedly were "quite violent" (Buffalo *Commercial Advertiser:* "The Earth-

quake," 21 Oct 70, 3; Buffalo *Express:* "The Earthquake," 21 Oct 70, 1; "Another Earthquake!" 21 Oct 70, 2; "The Earthquake," 22 Oct 70, 1).

[3]In addition to Edward: Julia Curtis Twichell, born on 9 January 1869, and Susan Lee Twichell, born on 15 October 1870. Ultimately the Twichells had nine children, the last born in 1884 ("Hartford Residents," Twichell Family, 1).

To Jesse C. Haney
14 November 1870 • Buffalo, N.Y.
(MS: CtHSD)

Buffalo, Nov. 14.

My Dear Haney:[1]

Can't meddle with the Almanac business with a clear conscience—have had heaps of offers, but that belongs to Josh & I won't touch it.[2]

I inclose picture. I don't mind being caricatured myself, but don't put in my baby.[3] If I was sure it was going to live, I wouldn't care, but its health is so precarious that I hardly dare utter a pleasantry about the little fellow lest he pass from us & leave it looking ghastly in print.

Good luck go with you & long life attend you.

Yrs Truly

Sam[l]. L. Clemens.

[1]Haney (1829–1901) wrote and published handbooks on authorship, shorthand, memory enhancement, stammering cures, ventriloquism, horseshoeing, soap-making, and bartending. He also edited and published humor magazines, including, currently: *Nick Nax for All Creation,* the *Comic Monthly, Merryman's Monthly,* and *Haney's Journal* ("Death List of a Day," New York *Times,* 6 Aug 1901, 7; Mott 1938, 43, 180 n. 120, 183–84, 185 n. 132; "Rare Chance!" *Galaxy* 11 [Jan 71]: "Galaxy Advertiser," 14).

[2]See 13 Oct 70, 26 Oct 70, and 31 Oct 70, all to Bliss.

[3]The enclosed photograph has not been found, but was probably taken either in May or July (20? May 70 to Paige; 8 July 70 to OLC, n. 3). Haney published a "capital caricature" of Clemens, presumably based on the photograph, in the December 1870 number of the *Comic Monthly* ("Mark Twain," *Galaxy* 11 [Jan 71]: "Galaxy Advertiser," 14). No copy of the magazine has been found.

To Charles J. Langdon
14 November 1870 • Buffalo, N.Y.
(MS, draft telegram: CU-MARK)

Buf. Nov. 14/70.

Chas. J. Langdon,
        Elmira.
We are well & strong. Ł Send them along, Charley.

Clemens.[1]

3134.[2]

[1] Langdon responded on 15 November: "Your telegram is recd. *I* think mother will come before if you so choose. I have not spoken to her about it but I heard her say the other day that she had a mind to go. Ida will come as I have often told you. In fact send for any body in the family & they will gladly come to you" (CU-MARK).

[2] The telegram's record number, jotted down by Clemens.

To T. B. Pugh
14 November 1870 • Buffalo, N.Y.
(MS: Fox)

⊂c⊃

Buffalo, Nov. 14.

My Ɯ Dear Mr. Pugh =

I have a stronger desire to lecture again in Philadelphia than in any other city, not even excepting Boston itself. But piles & piles of money couldn't seduce me away from home this season! [1]

I'm a wet nurse, now, & I like it! We have got a baby & we don't want any more money nor any more glory either! Count us *out*, Mr. Pugh!

Yrs Sincerely,
        S. L. Clemens.

[1] Thomas Burnett Pugh (1829–84) was a native of Unionville, Pennsylvania, where while still a teenager he had been an ardent Abolitionist, working "with his father in rescuing slaves and passing them northward." Pugh became a Phil-

adelphia publisher and bookseller and then a lecture manager. He was instrumental in promoting Anna E. Dickinson in the early and mid-1860s and then, in 1869, founded his "Star Course" of lectures at the Academy of Music, an annual series that became "the leading intellectual institution of Philadelphia." Through it, Pugh "did more to popularize elevated entertainments; did more to keep the best always first; did more to encourage growth of intellectual life, of genius, of wit, of artistic refinement, of general education, than any manager of public entertainments whose name is recorded in the history of Philadelphia" ("Obituary. T. B. Pugh," clipping from unidentified paper, 6 June 84, in Star Course scrapbook, Philadelphia Academy of Music Archives, PH in CU-MARK, courtesy of JoAnne E. Barry). Clemens had lectured for Pugh on 7 December 1869 (*L3*, 415, 416 n. 1).

To Mary Mason Fairbanks
19 November 1870 • Buffalo, N.Y.
(MS: CSmH)

Saturday

Dear Mother:

What the "F‚at C‚ontributor" needs is not words‚, but *ideas*. Furnished with the latter, ‚he‚ appears to know as many words as anybody. You perceive by the enclosed that I have helped him to *one*. I notice on ‚an‚ average of ~~tw~~ once a month, that I have been unintentionally & unknowingly ~~con~~ pumping an idea into the head ‚of one or another‚ of the ~~family of acknowledged~~ ‚village‚ "humorists" of the land. And when I furnish them an idea & also a *model*, their article is bound to be *copied* if they stick to the model close enough. Why even the "Fat Contributor" is copied when he stays faithfully by his model & ventures on no disastrous originality.[1]

Do you know, a Philadelphia imbecile by the name of "John Quill" made quite a ~~weighty local reputation in Ameri~~ reputation for himself simply by printing articles of mine with his name to them. But when I objected, he foolishly tried to ~~write~~ write *original* articles; & lo & behold you he passed out of the ~~liera~~ literary world on his first one just as gently ~~a~~ & as peacefully as ever a dead man was toted out on a shutter.[2]

In a hurry

Yrs
Mark.

We are doing finely—baby boards ½ with his mother now, half the time. I guess I shall write tomorrow.

P. S. On second thoughts, I *publish* the article, ~~Mon~~ next Monday or Tuesday, with the added headline *"Plagiarized."* Will you copy it with that added line? ~~{try~~ I am so deliciously tempted to print this letter![3]

---

[1]Clemens had personally arranged the Buffalo *Express*'s exchange agreement with the Cincinnati *Times* as a favor to Alphonso Miner Griswold, the *Times*'s city editor (*L3*, 324). As a result he saw Griswold's "Hints to Farmers," which seemingly echoed his own "How I Edited an Agricultural Paper Once" (SLC 1870pp, 133–35). The enclosed clipping of Griswold's article does not survive, nor has a file of the Cincinnati *Times* been found, but see note 3.

[2]See 26 Apr 70 to Fuller, n. 4.

[3]The Buffalo *Express* reprinted Griswold's article on page two on Monday, 21 November:

HINTS TO FARMERS.

PLAGIARIZED.
BY THE "FAT CONTRIBUTOR."
[Written for the Cincinnati Times.]

Now that the Winter is approaching, it would perhaps be as well to discontinue haying, and turn your attention to putting in your fall saw-logs. No farmer can consider his fall work complete until he has his cellar well supplied with saw-logs. Seated around the blazing hearth of a Winter's night there is not fruit more delicious.

A correspondent asks us what we think of late plowing. Plowing should not be continued later than ten or eleven o'clock at night. It gets the horses in the habit of staying out late, and unduly exposes the plow. We have known plows to acquire springhalt and inflammatory rheumatism from late plowing. Don't do it.

To another correspondent who wants us to suggest a good drain on a farm, we would say a heavy mortgage at ten per cent. will drain it about as rapidly as anything we know of.

When you make cider select nothing but the soundest turnips, chopping them into sled length before cradling them. In boiling your cider use plenty of ice, and when boiled hang it up in the sun to dry.

A pick axe should never be used in picking apples. It has a tendency to break down the vines and damage the hive.

In sowing your Winter apple jack a horse rake will be found preferable to a step ladder. Step ladders is liable to freeze up, and are hardly palatable unless boiled with sugar.

In cutting down hemlock trees for canning select the largest. Don't throw away your chips, as they make fine parlor ornaments encased in rustic frames of salt and vinegar.

The coming cold weather should suggest to the humane farmer the necessity for a good cow-shed. The following is a receipt for making a good cow-shed: Pour a pailful of boiling hot water on her back, and if that does not make a good cow-shed—her hair— we are no prophet to anybody.

Now is the time for planting your Winter hay. The pink-eyed Southdown is probably the best variety, as it don't need poling and begins to lay early.

The *Express* did not print Clemens's letter, nor did the Cleveland *Herald* "copy" the *Express*.

To Olivia Lewis Langdon
19 November 1870 • Buffalo, N.Y.
(MS: CtHMTH)

(c)

Buf. Nov. 19.

Dear Mother:

Thank you ever so much for the apples, Lang. says they are perfectly bully—& I endorse it & so does Livy.

Please tell Charley to send me a pair of those suspenders from Covell, Fay & Co.'s[1] that require only *4 buttons,*—2 on each side & two behind—send 'em COD.

Now mother, you must hurry & get strong enough to be here on
Thanksgiving Day[2]—& *sooner* if you can, for Livy is very lonely. She lets
me go up to the study & work, (which I ought not to do & yet I am so
dreadfully behind hand that I get blue as soon as I am idle)—I go up
there & Livy sits lonely all day, for the room is dark & she cannot read—
& most of the time Mrs. Smith is out in the kitchen with the baby.

Got Hattie's letter & soap.[3] Thanks.

We will wait a while & if that letter to Grandma don't come back to
me I will copy & send it again. Could Charley ask the ₱ Postmaster at
Elmira to help trace it? I will drop the Buffalo P.M. a line. I sometimes
misdirect letters, but I can almost swear that this was distinctly directed
to "*Mrs. Eunice Ford, Elmira, N. Y.*"[4]

Lovingly Yr son

Sam*l*.

[1] The Elmira haberdashery owned by Edward Covell and Cyrus W. Fay (Boyd
and Boyd, 90).

[2] Thursday, 24 November.

[3] Possibly from Harriet Lewis (11 Nov 70 to Ford, n. 4).

[4] It is not known whether the surviving 11 November letter to Eunice Ford
was Clemens's original or a second copy.

To Susan L. Crane
19–20? November 1870 • Buffalo, N.Y.
(MS: CU-MARK)

[Sue, please return this to me.]

S.L.C.

Two Views of Langdon Clemens Thinking.

Two Views of Langdon Clemens asleep.

[*new page, in pencil:*]

~~10~~ 11 days old.
Measurements of the Baby, in inches.

———

Length 16.
Round hips 6½

Around Waist, 8½
"   Abdomen 9½ (over thick bandage.)
Around Bust 10.

Langdon Clemens

At 13 days

Around ~~writs~~ wrist—2
"   Ancle   2¼
Length of foot   ~~2½~~ 2¼

To Charles J. Langdon
20 November 1870 • Buffalo, N.Y.
(MS: CtHMTH)

Buf. 20.

Dear Bro ~~Chal~~ Charley:

We thank you ever so much for the shoes, for the baby was about out. They are not quite high enough in the instep, but the baby is ignorant & does not know that that is a defect. We will keep it quiet. The first time the baby saw the shoes he said:

"Skcull those things right over here, for I am ~~g~~ about tired going barefooted in ˄the˄ winter time, ~~like a~~ you bet your life!"

I said: "My son, slang is a thing I will *not* permit in this house."

And he replied:

"I do not wish to have any words with you, ~~old man,~~ father, but ~~if~~ whenever you find that the nature of my conversation is not suited to your appetite, ~~you~~ suppose you get up on your ear & take a walk 'round the block."

I cannot think ~~h~~ where the child got its unhappy ~~disposition~~ proclivity for slang, for from the beginning it has been my earnest endeavor to make its speech as free from anything of that kind as my own. Sometimes in the bitterness of my heart I say, "*Why* did I let him run with Susie[1] so much?"

Ellen's ~~moth~~ money was here a week before I knew anything about it—so it is all right.[2]

We *do* want Mother to hurry & come.

With great love to you all,

> Yr Bro
>
> Sam.

We sent back the deed—did you get it?[3]

[1] Crane.

[2] Ellen White, the Clemenses' housekeeper and cook, had formerly been a Langdon family servant in Elmira (6 Feb 70 to Bowen, n. 5). The payment to her has not been explained.

[3] Langdon had enclosed two deeds in his letter of 15 November 1870 to Clemens. Both evidently pertained to "some Property on R.R. Ave. adjoining the Boot & shoe manf. of D Atwater & Co," which Elmira grocer Delos Holden had purchased from Jervis Langdon, under a mortgage calling for payments of "$500. per annum with interest semi annually" (CU-MARK). One deed required Olivia Clemens's signature, as one of Langdon's heirs; the other required Clemens's signature, as one of the executors of his estate. Neither is known to survive.

To Orion Clemens
21? November 1870 • Buffalo, N.Y.
(MS: NPV)

[*on back of letter as folded:*]

I hope you will pack up & leave for Hartford *instantly* & finally.

> Yr Bro.
>
> Sam.

Be hasty. Be quick. Sell out *clean*, in St. Louis. Leave nothing for other people to attend to.

Livy & child doing tolerably.

~~Don~~ Shall you want the money?[1] If so, say it.

> { 149 Asylum St[r].[2]
> { Nov. 18. 1870

D[r] Clemens,

Have I been so stupid, as not to say to you I ∥ expect your brother *so far as we are concerned*. I thought I had said so or as much, & was waiting for report, daily as to his time of arrival &c—

He tells a good yarn in the slip sent.[3] We will give him scope for his talent here—

Wish he had been here for 10 days past. I have had a newspaper fight with Burr & Co. & all his backers over *U. Races* & have had to do it single handed, & think I came out in good standing— Another pen would have done better no doubt, had it had an experienced hand like your brother, at the end of it.[4] Wrote you yesterday— Frank says his baby is all right— so far *as heard from possibly has gained "an ounce"*[5]

> truly
>
> Bliss

[1] For travel expenses (5 Nov 70, 11 Nov 70, both to OC).

[2] The address, in Hartford, of the American Publishing Company.

[3] Possibly a clipping from the St. Louis *Missouri Democrat*, where Orion was employed. Nothing by him has been identified in the paper, however.

[4] The dispute was over American publication of John George Wood's *The Natural History of Man* (London: George Routledge and Sons, 1868–1870). The American Publishing Company had issued it as *The Uncivilized Races, or Natural History of Man* (1870)—with authorization, and printing plates, from Routledge and Sons, who wished to counter the cheap, pirated edition previously issued by John B. Burr and Company, another Hartford firm, as *The Uncivilized Races of Men in All Countries of the World* (1870). The rivals argued their editions' legitimacy, accuracy, and completeness in a series of letters to the Hartford *Courant:* "An Explanation Called For," 10 Nov 70, 2; "The Exact Truth," 11 Nov 70, 2; "A Bit of Bitter Truth," 14 Nov 70, 2; "Truth Versus Humbuggery," 15 Nov 70, 2; "'The Uncivilized Races of Men,'" 16 Nov 70, 2; "Our Last Shot," 17 Nov 70, 2; "The Uncivilized Races of Men," 18 Nov 70, 2; "The War of the Races," 19 Nov 70, 2; "The Uncivilized Races of Men," 21 Nov 70, 2. The first of these, signed "Justice" and offering an ostensibly disinterested comparison, seems to have been Bliss's stratagem for provoking the debate that followed. On 16 December 1870 the *Courant* printed Routledge and Sons' summation of its position, accompanied by Burr and Company's formal retraction of the charges of "misrepresentation, fraud and bribery" it had levied against the English publishers ("'The Uncivilized Races'—A Card," "A Card to the Trade and Public of the United States of America," Hartford *Courant*, 16 Dec 70, 2; Geer 1870, 72, 435; "New Books," *Author's Sketch Book* 1 [Nov 70]: 3).

[5] Newlyweds Frank and Frances Bliss had their first child, Elisha French Bliss, on 23 June 1871 (15 Sept 70 to Bliss and French, n. 2; "Hartford Residents," Bliss Family, 1).

To Elisha Bliss, Jr.
22 November 1870 • Buffalo, N.Y.
(MS: CtY-BR)

Buffalo, Nov. 22.

Friend Bliss:

Please send this beggar a cheap copy of the book & paste the enclosed into it.[1]

Have instructed my brother [to] get to Hartford with all convenient dispatch. Frank's "ounce" is not bad for a novice.

Yrs

Mark.

✉———————————————————————————————

[*letter docketed:*] √ [*and*] Mark Twain | Nov 22/70 | Author

[1] Presumably an autograph for insertion in *The Innocents Abroad*. The beggar has not been identified.

To Charles Henry Webb
26 November 1870 • Buffalo, N.Y.
(MS: ViU and MoSW)

Buf. Nov. 26.

Friend Webb—

Business first. I could not consent to a new edition of the J. F. any time within two or three years without ₩ vitiating my contracts with my present publishers & creating dissatisfaction. I would have issued the Galaxy (they belong wholly to me) & other sketches, in a couple of volumes, before this, but for the reason abovementioned.[1] But when I go down to New York in the spring I want to look the whole J. F. matter over, & ~~if there is anything fairly & strictly owing~~ whatever is fair & right, I am perfectly willing to do. ~~But in~~

I have been very much ashamed of myself several times for getting

in a passion & hiring a lawyer & making myself th[o]roughly uncomfortable when there was no occasion for it—but I hold that a man has *got*
to make an ass of himself once a year anyhow, & I am sure I went along
intelligently enough the *balance* of last year. I was very sorry, though, ~~to
make trouble~~ that I made trouble with a friend, because that is folly of
~~som~~ such a particularly low grade.[2]

I ~~$~~ had seen the letter about your marriage, for it was copied every-
where & I am cordially glad you are out of the ~~chilly~~ ͺlist of theͺ unwise,
& one of *us*.[3] Like you, I lost ten or fifteen years of married life just by
sheer carelessness in not getting married ten or fifteen years sooner, but
I went according to my lights, & what more could a man do. But I am
making up for it now. I never write a line for my paper,[4] I do not see the
office oftener than once a week, & do not stay there an hour at any time,
& I never go out of the house, except for exercise, one hour twice a day.
So I see nobody but my wife & visiting friends from a distance. [But we
are not absolutely lonesome, because, including the servants, we have
eleven in the family just now.][5] Housekeeping is perfectly jolly, so long
as you & your wife cordially agree on a visitor before he is invited, & I
tell you we are always mighty particular to look to that. Wherefore I am
enabled authoritatively to invite you & Mrs. Webb to ~~rum~~ run up here
& spend a week with us as soon ~~you~~ as we get the decks clear again & you
can make it convenient. I work in my particular den, from 11 AM till 3
P.M., rain or shine—but the rest of the day & night I'll help Mrs. C.
entertain you all I know how. I thank you for your invitation to drop in
at 155 Madison ave., & shall promptly do so when in town.

Now *why* did you persist in publishing with Carleton? That snob.[6]

Indeed Harte *does* soar, & I am glad of it, notwithstanding he & I
are "off," these many months. It happened thus. Harte read all the MS
of the "Innocents" & told me what passages, paragraphs & *chapters* to
leave out—& I followed orders strictly. It was a kind thing for Harte to
do, & I think I appreciated it. He praised the book so highly that I
wanted him to review it *early* for the Overland, ~~so that I could~~ & help
the sale out there. I told ~~the~~ my publisher. He ordered Bancroft to send
Harte a couple of books before anybody else. Bancroft declined! I wrote
~~a not~~ Harte & enclosed an order on Bancroft for 2 book[s] & directing
that the bill be ~~sent~~ deducted from my publishers returns or sent to me.
Mr. Bancroft *"preferred the money."* Good, wasn't it? [He wrote me the
other day, asking me to help get him agency for my new book for Pacific

& the Orient—which I *didn't.*] Well, sir, Harte wrote me the *most daintily contemptuous & insulting letter you ever read*—& what I want to know, is, where *I* was to blame? How's that?[7]

Dinner is ready. We offer our warm regards & congratulations to you & Mrs. Webb.

Ys

Clemens.

✉—————————————————————————————

Personal. | C. H. Webb Esq | Care E. P. Dutton & Co | 713 Broadway | New York.[8] [*postmarked:*] BUFFALO N.Y. NOV 27

[1] In October 1870 existing contracts with the American Publishing Company had forced Clemens to abandon a sketchbook he hoped to give to the publishers of the *Galaxy* (13 Oct 70, 26 Oct 70, 31 Oct 70, all to Bliss).

[2] Clemens's grievance concerned *The Celebrated Jumping Frog of Calaveras County, And other Sketches,* published by Webb in 1867, but nothing is known of the legal action he apparently initiated in 1869 and abandoned in early 1870 (22 Jan 70 to Bliss, n. 5). He did not wait until the spring of 1871 to look into the Jumping Frog matter again; instead he met and came to terms with Webb in New York in December 1870 (17 Dec 70 to Fairbanks; 22 Dec 70 to Bliss).

[3] The letter about Webb's 11 October 1870 marriage to Elizabeth W. Shipman, of Brooklyn, has not been identified.

[4] See 27 Mar 70 to the Langdons, n. 5.

[5] In addition to Clemens, Olivia, and Langdon, five servants and two probable visitors can be identified as current members of the Buffalo household: coachman Patrick McAleer; housekeeper and cook Ellen White; the unnamed replacement for Harriet, the maid fired on 15 April; "Auntie" Smith, Langdon's nursemaid; Mrs. Brown, Langdon's wet nurse; and Olivia Lewis Langdon and Ida Langdon, recently invited (16 Apr 70 to Crane; 11 Nov 70 to Ford; 14 Nov 70 to Charles J. Langdon; 19 Nov 70 to Olivia Lewis Langdon).

[6] In February 1867 George W. Carleton offended Clemens in rejecting the *Jumping Frog* book, which Webb published about three months later (*L2,* 12-14, 19 n. 2). Carleton published four of Webb's books: *Liffith Lank; or, Lunacy* (1866), *The Wickedest Woman in New York* (1868), *Parodies* (1876), and *Sea-weed and What We Seed: My Vacation at Long Branch and Saratoga* (1876).

[7] Harte's letter to Clemens is not known to survive. Hubert H. Bancroft did not continue as the American Publishing Company's West Coast representative: the agency for *Roughing It* went to Anton Roman, another San Francisco bookseller and publisher. (Bancroft's letter of "the other day" probably was the one Clemens received from him in October: see 8–13? Oct 70 to Bliss.) Harte's assistance in revising the manuscript of *The Innocents Abroad,* resulting in extensive deletions and other alterations, is fully discussed in Hirst 1978, 1–34. His long review of *Innocents,* which appeared in the *Overland Monthly* for January 1870, found the book to be an exception to the poor stuff usually issued by subscription publishers, "a joyous revelation—an Indian spring in an alkaline literary desert" proving that "Mr. Clemens deserves to rank foremost among American humor-

ists" (Harte 1870a, 100, 101). Clemens conceivably influenced, as repayment, the Buffalo *Express*'s flattering notice, on 30 April 1870, of the "exquisite art" of Harte's *The Luck of Roaring Camp, and Other Sketches* (Boston: Fields, Osgood and Co., 1870), but he almost certainly did not write it ("New Books," 2). Harte was "soaring" in November 1870 as a result of "Plain Language from Truthful James" (sometimes also called "The Heathen Chinee"). First published in the *Overland Monthly* for September 1870 (Harte 1870b), the poem was reprinted in newspapers and cheap broadsides, throughout the United States and abroad, and "like a popular song or a vaudeville joke became the property of the man in the street"—although Harte thought it "the worst poem I ever wrote, possibly the worst poem anyone ever wrote" (George R. Stewart 1931, 179–81). Soon after, Harte turned down an appointment as "Professor of Recent Literature and Curator of the Library and Museum" at the University of California in Berkeley, for an annual salary of $3,600, a refusal that was widely reported. In early 1871 he went east, in order to exploit his fame there: see 3 Mar 71 to Riley, n. 6 (Hart 1987, 419–20; Thomas, 1:162–63; Bierce; *San Francisco News Letter and California Advertiser:* "Journalistic Muffs," 27 Aug 70, 8; "Mr. Frank Bret Harte . . . ," 24 Sept 70, 5; Elmira *Advertiser:* "Personal," 28 Sept 70, 4; Pittsburgh *Gazette:* "Generalities," 29 Sept 70, 1).

[8]Webb's business address until around May 1872. Nothing has been learned of his responsibilities at Edward P. Dutton and Company, booksellers and publishers chiefly of religious and juvenile books, but the firm helped promote the adding machine he patented in 1868 (*Seventy-five Years*, 34–37, 39; Wilson: 1869, 316, 1153; 1870, 340, 1268; 1871, 324, 1204).

To John Henry Riley
27 or 28 November 1870 • Buffalo, N.Y.
(Transcript: Riley to SLC, 30 Nov 70, CU-MARK)

. . . .

Will You Go?[1]

. . . .

[1]This inquiry—first proposing the trip discussed in 28 Nov 70 and 2 Dec 70 to Bliss and in 2 Dec 70 to Riley—survives in Riley's reply (2 Dec 70 to Riley, n. 1).

To Elisha Bliss, Jr.
28 November 1870 • Buffalo, N.Y.
(MS: CU-MARK)

Private & Conf.   [Copy.]

Buf. Nov. 28.

Friend Bliss:

My brother expects to start east in about 6 or 8 days.

I have put my greedy hands on the best man in America for my purpose & shall *start him to the diamond fields of South Africa within a fortnight,, at my expense.*[1]

I shall ,write, a book of his experiences for next spring, (600 pp 8vo.,) ,spring of '72, & write it jo just as if I had been through it all myself, but will explain in the preface that this is done merely to give it life & sparkle. & reality.

That book will have a perfectly awful ,beautiful, sale.

1. NOW Sir, WILL YOU PAY ,ME, 10 PER CENT COPYRIGHT ON IT,?

2. Will you advance me a thousand dollars, ,(or $1,500 if it should be necessary,), now, for this purpose, with this distinct understanding, viz: That if the thing works & I manage to write the book on the diamond adventures, you are to deduct all of that thousand ,or $1,500, dollars from the first quarter's sales of said book; but if the project fails & I can't get a book out of it, then you ,are, to lose half of the thousand ,or fifteen hundred, dollars & I to lose the other half.

Say yes or no quick, Bliss, for I can this thing is brim-full of fame & fortune for both author [&] publisher. Expedition's the word/,, & I don't want any timidity or hesitancy now., Hang it I can find you as many as several publishers[2]

But whether my pro project & my terms find favor in your eyes or not, *I* am perfectly satisfied with the scheme & my man will be packing his trunk by this time tomorrow. And in another 24 hours he will be full freighted with my minute instructions & will have his name to the contract & off for Africa within a fortnight, as I said.[3]

Yrs Truly
S. L. Clemens.

Keep all this a secret, even from Frank himself, now & henceforth—for I don't want to furnish some other Hartford publisher with an idea, though I would really care „no„ more than about 2 figs for his opposition. But keep it a secret. It is best to do it.

Mrs Fairbanks (my best critic) likes my new book WELL, as far as I have got.

P. S. I don't care two cents whether there is a diamond in all Africa or not—the adventurous narrative & its wild, new fascination is what I want.

[*on back of page 1 as folded:*]

Confidential.

---

[1] Diamonds were discovered in South Africa, on the banks of the Vaal River, in the spring of 1870, with subsequent rich finds reported in September and October (Appleton 1873, 1–2; "The Diamond Land," Buffalo *Express*, 15 Oct 70, 2–3; "The African Diamond Fields," New York *Tribune*, 1 Nov 70, 4; "A New Golconda. The Diamond Fields of South Africa," Buffalo *Express*, 11 Nov 70, 2). Clemens's proxy there was to be John Henry Riley, qualified by his experience as a journalist (8 July 70 to OLC, n. 2), and also by attributes Clemens elaborated in "Riley—Newspaper Correspondent," in the *Galaxy* for November 1870:

> Riley is full of humor, and has an unfailing vein of irony which makes his conversation to the last degree entertaining (as long as the remarks are about somebody else). But notwithstanding the possession of these qualities, which should enable a man to write a happy and an appetizing letter, Riley's newspaper letters often display a more than earthly solemnity, and likewise an unimaginative devotion to petrified facts, which surprise and distress all men who know him in his unofficial character. He explains this curious thing by saying that his employers sent him to Washington to write facts, not fancy, . . . What a shame it is to tie Riley down to the dreary mason-work of laying up solemn dead-walls of fact! He does write a plain, straightforward, and perfectly accurate and reliable correspondence, but it seems to me that I would rather have one chatty paragraph of his fancy than a whole obituary of his facts.
>
> Riley is very methodical, untiringly accommodating, never forgets anything that is to be attended to, is a good son, a staunch friend, and a permanent, reliable enemy. He will put himself to any amount of trouble to oblige a body, and therefore always has his hands full of things to be done for the helpless and the shiftless. And he knows how to do nearly everything, too. He is a man whose native benevolence is a well-spring that never goes dry. He stands always ready to help whoever needs help, as far as he is able—and not simply with his money, for that is a cheap and common charity, but with hand and brain, and fatigue of limb and sacrifice of time. This sort of men is rare. (SLC 1870hhh, 726–27)

Pinholes in the manuscript of this letter suggest that Clemens enclosed a clipping or clippings—possibly information about South Africa, for example "The South African Diamond Field," (Buffalo *Express*, 28 Nov 70, 2). He did not enclose his sketch about Riley, which he first recommended to Bliss in his letter of 20 December.

[2] Bliss replied on 30 November (CU-MARK):

Dear Clemens,

Yours ,just, recd. Yes we will go in, on that game— You dont think I am very timid do you— I never was called that—

But I want to tell you what I think is fair, between us.

I shall be short & plain—

First, I know well ,that, people offer you big percentages, all right,—but they cant afford to pay 10%—no man can. On your Book, had we paid 10% we should not have made *$5000*—this is true—I can show you figures— Now then I say this frankly, to you & then leave it for you to say whether it shall be 7½ or 10%— Look at it a minute. We are paying agts *all good ones 50%* we pay our general agts 55% some 60%, to keep them— a book at 3.50 55% off, gives us 1.57½—the book costs us about 1.00 without any copyright. Cost of Plates, or any other expenses, 7½% copyright, is about 25cts—nearly $1.25 cost of Book, giving us a small profit. At 50% it gives us 50cts profit, pay *$10,000* for plates & engravings, to start, pay for adverts, office exs &c & unless a man sells a pile he will lose money. This is a plain show, no matter how others figure— It is truth— Another point. Should the man not succeed & the book fail—why not have it understood some other subject agreed on by us shall take its place & a book come anyway if you like   Is this unfair? That is all— Shall we put it in this light— A *Book* to be *written* by you to follow the next, soon as possible & politic   Terms &c same *as next book* as agreed, in contract.

Subject   Diamond Land or *some other mutually agreeable—$1000, to $1500* advanced ,by us, to come out of copyright on first sales. (if this suits you)

Will this suit you? Aint it fair? I am with you heart & hand, & want to go in of course—& give you my ideas—of right & wrong— If you dont *see it*—say where & how it should be, but please "put yourself in our place" & decide it—

If this basis seems fair to you telegraph *all right* & whatever else you want to say. If it dont telegraph wherein it is not—& I will reply. When do you want the Cash? *It will be ready.*

Please consider this thing settled between us   someway & I will if necessary come out & see you & fix it at once as I know we can—but lets get on by tel & letter if possible.

                                                                    truly
                                                                    Bliss

We are printing more & selling more than all Hartford Pub. put together   *Sure* Understand the 10% matter I leave to you, but you know I tell you frankly what subscription houses can afford, & I know

[*letter docketed by Clemens:*]

                              Bliss's No. 1.

                              It is in answer to this.┬f
[*on envelope:*] Diam. Correspondence. | Bliss & Clem. both.

[*in pencil:*]
Redpath
Shillaber
Orion
Bliss
Ma
Webb

Dan
Mrs. Fairbanks
Stoker ⎱
Gillis ⎰ Sonora
Cal. Higbie.
Geo. W. Curtis.
Gray

Clemens replied to Bliss's letter on 2 December. He probably made this entire list well before he used this envelope to preserve their initial diamond mine correspondence. By late November he had already written to James Redpath (12 November), Orion Clemens (5 November, 11 November, 21? November), Bliss (5 November, 7 November, 22 November), Charles H. Webb (26 November), and Mary Mason Fairbanks (5 November, 7 November [telegram; not extant], 19 November). November letters to Benjamin Shillaber, Jane Lampton Clemens, Daniel Slote or Dan De Quille, Richard Stoker, James N. Gillis, Calvin H. Higbie, *Harper's Weekly* editor George W. Curtis, and David Gray are not known to survive. Stoker, Gillis, and Higbie all were potential sources of information for *Roughing It*—as was Dan De Quille (William Wright), who, however, Clemens apparently had in mind in conjunction with the diamond mine book (2 Dec 70 to Riley, final postscript). Some of the missing letters may have announced, or acknowledged congratulations upon, the birth of Langdon Clemens.

[3] Clemens's satisfaction was not tempered by the failure of a previous collaboration, with Darius R. Ford—or by the fact that Riley had not yet agreed to go (22 Jan 70 to Bliss, n. 2; 27 Mar 70 to the Langdons; 2 Dec 70 to Riley).

To Warren L. Brigham
1 December 1870 • Buffalo, N.Y.
(MS: MBAt)

Buffalo, Dec. 1

Dear Sir:

I am sorry indeed that I did not see you, & glad, at the same time that you did not make the long trip out to my house & *then* fail, as—a thing apt to occur because folks are apt to come in the daytime & I don't let anybody in, then! But I'm a sociable creature at night when work is done.

But work is piled on me in toppling pyramids, now—which figure represents a book which I am not getting out as fast as I ought—& I am obliged to say that I could not take half a column more on any terms. I would like exceedingly well to write for the Gazette (the only Weekly paper I ever wanted to own,) but as we steamboatmen used to say, "I've got my load."[1]

Yrs Truly

Sam*[1]*. L. Clemens.

[1] Warren Luther Brigham (1846–80) apparently began his journalistic career in 1867 with the Boston *Saturday Evening Gazette,* moved to the Boston *Advertiser* in 1868, then to the Boston *Courier* in the summer of 1870, and was again with the *Gazette* when he wrote Clemens in November. The *Gazette,* founded in 1814, was "an excellent paper of its kind, with its theatrical and other reviews, its amusing tales, its humor, and its 'lighter gossip of Boston life'" and its penchant for "racy western material" (Mott 1938, 35, 121; Lisa Backman, personal communication; *Boston Directory:* 1870, 111; 1871, 115).

To Elisha Bliss, Jr.
1? December 1870 • Buffalo, N.Y.
(MS: CU-MARK)

Dear Bliss—

Here is a half-forgotten friend of mine whose husband stood high in Nevada, & whose brother-in-law, Sunderland, was worth half a million when I saw him last. But the husband got lost in the desert & the cuyotés ate him; & presently the sharpers of the stock-board ate the brother-in-law—& behold the widow![1]

Write her, but don't tell her I sent you her letter.[2]

Ys

Mark.[3]

[1] Neither the widow nor her husband has been identified. The brother-in-law, Thomas Sunderland (b. 1820 or 1821, d. 1886), a native of Indiana, studied law in Iowa and then practiced in Hannibal, Missouri, before going to California in 1849. After trying his hand at gold mining, he was an attorney in Sacramento, then moved to Virginia City, Nevada Territory, where he established a lucrative law practice and in the early 1860s was in partnership with Clemens's friend Alexander W. Baldwin. Sunderland continued to practice law in Virginia City through most of the 1870s. Although unsuccessful as a railroad promoter in 1868, he does not seem to have suffered any irreparable losses at the hands of

stock "sharpers." On the contrary, he reportedly made enormous profits, total-
ing far in excess of "half a million," from his various Nevada mining interests
(anonymous biographical sketch, CU-BANC; *L1*, 280 n. 11; "Obituary Notes,"
New York *Times,* 11 Oct 86, 5; Kelly 1863, 285–86; Knight, 300; Angel, 280,
338; *Storey,* 221, 244).

² The letter, which does not survive, may have requested an agency for the
book Clemens was writing—known in Nevada to be about his western experiences (28? Sept 70 to Goodman).

³ Bliss replied on 3 December (CU-MARK):

Friend Clemens,
   "Little madam" is a brave one— What a magnet for the women you are—
"From the North & the South the East & the West" they come to do homage"   Am
looking for your brother daily. Have been in a stew—all day looking for a dispatch ~~from
you~~ & none ~~have e~~ has come from you— Did my letter reach you—& have you replied?— Am anxious to hear, as I suppose the matter requires prompt action— Do you
demur to my argument? Trust to hear from you soon—about it—& know how you
feel— Hope you did not think me over sharp—now did you?
   Let me hear from you if mine is not recd, telegraph.
                                                                         truly
                                                                         Bliss

[letter docketed by Clemens:]

                    Bliss:
                    ――――――

                    ~~Not~~ Simply an urgent & uneasy letter of inquiry.
                    ――――――

                    Rec'd Dec. 6/70.

The next letter was the one Bliss was anxiously awaiting, a response to his proposal of 30 November (28 Nov 70 to Bliss, n. 2).

To Elisha Bliss, Jr.
2 December 1870 • Buffalo, N.Y.
(MS: Craven)

ˌ[Copy.]ˌ¹

   ˌDon't overlook the ~~P. S. S.~~ Post Scripts.

                                                             Buf. Dec. 2.
Friend Bliss:
   I'll tell you what I'll do. I'll not take advantage of your ~~perm~~ con-
sent to pay me 10 per cent, but I'll do this.² You're to pay me *8½ per cent,*

& advance me ~~three tho~~ another thousand dollars (in addition to the fifteen hundred,) any time I demand it during 1871, this thousand *also* to come out of my first earnings on the African book. ˏOVER.

[I have been looking into the matter, & my man *might* need more than the $1500, though I'll not demand the extra $1,000 from you, unless he demands it of *me*, by & bye.]ˏ And further:

If my man don't get back & I can't write the African book for you, I'll write you a 600 page 8vo. book *in place of it*, which you are to pay me 8½ per cent copyright on & you to subtract all that $1500 or $2500 from ʄ my first receipts on *that* book.

How's that?

ˏ1.ˏ Don't you see? You get a *book*, in any event.

2. You pay 8½ p. cent. copyright in any event.

3. I ~~lose~~ *alone* risk that advance-money on my man. If nothing comes of it, I lose it *all*, you *none* of it.

~~That extra~~

I would not publish a book through you (or any other person) at a copyright which I believed would preclude your getting your fair & full share of the profits of the enterprise.

Write or telegraph.[3]

~~Ys Yrs~~ ˏYrs.

S. L.ˏ Clemens.

P. S. Keep this whole thing a dead secret—else we'll have somebody standing ready to launch a book right on our big tidal wave & swim it into a *success* when it would otherwise fall still-born.

P. P. S. If this suits, ~~preserve~~ draw a written contract, or else take proper measures to make this fully & legally binding on both of us in its present form.[4]

Clemens.

[1] See the textual commentary.

[2] Bliss had actually rejected Clemens's request for a ten percent royalty on the diamond mine book—while pretending to defer to his judgment in the matter (28 Nov 70 to Bliss, n. 2).

[3] Bliss's 5 December telegram reached Clemens the following day: "All right to go ahead will write tomorrow" (CU-MARK). His follow-up letter of 6 December is not known to survive.

[4] On 6 December Bliss drew up a contract formalizing the terms Clemens proposed (Appendix E). He probably enclosed it in his letter that day. Clemens did

not see it until 17 December, when he returned to Buffalo after a week in New York City (Bliss to SLC, 20 Dec 70, CU-MARK).

To John Henry Riley
2 December 1870 • Buffalo, N.Y.
(MS and transcript: CU-MARK and NN-B)

ₐ[Preserve this letter.]ₐ

Buf. Dec. 2.

Dear Riley:

Your letter has come, & I have "reflected." I had already done that *I* a good deal & so my mind is not altered.[1]

You know right well that I would not have you depart a hair from any obligation, ~~either~~ for any money. The boundless confidence I have in you is *born* of ~~un~~ a conviction of your integrity in small as well as great things. I know plenty of men whose integrity I would trust to *here*, but not off yonder in Africa.

I do not want you to dishonor any obligation, but I want you to write instantly to the Alta & the other papers saying, "I am offered a rare opportunity to permanently better my fortunes, & therefore I have appointed so & so to be your correspondent in my place*,*, provided you approve; otherwise please instruct me by return mail how next to proceed."[2] Of course you can elaborate this, but is the idea correct?—that is, providing there is nothing graver or more binding than usually exists between publisher & correspondent. If these publishers can *discharge* you when they please, just as *I* they can discharge their local reporter when they please, you are doing nothing wrong if you give them a fortnight's warning & do all you can to leave your place satisfactorily supplied.

But if your understandings are *stronger*, you cannot thus *give them notice*, but you can ask them *t* as a perfectly reasonable favor, to *release you* with all convenient dispatch. None of these propositions of mine have in them any taint of dishonor.

As for Sutro, his big heart will simply ∅ jump up & say, "By — Riley, don't stop a minute for my matters—if it's the best thing for you *I* won't stand in your way."[3]

That Cole & Carter will "rely on your aid" is an obligation only this far: if they can *insure* you better results than ~~Africa offers~~ some other field offers, then *in a business way* they are entitled to rely on your aid. If you are in debt to them for past favors ~~not~~ predicated tacitly upon your aid in this session, then you are ~~in~~ *morally* bound. But in any case your simple request with ~~sta~~ averment that you see an unusually promising chance for you ought to secure their instant & cordial acquiescence.[4]

As to your committees. By a vote, your committees can discharge you. By a vote they can decline to re-elect you, after all your long service. If they could greatly better themselves, it would not only be their fair & just *policy* to do one of these things, but their ,official, DUTY to do it. But if I engage you to go to Africa for 3 or 6 months, ~~w~~ for wages, for me, I can *not* discharge you,, till your time is up,, no matter whether you suit me or not.

But take no snap judgment on the committees, either. Let them choose a clerk, & do you diligently instruct ,him, while you get ready for Africa.[5]

You have certain *moral* obligations resting upon you toward all these parties you have mentioned—& also some less strenuous *business* ones. But in both cases they are doubtless such as an earnest *request* from you would cheerfully cancel.

Now I come to business.

This thing is the pet scheme of my life. As follows:

1. I to pay your passage both *to & from* the South African diamond fields.

2. You to skirmish, ~~prof~~ prospect, work, travel, & take ~~min t~~ pretty minute notes, with hand & brain, for ~~3 or 6 months~~ 3 months (~~or 5 or 6 if necessary,~~) I paying you a hundred dollars a month, for you to live on. [Not more, because sometimes I want you to have to ~~sku~~ shin like everything for a square meal—for *experiences* are the kind of book-material I want.]

3. If you *should* pick up $5,000 worth of diamonds, ~~you~~ (within the specified time,) you to pocket that.

4. If you *should* make more, ,(in any way whatever,), before returning here (~~either during or subsequent to the specified 3 or 6 months,~~) you to send me *half* of that *surplus*—after first securing your $5,000 all right.

5. You to overstay the 3 months on no other condition ,than, that

you pay me $5,000 a month *in advance* for each month so overstaid, & divide earnings with me beside*l*. [Oh, I guess you'd *better* come home for a while & persuade me to drop No. 5, at least.]

6. You to use these manifold-paper diaries ⨇ so that you can every day or every few days write two journals at once, & mail one to me & preserve the other carefully yourself.[6]

7. You are to write no *l* newspaper letters while gone, & write no private letters without taking care that their contents shall be kept out of print. [I want to lay all the ropes thoroughly & then *spring* this book on the public.] I don't want other publishers to have a chance to come the usual pitiful game—i. e., come out with an opposition book which rides into grand prosperity on the tide of the other's success, instead of falling still-born, as it would if left to itself.] ‸This to be a *secret* expedition while in progress, but to be a frightfully celebrated one 6 months afterward, ‸not only here but‸ in every language ~~on ear~~ in civilized Europe.]‸

8‾

8. You to come to my house at the end of your labors, & live with me, at $50 a month & board, (I to furnish the cigars,) from 4 to 12 months, till I have pumped you dry—for‸, the purpose of‸ your diary is to keep *you* ‸(as well as me,)‸ bright & inspire your tongue every morning when you ~~sit~~ take a seat in my study. You are to talk one or two hours to me every day, & *tell* your story—& the rest of the day & night you can do what you please with—& at 3 P. M., I shall always quit work too. With your diary by me I shall be able to write without mistakes after you are gone out ~~for~~ walking or driving.

9. At no time within five years are you to write or publish a book *about Africa or its diamond fields*. [This will fool rival publishers, too.]

==========

All the above is for *my* ~~m~~ benefit. But *some* shall enure to you‸, in case you follow my ~~plam~~ plan. Thus:

1. You see an interesting part of the world, & one upon which the *y* eyes of the ~~wo~~ whole world are ~~gazing~~ centred.

2. It don't cost you a cent to go or come, nor give you a chance to starve while there.

3. It *does* give you a chance to pick up a fortune in 3 months—the very same chance that thousands would be glad to take at their *own* expense.

4. I should write the book as if *I* went through all these adventures myself—this in order to give it snap & freshness. But would begin the ~~Chapter~~ book by saying: "When Daniel de Foe wanted to know what life on a solitary island was like, & doubted whether he ~~cou~~ was hardy enough to stand it himself, he sent the ingenious Robinson W. Crusoe; & when I wanted to know all about ~~the~~ wild life in the diamond fields & its fascinations, ~~I sent the~~ & could not go myself, I sent the ingenious Riley. Now Riley, having returned from his pilgrimage, sits down night & after night & tells his story & when he has finished I set it down from memory—~~not getting the ex~~ not caring so much about the exact language as about the *spirit* of the narration, of course—but using his language when it suits me, & when it suits me putting words of my own to his ideas, fancies & adventures—& just as often the one as the other. In all cases it is Riley speaking, whether the children of his mind appear in the clothing wherein they issued from the door of their nursery, or have doffed a cap or changed a stocking here & there. And to begin, Riley says: "I left New York on board, etc., etc., etc."

Do you see? And I'll hurl in a parenthesis of my own, occasionally, in brackets,—a comment on you or descriptive remark or anecdote about you, or fancy portrait of you in various circumstances of the voyage or adventures in the mines—& do these things so guilelessly that before the reader knows it he is perishing to see *Riley*.

Then my object is accomplished & my game's made! Because thus I can slam you into the lecture field for life & secure you ten thousand dollars a year as long as you live, & all the idle time you want, to loaf & travel in or raise a family. I mention lecturing without any fears because you were born for the platform—you were intended to stand before an audience, & not smile or make a gesture, but simply talk quietly along in a conversational voice & fashion & make them deal out laughter & applause in avalanches. And I mention lecturing with [no] misgivings that you may object, for the reason that I do not take you to be a man either afraid or ashamed to undertake a responsibility which another man would dare.

I would want to "coach" you, thoroughly, drill you completely (for it took me 3 or 4 years to learn the *dead sure* tricks of the platform, but I could teach them to you in 3 or 4 weeks so that when you stepped on a stage you would not be wondering within yourself whether you were going to vanquish the audience, but would absolutely *know* you would do it.)

When you got to Boston or Philadelphia, (either you pleased,) I would introduce you to the audience (provided you wished it,) or follow you with a paragraph, & if it wasn't a good advertisement I want to know why?

5. You should infallibly begin your lecture career at $75 to $150 a night, & in your second lecture season (with the same old lecture,) you should have engagements enough to keep you talking right along for seven months, if you wanted to.

6. In your "off" months you could travel to some quaint country & get up a new lecture about it, & issue a profitable book through my publisher, well aware that your celebrity would give it a great sale—but I'd *rather* that you went at my expense every time & let *me* have the book, old boy.

7. If you never lecture, & never make anything in the diamond land (over ~~$0~~ $5,000) you'll not owe me anything. But if you *do* lecture, then you can pay me back your expenses, *in your second or third season*, provided your lecturing is the success I have promised it will be, but *not otherwise*.

Finally.—

1. You don't get a cent out of the book. But,
2. You *may* pick up $50,000 in the mines. And,
3. In 5 years of lecturing you *shall* receive $50,000 if you'll lecture.
4. ~~4.~~

Pull & all haul my scheme as you please—criticise as you will, it's as sound as a drum—there isn't a leak in it. I'm *bound* to make money out of it if you get back, & you are *bound* to make money lecturing if you *will*.

For the certain & assured prosperity of us both, there needs not to be a solitary (or solitaire) diamond in all Africa, ~~& I am not~~—what we want is to tell in the book & on the platform how lively a time we ~~have~~ had *hunting* for them.

But I ~~ure~~ *urge* upon you, "Expedition's the word!" Clear & out *now*, & let us publish the FIRST book & take the richest cream & deliver the freshest & newest & most fascinating picture of this rush, & not come lagging in second or third or fourth, on a publi~~csh ho~~ whose appetite has begun to lose its grand ravenousness. *Now* is the time to start—strike while the iron is hot. Sail hence, New Year's;~~-/~~

10th Jan. arrive England.

30th "   "   Natal.

Feb. Mch. Apl. in Africa.

Sail May 1, reach here June 30.

July, Aug., Sept., Oct., you talk & I write.

Nov., Dec. & Jan., the book in press & printing 50,000 copies before one is issued,; ~~& all as ely as possible.~~ Agents taking 50,000 subscriptions in the meantime. And in the meantime let ~~them~~ ˄the publishers˄ ~~start~~ scratch for all the oppositions books they want to—I'll launch the Riley book Feb. 1, 1872, & sweep the world like a besom of destruction (if you know what that is.)[7]

˄~~Feb. &, March & April I'll~~ ˄¶ During Feb., I'll˄ drill you in your lecture.

˄March, Apl.,˄ May, ~~June, July,~~ send you traveling, if there's nothing better to do, & let you get me another book & return & fill me up.

June, July, Aug & Sept., you talk & I write.

Middle of October, you begin & lecture till first of next April or May & then go to Cal & talk in San F at $1200 or $1500 a night.[8]

There isn't a solitary thing in this entire programme that cannot be carried out *to the very letter,* if you will *lecture.* I don't say if you *can,* but if you *will.* I'll make you make some of the "humorous" lecturers very sick.

But *hurry,* now. There is no single moment of time to lose. If you could start *now,* it would be splendid—we'd gain a months—but I know you'll have to have 2 or 3 weeks in which to fairly & honorably release yourself from your ~~se~~ ˄existing˄ business ~~bu~~ ties. Run up here as soon as you can, & let's talk it all over. ~~Com~~

Commence, now, Riley, & post yourself as to expenses, & let me know. I say nothing about posting yourself about other matters needful ~~for~~ to know, because I know your habits of mind.

Hang it, I'll have you so well known in 18 months that there will be no man so ignorant as to have to ask "Who is Riley?"—& that will stab Fitz Smythe to the ~~ha~~ heart![9]

Answer.[10]

> Yr friend
> Sam'. L. Clemens.

℗ P. S. Mind you keep the secret absolutely. One don't have such a valuable one entrusted to him every day.

P. S. If *you* couldn't, I had my eye on Dan de Quille, but I sort of doubt if poor old Dan could [take] a right big interest in *any*thing, now.[11]

✉———————————————————————————————

Private.

J. H. Riley, Esq

P. O. Box 75

[Please return to   }   **Washington**

Sam*¹*. L. Clemens,   }   D. C.

Buffalo, if it miscarries.

[*postmarked:*] BUFFALO N.Y. DEC 3

[1] Clemens responded to the following letter (CU-MARK):

(JR)

Washington, D.C.,
Nov. 30ᵗʰ 1870.

Friend Clemens

Last night I dreamed "three times in succession" that I dwelt and delved in the Diamond fields of South Africa, and fairly reveled in the Republic of the Transvaal (wherever that may be)—furthermore that that I had been eminently successful in finding and buying the precious gems, some of which outrivalled the *Koh*-i-*nor* in size, weight and water, and outshone the Great Hoggarty Diamond in brilliancy. And lo and behold, this morning comes your letter!

How I would [have] liked to have been able to pack right up and start from the word "go". I am "mighty willin" but not ready. And so after duly considering the subject, and carefully weighing the *pros* and *cons* I telegraphed the following "at your expense":—

"Yes—at the close of session. Will write. Would rather talk. Pass is good yet. Can start to-morrow evening. Shall I? Answer". Charges $1.50 for that with orders to C.O.D.

Waiting a reply I am writing you, with thanks for your kind consideration for my welfare and assuring you that I would really like to go. I am somewhat of an expert in precious stones, thanks to that poor old Brazillian Diamond Hunter whom I befriended in the Cal. mines, years ago; have a taste that way and thanks to my early experience in the gold fields and in Mexico and Centro-America am a good campaigner and know how to take care of myself and others. Besides which a residence of five years in the District of Columbia should certainly fit a man for South Africa, North Africa or the Interior of Africa. All of which is respectfully submitted. But—why did the idea not enter into your head or my head, or the pair of cabbage-heads when I was with you in Buffalo? And I would have said YES to your query "Will You Go?" at once. Now, I consider that I am to a certain extent compromised to remain here through this session for I know that Senator Cole, Sutro, Judge Carter and others will rely upon my aid in their matters and apart from my engagement with the ALTA I have agreed to correspond with two other Cal. newspapers during the session; and this only one short week ago.

Then there are my two Committees—before which there remains much unfinished business which "went over" during the last session—and with which no new man taking my place as Clerk, could attend to so well as I, and it would not be right for me to leave at this time. Were I [to] go to Africa, to the diamond fields, or to Peru, to the coal mines, for you, I am sure you would not like me to fly off somewhere else just because the impulse seized me or a better offer were made me to go elsewhere. No—I cannot do it even though to "stick" should result to my disadvantage. But if there is no actual haste in the matter *I can go* after close of the session say as soon as you like after the fourth of March next. Who cares if there are "four hundred waggons on the Pnielside". Why when I get there with my waggon I'll drive in on the near side or the off side and thus secure a positive advantage—especially when it is time to leave. So wait for the "Ides of March" or fix a date to correspond to 'em, and I'll go.

Yours truly
J. H. Riley.

Your injunction of secresy is heeded most religiously.

Riley had come to Buffalo on 30 October, registering at the Mansion House hotel ("Hotel Arrivals," Buffalo *Express*, 31 Oct 70, 4). Pniel, South Africa, was about thirty miles east of Cape Town.

[2] Riley chose George Alfred Townsend to assume his San Francisco *Alta California* correspondence, and perhaps his other, unidentified, newspaper commitments as well. Townsend (1841–1914), by this time a playwright, poet, biographer, and lecturer, had been a Civil War correspondent for the New York *Herald* and the New York *World*, and, since 1867, Washington correspondent of the Chicago *Tribune*, the Cincinnati *Enquirer*, and other papers. His letters were highly regarded for their humor, wisdom, and keen observation. He, Riley, and Clemens had shared a house in Washington during the winter of 1867–68 (Riley to SLC, 6 Dec 70, 31 Dec 70, CU-MARK; "G. A. Townsend, Journalist, Dead," New York *Times*, 16 Apr 1914, 9; *L2*, 196 n. 1).

[3] Adolph Sutro (1830–98), another mutual friend of Clemens and Riley's, was in Washington in December 1870 to protect and advance his congressional franchise, granted in July 1866, to build a tunnel through Mount Davidson in Nevada to facilitate access to the Comstock lode. Construction had begun in October 1869 and the main tunnel was completed in 1878. Two years later Sutro sold his shares in the Sutro Tunnel Company and turned his attention to real estate investments in San Francisco (see *RI 1993*, 684–85). As clerk to the House Committee on Mines and Mining, Riley was well placed to be of assistance to Sutro (Adolph Sutro, 31–32).

[4] Cornelius Cole, senator from California, was an acquaintance of Clemens's (6 July 70 to OLC, n. 1). He served on the Senate Committee on Appropriations and the Senate Committee on Public Buildings and Grounds, neither of which employed Riley as clerk (Poore: 1870, 56, 57, 67; 1871, 57, 58, 68). "Carter" probably was David Kellogg Cartter (1812–87), chief justice of the Supreme Court of the District of Columbia since 1863.

[5] Riley was anxious to arrange his clerkships before the convening of the third session of the Forty-first Congress (5 Dec 70–3 Mar 71), but did not complete his arrangements until after the session had begun. By the end of December he had turned his clerkship of the House Committee on Mines and Mining, and possibly his second, unidentified clerkship, over to still another of his and Clemens's mutual friends, James Rankin Young, former head of the New York *Tribune*'s Washington bureau, now correspondent for the New York *Standard* and two Philadelphia papers, the *Post* and the *Star* (*L3*, 228, 230 n. 6; *BDUSC*, 187; Riley to SLC, 31 Dec 70, CU-MARK; Boyd 1871, 387; Poore: 1870, 122; 1871, 128).

⁶Riley's surviving notes are carbon copies torn from such a diary (3 Mar 71 to Riley, n. 1).

⁷A broom, as in "I will also make it a possession for the bittern, and pools of water: and I will sweep it with the besom of destruction, saith the Lord of hosts" (Isaiah 14:23).

⁸Clemens had earned about sixteen hundred dollars when he lectured in San Francisco on 14 April 1868 (*L2*, 209 n. 2).

⁹Evidently Riley shared Clemens's antagonism toward Albert S. Evans ("Fitz Smythe"): see 28 Jan 70 to Bliss, n. 1.

¹⁰Riley first responded on Monday, 5 December, with a telegram that Clemens received the following day: "Long letter rec'd   Plan approved   Will get ready to go" (CU-MARK). On 6 December he sent a follow-up letter, tentatively accepting Clemens's invitation to Buffalo: "I shall try and get leave of absence till Monday next, and in the event of succeeding will start to-morrow (Wednesday) or say Thursday evening, at furthest, so that you may look for me at the Mansion House on Thursday or Friday night—to return on Monday next. I guess when I'm all ready to start for Buffalo, I'll telegraph you to that effect" (CU-MARK). Instead Riley and Clemens met in New York City around 14 December (13 Dec 70, 20 Dec 70, both to Bliss).

¹¹William Wright (Dan De Quille) may have been incapacitated by the alcoholism that occasionally resulted in his temporary imprisonment and discharge from the Virginia City *Territorial Enterprise* (Doten 1973, 2:1071, 1087, 1119). Joseph T. Goodman had probably informed Clemens of Wright's circumstances. Goodman and Clemens clearly were corresponding in 1870, but except for a paraphrase of one of Clemens's letters (28? Sept 70 to Goodman) the correspondence has not been found.

To James Redpath
3 December 1870 • Buffalo, N.Y.
(MS: WU)

Buffalo, Dec. ⨍ 3.

Friend Redpath—

Joe Larned, (my partner & chief editor) has written an article on "Heat," ~~in our~~ & today he will send you a dozen copies of our paper containing it. I told him I would ask you to ~~talk~~ take pains, from time to time, ~~ap~~ as opportunity offered, to talk a few minutes with a scientific man, till his curiosity was excited & then make him read the article & see ~~what~~ whether ~~he~~ his verdict favored its being a fallacy or whether it made it something better. Joe thinks it is either good & sound & ~~trut~~ true, or else the wildest & unworthiest lunacy, one or the other. When I tell you that he has devoted the off-hours of a laborious editorship of a morning paper ~~to the~~ to faithful work on this thing *for* ~~thee~~ *three years*, you will feel as I do, viz., that if you & I can do such a man a kindness, we will cheerfully do it.[1]

Yrs

Mark

P. S. Considering the strain I took (for a lazy man, & for pure love of shoving a genius into the light of the national sun who ~~wh~~ had been wasting itself in the obscurity of Nevada sagebrush) to make Tom Fitch acquainted with you & get you to confer on him fame & fortune, I think he might drop me a line to tell me how he came out ~~th~~ on the 29[th.] I have seen no Boston papers.[2]

But whether he succeeded or not my anxiety is not moved or ~~str~~ stirred—because I know he *can* succeed, & superbly, too. It is in him. If he has not made a hit this time, ~~let~~ work him up & sail him in again & he *will* make one. Then put him [in] Pugh's course,[3] & in the big courses of all the big cities *for nothing*, this winter, without fooling around with 20 & ~~50-~~ ‚30-‚dollar engagements as I before proposed, & he can ~~wall~~ walk over the course next year.

Yrs in a hurry

Mark.

P. S. My ‚Saturday Review fraud fooled *some* of the boys, anyway.[4]

✉—————————————————————————

[*letter docketed:*] BOSTON LYCEUM BUREAU. REDPATH & FALL. DEC 10 1870 [*and*] Mark Twain | Buffalo N.Y. | Dec. 3 '70

[1] Larned filled more than three columns in the Buffalo *Express* of 3 December with his challenge to "the received hypothesis" that "Heat is some mysterious state of invisible motion imparted to the ultimate atoms of matter." He suggested instead that it was "*the variable degree of density or tension in which the so-called 'æther' that occupies all inter-molecular as well as all inter-planetary spaces is existing in the matter!*" (Larned 1870f).

[2] See 10? July 70 to Redpath and 10? July 70 to Fitch. Fitch's 29 November lecture on "The Coming Empire"—to a full house at Tremont Temple, in the Boston Lyceum Bureau course—was chiefly a paean to California and Nevada. The Boston *Morning Journal* observed that "Bostonians fully coincided in the opinion expressed by the author of 'The Innocents Abroad'" that "'they never listened to anything so delightful before'" ("'The Coming Empire,'" 30 Nov 70, 2). The Boston *Advertiser* remarked: "Mr. Fitch's eloquence, though rather florid, is impressive, and he has a keen sense of humor with a happy knack of expressing it. Indeed, it is easy to see why Mark Twain likes him" ("'The Com-

ing Empire,'" 30 Nov 70, 2). Redpath's promotional magazine for the 1871–72 season reported that during Fitch's two-week 1870 tour he also spoke "at Attleboro', Westboro', Middleboro', West Medway, Newtonville (Mass.), Biddeford (Maine), and Manchester (N.H.); from all of which places, the Bureau received eulogistic accounts of his success" (*Lyceum* 1871, 27).

³See 14 Nov 70 to Pugh.

⁴After learning from the Boston *Advertiser* ("Perhaps the most successful flights . . . ," 22 Oct 70, 2) that *The Innocents Abroad* had been reviewed by a literal-minded critic in the London *Saturday Review* of 8 October 1870 ("The Innocents Abroad," 30:467–68; reprinted in Anderson and Sanderson, 39–43), Clemens wrote "An Entertaining Article," for his December 1870 *Galaxy* "Memoranda." It included a long burlesque review calling *Innocents* a work of "imposing insanity" and "a deliberate and wicked creation of a diseased mind," which Clemens passed off as the *Saturday Review* notice. In "A Sad, Sad Business," part of his January 1871 "Memoranda," he confessed to the hoax and printed specimen commentaries from newspapers taken in by it (SLC: 1870nnn, 876–78; 1871b, 158–59).

NO LETTERS are known to survive between 3 and 11 December 1870. Although the illness and death of Emma Nye and the birth of Langdon Clemens had impeded Clemens's progress on *Roughing It,* and although he had already distracted himself with his scheme for an African diamond mine book, he now found the time for yet another literary project. On 7 or 8 December he telegraphed Isaac E. Sheldon and Company, publishers of the *Galaxy,* proposing a holiday publication. He had previously wanted to publish a sketches volume through Sheldon and Company, but was frustrated when Elisha Bliss invoked a prohibitory clause in the 15 July 1870 *Roughing It* contract. Now he apparently planned to circumvent that contract by making the proposed work a pamphlet, a ploy that Bliss resented. Sheldon and Company was quick to respond. On 9 December the firm telegraphed Clemens twice, first to say "We will publish it & give you half of all profits," and then to offer a royalty of "Fifteen pr ct on retail" as an alternative (CU-MARK). A letter followed that same day, confirming the offers and recommending the royalty, which Clemens ultimately chose, as "much better for you than any copyright we could name, if the book proves a success." It also urged haste:

> It is now of course late in the season to get out a book and there are always delays we can never calculate on, as each step in the process of manufacturing

is made, but we can get it out as soon as anyone, and should not lose a moment. (CU-MARK)

Probably on the night of 9 December Clemens "shot off to New York," arriving the following morning (17 Dec 70 to Fairbanks). His presence was quickly noted: the New York *Herald* reported that "Mark Twain, the great humorist, has come to the city from Buffalo, and is now stopping at the Albemarle Hotel" ("Personal Intelligence," 11 Dec 70, 6), and the New York *Tribune* listed him among its "Prominent Arrivals" (12 Dec 70, 8).

On 10 December Clemens must have begun conferring with Sheldon and Company about the pamphlet—published as *Mark Twain's (Burlesque) Autobiography and First Romance,* but not until March 1871—and in the succeeding days tried to speed its production by locating Edward F. Mullen, an illustrator he wanted for it. Also on 10 December, or soon after, he met with Charles Henry Webb to resolve their differences over *The Celebrated Jumping Frog of Calaveras County, And other Sketches.* Clemens received an accounting of the costs of production and a report of the sales since 1867 and bought the copyright back from Webb.

But business did not occupy all of Clemens's time in New York. At the Albemarle, a "very elegant hotel" at 1101 Broadway, at the junction of Fifth Avenue and Twenty-fourth Street, Clemens enjoyed a respite from domestic concerns and "smoked a week, day & night" (Miller, 70; 19 Dec 70 to Twichell). He may have attended "Dan Bryant's new minstrel hall on the north side of 23rd Street, west of Sixth Avenue," where on 11 December a dramatization of his Jumping Frog story, starring "Little Mac," a dwarf, in the title role, went on the bill (Odell, 9:76–77). Called an "attractive feature" by the New York *Herald,* the skit was performed throughout the remainder of December and was reprised in April 1871 (New York *Herald:* "Music and the Drama," 12 Dec 70, 5; "Amusements," 10–31 Dec 70; Wilson 1870, 30). It is unlikely that Clemens authorized this production, but its evident popularity conceivably influenced his determination to exploit the story anew.

Clemens also visited with New York friends, among them fellow journalists Whitelaw Reid, John Hay, and possibly John Rose Greene Hassard, all of the New York *Tribune.* In 1905 he recalled a conversation with Hay that must have occurred at this time, although he could place it only "in 1870 or '71." They discussed the charge of imitating Bret Harte that had been leveled against Hay, who on 19 November had published "Little-Breeches," the first of his "Pike County Ballads," in the *Tribune* (John M. Hay 1870). Clemens remembered that their meeting enabled him "incidentally" to get "acquainted with Horace Greeley":

> It was difficult to get an interview with him, for he was a busy man, he was irascible, & he had an aversion to strangers; but I not only had the good fortune to meet him, but also had the great privilege of hearing him talk. The Tribune was in its early home, at that time, & Hay was a leader-writer on its staff. I had an appointment with him, & went there to look him up. I did not know my way, & entered Mr. Greeley's room by mistake. I recognized his back, & stood mute & rejoicing. After a little, he swung slowly around in his chair, with his head slightly tilted backward & the great moons of his spectacles glaring with intercepted light; after about a year—though it may have been less, perhaps—he arranged his firm mouth with care & said with virile interest—
> "Well? What the hell do *you* want!" (SLC 1905, 5–6)

Both the conversation with Hay and the encounter with Greeley probably occurred on 11 or 12 December, when Clemens brought the *Tribune* the manuscript of the next letter (26 Oct 70, 22 Dec 70, and 3 Jan 71 to Bliss; 26 Dec 70 and 31 Dec 70 to Reid; 27 Jan 71 to Sheldon, n. 1; *RI 1993*, 823–26).

To the Editor of the New York *Tribune*
11 December 1870 • New York, N.Y.
(New York *Tribune*, 13 Dec 70)

To the Editor of The Tribune.[1]

SIR: Mr. R. C. Gridley, widely known upon the Pacific coast, died at Paradise, Cal., November 24, of neuralgia of the heart. Mr. Gridley was one of the early emigrants to the Californian gold-fields, &, during his twenty years' residence, maintained an enviable reputation for integrity, benevolence, & enterprise.[2] His name was familiar to the nation during the days when fairs & such enterprises, in behalf of the Sanitary fund,[3] were common, in consequence of his efforts in aid of that charity with the once famous "Sanitary flour sack." He had engaged to carry a 50-pound sack of flour from one end of the town of Austin, Nevada, to the other, in case an approaching election went against his political party. His party lost the election, & Mr. Gridley made good his word. When he had completed his task, he put up the flour at auction, for the benefit of the United States Sanitary fund. The buyer immediately ordered that it be sold again for the fund. Mr. Gridley sold it again, & continued to sell & resell it till it had brought $800, gold. The news spread far & wide, & other towns called for Mr. Gridley & the flour sack. He left his partner in charge of his business[4] & started with the sack, & in every town was received with bands of music & by the citizens in mass. In one day, in Virginia City & its suburbs (17,000 inhabitants), the sack sold for $30,000, gold.[5] Mr. Gridley sold it in the large towns & cities of California, & then brought it East, & sold it over & over again here;[6] &, finally, after selling it at the Mississippi Valley Fair, at St. Louis, for a great sum, it was made into small cakes there, & these were sold at extravagant prices.[7] This long & tedious expedition, undertaken & carried through to the end with whole-hearted zeal, albeit there was no dollar of remuneration in it for Mr. Gridley, is the best exemplar of the generous nature of the man, & also of his great energy.[8]

S. L. C.[9]

Albemarle, Dec. 11, 1870.

[1] Horace Greeley, the founder of the New York *Tribune,* had been its chief editor for nearly thirty years. In writing to the paper Clemens customarily directed his letters to Whitelaw Reid, the managing editor since 1869.

[2] Reuel Colt Gridley (b. 1829) had been one of Clemens's Hannibal schoolmates. For Clemens's on-the-spot account of the events he here recalled for the *Tribune,* see *L1,* 281–84. He reworked this material in chapter 45 of *Roughing It* (*RI 1993,* 294–98).

[3] The United States Sanitary Commission and the Western Sanitary Commission, established in 1861, were the two major organizations that raised funds for the care of sick and wounded Union soldiers. During the next five years they raised more than $24 million in cash and supplies (*L1,* 284 n. 3).

[4] Gridley, Hobart, and Jacobs, an Austin grocery firm (*L1,* 285 n. 10).

[5] Actually about $23,200 in gold; the day was 16 May 1864 (*RI 1993,* 661–62).

[6] Gridley auctioned the flour sack twice in Sacramento and once in San Francisco; his eastern auctions have not been identified (*RI 1993,* 663–64).

[7] Pamela Moffett was among the women supporting the Mississippi Valley Sanitary Fair, which was held in St. Louis in May and June 1864 and raised some $600,000. Gridley did not take the sack to St. Louis until the summer of 1865, however. The scheme to bake the flour into cakes, possibly first conceived by Clemens himself, was never carried out (*L1,* 282–83; *RI 1993,* 664).

[8] Estimates of the total Gridley raised range between $40,000 and $275,000 in gold. In *Roughing It* Clemens put it at "a hundred and fifty thousand dollars in

greenbacks." Given the fluctuating value of the greenback, that probably was the equivalent of, at most, about $87,000 in gold (*RI 1993*, 298, 662, 664).

[9] For another instance of Clemens's obscuring his identity when making a "serious" public statement, see 29 Apr 71 to Reid.

To Elisha Bliss, Jr.
13 December 1870 • New York, N.Y.
(Paraphrase: Bromer, item 10)

10. CLEMENS, SAMUEL L. **Four page ALs,** signed "Clemens" with the postscript signed "Mark" to "Friend Bliss" (his Hartford publisher Elisha Bliss), Dec. 13, [1870]. The letter discusses a scheme of Clemens' to write about the diamond rush in South Africa.[1]

[1] It also summoned Bliss to New York City for further discussion. He arrived by the morning of 14 December ("Morning Arrivals," New York *Evening Express,* 14 Dec 70, 3). Although John Henry Riley also met with Clemens around this time, he and Bliss may not have become acquainted (20 Dec 70 to Bliss).

To Elisha Bliss, Jr.
per Telegraph Operator
17 December 1870 • Buffalo, N.Y.
(MS, copy received: NN-B)

THE WESTERN UNION TELEGRAPH COMPANY.

2059

DATED ___Buffalo N.Y._____ 187 0_____

RECEIVED AT ___3 20 Dec 17_____

TO ___E. Bliss Jr._____
149 Asylum St.

Got homesick. Will come shortly with sketches & manuscript.[1] Send me right away New York draft for fifteen hundred dollars payable to James H. Riley.[2] He starts in ten days.

Saml L. Clemens

29 pd N

[telegram docketed:] √ *[and]* Mark Twain | Dec 17/70

[1] The sketches were for a volume that Clemens and Bliss must have discussed in New York; their 29 December contract for it is transcribed in *ET&S1*, 435. The manuscript was a sample of *Roughing It*.

[2] Actually John Henry Riley. See 20 Dec 70 to Bliss, n. 3.

From Samuel L. and Olivia L. Clemens
to Mary Mason Fairbanks
17 December 1870 • Buffalo, N.Y.
(MS: CSmH)

(c)

Buf. 17th.

Mother dear, I am so sorry that things have interfered over & over again to keep me from writing you. As soon as you left[1] I found myself in a perfect crush & jam of literary work,[2] & I said to myself that everything must give place now to sheer downright labor—& so I stuck to it with all my might, even when I knew I ought to be giving more time & cheer to Livy and mother[3]—& mind you I would not even reply to pressing business letters. ~~But~~ And just as your last letter arrived I shot off to New York to issue a pamphlet, & staid over 7 days—just got back this minute, & wouldn't even delay to have half a talk with Livy, who is sitting here applauding me & urging me to not stop till Mother Fairbanks is ~~thou~~ thoroughly satisfied that she *must* write herself "Mother" Fairbanks. But she is hurrying me, too (kissing me all over the head so boisterously that *I* my pen misses the switch & goes off the track every now & then.)

The baby is doing well, now, but they tell me he was dangerously ill yesterday & they came near telegraphing me to hurry home.

I sent Allie our little wedding offering from New York yesterday (the two Sistine ~~cubs~~ ,cherubs, ~~with~~ resting their elbows on a bench & smiling up at the Madonna,.) One of the ~~cubs~~ ,cherubs, is to represent

Livy's loving wishes for the blessed couple, & the other is to represent mine to the best of his ~~smile~~ small ability.

We got the wedding invitations to-day, & I think ~~d~~ Dan Slote, Charley & I, will go to Cleveland together. Dan told me to telegraph him, & I shall.[4]

I bought my "Jumping Frog" copyright back again from Webb. Am going to melt up the plates. I gave him his indebtedness ($600,) & $800 cash beside, for ~~the~~ his share of the copyright & right of publication. Think of *purchasing* one's own property after never having received one cent ~~on~~ from the publication![5]

Well, mother dear, I'll close, now, & try hard to do better in future. For even if we do neglect other friends & correspondents we have the very strongest desire & determination *not* to neglect *you*, ever any more. "God bless us, every one."[6]

Good bye.

Yr Son

Saml.

We are glad to get the Youth back again, dear Mother Fairbanks, I do assure you— and feel as if we never wanted to let him go again— Mother and I often speak of you and you well know that the words are loving ones— Love and all good and pleasant wishes to Allie, and kind regards to the rest of your household including Mr Gaaylord. Always with love yours

Livy.

[1] See 7 Nov 70 to Langdon, n. 3.

[2] Including the *Galaxy* "Memoranda" for January 1871, work on *Roughing It* and the planned volume of sketches, production of the *(Burlesque) Autobiography* "pamphlet," and promotion of the scheme for a diamond mine book.

[3] Olivia Lewis Langdon had been visiting since around 24 November (19 Nov 70 to Langdon).

[4] Clemens attended Alice Holmes Fairbanks's wedding in January, but it is not known if he was accompanied by Slote and Langdon (12 Jan 71 to OLC).

[5] See 22 Dec 70 to Bliss.

[6] Apparently the Clemenses were reading "A Christmas Carol."

To Joseph H. Twichell
19 December 1870 • Buffalo, N.Y.
(MS: CtY-BR)

(*c*)

Buf. 19th.

Dear J. H.—

All *is* well with us, I believe—though for some days the baby has was ˏquiteˏ ill. We cond consider him nearly restored to health now, however. Aský my bo brother about us—you will find him at Bliss's publishing office where [he] is gone to edit Bliss's new paper,—left here last Monday.[1] Make his & his wife's acquaintance. Take Mrs. T. to see them ʄ as soon as they are fixed.

Livy *is* up, & the prince keeps her busy & anxious these latter days & nights, but I am a bachelor up stairs & don't have to jump up & get the soothing-syrup—though I would as soon do it as not, I assure you. [Livy will be almost certain to read this letter.]

Tell Harmony (Mrs. T.) that I *do* hold the baby, & do it pretty handily, too, although with occasional apprehensions that his ʄ loose head will fall off. I don't have to quiet him—he hardly ever utters a cry. He is always thinking about something. He is a patient, good little baby. And

Smoke? I *always* smoke from 3 till 5 on Sunday afternoons—& in New York the other day I smoked a week, day & night. But when Livy is well I smoke only those 2 hours on Sunday. I'm "boss" of the habit, now, & shall never let it boss me any more. Originally, I quit solely on Livy's account (not that I believed there was the faintest *reason* in the matter, but just as I would deprive myself of sugar in my coffee if she wished it, or quit wearing socks if the she thought them immoral), but & I stick to it yet on Livy's account, & shall always continue to do so, without a pang.[2] But somehow it seems a pity that *you* quit, for Mrs. T. didn't mind it if I remember rightly. Ah, it is turning one's back upon a kindly Providence to spurn away from us the good creature he sent to make the breath of life a *luxury* as well as a necessity, *enjoyable* as well as useful, to go & quit smoking when there ain't any sufficient excuse for it. Why my old boy, when they used to tell me I would shorten my life ten years by smoking, I they little knew the devotee they were wasting their puerile words upon—they little knew how I trivial & valueless I would regard a decade that had no smoking in it! Ha! But I won't persuade you, Twichell—I won't until I see you again—for but *then* we'll smoke for a week together & then shut off again.

I would have gone to Hartford from New York last Saturday[3] but I got *so* homesick I couldn't. But maybe I'll come soon. [Can you keep a secret? Among other reasons, I would have had to stay at Bliss's— wouldn't let me go to the hotel—why didn't you offer me bed & board? I'm expecting to run over there in a couple of weeks.] ‚or more.]‚

No, Sir, *catch* me in the metropolis again, to get homesick.

I didn't know Warren Warner had a book out.[4]

We send oceans & continents of love—I have worked myself down, to-day.

> Yrs always
> Mark.

[1] On 12 December, that is, while Clemens was in New York.
[2] See 13 Jan 70 to OLL.
[3] December 17.
[4] *My Summer in a Garden* (3 Jan 71 to Twichell, n. 1).

To Elisha Bliss, Jr.
20 December 1870 • Buffalo, N.Y.
(MS: Christie's)

> Buf. Dec. 20.

Friend Bliss

Have just read over, approved & signed that contract, & it will go to you to-night.[1]

Riley is my man—did I introduce him to you in New York? He sails Jan. 4 for Africa. Just read about him in my Galaxy Memoranda for a month or two ago—have forgotten which month, but it is headed "Riley—Newspaper Correspondent."[2] Riley is *perfectly* honorable & reliable in every possible way—his simple promise is as good as any man's oath. I have roomed with him long, & have known him years. He has "roughed it" ~~it~~ ˄in˄ many savage countries & is as tough as a pine-knot. He is the very best man in the entire United States for this mission—& when he comes back & tells me his story in my study (for he is a splendid talker,) I'll set it down red hot, & that book will just make the "Innocents" sick! ⟨He is to talk to me 2 hours a day, ~~till I have~~ week after week & month after month till I have pumped him entirely dry, I boarding him free in my house & paying him $50 a month beside. I'll get *two* 600‑page books out of his experiences, see if I don't. And if you make the first one go, we won't have any trouble about who shall publish the second one. I mean to keep Riley traveling for me till I wear him out!

All this is "mum."

Yrs Clemens

P. S. When I ~~teel~~ tel[e]graphed you to send the check for $1,500 it didn't occur to me that maybe you'd rather have the contract signed first, but that was just like my thoughtlessness. But send the check to me on New York, *made payable to the order of J. H. Riley*, & I will forward it to him at Washington, as he desired me to do. If you haven't sent it yet, you may make it in *two* drafts,[3] one for $100⁰⁰ and one for $1,400⁰⁰.

How is my brother getting along, & what sort of a home has he gone into?[4]

Mark.

✉—————————————————————————

[letter docketed:] Mark Twain | Dec 20/70 | Author

[1] The contract for the South African diamond mine book (2 Dec 70 to Bliss; Appendix E).

[2] See 28 Nov 70 to Bliss, n. 1.

[3] Bliss's letter of 20 December crossed in the mail with Clemens's:

> We send you to day our check on New York for Fifteen Hundred Dolls, payable to your order, & you can endorse it over to anyone you choose to. . . . Did you find the contract at Buffalo on your return & is it all right. If so sign & return at your convenience— . . .
>
> Please acknowledge receipt of check &c. Let me know about Mss. & also about the sketches & come on & have a talk if possible. (CU-MARK)

The check was on the Tenth National Bank, in New York (NN-B). On 22 December Clemens endorsed it to Riley and enclosed it in a letter that went first to Washington and then by 26 December reached Riley in Philadelphia, where he

was visiting his mother (Riley to SLC, 26 Dec 70, 31 Dec 70, both in CU-
MARK).
    [4] See 5 Jan 71 to Bliss, n. 3.

To ~~Edward T. Howard~~
To A. Francis Judd
20 December 1870 • Buffalo, N.Y.
(MS facsimile: CtY-BR)

(LLC)

                                                            Buffalo, Dec. 20.

Friend ~~Howard—~~
        Judd—[1]
    (Your letter made me think of Ned Howard, & unconsciously I
wrote the name.) I don't think an enormous deal of Howard, though
that's nothing against *him*, ~~oc~~ of course. Tastes differ, & 200 miles mule-
back in company is the next best thing to a sea-voyage to bring a man's
worst points to the surface. Ned & I *like* each other, but we don't *love*, &
we never did. I like to talk with him, & I buy little jewelry trifles there,
but we don't embrace—I would as soon ¢ think of embracing a fish, or
an ~~icl~~ icicle, or any other particularly cold & unemotional thing—say a
dead stranger, for instance.[2]
    Our wedding cards brought exceedingly pleasant notes from 2 little
favorites of mine, the Spencer girls, at Benicia.[3]
    I do wish you *had* spent a day or two with us in Buffalo, & I beg that
you *will* when you come again. I love to see people from the Islands notwithstanding I conducted myself so badly there & left behind me so
unenviable a name.[4] But then you know they honor Harris there, & so
while that continues the preferable distinction is to stand *dis*honored,
maybe. I never stole anything in the Islands—and ah, me, I wish Harris
could say as much![5]
    I am under contract to write 2 more books the size of Innocents
Abroad (600 pp 8vo.) & after that I am going to do up the Islands &
Harris. They have "kept" 4 years, & I guess they will keep 2 or 3 longer.[6]

Have sold 82,000 copies of the Innocents in 16 months—the largest sale of that size book ever made in America in the same length of time. It still sells 2 to 3,000 a month & will so continue for a long time.[7]

Yes, the statement that you mention about the white children of the Islands having never borne a stain in any instance on their good name was in my lecture & has been pretty well disseminateḑion through the United States.[8]

[*one half of MS page missing*]

⊠————————————————————————————

ˏIf this isn't postage enough, it don't make any difference, because I have a private understanding with his Majesty Kamehameha V., whereby and "Harris."ˏ[9]

————————————————————————————

A. Francis Judd Esq
Honolulu
H. I.

[*across envelope end:*] Return to Mark Twain | Buffalo, U. S. [*postmarked·*] BUFFALO N.Y. DEC 21 [*and*] SAN FRANCISCO PAID ALL DEC 31

[1] Albert Francis Judd (1838–1900), the son of Gerrit Parmele Judd, Hawaiian missionary and statesman, became attorney general of the Hawaiian Islands in 1873, a member of the Hawaiian supreme court the following year, and served as its chief justice from 1881 until his death. His letter to Clemens does not survive. Clemens's acquaintance with the Judd family, largely undocumented, dated from 1866 (*L1*, 333–56; *N&J1*, 91–237).

[2] Edward Tasker Howard (1844?–1918), of New York and San Francisco, had been Clemens's reluctant travel companion in Hawaii in June 1866. Howard was now a jeweler in New York: see *L1*, 346 n. 10, and Austin, 250–54 (both misidentifying Howard as an Englishman), and *RI 1993*, 736–37.

[3] Nellie and Katie Spencer were the daughters of Thomas Spencer, a merchant and ship chandler at Hilo, Hawaii, who apparently hosted Clemens and Howard in June 1866. In Benicia, California, the girls may have attended Mills Seminary for women, forerunner of Mills College (*N&J1*, 133; Austin, 203; *MTH*, 15, 77–78; Hart 1987, 26, 321).

[4] This bad behavior has not been documented. Although on at least one occasion Clemens "made Honolulu howl" (*L3*, 359), opinion of him seems to have been favorable: see for example, Austin, 250–54, and *MTH*, 134, 151–52.

[5] Charles Coffin Harris (1821–81), from New Hampshire, was the Hawaiian minister of finance and the most influential advisor to King Kamehameha V.

Clemens ridiculed Harris, who was pompous and overweening but not dishonest, in letters to the Sacramento *Union* (*N&J1,* 119 n. 35; SLC 1866c, e–f).

⁶The Hawaiian Islands and Harris only had to "keep" until July 1871, when, using some of his Sacramento *Union* letters and the manuscript of an abortive 1866–67 book on Hawaii, Clemens prepared most of what became chapters 62–77 of *Roughing It* (chapters 67 and 68 included attacks on Harris). Then in January 1873 he published two letters about Hawaii in the New York *Tribune,* in the second of which he excoriated Harris still again. In 1884 he began a Hawaiian novel; the fragments that survive in the Mark Twain Papers do not refer to Harris (*RI 1993,* 463–64, 469, 718, 815, 862–63; SLC 1873c–d; *N&J1,* 104–5).

⁷Sales of *The Innocents Abroad* through its first fifteen months, or five quarters (30 July 69–31 Oct 70) totaled about 74,500 copies. By the end of the sixth quarter (1 Nov 70–31 Jan 71) the total had reached about 82,524 (5 Aug 70 to Bliss, n. 1; 7 Nov 70 to Bliss, n. 1; 15 Feb 71 to Bliss, n. 1).

⁸Clemens had begun disseminating some form of this statement with his very first Sandwich Islands lecture, in San Francisco on 2 October 1866, when he paid "an exceedingly glowing tribute to the missionaries" ("Editorial Gossip," San Francisco *Sunday Mercury,* 7 Oct 66, clipping in Scrapbook 4:33–34, CU-MARK). In 1867, Henry M. Stanley, reporting for the St. Louis *Missouri Democrat,* transcribed the version Clemens used in his lecture on 26 March:

> There are 3000 whites there, mostly Americans, and they are still increasing. They own all the money, control all the commerce, and own all the ships. They have a constitutional monarchy but they have no constitution, and the monarchy is only an empty name. . . . In education, refinement and culture, the sons and daughters of our missionaries there need not be ashamed to compare themselves with their brothers and sisters in the United States. (Stanley)

Lecturing in New York on 6 May 1867, Clemens "gave the American missionaries great credit for their work in civilizing and converting the Islanders, and spoke of the singular fact that the descendants of these missionaries have no stain upon their moral character, being exemplary citizens" ("Mark Twain's Lecture," New York *Times,* 7 May 67, 5). Then, on his eastern tour of November 1869–January 1870 with "Our Fellow Savages of the Sandwich Islands," Clemens reprised the statement, for example as reported by the Hartford *Courant* of 24 November:

> There are about three thousand white people in the islands; they are mostly Americans. In fact they are the kings of the Sandwich Islands; the monarchy is not much more than a mere name. These people stand as high in the scale of character as any people in the world, and some of them who were born and educated in those islands don't even know what vice is. ("Mark Twain's Lecture," 2)

(*L1,* 361; *L2,* 40–44; *L3,* 483–86; 1 Feb 94 to Frank Fuller, CtY-BR; AD, 20 Nov 1906, CU-MARK).

⁹Lot Kamehameha (1830–72) reigned as Kamehameha V from 1863 until his death. Clemens had planned to meet him in April 1866, but apparently did not do so (*RI 1993,* 717). The postage—a three-cent pre-stamped envelope, covering the basic domestic rate, to which Clemens added a three-cent stamp—was correct, as the San Francisco postmark indicates (Meyer et al., 84).

To Elisha Bliss, Jr.
22 December 1870 • Buffalo, N.Y.
(MS: CtY-BR, ViU, Axelrod)

Buffalo, Dec. 22/70.

Friend Bliss:

This is to acknowledge receipt of the fifteen ¢ hundred dollars for the foreign expedition. Thanks.

ᴀSam*ˡ*. L. Clemensᴀ

The contract has gone to you, approved & signed. Send me one.

You'd better go to canvassing for the vol. of sketches *now*, hadn't you? You must illustrate it—& mind you, the man to do the choicest of the pictures is Mullin—the Sisters are reforming him & he is sadly in need of work & money. Write to Launt Thompson the Sculptor, (Albemarle Hotel, New York) about him. I did ᴡ so want him for that satire but didn't know he was sober now & in hospital.[1]

Make out a contract for the sketch-book (7½ per cent.) & mail to me.[2]

I think the sketch-book should be as profusely illustrated as the Innocents.

To-day I arranged enough sketches to make ~~200~~ 134 pages of the book (200 words on a page, I estimated—size of De Witt Talmage's new book of rubbish.)[3] I shall go right on till I have finished selecting, & then write ań new sketch or so. One hundred of the pages selected to-day are scarcely known.

I bought my Jumping Frog from Webb,—gave him what he owed me ($600⁰⁰,), and $800 cash, & 300 remaining copies of the book, & also took $128 worth of ~~fresh~~ unprinted paper off his hands.[4]

I think of a Jumping Frog *pamphlet* (illustrated) for next Christmas—do you want it?[5]

Ys Ever
Mark

[*letter docketed by Bliss:*] Write L. Thompson sculptor about Mullins Albemarle Hotel [*and, in another hand:*] √ [*and*] Mark Twain | Dec 22/70 | Author

[1] Edward F. Mullen had contributed illustrations to humorous books by three of Clemens's contemporaries: *"Drifting About"; or, What "Jeems Pipes, of Pipesville," Saw-and-Did* (New York: G. W. Carleton, 1863), by Stephen C. Massett; *The Life and Adventures, Songs, Services and Speeches of Private Miles O'Reilly* (New York: G. W. Carleton, 1864), by Charles G. Halpine; and *Artemus Ward; His Travels* (New York: G. W. Carleton, 1865), by Charles Farrar Browne. The satire Clemens had wanted Mullen for was "The House that Jack Built," an attack on the promoters of the Erie Railroad, in *Mark Twain's (Burlesque) Autobiography and First Romance*. (It instead featured cartoons by Henry Louis Stephens.) Bliss, who had been dissatisfied with Mullen in the past, agreed to use him again (see note 5, below, and 4 and 5 Jan 71 to Bliss, n. 4). Launt Thompson (1833–94), whose studio was at 51 West Tenth Street, was temporarily living at the Albemarle Hotel between lodgings (Hamilton, 189–90, 208, 210; Wilson: 1870, 1200; 1871, 1142).

[2] Bliss sent Clemens a copy of the signed diamond mine book contract (Appendix E) and a draft sketch book contract (*ET&S1*, 435) on 29 December.

[3] Talmage, whose writing Clemens had ridiculed in the May 1870 *Galaxy* (30? Apr 70 to Converse, n. 1), had published his first book, *Crumbs Swept Up*, a popular collection of instructive tales, anecdotal essays, and travel articles, in the fall of 1870.

[4] Clemens's copy of a statement from New York printer and binder Samuel W. Green, itemizing work done for Charles Henry Webb on *The Celebrated Jumping Frog of Calaveras County, And other Sketches*, survives in the Mark Twain Papers. Dated 10 December 1870, and prepared for Clemens and Webb's negotiations in New York, it shows that 4,076 copies of the *Jumping Frog* book were bound between 30 April 1867 and 21 October 1870, with an additional 250 copies remaining in unbound sheets. The statement does not indicate the cost to Webb for printing or binding. Nor does it mention the 50 bound copies that apparently remained unsold. Since Clemens's royalty probably was 10 percent of the retail price ($1.00 paperbound, $1.50 cloth), the total amount owed to him—discounting the unsold books, and not allowing for review copies—would have been between $377.60 and $566.40 (Wilson 1870, 469; *L2*, 48–49, 53; *ET&S1*, 545 nn. 43, 44).

[5] Bliss replied on 28 December (misdating his letter 29 December; CU-MARK):

Friend Clemens,
    Yours of 22nd rec'd. Glad to hear you are progressing with the *Books*— I believe I wrote you I would copy this contract the next day after I wrote you & send you Well I think I did—not do as I agreed this time— The fact is I have been so busy with your brother &c getting things ready for paper &c I have not had a moment to do it— Have waited 2 or 3 days past to do it & send with this reply, & now dont send it. Well I will do it to night before I go to bed & also make out the contract for the *Sketch book* & send *both tomorrows' mail*—but dare not delay writing you longer. Yes we will have Mullen illustrate the sketch book all right. Glad you have the Jumping Frog, in your own hands, but think he got the *big end of a loaf* He ought to have sold you the plates for what he owed you.
    Dont you think Jumping Frog would be a big thing in the sketch book? Seems to me it will do you as much good there as anywhere & pay you best— Think strongly of it, & see if you dont think it will be best to put it in there— By the way where are the plates & dont you want the book sold as it is—think we could sell a good many without making

a noise—if you dont put it in Sketch book— *Yes we want it in the pamphlet*, or at least talk it over with you before you let it go, if you use it this way. Are you coming on? Will canvass for Sketch book as soon as Prospectus is ready for it. Will send Contracts to-morrow. Excuse my past ~~lies~~ failures.

> Truly
> Bliss

On 29 December, in his letter enclosing the sketchbook contract, Bliss asked Clemens to revise his old sketches and include some new ones so that "a new copyright" could be secured on the volume (CU-MARK). The contract for it made this a requirement (*ET&S1*, 435). For Clemens's plans for the plates of the *Jumping Frog* book, see 17 Dec 70 to Fairbanks. He responded to Bliss's Jumping Frog proposals and submitted some portion of the sketchbook contents in early January 1871 (3 Jan 71, 4 and 5 Jan 71, both to Bliss).

To Francis P. Church
23 December 1870 • Buffalo, N.Y.
(Mott 1957, 366–67)

Dec. 23.

Oh, please don't fail to get this delicious thing in—now *don't*. Don't wait to ask the Sheldons whether they'll back me for $1,000—I hereby give them authority to secure themselves amply by means of my share of my pamphlet which they are about to publish.[1] Or let them call for the *money* if it is won, & I'll furnish it instantly. I've got these *Enquirer* idiots just where I wanted *some*body—don't you see why? Because half of the people don't know now whether to believe I wrote that thing or not, or whether it *was* from the *Review,* or whether it is all a sell, & no criticism ever *was* in the London paper. Now, over the shoulders of this Cincinnati fool, I'll make the whole thing straight.

Don't let that paragraph get lost for your life.

I've got the *original* London *Saturday Review of Oct. 8 with the silly original critique in it right under my nose at this moment*—& I'll lock it up till that idiot *dares* to call for it—which he never will![2]

¹*Mark Twain's (Burlesque) Autobiography and First Romance.* The "delicious thing" was the manuscript of "A Falsehood": see the next note.

²Reacting to Clemens's "An Entertaining Article" (3 Dec 70 to Redpath, n. 4), the Cincinnati *Enquirer* of 17 December had remarked:

> MARK TWAIN at last sees that the *Saturday Review's* criticism of his *Innocents Abroad* was not serious, and he is intensely mortified at the thought of having been so badly sold[.] He takes the only course left him, and in the last *Galaxy* claims that *he* wrote the criticism himself, and published it in the *Galaxy* to sell the public. This is ingenious, but unfortunately it is not true. If any of our readers will take the trouble to call at this office we will show them the original article in the *Saturday Review* of October 8, which, on comparison, will be found to be identical with the one published in the *Galaxy.* The best thing for MARK to do will be to admit that he was sold, and say no more about it. ("Notes and Notions," 4)

In "A Falsehood," in his *Galaxy* "Memoranda" for February 1871, Clemens reprinted the *Enquirer* item and issued the following challenge:

> If the "Enquirer" people, through any agent, will produce at THE GALAXY office a London "Saturday Review" of October 8th, containing an "article which, on comparison, will be found to be identical with the one published in THE GALAXY," I will pay to that agent five hundred dollars cash. Moreover, if at any specified time I fail to produce at the same place a copy of the London "Saturday Review" of October 8th, containing a lengthy criticism upon the "Innocents Abroad," entirely different, in every paragraph and sentence, from the one I published in THE GALAXY, I will pay to the "Enquirer's" agent another five hundred dollars cash. I offer Sheldon & Co., publishers, 500 Broadway, New York, as my "backers." . . .
>
> In next month's GALAXY, if they do not send the agent and take this chance at making a thousand dollars where they do not need to risk a single cent, they shall be exposed. I think the Cincinnati "Enquirer" must be edited by children. (SLC 1871f, 319)

On 19 January 1871, shortly after the February *Galaxy* issued, the *Enquirer* responded:

> WE fear that our relations with "MARK TWAIN" are becoming serious. We used to consider him a funny man, but we find him as matter-of-fact as a last-year's bird's-nest. . . .
>
> Mr. TWAIN published in the *Galaxy* what purported to be a review of his "Innocents Abroad," taken from the *Saturday Review.* He treated it with great gravity, and we professed to believe that he had been sold. The Hon. Mr. TWAIN laughed at us, and declared upon his word of honor that he had written it himself. As he had lied about it in the first place we thought that there would be no harm in doing a little additional lying, and therefore we asserted that the article in question *did* appear in the *Saturday Review* of October 8, and offered to show it to any inquiring person who might call at our office. Nobody ever called. . . . Now we have Mr. TWAIN in the *Galaxy* copying our article, and crying in a loud voice . . .
>
> Now, this is all bosh. As MARK TWAIN never told the truth in his life, how are we to know that he is not lying about his inordinate desire to gamble? . . . We are not to be "bluffed." We deputize GEORGE, the COUNT JOANNES, to defend us in this matter. If he is convinced that our position is tenable, and that the *Saturday Review,* of October 8, will bear us out, he is authorized to cover any money which he finds in the hands of SHELDON & CO. to the credit of MARCUS AURELIUS TWAIN. As for Mr. TWAIN's threat of exposure, we care nothing. . . . Mr. TWAIN ought to have more respect for his infant son than to be making a "noodle" of himself. Upon the whole, we have about concluded that the "Memoranda" of the *Galaxy* is edited by a lunatic. ("Notes and Notions," 4)

The *Enquirer's* proposed representative was George Jones (1810–79), a self-aggrandizing lawyer and actor who used the stage name "Count Joannes" and was a figure of ridicule in both of his professions. Clemens let the matter drop: he did not publish "Memoranda" in the March *Galaxy* and made no mention of the *Enquirer* in the brief final "Memoranda" he published in April (Joseph, Squires, and Louis, 510; Bryan, 1:681; Odell, 7:546, 583, 605–6, 9:28, 10:72, 388–89; "Joannes," New York *Tribune*, 14 Jan 71, 4).

To Eunice Ford
25? December 1870 • Buffalo, N.Y.
(MS: CtHMTH)

Christmas, 1870.

Dear Greatgrandma:

With this I send you a loving Christmas present to remind you that it at this season of all seasons of the year when babies are important & their acts of great honor & significance, *this* baby recognizes & approves of his greatgrandma—entirely & completely.

This present is a small personal friend of mine who has gotten over his crimson period, his yaller period & his red-gum period & has bleached out & taken a good complexion.[1]

He has a good many ve virtues, but his chiefest one is his mannerly & attractive quietness. He never speaks till he is spoken to—and even then he don't answer right off. Merry Christmas to you & a great deal of love.

> Your greatgrandson
> Langdon Clemens.

[1]A photograph of Langdon Clemens may have accompanied this letter, although no such early image has been identified. Possibly, however, the enclosure was a drawing, similar to the ones Clemens had recently done for Susan Crane (19–20? Nov 70 to Crane).

To Alfred B. Crandell and Other Members
of the Farmers' Club
26 December 1870 • Buffalo, N.Y.
(MS: Karanovich)

Buffalo, Dec. 26.

Gentlemen:

I thank you very much for your invitation to the Agricultural dinner, & would promptly accept it & as promptly be there but for the fact
that Mr. Greeley is very busy this month & has requested me to clandestinely continue, ₐfor him,ₐ in the Tribune, ₓfor him,ₓ the articles
headed "What I Know about Farming." Consequently the necessity of
explaining to the readers of that journal *why* buttermilk cannot be manufactured profitably ₒₜ ₒᵤₜ ₒf at 8 cents a quart out of butter that costs
60 cents a pound, compels my stay at home until the article is written.

With reiterated thanks, I am—

Yrs Truly

Mark Twain[1]

[1]Crandell later added the following commentary, beneath the signature:

Explanatory:

As Secretary of the New York Rural Club—Horace Greeley President—I was
instructed to invite Mark Twain to one of our dinners. This is his reply. Time must have
been about 1871.

A. B. Crandell.

He misremembered somewhat. The dinner was a 5 January 1871 reunion, at the
Metropolitan Hotel, for a "number of members of the Farmers' Club of the
American Institute, who made a trip to California together last Summer" ("The
New-York Farmers' Club," New York *Tribune,* 6 Jan 71, 8). The secretary of the
Farmers' Club was J. W. Chambers, not Crandell; the club's president was Na-
than C. Ely, not Horace Greeley. Greeley—whose "What I Know of Farming"
appeared weekly in the New York *Tribune* throughout 1870—was president of
the parent American Institute of the City of New York, founded in 1828 to promote advances in "agriculture, commerce, manufactures, and the arts" (Lossing, 169, 171; Wilson 1870, "City Register," 42, 43). Possibly Crandell—identified by Albert Bigelow Paine as "A. B. Crandall, in Woodberry Falls, N. Y."
(*MTL,* 1:180)—was *its* secretary. He was one of the speakers at the Farmers'
Club dinner. Clemens's letter of regret was among several that were read.

To John R. Drake
26 December 1870 • Buffalo, N.Y.
(MS: CtY-BR)

Buf. Dec. 26.

J. R. Drake, Esq
Dr Sir:

I will with pleasure forward to your brother the items he desires, at my earliest convenience.[1]

Yrs Truly
Saml. L. Clemens.

---

[1] John Robert Drake (b. 1830), who worked for the Buffalo patent agency of
Burke, Fraser, and Osgood, lived at 366 Delaware Avenue, two blocks from the
Clemenses. Clemens's next letter was to Drake's brother (*Buffalo Directory:*
1870, 17, 342, 580; 1871, 322, 611; 1872, 266, 305; Samuel Gardner Drake).

To Francis S. Drake
26 December 1870 • Buffalo, N.Y.
(MS: NN-B)

Buffalo, Dec. 26.

F. S. Drake, Esq
Dr Sir:

I have received your note, through your brother, & enclose the ʄ within.
There is ń really no biography *to* my career.

I have put in the only striking thing that occurs to me,—viz., that
I fully expected the "Jumping Frog["] to sell 50,000 copies & it only sold
4,000;[1] & I only expected the "Innocents" to sell 3,000 copies but it as-
tounded me by selling 85,000 copies in ˏ*within*ˏ *16 months*—which, I am
told, is the largest sale of a *four-dollar* book (price $ is $3.50 to $5—$4
about the average) ever achieved in America in so short a time.[2] *That* is
the only thing in my life that seems to me remarkable enough to merit
public attention—

Besides, my idea is, that you only desire the mere name & one or
two items—for your full biographies must be necessarily given to the
men of *permanent* fame, like our generals & ~~chei~~ chief poets &
historians.[3]

Ys Truly

Sam*ˡ*. L. Clemens.

[1] See 22 Dec 70 to Bliss, n. 4.
[2] See 20 Dec 70 to Judd, n. 7.
[3] Francis Samuel Drake (1828–85) was preparing the first edition of his one-
volume *Dictionary of American Biography, Including Men of the Time* (1872).
Drake used Clemens's enclosure for the following entry, which was shorter than
those for Artemus Ward, Josh Billings, and Petroleum V. Nasby:

> **Clemens,** SAMUEL LANGHORNE, "Mark Twain," humorist, b. Florida, Munroe
> Co., Mo., 30 Nov. 1835. Entered journalism in Virginia, Nevada, in 1862; continued
> in it 3 years there, 3 years in San Francisco, and one in Buffalo. Author of "The Jumping
> Frog, and other Sketches," 12mo, 1867; "The Innocents Abroad," 8vo, 1869, of which
> 100,000 copies have been sold in two years. Contrib. of humorous sketches to "The
> Galaxy," 1870–1. (Francis Samuel Drake, 195)

Sales of *The Innocents Abroad* reached 100,000 around July 1872 (Hirst 1975,
326).

To Whitelaw Reid
26 December 1870 • Buffalo, N.Y.
(Transcript and MS: New York *Tribune*, 29 Dec 70, and DLC)

Mark Twain will publish a burlesque autobiography, in pamphlet
form, in a few days, through Sheldon & Co.

Buffalo, Dec. 26.

Friend Reid:

I would like it very much if you would put the above item into your
column of little floating paragraphs & general notes. As the thing is not
known to anybody, it is a fair & legitimate item of literary news, & so it
is not unpardonable in the subscriber to ask you to print it.[1]

Merry Christmas & a happy New Year to you! I have had the one,
in unexampled magnificence, & so am ready to hail the other.

Was exceedingly sorry I did not get to dine with you—& scarce even see you. I sent you a voluminous explanatory telegram just before taking the cars—which I hope you rec'd.[2]

Yrs ~~Mark~~ fa[i]thfully

Mark.

[1]Reid obliged, cutting Clemens's "item" from this letter to use as printer's copy for the "Personal" column of the New York *Tribune* of 29 December 1870 (4). The text included here has been restored from the paper, although it may not be exactly as Clemens originally had it. On 1 January 1871, Reid wrote to him: "I gave your paragraph out and think it has appeared. I'm heartily glad to be able to render a service—if so trifling a thing deserves that name" (DLC). As Clemens and Reid intended, the announcement was immediately copied by other papers, for example: the Elmira *Advertiser* ("City and Neighborhood," 30 Dec 70, 4); the Buffalo *Courier* ("Personal," 31 Dec 70, 1); the Buffalo *Express* ("It is mentioned . . . ," 31 Dec 70, 2); and the Hartford *Courant* ("Personal," 31 Dec 70, 2). Unfortunately, the publicity was premature, for on 29 December Isaac E. Sheldon wrote to Clemens:

> I think the book will do quite as well 6 or 8 weeks from this time as it could now. During the month of Jan almost every bookseller is engaged on his inventory. I think however that it is best to get the book ready just as fast as possible; even if we hold them for a time after they are all made. There always are delays in getting a book ready. The engrav[ings] are promised for the end of this week. It will be next Tuesday [3 January 1871] before we can put them into the stereotypers hands & begin on the plates. (CU-MARK)

Sheldon promised to send an advertising circular "to every bookseller"—as soon as he and Clemens agreed to "the exact day of publication & the price." On Saturday, 31 December, ahead of schedule, he sent Clemens "proofs of all the cuts," that is, the electrotyped illustrations (CU-MARK). Setting a price was a matter of some contention, however (27 Jan 71 to Sheldon). *Mark Twain's (Burlesque) Autobiography and First Romance* was finally published in March 1871.

[2]On 15 December Reid had written to Clemens at the Albemarle Hotel:

> I have been waiting all the week for you to make your appearance, and here it is Thursday night. Please you send me word by the bearer that you will dine with me tomorrow (Friday) evening at half past 6 o'clock at the Union League Club. If you will say yes, I'll have one or two friends, not more, to meet us over a quiet bottle of wine. (DLC)

Clemens's "voluminous" telegram in reply is not known to survive. In his 1 January 1871 letter, Reid remarked: "I got your dispatch in time to send word to a friend or two I had asked not to come. Better luck next time" (DLC). The Union League Club was founded in 1863 to support the North during the Civil War and afterward turned its attention to political and social reform. Its headquarters were currently "in a fine mansion on the corner of Twenty-sixth Street and Madison Avenue" (Lossing, 748–52).

To Whitelaw Reid
31 December 1870 • Buffalo, N.Y.
(MS and transcript: DLC and New York *Tribune*, 4 Jan 71)

Buf. ~~30~~ 31ˢᵗ· Dec.

Friend Reid—

They are bound to make a flaming success of Surratt if these fool mayors & revenue officers do not stop making catspaws of themsel*f*ves for Surratt's manager (for I am ~~perfectly~~ satisfied that his manager is at the bottom of the whole thing.)

I This article would place me under my own commendation but for the fact that a notoriety based on tranquil contempt with no *p* bitterness visible in it is about as damaging as telegraphic betrayals of empty lecture-halls.

We are all well at home, & beg that you will visit us & the Falls when you can, & let us entertain you a day or two & make you acquainted with David Gray.[1] Please remember me to Mr. Hazard[2] & Col. Hay.[3]

In case you don't want this article it will be not the slightest offense in the world to leave it out, but I *would* take it as a great favor if you will then return it to me (I enclose stamps) for I have written it on *principle* & have sacrificed to it half a day which I could not nearly as well spare as I could the best suit of clothes I have got in the world.

Ys faithfully
Clemens.

[*enclosure:*]

To the Editor of The Tribune.

Sɪʀ: John H. Surratt's manager evidently understands his business, or else Surratt is fortunate above the average of snubbed & struggling would-be lecturers—for every day the newspapers reveal to the people that the gentleman is being *persecuted*. I am of the lecturing guild, Sir, & am aware that the cheapest & the surest way to get an undesired or unknown person splendidly before the public & crowd his houses, is to get somebody to *persecute* him. There are other ways, but this is the surest. One of the most courted lady-lecturers of the day owes by far the largest half of her profitable notoriety to a dreadful platform failure, which procured for her such an avaianche of newspaper scorn & rebuke that she became known (& sympathized with) all over the land in a single day. Another of the most courted lady-lecturers of the day is soaring along on a lucrative notoriety nine-tenths of which is the result of industriously-supplied two-line personal items telling how she wore her hair at Long Branch.[4] So you see how easy it is to excite the public interest in an individual, & fill that individual's lecture-halls for him. Do you not perceive that Mr. Surratt, who cannot at present induce more than a hundred people to listen to him, is on the high road to a notoriety which in a very little while will cram the largest halls in America with people eager to see the new wonder & hear him? Indeed he is on that very high road.

Mr. Surratt's manager, I fancy, is deliberately procuring this persecution, & the deep old fox knows that it is exactly the sort of advertising he needs. It is a hundred thousand times more effective than commonplace commendation in the dramatic column, which makes not the least impression upon the reader. When the telegraph recently spread it over the country that Mr. Surratt had an audience of only a hundred & fifty to hear him at Cooper Institute it was a most damaging thing. Six more such announcements, unaccompanied by any saving persecution, would have hurried the lecturer Surratt beyond the hope of resurrection; but at a lucky moment there was talk of his arrest (incited by his manager, no doubt), & next there was a story that Attorney-General Holt once offered to save Mrs. Surratt, & set her free, if the son would take her place, & *the son refused,* (more, acute managerial invention, no doubt),[5] & next came the announcement that Surratt's Baltimore lecture was interfered with by his arrest on a charge of non-payment of a trifling tobacco tax years ago (this official persecutor being a guileless catspaw of that manager, without the shadow of a doubt); & now at last comes the announcement that the Mayor of Washington has warned Surratt against driving the people of the capital to extremities by attempting to lecture there, & immediately the meek & law-abiding Surratt takes in his sign & closes his hall (the entire thing a crowning triumph of that manager's inventive genius, without question)![6]

If it is desired to make John H. Surratt a prodigious success as a lecturer & give him an income of $25,000 a year, it is only requisite that mayors, revenue officers, & hall proprietors continue to stand in front & persecute the lecturer while the ingenious manager stands behind & pulls their strings—& it is further only necessary that the telegraph people get knowledge of the said persecution (a thing which the said manager will attend to). But if it is desired that Mr. Surratt drop entirely out of the public notice in three short weeks, it is only necessary to *let him alone* & cease to make public mention of him. His little candle would straightway begin to burn weaker & weaker, & the "cabbage head" would begin to develop more & more prominently on its top, & presently the poor thing would flicker out & pass away in a film of smoke, leaving nothing behind but an evanescent stench. Am I not right?

MARK TWAIN.

Buffalo, Dec. 29, 1870.

---

¹"I heartily wish I could accept your very tempting invitation to Buffalo," Reid replied on 3 January. "By the way every body speaks cordially of David Gray, and some time I hope to have the pleasure of meeting him" (DLC).

² John Rose Greene Hassard planned to enter the priesthood, but instead became a journalist, biographer, and editor, spending the greatest part of his professional life at the New York *Tribune,* chiefly as music critic (*L2,* 175 n. 2).

³ John Milton Hay (1838–1905) spent most of the 1860s as, successively, assistant private secretary to Abraham Lincoln, an army officer (colonel in 1865) on assignment to the White House, secretary to the American legation in Paris, the American chargé d'affaires at Vienna, and secretary to the American legation in Madrid. Since the fall of 1870 he had been employed as an editorial writer and night editor for the *Tribune.* Apparently Clemens had last talked with him, at the paper's offices, on 11 or 12 December (see pp. 269–70), but it is not known exactly when they first met. In an Autobiographical Dictation of 31 January 1904, Clemens recalled a "Sunday morning, twenty-five years ago," when "Hay and I had been chatting and laughing and carrying-on almost like our earlier selves of '67" (CU-MARK; in *MTA,* 1:232–38, as "A Memory of John Hay"). And after Hay's death on 1 July 1905, Clemens issued a statement in which he remarked that "My friendship with Mr. Hay & my admiration of him endured 38 years without impairment" (*MTB,* 3:1249). An Autobiographical Dictation of 16 February 1906 lends indirect support to 1867 as the year of their meeting. There Clemens recalled that David Gray, of the Buffalo *Courier,* whom he had met in Buffalo in August or September 1869, became an "intimate friend, through his intimacy and mine with John Hay" (CU-MARK, in *MTA,* 2:118). In an Autobiographical Dictation of 27 August 1907, however, Clemens asserted that Hay and Whitelaw Reid "were salaried members of the New York *Tribune* staff when I first knew them" (CU-MARK†). That was certainly true of Reid, who joined the paper in 1868, and was acquainted with Clemens by June 1869. But while Clemens and Hay *might* have met only after Hay became Reid's *Tribune* subordinate in the fall of 1870, no convincing date between then and 11 December has been identified. Nor is there evidence of a meeting during one other possible period, October 1868–July 1869, while Hay was in the United States between European postings. In the absence of definitive information, then, 1–2 February 1867 and 23 February–3 March 1867, when Clemens and Hay were in New York City, and 4–8 June 1867, when Clemens and perhaps Hay were there,

seem the most likely periods for their initial meeting ("Personal," New York *Tribune*, 2 Feb 67, 2; Thayer, 1:245, 272–73, 278–80, 314–16, 335–36; Clara Louise Hay, 375; *L2*, 1–2, 10–18, 49–62; *L3*, 265 n. 1).

[4]Both of Clemens's allusions *could* be to Olive Logan, who was promoted relentlessly by means of "personal items" (8 Jan 70 to OLL [1st], n. 3) despite the embarrassing failure of her "Stage Struck" lecture in Boston's Music Hall on 5 November 1868, when those of her audience "near the doors soon struck for home." That fiasco was still drawing comment a year later ("Brief Jottings," Boston *Evening Transcript*, 5 Nov 68, 2, 6 Nov 68, 2; "Miss Olive Logan . . . ," Washington *Morning Chronicle*, 25 Oct 69, 2). It is likely, however, that the second lecturer was Kate Field, who also was regularly followed in the press and whose current lecture, on Charles Dickens, was quite popular, although Clemens was unenthusiastic about it (30 Jan 71 to Redpath, n. 3). Long Branch, New Jersey, was a popular summer resort on the Atlantic (Hall, 130).

[5]Joseph Holt (1807–94), actually judge-advocate general of the army, prosecuted the Lincoln assassins before a military commission. He was accused of suppressing the commission's recommendation of clemency for Mary Surratt (see note 6). The "story" Clemens retells here apparently was apocryphal.

[6]John H. Surratt (1844–1916) was tried in 1867 for participating in John Wilkes Booth's conspiracy to assassinate Lincoln, but was released after the jury was unable to reach a verdict. His mother, Mary (b. 1817), keeper of the boardinghouse where Booth planned the crime, was found guilty of the same charge and hanged in 1865, despite a lack of evidence, while Surratt himself was hiding in Canada. In December 1870 Surratt, managed by a Mr. Corbyn (or Crobyn), otherwise unidentified, had a brief season on the eastern lyceum circuit. Appearing before audiences of 100–300, he discussed his activities as a Confederate spy, defiantly admitted his part in Booth's initial plan to abduct Lincoln but professed ignorance of any assassination scheme, and denied abandoning his mother, alleging that he had been assured she could not be convicted. Surratt lectured without incident in Rockville, Maryland, on 6 December, and at New York's Cooper Institute, on 9 December, but was arrested after a 29 December lecture in Baltimore—for not having paid his license as a tobacco dealer there two years earlier. Friends claimed that the arrest was made to prevent his fourth appearance, scheduled for Washington, D.C., on 30 December. Washington Mayor Matthew G. Emery asked Surratt, free on bail, to cancel that lecture, for fear it might prompt a public disturbance. Surratt's compliance was not entirely voluntary. He was forced to take in his sign, or at least alter it, when, in succession, several Washington halls were refused to him. Last-minute arrangements were made for him to speak in a saloon, and a small audience gathered there, but he failed to show up. Thus ended his platform career (Chamlee, 531–38; New York *Tribune:* "John H. Surratt on the Platform," 8 Dec 70, 5; "Home News," 10 Dec 70, 5; "Arrest of John H. Surratt," 30 Dec 70, 1; "Washington," 31 Dec 70, 3; "Surratt Once More," 2 Jan 71, 5; New York *Times:* "John H. Surratt at the Cooper Institute," 10 Dec 70, 5; "Washington," 31 Dec 70, 1; Buffalo *Express:* "Washington," 26 Dec 70, 1).

To Joseph H. Twichell
3 January 1871 • Buffalo, N.Y.
(MS: Craven)

Buf., ≠ 3ᵈ.

Dear J H—

I tell you it is ~~perfectly~~ magnificent!——rich, delicious, ~~me~~ fascinating, brim full of meat,—the humor ~~is~~ transcends anything I have seen in print or heard from a stage this many a day,—& every page glitters like a cluster-pin with many-sided gems of fancy—Warner's book I mean—it is splendid.[1] But I haven't dressed yet—the barber is waiting to shave me, Livy & the rest of the family[2] are clamoring for breakfast & it does seem that a body can't sit down in his shirt-tail to drop a friendly line to a friend without all the elements "going for" him.

All well here. Hope same to you & yrs. Happy N. Y.ʳ & all that. Gd bye—

Ys

Mark

[1] Twichell had told Clemens in December about *My Summer in a Garden*, which gathered Charles Dudley Warner's humorous essays about a small farm, previously published in the Hartford *Courant*. Warner's first book, it was an immediate success, selling out the first printing by mid-December, within three weeks of publication (19 Dec 70 to Twichell; Lounsbury, xiv–xvi; Hartford *Courant:* advertisement, 28 Nov 70, 2; "Brief Mention," 17 Dec 70, 2).

[2] Including Olivia Lewis Langdon, who had arrived for a visit of nearly two months in late November 1870 (19 Nov 70 to Olivia Lewis Langdon; 20 Nov 70 to Charles J. Langdon; 25 Jan 71 to Day).

To Elisha Bliss, Jr.
3 January 1871 • Buffalo, N.Y.
(MS: CU-MARK)

(LLC)

Buf. Jan 3.

Friend Bliss—

No, if this pamphlet[1] pays, I want to is you to issue Jumping
Frog *illustrated*, along with 2 other sketches for the *holidays* next year.
I've paid high for the Frog & I want him to get his price back by himself.
The Sketch Book will be good enough without him.[2]

Name the Sketch book *"Mark Twain's Sketches"* & go on canvassing
like mad. Because if you don't hurry it will tread on the heels of the *big*
book next August.[3] In the course of a week I can have most of the matter
ready for I you I think. ᴧAm working like sin on it.ᴧ

Yrs

Clemens

[1] *Mark Twain's (Burlesque) Autobiography and First Romance.*
[2] See 17 Dec 70 to Bliss, and 22 Dec 70 to Bliss, n. 5. Clemens did not publish
a Jumping Frog pamphlet in 1871, but in 1874 included the story in *Mark
Twain's Sketches. Number One* (New York: American News Company), a paper-
covered booklet. The sketchbook he was assembling at this time, which did not
include the Jumping Frog, was repeatedly postponed. The contract for it was
not fulfilled until 1875, with *Sketches, New and Old,* which included "The
'Jumping Frog.' In English. Then in French." For an account of Clemens's
sketchbooks of this period, see *ET&S1,* 555–653.
[3] Clemens's (still untitled) book about his western years. *Roughing It* was not
in fact published until February 1872.

To Elisha Bliss, Jr.
4 and 5 January 1871 • Buffalo, N.Y.
(Transcript, paraphrase, and MS: AAA 1927a,
lot 244, and CU-MARK)

Jan. 4.

[*paraphrase: to Mr. Bliss of the American Publishing Co. . . . . stating he is
sending him the Mss. for these "Sketches" and writing that he wants*] the one

about the liar to be first one in the book;[1] [*paraphrase: Also, that he wants his brother to make copies of the "Sketches" before they are sent to the artist.*][2]

P. S.

Buf. Jan. 5.

Dear Bliss =

The curious beasts & great contrasts in this Pre-duluge article[3] offer a gorgeous chance for the artist's fancy & ingenuity, I think.

Send both sketches to Mullen—he is the man, to do them, I guess. Launt Thompson, Albemarle Hotel, will find him when wanted.[4]

Yrs

Mark.

[1] One of two manuscripts enclosed here, this sketch concerned a spectacular liar Clemens had met in the Sandwich Islands in 1866. He soon withdrew the manuscript, however, deciding to publish it as "About a Remarkable Stranger" in the April 1871 *Galaxy*. The manuscript does not survive (22 Feb 71, 4 Mar 71, both to OC).

[2] Orion finished making these security copies, which have not been found, during the second week of January (OC to SLC, 25 Jan 71, CU-MARK).

[3] An offshoot of, or selection from, the Noah's Ark book that Clemens had been working on for almost five years and that Bliss had been privy to at least since January 1870. Clemens had first broached the idea for an article on the subject in a letter to his sister in August 1869. He called this sketch "Pre-flood show" in the draft table of contents he prepared for the sketchbook, probably sometime in December 1870. He soon retrieved this manuscript as well: it has not been found, and was never published (22 Jan 70 to Bliss; *L3*, 312; *ET&S1*, 574–79; 22 Feb 71 to OC).

[4] On 25 January, Orion wrote Clemens that Bliss was in New York, searching for Mullen, as Clemens had suggested (22 Dec 70 to Bliss). Having employed Mullen as one of the illustrators of Albert D. Richardson's *Beyond the Mississippi* (1867), Bliss was reluctant to rehire him, put off by Mullen's pawning of wood blocks to buy whiskey, and his "charging fancy prices." But, Orion reported, Bliss promised "to get him to do some of the work" (CU-MARK). After the western book (*Roughing It*) displaced the sketchbook later in January, Bliss hired Mullen to help illustrate it (*RI 1993*, 857–58).

To Elisha Bliss, Jr.
5 January 1871 • Buffalo, N.Y.
(MS: MGlHi)

Buf. Jan. 5.

Friend Bliss—

I wish you would make the theatre give my brother & his wife season-passes—& you can puff & advertise in return. ˌHe's an editor now & entitled to courtesies.ˌ It will keep them in good spirits to go often to the theatre, & besides I want him to get drawn away from thought, & have a bracing & revivifying relaxation from his long siege of hard night work.[1]

Will you do it?[2]

Ys

Clemens.

I am glad you have made the place so pleasant to my brother—he & wife talk gratifiedly.[3]

---

[1] See 31 Oct 70 to Bliss and 5 Nov 70 to OC.

[2] Hartford's two theaters were Allyn Hall and Roberts' Opera House. During the 1870–71 season, each booked a variety of events: Allyn Hall mainly concerts and lectures, Roberts' Opera House theatrical and operatic performances (advertisements in Hartford *Courant*, 1870–71 passim). No evidence has been found that Bliss carried out Clemens's suggestion.

[3] Orion, accompanied or soon followed by Mollie, arrived in Hartford in mid-December 1870 to assume the editorship of the *American Publisher*, taking temporary lodgings. Bliss wrote Clemens on 20 December: "Your Brother is here & we are getting at work in earnest" (CU-MARK). No gratified letters from Orion or Mollie to Clemens are known to survive from December 1870, but by late January they had moved to "Pierson's, next door to Bliss's"—that is, to C. W. and David Pierson's boarding house at 263 Asylum Street, where they remained until early July (OC to SLC, 25 Jan 71, 4 July 71 [CU-MARK]; MEC to SLC, 4 July 71 [CU-MARK]; Geer 1871, 193).

From Samuel L. and Olivia L. Clemens
to Mary E. (Mollie) Clemens
5? January 1871 • Buffalo, N.Y.
(MS: NPV)

[first two MS pages (about 200 words) missing]

don't know but I will. I would like to d̶o̶ drop in on Bliss, too, since he
has got into his new house.[1]

Tell Orion I'll bet he is right & Bliss wrong—brief introductories
are *best.* Make them short & m̶e̶ fill them full of *meat,* is the trick.[2]

Ŧ Rev. Mr. Twichell may be justly described without flattery to be
a bully boy with a glass eye (as the lamented Josephus phrases ͺitͺ in his
Decline & Fall of the Roman Empire) ͺ—so is his wife—ͺ& I wrote him
to call on Orion & get acquainted—which he s̶a̶i̶d̶ says he will just as soon
as a press of botherations gives him a chance.[3] Both of you *go slow*—don't
hurry in the matter of making friends, & don't get impatient. Making
friends in Yankee land is a slow, slow business, but they are friends
worth having when they *are* made. There is no section in America f̶i̶t̶ half
so good to live in as splendid old New England—& there is no city on
this continent so lovely & lovable as Boston, almost in sight of which it
is now your high privilege to live.

The baby's weight has increased to 7½ pounds & his personal comeliness in proportion. I f̶e̶d̶ feel that I can say without exaggeration that
he is h̶u̶m̶p̶i̶n̶g̶ ͺ(our little boy never humps. Livy)ͺ ͺhumpingͺ himself.[4]

B̶l̶e̶s̶s̶ ̶m̶y̶ ̶s̶o̶u̶l̶
Good bye

                                                                    Yrs
                                                                    Sam.

[in ink:] P. S. Have written Bliss & asked him to get Orion ͺ2 season passes
to theatre.

[1] Bliss had moved from 273 to 265½ Asylum Street by July 1870. Clemens's
last known visit to Hartford was in December 1869. A desire to avoid Bliss's
hospitality had been one of his reasons for staying away (19 Dec 70 to Twichell;
L3, 439; Geer: 1869, 55; 1870, 57).

[2] Orion and Bliss were planning the editorial content of the *American Publisher.* The general "introductories" ultimately published were brief and item-

ized the sort of "useful information" that readers could expect to find. A contemplated "elaborate apology for 'Number One'" was abandoned (OC 1871c–d).

[3] Orion reported to Clemens on 25 January: "Twitchell and his wife called on us before we moved. He had previously called on me at the office. Mollie and I like them both very much" (CU-MARK). According to an 1872 article on contemporary expressions, "'Bully' is a term of commendation applied in a patronizing way among the vulgar, and means very fine. A more extensive phrase is 'A bully boy with a glass eye'" ("Popular Phrases," Chicago *Tribune*, 1 Jan 72, 1). Clemens again attributed the term to the historian Flavius Josephus in chapter 22 of *Roughing It* (*RI 1993*, 147).

[4] Clemens retraced "humping" in ink (Olivia had canceled it) when he added his postscript.

To John M. Hay
6? January 1871 • Buffalo, N.Y.
(Paraphrase: Joseph Bucklin Bishop, 777, and Thayer, 1:375)

On the first appearance of "J. B.," Mark Twain wrote to me, saying that I was all wrong making him an engineer,—that only a pilot could have done what I represented him as doing.[1]

[1] Hay's poem "Jim Bludso, (of the Prairie Belle.)"—about the engineer of a burning steamboat who dies while keeping his vow to "'hold her nozzle agin the bank / Till the last galoot's ashore'"—appeared in the New York *Tribune* on 5 January (John M. Hay 1871). On 9 January Hay replied to Clemens's criticism (CU-MARK):

Please send the inclosed by return mail

Astor House

Private   January 9. 1871

My Dear Mr Clemens

I owe you many thanks for your kind letter. I think the pilot is a much more appropriate and picturesque personage and should certainly have used him except for the fact that I knew Jim Bludso and he was an engineer and did just what I said—as was related to me by a common friend last fall. But I care nothing for that exceptional fact—it would be better to make him a pilot, and why cant I alter it in the Weekly, which is most read and copied by country papers. I send you the proposed change for your criticism—if you approve, I will launch it so, and let the two versions fight it ought ,out, & we will bet on the Pilot.

The opposition is getting beaten out I think. Some of the heathen still rage furiously and their words of their mouths are "ribaldry" "plagiarism B. H" and "vulgar blasphemy." But there are compensations. "The Atlantic" and Harpers and the Aldine have all asked me for some more foul vulgarity—and alack! I have not time to write it.

My love to David to whom I will soon write.

A charming family, Clarence Seward's to wit, have made me promise to bring you to them some day—so give me an hour when you come again.

> Yours faithfully
> John Hay

The mutual acquaintances Hay alluded to were Bret Harte and David Gray. Clarence A. Seward (1828–97), nephew and adopted son of William H. Seward, was a former judge advocate general of New York State, a Civil War veteran, and currently a lawyer in New York City. On the back of Hay's letter, Clemens wrote: "Col. John Hay with poem 'Jim Bludso.'" His response to Hay's proposed revision is not known, nor has the weekly *Tribune*'s reprinting of it been found, but in the version of the poem Hay collected in *Pike County Ballads and Other Pieces* later in 1871 Jim Bludso remained an engineer. On 14 January Hay wrote again, turning down Clemens's offer of a partnership in the Buffalo *Express* and remarking:

> I cannot forbear telling you how much I have been encouraged and gratified by your generous commendation of my verses. I have sometimes thought that the public appreciation was a compound of ignorance and surprise—but when you, who know all about the Western life and character, look at one of my little pictures and say it is true, it is comfortable beyond measure. (CU-MARK)

To Earl D. Berry
6 or 7 January 1871 • Buffalo, N.Y.
(MS: ViU)

472 Delaware.

Mr. Berry—please see to it that the concert in aid of the Soldiers' orphans, has a generous publicity. Let it have all the noise possible[1]—— ~~even though it be at the~~

> Yrs Truly
> Sam*l*. L. Clemens.

ⓒ | Mr. Berry | City Editor | "Express."

[1] The National Orphans' Homestead was established at Gettysburg in 1865 as a home for orphaned children of the Union dead. On 23 December 1870, an editorial in the Buffalo *Express* had endorsed local efforts to collect donations for this "great charity" ("Soldiers and Sailors' National Orphans' Homestead," 4). Now its Buffalo supporters planned a benefit concert by the "poet, composer, and vocalist" James Gowdy Clark, to be held in the North Presbyterian Church on 12 January. The *Express*'s first notice of this event appeared on the morning

of 6 January: "The homestead has never been in such pressing need of help as at the present time. Let all benevolent citizens remember this" ("The National Orphans' Homestead," 4). Although Clemens could have written this request to his city editor almost any time in early January, it seems most likely that it was a response to the 6 January notice. The letter was hand delivered to the *Express* office probably on Friday or Saturday, 6 or 7 January. Berry apparently acted on Clemens's instruction on Monday, 9 January, for the first of four subsequent notices appeared the following day (Buffalo *Express:* "Don't Forget the Orphans of Soldiers," 10 Jan 71, 4; "The Orphans' Homestead Concert," 11 Jan 71, 4; "The Orphans Homestead Concert," 12 Jan 71, 4; "Clarke's Concert," 13 Jan 71, 4; *NUC*, 111:21–22; *L3*, 296–97 n. 2).

To Olivia L. Clemens
12 January 1871 • Cleveland, Ohio
(MS: CU-MARK)

~~Wednes~~Thursday

1 A.M.

Livy Darling—

Just a line to say that I have seen our dearest experience duplicated to-night—a gloriously happy bride & bridegroom & two thoroughly satisfied families & a host of friends.[1] ~~I~~

I ~~was~~ got a piece of wedding candy saved up for Langdon & lost it. Was going to get some wedding flowers to send to you, & presently of her own volition Mrs. Severance got them *for* me & pressed them in a book. I will try & not forget to enclose them in this letter. We are to take tea with Mrs. S. tomorrow—at least I am.[2]

They were all delighted with our & mother's presents. ~~I~~ But I am sure they think *ours*[3] was only a *Christmas* gift. I shall tell them better.

About four to six or seven hundred people have asked after your & the cub's health & the latter's progress.

(The reason your letter[4] wasn't *news* to me this morning, sweetheart, was because I slipped up into the study & read ~~if~~ it long before I left home!)

Mrs. Fairbanks ~~was~~ wants us to spend the summer with them here at their new & beautiful place (which I am to visit tomorrow.)[5]

I like ~~all~~ the Gaylords, "Willie" included.[6]

I *wish* I could see you & the dear little cubbie to-night, I do.

Give my warm love to our mother & our boy—& unto you I send a world of affection & many, many loving kisses—

And so, with a God bless you, my own darling, I will now to bed—for I am a stranger to sleep, by this time.

Sam.

✉—

Mrs. S. L. Clemens | 472 Delaware st | Buffalo | N. Y. [*postmarked:*] CLEVELAND O. JAN 12

[1] On the evening of Wednesday, 11 January, Alice Fairbanks and William H. Gaylord were married by the Reverend W. H. Goodrich at the Fairbanks home. Clemens had arrived in Cleveland at the earliest on 9 January, possibly accompanied by Charles Langdon and Daniel Slote (Cleveland *Plain Dealer,* 13 Jan 71, 2; 17 Dec 70 to Fairbanks).

[2] The flowers prepared by Emily A. Severance were enclosed.

[3] See 17 Dec 70 to Fairbanks.

[4] Not known to survive.

[5] The Fairbanks house, at 221 St. Clair, had sustained two fires in 1869. The new home, built during 1870 within view of Lake Erie in East Cleveland, was called "Fair Banks" (*L3,* 86, 168; Mary Mason Fairbanks, 354; *Cleveland Directory:* 1870, 127; 1871, 162).

[6] In 1879, after Mary Mason Fairbanks had become disillusioned about William Gaylord, Clemens acknowledged that he thought him a fool (15 May 79 to Fairbanks, CSmH, in *MTMF,* 230).

To Charles Henry Webb
14 January 1871 • Buffalo, N.Y.
(MS: MoSW)

Buffalo, Jan 14.

Dear Webb—

I dassent. I made up my mind *solidly* day before yesterday that I would draw out of the Galaxy with the April No. & write no more for any periodical—except, at long intervals a screed that I happened to dearly *want* to write.[1]

Yes *sir*—King William was a mistake & a big one, for it was repeating ~~my~~ a joke—but the way of it was that the idea ~~of doing~~ ſ of burlesquing the Galaxy portraits was in my head long before the Map, & so I did not recognize the injudiciousness as clearly as I would have done had not that been the case. But it was a big mistake.[2]

Carleton & I can't trade, under *any* circumstances.[3]

Every Saturday accuses me of writing "a ~~some~~ feeble imitation" of Bret Harte" in the shape of a euchre rhyme about threes & a flush. A pretty grave charge. Mr. "Hi. Slocum" is the habitual plagiarist who did it. So let ~~my~~ us sorrow together,, over these Every Saturday villainies.[4]

I've been off holidaying *another* week—at a Cleveland wedding[5]— & now you bet you I am going to place my nose in contact with the grindstone & *keep* it there.

Please give my kindest regards to Mrs. Webb.

> Yr friend
> Sam'. L. Clemens.

[1] Webb, whose letter is lost, was neither editing nor publishing a periodical at this time. Between 7 January and 11 February 1871, however, as "John Paul," he contributed a weekly column entitled "Things" to *Every Saturday*, published in Boston by James R. Osgood and Company. He may have been acting on behalf of Osgood or George W. Carleton, his own publisher.

[2] For Clemens's map of the "Fortifications of Paris" and his portrait of William III of Prussia, see 22 Sept 70 to Bliss, nn. 1 and 2, and 18 Oct 70 to Church, n. 1. He continued to regret the similarity of the two satires: for an 1874 reprinting, he deleted his bogus "Commendations of the Portrait," saying "Leave this out— it is only a repetition of the 'Commendations' attached to the 'Map of Paris'"; and he entirely omitted the sketch from later reprintings of his work (SLC 1873b, 586).

[3] See 26 Nov 70 to Webb, n. 6.

[4] "Three Aces: Jim Todd's Episode in Social Euchre" appeared in the Buffalo *Express* on 3 December 1870 (2)—attributed to "Carl Byng," not to "Hy Slocum." On 7 January, *Every Saturday* had carried the following note by editor Thomas Bailey Aldrich: "Mark Twain's versified story of the 'Three Aces' seems to be a feeble echo of Bret Harte. The 'Truthful James' vein is one that can be worked successfully only by the owner of the 'claim'" ("Literary Items," n.s., 2:19). The 14 January issue of the magazine, which Webb may have seen in proof but too late to correct, committed a similar "villainy," attributing to Harte the founding of the *Californian*, which it called "an unsuccessful newspaper enterprise of his own" ("Mr. Francis Bret Harte," n.s., 2:43). On 28 January, *Every Saturday* published Webb's protest that he, not Harte, had established the *Californian*, and that he, "more than any other was prominently and personally identified with the paper," which had successfully contributed "towards elevating the tone of Californian journalism and developing the brilliancy which has since burst from the Western horizon" (Webb 1871; *L1*, 314 n. 5; *RI 1993*, 699).

[5] The previous holiday was 10–17 December, spent in New York City, part of the time with Webb (see p. 269).

To the Editor of *Every Saturday*
(Thomas Bailey Aldrich)
15 January 1871 • Buffalo, N.Y.
(MS: MoSW)

(LLC)

To the Editor of Every Saturday:[1]

You stated, ~~two or three weeks ago,~~ ˄in a recent issue,˄ that I have written "a feeble imitation of Bret. Harte's Heathen Chinee," in the shape of ȁ certain rhymes about a euchre game that was turned into poker & a victim betrayed into betting his all on three aces when there was a "flush" out against him. Will you please correct your misstatement, inasmuch as I did not ˄write˄ the ~~wr~~ rhymes referred to, ~~to~~ nor have anything whatever to do with suggesting, inspiring, or producing them? ˄They were the work of a writer who has for years signed himself "Hi. Slocum.",˄ I have had several applications from responsible publishing houses to furnish a volume of poems after the style of the "Truthful James" rhymes. I burned the letters without answering them, for I am not in the imitation business.

Yours Truly
~~Sa~~ Mark Twain.

Buffalo, Jan. 15.[2]

---

[1] Thomas Bailey Aldrich (1836–1907), whom Clemens did not actually meet until late in 1871 (1 Nov 71 to OLC, n. 3). Aldrich was born and educated in Portsmouth, New Hampshire, which served as the setting for many of his literary works. In 1852, lacking the funds to attend Harvard (a consequence of his father's death in 1849), he moved to New York to work as a clerk in his uncle's business. Almost immediately he began to publish poems in various journals, eventually joining the editorial staffs of the *Evening Mirror, Home Journal,* and *Saturday Press.* During 1861–62 he served as Civil War correspondent for the New York *Tribune* and, briefly in 1863, as managing editor of the *New York Illustrated News.* In 1865, having published several books of poetry and short stories (the first in 1855), he married Lilian Woodman and moved to Boston, where James R. Osgood had offered him the editorship of *Every Saturday,* a post he held from 1866 to 1874. In 1869, he published *The Story of A Bad Boy,* about which Clemens remarked to Olivia Langdon: "I could not admire the volume much" (*L3,* 440; Wolf, 43–46; Price, 4–5; Greenslet, 15–16, 56, 58, 76). Clemens and Aldrich enjoyed a lifelong friendship.

[2] Aldrich published this letter, without its dateline, in the 4 February issue of *Every Saturday,* explaining that

> the poem entitled "The Three Aces," with Mark Twain's signature attached as author, appeared in several of our New York exchanges. That was our only authority for attributing the verses to him. We are very glad that he did not write them, for the rhymes lack that freshness and brilliancy which Mark Twain has taught us to expect in his writings. (Aldrich 1871)

Some newspapers did assume that Hy Slocum and Carl Byng (author of "The Three Aces") were alternative pseudonyms for Mark Twain, and therefore reprinted their sketches from the Buffalo *Express* as if they in fact were his. For example, see: "A Humorous View of the Farmers' Club. Mark Twain's Report of the Proceedings," Pittsburgh *Gazette,* 7 Dec 70, 2, reprinting Byng 1870a; and "Mark Twain on Yaller Dogs," San Francisco *Golden City,* 19 Dec 69, 2, reprinting Slocum 1869m.

To Thomas Bailey Aldrich
22 January 1871 • Buffalo, N.Y.
(MS: MH-H)

Buffalo, Jan. 22.

Dear Sir:

Please do not publish the note I sent you the other day about "Hy. Slocum's" plagiarism entitled "Three Aces"—it is not important enough for such a long paragraph.[1] Webb writes me that he has put in a paragraph about it, too—& I have requested him to suppress it.[2] If you would simply state, ~~without any fuss~~ in *a line & a half* under "Literary Notes" that you mistook one "~~Hy. Slocum~~" (no, it was one "*Carl Byng,*" I perceive) "Carl Byng" for Mark Twain, & that ~~the form~~ it was the former who wrote the plagiarism entitled "Three Aces," I think that would do a fair justice without any unseemly display. But it *is* hard to be accused of plagiarism—a crime I never have committed in my life.

Ys Truly

Mark Twain.

I have just crossed Mr. Carl Byng & Mr. Hy. Slocum *both* off ~~my~~ the "Express's" list of contributors (for their ~~own good~~ **own good**—for everything they write is straightway saddled onto *me.*)[3]

[1] Aldrich replied on 25 January: "It is too late for you to attempt to prevent me doing you justice! About 42000 copies of your note, with my apology nobly

appended, are now printed, and we hope to have the rest of the edition off the press by to-morrow night. In the next No. of E. S. I will withdraw my apology, if you say so!" (CU-MARK).

²This exchange of letters with Webb has not been found. None of Webb's final "Things" columns—in *Every Saturday* for 28 January, 4 February, and 11 February—mentioned the matter.

³Sketches by Carl Byng appeared irregularly in the Buffalo *Express* between 12 November 1870 and 28 January 1871. A statistical comparison of the Byng texts with known texts by Mark Twain has suggested that Clemens did not write the Byng pieces, and that they may have been the work of Clemens's partner, Josephus N. Larned (Gillette 1984, 2–3, 13–16). Larned may also have written the sketches by Hy Slocum that had appeared in the *Express* between 31 March 1868 and 8 October 1870. For all known articles by Byng and Slocum, see References (Byng 1870a–f, 1871a–b; Slocum 1868a–d, 1869a–p, 1870a–t; McCullough 1969, 1971, 1972).

To James Redpath
22 January 1871 • Buffalo, N.Y.
(MS: NN-B)

Buffalo, Jan. 22.

Friend Redpath—

I left the article with the Cleveland Herald people & told them not to print it for ten or twelve days. It is good, Redpath, & is se but I believe you could ₐhaveₐ been a little severer without seeming ill-natured or damaging the g̸ influence of the article,—don't you think so?[1]

Are you going to lecture Gough in California?[2] If so, take the advice of Ꜳ the only lecturer that ever *did* make 3 distinct lecturing tours in California,[3]—& that advice is, lecture him *3 nights in succession* (& so *advertise* it,);—then talk him 2 successive nights in Sacramento,—1 night (or possibly 2,) in Virginia City ₦ Nevada (provided you can get a church—for they *won't* go to that nasty theatre,.)[4] Then return & talk him 2 (or 3 successive nights again in San Francisco. There you are! If any body says "Go to San Jose, Petaluma, Grass Valley, Nevada City, Marysville, Carson City," or any *other* camp on the coast, tell them Artemus Ward & Mark Twain both *lost money* in each & every one of those places.[5] But six nights in Platt's Hall, San Francisco are the only ones in the ten that I would give you my old boots for—but they are worth close onto $8,000 gold, clean profit—more than that, if you charge 50 cents extra for reserved seats (which ought to be done—& you'll have from 500 to 1,000 $1.50 seats, that way.) I've ~~had s~~ had 1,400 reserved seats ˌ(all the *seats* there are in it,)ˌ in Platt's Hall—sold them all in 5 hours,⁾ & closed the box office at 3 P.M.⁾—but did *not* charge extra—being a fool—simply charged a dollar a ticket. But a man *must* have reserved seats there, whether he charges extra or not—it's the only good way.⁶

But maybe you ain't going to take Gough there, after all—well, put this letter where you can find it again when you *do* talk somebody there. Nasby would have a big run there.

Yrs Ever
Mark.

[letter docketed:] BOSTON LYCEUM BUREAU. REDPATH & FALL. JAN 7 23 1871 *[and]* L | *[rule]* *[and]* Mark Twain | Buffalo | Jan 22 '71

¹Redpath was planning a series of articles about lecturers, and had submitted the first—a thinly disguised exposé of Olive Logan and William Wirt Sikes—to David Ross Locke (Petroleum V. Nasby), editor and part owner of the Toledo *Blade*. Locke sent it to Clemens on 7 January, remarking: "I think it is good, but whether it had better go in the Galaxy or not is the question. Do with it as you like. If you dont use it for the Galaxy send it back to me & I will shove it into some daily in the west[.] The thing must be ventilated" (CU-MARK). Clemens instead brought it to Cleveland on or shortly after 9 January and gave it to Mary Mason Fairbanks for the Cleveland *Herald* (8 Jan 70 to OLL [1st], n. 3; 26 Jan 71 to Fairbanks; 30 Jan 71 to Redpath).

²John Bartholomew Gough (1817–86), a very successful temperance lecturer, took the total abstinence pledge in 1842, began lecturing in 1843, and published an autobiography before he was thirty. By 1853 he was so well known as a lecturer that he was summoned to England by the London Temperance League. Redpath's article mentioned Gough, but he did not join the Boston Lyceum Bureau roster until the season of 1872–73. In the spring and summer of 1871, however, under the aegis of the American Literary Bureau (of New York), Gough did tour California successfully (*Lyceum* 1872, 3, 15–17; Boston *Evening Transcript:* "Personal," 31 May 71, 2; "John B. Gough . . . ," 19 June 71, 2; "Lectures and Lecturers," 19 July 71, 2).

³Clemens first toured California and Nevada towns in October and early November 1866, made a second brief tour within California in November and early December of that year, and in April 1868 returned for a third tour that in part retraced his original route (*L1*, 361–70; *L2*, 205–14; *RI 1993*, 744, 745).

⁴On both his first and third tours Clemens lectured once at the Metropolitan Theatre in Sacramento—in October 1866 to "one of the finest audiences" and in April 1868 to a "crowded" house ("Mark—His Mission," Sacramento *Bee*, 12 Oct 66, 3; "Mark Twain's Lecture," Sacramento *Union*, 18 Apr 66, 3). As a re-

porter in 1863 he had described the new Maguire's Opera House in Virginia City (with seating for sixteen hundred) as a "spacious and beautiful theatre . . . exactly after the pattern of the Opera House in San Francisco" (SLC 1863). But Maguire's (later Piper's) soon became known as drafty and cold. In 1863 a patron of Artemus Ward's lecture said that "Every joke got off by the lecturer was not only heard but seen in a jet of vapor" (Watson, 131–32, 228; Rodecape, 142). Even so, Clemens's October 1866 lecture there was well attended: "all the available space for extra seats and standing room was occupied" (Doten 1866). For his April 1868 lectures, on two successive nights, the house was not at capacity, but was full enough for the Virginia City newspapers to report a "crowded" house and a "very large and fashionable audience" ("Mark Twain," Virginia City *Trespass*, 28 Apr 68, 3; "Mark Twain's Lecture," Virginia City *Territorial Enterprise*, 29 Apr 68, 3; *L3*, 106 n. 2).

[5] During his 1863 tour of the West, Artemus Ward lectured in many of the towns Clemens later toured, among them San Jose, Grass Valley, Nevada City, Marysville, and Carson City. According to Edward P. Hingston, Ward's manager, travel and other expenses left little or no profit, and sometimes caused a net loss. Although Clemens's similar experiences in 1866 made him doubt that he could make an 1868 tour of the West even pay expenses, he did end his 1868 campaign with a profit (*L2*, 128; *L3*, 261 n. 2; Hingston, 316–28, 337–40, 374–77, 391–96, 408–9, 416).

[6] Platt's Music Hall seated eighteen (not fourteen) hundred and was, at the time of its opening in 1860, San Francisco's largest concert hall. Artemus Ward filled it for his 1863 lecture, and Clemens delivered one of his Sandwich Islands lectures there to a "large audience" during his second 1866 tour ("Mark Twain's Lecture," San Francisco *Evening Bulletin*, 17 Nov 66, 5; Estavan, 15:224–26; Hingston, 299). In April 1868, for the first of two lectures at Platt's Hall, reserved seats were priced at one dollar, bringing in, Clemens reported, "a little over sixteen hundred dollars in the house—gold & silver" (*L2*, 212). The following night's lecture, added at the last minute, drew a "fair but not crowded house" ("Platt's Hall," San Francisco *Dramatic Chronicle*, 16 Apr 68, 3). Clemens's final San Francisco lecture, at the Mercantile Library Hall on 2 July 1868, sold out ("'Mark Twain's' Lecture To-night," San Francisco *Alta California*, 2 July 68, 1; "Mark Twain Last Night," San Francisco *Examiner*, 3 July 68, 3; *L2*, 8–9 n. 1).

To Elisha Bliss, Jr.
24 January 1871 • Buffalo, N.Y.
(MS: Axelrod)

Buf. 24[th.]

Friend Bliss—

Orion says you hardly know whether it is good judgment to throw the Sketch Book on the market & interfere with the Innocents. I believe you are more than half right—it is calculated to do more harm than good, no doubt. So if you like the idea, suppose we defer the Sketch Book till the *last*. That is, get out the big California & Plains book first of August; then the Diamond book first March or April 1872—& *then* the Sketch book the following fall. Does that strike you favorably? If so, write out the contract in that way & forward it. By that time I can write a great many brand new sketches & they'll make the book sell handsomely—& by that time, too, some of the best of the *old* sketches will be forgotten & will read like new matter.

Drop me a line on it.[1]

Ys
Clemens.

✉───

[letter docketed:] Mark Twain | Jan 24/71

[1] Orion had first reported Bliss's opinion to Clemens in a letter (now lost) written between 8 and 14 January. Clemens had in turn replied in a letter, also lost, that arrived in Hartford while Bliss was in New York City (from 16 to 23 January) trying to find and hire Edward Mullen to illustrate the sketchbook. Orion waited for Bliss to return before replying for him, on 25 January, to the mid-January letter. No direct reply to Clemens's present follow-up is known to survive, or was perhaps needed, since Orion's 25 January letter must have arrived shortly after Clemens sent it. Orion wrote, in part:

> About the sketch-book interfering with the Innocents—Bliss says he is going on with the sketch-book, and you will see which is right. The substance is that it the new book will outsell the old one, and few people want to buy two books from the same author at the same time. (CU-MARK)

Bliss soon agreed to the proposed new order for the three projects already under contract, although the contracts themselves were not revised. *Roughing It* was not published until February 1872; the diamond mine book was never written; and the sketchbook was postponed until 1875, finally issuing as *Sketches, New and Old*.

To C. F. Sterling
24 January 1871 • Buffalo, N.Y.
(MS: ViU)

Buffalo, Jan. 24.

Dear Sir:

It isn't any hardship to receive a letter like yours, nor to write & say thank you, & right cordially, too, for it.[1]

I know that Tifft House—& I never could understand why they make such invidious distinctions & show such a mean partiality, these Buffalo people, in always ~~callin~~ referring to that place out yonder in the extreme edge of town as *the* poor-house, just as if the Tifft warn't in existence.[2]

Yrs Sincerely
Mark Twain.

[1] In his letter Sterling had alluded to Mark Twain's recent complaint about the burden of letter writing—"One of Mankind's Bores," in the February *Galaxy* (SLC 1871f, 318–19):

Birmingham Ct.
Jan. 21. 1871.

Dear Mark,

      I don't care if letters *are* a bore to you either to answer or receive, I've had so much amusement from your travels, memoranda, &c. I want to thank you for it and I'm going to do it. Accept then the hearty gratitude of one who feels indebted in a higher degree than his subscription to the Galaxy or purchase of "The Innocents Abroad" cancels. Sometimes I think the balance between you writers and we readers is most unfair and while you are racking your brains to amuse us, we in our selfishness swallow it all and also all amusing things that happen to us. That you too may have a little smile let me tell you how they do things in Buffalo.

      Stopping there one night a few weeks since I went to the 'Tift House' called the nicest I was told. Going up to my room I, as is my invariable custom felt of the bedding to see if there was sufficient to keep me warm as it was during one of the cold spells we have recently had. Found sheet, one blanket and white spread. Coming down I asked the clerk to put more bedding on 106. "Certainly sir." Going up to bed about 11.30 I found a blanket nicely spread over the outside. Still feeling doubtful as to quantity I felt again and found the *blanket had changed places with the counterpane and there was precisely the same* amount as at first. You will appreciate this as you know the style they spread at the "Tift House" and prices they charge. Don't imagine I send this for publication. Tis for *you* to laugh at.

Truly Yours,
C. F. Sterling

(CU-MARK)

Clemens noted on Sterling's letter:

Jan. 24, 1871.

Received on a low spirited day, & preserved for the comfort it brought.

[2] The Tifft House, one of Buffalo's most prominent hotels, opened in 1865. Clemens knew it well, having stayed there during his first visit to Buffalo in July 1869. In February 1870 some of the wedding guests who accompanied him and Olivia to Buffalo took rooms there. The "poor-house" probably was the Home for Aged and Destitute Females on Rhode Island Street, maintained by Buffalo's Church Charity Foundation (Severance, 177–78; *L3*, 281 n. 4; *Buffalo Directory* 1871, 53).

From Olivia L. and Samuel L. Clemens
to Alice Hooker Day
25 January 1871 • Buffalo, N.Y.
(MS: CtHSD)

Buffalo Jan 25th 1871

Alice dear

You were so very good to write me again when I have been so remiss about writing you—but you must know that I have had very much to keep me from writing—[1]

I often feel since Father left us, that he was my back bone, that what energy I had came from him, that he was the moving spring— It seems to me that all who have lived by the side of so noble and self sustained a life as his was must feel so—and you know how he carried us all along, by his strength and cheer— Truly a great light went out of our home— Father used to speak often of you during his sickness—particularly of the letter to him, in which you spoke of his being your babies Grandfather, he wanted me to answer that letter and tell you that he should have written himself if he had been able—[2]

I dread very much my first visit at home— I know that I shall realize more than I possibly can away from there that Father has left us never to return any more—

The picture of baby and Mother which you sent me was so very sweet and prettie. I do ~~pris~~ prize it very highly—[3]

Shall I explain to you how I come to be writing you with a pencil? I am at this present time seated in a private room of the General Hospital in Buffalo— I with my baby near me— I had not food enough for the little one, we tried feeding him but that did not do at all, so we were obliged to look for a wet nurse— At last we found one here at the Hospital, she is a nice person and is well reccommended—she is not yet able to be moved, so every day, baby, nurse, and I come up here and spend the day returning home at night—

It is about the forlornest place that ever you saw, but you know we can do almost anything for the dear little ones—

I have had a great aversion always to wet nurses, but all told me that I could not nurish him myself, and the Dr. said that it would be very unsafe for me to ˎlet himˎ go into the Summer on the bottle— So after much battleing I yielded—[4]

How delighted I shall be when we can bring our two little one[s] together, ~~and exhibit~~ shall we not both be proud Mothers—

Sue is not with me now— Mother was with ʄ me for about two months, but she has now returned home,[5] so Mr Clemens baby and I are alone again, our lives are very quiet happy lives, even in spiteɖ of the great sorrow that is almost constantly present to us—

I did hope to study some this Winter and I may possibly still, but I find hands and heart so full that I seem to have little leisure— Are you studying any?—[6]

Mr Clemens and I read with a great deal of pleasure Mr Warners book— I came very near writing Mrs Warner and telling her of the two or three exceedinglyˎ pleasant evenings that the book gave us—[7]

Write me again and tell me more= I was so very ~~sorry~~ ˎmuch disapointed,ˎ that I was not able to have your Mother[8] make her intended visit to me— Will she not be coming this way again before very long?ˎ— ~~Can~~

I am so very sorry for Mary— It seems *too bad* that all her exquisite little things are gone— I can hardly believe it—her home was so full of ~~exqu~~ delicate, dainty bits, of all kinds—[9] Give my love to her please, and tell her that if it were possible I would wish her a home that should seem twice as ~~car~~ charming, and twice as much like some fairy palace—

Can you realize that dear Emma Nye has gone from us? I feel often, in thinking of both Father and Emma, as if I would write them of this and that—

I hope that you will come to me with Husband and baby next Spring—can you not?—

I must not write more— I wish you *could* see my baby— I consider him such a sweet little ~~baby~~ ˎboyˎ—

With kind regards to Mr Day, and a loving kiss for little Alice[10]   I am as always your loving friend

                                        Livy Langdon Clemens

The very first time I get a chance, I am coming to Hartford to beg Mrs. Hooker's pardon for sending her such an absurdly curt dispatch— for I did not *want* to send such a message to her. The hurry was very

great—not a single instant to spare—& so I started the messenger off
with a telegram of a single sentence when I could have been much politer
if I had had another half minute to write more in.[11]

Yr friend

Sam*l*. L. Clemens

[1] Olivia may not have written since 6 June 1870, when she congratulated Day
on the 8 May birth of her first child, Katharine Seymour Day (CtHSD; "Hartford Residents," Day Family, 3).

[2] Olivia had written Day about Jervis Langdon's illness on 31? May 1870
(CtHSD), undoubtedly prompting the letter to him, now lost. Langdon died a
little more than two months later.

[3] The photograph has not been found.

[4] The Buffalo General Hospital was on High Street between Elm and Oak,
about half a mile from the Clemenses' house. The unidentified woman, recovering from the birth, or possibly the loss, of her baby, was Langdon Clemens's
second wet nurse; his first, Mrs. Brown, had apparently been let go when Olivia
put him "on the bottle." The doctor was Andrew R. Wright (Severance, 200;
Buffalo Directory: 1870, map; 1871, 50, 285; 11 Nov 70 to Ford, n. 5).

[5] Susan Crane had spent the first two weeks of November 1870 in Buffalo and
returned by 31 January; Olivia Lewis Langdon had arrived just before Thanksgiving (12 Nov 70 to the Twichells; p. 325; 19 Nov 70 to Langdon; 17 Dec 70 to
Fairbanks).

[6] Before their marriages, Olivia and Alice had used their correspondence to
stay informed about each other's studies. In addition to readings in history and
literature, Olivia had studied French "with the nuns" in 1868, and that year and
the next she studied "Natural Philosophy" and chemistry under Professor Darius R. Ford (OLL to Alice Hooker, 29 Sept 68, CtHSD). Alice had studied music
and French, and on 8 March 1868, after a hiatus in their correspondence, Olivia
had written jokingly, "I want to . . . learn whether you have mastered the Greek
alphabet! Whether you read German fluently, and draw superbly. Paint in
watter collors with origanality— Whether you expect to exhibit in the next annual exhibition at the Academy or if not what your plans are?" (CtHSD; OLL
to Alice Hooker, 26 May 67, 7 June 67, 17 June 67, 30 Oct 67, 8 Aug 68, 3 Mar
69, all in CtHSD; *L3*, 4, 6–7 n. 6, 181, 182–83 n. 6).

[7] Charles Dudley Warner's *My Summer in a Garden*. Olivia knew his wife, the
former Susan Lee, a Nook Farm neighbor and friend of the Hooker family's,
and had doubtless seen her at the wedding of Alice Hooker and John Day in June
1869 (3 Jan 71 to Twichell, n. 1; *L3*, 270, 404, 407 n. 3).

[8] Isabella Beecher Hooker, the spiritualist and women's rights advocate (*L2*,
146 n. 4).

[9] Alice's older sister, Mary, was married to Henry Eugene Burton, a Hartford
lawyer. On 27 December 1870, a fire had destroyed their cottage on Forest
Street. "The furniture in the dining room and parlor was nearly all lost, together
with the pictures, bronzes, books and ornaments—in short nearly everything
that makes 'home.' A portion of the silver that had been upon the breakfast table

was saved; the rest of it was melted. The furniture from one chamber was saved, together with some clothing, but the most expensive portion of female wearing apparel was burned" ("Fire on Forest Street," Hartford *Courant*, 28 Dec 70, 2; *L3*, 143 n. 11).

   ¹⁰A second child, named Alice, was not born to the Days until 3 January 1872. Olivia may have meant to suggest that eight-month-old Katharine was her mother in miniature ("Hartford Residents," Day Family, 3).

   ¹¹The telegram, probably cancelling Isabella Beecher Hooker's visit, is not known to survive.

To Mary Mason Fairbanks
26 January 1871 • Buffalo, N.Y.
(MS: CSmH)

Home, Jan. 26.

Dear Mother:

   Tell Bone & Benedict¹ that the article is by James Redpath of Bleeding Kansas fame² (now proprietor of the big "Boston Lyceum Bureau")—the best posted man in the land on lecturers. Now that I come to think of it, the article is "*by a retired lecturer,*" or something of that kind, which pretty plainly points to me. If the next one passes through my hands I will see that ~~is~~ it is "*by the boss of a late lecture bureau*" or something like that. *I* couldn't dare to write about my own guild, that way. ~~And~~ It would be like blackguarding one's own family.³

   Well, it seems the Moffett children can't come—I enclose letter. We are very very sorry, & yet we don't dare to expose the cub to any more influences calculated to keep him up nights.⁴ He did well, last night—was peaceable, & I let him off & didn't "go for" him with Dewees' Mustang Liniment.⁵ Tell Mollie to never mind the absence of the Moffetts—*we'll* entertain her, & we'll get her to help entertain the baby.⁶

   Yes, you sent the wedding cards by me. Livy & Lang. know all about the pretty summer trip, & are calculating very strongly on it.

   Remembering the hatchet, I am your own moral son, which cannot tell a lie, when a body is looking straight at him

—⟞⟝—

Sam*ˡ*.

[*one MS page (about 70 words) missing*]

shovel in some solid facts to balance the nonsense;—namely: Livy & the girl & the baby spent another day at the hospital, today & let Langdon nurse a patient there. We are all back home, now. We are to keep this up until next Monday, & then the woman can be moved here.

Trot Mollie along on time. Also make the bride & groom be *sure* to stop.[7]

Yr Son

Sam[l].

[1] Publishers of the Cleveland *Herald*. John Herbert Aloysius Bone (1830–1906), born in Cornwall, England, moved to Cleveland in 1851 and soon began contributing to the *Herald*. He published his first book, *Stories and Legends; With Other Poems*, in 1852, and in 1857 joined the staff of the *Herald*, where he remained for nearly thirty years, producing lead articles and editorials and becoming known as "a veritable encyclopedia of knowledge and a writer of ability" (Rose, 471). George A. Benedict was editor-in-chief and one of the proprietors of the *Herald*, the partner of Abel W. Fairbanks. Clearly Clemens referred to him and not to his son, George S. Benedict, also a partner and the paper's business manager, who died in a train wreck on 6 February 1871. Clemens's acquaintance with the Benedicts dated from late 1868 and early 1869, when he was considering the purchase of an interest in the *Herald* (Coyle, 66; "Death of George S. Benedict," Cleveland *Herald*, 8 Feb 71, 2; *L2*, 360; *L3*, 49, 69, 85 n. 2, 195, 277 n. 1).

[2] Redpath had been a crusading abolitionist, famous for his advocacy and personal bravery, as well as his periodic dispatches from Kansas Territory to the New York *Tribune* between 1854 and 1859, during the strife between pro- and anti-slavery factions. In 1859 and 1860 he published three influential books, each in part about Kansas: *Hand-book to Kansas Territory and the Rocky Mountains' Gold Region; The Public Life of Capt. John Brown*, which sold over 40,000 copies by the mid-1870s; and *The Roving Editor: or, Talks with Slaves in the Southern States*, which included a verbatim history of the first slave kept in Kansas. Redpath dedicated *The Roving Editor* to John Brown: "You went to Kansas, when the troubles broke out there—not to 'settle' or 'speculate'—or from idle curiosity: but for one stern, solitary purpose—*to have a shot at the South*. So did I" (Redpath 1968 [1859], iv; Horner, 40–99 passim; "James Redpath," in *Lyceum* 1876, unnumbered prefatory page; *L3*, 217–18 n. 8).

[3] See 30 Jan 71 to Redpath.

[4] The enclosure, probably a letter from Pamela Moffett describing an illness Annie and Samuel had had recently, is not known to survive.

[5] William Potts Dewees (1768–1841), a pediatrician, was the author of *A Treatise on the Physical and Medical Treatment of Children* (1825), which included prescriptions for colic and other infant ailments. Mustang Liniment, used to treat horses, was not one of Dewees's nostrums (Carson, 58).

[6] While in Cleveland earlier in January (12 Jan 71 to OLC), Clemens must

have invited fourteen-year-old Mollie Fairbanks to Buffalo, promising that the Moffett children would be there as well. There is no evidence that she came.

[7]It is not known if Alice and William Gaylord—presumably on, or about to begin, their honeymoon—visited Buffalo.

To Thomas Bailey Aldrich
27 January 1871 • Buffalo, N.Y.
(MS: MH-H)

472 Delaware st.
Buffalo, Jan. 27.

Dear Mr. Aldrich—

No indeed, don't take back the apology! Hang it, I don't want to abuse a man's civility merely because he gives me the chance.[1]

I hear a good deal about doing things on the "spur of the moment"—*I* invariably regret the things I do on the spur of the moment. That disclaimer of mine was a case in point. I am ashamed every time I think of my bursting out before an unconcerned public with that bombastic pow-wow about burning ~~poor~~ publishers' letters, & all that sort of imbecility, & about my not being an imitator, &c. Who would find out that I am a natural fool if I ~~keep~~ kept always cool & never let nature come to the surface? Nobody.

But I did hate to be accused of plagiarizing Bret Harte, who trimmed & trained & schooled me patiently until he changed me from an awkward utterer of coarse grotesquenesses w̸ to a writer of paragraphs & chapters that have found a certain favor in the eyes of even some of the very decentest people in the land—& this grateful remembrance of mine ought to be worth its face, seeing that Bret broke our long friendship a year ago without any cause or provocation that I am aware of.[2]

Well it *is* funny, the reminiscences that glare out from murky corners of one's memory, now & then, without warning. Just at this moment a picture flits before me: *Scene*—private room in Barnum's Restaurant, Virginia, Nevada; present, Artemus Ward, Joseph T. Goodman, (editor & proprietor Daily "Enterprise"), & "Dan de Quille" & myself, reporters for same; remnants of the feast thin & scattering, but ~~empty bottles~~

such tautology & repetition of empty bottles everywhere visible as to be offensive to the sensitive eye; time, 2.30 A.M.,[3] Artemus thickly reciting a poem about a certain infant you wot of,[4] & interrupting himself & *being* interrupted every few lines by poundings of the table & shouts of "Splennid, by Shorgzhe!" Finally, a long, vociferous, poundiferous & vitreous jingling of applause announces the conclusion, & then Artemus: "Let every man 'at loves his fellow man & 'preciates a poet 'at loves *his* fellow-man, stan' up!—stan' up & drink health & long life to Thomas Bailey Aldrich!—& drink it *stanning!*" [On all hands fervent, enthusiastic, & sincerely honest attempts to comply.] Then Artemus: "Well— *consider* it stanning, & drink it just as ye are!" Which was done.

You must excuse all this stuff from a stranger, ~~but~~ for the present, & when I see you I will apologize in full.

Do you know the prettiest fancy & the neatest that ever shot through Harte's brain? It was this: When they were trying to decide upon a vignette for the cover of the *Overland*,[5] a grizzly bear (of the arms of the State of California) was chosen. Nahl Bros.[6] carved him & the page was printed, with him in it, looking thus:

As a bear, he was a success—he was a good bear. But then, it was objected, that he was an *objectless* bear—a bear that *meant* nothing in particular, signified nothing,—simply stood there snarling over his shoulder at nothing—& was painfully & manifestly a boorish & ill-natured intruder upon the fair page. All hands said that—none were satisfied. They hated badly to give him up, & yet they hated as much to have him there when there was no *point* to him. But presently Harte took a pencil & drew these two simple lines under his feet & behold he was a magnificent success!—the ancient symbol of Californian ~~save~~ savagery snarling at the ˌapproachingˌ type of high & progressive Civilization, ᴖᴜ the first Overland locomotive!:[7]

I just think that was nothing less than inspiration itself.
Once more I apologize, & this time I do it "stanning!"

Yrs Truly

Sam[l]. L. Clemens.

[1] See 22 Jan 71 to Aldrich, n. 1.

[2] See 26 Nov 70 to Webb.

[3] In 1863 the Barnum Restaurant, at the corner of North B and Sutton streets, in Virginia City, was several blocks from the *Territorial Enterprise*'s new offices on South C Street (Kelly 1863, 172; *RI 1993*, 658). The *"Scene"* Clemens described must have occurred between 18 and 29 December 1863 (very possibly on Christmas Eve), while Artemus Ward was in Virginia City to lecture (*L1*, 266, 269–70 n. 5).

[4] Ward was undoubtedly reciting Aldrich's sentimental "Ballad of Babie Bell." The poem first appeared in the New York *Journal of Commerce* in 1855 and, according to Aldrich's earliest biographer, "swept through the country like a piece of news," being "reprinted in the 'poet's corner' of the provincial press from Maine to Texas" (Greenslet, 26). Aldrich first collected it in *The Ballad of Babie Bell, and Other Poems* (1859).

[5] Harte was the first editor of the *Overland Monthly*, which began publication in July 1868 in San Francisco. Modeled after the *Atlantic Monthly*, it was immediately successful both in the East and West, and it brought Harte fame by disseminating some of his best work (George R. Stewart 1931, 157–59; *L3*, 321 n. 1).

[6] Charles Christian Nahl (1818–78) and Hugo Wilhelm Arthur Nahl (1833–89), half-brothers born in Germany, had settled in California in 1851. After working a short time as gold miners, they became partners in a San Francisco art and photography studio. Charles, an illustrator and lithographer as well as a painter, designed the bear on the California state flag. Arthur, a painter, illustrator, engraver, and pioneer photographer, designed the state seal (Samuels and Samuels, 341–42).

[7] Clemens carefully cut apart a single *Overland Monthly* vignette and pasted the segments to the pages of his letter just as they appear here (reproduced actual size). His pains were repaid when Aldrich replied (CU-MARK):

JAMES R. OSGOOD & CO. PUBLISHERS BOSTON. LATE TICKNOR & FIELDS, AND
FIELDS, OSGOOD, & CO. NO. 124 TREMONT STREET, BOSTON.
NEW YORK OFFICE, NO. 713 BROADWAY.

BOSTON Feby 9ᵗʰ 18 71

Dear Mr. Clemens,

I have been a long while acknowledging the receipt of your cheerful letter; but you understand how a man who writes perpetual 'leaders' sometimes finds that the pen he uses for his private correspondence weighs about a ton. Now and then I kick over my personal inkstand; but I have just set it up on end and refilled it, in order to thank you for your entertaining pages. I am glad that I accused you of "The Three Aces", and ruffled your feelings, and caused you to tell me about poor Artemus Ward, and how the Overland got so striking a design for its cover. Really, that is the best bear story I ever heard. All this would 'nt have happened if I had not wronged you. Mem: Always abuse people.

When you come to Boston, if you do not make your presence manifest to me, I 'll put a ¶ in "Every Saturday" to the effect that though you are generally known as Mark Twain, your favorite nom de plume is "Barry Gray." I flatter myself that will bring you.

Yours very truly,
T. B. Aldrich.

"Barry Gray" was the pseudonym of genteel humorist Robert Barry Coffin (1826–86), who, like Aldrich, had been associated with the New York *Home Journal* in the late 1850s.

To Elisha Bliss, Jr.
27 January 1871 • Buffalo, N.Y.
(MS: CU-MARK)

Buffalo, Jan. 27.

Friend Bliss:

Tell you what I'll do, if you say so. Will write night & day & send you 200 pages of MS. every ~~well~~ week (of the big book on California, Nevada & the Plains) & ~~place~~ finish it all up the 15ᵗʰ of April if you can without fail *issue* the book on the 15ᵗʰ of May,—putting the sketch book over till another time. For this reason: my popularity is booming, now, & we ought to take the very biggest advantage of it.

I have to go to Washington next Tuesday & stay a week, but will send you 150 MS pages before going, if you say so. It seems to me that I would much rather do this. *Telegraph* me now, right away—don't wait to write. Next Wednesday I'll meet you in N. Y—& if you can't come there I'll run ~~if~~ up & see *you*.[1]

You could get a *cord* of subscriptions taken & advertising done be-

tween now & April 15. I have a splendid idea of the sagacity of this
proposition.

    Telegraph me right off.

Yrs

Mark

[*letter docketed:*] √ [*and*] Mark Twain | Jan 27/71

[1] Clemens left for Washington, via New York, on Tuesday, 31 January. Bliss
evidently telegraphed that he would meet him in New York and Clemens responded with a telegram naming the time and place (31 Jan 71 to Bliss; p. 325).
Probably among the matters they discussed was Bliss's request that Clemens stop
writing for the *Galaxy*, published by Isaac Sheldon and Company, and instead
contribute to the *American Publisher,* a proposal Orion had outlined in his letter
of 25 January:

> Bliss says you must make Sheldon pay you $5,000 if you write another year; that he
> will pay you that to write ~~for~~ exclusively for this paper, if you will give him all your
> books, which he thinks you ought to do—let him do all your publishing, and just write
> books and for the paper. (CU-MARK)

Bliss's offer was prompted in part by an encounter with Sheldon (see the next
letter). The amount was $3,000 more than Clemens had accepted for a year's
Galaxy "Memoranda."

To Isaac E. Sheldon
27 January 1871 • Buffalo, N.Y.
(MS paraphrase: CU-MARK)

Jan. 27-71

I wrote She[l]don to-day ~~that~~ protesting against a higher price than 25
cents for the pamphlet.[1]

[1] Clemens himself made this note of his letter, now missing, on the envelope
of the 25 January letter from Orion. Orion reported that in New York Bliss had
seen Sheldon, who was preparing to issue *Mark Twain's (Burlesque) Autobiography and First Romance:*

> Sheldon told him it was to be a 50 cent pamphlet & 75ᶜ in muslin. Against that Bliss
> protests. . . . He says if you let that be printed in muslin he will not come down on you
> with the contract, but he will always feel like you hav[e]n't treated him right. His com-
> pany enjoys the prestige of being the sole publishers of Mark Twain, which they use
> with their agents, and the advantage of this prestige they will lose if a book of yours

comes back pu out published by somebody else. He ridicules Sheldon's talk of expensive cuts, saying those in the Innocents cost $60 a page—the full page cuts. . . .

Bliss is anxious that my letter should not show any feeling on his part in regard to the Sheldon pamphlet. (CU-MARK)

Clemens's 15 July 1870 contract for *Roughing It* with the American Publishing Company stipulated that he was "not to write or furnish manuscript for any other book unless for said company during the preparation & sale of said manuscript & book" (Appendix E). The muslin binding and the price, Bliss felt, would turn the pamphlet into a book. Clemens's letter, together with a discussion he had with Sheldon in New York on 1 February, led to an agreement by which Sheldon was to publish only seventy-five copies of the *(Burlesque) Autobiography* in muslin. But Sheldon seems not to have abided by that agreement, and the pamphlet issued in March in both paper and cloth bindings, priced at forty and seventy-five cents respectively, without limit on the number of cloth copies (*ET&S1*, 565; "Mark Twain's New Book," *Galaxy* 11 [Apr 71]: verso of "Contents"; Sikes).

To Willard McKinstry
28 January 1871 • Buffalo, N.Y.
(MS: ViU)

Buffalo, Jan. 28.

W. McKinstry, Esq

Dear Sir:

I thank you very much indeed for your kind invitation to attend the celebration of an event which, in this country (yes, in *any* country,) is so unusual as to well deserve to be termed *remarkable*—& that, too, with emphasis,—the fifth fiftieth birth-day of a newspaper! We are accustomed to contemplate the sixty-six the seventy years of the *New York Evening Post* & the one hundred & six years of the Hart *Connecticut Courant* with a sort of awe-inspired veneration—& here you come startling us with a half-century veteran reared in a western village! I doff my hat to the hale patriarch, & record the hope that the *Fredonia Censor* may still be hale at a hundred & fifty![1]

Sincerely regretting my inability to be present f at the dinner, I am

Ys Truly

Mark Twain.

[1] Willard McKinstry (1815–99), publisher and editor of the Fredonia *Censor* since 1842, whom Clemens had probably met when he lectured in Fredonia in

January 1870, had sent a printed invitation to a fiftieth anniversary supper in honor of the paper's founder, Henry C. Frisbee (1801–73). The *Censor* published Clemens's letter on 8 February, along with similar communications from Horace Greeley of the New York *Tribune*, David Gray of the Buffalo *Courier*, and others. Clemens's mother and sister had been living in Fredonia since April 1870 (*Chautauqua County*, 2:107–9; "The Semi-Centennial Anniversary of the Fredonia Censor," Fredonia *Censor*, 8 Feb 71, 1).

To James Redpath
30 January 1871 • Buffalo, N.Y.
(MS: MH-H)

Buf. 30.th

Dear Redpath—

I may talk a little (only in New England) next fall, but all the chances are in favor of my not doing anything of the kind. We'll see.

I suppose that article of mine on Rev. Sabine will be made to damage me a good deal, through the manipulations of these religious editors. Do not you think so?[1]

I have ~~g~~ just received the enclosed from Cleveland (Herald.) You must alter the authorship of the other ones ~~to "lec~~ "*reformed lectur*ESS"—~~be~~ otherwise the whole thing will be saddled on to me by these fair *f* victims.[2]

I stumbled in awkwardly & unexpectedly enough ~~or~~ on Kate Field at a private house yesterday, & introduction followed.[3]

I don't know anything about the lecture-capacities of towns east of Nevada—never tried them.

Yrs

Mark

☞ I hope to drop in on you in 2 or 3 ~~weeks.~~ months.

P. S. The Cleveland Herald wants the next one rushed along—send it to me.

[*letter docketed:*] BOSTON LYCEUM BUREAU. REDPATH & FALL. FEB 6 1871 [*and*] L | [*rule*] [*and*] Mark Twain | Buffalo N.Y. Jan. 30 '71 [*and*] BOSTON LYCEUM BUREAU. REDPATH & FALL. FEB 20 1871

[1] William T. Sabine (1838–1913), rector of New York's fashionable Episcopal Church of the Atonement and later bishop of the Reformed Episcopal Church, had refused to perform funeral services for George Holland (b. 1791), a popular comic actor who died on 20 December 1870 "without a stain on his name." Sabine explained that he "did not care to be mixed up" in Holland's funeral since theaters did not teach "moral lessons." Public outcry against Sabine was widespread and severe. The New York *Times* called him "only a stripling in years" who "has through his short course of life nursed only the most intolerant of principles associated with insolence, bigotry and ignorance" (New York *Times:* "Mr. George Holland," 22 Dec 70, 4; "Pharisaical Delicacy," 29 Dec 70, 1; "Rev. Sabine and Public Opinion," 31 Dec 70, 2). In the February 1871 *Galaxy*, Mark Twain joined the attack, calling Sabine a "crawling, slimy, sanctimonious, self-righteous reptile" and noting that:

> It is almost fair and just to aver (although it is profanity) that nine-tenths of all the kindness and forbearance and Christian charity and generosity in the hearts of the American people to-day, got there by being filtered down from their fountain-head, the gospel of Christ, *through dramas and tragedies and comedies on the stage, and through the despised novel and the Christmas story, and through the thousand and one lessons, suggestions, and narratives of generous deeds that stir the pulses, and exalt and augment the nobility of the nation day by day from the teeming columns of ten thousand newspapers*, and NOT from the drowsy pulpit! (SLC 1871f, 320–21)

[2] The actual enclosure does not survive, but it was certainly a clipping of Redpath's article in the Cleveland *Herald* (transcribed in Appendix B from the *Herald*). Redpath *was* a former lecturer, having performed for two years "exclusively under the management of Irish land leagues, Irish benevolent societies, or of Catholic Churches" (Eubank, 290). No further articles by him have been found, however, very likely because he published none, fearing that if his authorship were discovered it would undermine his Boston Lyceum Bureau. In fact, Olive Logan, one of the "fair victims," and her husband-to-be, Wirt Sikes, both of whom had been represented by the bureau in 1869–70 and 1870–71, severed their connection with it before the 1871–72 season was announced (Eubank, 295–97). By late 1871, Logan had taken out the following public notice:

> **"NICE YOUNG MEN."**
> I am forced, by the continued impertinent intermeddling of unscrupulous so-called "Bureaux," to announce that I shall in future refuse to answer any letters or applications which come to me through these obtrusive "middle-men." Committees must apply directly to me, or be met with silence.
>
> **OLIVE LOGAN,**
> **55 West Ninth-st., N. Y. City.**

(Chicago *Evening Post*, 16 Dec 71, 4)

[3] Kate Field (Mary Katherine Keemle Field, 1838–96), the well-known journalist and the author of *Adelaide Ristori* (1867), *Planchette's Diary* (1868), and *Pen Photographs of Charles Dickens's Readings* (1868), had made her platform debut in 1869 (Whiting, 211). She was evidently one of the lecturers alluded to in Redpath's first article and probably the intended subject of a later one. Field appeared in Buffalo on 30 January 1871. The next day the Buffalo *Express* reported:

> Miss Field delivered her lecture on Charles Dickens, last evening, at St. James Hall, to a fair audience—to an audience larger in fact than is often obtained by an independent lecturer [that is, one not sponsored by the local lyceum society]. Of the merits of the

lecture we shall only say that our criticism of it, if we undertook one, would hardly be as unstinted praise as we have found lavished upon Miss Field's discourse in many of our exchanges. ("Miss Kate Field's Lecture," 31 Jan 71, 4)

Clemens may have written, or at least inspired these remarks, for he was consistently contemptuous of Kate Field's platform abilities, even though he was not unsympathetic to her. In an autobiographical sketch about his lecture days, written in 1898, he recalled:

> Kate Field had made a wide spasmodic notoriety in 1867 by some letters which she sent from Boston—by telegraph—to the *Tribune* about Dickens's readings there in the beginning of his triumphant American tour. . . . By & by she went on the platform; but two or three years had elapsed & her subject—Dickens—had now lost its freshness & its interest. For a while people went to see *her,* because of her name; but her lecture was poor & her delivery repellantly artificial; consequently when the ˏcountry'sˏ desire to look at her had been appeased, the platform forsook her.
>
> She was a good creature, & the acquisition of a perishable & fleeting notoriety was the disaster of her life. (SLC 1898a, 8–9)

To Elisha Bliss, Jr., or Francis E. Bliss
per Telegraph Operator
31 January 1871 • Buffalo, N.Y.
(MS, copy received: CU-MARK)

THE WESTERN UNION TELEGRAPH COMPANY.

1257

DATED   Buffalo NY   187 1

RECEIVED AT   200   Jan. 31

TO   E. Bliss or Frank 149 Asylym St

Have an appointment at Grand Hotel eleven tomorrow can you be there at noon[1]

Clemens

14 pd.

[*telegram docketed:*] √ [*and*] Mark Twain | Jan 24/71[2]

[1] The eleven o'clock appointment was with Isaac E. Sheldon or Francis P. Church, or both. In his subsequent meeting with Elisha Bliss, Clemens probably reported on his progress on *Roughing It* and answered Bliss's objections to his commitments to Sheldon (27 Jan 71 to Bliss, n. 1; 27 Jan 71 to Sheldon, n. 1).

[2] Bliss's clerk misread the telegram's date, which was poorly written.

NO LETTERS are known to survive between 31 January and 9 February 1871. On 31 January Clemens left Susan and Theodore Crane in Buffalo with Olivia, and went to New York for two days, 1 and 2 February, stopping at the Grand Hotel. There he met with Elisha Bliss, Francis P. Church, and probably Isaac E. Sheldon. He and Church worked out the terms of his planned withdrawal from his monthly *Galaxy* "Memoranda," and persuaded Whitelaw Reid, of the New York *Tribune*, to report the results on 2 February:

> Mark Twain threatens to cease writing periodically. He says trying to think how he shall be funny at a certain date, is very melancholy; keeps him awake at night; prompts him to commit suicide, run for Congress, or describe in print his reminiscences of distinguished men whose funerals he has had the pleasure of attending. With the April number of *The Galaxy* it is therefore understood that he will make his bow, and retire from this field of his triumphs. He will still, however, contribute to its further glories, as occasion and inspiration may allow. ("Personal," 5)

Church also prepared a more detailed paragraph for the *Tribune*, which published it the next day:

> MARK TWAIN, who has been spending a few days quietly in New-York, left last night for Washington. He has arranged with Mr. Church, the Editor of *The Galaxy*, a transformation of his department. In the May number, for "Memoranda" will be substituted a humorous department to which widely-known writers will contribute, in addition to Mark Twain, who desires to be released from carrying on his unaided and already overloaded shoulders the heavy burden of a whole department. He will still remain, however, the leading and frequent contributor to the new one, the only magazine articles he will write being those he is to furnish *The Galaxy*. ("Personal," 3 Feb 71, 5)

Clemens arrived in Washington, D.C., on the night of 2 February or early the next morning and registered at the Ebbitt House. Already at the Ebbitt House were several other Buffalo residents, including Josephus Larned, who was overseeing the publication of a trade report he had written. By 7 February David Gray was also in town.

The impulse for Clemens's trip was the delay in Jervis Langdon's lawsuit against Memphis, Tennessee, initiated in 1869, for non-payment of a five-hundred-thousand-dollar street paving bill. With Langdon's death in 1870, the affairs of the estate had been thrown temporarily into a crisis, which Clemens described in a 1906 Autobiographical Dictation:

> [Talmage Brown] had paved Memphis, Tennessee, with the wooden pavement so popular in that day. He had done this as Mr. Langdon's agent. Well managed, the contract would have yielded a sufficient profit, but through Brown's mismanagement it had ~~nearly~~ ˌmerelyˌ yielded a large loss. With Mr. Langdon alive, this loss was not a matter of consequence, and could not cripple the business. But with Mr. Langdon's brain and hand and credit and high character removed, it was another matter. . . . His agents were usually considerably in debt to him, and he was correspondingly in debt to the owners of the mines. . . . A careful statement of Mr. Langdon's affairs showed that the assets were worth eight hundred thousand dollars, and that against them was merely the ordinary obligations of the business. Bills aggregating perhaps three hundred thousand dollars—possibly four hundred thousand—would have to be paid; half in about a month, the other half in about two months. The collections to meet these obligations would come in further along. (AD, 23 Feb 1906, in *MTA*, 2:135–36, with omissions)

Clemens now hoped to revive the stalled legislation he had first tried to advance, with limited success, in July 1870 (6 July 70, 8 July 70, both to OLC). His present effort was summarized, in a letter to the Chicago *Tribune*, by his friend George Alfred Townsend, who also described a literary collaboration probably plotted during several convivial dinners:

BUFFALO'S ABROAD

The venerable Mark Twain came to Washington a few days ago to have Tennessee divided into two Judicial Districts. It appears that the city of Memphis stands indebted to an estate, of which he is an executor, in the sum of three or four hundred thousand dollars, but that, owing to the long docket in the Tennessee District, the case is never reached for adjudication. He wants the district cut into "twain," but even the great humorist sometimes fails in politics, and, after three days' hopeless meandering in that great bourse of the Capitol, Mark gave the town his blessing, and hastened to Buffalo. He is said to be writing a comic Bible, with Samson for the central character, and he makes his hero bring down the house, hitting the Philistines hard. The ascetic David Gray, editor of the Buffalo *Courier*, furnishes some chapters in this book on the Song of Solomon, and the Rev. J. N. Larned, of the Buffalo *Express*, institutes some happy comparisons between Canada and the land of Canaan. Buffalo deserves the cognomen of "the comic city of the Western hemisphere." (Townsend 1871b)

A note from 1870–71 evidently provides the working title for the "comic Bible": "Samson Humorist" (CU-MARK).

Meanwhile, in Buffalo, Olivia had fallen ill with what was eventually diagnosed as typhoid fever. On 3 February she wrote Pamela Moffett, "I am not feeling well today" (NPV), and by 6 February she was so ill that Susan Crane wrote Clemens in Washington (CSmH):

> Buffalo.
> Mon Feb 6. 1871
>
> Dear Mr Clemens.
>
> Livy has consented to allow me to write you that she is not well, and has not been since you went away.
>
> She has had some fever, no appetite, no power to sleep, & ~~great depression of spirits.~~ ˏLivy did not like that, so I did not say it.ˏ This although she has kept about every day & this morning is up when I think she is far from able to be.
>
> The Dr has seen her twice, giving her some vigorous remedies and said that she must not have the baby at night, and for three nights the girls have cared for him. He is doing quite well now although he has not been well. & it is the anxiety in part which has worn Livy. The Dr thinks her nervous system has been overtaxed & her stomach has been deranged thereby.
>
> Now why I write is this—or why Livy allows me to write— If your business would take you over into next week Livy feels that it would be almost unendurable but if your knowing these facts, would help you to close it this week, or defer it, she is willing to have you know how she is.
>
> Of course she knows that you will come as soon as possible any way, but rather than have you remain until next weekˏ she would ~~rather~~ have you give up the business. She would rather give up her interest in Memphis.
>
> If you will dispatch as soon as this is rec^d we will tell you just how Livy is at that time. She did not wish to alarm you with a dispatch now & there really is no need of it now.
>
> You may trust to my letting you know the truth—
>
> Theodore goes home this afternoon & I shall take as good care of Livy as she will allow me, but she is not very good to be taken care of. Do not be worried. I think Livy will be better but I wanted to feel that we were not keeping you entirely in the dark.
>
> Affectionately Yours
> Susie L Crane

Before receiving this letter, Clemens had independently telegraphed his plans to Buffalo, for Sue Crane noted on the envelope "Feb 6 | PS—1 AM | Your Dispatch rec^d and answered." (Neither Clemens's telegram nor Crane's answer survives.) On 7 February, Clemens visited Mathew Brady's studio, where he was photographed with Gray and Townsend (Horan, 404 illustration; see p. 571 for a reproduction of one of the photographs from that sitting), and later attended a dinner reported in the

Washington *National Republican:* "Hon. S. S. Cox gave a dinner to Mark Twain, at Welcker's on Tuesday evening, at which were present Hon. Charles E. Eldridge, Mr. Gray, of the Buffalo *Courier,* Donn Piatt, George Alfred Townsend and W. W. Warden, as representative(?) Washington correspondents" ("Our Fashionable Society," 9 Feb 71, 1). Welcker's restaurant was called by one reporter "one of the best restaurants in the world," and its proprietor was noted for furnishing "all the big dinners and suppers, whose beauty and elegance and cost so often astonish the people at the Capitol" (Ramsdell 1871b). Charles Augustus Eldredge (1820–96), a lawyer, had been a Democratic congressman from Wisconsin since 1863. William W. Warden, also a lawyer, was a correspondent for the Boston *Post,* the Philadelphia *Day,* and the Richmond (Va.) *Dispatch.* Donn Piatt (1819–91) was a veteran correspondent of several newspapers and currently Washington correspondent for the Cincinnati *Commercial.* He, in partnership with Townsend, had just bought a two-thirds interest in the weekly Washington *Sunday Herald,* which they transformed into a new weekly, *The Capital.* In describing the Cox dinner, Piatt remarked:

> This was my first meeting with Mark Twain. . . . He is not only careless about his clothes, but he is positively ignorant on the subject, and labors under the impression that the garment that hangs so loosely upon his shoulders is a coat. From under his bushy hair his face peers out, presenting a square, well-proportioned forehead, keen gray eyes, and hooked nose, a well developed mouth, exhibiting a good deal of decision, and a chin that rounds out, supporting the whole, in no part of which will you find a particle of the humor for which he is distinguished. His face, on the contrary, is a sad one, and when all are in roars about him he continues in a state of dense solemnity. . . .
>
> It is quite impossible for him to produce in his conversation a serious effect. The exceedingly droll quaintness of his solemn countenance, added to the drawl of his voice, makes one laugh when the speaker is really striving to be serious. . . .
>
> I am told by those who know him well that he is a very kind hearted fellow. He has generous impulses and a gentle, patient nature. We had an illustration of his affection, for unfortunately in the midst of the dinner he received a telegram telling him of the sickness of his wife, and he was forced to leave upon the next train. Mr. Barry [i.e. David] Gray, a gentleman who has written some of the most beautiful and quaintest poems of the day, left with him. This blank at the table brought our dinner to an abrupt termination. I was very sorry, not only on account of the cause for Mr. Clements' leaving, but the lost opportunity for becoming better acquainted with him. Regarding Mark Twain as a

man equal to Hood, and one whose humor is producing so marked an effect upon our literature, I was anxious to know him personally. He and Bret Harte are the two men of all others one would go the greatest distance to look into and study. (Piatt 1871a)

The telegram was from Susan Crane, who, concerned about the increasing severity of Olivia's illness, was unable to wait for Clemens's response to her letter of 6 February. It brought him back to Buffalo, doubtless by the morning of 8 February ("Morning Arrivals," New York *Evening Express*, 1 Feb 71, 3; "Personal," New York *Tribune*, 3 Feb 71, 5; Townsend 1871a; Casual; "Personal," Washington *National Republican*, 19 Jan 71, 2; "Personal," Washington *Evening Star*, 4 Feb 71, 4; "George Alfred Townsend and Donn Piatt . . . ," Washington *National Republican*, 11 Feb 71, 2; Boyd: 1871, 363, 369; 1872, 478; *BDUSC*, 956; Poore 1870, 122; "Personal," Buffalo *Courier*, 26 Jan 71, 1; *L2*, 196 n. 1).

To Louis Prang and Company
9 February 1871 • Buffalo, N.Y.
(MS: MoKHC)

Buffalo, Feb. 8̸ 9.

L. Prang & Co

    Gentlemen:

The chromo came, & I did not notify you because I hoped to get time to write & print a notice, but no time ever comes to *me*, ~~except~~ ₍By all odds it is the pleasantest & happiest & *truest* picture I have seen for many a day. It holds the place of honor in my study.[1]

    This is all in haste. I am simply out of the sick room for a moment's rest & respite. My ~~wife's life (a year & 7 days married) is only hanging by a thread.~~ ₍wife is seriously & I am afraid even dangerously ill.₎[2] You will excuse my long delay in responding to your kind compliment.

Yrs Truly

S̶a̶ Mark Twain

¹The chromolithograph perhaps was one of Prang and Company's "latest publications"—"Mt. Chocorua" and "North Conway Meadows," reproduced from paintings by Benjamin Champney (1817–1907), a well-known landscapist (advertisement, *Every Saturday,* n.s., 2 [4 Feb 71]: 112). The present endorsement was Clemens's substitute for the contemplated notice.

²With typhoid fever, probably diagnosed already although not identified in Clemens's extant letters for nearly two weeks (22 Feb 71 to Reid). The disease had taken Emma Nye's life in September 1870.

To Unidentified
13 February 1871 • Buffalo, N.Y.
(MS: ICU)

OFFICE "EXPRESS" PRINTING CO.

BUFFALO, Feb. 13 187¢ I.

DEAR SIR:

    IN ANSWER I AM OBLIGED TO SAY THAT IT WILL NOT BE POSSIBLE FOR ME TO ACCEPT YOUR KIND INVITATION. I SHALL NOT BE ABLE TO LECTURE AGAIN DURING THE PRESENT SEASON. THANKING YOU KINDLY FOR THE COMPLIMENT OF YOUR INVITATION, I AM

                YOURS TRULY,

                    SAM'L L. CLEMENS.

                    ["MARK TWAIN."]

AGENTS:

BOSTON LYCEUM BUREAU,

20 BROMFIELD STREET,

BOSTON.

P. S. Am sorry to say that I am clear out of the lecture field, & neither riches nor glory can tempt me!

                Yrs Truly

                S. L. Clemens

To Elisha Bliss, Jr.
15 February 1871 • Buffalo, N.Y.
(MS: CU-MARK)

Buffalo, Feb. 15/71.

Friend Bliss—

This is to acknowledge receipt of your check for $1,452.62—copyright on sales of Innocents Abroad for quarter ending Jan. 31. The sales keep up amazingly.[1]

Riley sailed finally from London Feb. 1. It is a thirty-day voyage. ~~We I *must* have & *will* have~~ ⫟ He had plenty of company—every ship goes full. He sends me London papers which reveal to me that we are all asleep over here. ~~But I'll see~~ But that is all the better for me. I mean to print *nothing—* beforehand, but let the book be a booming surprise.[2]

Tell Orion that we cannot tell what the result is going to be. Sometimes I have hope for my wife,—so I have at this moment—but most of the time it seems to me impossible that she can get well. I cannot go into particulars—the subject is too dreadful. I thank him & Mollie for their kind offers.[3]

Ys

Clemens

✉—————————————————————————

[*letter docketed:*] √ [*and in ink:*] Mark Twain | Feb 15/71

[1] The check, sent by Frank Bliss on 13 February (letter and statement in CU-MARK), was for royalties on sales of 8,024 copies during the sixth quarter (1 Nov 70–31 Jan 71), an improvement over the fifth quarter, but not as good as the fourth (5 Aug 70 to Bliss, n. 1; 7 Nov 70 to Bliss, n. 1).

[2] Riley had left New York for Liverpool on 7 January on the *City of Brussels*. He wrote on 22 January from London that he planned to sail on the *Gambia* on 1 February and arrive in Natal, on Africa's east coast, in "30 to 35 days" (CU-MARK). But the *Gambia* did not depart English coastal waters until 11 February and after a difficult fifty-day voyage, Riley disembarked early in Cape Town, on the west coast, on 23 March. He noted in his "Memoranda": "Your correspondent wouldn't ~~take~~ repeat (with the risks) another such a voyage at sea for one hundred thousand dollars" (Riley, 10, 11, 14, 17, 18; advertisement for *Gambia*, London *Times*, 1 Feb 71, 2). The "London papers" do not survive, but

presumably were clippings describing the South African diamond discoveries and the rush to the fields.

[3] No letters offering assistance are known to survive.

To Jane Lampton Clemens and Family
17 February 1871 • Buffalo, N.Y.
(MS: NPV)

Buf. 17th

Dear Folks—

By means of opiates we have given Livy 2 nights rest & sleep, & she seems better, but ~~is~~ still is very low & very weak. She is in her right mind this morning, & has made hardly a single flighty remark.[1]

She is greatly concerned about Sammy's eyes, & urges me to write at once & tell you not to try any but the oculist of the highest reputation in the land, whoever he may be. She don't like the idea of going to the country village of Rochester—thinks the best oculists must of necessity gravitate to New York & Boston—which is good reasoning, but they have to *come* from the country villages originally & maybe you have found such an one in Rochester. I do hope so, if the trade is made.[2] But if not, suppose you take him to Hartford & stop with Mollie while Orion ~~tak~~ (after inquiring of Twichell, D[r.] Taft[3] etc.,) goes with him to Boston or New York.

I owe ma $300 since Jan 1. Let her take the enclosed order to Mr. Clement's bank, & let them place $300 to her credit in lieu of it.[4]

Ys

Sam

[1] Since Olivia first had symptoms of typhoid fever on 1 or 2 February, she was now in the third week of her infection. Typhoid was understood to be linked somehow to "insanitary conditions in house drainage, water supply, &c." and, more specifically, to be transmitted by contaminated drinking water or milk. Symptoms typically lasted for a month, although sometimes as long as three months, often with prolonged relapses. First symptoms were known to begin "somewhat insidiously. Indeed, it is no uncommon thing for patients with this

fever to go about for a considerable time after its action has begun. The most marked of the early symptoms are headache, lassitude, and discomfort, together with sleeplessness and feverishness, particularly at night." By the second week, patients had high fever, spots, diarrhea, vomiting, severe abdominal pains, intestinal hemorrhages, and enlarged spleen and liver. By the third week, "nervous disturbance is exhibited in delirium, in tremors and jerkings of the muscles." The diet recommended was milk, barley water, and broths, and during convalescence

> largely milk and soft matters, such as custards, light puddings, meat jellies, boiled bread and milk. . . . Such drugs as quinine, salicin, salicylic acid, and salicylate of soda, kairin, antipyrin, antifebrin, &c. . . . may frequently break in upon the continuity of the fever, and by markedly lowering the temperature relieve for a time the body from a source of waste, and aid in tranquillizing the excited nervous system. (Affleck, 23:678–80)

When drugs failed to lower temperature, cold baths and massage were sometimes recommended. By the early 1880s, a bacterium, *Salmonella typhi*, was identified as the cause of the disease (Ziporyn, 72–73). By 1890, the death rate from typhoid fever was estimated at about twelve percent of cases.

² The Rochester physician has not been identified. Samuel E. Moffett's infirmity probably was related to a nervous disorder that he evidently suffered at least through late 1872 (11 June 71 to JLC; 21 June 71 to OC and MEC; 26 Nov 72 to JLC and PAM, NPV). Clemens later recalled:

> As child and lad his health was delicate, capricious, insecure, and his eyesight affected by a malady which debarred him from book-study and from reading. This was a bitter hardship for him, for he had a wonderful memory, a sharp hunger for knowledge. School was not for him, yet while still a little boy he acquired an education, and a good one. He managed it after a method of his own devising: he got permission to listen while the classes of the normal school recited their abstruse lessons and blackboarded their mathematics. By questioning the little chap it was found that he was keeping up with the star scholars of the school. (AD, 16 Aug 1908, CU-MARK, in SLC 1923, 352)

³ Cincinnatus A. Taft (1822–84), Hartford's leading doctor, was an 1846 graduate of the College of Physicians and Surgeons of New York. He practiced homeopathy, "although he exercised a certain eclectic independence, which looked rather to cure than to creed, and was not entirely within the limitations of any one 'school'" ("The Death of Dr. Taft," Hartford *Courant*, 27 June 84, 1). He became the Clemens family physician after they moved to Hartford (4 Dec 71 to OLC).

⁴ Clemens had sent a draft for $300 directly to the Fredonia bank in June 1870. Presumably he had met Clement in Fredonia in early October 1870 (25 June 70 to JLC and PAM; 4 Oct 70 to Redpath, n. 1).

To Fannie Dennis
17 February 1871 • Buffalo, N.Y.
(MS: Axelrod)

Buffalo, Feb. 17/71.

Miss Fannie Dennis:

   Brooklyn:

   To write an autograph is no trouble at all, when a body is used to it, but I never have tried to add a "sentiment" in my life, & so I assure you it comes awkward enough.[1] Therefore, let us ~~judge~~ just dodge the difficulty entirely & make use of somebody else's sentiment. Now *I* always admired that neat & snappy thing which good old John Bunyan said to the Duke of Wellington: "Give me liberty, or give me death!" ~~It~~ Isn't it pretty?

Very Truly Y^rs
Saml. L. Clemens
Mark Twain. ⎫

[1] Dennis's autograph request is not known to survive. She has not been further identified.

To Orion Clemens
22 February 1871 • Buffalo, N.Y.
(MS: CU-MARK)

Buf. 22^d

My Dear Bro—

   Return to me, per express, the "Liars" & the other 2 sketches—right away.[1]

   Livy is *very, very* slowly & slightly improving, but it is not possible to say whether she is out of danger or not—but we all consider that she is *not*. I have a non-resident physician in the house, hired at fifty dollars a day—(but this you are not to repeat.)[2]

Yrs

Sam.

[1] Two of these sketches have been identified (4 and 5 Jan 71 to Bliss, nn. 1, 3; 4 Mar 71 to OC, n. 1).

[2] Rachel Brooks Gleason (1820–1905) had come from Elmira, most likely in mid-February, to temporarily supplant Andrew Wright as Olivia's physician. A teacher until her marriage in 1844 to Dr. Silas O. Gleason (1818–99), she was one of the first women admitted to the Central Medical College in Rochester, where, studying under her husband, she received her degree in 1851. The Gleasons opened the Elmira Water Cure on East Hill in 1852, where Rachel thereafter treated several Langdon family members and friends. Her 1870 book, *Talks to My Patients: Hints on Getting Well and Keeping Well,* which dispensed medical and practical advice for women from childhood through menopause, was currently enjoying great success, having gone through five printings in its first year (Cotton, 20–21; Willard and Livermore, 322; Kirk, 1:677; 14 Mar 71 to Fairbanks). The Water Cure was temporarily closed by the Gleasons "for a few months, to afford them rest," and reopened on 1 May 1871 ("Elmira Water Cure," Elmira *Advertiser,* 29 Apr 71, 4). Rachel Gleason probably remained in Buffalo until early March, when Olivia's condition began to improve.

To James Redpath
22 February 1871 • Buffalo, N.Y.
(MS: MH-H)

Buffalo, 22[d].

Dear Redpath—

In haste—

[Mem. Wash[n] born this day.]

They keep writing me from Cleveland to send along the next article—so let's have it—but *do* find some other author than "A Retired Lecturer"—it points right at me*,*, old boy.[1]

Yes, you be sure & call when you come here. Nasby was here yesterday, enormously fat & handsome. We had a pleasant talk but I

couldn't offer him the hospitalities because my wife is very seriously ill
& the house full of nurses & doctors.²

    Love to Fall.

    In a hurry

Yrs

Mark.

[*letter docketed:*] BOSTON LYCEUM BUREAU. REDPATH & FALL. APR 5 1871 [*and*] L
| [*rule*] [*and*] Mark Twain | Buffalo N.Y. | Febry 22 '71

  ¹See 26 Jan 71 to Fairbanks and 30 Jan 71 to Redpath.

  ²Redpath's letter proposing a Buffalo visit is not known to survive. Nasby (David Ross Locke) was in Buffalo to deliver a lecture entitled "In Search of the Man of Sin" on 21 February at St. James Hall, for the Buffalo chapter of the Grand Army of the Republic's charity fund. It was he who had sent Redpath's first article about lecturers to Clemens. Locke's wife had been seriously ill with typhoid fever in January ("Petroleum V. Nasby, This Evening," Buffalo *Commercial Advertiser*, 21 Feb 71, 3; "Lecture Course," Buffalo *Courier*, 21 Feb 71, 3; 22 Jan 71 to Redpath, n. 1; Locke to SLC, 7 Jan 71, CU-MARK).

To Whitelaw Reid
22 February 1871 • Buffalo, N.Y.
(MS: DLC)

Buffalo, 22ᵈ.

Friend Reid:

    I thank your heartily for saving me that gratuitous ~~offense~~ ₐsnubₐ in the Tribune, & shall be glad to choke a slur for you if I ever get a chance. I guess this emanated from some bummer who owes me borrowed money & can't forgive the offence.¹

    My wife is still dangerously ill with typhoid fever, & we watch with her night & day hardly daring to prophecy what the result will be.

    Warm regards to Hay & Hazard.²

Yrs Ever

Mark.

  ¹Reid's letter to Clemens is lost and nothing is known of the "slur" he intercepted.

  ²John Hay and John Rose Greene Hassard.

To E. C. Chick
26 or 27 February 1871 • Buffalo, N.Y.
(Paraphrase: James Sutton to SLC, 2 Mar 71, CU-MARK)

As to the other ~~sketch~~ ‸"thing"‸ we are not anxious to have it, especially when we learn that "it is too long, as it stands,⸓ to be modest."[1]

[1] Edson C. Chick was managing editor of the *Aldine*, a graphic arts and literary magazine published by James Sutton and Company, New York. Chick had solicited a picture of Clemens and an autobiographical sketch to accompany it for the April 1871 issue. Clemens sent a print of Mathew Brady's July 1870 photograph, but not the sketch, by 23 February, when Chick wrote him, "I send you today copies of Mch 'Aldine'. Having made the announcement ‸of portrait‸ we are anxious for copy. . . . Please let us know at once on what day we can *depend on* copy, or send copy itself" (CU-MARK). Clemens replied on 26 or 27 February with a telegram (now lost), evidently saying that he was then mailing the autobiography with a cover letter. The letter, which offered an additional sketch, survives only in the words quoted by Sutton, who replied for Chick on 2 March, accepting the first "charge of pepper" (the autobiography), but declining the offered sketch (CU-MARK). "An Autobiography," with an engraving of the Brady photograph, appeared in the April *Aldine* (SLC 1871g). Chick continued with the *Aldine* until it ceased publication in 1879, after which he worked for a time as a theatrical and art critic for Frank Leslie's publications. He was later twice committed to asylums for the insane, first in New York, where he was discharged as "incurable but not dangerous," and again in 1888 in Taunton, Massachusetts ("An Insane Journalist," New York *Times*, 19 Apr 88, 1; Mott 1957, 410–12; 8 July 70 to OLC, n. 3; Chick to SLC, 27 Feb 71, CU-MARK; "The Aldine Dinner," New York *Tribune*, 16 Mar 71, 5).

To John Henry Riley
3 March 1871 • Buffalo, N.Y.
(MS: NN-B)

Buffalo, March 3.

Dear Riley:

Your letters have been just as satisfactory as letters could be, from the day you reached England till you left it again.[1]

I have come at last to loathe Buffalo so bitterly (always hated it) that yesterday I advertised our dwelling house for sale, & the man ~~co~~ that comes forward & pays us what it cost a year ago, ($25,000,) can take it. ~~I~~ Of course we won't sell the furniture, at *any* price, nor the horse, carriage or sleigh.[2] I offer the Express for sale also, & the man that will pay me $10,000 less than I gave can take *that*.[3]

We have had doctors & watchers & nurses in the house *all* the time for 8 months, & I am disgusted. My wife came near dying, 2 weeks ago.[4]

I quit the Galaxy with the current number,[5] & shall write no more for any periodical. Am offered great prices, but it's no go. Shall simply write books.

Do you know who is the most celebrated man in America to-day?— the man whose name is on every single tongue from one end of the continent to the other? It is Bret Harte. And the poem called the "Heathen Chinee" did it for him. His journey east to Boston was a perfect torchlight procession of eclat & homage. All the cities are ~~contend~~ fussing about which shall secure him for a citizen.[6]

I mean to store our furniture ~~until I can~~ ˌandˌ build a house in Hartford just like this one.

Was in Washington nearly a month ago. The Sutro accused me of sending you abroad. So did George Alfred T.[7]

The latter says Ramsdell went to San Domingo with the U.S. Commissioners for the NY Tribune, & left Washington when his wife was within *2 days* of her confinement[8]—& G.A.T. says the Row boys will give him the cold shoulder when he gets back.[9]

God speed you, old boy—I must run back to my wife—she is not well yet by any means.

Ys Ever
Mark.

[1] In his 22 January letter from London, the only one to survive from his African excursion, Riley enclosed "Memoranda of trip thus far, believing that I have jotted down quite sufficient to talk on for the mere stepping-stone to the long trip to come" (CU-MARK). That enclosure probably included at least the first two of the extant sixteen pages of Riley's "Memoranda," detailing his transatlantic voyage, his sojourn in Liverpool, and his arrival in London (Riley). To date Clemens had evidently received seven more pages (only four of which survive) enclosed in letters Riley wrote before his departure from England.

[2] The furniture was worth "$10,000 or $12,000," the horse, carriage, and sleigh between $3,000 and $7,000 (6? Feb 70 to McComb, n. 2).

[3] Clemens had difficulty disposing of his one-third interest in the *Express*. He had paid Thomas A. Kennett $15,000 of the full purchase price of $25,000 in

August 1869, $12,500 of it advanced by Jervis Langdon. In August 1870 he probably paid Kennett an additional $2,500. Then, on 1 March 1871, with a $7,500 debt to Kennett remaining, Clemens drew up and signed a contract to transfer his holdings to one of his partners, George Selkirk, with Selkirk to pay him $15,000: $1,000 upon execution of the contract and the rest over five years. Selkirk apparently could not make the first payment until mid-April, when the contract was activated. Under its terms, Clemens remained responsible for the obligation to Kennett, paying him $2,500 plus interest in August 1871 and again in August 1872, leaving $2,500 to be paid. Meanwhile the terms of Selkirk's financial obligations to Clemens changed as a result of his own partial transfer of ownership in the Express Printing Company, although in early 1873 Clemens still expected payment from him. By early 1878, almost seven years after he signed the contract with Selkirk, Clemens still had not received complete payment. Of the $12,500 Clemens owed to Jervis Langdon, he evidently began paying Langdon before the end of 1869, and completed payment to J. Langdon and Company by 28 December 1871 (Selkirk to SLC, 17 Jan 78, CU-MARK; *L3*, 294 n. 2; 7 Jan 70 to Fairbanks, n. 6; 2 and 3 Mar 70 to Langdon, n. 4; 1 Apr 70 and 16 and 17 Apr 70, both to the Langdons; 23 Apr 70 to Bliss; contract of 1 Mar 71 between Selkirk and SLC, CtHMTH; Kennett to SLC, 13 July 72, CU-MARK; 6 Aug 72 to Charles M. Underhill, NN-B; Theodore Crane to SLC, 16 Aug 72, CU-MARK; 22 Mar 73 to Josephus N. Larned, NBuHi; Smith, 339; Charles J. Langdon to SLC, 7 Jan 78, CU-MARK; 28 Dec 71 to OLC).

⁴The essence of Clemens's public explanation for leaving Buffalo. For example, on 2 May the Washington *National Republican* reported on "good authority" that Mark Twain "was induced to sell his interest in the Buffalo *Express* solely on account of the health of his wife, who, we are sorry to hear, is extremely delicate. These steps were taken by him on the advice of his physicians" ("Mark Twain . . . ," 2).

⁵The April (not the March) issue of the *Galaxy*, which was to carry Clemens's "Valedictory" and two sketches for his final "Memoranda." See 4 Mar 71 to OC, n. 2.

⁶Harte's poem had achieved enormous popularity in the fall and winter of 1870. Taking advantage of this sudden fame, Harte decided to go east. He turned down the offer of a professorship at the University of California in Berkeley (for an annual salary of $3,600). And he failed to negotiate satisfactory terms to remain as editor of the *Overland Monthly*, which he had edited since 1868. On 2 February 1871, he left San Francisco for Boston, where he planned to sign a contract with James R. Osgood and Company. The New York *Evening Express*, complaining that accounts of Harte's journey resembled "a royal progress," noted that "the papers have been deluged with telegrams and private communications in regard to the movements of the gentleman from California" ("Movements, Doings, Etc.," 21 Feb 71, 2). In Chicago, Harte was urged to remain as editor and part owner of the *Lakeside Monthly* at a salary of $5,000. Instead he continued his journey to Boston, where he was given an extravagant welcome on 25 February. He stayed with William Dean Howells and on his first day met "among others, Louis Agassiz, Henry W. Longfellow, James Russell Lowell, Oliver Wendell Holmes, Ralph Waldo Emerson and Richard H. Dana, Jr." ("Personal," Buffalo *Courier*, 7 Mar 71, 1). Soon after, he signed a year's contract for $10,000 to write exclusively for Osgood's publications (26 Nov 70 to Webb, n. 7; "Don't Be Rash, 'Bret,'" *San Francisco News Letter and California Adver-*

tiser 20 [21 Jan 71]: 8; "Personal Paragraphs," Hartford *Courant,* 14 Feb 71, 2; "Bret Harte to Become a Chicagoan," Buffalo *Courier,* 15 Feb 71, 1; "Literary," New York *Evening Express,* 11 Mar 71, 1; Thomas, 1:167, 169; Merwin, 222–23, 232; Weber, 120).

[7]Clemens had seen both Adolph Sutro and George Alfred Townsend while in Washington on Langdon family business in early February. Although he had sworn Riley to secrecy about the diamond mine scheme, Riley had good reason to speak, at least in general terms, to both Sutro, who had informally employed him for several years, and to Townsend: "I have not said a word to anyone about the matter, and only spoke to Sutro of my having almost decided to accept of a position that might take me away from here at the holidays, and to Geo. Alfred Townsend about doing the corr[es] for the ALTA in case I have to go away from here for a few months" (Riley to SLC, 6 Dec 70, CU-MARK). See 2 Dec 70 to Riley, nn. 1–3.

[8]Hiram J. Ramsdell (1839–87), whom Clemens had known since the winter of 1867–68, was currently a correspondent for the New York *Tribune.* Originally from Laona, New York, he was an editor of the Wellsboro (Pa.) *Agitator* by his early twenties, served three years in the Sixth Pennsylvania Reserves during the Civil War, and came to Washington in 1866. After serving as James Rankin Young's assistant in the *Tribune*'s Washington bureau, he became a correspondent for the Cincinnati *Commercial* and other newspapers, returning to the *Tribune* bureau again under Zebulon L. White. In 1869 negotiations had begun for annexation of the Dominican Republic (San Domingo or Santo Domingo), but on 30 June 1870 the Senate rejected President Grant's proposed treaty toward that end. In January 1871, while Dominican supporters and opponents of annexation were at war, Grant complied with a congressional directive and dispatched a three-member commission to the island to report on conditions there and on prospects for future annexation. Ramsdell was one of several correspondents who accompanied the mission, which left New York on the *Tennessee* on 17 January and returned to the United States on 26 March. It is not known whether either of his two children was born before his return. Ramsdell soon became world famous when, during secret deliberations, he and Zebulon L. White transmitted the text of the Treaty of Washington between Great Britain and the United States to the *Tribune,* which embarrassed both governments by publishing it on 11 May 1871. Ramsdell refused to divulge his source at a Senate hearing (Poore 1870, 122; *L2,* 196 n. 1; Ramsdell 1871a, 1; Appleton: 1873, 675–77; 1875, 654–68; "The Treaty of Washington," New York *Tribune,* 11 May 71, 1, and 17 May 71, 1; "Death of Mr. Ramsdell," Washington *Critic,* 26 May 87, 1).

[9]Townsend was himself one of the "Row boys" or correspondents on Washington's newspaper row, much of which was owned by C. C. Willard, the proprietor of the Ebbitt House, "of whom the Herald, the Tribune, the Times, the World, the Gazette and the Commercial rent their offices in this city. In addition to these papers, there are represented on the 'Row' four Boston papers, three or four Chicago papers, three Philadelphia papers, two or three Cincinnati papers, two St. Louis papers, two Baltimore papers, three or four New York papers, and many others" (Ramsdell 1871b).

To Orion Clemens
4 March 1871 • Buffalo, N.Y.
(MS: NPV)

Buffalo, 4th

My Dear Bro:

What I wanted with the "Liar" sketch, was to work it into the California book—which I shall do. But day before yesterday I concluded to go out of the Galaxy on the strength of it—& so I have turned it into the last Memoranda I shall ever write & published it as a "specimen chapter" of my forthcoming book.[1]

I have written Church the Galaxy people that I will never furnish them another article, long or short, for any price but $500⁰⁰ cash—& have requested them not to ask me for contributions any more, even at that price. I hope that lets *them* out, for I will stick to that.[2]

Now do try & leave me clear out of the Publisher for the present, for I am endangering my reputation by writing *too much*—I want to get out of the public view for a while. I will am still nursing Livy night & day & *cannot* write anything. I am nearly worn out. We shall go to Elmira ten days hence (if Livy can travel on a mattrass then,) & stay there till I have finished the California book—say three months. But I can't begin work right away when I get there—*must* have a week's rest, for I have been through 30 days' terrific siege. That makes it after the middle of March before I can go fairly to work—& then I'll have to hump myself & not lose a moment. You & Bliss just put yourselves in my place & you will see that my hands are full & *more* than full. When I told Bliss in N. Y. that I would write something for the Publisher *I* could not know that I was just about to lose FIFTY DAYS. Do you see the difference it makes? [*in margin:* The Publisher is a gallant success, & a credit to you.][3]

Just as soon as ever I can, I will send some of the book MS., but right in the be first chapter I have got to alter the whole style of one of my characters & re-write him clear through to where I am now. It is no fool of a job I can tell you, but the book will be greatly bettered by it. Hold on a few days—four or five,—& I will see if I can get a few chapters fixed & send to Bliss.[4]

I have offered ~~the~~ this dwelling house & the Express for sale, & when we go to Elmira we leave here for good. I shall not select a new home till the book is finished, but ~~writing a book, & reap if it proves to be a poor book~~ we have very little doubt that Hartford will be the place. We are almost certain of that.

Ask Bliss how it would do to ship our furniture to Hartford, rent an upper room in a building and ~~st~~ unbox it & store it there where somebody can frequently look after it. Is not the idea good? The furniture ~~it~~ is worth $10,000 or $12,000 & must not be jammed into any kind of a place & left unattended to for a year.[5]

The first man that offers $25,000 for our house can take it—it cost that.

What are taxes there? Here, all bunched together, of all kinds, they are 7 per cent—simply *ruin*. *Personal* property (city) tax is 4½ PER CENT here,—& we have ,$55,000 or, $60,000 worth of personal property. On real estate it is a trifle easier—but you can see how they would scorch us if we staid here. We have not paid this personal tax & when it is *due* we shall no longer be citizens.[6] Don't let any of this stuff get into the papers—mind & be careful about that. It would make me smell pretty loud here.

The things you have written in the Publisher are tip-top.[7]

In haste

Yr Bro

Sam.

[1] The "Liar" sketch was about Francis A. Oudinot (1822?–71), whom Clemens had met on the island of Maui in 1866. In returning the manuscript at Clemens's request (22 Feb 71 to OC), Orion seems to have asked about his brother's plans for it, perhaps because Bliss had already commissioned some illustrations for the sketchbook (24 Jan 71 to Bliss, n. 1). Clemens's decision to publish the sketch in the April *Galaxy* ("About a Remarkable Stranger: Being a Sandwich Island Reminiscence") followed his quarrel with Francis P. Church over when and how to announce his withdrawal from the magazine (see note 2). When he wrote this letter, he knew that the sketch would follow his "Valedictory" and a "postscript" to the "Valedictory" that he had added sometime early in February and that he first expected to appear in the March issue. The postscript was probably "My First Literary Venture," which Clemens characterized as something that "dropped from my pen of its own accord and without any compulsion from me, and so it may as well go in" (SLC 1871h, 615). On or about 2 March, Clemens sent Church "About a Remarkable Stranger," providing the following introduction:

[On second thoughts I will extend my MEMORANDA a little, and insert the following chapter from the book I am writing. It will serve to show that the volume is not going to be merely entertaining, but will be glaringly instructive as well. I have related one or two of these incidents before lecture audiences, but have never printed any of them before.—M. T.] (SLC 1871h, 616)

Later in the year he revised the sketch for *Roughing It,* chapter 77 (*RI 1993,* 526–31, 739–40, 1015–16).

²Clemens wrote this (now lost) letter to the "Galaxy people" shortly before he sent them "About a Remarkable Stranger"—that is, sometime after 21 February (when the March *Galaxy* was available in western New York) but no later than 1 March, since Church replied to it on 2 March. Beginning on 8 February there had been at least eleven telegrams and letters exchanged between Clemens, Church, and Isaac E. Sheldon, but texts for Clemens's letter and three telegrams have not been found. Their existence and general import, however, can be inferred from Church's and Sheldon's replies (all in CU-MARK). Returning from Washington to find Olivia gravely ill, Clemens telegraphed Church on 8 February to ask that the "Memoranda" department be omitted from the March *Galaxy,* leaving (as he thought) only his notice of withdrawal, or "Valedictory," the text of which he and Church had worked out in New York on 1 February, but to which he had recently sent a postscript, probably "My First Literary Venture." He also asked that Sheldon delay publication of the *(Burlesque) Autobiography.* On the afternoon of 9 February, Church replied by telegraph: "All galaxy gone to Press impossible to do it notice of withdrawal not in department generally so quiet it need not disturb you my heartiest sympathy." The same day he amplified the telegram in a letter:

> My dear Mark:
>   Your dispatch came too late. The Galaxy had already gone to press days before, and it was impossible to please you by leaving out the department.
>   You know, my dear fellow, I would do whatever I could to meet your wishes at such a time.
>   I will tell Sheldon to stop the book.
>   Dont trouble yourself about Memoranda. It is quiet & not so utterly incongruous as you think. I left out the notice of withdrawal, thinking it better for both of us that it should rest until April, & not hearing in time from you about the postscript.

After speaking to Sheldon, however, Church wrote a second letter:

> My dear Mark:
>   Since sending my letter & telegram of this afternoon I have found after consultation with Sheldon that by delaying & reversing things generally I can leave out memoranda & gratify your wish and my desire to please you.
>   It is making a ~~row~~ great trouble in the printing office, but as it *can* be done, it *shall* be done. I supposed it was impossible.
>   I hope your fears are not to be realized. But I can only hope & wish for the best.

Having as yet received only Church's telegram, Clemens telegraphed a second time, perhaps to ask that some explanation of his situation be included in the front matter of the magazine. But on 10 February Church wrote in reply:

> I have your last telegram, but I have already written that I succeeded in stopping Memoranda.
>   It will delay the Galaxy several days, but I keenly appreciate your feelings & honor you for it. I hope I should feel so myself under similar circumstances.

Sheldon also wrote on 10 February to "Friend Clemmens":

> I have spent all the afternoon in arranging to leave your department out of the March no & I assure you it has been no light task. It was part of a form on the press & all that comes after it in the March no had to be fixed over. Aside from the expense, it will cause us several days delay, which is peculiarly unfortunate as we were very much behind on this number. . . .
>
> The pamphlet I can hold a few days if you desire it, but a few samples of it have got out. I might hold the Editors copies back, while the distant orders are on their way by freight lines & they will not reach their destination for some time to come. Of course it is universally understood that this book was written long ago & has been in the press for some time.

Probably after receiving at least Church's two letters of 9 February, Clemens telegraphed a third time, on 10 or possibly 11 February, asking that an explanation of the absence of "Memoranda" be inserted in the March *Galaxy*. On 11 February, Sheldon responded by letter:

> Your telegram just rec'd.
> I write to you this morning.
> A note is inserted in the Nebulae & also in Table of Contents giving the reason why your Memoranda is not in this time.

The note was inserted at the end of "Nebulæ," the *Galaxy* editor's own department, which always occupied the final pages of each issue: "*The friends of* MR. CLEMENS (*Mark Twain*) *will share our regret that the sudden and alarming illness of his wife deprives us this month of his usual contribution to 'The Galaxy'* " (*Galaxy* 11 [Mar 71]: 478; no copy of the March issue has yet been found with the table of contents intact). On or soon after 21 February, Clemens saw the published note, which seemed to him to imply that his "usual" contributions would *resume*, rather than cease, in April, probably because he remembered the 3 February notice in the New York *Tribune* that promised his continuance as "leading" contributor (see p. 325). He complained in his lost letter to "the Galaxy people," and also made several other demands that can be inferred from Church's reply on 2 March:

> My dear Mark:
>   You certainly didn't read the notice announcing the omission of the March Memoranda aright. I only said that the department would be continued as usual "*next month*[.]" I had no idea of committing you to its indefinite continuance. Indeed that item explaining the whole matter which we got Reid to put in I had sent all over. My only thought was to indicate that the absence of this month's Memoranda didn't mean its discontinuance with that number. I thought that it was best to say some thing of the sort to show that it was an accidental omission only. Otherwise there would have been plenty of people to say it was only a manufactured excuse for giving up Memoranda.
>   I thought it was understood that your farewell was to go in & with it your postscript & then some words of mine, there or elsewhere in the magazine.
>   Now, only think of it. What better could I have done? And remember that notice & all had to be written in a minute, for there was no time to think. But I still cannot think I did wrong.
>   I will say some thing of the close of Memoranda this month, but I hardly know what to say.
>   Of course, my dear fellow, I shall not keep the name Memoranda. I had no idea of it.
>   Why not send me word to put in the Farewell? You see it was intended for either March or April anyway, and we were in doubt (you & I) as to whether it was best to have

it in the last or next to last month. I am afraid however it will be too late for you to get this, & me your answer in time.

And can't you work up some thing to start the new department—why not one of the things already in type? But I will have the plates of those pages destroyed, so that they need never arise to bother you if you dont want them.

Dont let us quarrel nor shall we, if I can help it by doing the square thing.

By 4 March, Clemens had been sufficiently appeased by Church's letter to allow publication of the "Valedictory" with its "postscript," as well as "About a Remarkable Stranger." Clemens did not immediately contribute to the new department, but in April or May he gave its editor, Donn Piatt, the first of two small contributions (27 Mar 71 to Piatt, n. 1).

[3] Orion had sent the first number of the *American Publisher*. Clemens's contribution was "A Question Answered," an excerpt from the first of six "Answers to Correspondents" columns he published in the *Californian* in 1865, and in 1867 reprinted, in part, in *The Celebrated Jumping Frog of Calaveras County, And other Sketches*, from which Orion supplied the text. Orion's editorial commentary explained that "very dangerous illness in his (Mr. Clemens's) family" prevented something more current. On the strength of a telegram from Clemens (now lost), Orion also promised "a contribution from him in the next number" (OC 1871b; SLC 1865a–f, 1867a, 45–48). Having made that commitment in print, Bliss and Orion were alarmed by Clemens's casual desire to be left out of the next issue as well. On 7 March, perhaps before he saw Clemens's letter, Bliss wrote: "We trust you will not disappoint us this month[.] We have made a good start & got well underway & we want to keep on steadily. Send us on as soon a[s] possible something good for it" (transcript in CtHMTH). The following day Orion was more insistent (11 and 13 Mar 71 to OC, n. 1). Clemens dated the fifty lost days from his 1 February meeting with Bliss in New York. He underestimated the time it would take him to finish *Roughing It*.

[4] Clemens had drafted at least the first eight or nine chapters, plus chapter eleven and some later sections. The character he planned to rewrite was "almost certainly the narrator himself," and, as the next letter shows, he finished this revision as predicted (*RI 1993*, 818–19, 822, 827, 834–35, 838).

[5] See 11 and 13 Mar 71 to OC, n. 1.

[6] Even if Clemens included the price of the house in his estimate, it is unclear how he arrived at the figures of $55,000 or $60,000 of personal property. Taxes at 4½ percent on those amounts would be $2,475 or $2,700; taxes at 2½ percent on $25,000 for the house alone would be $625. Before leaving Buffalo, the Clemenses did pay a city tax bill of $222.25, including interest and special fees, which was a far smaller amount than Clemens anticipated here. The total of all "National, State, county and municipal taxes" they paid in 1870 was $797 ("Income Tax, 1871," draft of return by SLC, Mar 71, CU-MARK; "City Tax, 1871," receipt to OLC, 27 Sept 71, CU-MARK). On 8 March, Orion reported that Bliss "says he wrote you about the taxes—that they are 1½ per cent" in Hartford (CU-MARK).

[7] Orion had evidently marked his own contributions in the copy of the *American Publisher* that he sent to Clemens, which does not survive. They included— presumably in addition to much of the editorial matter—"The American Publisher's Proclamation," a long introductory sketch about a genie who promises to "girdle the earth in thirty minutes; traverse either pole; dive to the centre of

the globe; walk under the ocean; fly above the clouds; or make excursions into genii land or fairy land" to gather materials for "the children's department of this paper" (OC 1871c; OC 1871a–b, d; Bliss to SLC, 15 Mar 71, CU-MARK).

To Orion Clemens
9 March 1871 • Buffalo, N.Y.
(MS: PBL)

Buf. 9[th,]

Dear Bro:

Tell Bliss "all right"—I will try to give him a chapter from the *new* book every month or nearly every month, for the Publisher. ~~I have g~~

I have got several chapters (168 pages MS.) revised & ready for printers & artists, but for the sake of security shall get somebody to copy it & then send the original to him.[1] Thank him for promising to take care of our furniture.

Yrs
Sam.

[1] One hundred sixty-eight pages would have taken Clemens through "the conjectured end of chapter 8, the pony-express incident" (*RI 1993*, 835, 838–40).

To Samuel S. Cox
9 March 1871 • Buffalo, N.Y.
(MS: CtHMTH)

Buffalo, 9[th,]

Dear Cox—

Thanks for Knott's speech—it is first rate.[1]

At last my wife is clear out of danger & mending tolerably fast. We send our love to you & yours.

Remember us to Geo. Alfred Townsend & Don Piatt. David Gray & I took a strong liking to Piatt,—& it was a great pity that he was suffering so with the neuralgia & I had such depressing news from home. We'd have had a royal time at this that dinner of yours.[2]

We are selling our dwelling & everything here & are going to spend the summer in Elmira while we build a house in Hartford. Eight months' sickness & death in one place is *enough* for

Yrs Truly

Sam[l]. L. Clemens

P. S. If you'll drop in any time at the Langdon homestead we'll find bed & sustenance for you & Mrs. Cox, *sure*.[3]

---

[1] James Proctor Knott (1830–1911) was a Democratic congressman from Kentucky. His satirical speech to the House on 27 January, in mock support of a Minnesota railroad project, was widely reprinted. Cox probably sent Clemens a clipping of "St. Croix and Bayfield Railroad," from page one of the Washington *Globe* of 29 January (*BDUSC*, 1323–24; *Congressional Globe* 1871, "Appendix," 3:66–68).

[2] For Cox's dinner, see pp. 327–29. Piatt was described by a fellow correspondent for the Cincinnati *Commercial* as "one of the institutions of Washington":

All men seem to know, or know of him. He has grown to be one of the celebrities of the land. Many fear or dislike him for what he has written, and many love and respect the man for his inherent good qualities and genuine kindness of nature. Knowing him only through his writings, we had formed the impression that all the milk of human kindness in the man, by some mysterious process, had been changed into wormwood and gall, and was oozing out at the end of his fingers in the form of the bitter D. P. letters to the Commercial. But we have learned here some new phases of the man's character. Many who know him well—and among others George Alfred Townsend—have told us that Piatt was one of the most kind and genial men they had ever known—one of the most unselfish and generous—doing more individual favors to poor devils who had no claims upon him; securing by persevering personal effort more places for wounded and worthy soldiers than any man in Washington; that he is a man of the very largest human sympathy, and that his heart was as easily touched by a tale of real suffering or wrong as a child's. . . . Piatt is no Bohemian in any sense of the word; is not dependent upon his pen for support; lives at the Arlington, we are informed, very elegantly upon his own means, and is in all senses an independent writer. One thing is certainly to be conceded: that wrongs and frauds, the jobs of Washington, so indescribably corrupt and infamous, receive no mercy at his hands. And for the battles which he has often fought in the interests of the people against politicians, tricksters and jobbers, and against their corrupt schemes, the country owes him a debt of gratitude. (Cincinnati)

[3] Cox had been married to the former Julia Buckingham, of Zanesville, Ohio, since 1849. They had no children ("Congressman Cox Dead," New York *Times*, 11 Sept 89, 5).

To Orion Clemens
10 March 1871 • Buffalo, N.Y.
(MS: NN-B)

Buf. 10th.

Dear Bro:

Have just sent out 160 MS pages of my book to be copied[1]—shall have it back next Tuesday. Then I will ship it to Bliss & mark a chapter to be transferred to the Columns of the Publisher.[2]

We must store all our furniture—that will be the best plan, for the reason that it will not be needed by us for at least 2 years—I mean to take my time in building a house & build it *right, &* —even if it does cost 25 per cent more.

So whenever the present house is sold we will box & ship the furniture to Bliss & let him rent a place & such as he describes, to store it in.[3] I am very much obliged to him indeed. We won't take less than $25,000 for the house, though, & so it may take us 6 months or a year to sell it (though we expect to sell it *soon.*)

Please sit down right away & torture your memory & write down in minute detail every fact & exploit in the desperado Slade's life that we heard on the Overland—& also describe his appearance & conversation as we saw him at Rocky Ridge station at breakfast. I want to make up a telling chapter from it for the book—& will put in it in the Publisher too, as soon as the agents begin to canvass.[4]

Ys

Sam

Love to Mollie,

---

[1] Clemens must have sent the entire 168 pages he had just promised (9 Mar 71 to OC), for the pages sent clearly included "The Old-Time Pony-Express of the Great Plains," which at this time probably ended chapter 8 in the manuscript of *Roughing It* (*RI 1993*, 835, 838–40; 20 Mar 71 to Bliss and OC).

[2] See 17 Mar 71 to Bliss, and 20 Mar 71 to Bliss and OC.

[3] See 11 and 13 Mar 71 to OC, n. 1. In September Clemens insured the furniture for $20,000 and shipped it to Hartford (27 Nov 71 to OLC, n. 1).

[4] Orion responded on 11 March, characterizing his extended, circumstantial account of the notorious Slade as "all I can remember—and more than I recollect

distinctly or feel entirely certain of—trusting that it would be practically near enough correct" (CU-MARK, in *RI 1993*, 778–81). Before 18 March Clemens used most of Orion's information to complete chapter 10 of *Roughing It* (*RI 1993*, 835–36; 15 Sept 70 to the postmaster of Virginia City, nn. 2–4; 20 Mar 71 to Bliss and OC).

To Orion Clemens
11 and 13 March 1871 • Buffalo, N.Y.
(MS: CU-MARK)

_ʌSaturday,_ʌ
Buf. 11th.—

N̸ Now why do you & Bliss go on urging me to make promises? I will not keep them. I have suffered damnation itself in the trammels of pe-riodical writing and I will *not* appeʄar once a month nor once in *three* months, ~~either.~~ in the Publisher nor any other periodical.[1]

You shall not advertise me as anything more than an *occasional* con-tributor—I̸ & I tell you I want you to let me choose my own occasions, too.[2]

You talk as if I am *responsible* for your newspaper venture. If I am I want it to stop right here—for I ~~will be damned~~ ʌdarned, if Iʌ am ʌnotʌ going to have another year of harassment about periodical writing. There isn't money enough between hell & Hartford to hire me to write once a month for *any* periodical. I would do more to advance Bliss's in-terests than any ~~ma au~~ other man'sʌ in the world, but the more I turn it over in my mind how your & Bliss's letters of yesterday are making the Publisher a paper which the people are to understand is Mark Twain's paper & to sink or swim on his reputation, the more outrageous I get.

Why, confound it, when & how has this original little promise of mine (to "drop in an occasional screed along with the Company's *other* authors,")[3] grown into these formidable dimensions—whereby I am the *father & sustainer* of the paper & you ʌhaveʌ actually committed your-selves, & me too with advertisements looking in that direction?

Let this cease, ~~until I see you or Bliss & have another talk face to face.~~ Say nothing more about my appearing in the paper on any other footing than occasionally, like the other authors.

Curse it, man, ~~if I had known that~~ I would not have had it published around that I was staking my reputation as the sponsor of a new journalistic experiment for $30,000 *cash*—& ~~by the living God~~ ˄yet˄ the thing is being done free gratis for nothing!˄—I mean without˄ any real & tangible contract.˄

Make me the very smallest among the contributors—the very seldomest I mean—& in that way give me some *weight*. Haven't I risked cheapening myself sufficiently by a year's periodical dancing before the public but must *continue* it?

I lay awake all last night aggravating myself with this prospect of seeing my hated nom de plume (for I do loathe the very sight of it,) in print *again* every month.

~~I am plainly & *distinctly* committed, by those shuffling gentlemen of the Galaxy for "*frequent*" articles⁴—& I tell you I wouldn't write them a single paragraph for twenty-five dollars a *word*. Keep that to yourself, but it is so.~~ ˄[About Galaxy—scratched it out.]˄

I don't want to even see my *name* anywhere in print for 3 months to come. As for being the high chief contributor & main card of the Publisher, I won't ~~her~~ hear of it for a single moment. I'd rather break my pen & stop writing just where I am. Our income is plenty good enough without working for more; & sometimes I think I'm a sort of fool for going on working, anyhow.⁵

Now whenever you mention my name in connection with the paper, ⫽ put "*occasional* contributor" after it & don't you intimate that I am anything, more.

I ⫽ must & will keep shady & quiet till Bret Harte simmers down a little⁶ & then I mean to go up head again & *stay* there until I have published the two books already contracted for & just one more beside, which latter shall make a ripping sensation or I have overestimated the possibilities of my subject.⁷

Now write me something pleasant—& drop me back where I belong—as an *occasional* contributor. I can produce more than one letter from Bliss ~~saying~~ ˄intimating that˄ he would pay me $5,000 a year for *regular* contributions⁸—& I *never took him up*—yet in your letter you say:

"Put yourself in our place. A new enterprise in which Twain was to be a feature & so widely advertised. Are you going to kick the pail over?"

You had a perfect right to advertise me widely as an occasional contributor, but none to make ~~I~~ me ~~the~~ responsible for the life or death of the paper. Yet you say:

"Squarely ~~rh~~ we *must* have something from you or we run the risk of going to the dickens"—

Simply puts the responsibility on my shoulders when I have tacitly refused to do the thing for $5,000 a year.

And in your next sentence you say "we must have something every month."

Clearly this is all wrong. Please to put yourself in *my* place.

The man who says the least about me in any paper for 3 months to come will do me the greatest favor. I tell you I mean to *go slow.* I will "top" Bret Harte again or bust. But I can't do it by dangling eternally in the public view.

~~Taking~~

Take all I have said kindly—impatiently, perhaps, but not ill-naturedly, toward either you or Bliss.

Ys

Sam

P. S. Shall ship some book MS. next, Wednesday;[9]
[*new page:*]

MONDAY.

I have left this letter two days "to cool"—in order to see if my mind remains the same about it.

I find that it *does* remain the same, only *stronger.* The more I think of it the more I feel wronged. After my Galaxy experience I would not *appear* (originally or otherwise,) in any paper once a month for $7,000 a year.[10]

Now *why* did you suppose I would appear *constantly* in The Publisher under a mere vague understanding that I was to be *paid* for it? (for I NEVER promised it.)

Is it because I am under obligations to the Am. Pub. Co.? ~~That~~ To decide that, it will be necessary to *examine the accounts & see which of us has made the most money out of the other.*

When Bliss agreed, once, to *stand* a high royalty on a book contract we were making, I receded *voluntarily,* & put the per centage *a good deal lower.*[11]

I have never tried to crowd the Co.—but here the Co. is trying very decidedly to crowd *me.*

I never will enter into even the most trifling business agreement hereafter without having it in writing, with a revenue stamp on it.

I want you to *right* me, now, as far as you can, & do it without any delay. Drop all advertisements about my writing *"exclusively"* for the Publisher, for I want no manacles on me. And put this paragraph in PROMINENTLY:

Correction.

I notice an

An item has appeared in several of the papers to the effect that I am to write <u>regularly</u> for ʧhe <u>Publisher</u>. It would be wrong to let this error go uncorrected. I only propose to write <u>occasionally</u>—nothing more,ᴀ—& shall doubtless appear less frequently than any other contributor.ᴀ

Mark Twain.

If you alter or leave out that paragraph I shall publish it elsewhere.[12]

Now I am heartily sick of this whole subject & do not want to hear another word about it. Write me on anything else you please, but drop this & drop it entirely—never to be touched upon again.[13]

If you had not spread it abroad that I am to write, I would ask you to remove my name wholly from the list of contributors.

Yrs

Sam

[1] Clemens was replying to two letters from Bliss and one from Orion. Bliss had written on 7 March and again, more urgently, on 8 March (see 4 Mar 71 to OC, n. 3, for the first letter; the second is lost). Orion had written on 8 March (CU-MARK):

> My Dear Brother:–
>   Your very welcome letter contains a great deal of pleasant information.
>   1. That Livy will soon be well enough to move.
> And 2. That we may look for you as a resident of our city. Bliss says he will furnish the information about taxes. I will see him when he comes in and get the figures unless he is going to write you the information himself. He says if you will only write we will take care of your furniture and it shan't cost you anything. He knows an upper story, new and free of bugs, that can be rented cheap. Besides, we will hunt up any information you want, and do anything else you want done, if you will only write. He is in earnest. He is decidedly worked up about it. He says, put yourself in our place. A new enterprise, in which "Twain" was to be a feature, and so widely advertised. He receives congratulations in New York at the Lotus Club that you and Hay are to write for the paper. Everybody likes it. It starts out booming. Are you going to kick the pail over? Think

of yourself as writing for *no* periodical *except* the Publisher. "Have you seen Twain's last?" says one. "It's in the Publisher." He goes and buys it because there is no other chance to get it. It gives us prestige. Look how it helps me. I should be an editor with something to edit. This "Publisher" may as well be built up into something large as not. With a great circulation, giving only once a month a taste of "Twain," to whet people's appetites for books, it acts as an advertisement, and we have an incentive to "write up" "Twain," so far as his own efforts leave us anything in that way to do. Under these circumstances, with your pen withdrawn from the Galaxy, and held aloof from small books, and confined to the larger and more elevated description worthy of your mettle, and writing *only* for us, who publish a paper as a branch of your publisher's enterprise, you would not be writing too much nor too little, but just exactly enough. Squarely, we *must* have something from you or we run the risk of going to the dickens. Bliss says he will pay you, but we must have something every number. If you only give us a half column, or even a quarter of a column—a joke or an anecdote, or anything you please— but give us *something,* so that the people may not brand us as falsifiers, and say we cried "Twain," "Twain," when we had no "Twain." If you don't feel like writing anything, copy something from your book. Are you going to let the Galaxy have a chapter and give us nothing? If you don't feel like taking the trouble of copying from the book say we may select something. We shall have time enough if you send some chapters in four or five days, as we ˏyouˏ proposed. If you prefer it I will hunt out something from my old file of Californians and send it to you to revamp. That paper never had much circulation east.

Junius Henri Browne and Signor Blitz have books under way. In the first number of the Publisher you may have noticed articles without other than the usual credit, "by Junius Henri Browne," and "By Signor Blitz." These were simply extracts from their forthcoming books, put in as original communications for our paper. Why can't we do that with your book?—that is, when we all get in a tight place like the present.

Mollie suggests another plan of taking care of your furniture. If a house were rented in which the best could be stored and leave a few rooms in which we could "keep house," using the plainest things, the furniture might be better taken care of and better guarded against the only accident outside of insurance policies—stealing. Fix it to suit yourself and we will attend to it carefully any way you want it done.

Do not understand that we fail or slacken in sympathy for you. We appreciate the sad fact that you have been sorely tried by an affliction which brought with it the shadow of a gigantic and irreperable shadow sorrow, brought it close enough to chill you to the marrow; we do appreciate your exhaustion, your prostration, and the fearful strain it would be to you to attempt now to write for us. I could not have found it in my heart to insist now on the imposition of the least labor upon you if it had not been for the very serious moment the matter is to us—and even then we only *insist* so far as to request the privilege of copying a little from your book, or using other compositions without present labor to you.

Bliss wants me to say (he read the preceding except the paragraph in relation to Mollie's proposition) that he was so much troubled about the prospect of not getting you into our next two numbers that he may have forgotten to express the earnest sympathy he feels for you, and wishes me to convey the expression of it to you. He says he laid awake till 2 o'clock last night thinking of your com[m]unications for the paper, and of the amount of work he had before him between now and the first of April. He says he wrote you about the taxes—that they are 1½ per cent.

Mollie and I go to-night to a children's party at Bliss'—75 invited, and to-morrow at 6 to tea with a fine lady on Elm Street—Mrs. Sargent. She means to have Hodge and his wife also. Hodge is pastor of our church (Presbyterian) and has had us at his house twice to dinner on Sunday—as we have a long walk. Hodge's wife has translated some Swiss tracts, which have been published by the Dutch Reformed Church. She has a sister married to Colgate of soap celebrity, and the great telegraph inventor, Morse, is her uncle. She says her Uncle Sidney (five years younger than ~~Morse~~ ˌthe telegraph inventorˌ is an enthusiastic inventor, but very quiet, says little, and slowly perfects his inventions. For one he has been offered a hundred thousand dollars by the United States. He refused. He has another under way (though I suppose this is confidential) a new motive power designed to cross the Atlantic in 24 hours. Singular coincidence that it should be so near in the line of what I am trying to do—he working at the engine and I at the wheel—and that without my giving her any more of a hint than that I was merely trying to invent *something*, she should say that her brother was such a lover of inventions, if she should tell him there was an inventor here wanted his advice it would be her best chance to get him here. My love to Livy and the baby,

Your Bro.,
Orion.

Clemens wrote on the envelope, "Still urging MSS."

[2] The first issue of the *American Publisher* had advertised Mark Twain as "among the contributors engaged for this paper" ("Our Contributors," *American Publisher* 1 [Apr 71]: 4). During its twenty-one-month run, the magazine printed pieces by him on fourteen occasions. In all but three instances (SLC 1871m, o–p), these were extracts from published work: *The Innocents Abroad*, *Roughing It*, and earlier writings (SLC 1871i, k, r–s, 1872d–j). The *Publisher* regularly included among its fillers anecdotes attributed to Mark Twain and notices about him.

[3] If Clemens made the promise in a letter, it has not been found.

[4] Clemens may have had in mind the New York *Tribune*'s 3 February report that, even after abandoning his "Memoranda," he was still to be a "leading and frequent contributor" to the *Galaxy* (see p. 325).

[5] In calmer moments Clemens did not consider relying solely on his wife's income: see 16 and 17 Apr 70 to the Langdons, n. 4, and 26 Oct 70 to Bliss.

[6] See 3 Mar 71 to Riley, n. 6.

[7] Clemens had already contracted for three books: *Roughing It;* the volume of sketches; and the South African diamond mine collaboration with John Henry Riley, which he expected would cause a "ripping sensation."

[8] These letters are lost, but see 27 Jan 71 to Bliss, n. 1.

[9] That is, 15 March. Clemens did not send the manuscript until Saturday, 18 March (20 Mar 71 to Bliss and OC).

[10] Clemens had stipulated a salary of two thousand dollars for his year's contributions to the *Galaxy* (11 Mar 70 to Church; 11 Mar 70 to Bliss).

[11] See 2 Dec 70 to Bliss.

[12] This notice did not appear in the *American Publisher* and it has not been located elsewhere.

[13] Bliss's 15 March reply is transcribed here in full. All but one page of it is in CU-MARK. Page 10 has been recovered in part from an independent transcript of the letter (ViU) made before Clemens enclosed page 10 in his reply to Bliss: see 17 Mar 71 to Bliss, n. 6.

Friend Clemens. Your brother has handed me your letters— I cannot conceive what we have done to draw your fire so strongly— I believe some misapprehension exists on your part of the position—& although you interdict the subject, I cannot let it drop without a reply,— If I overpressed you to write *monthly* for us, I am sorry[.] I ~~did so~~ denied all intentions to do it at the time—& intended merely to set forth the advantages it would be to us & your brother to have you do it— You say in *yours* "*drop all advertisements about my writing* EXCLUSIVELY *for the Publisher*"

Will you do me the favor to say whether you have seen any advertisements of ours to that effect? We have never made use of this word in any shape, hinted or said such a thing that we are aware of: Again you say, "*Say nothing more about my appearing in the paper on any other footing than occasionaly like the other authors*" Have you ever seen anything from us that has placed you in any different position—or thrust you prominently forward. In every advt. or card issued by us your name has appeared *with the others*—& nothing said specially about you— The only special mention made of you by us to my knowledge, was in the excuse for articles last issue, which your brother wrote & inserted on strength of your telegram & says he sent you copies of the paper, ~~naming which~~ pointing out the articles he wrote—& that you did not demur to anything—but wrote "The 'Pub." was a splendid success" I send you enclosed the only *advertisements* or *cards*—or *items*—or *anything else* we ~~have~~ had inserted or used up to *last Friday* either in our paper or elsewhere— You will note that nothing is inserted as to your writing exclusively or in any other way for us, but simply assume you as a contributor with the rest— *We have in no way intimated* that you was *sponsor* or *father to the* paper or that you had any connections with it except as above *in common with other authors & contributors.* In what manner then had we erred, or done unjustly towards you—or "wronged" you—? Writing you as a friend I spoke freely in my last, not supposing I was writing to one who would scan every word closely as if written by a stranger— I begged excuse at the time for any seeming overpressing, assuring you I intended none I spoke of your name as a "right bower" not intending it to ˏbeˏ understood we had held ~~up it~~ ˏyou upˏ in that form to the public— Nothing has been said outside ~~of~~ ˏonˏ the subject except what appears in ~~five~~ ˏfourˏ of our advts. ˏ& indˏ— Should the Publisher go down tomorrow I know of no manner in which your name could be identified with it— We know of no way it is effected by your reputation, except so far as the fact of ~~contr~~ your contributions might aid its sale like those of any other contributor— I repeat in no moment have you been put forward of other authors, except so far as in our lists your name was *properly* ˏ(if at all)ˏ *put first.* I say up to last Friday nothing but the 3 cards & advts. marked *1. 2. & 3* had appeared or been used & no other mention made of you to our knowledge— Wishing to advertise our paper in the Country papers, however we got up the little yellow ticket enclosed—& without intending to assert that you or anyone else had agreed to write for every issue of the paper, but that you & the others named were *parties engaged by us & paid, for articles,* we used the word *regular contributors* We used it in contradistinction to *voluntary, transient—unknown* or *unengaged* contributors—whose articles are "coming in"— We did not mean to promise that an article from each of these named in the advt. would appear in *each issue*— I may have been unfortunate in the selection of the word, but of ˏsoˏ little importance did I attach to the word regular that your brother & myself had forgotten it was in, until we looked it up last night to *scan it* We read your letter of the 9th on Friday in which you say "all right",! *I will try to give him" (Bliss) "a chapter from the new book every month or nearly every month for the Publisher"* I then sent off some of the papers to the press, (the Country press or small, city papers) with the slip enclosed— I had no doubt in my own mind we had full authority to use your name in the sense we intended to— Some of these tickets have gone to N.E. papers & in to N.Y. State to some portions of the press.
I cannot imagine that that advt. is what has caused the severe tone of your letter—as I hardly think you could have seen it—when yours was written— No paper could have recd it & inserted it by Saturday—even if they had got their copy of it— Hence I am entirely in the dark as to the reasons why you fancy anything has been said or done by us to make you responsible for the success or non success of this paper. Why you feel that you are ~~offering with~~ staking your reputation on it—or acting as sponsor or where you get the idea we are so publishing or know of its being so published. We have seen no notice of our paper *referring to you* in any way, or connecting you with it, except sometimes mentioning the *editor as your brother*— Is it possible that some have inferred

from that, you was connected with it, & have so stated—such statements meeting your eye? none have come to our notice—
Now then it seems to us, (your brother & myself) that you have seen something in the papers we know nothing about, & that you imagine *we* have done it—& that taken in connection with our letters you imagine that we are intending to rely on you, lean heavily on you & give out that you are *virtually running this paper*

This is all wrong. We supposed you would write & furnish us with some little articles—enough to give us the power to quote you as a contributor—that this would be great help to us & aside from that we expected nothing— We announced you as a contributor holding an article in our hands from you for first paper— You withdrew this after the paper had progressed & was to send something else— At the last moment it failed to come—(the excuse was *amply sufficient*)   You telegraphed us to make excuse, we did so, stating you would give us something next number. You saw this in the paper, our list of contributors with your name in, & no demur that I am aware of. Then comes a letter saying you could not write [for] us. In reply, I attempted to show you our position the *present* one *not the future* & how it would effect us to not have an article next issue— People are so ready to believe all to be humbugs. We wanted to avoid this reputation for our paper! As to the future we took occasion to name our wishes—pointed out advantages &c. stating I did not wish to overpress the matter & hoped you would not consider I did— Receive in reply, ˏto the effectˎ All right you will do one of the things I propose, in a measure at least, & I suppose all was understood—this was followed by one written the 10ᵗʰ stating something very similar—when on the 11ᵗʰ your tone changes & your last is written, & endorsed on the 13ᵗʰ   We show you fairly all that we have done— What is wrong in it? Please point it out to us, & say in what instance or in what manner we have disconnected you from the other authors & contributors, or made you more prominent—or in any way thrown any responsibility of the paper, or its success on you—except so far as the first forthcoming number is concerned ⅍ that seems ̶i̶n̶ ˏin a˄ position when aid from you is almost necessary for our reputation & character—whether we are entitled to that aid we leave for you to judge— As to remuneration for what you should do, I have told your brother which I suppose he has told you that we would pay you well for all you wrote for usˏˎˏ & I so stated to you in N.Y.ˎ   I should expect you to set your own price & should pay it— I have asked all to put their own price on articles, ̶w̶h̶e̶r̶e̶f̶o̶r̶e̶ & all have done so & been paid promptly. Your brother may have been ˏsoˎ influenced by my seeming distress at the position of affairs—that he wrote more strongly than absolutely necessary. He read the letter to me & I suggested no changes, paying but little attention except to its general tenor— I did not mean him to convey any idea to you that our paper's success ˏabsolutelyˎ depended upon your future writing for us, but that ̶t̶h̶a̶t̶ ˏitˎ was in a manner the condition ˏof affairsˎ so far [as] an article for next issue was concerned as it involved a promise from us, made as your brother & I both supposed, fairly—

The *monthly* contributions—was a matter to furnish far ahead—on which the public had no powers as we have solicited no subscribers yet, & for 3 months we wish to do all we promise. In this next issue, we shall show our plansˏ, we shall mention the fact that after another issue we shall charge for the paper, that we shall have for contributors such & such writers &c &c Our present advts. are only for *the 3. months* nothing more— We can honorably place your name before or behind as you may desire & wish—& this brings me to the Card you send[.] [*from transcription of missing page 10:*] The insertion of that conveys the idea of misunderstanding & [antagonistic] feeling between us[.] Is it wise to give birth to this? It insinuates also an unfairness in [what has been said] If you wish anything said after they [have read it, it requires] up on our part a direct assertion as to what we have said & done [W]ould it not be best to say ourselves that "Mark Twain ret[ires] from the Galaxy & [his] monthly contribut[ion] in the "M[emoranda]" and also from most other periodical literary [tasks to devote] h[i]s time to the publication of his forthcoming book. He will appear [in] & will [write for the Publisher as an] occasional contributor."

Would not this place you right before the public & do us no harm as [t]he adv[s]. of the public paper will be seen only in small [Country] paper[s] as they were intended only for such & the word regular if not proper ther[e] will do you no damage if you do not wish. We can insert your name among contributors as now or add [*MS continues:*] occasional if it adds anything to it—in meaning—or we can after 3 mos strike your name out altogether if you wish it, although we should much regret to do so, & hope you will not require it—

We think, that, as in our paper you never have been ,never, announced in anyway other than as the others have, under the head of *contributors* no explanation or correction is required— Any items as to your future movements in other papers are hardly worth replying to so long as they are not dishonorable to you— They are read & pass out of sight— Nothing we have said, or done imposes on you any *monthly contributions* or on us the obligation to furnish them— You are on the same platform with the other authors—have not been claimed as our writer exclusively—have not in any way by us been identified with the paper except as a contributor, same as the rest. Then why the necessity of stirring it up,? It injures us without doing you any service whatever— If you do not wish to write for us dont do it—we shall endeavor to get on as without your name—& think we shall—but we do think you should at least lift us from the a[w]kward position we are in about our promise for next number—& if you will say whether you are willing your name should stand as a contributor—in the list among others as it does now in the paper, or in what shape you want it—we will arrange it to suit—or & if you wish any explanation of anything said by us, will not such as are properly written out & arranged answer all purposes.

Please excuse my lengthy epistle—I will be brief hereafter as possible—& let me hear from you in reply.

> Very Truly
> E Bliss Jr

The three enclosures of advertisements mentioned by Bliss have not survived.

To Susan L. Crane
12 March 1871 • Buffalo, N.Y.
(MS, not sent: CU-MARK)

Buf, Sunday[1]

Dear Susie:

Clara is splendid!—but you knew that before. We all get along handsomely.

[1] Presumably Clemens abandoned, or misplaced, this beginning to a letter only shortly before he wrote the next one.

To Susan L. Crane
14 March 1871 • Buffalo, N.Y.
(MS: CU-MARK)

Buf. 14th

Dear Susie:

I hold Livy up, now, & she *goes through the motions* of walking—
from the bed to the chair—& sits there 2 hours at a time. I don't *lift* her
into the sitz bath or out of it any more—merely help her.

I have talked to the wetnurse, the D^r. has talked to her & Miss Clara
has talked to her—& so between us we have drilled her into a good officer. We like her better than at first. She has willingness, plenty of it,
but no sense—I mean no judgment. She goes on dressing the cubbie
serenely, & never bothers about his frantic crying.[1]

Sarah got at loggerheads with her—& next ~~she ref refused~~ I found
she had for a week been leaving Emily to take the *whole* care of the baby
at night. So I discharged Sarah. She didn't want to go at all, & was ready
to make good promises for the future, but I thought it best that she
should go—& to tell the truth I couldn't cheerfully stand that breaking
of my own express order (to sleep in the same room with the wet nurse.)

I hired Susy ¢ to come back that same day—got her to compromise
with her employer & come here several days before her time was up.
Margaret was staunch & true, & a ready help through all the fuss.[2]

I make them keep the cubbie in the library altogether, now, & reg-
ulate the ~~place~~ temperature with a thermometer. It is high treason to take
him into the kitchen upon any pretext, & misprision of treason to even
refer to the kitchen in his presence.

Miss Clara is perfectly splendid—but you know that. Livy drinks
ale, now, for a tonic—suggested it herself, & the D^r., as usual, agreed.
She was as tight as a brick this afternoon (as the historian Josephus would
say.) She talks incessantly, anyhow, so the ale hadn't any the advantage
of her there, but it made her unendurably slangy, & that is what we
grieved for.

We play cards a great deal—cut-throat ~~Eur~~ Euchre.

Susie dear, can you correctly pronounce any ~~one~~ two of these italicised words without referring to a dictionary?

"He was an *aspirant* after the *vagaries* of the *exorcists*, & a *coadjutor* of the *irrefragable* yet ~~exqu~~ *exquisite farrago* on the *subsidence* of the *italicised finale*." (Webster *is* an old fool—(Livy's permission.)

We *all* join in sending a great tidal wave of affection sweeping down upon you where ever you are[3]—not to ~~dro~~ bury you & drown you, but to bear you upward & onward to any & all happinesses that you may seek, and any & all ambitions you shall aspire to, by the will of God. Amen.

Livy & I have had a long & pleasant talk about Mrs. Corey,[4] & I have drawn a picture of the baby's foot for her—chose the foot because it *happened* so, not because it was worthier of his father's art than any other feature of him.

The cubbie is not well, & Livy thinks D[r.] Wright will help us lose him if he can ‸get‸ ten days more to do it in. I wish we were in Elmira, for I think a good deal as Livy does. It will be hard, *very* hard to go & discharge Wright & take another physician, & yet we have got to do it if the baby gets really sick.

Very lovingly, & ever & ever so gratefully Yours, Susie, for your long & exhausting service here when your own health demanded your absence. (Shall we *ever* be able to repay it to either you or to Theodore your other ~~see~~ self?[)]

Sam[l.]

[1] The wet nurse, recently hired, was a replacement for the woman who had begun nursing Langdon at Buffalo General Hospital and had moved into the Clemens household around 30 January. The doctor was Andrew Wright, mentioned by name for the first time in the penultimate paragraph of this letter. Olivia's close friend Clara Spaulding had come to assist her convalescence probably around 10 or 11 March, replacing Susan Crane, who returned to Elmira around the same time (25 Jan 71 to Day; 26 Jan 71 to Fairbanks; 11 Nov 70 to Ford, n. 5; 22 Feb 71 to OC, n. 2; 14 Mar 71 to Fairbanks).

[2] None of the four nurses has been further identified; Margaret, however, remained with the family until May 1872 (17 May 72 to Annie Moffett, NPV).

[3] Susan Crane, suffering from a chronic throat ailment, had been advised to leave Elmira for a warmer climate (see the next letter). She and Theodore had spent the winter of 1868–69 in the South for the same reason (*L2*, 287 n. 3, 299 n. 1; *L3*, 182 n. 2, 212).

[4] Ella J. Corey, Olivia's Elmira friend (*L3*, 243 n. 4, 506 *caption*, 508).

To Mary Mason Fairbanks
14 March 1871 • Buffalo, N.Y.
(MS: CSmH)

Home, 14th.

Dear Mother:

If we haven't much to tell, we at least haven't any bad news among it.

We have a wet nurse with plenty of milk, now, & a supplemental nurse that is handy & loves the baby. We have discharged two nurses lately, whom we had in place of these.

Mrs. Dᵣ· Gleason left here when Livy was decidedly & distinctly out of danger & then Susy Crane staid till ⁂ 3 or 4 days ago[1] when Livy had become wonderfully better & hungrier & chattier & cheerfuller, & departed for Elmira, Clara Spaulding relieving her. Clara is here yet. We play 3-handed (cut-throat) Euchre & other games, although Livy lies in bed. Livy sits up 2 or 3 times a day an hour to 2 hours at a time but cannot walk a step (& won't for a month, *I* think, tho' she puts it 10 days.)

We leave for Elmira as soon as she can travel, & the agents may take their own time about selling the house.

We spent the most of this morning-hour talking about you and re-hearsing gratefully the fact that ~~she~~ you have dropped affairs of the highest importance more than once to come & cheer & help & comfort us in our great need[2]—& I don't believe anybody has so good a friend & mother ~~& y~~ as you are to us, or one who is so loved, & whose motherly ways & deeds are ~~so~~ more ⁂ gratefully remembered & sincerely ~~appe~~ appreciated.

Susie is to go South immediately. Her physicians say⁄ that with great care she may live a good while, but that it is *imperative* that she spend her Springs South.

⁄Charley is pining for Europe again, & I think a majority vote can be polled to let him go. He is to[o] uneasy & spasmodic to be of the fullest comfort or usefulness, either, at home.

Go on "fixing up" out at "Faro-Bank,"[3] for we are personally interested. We look forward to a two or three weeks of genuine comfort & placid satisfaction there in the summer.

Love to all the old household & the new branch.[4]

Lovingly

Yr Son

[1] Susan Crane's arrival, in late January when she and Theodore came for a visit, had preceded Dr. Gleason's by two or three weeks (pp. 325, 327; 22 Feb 71 to OC).

[2] Apparently Mrs. Fairbanks had visited in October as well as November 1870 (5 Nov 70 to OC, n. 5; 7 Nov 70 to Langdon, n. 3).

[3] Fair Banks, Mrs. Fairbanks's home.

[4] Alice Fairbanks Gaylord and William H. Gaylord, married on 11 January.

To Jane Lampton Clemens and Family
15 March 1871 • Buffalo, N.Y.
(MS: NPV)

Buf. 15.

Dear Folks—

Livy sits up 2 hours at a time, but can't walk yet. The first time she can walk across the floor we shall leave for Elmira to spend Spring & Summer, & eventually shall go to Hartford to live,—about 2 years from now—shall travel in the meantime, maybe. Have put up the printing office & our house for sale.

Susie Crane has gone home to go South, & Clara Spaulding is here helping me nurse Livy.

Love to all

Sam

To James Redpath
15 March 1871 • Buffalo, N.Y.
(Transcript and paraphrase: *National Book Auctions*, lot 157)

Buf., 15.

Dear Redpath—

[*paraphrase: About one-hundred-fifty words in Mark Twain's hand-writing offering to lecture in N. E. for $150.00 but for*] not less than $250.00 in Boston. [*paraphrase: Interesting letter to his agent, requesting a speaking tour. He asks that the matter be hushed in the meantime, and that he, reluctantly, would speak because of a contemplated enterprise, but in Boston he wants more money!*]][1]

Mark.

[1]Clemens first intimated the possibility of a limited fall lecture tour in his 30 January letter to Redpath. It wasn't until 15 March, three days before he left Buffalo for good, and with Olivia definitely on the mend, that he could have written at least tentatively confirming that intention. The "contemplated enterprise" has not been identified.

To Orion Clemens
15–18 March 1871 • Buffalo, N.Y.
(MS: CU-MARK)

Buf. 15.

My Dear Bro:

I am sorry to ever have to read anybody's MSS, it is such *useless* work—the Great Public's is the only opinion worth having, & you can't get that by applying a fire-assay to a random specimen of it.

My opinion of a children's article is wholly worthless, for I never saw one that I thought was worth the ink it was written with, & yet you know & I know that such literature is marvelously popular & worth heaps of money.[1]

What *can* my criticism be worth? I find that you are just like everybody else—can put your *heart* into a letter (naturalness, that pearl of price, follows by inexorable law,) when it is a *private* one, but the moment you set out to p̶ write a *public* letter you forget that the Public is simply a multiplication of the poor, common, human Private individual—you forgø̶et that & look upon it as a vast, vague, unreal Shape, of some mysterious kind, & so you mount a high horse & a dismally *arti-/ficial* one, & go frothing in a way that nobody can ~~poss~~ understand or sympathize with. Your ʜ̶ *heart & soul* &̶ are not in this article. Then you certainly can't get anybody else's into it. Your *private* letter to me stirs me—& would enlist the instant interest of the veriest stranger—consequently it is a good & ~~valu~~ worthy literary production—& the other isn't.

Now that is only my *opinion*—Mollie's is on the other side & is really worth *more* than mine, since I have ˄no˄ love for children's literature. Therefore, toss my opinion to the winds & hold fast to the more worthy one.[2]

~~But I tell you this. It is the only infallible rule in literature, too: If you are~~ Your heart & soul *must* ~~be in your work—~~*any*~~ work—to achieve success with it.~~

~~If you were to set out to write to Mollie (at a distance & unacquainted with~~ ˄If you were to set out to write to Mollie (at a distance & unacquainted with˄ ~~the matter,) an outpouring of your heart upon the~~ ~~your experiences in Bliss's office, knowing that no eye would see it but hers & hence you need not mince anything, don't you know it would be a readable article? Of course it would.~~

~~But my opinion is worth infinitely less than Mollie's about this article. Let that comfort & encourage you.~~

At any other time your experiences there would distress me greatly—but ~~for~~ I am & have been for weeks so buried under beetling Alps of trouble that yours look like little passing discomforts to me˄—molehills. [And yet I know very well that ~~every~~ ˄each˄ individual's troubles are stately from *his* point of view.]

I am the worst man in the world to send MS to. Now don't repeat that. It hurts me a hundred times more to give ɑ̶ a disparaging opinion than it can hurt the writer to receive it. Considering that you have read my article in the Galaxy on this very subject, I should have thought you would ~~have~~ sparеd̶ me.[3]

I am simply half-crazy—that is the truth. And I wish I was the other half.

$ Yrs

Sam^*l·*

[*new page:*]⁴

If the Introductory pages are THE *feature*, leave out the rest.

If the portraits of the grotesque monsters are THE feature, leave out the rest.

If the sea-story is the feature, leave ~~the ev~~ out everything else.

~~Let there be consistency *somewhere*~~

Perhaps you will say that the *object* & consistency of ~~the~~ these apparently irreconcilable unnecessities will appear in the subsequent chapters—in which case I have nothing more to say—but if it strikes me as strained & incoherent, it might strike others so.⁵

But lay this away (never destroy MS.) for 3 months & then read it & see if you can't better it. Meantime write about some invention of somebody's that you are filled with admiration of, or which you thoroughly despise—write about something that you *feel*.

———————————————————————————

Mrs. Mollie Clemens | 149 Asylum st⁶ | Hartford | Conn [*postmarked:*] BUFFALO N.Y. MAR 18 [*docketed by OC:*] Criticism

¹ This letter replied to Orion's 13 March request for an evaluation of the children's story he was writing for the *American Publisher.* Orion had been wounded by Elisha Bliss's dismissive response and resented Bliss's insistence that he confine himself to clerical tasks (13 Mar 71 to SLC, two letters, CU-MARK).

² Orion reported that

> Mollie thinks it good and suitable for children. . . . But I doubt the suitableness of this story for children, and am inclined to think Bliss is right in thinking he can get plenty of people to write better for children. If you think with Mollie please send it right back for the children's department of the Publisher. . . . If you think that with the alterations noted it will do for some paper or magazine please send it—and if you don't like it at all throw it in the fire. (13 Mar 71 to SLC [2nd], CU-MARK)

³ In "A General Reply," in his November 1870 *Galaxy* "Memoranda," Clemens had observed:

> Every man who becomes editor of a newspaper or magazine straightway begins to receive MSS. from literary aspirants, together with requests that he will deliver judgment upon the same. And after complying in eight or ten instances, he finally takes refuge in a general sermon upon the subject, which he inserts in his publication, and always afterward refers such correspondents to that sermon for answer.

The "public sermon" he then proceeded to "construct" stressed the necessity of serving an uncomplaining and unremunerated literary apprenticeship in order to achieve recognition from the public, "the only critic whose judgment is worth anything at all" (SLC 1870hhh, 732–33).

[4]Clemens may have added the following remarks as late as 17 or 18 March, just before mailing the letter.

[5]"The American Publisher's Proclamation," in the first *American Publisher*, promised Orion's children's story. In addition to a genie and a grotesque fisherman, the proclamation alluded to the other "irreconcilable unnecessities" Clemens catalogued here (OC 1871a). Orion's plans for continuing the tale included the introduction of "Mother goose and her gander and the man in the moon; and after that the return of the giant armed and dressed after waking up the other genii from their very long sleep" (13 Mar 71 to SLC [2nd], CU-MARK).

[6]The office of the American Publishing Company. Clemens evidently sent his letter there because he did not have the exact address of Orion and Mollie's boarding house. By directing it to Mollie, he could insure that no one at the firm but Orion would open it.

To Elisha Bliss, Jr.
17 March 1871 • Buffalo, N.Y.
(MS: NN-B)

Buf. Mch. 17.

Friend Bliss:

Out of this chaos of my household I snatch a moment to reply.[1] We are packing up, to-night, & tomorrow I shall take my wife to Elmira on a mattrass, ~~with~~—for she can neither sit up nor stand,—& will not for a week or two. It is a great risk, but the doctor[2] agrees that the risk is just as great to have her stay here & worry herself to death with two ~~jun~~ child= nurses whom she cannot look after, & who neglect her sick child. In three whole months I have hardly written a page of MS. You do not know what it is to be in a state of absolute frenzy—desperation. I had rather die twice over than repeat the last six months of my life.

Now do you see?—I want *rest*. I want to get clear away from all hamperings, all harassments. I am going to shut myself up in a farm-house alone, on top an Elmira hill, & *write*—on my book.[3] I will see no company, & worry about nothing. I never will make another promise again of any kind, that *can* be avoided, so help me God.

Take my name clear out of the list of contributors, & never mention me again—& then I shall feel that the fetters are off & I am free. I am to furnish an article for your next No. & I *will* furnish it—that is just the way I ~~make~~ ruin myself—making promises. Do you know that for *seven weeks* I have not had my natural rest but have been a night-&-day sick=nurse to my wife?—& am still—& shall continue to be for two ~~we~~ or three weeks longer———yet must turn in now & write a damned *humorous* article for the Publisher, because I have *promised* it—promised it when I thought that the vials of hellfire bottled up for my benefit *must* be about emptied. By the living God I don't believe they ever *will* be emptied.

The MS I sent to be copied is back but I find nothing in it that can be transferred to the Publisher—for the chapter I intended to use I shall tear up, for it is simply an attempt to be ~~full~~ funny, & a failure.[4]

ᴵ When I get to Elmira I will look over the *next* chapters & send something—or, failing that, will write something—my own obituary I hope it will be.

As to where I got the idea, &c &c &c—got it from Larned & Gray & other friends who got ~~if~~ it from papers—never saw it myself—but you say truly that a newspaper rumor is binding on nobody.[5] I see easily enough that your advertisements haven't anything in them that I can find any fault with—nothing at all. So I was wronging you—not you me.

I like this editorial notice on your page 10 very well—if you think well of it still, ~~& if you think~~ put it in & leave out the notice I sent you.[6]

If I *dared* fly in the face of Providence & make one ˏmoreˏ promise, I would say that if I ever get out of this infernal damnable chaos I am whirling in at home, I will go to work & amply & fully & freely fulfill some of the promises I have been making to you—but I don't dare! Bliss—I don't dare!

I believe if that baby goes on crying 3 more hours this way I will butt my frantic brains out & try to get some peace.

Yours, in *perfect* distraction—

Samᴵ L. Clemens.

~~PS. When~~

[*letter docketed:*] √ [*and*] Mark Twain | March 17/71

[1] To Bliss's letter of 15 March (11 and 13 Mar 71 to OC, n. 13).
[2] Andrew Wright.
[3] Beginning in 1871, the Elmira residence of Susan and Theodore Crane, named Quarry Farm by Thomas K. Beecher after an abandoned slate quarry

near the house, provided an annual writer's retreat for Clemens. Jervis Langdon had bought the land and "plain little wooden house" on East Hill overlooking the Chemung River in May 1869, as a family retreat. The house, enlarged and by 1871 the year-round residence of the Cranes, had been bequeathed to Susan by Langdon. The Cranes continued to make improvements and buy surrounding land, eventually holding 250 acres. The Clemenses usually spent their summers there, and sometimes began their stay in the spring, although in 1871 the family first stayed at Mrs. Jervis Langdon's house in central Elmira, with Clemens going up to the farm to write. The famous octagonal study that Susan Crane built for him was not in place until 1874, however (Ida Langdon, 53–54; "City and Neighborhood," Elmira *Advertiser,* 21 May 69, 4; Park; Jerome and Wisbey 1977, 6–7; Wisbey 1985, 4; Jervis Langdon).

[4] The chapter Clemens intended to tear up was possibly a detailed description of Overland City, mentioned at the end of the published chapter 6 of *Roughing It* as "the strangest, quaintest, funniest frontier town that our untraveled eyes had ever stared at and been astonished with." He probably did not remove it at this time, however (*RI 1993,* 40, 837–38). As the next letter indicates, he soon changed his mind about an excerpt for the *American Publisher.*

[5] No newspaper notices implying Clemens's sponsorship of or exclusive publication in the *American Publisher* have been found.

[6] Clemens enclosed manuscript page 10 of Bliss's 15 March letter, on which Bliss had drafted the "editorial notice": see 11 and 13 Mar 71 to OC, n. 13. It was never used, however, and Mark Twain continued to head the *American Publisher's* regular roll of "contributors engaged for this paper" until the May 1872 issue. He then disappeared from the list and Orion Clemens, who had been fired (or resigned) in March, ceased to be designated editor on the masthead (see *RI 1993,* 877–79).

To Elisha Bliss, Jr., and Orion Clemens
20 March 1871 • Elmira, N.Y.
(MS: CU-MARK)

P. S. ~~Even~~ Before the book is printed I shall write that bull story over again (that precedes the pony) or else alter it till it is good—for it *can* be made good—& then you can put *that* in the Publisher too, if you want to.[1]

Yrs. Clemens

You got the Book MS, of course?[2]

(c)

Elmira, 20th.

Friend Bliss:

We are all ~~hear~~ here, & my wife has grown weak, stopped eating,

& dropped back to where she was two weeks ago. But we've all the *help* we want here.

Here is my contribution (I take it from the book,) & by all odds it is the finest piece of writing I ever did. Consequently I want the people to *know* that it is from the book:

Head it thus, & go on:

The Old-Time Pony-Express
of the Great Plains.

═══════

(small type) [Having but little time to write volunteer contributions, now I offer this in chapter from ~~444~~

By Mark Twain.

(small type.) [The following is a chapter from Mark Twain's forthcoming book & closes with a life-like picture of an incident of Overland stage travel on the Plains in the days before the Pacific railroad was built.— —[Ed. Publisher.

[From along about the 160th to 170th page of the MS.] It begins thus:

"However, in a little while all interest was taken up in stretching our necks & watching for the pony-rider" &c.—Go on to end of chapter.[3]

Refer the marginal note to Orion, about postage. ~~But I~~ I feel *sure* I am wrong, & that it *was* FOUR Dollars an ounce instead of TWO— —make the correction, if necessary[4] READ PROOF VERY CAREFULLY, ORION —you need send none to me.

---

[1] The story of George Bemis's treeing by a "wounded buffalo bull" ultimately began chapter 7 of *Roughing It*. In the printer's copy manuscript, it must have made up the first half of chapter 8, immediately preceding the pony express incident (see note 3; *RI 1993*, 42, 576, 840).

[2] Almost certainly on 18 March, the day the family left Buffalo for Elmira, Clemens sent not only the eight chapters of manuscript (168 pages) for which he had made a security copy, but the following three, altogether comprising about 258 pages, or what was then chapters 1–11 (*RI 1993*, 837–40). He had expected to send at least the first eight chapters on 15 March (9 Mar 71, 11 and 13 Mar 71, both to OC; 17 Mar 71 to Bliss).

[3] Having already sent the printer's copy manuscript of what then constituted the first eleven chapters of *Roughing It*, Clemens must have enclosed his security

copy of the pony express incident with this letter. The chapter divisions in the printer's copy manuscript were different from those of the published book, however, and the incident, which makes up the first half of chapter 8 as published, was evidently the last half of chapter 8 in the manuscript, as this letter implies. Clemens must have drawn the text he so accurately quotes from his security copy, but he could only approximate the page numbers of the original, since the copy did not reproduce them (*RI 1993*, 839–40). The *American Publisher* used Clemens's title and byline but modified his editorial note (all shown here as Clemens marked them for the printer) to read "[The author sends us for this issue the following from his forthcoming book, being a life-like picture of an incident of Overland stage-travel on the Plains, in the days before the Pacific Railroad was built.—ED. PUBLISHER.]" (SLC 1871k).

⁴The marginal note must have been on one of the enclosed pages of the security copy manuscript. The *American Publisher* text retains Clemens's original reading that the express rider's "literary freight was worth *two dollars an ounce*," but chapter 8 of the first edition of *Roughing It* reads "*five dollars a letter*," the result of Orion's correction (SLC 1871k, 1872b, 71). Clemens's original figure was correct. Although the fee had initially been set at five dollars per half ounce, plus ten cents postage, when the pony express service began in April 1860, it had dropped to four dollars per ounce by July 1861. By late July, when the Clemens brothers began their journey across country by stage, it had been further reduced to two dollars an ounce (*RI 1993*, 582–83, 936).

To Donn Piatt
27 March 1871 • Elmira, N.Y.
(Transcript and paraphrase: Benjamin 1947, item A 1438)

J. LANGDON,	OFFICE OF J. LANGDON & CO. MINERS AND DEALERS IN
J. D. F. SLEE,	ANTHRACITE AND BITUMINOUS COALS. 6 BALDWIN ST.
T. W. CRANE,	
C. J. LANGDON.	ELMIRA, N.Y., Mar. 27 1871.

. . . . .

If my letter should make trouble between you & Church & you should divulge to him that opinion of mine (a thing which you have every right to do, since it was no secret,) might he not sue me for damages? If he would only try to whip me, I wouldn't mind it, but a libel suit . . . Lord bless me! [*paraphrase: He therefore suggests that Piatt keep Clemens's opinions*] rather in the background . . . unless you feel that it is really necessary to use them in your own defence. [*paraphrase: Clemens had been connected with the Galaxy, and Church owed him*] about 3 months back pay.[1]

.   .   .   .

[1] Piatt had been asked by William and Francis Church to edit a department in the *Galaxy* to replace Mark Twain's "Memoranda." At this time he was negotiating his salary, and had evidently asked Clemens about his experiences with the Churches. Clemens had replied with a (now missing) letter, frankly venting his irritation with them. He had second thoughts, however, and wrote the present letter, to which Piatt responded the next day (CU-MARK):

"THE CAPITAL," NO. 428 ELEVENTH STREET,

WASHINGTON, D. C. March 28 18 71

My dear fellow

Your letter is perfectly safe in my hands—stop to make it so I have just put it in the stove altho' I wished to retain a confidential letter written by one I like and admire much as I do you

I am very glad to hear that your dear wife is convalescent and I hope with you that she will soon be well.

I told the Churches I could not take the responsibility of that Dpt for any such sum as the one offered—so they came down and agreed to my demand.

Now I wish on my account you would reconsider your determination and help me a little. I find in print some very capital things from you that you ordered out—now cant you give me some of them?

So soon [as] the Church signs an agreement with me I am going to throw over letter writing and devote myself to editing and book making— We ought to make a shove for an international copy right. The literary and other brain of the country ought to be sufficient to accomplish this

Where are you to be this summer— I propose taking my wife to the Sea side— Narragansett Rhode Island— Cant you

Yours sincerely
Donn Piatt

The April issue of the *Galaxy* carried Mark Twain's final "Memoranda." It also announced Piatt's new department, which by May was titled "The Galaxy Club-Room," and called for additional contributors. Piatt negotiated an annual salary of five thousand dollars, three thousand more than Clemens had received ("*As Mark Twain* . . . ," 11:618; "Personal," Buffalo *Courier*, 8 May 71, 1). In his first column he acknowledged his predecessor as follows:

I suppose that Mark Twain, our greatest humorist, could have written twice twelve articles of the most charming character had he been left to himself in their production. I never knew a man who had such a propensity to look upon the ludicrous side of things, and such an unlimited supply of grotesque fun; but the fact that a department had been assigned to him in a magazine, and a world advertised in advance that once a month a certain amount of wit and humor would be forthcoming, ended by paralyzing his hand and drying up all his prolific sources of entertainment. . . . Now with this fact before me, I wish it clearly understood that I am only the presiding officer of this GALAXY CLUB ROOM, and not, as was Mark before me, the author of a department. If, in the thirty days preceding the printing, I can gather up from other brains enough to make these pages entertaining, my efforts will be a success; otherwise they will be a failure. (Piatt 1871b, 752)

Before the end of May, Clemens contributed a single-page manuscript, which Piatt edited and published, unsigned and unattributed, as "TO A CORRESPON-DENT" in the July "Club-Room." The manuscript reads:

Answers to Correspondents:

<u>Agricultural</u> <u>Inquirer</u>.—No, you are wrong. The sand is *not* put in a chicken's craw for the purpose you name. Why do you continue to grope along in agricultural darkness & ignorance? Why do not you read authorities, & inform yourself. A glance at Mr. Greeley's great work on What he Knows ↓About Farming would have taught you that the sand is put in the chicken's craw for ballast.

Saml. L. Clemens ⎫
Mark Twain. ⎭

(SLC 1871j†)

To John Henry Riley
27 March 1871 • Elmira, N.Y.
(MS: CtY-BR)

J. LANGDON, MINER & DEALER IN ANTHRACITE &
BITUMINOUS COAL   OFFICE NO. 6 BALDWIN STREET

ELMIRA, N.Y. Mch 27 186 71

Dear Riley:

My wife has been very sick for two months. So I moved her hither on a mattrass & she is slowly recovering, though still in bed. We shall remain here 2 or 3 months, & eventually will move to Hartford & build—though we'll not build for the next 18 months likely. We shall ₐsellₐ the newspaper & the Buffalo dwelling, but retain the furniture.

I have nothing new to tell you, & am simply writing to let you know I am not dead. I delight in the anticipation of an African letter from you in the course of two or three weeks.

Give my love to the niggers.

Ys 𝑇 Ever
Mark.

To Orion Clemens
4 April 1871 • Elmira, N.Y.
(MS: CU-MARK)

Elmira, Apl 4.

Dear Bro:

In moving from Buffalo here I have lost certain notes & documents—among them ~~the~~ what you wrote for me about the difficulties of ~~g~~ opening up the Territorial government in Nevada & getting the machinery to running. And now, just at the moment that I want it, it is gone. I don't even know what it was you wrote, for I did not intend to read it until I was ready to use it. ~~Do~~ Have you time to scribble something again, to aid my memory. Little characteristic items like Whittlesey's refusing to allow for the knife, &c are the most illuminating things—the difficulty of getting credit for the Gov't—& all that sort of thing. Incidents are better, any time, than dry history. Don't tax yourself—I can make a little go a great way.[1]

Baby in splendid condition. Livy as feeble as ever—has not sat up ~~by~~ but once or twice for a week.

Ys T

Sam

Is Bliss doing anything with the MS I sent? Is he thinking of beginning on it shortly?[2]

---

[1] In his 11 November 1870 letter to Orion, Clemens had acknowledged receipt of his "full Nevada notes." The present request for details of the territorial government's difficulties, prominently discussed in what became chapter 25 of *Roughing It*, indicates that Clemens was preparing to write that chapter, although much of the material intervening between it and chapters 1–11, which he had sent to Bliss on 18 March (20 Mar 71 to Bliss and OC, n. 3), was incomplete or still in draft form. As Nevada territorial secretary, Orion had had to justify expenses to obtain disbursements from Elisha Whittlesey (1783–1863), first comptroller of the Treasury Department. Whittlesey's office disallowed the purchase of several of the sixteen pocket knives Orion had purchased out of his own salary for the members and staff of the second Territorial Legislature (*RI 1993*, 168–71, 619–23, 842–46).

[2] The *Roughing It* contract specified that the American Publishing Company agreed "to commence operations at once upon receipt of manuscript, & to push it through with all the dispatch compatible with its being well done in text & illustrations" (Appendix E).

To Thomas Nast
4 April 1871 • Elmira, N.Y.
(MS: ViU)

Elmira, Apl. 4.

My Dear Nast:[1]

I like that ~~old~~ "Beef Contract" article of mine as well as anything I ever wrote, & it is very popular in Washington on account of its satire on clerkly airs & official circumlocution. I published it in the Galaxy just about a year ago—you will find it in the Number for May 1870 I think. It is entitled "The Facts in the Case of the Great Beef Contract."[2]

I am glad your Almanac promises so well, & I assure you I earnestly wish you a ~~word~~ world of success with it.

Yrs Sincerely

Saml. L. Clemens

---

[1] Thomas Nast's fame as an illustrator and political caricaturist was well established in the fall of 1867, when he first met Clemens and, as Clemens later recalled, proposed a joint lecture tour "when I was unknown" (12 Nov 77 to Nast, NN-B, in *MTL*, 1:311). Nast (1840–1902) had come to New York at the age of six from his native Landau, Germany. After attending the Academy of Design, he sold his first commercial illustrations in 1855 to *Frank Leslie's Illustrated Newspaper*, published his first political cartoons in the late 1850s in *Harper's Weekly*, and traveled in the United States and Europe in 1859–61 for the *New York Illustrated News* and other periodicals, illustrating such occurrences as John Brown's funeral and Garibaldi's revolt. Hired by *Harper's Weekly* in 1862 as a staff artist, his cartoons endorsing emancipation and supporting the North's vigorous prosecution of the Civil War inspired Lincoln to call him "our best recruiting sergeant" (*DAB*, 13:392). After the war, he remained with *Harper's Weekly*, where he published political cartoons almost continuously, focusing especially on the failures of Reconstruction and on the need for political reform in New York City. In 1870 he and *Harper's* launched a campaign against William Marcy Tweed and Tammany Hall that continued through 1871, arousing the public outrage that resulted in Tweed's arrest on criminal charges on 7 November. Nast also illustrated several books, including Mary Mapes Dodge's *Hans Brinker: or, The Silver Skates* (1866), Petroleum V. Nasby's *Ekkoes from Kentucky* (1868), and Henry William Pullen's *Fight at Dame Europa's School* (1871) ("Thomas Nast," *Harper's Weekly* 15 [26 Aug 71]: Supplement, 803; "The Great American Cartoonist," *Harper's Weekly* 46 [20 Dec 1902]: 1972; "Death of Thomas Nast," New York *Times*, 8 Dec 1902, 1).

[2] Nast had asked permission to reprint something by Clemens in his forthcom-

ing *Th. Nast's Illustrated Almanac for 1872*, the first in a series of such annual booklets he published through Harpers (Nast). On 24 April 1871, he replied to the present letter:

> My dear Mr Clemens
>
> The "beef contract" is very good, but I do not think it is as suitable for my almanac, as some of your other things, for I must bear in mind that I cater for the children in my almanac as well as the big folks, so I think, that "the good little boy who never prospered," or "advice to little girls," or "the late Benjamin Franklin," would suit me better, therefore, if you will graciously accord me your permission to use any of the aforesaid, I shall be happy to avail myself of it.
>
> The "beef contract," would make a good pamphlet I think by itself, with illustrations, got up like one I send you "The fight in Dame Europa's school," a good many of your other things too, ought to be illustrated.
>
> How does the idea strike you and upon what terms would you go into such a speculation?
>
> Must I see the Galaxy proprietors on the subject, of the almanac article? (CU-MARK)

"Advice for Good Little Girls" was available in the *Jumping Frog* book. Both "The Story of the Good Little Boy Who Did Not Prosper" and "The Late Benjamin Franklin" appeared in the *Galaxy* (SLC: 1867a, 164–66; 1870dd, 724–26; 1870pp, 138–40; *ET&S2*, 243–45). Clemens replied almost immediately: see 27? Apr 71 to Nast.

To Robert M. and Louise M. Howland
6 April 1871 • Elmira, N.Y.
(MS: CU-MARK)

Elmira, Apl. 6.

Dear Bob & Lou:

We were *very* glad to get the pictures, indeed. They are excellent. My wife is never tired of talking about Lou, & admiring her. I never knew her to take such a strong liking to any stranger before.[1]

The baby is perfectly strong & hearty, but his mother cannot yet stand on her feet. She progresses only very slowly. Love to you both.

Yrs Ever
Sam.

P. S. Never been able to get my little family into a photograph gallery yet—but hope to some day, & then we'll remember you.[2]

---

[1] Olivia had met both Robert and Louise Howland during their brief visit to Buffalo, evidently sometime between 1 and 6 or 12 and 21 June 1870. More than a year later she recalled that visit in a letter to Robert Howland that she wrote for Clemens (1–6 or 12–21 June 70, 20 Nov 71, both to Howland). The photo-

graphs the Howlands sent have not been located. Robert Howland figures as "Bob H——" in chapter 21 of *Roughing It,* which Clemens probably wrote in early April (*RI 1993,* 145, 842).

[2] Olivia repeated this promise in November but apparently was never photographed with Langdon (20 Nov 71 to Howland).

To Isaac E. Sheldon
6 April 1871 • Elmira, N.Y.
(MS, Clemens's copy: CU-MARK)

Elmira, Apl. 6.

Friend Sheldon:

I am glad you agree with me. I begin to think I can get up quite a respectable novel, & I mean to fool away some of my odd hours in the attempt, anyway. You intimate that the present pamphlet don't give a man his money's worth, considering the price. I feared that that was so, at first—but you said 40 cents was the cheapest it could be sold at.[1]

Concerning that copyright, Sheldon, I want to protest against the first payment being put off till Aug. 1$^{st.}$ You ought to make me a return the first of June, & another the 1st of Sept. For you to use my money five or six months without my consent & without interest is not exactly fair, & so I hope you will depart from your custom in this instance. It isn't a matter of sufficient importance, on either side, to worry about or get ruffled over, but my suggestion is entirely just & fair, & so I think yours is the side that ought to yield this time.[2]

Ys

Clemens.

[1] Clemens was replying to the following letter from Isaac E. Sheldon (CU-MARK):

SHELDON & COMPANY, PUBLISHERS AND BOOKSELLERS, 677 BROADWAY, AND 214 & 216 MERCER ST., NEW YORK. OFFICE OF THE GALAXY.

NEW YORK, Apl 4th 187 1

M   Friend Clemmens

Your favor of Apl 3rd is at hand. I rec'd also a few days since yours of Mar 22nd. Inclosed find a contract as you desire. It is just like the one you sent except that settlements are made 1st of Aug & Feb each year. At these times we make up a/cs of copyright in all our books.

The returns for copyright, after the first settlement, will of course not be large, as a book like this has its main sale at once. As regards the story, I like the idea & it would sell well if it were a good story & had a quiet vein of humor as well as the tragic interest of a story. I do not see why you could not write such a story. If you feel in the spirit of it I should certainly make the attempt. We had better give the public enough for the money next time. I like to have every one satisfied

> I am Truly Yours
> Isaac E Sheldon

Both of Clemens's earlier letters to Sheldon are lost, but in the first one (22 March) he presumably sent Sheldon a formal contract for the *(Burlesque) Autobiography* to replace their December 1870 agreement by letter. Sheldon in turn enclosed the following, also dated 4 April:

> This memorandum certifies that before publishing Mark Twains pamphlet "Autobiography and First Romance" we agreed to pay him a royalty of *six cents* on every copy sold. Said agreement is still in force—and we further agree to make a full statement to him of sales every first of August and first of February and accompany the same with the amount of money due him.

> Signed
> Sheldon & Co

On the envelope of Sheldon's letter Clemens wrote: "Answered Apl. 6. protesting." Then he added: "Copy of ANSWER ENCLOSED."† (That copy is transcribed here; the document actually sent to Sheldon has not been found.) Clemens's second letter (3 April) was evidently about the "story" he planned to write. This was probably the book he had earlier hoped to undertake with David Gray, but more recently with Joseph T. Goodman, who had been in Elmira since 24 March and had read and praised part of the manuscript for *Roughing It* (18 Apr 71 to OC, n. 2; 30 Apr 71 to OC, n. 5).

[2] It is not known whether Clemens's protest was effective.

To Orion Clemens
8, 9, and 10 April 1871 • Elmira, N.Y.
(MS: CU-MARK)

Elmira, Apl. 8.

Dear Bro:

If I don't add a postscript to this, tell Bliss to go ahead & set up the MSS & put the engravers to work.[1] My copy is down at the house & I am up here at the farm, a mile & a half up a mountain, where I write every day.[2]

I am to the ~~6~~ 570th page[3] & booming along. And what I am writing now is so much better than the opening chapters, or the Innocents Abroad either, that I do *wish* I could spare time to revamp the opening chapters, & even write some of them over again.

I will read the bull story when I go down, & see whether it will do or not. It don't altogether suit me, but ~~maybe I shan't~~ I shall alter it *very little,* anyway. I don't want it to go in the same number of the paper with the pony sketch. Mind, I never want two articles of mine in the same number. Put it in the next if you choose.

Ys

Sam.

We carried Livy to the barouche, today, & she rode around the block twice.

———᳝᳝᳝———

Tell Bliss to hatch up lots of pictures for the book—it is going to sell bully.

[*new page:*]

P. S.

Leave out the yarn about Jack & "Moses." It occurs about 117th page. ~~Stop~~ ˌClose˒ the chapter with theˌse˒ words "and when they tried to teach a subordinate anything that subordinate generally "got it through his head"—at least in time for the funeral.["]⁴

———᳝᳝᳝———

Accompanying this, is the bull story, altered the way I want it. Don't put it in till about the fourth No. of the paper.

OVER.

Tell Bliss to go ahead setting up the book just as it is, making the corrections *marked in purple ink,* in some 20 or 30 pages which I shall mail to-nightˌ—possibly in this envelop.⁵

Ys

Sam

P. S.—Monday—Am to 610th page, now.⁶

———᳝᳝᳝———

<hr />

¹Clemens's anxiety to see production begin on the first eleven chapters of his western book—long before he had completed writing it—made him misspeak. Bliss's first step would be to commission drawings from the *illustrators,* and only then to hire engravers to produce woodblocks.

²While Clemens was working at Quarry Farm, the other members of his household remained at Mrs. Jervis Langdon's home in Elmira proper (17 Mar 71 to Bliss, n. 3).

³That is, about to the end of chapter 24 of *Roughing It* (*RI 1993,* 814, 842).

⁴Clemens had told this "yarn" about *Quaker City* passenger Jack Van Nos-

trand (the "'Moses Who?' story") in at least three of his "American Vandal Abroad" lectures in 1868–69 (*L2*, 298, 299 n. 2; *RI 1993*, 581). He added this instruction to Orion in the evening after returning to the Langdon house, where he could reread his security copy of the first eight chapters of the manuscript. The change proposed here was not ultimately adopted in chapter 6 of *Roughing It* (*RI 1993*, 847–48).

⁵After revising (and apparently lengthening) the story about Bemis and the buffalo on his security copy of what was then chapter 8, Clemens must have enclosed it in this letter. Since he did not mail the letter until 10 April, however, he probably did not separately mail the "20 or 30 pages" with their corrections "to-night" (9 April), but rather sent them with the letter. None of the actual enclosures has survived, but for a discussion of their possible content, see *RI 1993*, 848–49.

⁶By 10 April, when he wrote this final postscript, Clemens had reached about the beginning of chapter 27, his account of his journey to Humboldt County, Nevada Territory (*RI 1993*, 814, 847). On 12 April he went to New York, where he remained for at least two days. His business there has not been identified, but he might well have met with Isaac Sheldon to follow up on his letter of 6 April, or with Francis P. Church to arrange for his final payment for the *Galaxy* "Memoranda" (27 Mar 71 to Piatt; "Prominent Arrivals," New York *Tribune*, 13 Apr 71, 8; "Morning Arrivals," New York *Evening Express*, 13 Apr 71, 3).

To Orion Clemens
18 April 1871 • Elmira, N.Y.
(MS: CU-MARK)

Elmira, Apl. 18.

My Dear Bro:

Since Knox has printed a similar story ~~(so~~ (the same "situation" has been in print often—men have written it before Knox & I were born,)— let the Bull story alone until it appears in the book—or at least in the "specimen" chapters for canvassers. That is to say, Do not put it in the paper, *at all*. I cannot alter it—too much trouble.¹

Joe Goodman is up here at the farm with me—will come up every day for 2 months & write a novel.

He is going to read my MSS critically.²

Livy just the same—no better, no worse.

Yrs

Sam.

P. S. No—I won't print Jack & Moses. I may lecture next winter, & in that case shall want it.[3]

Mind you, I do ˏmustˏ not appear in the paper oftener than bi= monthly, in *any* case.

[1] Replying to the previous letter, Orion (in a letter now lost) had warned Clemens of a resemblance between his Bemis buffalo story and a story by Thomas Knox, possibly in *Overland through Asia* (1870), published by the American Publishing Company. But nothing in that book is persuasively like Clemens's story, and indeed, on 22 April, Bliss himself wrote Clemens "Your brother says he wrote you Knox had written up something similar to the Bull story—I never saw it & do not know anything about it. It ˏYoursˏ struck me *as a good thing, every way*" (CU-MARK, in *RI 1993*, 850).

[2] Goodman had arrived in Elmira on 24 March and stayed for several months. By 18 April he had almost certainly read much of what Clemens had written for his western book, either in the security copy for chapters 1–8 (which, except for the pony express anecdote mailed on 20 March, remained intact until 10 April) or in Clemens's own manuscript from chapter 12 onward (*RI 1993*, 840–42).

[3] Orion had evidently asked to print the "Jack & Moses" story (see the previous letter) in the *American Publisher.*

To Mary Mason Fairbanks
18 April 1871 • Elmira, N.Y.
(MS: CSmH)

Elmira, Apl. 18.

Dear Mother:

Am just starting to Buffalo to finish the sale of my "Express" interest.[1]

We do long to get out there with you, & we have high hopes on that head, too—but no *certainties,* on account of Livy's continued prostration. I find myself daily regarding her substantial recovery as farther & farther away. I cannot see that she has gained a single hair's breadth in 30 days. She is hopeful & confident—but what does she found it on? If I had her in your care a month she would get well, but you see it isn't possible.

Love to you all, & more ⹀ than all, to you, our Mother.

Sam*l.*

✉

Mrs. A. W. Fairbanks | Care "Herald" | Cleveland | Ohio. [*return ad-*
dress:] RETURN TO J. LANGDON & CO., ELMIRA, N. Y., IF NOT DELIVERED WITHIN
10 DAYS. [*postmarked:*] ELMIRA N. Y. APR 18

¹On 20 April, the Buffalo *Courier* reported that "'Mark Twain' was in the city
yesterday. . . . We learn that he has disposed of his interest in the *Express* to Mr.
George H. Selkirk, one of the previous proprietors of that paper" ("Personal,"
2). But see 3 Mar 71 to Riley, n. 3.

To Unidentified
18 April 1871 • Elmira, N.Y.
(MS: CtHMTH)

Elmira, Apl. 18.¹

Dear Sir:

The speech on "Woman" was delivered very early in January, 1868,
& was copied into all the papers during the month. A reference to files
of the period will unearth it. I have no copy—I wish I had.²

Yrs Truly

Sam*ˡ*. L. Clemens.

¹ This letter has been assigned to 1871 because Clemens is known to have used
stationery of its kind intermittently between 6 September 1869 and 29 June
1871, and because he was not in Elmira on 18 April in 1870.

² Delivered on 11 January 1868 before the Washington Newspaper Correspondents' Club, Clemens's response to the toast "Woman: The Pride of the
Professions, and the jewel of ours," was published from a phonographic tran-
script in the Washington *Evening Star* on 13 January 1868 (SLC 1868b). The
following reprintings have been located so far: "A Eulogy of Woman by 'Mark
Twain,'" New York *Evening Post*, 15 Jan 68, 1; "Woman. Mark Twain's Eulogy
of the Fair Sex," St. Louis *Missouri Republican*, 22 Jan 68, 3; "Woman—Mark
Twain's Opinion of Her," Virginia City *Territorial Enterprise*, 2 Feb 68, 1; "A
Eulogy of Woman by 'Mark Twain,'" San Francisco *Examiner*, 3 Feb 68, 1;
"Woman—Mark Twain's Opinion of Her," Oakland *News*, 10 Apr 68, 4; "Eulogy on Woman," *Excelsior Monthly Magazine* 1 (Aug 68): 99–100. Clemens sent
a clipping of the *Evening Star* printing to his mother on 14 January 1868, and a
clipping of the *Excelsior* printing to Elisha Bliss on 3 September 1868 (*L2*, 131–
32 n. 5, 155–57, 245 n. 1, 415–16).

To Mary Mason Fairbanks
26 April 1871 • Elmira, N.Y.
(MS: CSmH)

Elmira, 26th

Dear Mother:

My! how you startled us! And even as it is, we don't feel altogether comfortable about you. We shall feel a good deal *more* comfortable when we hear that you are out again. I shall, I assure you, for I have lately had experience of sick folks who were *going* to come right up, & but *don't* for an matter of two months. However, Livy is making progress in the last two or three days. She walks three or four steps, by holding on to a chair, & every day she rides a fl few blocks. She is bright & cheerful. We look forward to our Cleveland trip, for you will have a couple of months to get well in in the meantime, & that will do, won't it?

I am pegging n away at my book, but it will have no success. The papers have found at last the courage to pull me down off my pedestal & cast slurs at me—& that is simply a popular author's death rattle. Though he wrote an *inspired* book after that, it would not save him.[1]

We send a world of love to you all. Tell us how your hurts are, now.[2]

Lovingly
Saml.

[1] The only known "slurs" of recent date were reviews of *Mark Twain's (Burlesque) Autobiography and First Romance*. The Boston *Literary World* for 1 April 1871 commented:

> The prime difficulty that meets the critic is one of classification: he feels like a naturalist gazing upon Barnum's "What Is It?" Is it "fish, flesh, fowl, or good red herring"? The evidence is purely circumstantial, extraneous, and very unsatisfactory. The name of the author justifies the suspicion that the work is one of humor; but the book itself affords not the feeblest fibre of corroboration, and the suspicion is dismissed as unwarrantable. . . . We are sincerely sorry to see Mark Twain, who has done some admirable work, lending himself to a mere money-catching scheme like this. ("Mark Twain's Autobiography," 1:165)

Also in April, in Cincinnati, *The Eclectic: A Monthly Magazine of Useful Knowledge* wrote:

> It is well that the publishers put "Burlesque" in brackets on the title page, else many persons would scarcely have seen that the author intended to be peculiar. This making fun for so-much a page, and grinding it out monthly to meet the demands of publishers, is not usually very laughable. Indeed, on the contrary, the material has frequently a

funereal character that impresses one unpleasantly, as he wonders if the mental decrepitude does not presage early death. ("Book Notices," 3 [Apr 71]: 256)

[2] Mrs. Fairbanks's injuries have not been identified.

To Thomas Nast
27? April 1871 • Elmira, N.Y.
(Merwin-Clayton 1907a, lot 60)

Elmira

.   .   .   .

Take any sketch you please & you are the man to make the selection, because you can tell what will illustrate best[1]

.   .   .   .

[1] Clemens replied to Nast's letter of 24 April (4 Apr 71 to Nast, n. 2). He probably mentioned that the proprietors of the *Galaxy* had no control over either of the two *Galaxy* sketches Nast had wanted for *Th. Nast's Illustrated Almanac for 1872*. The almanac ultimately reprinted "The Late Benjamin Franklin" from the *Galaxy* and "Advice for Good Little Girls" from the *Jumping Frog* book, each accompanied by several drawings (Nast, 26–27, 47). Clemens's response to Nast's proposal of a separate pamphlet is not known, but no such pamphlet was published.

To Whitelaw Reid
29 April 1871 • Elmira, N.Y.
(MS and transcript: DLC and New York *Tribune*, 3 May 71)

Elmira, Apl. 29.

Friend Reid:

I have written this thing[1] for an *object*—which is, to make people *talk* about & look at, & presently ENTERTAIN the idea of commuting Rulloff's penalty.[2]

The last paragraph (as magnificently absurd as it se is,) is what I depend on to start the *talk* at every breakfast table in the land—& then the talk will drift into all the different ramifications of this case & first thing they know, they will discover that a regret is growing up in their souls that ~~such a~~ ˏtheˏ man is going to be hung. If the *talk* gets started once, that is sufficient—they'll *all* talk, pretty soon, & then the *acting* will come easily & naturally.

The last paragraph of the article is bully. Silly as it is, nobody can read it without a startle, or without having to stop & *think*, before deciding whether the thing is possible or not.

Now if you don't want this or can't print it now, I wish you would re-mail it to me, for I want to print it somewhere. Don't comment on it, unless you'd like to back up this brave ˏRedeemer for Science.

Ys

Clemens.

[*enclosure:*]

To the Editor of The Tribune.

SIR: I believe in capital punishment. I believe that when a murder has been done it should be answered for with blood. I have all my life been taught to feel in this way, & the fetters of education are strong. The fact that the death law is rendered almost inoperative by its very severity does not alter my belief in its righteousness. The fact that in England the proportion of executions to condemnations is only one to 16, & in this country only one to 22, & in France only one to 38, does not shake my steadfast confidence in the propriety of retaining the death penalty. It is better to hang one murderer in 16, 22, or 38, than not to hang any at all.[3]

Feeling as I do, I am not sorry that Rulloff is to be hanged, but I am sincerely sorry that he himself has made it necessary that his vast capabilities for usefulness should be lost to the world. In this, mine & the public's is a common regret. For it is plain that in the person of Rulloff one of the most marvelous intellects that any age has produced is about to be sacrificed, & that, too, while half the mystery of its strange powers is yet a secret. Here is a man who has never entered the doors of a college or a university, & yet, by the sheer might of his innate gifts has made himself such a colossus in abstruse learning that the ablest of our scholars are but pigmies in his presence. By the evidence of Prof. Mather, Mr. Surbridge, Mr. Richmond, & other men qualified to testify, this man is as familiar with the broad domain of philology as common people are

with the passing events of the day. His memory has such a limitless grasp
that he is able to quote sentence after sentence, paragraph after paragraph, & chapter after chapter, from a gnarled & knotty ancient literature that ordinary scholars are capable of achieving a little more than a
bowing acquaintance with. But his memory is the least of his great en-
dowments. By the testimony of the gentlemen above referred to, he is
able to *critically analyze* the works of the old masters of literature, &
while pointing out the beauties of the originals with a pure & discrimi-
nating taste, is as quick to detect the defects of the accepted translations;
& in the latter case, if exceptions be taken to his judgment, he straightway opens up the quarries of his exhaustless knowledge & builds a very
Chinese wall of evidence around his position.[4] Every learned man who
enters Rulloff's presence leaves it amazed & confounded by his prodigious capabilities & attainments. One scholar said he did not believe that
in the matters of subtle analysis, vast knowledge in his peculiar field of
research, comprehensive grasp of subject & serene kingship over its limitless & bewildering details, any land or any era of modern times had
given birth to Rulloff's intellectual equal.[5] What miracles this murderer
might have wrought, & what luster he might have shed upon his country
if he had not put a forfeit upon his life so foolishly! But what if the law
could be satisfied, & the gifted criminal still be saved. If a life be offered
up on the gallows to atone for the murder Rulloff did, will that suffice?
If so, give me the proofs, for, in all earnestness & truth, I aver that in
such a case I will instantly bring forward a man who, in the interests of
learning & science, will *take Rulloff's crime upon himself, & submit to be
hanged in Rulloff's place.* I can, & will do this thing; & I propose this
matter, & make this offer in good faith. You know me, & know my
address.

————, April 29, 1871.   SAMUEL LANGHORNE.

———

[*on back of letter as folded:*] Whitelaw Reßid Esq

[1]Clemens enclosed the manuscript (now lost) of a letter to the *Tribune,* which
published it on 3 May, under the heading "A Substitu[t]e for Rulloff. Have We
a Sydney Carton among Us?" (SLC 1871*l*). The *Tribune* printing supplies the
text of the enclosure printed here.
[2]On 11 January 1871, Edward Howard Ruloff (1819–71) was convicted of
murdering a clerk during the burglary of a Binghamton, New York, dry goods

store. He was sentenced to hang. Ruloff's trial and subsequent appeals—among them a tumultuous 5 April appearance in Elmira before the New York Supreme Court—revealed his thirty years of crime, including the murder of his own wife and child, all of which was widely reported in the newspapers. Much attention was also given to Ruloff's scholarly bent. He was an amateur medical practitioner and a self-taught lawyer who had regularly defended himself and his accomplices. He was also a professed linguist devoted to the completion of his treatise on "Method in the Formation of Language," which he had been subsidizing for years with the proceeds of his crimes. On 15 May 1871, the governor of New York turned down a last appeal for commutation of the death penalty and Ruloff was executed on 18 May (New York *Times:* "Edward Rulloff, Philologist and Murderer," "Verdict of the Jury," 12 Jan 71, 4, 8; "Rulloff," 23 Jan 71, 1; "Rulloff Doomed," 6 Apr 71, 5; Washington *Morning Chronicle:* "An Accomplished Criminal," 17 Jan 71, 3; New York *Herald:* "Rulloff, the Murderer," 13 May 71, 5, 17 May 71, 7; "Rulloff's Race Run," "Rulloff's Last Crime," 19 May 71, 3; New York *Tribune:* "Ruloff Hanged," 19 May 71, 1, 8; Wilson and Pitman, 473–74).

[3] Clemens's enclosure was in part an answer to the *Tribune*'s 25 April editorial opposing the death penalty for Ruloff:

> A man in this disordered state of mind is dangerous to the public peace, and should not be permitted to remain at large. But nothing is to be gained by killing him. He should be treated like any other violent madman, and confined under close and merciful surveillance. With his great power of application and method, he might be made of great use in the administration of a prison or an insane asylum, and a liberal portion of his time should be allowed him to develop his scheme of universal philology. ("What Should Be Done with Ruloff?" 4)

The source of Clemens's comparative statistics about executions remains unidentified.

[4] Richard Henry Mather (1834–90) was a professor of Greek and German at Amherst College and a lecturer on the Boston Lyceum Bureau's 1870–71 roster (*Lyceum* 1870, 3). After visiting Ruloff in prison, Mather told the Springfield (Mass.) *Republican* that Ruloff had said that

> many of the classical authors he knew by heart, and would try and repeat portions if I would suggest where he should begin. Thinking that something from the *Memorabilia* might be appropriate to his present needs, I suggested the third chapter, first book, where the sentiments of SOCRATES with reference to God and duty in their purity and exaltation approach so nearly to Biblical revelation; and he at once gave me the Greek. Other parts of the same work, as well as the *Iliad* of HOMER and some of the plays of SOPHOCLES, he showed great familiarity with. Then, in order to show his thoroughness, he criticised the common rendering of certain passages, and he did it with such subtlety and discrimination and elegance as to show that his critical study of these nicer points was more remarkable than his powers of memory; in fact I should say that subtlety of analysis and reasoning was the marked characteristic of his mind. ("Rulloff, the Murderer," New York *Times*, 23 Apr 71, 1)

Hiram Lawton Richmond (1810–85) studied medicine with his father. In 1834–35 he attended Allegheny College in Meadville, Pennsylvania, but took no degree. He then studied law and was admitted to the bar in 1838. He practiced at this time in Meadville and would soon be elected as a Republican to the Forty-third Congress (1873–75). The New York *Times* touched upon his connection with the Ruloff case in an editorial of 25 January 1871: "There is, however, some little danger that this interesting felon may impose upon the public pretty much as he imposed upon Mr. RICHMOND, of Meadville, Penn., with his conchological knowledge about the *spondylus spinosus,* and his anatomical talk about the zygomatic process, and the lamb[d]oidal suture" ("Recreations of a Murderer," 4). Surbridge has not been identified.

[5] The source of these remarks remains unidentified.

To Orion Clemens
30 April 1871 • Elmira, N.Y.
(MS: NPV)

Elmira, 30.

Dear Bro:

I do not wish to write on the subject of articles *any* more. Leave me out of the paper except once in ~~3~~ 6 months,, & don't write me anything more about it—either you or Bliss. I know that you both mean the very best for me, but you are wrong.

You both wrote me discouraging letters. Yours stopped my pen for two days—Bliss's stopped it for three. Hereafter my wife will read my Hartford letters & if they are of ~~the~~ the same nature, keep them out of my hands. The idea of a newspaper editor & a publisher plying with dismal letters a man who is under contract to write *humorous* books for them![1]

I sent Bliss MSS yesterday, ~~up to~~ about 100 pages[2] of MS[d].

Don't be in a great hurry getting out the specimen chapters for canvassers, for I want the chapter I am writing *now* in it—& it is away up to page 750 of the MS.[3] I would like to select the "specimen" chapters myself (along with Joe Goodman, who writes by my side every day up at the farm).[4] Joe & I have a 600-page book in contemplation which will wake up the nation. It is a thing which ~~David Gray &~~ I have talked over with David Gray a good deal, & he wanted me to do it right ~~& just~~ & well—which I couldn't without a ~~re~~ man to do the accurate drudgery and some little other writing. But Joe is the party. This present book will be a tolerable success—possibly an *excellent* success if the chief newspapers start it off well—but the other book will be an *awful* success.[5] The only trouble is, how I am to hang on to Joe till I publish this present book & another before I *begin* on the joint one.[6]

When is the selection to be made for the specimen chapters?

Ys

Sam

[1]Clemens had already responded briefly to Orion's letter (18 Apr 71 to OC). Bliss's 22 April letter read as follows:

Friend Clemens

I have been going to drop you a line for some days, but am so busy, I hardly get time to write anything except what is absolutely necessary. I want to say to you this. We go to work on Pros. Monday, & shall get it out very quickly— I fear your brother has written in a manner to give you wrong impressions of my views. I have said to him that the first part of a book alone, is not sufficient to make a proper prospectus of. I of course cannot get up full plate engravings, until I know the subject, & then it is well to have a variety of matter in it— I have not spoken of the position of affairs thinking it of no acc, but perhaps, it might be well to say, that standing where I do, with so many agents all over, coming in contact with the masses, I can feel the pulse of the community, as well as any other person; I do not think there is as much of a desire to see another book from you as there was 3 months ago. Then anything offered would sell, people would subscribe to anything of yours without overhauling or looking at it much. Now they will inspect a Prospectus closer, & buy more on the strength of *it*, than they would have done a few months ago.

Knowing this to be so, I feel particularly anxious to get out a *splendid Prospectus* one brim full of good matter, of *your own style*— I want to reawaken the appetite for the book—& know of no better means than to show them slices of a rich loaf, & let them try it   Consequently I said to your brother, "If he has anything *particularly fine* lets have it for *prospectus.*" Another thing is about having anything appear of yours or from your book in our paper. I fear you have got the impression that I am so interested in that that I wish to push & help it, even at the risk of doing you an injury— Now Friend Clemens be pleased to understand that the paper is always a secondary consideration with me— I have kept you & your book uppermost in my mind—& the paper has not had a thought that was not subservient to your book. It was started to help sell our books & to ventilate them &c &c   Now this is my proposed plan to rush your next book.— I did prefer to get out extracts of it & get just as much notoriety for them as possible— I proposed to do this very soon—& whet the peoples appetites for more of the same— Now then I supposed anything in our paper as coming from the book, should be of a superior quality & would be largely copied &c— We may be wrong, & we have this to say now, that to do away with any feelings of uneasiness (if they exist) on a/c of this paper if you wish & deem best that you do not be mentioned in its columns—in connection with it or with us, nothing from the book be published in it—we will accede to it cheerfully. We do not wish any jealousy to spring up on this matter at all— We doubt the expediency of your withdrawing, just at this stage of proceedings from public view entirely—yet we may be wrong. We think an occasional *Twainish* thing from you, would aid the future sale of the book— Something published from the book of a rich spicy nature & credited to it—would be a great help   Now there—I have wanted to say this much. I may have given advice not needed & not in place. I should not have pretended to have said as much, were it not I feel very anxious to make a great success of the book— & think I see clearly how to do it— I really wish to act every way best for our mutual interests, & no other way, & would prefer to drop the paper today where it is, rather than to have any dissatisfaction on its account arise   I have made selections from Mss. here for Pros. & if you have any choice *cuts* ,further along in the book, for it send them on & I will heave them in. . . . Your brother says he wrote you Knox had written up something similar to the Bull story— I never saw it & do not know anything about it. It ˏYours, struck me *as a good thing, every way. Your first chap. is splendid*—smacks of the old style— (CU-MARK)

In remarking on the diminished public "desire" for a book by Mark Twain, Bliss alluded to the damage done by the *(Burlesque) Autobiography,* a work he had opposed (27 Jan 71 to Sheldon, n. 1; 26 Apr 71 to Fairbanks, n. 1).

[2]That is, manuscript for chapters 12–15—which became chapters 12–14 and Appendixes A and B in *Roughing It.* The subjects were Clemens's journey through Utah, his arrival in Salt Lake City, and his encounters with Mormons and Mormon history. These chapters were the same ones that Clemens again claimed, three days later, to have mailed "yesterday" (3 May 71 to Bliss; *RI 1993,* 814, 851).

[3]Most likely chapter 34, the story of the landslide case hoax. Clemens had probably reached the end of it or the beginning of chapter 35 (*RI 1993,* 814–15, 851). Neither was used for the prospectus.

[4]In addition to his planned novel, Goodman might have been working on some of his poetry (10 Jan 70 to OLL [2nd]; 18 Apr 71 to OC)—or perhaps on *The Psychoscope: A Sensational Drama in Five Acts,* which he co-authored with Rollin M. Daggett, another Nevada friend of Clemens's, and published in Virginia City in 1871.

[5]The subject of the planned collaborative novel conceivably was Washington, D.C., where, in July 1870, Clemens had gathered material that he hoped to use in a book (8 July 70 to OLC; 17 or 24 Aug 70? to PAM).

[6]Clemens had contracted for two works to follow *Roughing It:* the South African diamond mine book and a volume of sketches (Appendix E; *ET&S1,* 435).

To Elisha Bliss, Jr.
3 May 1871 • Elmira, N.Y.
(MS: CU-MARK)

                                                         Elmira, May 3.
Friend Bliss:

My friend Ned House, of the N. Y. Tribune, is in Japan, & is writing a book that will read bully & sell ditto. ~~If you~~ His idea of illustrating it profusely with quaint Japanese wood cuts made by native artists is a splendid feature. If you want his book, let me know what royalty, &c, you will pay, & I will write him. ~~Or would your~~ If your own hands should be full you might publish it through your brother's house. I enclose the letter he wrote ~~the~~ to David Gray & me on the subject.[1]

My book is half done. I mailed you the 12th, 13th, 14th & 15th chapters yesterday, & before that I had sent you the previous 11 chapters. Let me know if they all arrived safely.[2]

This book will be pretty readable, after all; & if it is well & profusely illustrated it will crowd the "Innocents."

Ys

Clemens.

✉️

[*letter docketed:*] √ [*and*] Mark Twain | May 3/71 | Author [*and*] Sam'l Clemens | For Year *1871*

[1] Edward H. House's letter does not survive. Bliss responded enthusiastically to his proposal, first in a letter (now lost), which Clemens received by 15 May, and again in a postscript to his letter of 17 May (15 May to Bliss, n. 7). Although Bliss apparently reached an agreement with House two years later, the book was not published by the American Publishing Company or any of its subsidiaries, including the Richard W. Bliss Company (3 May 73 to Bliss, transcript at WU; House to Bliss, 25 Nov 73, ViU). House eventually published *Japanese Episodes* (1881), a book of Japanese travel, with James R. Osgood and Company of Boston, and *Yone Santo: A Child of Japan* (1888), an illustrated novel, with Belford, Clarke and Company of Chicago (Geer 1871, 226). See also 9 June 70 to Bliss, n. 3.

[2] See 30 Apr 71 to OC, n. 2.

To Henri Gerard
5 May 1871 • Elmira, N.Y.
(MS: NN-B)

Elmira, N. Y., May 5.

Master Henri Gerard,[1]
    Editor "Comet."

    I have hardly time to write a communication for the "Comet," but am cheerfully willing to comply with your request that I should state my opinion of the paper,—which is, briefly, that although it is the fruit of a boy's brain & a boy's enterprise, it is superior to some papers issued by men. The crisp brevity with which you dispose of that fellow Bismarck has a charm for me which the long leaders of the ponderous dailies lacks—but at the same time you should have a care how you risk embroiling your country in a foreign war. However, I will not say a word—give it to Bismarck & ~~lu~~ let us take the chances.

The "Comet" is a neat paper & a readable one; & it seems to me that it is a marked & excellent sign of the times to see boys forsaking rowdy amusements for the worthier pleasures of literary endeavor.

I wish to subscribe for nearly 3 copies of the "Comet," & therefore enclose $1. Please send one of them to "Master Sammy Moffett, Fredonia, N. Y." ₐAnd the other one toₐ

Yrs Truly
Saml. L. Clemens.
Elmira, N. Y.

[1] Possibly Henri Gerard of New York, who in 1915 ran a bookstore called Gerard's Literary Shop at 83 Nassau Street (*New York Directory*, 762, 2307).

To Elisha Bliss, Jr.
15 May 1871 • Elmira, N.Y.
(MS: ViU)

Elmira, Monday.

Friend Bliss:

Yrs rec'd enclosing check for $703.35. The old "Innocents" holds out handsomely.

I feel confident that House will make a most readable book. Shall write him what you say.[1]

I have MS. enough on hand now, to make (allowing for engravings) about 400 pages of the book—consequently am two-thirds done. I intended to run up to Hartford about the middle of the week & take it along; ~~but I am~~ because it has chapters in it that ought by all means to be in the prospectus; but I find myself so thoroughly interested in my work, now (a thing I have not experienced for months) that I can't bear to lose a single moment of the inspiration. So I will stay here & peg away as long as it lasts. My present idea is to write as much more as I have already written, & then cull from the mass the very best chapters & discard the rest. I am not half as well satisfied with the first part of the book as I am with what I am writing now. When I get it done I want to see the man who will begin to read it & not finish it. If it falls short of the Innocents in any respect I shall lose my guess.

When I was writing the Innocents my daily "stent" was 30 pages of MS & I hardly ever got beyond it; but I have gone over that nearly every day for the last ten. That shows that I am writing with a red-hot interest. Nothing grieves me now—nothing troubles, me, bothers me or gets my attention—I don't think of anything boo but the book, & don't have am an hour's unhappiness about anything & don't care two cents whether school keeps or not. It will be a bully book. If I keep up my present lick three weeks more I shall be able & willing to scratch out half of the chapters ov of the Overland narrative—& shall do it.

You do not mention having received my second batch of MS, sent a week or two ago—about 100 pages.[2]

If you want to issue a prospectus & go right to canvassing, say the word & I will forward some more MS—or send it by hand, special messenger. Whatever chapters you think are unquestionably good, we will retain of course, & so they can go into a prospectus as well one time as another. The book will be done soon, now. I have 1200 pages of MS already written, & am now writing 200 a week—more than that, in fact; during past week wrote 23 one day, then 30, 33, 35, 52, & 65,—part of the latter, say, nearly half, being a re-print sketch. How's that?[3]

It will be a starchy book, & should be full of snappy pictures—especially pictures worked in with the letter-press.[4] The dedication will be worth the price of the volume—thus:

To the Late Cain,
This Book is Dedicated:

Not on account of respect for his memory, for it merits little respect; not on account of sympathy with him, for his bloody deed placed him without the pale of sympathy, strictly speaking: but out of a mere humane commiseration for him in that it was his misfortune to live in a dark age that knew not the beneficent Insanity Plea.⁵

I think it will do.

Ys

Clemens.

P. S. The reaction is beginning & my stock is looking up. I am getting the bulliest offers for books & almanacs, am flooded with lecture invitations, & one periodical offers me $6,000 cash for 12 articles, of any length & on any subject, treated humorously or otherwise.⁶

✉───

[*letter docketed:*] Mark Twain | May 15/71 | Author⁷

¹Bliss's letter about House's proposal does not survive (3 May 71 to Bliss, n. 1). The royalty check was for seventh-quarter (1 Feb–30 Apr 71) sales of some 3,800 copies of *The Innocents Abroad,* well below sixth-quarter sales (15 Feb 71 to Bliss, n. 1; Hirst 1975, 318).

²What was then chapters 12–15 (30 Apr 71 to OC, n. 2; 3 May 71 to Bliss).

³"Clemens had clearly shifted to counting by equivalent pages" by the time he wrote this letter (*RI 1993,* 853). Equivalent pages were those containing revised clippings, each of which Clemens multiplied by a factor of four to reflect the larger number of words they contained. A total of 1,200 equivalent pages (equal at this point to about 1,100 real pages) would have put him close to the end of what became chapter 51. His increased progress over the preceding ten or so days was due both to his subject—his experiences as a reporter for the Virginia City *Territorial Enterprise*—and to his incorporating more clippings than before into this part of his manuscript. The six daily stints described here correspond roughly to what became chapters 44 (8 May), 45 (9 May), 46 (10 May), 47 (11 May), 48 and 50 (12 May), and 51 (13 May). See *RI 1993,* 853–54, for a detailed account of this stage of composition.

⁴Bliss employed at least three artists on *Roughing It:* True W. Williams, Roswell Morse Shurtleff, and Edward F. Mullen. He supplemented their work by borrowing engravings from other books, including five issued by the American Publishing Company and its subsidiaries: Albert D. Richardson's *Beyond the Mississippi* (1867 and 1869), Thomas W. Knox's *Overland through Asia* (1870), Nelson Winch Green's *Mormonism* (1870), Albert S. Evans's *Our Sister Republic* (1870), and Junius Henri Browne's *Sights and Sensations in Europe* (1872). For further details of Bliss's borrowings and the three artists' contributions, see *RI 1993,* 857–59.

⁵Possibly an allusion to a recent failed attempt to appeal the conviction of Edward H. Ruloff on the grounds of insanity. Having followed the Ruloff case closely (29 Apr 71 to Reid), Clemens would have known that on 12 May a two-man lunacy commission appointed by the governor of New York had declared Ruloff sane ("Ruloff. Report and Conclusions of Drs. Gray and Vanderpool," New York *Times,* 13 May 71, 8). Well before November 1871, when the first

prospectus for *Roughing It* issued, he supplanted this dedication with one to Calvin H. Higbie (*RI 1993*, xxiii, 637, 876).

[6] None of these offers has been further documented.

[7] Bliss replied to Clemens on 17 May:

Friend Clemens
        Your favor recd   Am glad to hear from you. Sorry to hear you are not going to call on us to day. However it may be for the best as I think you are in the mood to do good work, at which I *heartily rejoice*—
        Glad to know you are so pressed with overtures for work.
        We intend to do *our part* towards making your book, what it should be, viz in illustrations. We shall try to have just the kind in that will suit—& think we shall succeed. I think it would be well to have Prospectus out *soon as practicible* as agents are anxious for it—still lets have the *best stuff in it*. I have no doubt you have ample matter now to select from, therefore suppose you do as you suggest, send another batch on, of *selected* chapters if you think best & I will get right to work— Suppose you send on such a lot, marked with what in your opinion is particularly good, & let me then make up prospectus matter from it & get engraving for it under way.
        Send the Mss. by *express* it will come then safely. I will put *bully cuts* into it, such as will please you
        Think this will be the plan if it suits you— I assure you nothing shall be wanting on my part, to bring it out in *high style*—I reckon I can do it—
        Glad to see you are feeling in good spirits & it seems a little closer to get a line in your old vein.
        Your Bro. is well.
                                                    Truly
                                                    E Bliss Jr
I got your telegraph & didn't go to N. Y waiting to see you first [*in margin:*] Dont let any body else get House'[s] book! (CU-MARK)

The postscript suggests that Clemens also telegraphed Bliss on 15 or 16 May to say that he was not coming to Hartford as planned. Apparently Bliss had intended to meet Clemens in New York, perhaps in order to assign parts of his manuscript to illustrators, and then return with him to Hartford.

To Donn Piatt
15 May–10 June 1871 • Elmira, N.Y.
(Paraphrase: *Galaxy* 12 [Oct 71]: 588)

MARK TWAIN.—Your affecting letter notifying us that you have experienced religion in consequence of the solemn impression produced upon your mind by reading the manuscripts sent in for the jocular department is received, and contents noted. Your request that the rejected communications for the Club-Room may regularly be forwarded to you, to be perused as a precaution against backsliding, is gladly granted. A contract has been made with the Express Freight Company, on very advantageous terms, to deliver to your address "one bushel waste paper per diem," for the receipt and storage of which please arrange. We imagine that if you want to continue solemn, your case is settled.[1]

[1] Piatt was responsible for "The Galaxy Club-Room" in the May–July 1871 numbers of the magazine. During April or May, Clemens acceded to his first request for a contribution (27 Mar 71 to Piatt, n. 1). In his letter of acknowledgement (now lost) Piatt surely requested further contributions and possibly informed Clemens of his intention to soon give up the editorship of the "Club-Room." Clemens may have responded with this facetious letter—almost certainly after 15 May but before mid-June, by which time he would have seen the June and the July issues of the *Galaxy*. In the latter of these the "Club-Room" consisted largely of short, humorous items Piatt had gathered, many of them uninspired. Clemens's letter to Piatt was independent of his response to Francis P. Church's 13 June request for a contribution. Clemens sent "About Barbers" to Church for the August "Club-Room," ostensibly edited by Piatt, but probably prepared by Church, who explained in a note:

> *"The Galaxy Club-Room" will hereafter be, like the other departments of the magazine, under the direct charge of the Editor of "The Galaxy." Mr. Donn Piatt finding his time occupied by his new and successful journal, "The Capital," relinquishes his position of Presiding Officer . . .* ("The Galaxy Club-Room," *Galaxy* 12 [Aug 71]: 288)

By September, once he was convinced he would get no further contributions from Clemens, Church probably prepared this paraphrase of the letter to Piatt for the October "Club-Room."

NO LETTERS are known to survive between 15 May and 7 June 1871. During that three weeks Clemens at first continued work on *Roughing It*, perhaps attempting to keep up the pace he described in his 15 May letter to Bliss. Toward the end of the month, he evidently wrote to David Gray about plans for publication, announcing for the first time his intention to protect English copyright by simultaneous publication in England, and Gray ran the following item on page one of the Buffalo *Courier* of 31 May:

MARK TWAIN'S NEW BOOK.—Mark Twain's new book, same size and style as the "Innocents Abroad," and as copiously illustrated, will be published in the fall, and will appear simultaneously in England and America. Dealing as it does with certain hitherto unrecorded phases of western life, it will be of historic value, as well as aboundingly humorous.

Clemens interrupted his work to go to Hartford, perhaps stopping for a day or two at the St. Nicholas Hotel in New York ("Morning Arrivals," New York *Express*, 31 May 71, 3, listing a "Clemens J, Elmira"). After his arrival in Hartford on 1 or 2 June, he gave Bliss the third batch of manuscript, which probably consisted of what became chapters 15–35, 37–48, 50–51, and possibly two later chapters he thought suitable for the prospectus, 76 and 78 ("Brief Mention," Hartford *Courant*, 3 June 71, 2; *RI 1993*, 855). In addition, he spent time with Orion and Mollie, inspecting and discussing Orion's inventions, and visited with several Hartford friends, including the Twichells (Joseph Twichell had sent him a letter on 8 May that began, "Mark! Mark! dear friend of days gone by, whose delights we tasted in those happy though distant times when thou didst lodge with us and sit smoking at our fireside, where art thou?" [CU-MARK]). On 4 June he attended services at Twichell's Asylum Hill Congregational Church and had dinner with Connecticut Governor Marshall Jewell. On 5 or 6 June he rejoined his family at his mother-in-law's house in Elmira. He may then have begun work on what became chapter 54 of *Roughing It*, which opens with a reference to a news item that appeared in the New York *Tribune* of 3 June ("A Chinaman Stoned to Death by Boys," 1), but he apparently did not immediately resume his daily routine of going to Quarry Farm to write, and he soon put *Roughing It* aside entirely for another three weeks (7 June 71 to OC and MEC; 10 June 71 to Redpath and Fall; *RI 1993*, 369, 856; 27 June 71 [2nd], 29 June 71, both to OC).

To Orion and Mary E. (Mollie) Clemens
7 June 1871 • Elmira, N.Y.
(MS: CU-MARK)

Elmira, 7th

Dear Bro & Sister:

I forgot to explain to you that the reason I left you so abruptly at the church door Sunday, was because I wanted to see Gov. Jewell & tell him why I did not go to the hotel ⌃in Buffalo⌃ & offer him the hospitalities of our house, when he sent up his card, after having been so hospitably treated by him & his brother in Hartford—& after all, the talk fell on something else & I forgot it. I forgot it again at dinner Sunday evening, & left his house at last without mentioning the matter or even inquiring after his brother's health. However it is no difference. It will "keep."[1]

Did not go on the hill today & have not seen Pamela & Sammy.[2]

Livy is much stronger & the baby is flourishing.

I will try & recollect to enclose in this the brass chain I took from you. Livy thinks it is wonderful perseverance. I think the invention is marvellously ingenious & I hope it will be a great success. But I want the Anti-Sun-Stroke hat invented—it is possible, ~~&~~ useful, & worth a thousand wheels. It would have an enormous sale. Go at it at once. Mind, the hat must not *weigh* perceptibly more ~~that~~ than it does now.[3]

Yrs

Sam*l*.

Livy is much obliged for your dispatch but thinks you should not have paid for it.[4]

---

[1] Marshall Jewell, whom Clemens had known at least since mid-June 1869, was a prominent parishioner of the Asylum Hill Congregational Church. After a close and contested election, he had just begun his second of three terms as governor of Connecticut (1869–70, 1871–72, 1872–73). At least two of his six brothers—Pliny and Charles A.—also lived in Hartford, and were connected with the family firm of P. Jewell and Sons, "*Hide and Leather* Dealers, and Manufacturers of Leather *Belting*, Fire Engine and Factory Hose" (Geer 1871, 168). Which brother offered hospitality to Clemens (possibly when he spent "a pleasant day & a pleasant evening" in Hartford in late November 1869: see *L3*, 404) is not known. Marshall Jewell had subsequently come to Buffalo when the Clemenses could not receive visitors, perhaps while Emma Nye or Olivia was ill with typhoid fever (Mansfield, 20; "Gov. Jewell . . . ," Fredonia *Censor*, 17 May 71, 2; Geer 1871, 248; Sobel and Raimo, 1:180; *L3*, 269, 385).

[2] Pamela and Samuel Moffett had arrived from Fredonia for treatment at the Elmira Water Cure, which was on East Avenue at the bottom of East Hill, on the road to Quarry Farm (11 June 71 to JLC; Cotton, 36–37).

[3] In addition to his duties on the *American Publisher,* Orion was continuing to work on his inventions, one of them a project that had occupied him for a number of years, a paddle boat apparently employing a wheel and a chain mechanism. During the next several months, this project was inconvenienced by a Hartford clock-maker who was slow in manufacturing the chains necessary for a working model (OC to SLC, 8 Mar 71, 4 July 71, 18 Sept 71, 22 Sept 71, and OC to MEC, 14 Sept 71, all in CU-MARK). See also 12 June 70 to PAM, n. 6.

[4] Orion may have telegraphed the time of Clemens's projected arrival in Elmira.

To Bret Harte
7 June–28 September 1871 • Elmira, N.Y.
(MS: Craven)

·   ·   ·   ·

[enclosure:][1]

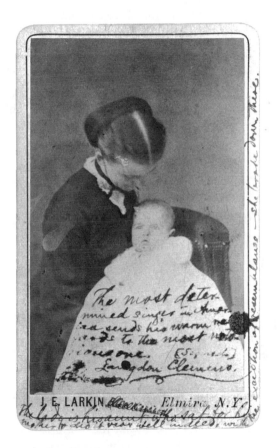

[1] The inscription on the photograph reads:

The most determined singer in America sends his warm regards to the most notorious one.

[Signed]
Langdon Clemens.

Elmira
J. E. LARKIN, Blacksmith ELMIRA, N.Y.
The lady is his aunt, who sat for his mother & did it very well indeed, with the exception
of resemblance—she broke down there.

In her photograph album, Olivia labeled another print of this picture of Langdon
and Susan Crane "Langdon Clemens 6½ months," indicating that John E. Larkin took it around 21 May 1871 (CSmH; Boyd and Boyd, 143). Olivia is not
known to have posed for a photograph with Langdon. Although she had been
"as feeble as ever" in April, by early June she was "much stronger" and could
have sat with him (4 Apr 71 to OC; 7 June 71 to OC and MEC). She did not,
possibly because Langdon soon became "seriously ill" (23 July 71 to Bowen).
By 28 September, shortly before the Clemenses moved to Hartford, they had
exhausted their entire supply of baby pictures, including the present one (28
Sept 71 to Lant). Clemens evidently enclosed the Larkin photograph (reproduced here at 100 percent of actual size from a print by Robert D. Rubic) in a
letter to Bret Harte (now lost) after they resumed good relations. Clemens had
campaigned for a reconciliation, sending letters to Charles Henry Webb and
Thomas Bailey Aldrich—Boston friends of Harte's—in which he extolled Harte
and explained their inadvertent falling out (26 Nov 70 to Webb; 27 Jan 71 to
Aldrich). He had thereafter either met with Harte in Boston or received a letter
(now lost) from him.

To James Redpath and George L. Fall
10 June 1871 • Elmira, N.Y.
(MS: NHi)

                                                        Elmira, June 10.
Dear Redpath & Fall:
        Without really intending to go into the lecture field, I wrote a
lecture yesterday just for amusement & to see how the subject[1] would
work up—but now that I have read it over I like it so much that I want
to deliver it.
        I want to impose a few stipulations if they strike you favorably &
you'll stand them:
        1. In whatever town I talk, I want the best price that that town has
ever paid Nasby—*except* it be a place thrown in here & there for the purpose of shortening travel between places. [*in margin:* Nasby will tell give
you transcript of his terms in the various places.][2]
        2. I want to stick to main railroad lines as a rule, avoiding out-of-
the way branches as much far as practicable.

3. I don't want to make any steamboat trips, or *any* stage or carriage trips of even 2½ miles—*2* miles is too much. To simplify it, I don't want *any* engagements OFF the railroads.

4. I don't want to lecture a single rod west of St. Louis in Missouri or Davenport Iowa,—nor south of Washington, D.C.[3] ‸OVER.

I would much rather talk for Pugh in Phila., & for the Correspondents' Club in Washington—think it well to talk for the latter at *half price,* making them understand that feature. Good card.‸[4]

{{ 5. I want to talk at least 12 times in good sized towns before I talk in a city—so as to get the hang of my lecture perfectly, you know.

6. If I am to talk in Brooklyn or New York, I ‸much‸ prefer that they should be the very last on the list.[5]

7. I am a bully good card in Philadelphia, Newark, Pittsburgh, Cleveland, & Detroit, & I want them to pay high prices.[6] ‸In Newark I would much prefer to talk for my same old society—the Clayonians—good boys.‸[7]

8.

8. Rondout, N. Y., is hard to get at & Trenton N. J., not agreeable—crowd both out with high prices.[8]

9. *I* think that out of New England I ought never to talk for less than $125, because I thereby escape one-horse towns, candle-lighted halls, & execrable hotels—though/ exceptions in order to put places close together are proper of course.[9] What /y do *you* think. ‸What does Nasby do?‸ Answer.

10. Is it well to go all over the country?—or would it be better to talk *only* in New England two of the months, & then put in the other two in the west, making Chicago the centre of operations & Cleveland & St. Louis the extremes of the circumference—& wholly leaving out ~~Pitts~~ New York, Philadelphia, Washington & everything, & simply **bridging** from New England to Cleveland by ~~simply~~ slamming in Elmira & Buffalo, or Pittsburgh. [*Mem.*—I want a big price in Buffalo if I talk there, which I ain't particular whether I talk there or not.][10]

Now by jings I *like* this latter idea of a 2-months N. England & a 2‌months western campaign—don't it strike you pleasantly? [*in margin:* If you ~~did~~ do this, you will need to specify the eastern & western months & so advertise, won't you?]

11. ~~It would so suit me entirely, though, to put Philadelphia along with Brooklyn & New York & make them my very *last* lectures, though~~

~~I traveled 500 miles to get there——but always remember I don't care 2 cents about talking in either place. I love Philadelphia, but I don't know anything about the other two places.~~

12. Give me all the appointments in New England that you can—[I wish it could occu fill up *all* the 3½ months ‚you hear *me*—‚]—I say 3½ because I don't suppose any courses open before middle of October.

13. Give me the very *shortest trips* you can, & Heaven will bless you. ‚[Three hours is a healthy stretch—six is FRIGHTFUL.[]]‚

~~14. Say—if you are posted~~

14.—Say—can't you, when making an appointment get the Society to name their best hotel, & then put it in my list, as Fall did several times before? Splendid thing.[11]

15.—Can't you get somebody to answer this letter in detail, please?

16.—Can't you file this letter away where Fall can refer to it when in doubt about particulars?

17. Is the form I enclose about the thing you want for announcement? Alter it to suit yourself—add to it—take from it—fix it the ‚way you‚ want it to read.[12]

Yrs Ever
Saml. L. Clemens.

Write me frankly about everything—I want all your views. Tell me of my errors.

P. S.—Say—why don't you ‚or Pugh‚ rent a popular hall in N. Y., & select the pick & choice of the lecturers ‚(say 5,)‚ & lecture EACH of them 5 to 10 nights *in succession* & just divide the *actual profits* with each after all expenses‚? Fifty ~~ni~~ successive nights could be put in, in that way, & you would clear $20,000 or $25,000. Don't you believe it? *I* do.

————————————————————————————————

[*letter docketed by Redpath:*] answered in part ☞ [*and*] BOSTON LYCEUM BUREAU. REDPATH & FALL. JUN 12 1871 [*and, in another hand:*] 6/23.71[13] [*and*] *Twain* Mark | Elmira, N.Y. | June 10 '71

[1] See note 12.

[2] Nasby's lecture fee, as much as $400 in large cities, had averaged $200 per engagement in 1870. Fees may well have been discussed when Nasby called on Clemens in Buffalo on 21 February 1871. Clemens was then already contemplating a new tour. As Nasby's agent, Redpath was, of course, fully apprised of his fees (22 Feb 71, 15 Mar 71, both to Redpath; "Personal," Hartford *Courant*, 18 Feb 70, 2; Harrison, 183; *Lyceum:* 1870, 3; 1871, 19).

³During his 1868–69 lecture tour, which included Illinois and Iowa, Clemens had lectured as far west as Iowa City, about fifty miles west of Davenport. His 1869–70 tour was limited to the northeastern states. In neither tour had he ventured farther south than Washington, D.C., or into Missouri at all (*L3*, 481–86). See 22 Jan 71 to Redpath for an account of Clemens's lecture tours in California and Nevada.

⁴Thomas B. Pugh, the Philadelphia lecture impresario, paid Clemens $250 for a 20 November 1871 lecture in his Star Course, a fee he received only one other time that season, in Boston, on 1 November (Redpath and Fall 1871–72, 3–6). Clemens was a favorite at the Washington Newspaper Correspondents' Club, which he had probably joined in late 1867. After delivering his widely reprinted reply to the toast to "Woman" on 11 January 1868 at a club banquet, he had promised to return with a formal lecture, but had not yet done so. During his 1871–72 tour, however, his Washington lecture was in the Grand Army of the Republic Course on 23 October, at an undiscounted fee of $150. He had previously spoken in that course on 8 December 1869 (18 Apr 71 to Unidentified; 28 June 71 to Redpath; SLC's receipt to Grand Army of the Republic, dated 23 Oct 71, ViU).

⁵Clemens lectured in Brooklyn on 21 November 1871, in the middle of his tour, and in New York on 24 January 1872, toward the end (see Appendix C for his full schedule).

⁶Newark and Pittsburgh paid Clemens $200; his usual fee was $125 or $150. He was not booked into Cleveland or Detroit (Redpath and Fall 1871–72, 5–6, 11–12).

⁷Clemens had lectured successfully for the Clayonians before what he called "a great audience" at the Newark Opera House on 9 December 1868 and again, less successfully, on 29 December 1869 (*L2*, 320–21, 323–24 n. 4; "Mark Twain Last Night," Newark *Advertiser,* 30 Dec 69, 2; "Mark Twain on the Sandwich Islands," Newark *Journal,* 30 Dec 69, 2).

⁸There was no direct train route to Rondout, over ninety miles north of New York City and across the Hudson River. Clemens had lectured there on 2 December 1868 and 12 January 1870 and would do so again in 1871. In Trenton he had lectured twice in 1869, delivering "The American Vandal Abroad" on 23 February and "Our Fellow Savages of the Sandwich Islands" on 28 December. The Trenton press evidently did not review the first lecture. The Trenton *True American* had called the second "one of the grandest humbugs of the day. However a man, and a printer at that, can have the cheek to go about the country retailing anecdotes as stale as some sausages, at $150 a night, is more than we can understand" ("An extended . . . ," 29 Dec 69, 3, in Lane). Actually, Clemens had received only $100 for his 28 December appearance. For his objection to Trenton, see 28 June 71 to Redpath. He did not lecture there during his 1871–72 tour (28 June 71 to Redpath; 20 July 71 to Fall; *L2*, 298, 300 n. 5; *L3*, 442 n. 1, 483, 485–86).

⁹Redpath eventually made engagements in several New England towns at lower fees: $100 for Brattleboro (Vermont), Milford, Andover, Malden, and Randolph (Massachusetts); and $110 for Great Barrington (Massachusetts), Exeter (New Hampshire), and Bennington (Vermont) (Redpath and Fall 1871–72, 1–6).

¹⁰The 1871–72 tour did not include Buffalo.

[11] Clemens's lecture itinerary did identify hotels in most cities, presumably those recommended by the local lyceum societies (Redpath and Fall 1871–72).

[12] The enclosure does not survive, but clearly was the draft of a publicity release about the new lecture—"An Appeal in behalf of Extending the Suffrage to Boys." See the next letter and 21 June 71 to Bliss for other, presumably similar announcements.

[13] Redpath's fist pointed to the earlier, stamped date. Neither his 12 June nor his 23 June reply is known to survive.

To David Gray
10 June 1871 • Elmira, N.Y.
(Paraphrase: Gray 1871a)

MARK TWAIN IN THE LECTURE FIELD.—Mark Twain is going to make a short lecturing tour in the early part of the coming season. Subject—"An Appeal in behalf of Extending the Suffrage to Boys." He says he thought he had retired permanently from the lecture field, but upon looking into things and finding that Woman is less persecuted, and is held in a milder bondage than boys, he thinks it incumbent upon somebody to "lift up a voice for the poor little male juvenile."[1]

[1] Clemens probably wrote this letter just after the preceding one to Redpath and Fall. Among the Boston Lyceum Bureau's lecturers on *women's* suffrage during the 1870–71 lecture season were: Susan B. Anthony, "The Woman Question"; the Reverend James Freeman Clarke, "Why should not Women Vote?"; the Reverend Robert Laird Collier, "Woman's Place"; the Reverend Rowland Connor, "The Subjection of Woman"; Anna E. Dickinson, "A new lecture on the Woman Question"; the Reverend Jesse H. Jones, "The Supreme Political Reform"; Mary A. Livermore, "The Reasons Why"; the Reverend W. H. H. Murray, "Woman's Suffrage: and what would be the result of it?"; Petroleum V. Nasby, "Struggles of a Conservative with the Woman Question"; and Judge Edwin Wright, "Woman Greater than her Aspirations" (*Lyceum* 1870, 2–4).

To Jane Lampton Clemens
11 June 1871 • Elmira, N.Y.
(MS: CU-MARK)

Elmira June 11
Dear Mother—[1]
 I saw Pamela
yesterday, & she seemed
to me about the same
she has been all the time
since she came here.   I

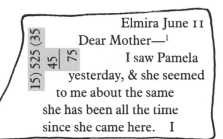

cannot discover that she
improves any great deal,
though I believe they[2]

in giving
the West,
the country p
the cuts
like to
With
to me to
iogra

contend that
she is really
improving,
& very steadily,
too.   Sammy

any des
& would
apers, sc

looks a good deal bet-
ter, I fancy. It seems
to me that he looks
hearty, healthy &
strong.   I   know
perfectly well that
some   of   that

phy" shown
be not un
your permi
reproduce
in my ab

nervous twitching about
the muscles of the face has
subsided.[3]   They have
moved into a room on the
first floor, & Pamela says
it was nearly necessary, ~~per~~

perhaps entirely so, that
she get on the lower
floor & save her strength
the tax of climbing the
stairs. Yesterday when
I was there she had just

received yours &
Annies letters a-
bout the debate
& the "Dunk gents."
We were glad indeed
that Annie acquitted
herself so well &
received such cor-
dial praise. Where
the other side man-
aged to find ar-
guments so

much convincing as or so
capable of able hand-
ling as to make
the negative of so
lame a question
win, is beyond my
comprehension.
They had not the ghost
of a chance, I
thought. I half
incline to the
belief that[4]

ry Truly
Vernol

the umpire let spread-eagle
declamation run away with his
calm judgment.   I sent these
letters to Orion, & also those
giving an account of the riot-
~~ous~~ otous proceedings of the
"Dunk roughs"—or was it
~~th~~   the "Dunk

the "Dunk gents?" Where is Dunk?[5]
I cannot find it on the map—
though ours ∮ is an old map, & has
many places left out & no
doubt this is one of them.
~~I am going~~   Your police
are doubtless like the police all over the

A. N. KELLOGG, PROPR
some illu
Autob
I. E.
"RAILROAD

world—mean, lazy,
worthless, cowardly thieves.
They acted, during & after your
riot, just as they would have
done in New York or any
other city in America.[6] N
I am going to start out in

Tru
October & lecture
as you may d
about 3 months or three
your consent, & w
& a half. My subject is:[7]
I shall be p

I expect to lecture first in New England 2 months
& then skip to Chicago & lecture a month in the west.
I may possibly talk in Elmira, Buffalo, Cleveland & Cincinnati as I go along. I think it is a
subject that will take—don't you? I have talked

with several people about it, & they say it is the best subject before the country to-day, & that if I can't do it
happy justice I can't do *any* subject justice.
Ma I will help Orion with any machine
he wants help on. When I was there the other day, we

decided that it was
best for him to peg
on along on this one
just as he is doing
until I see how
my new book is
going to pan out.
So he is working
away just the same
as before.[8]

Ma, I think it
likely that some men
are so consti-
tuted that

they will, under cir-
cumstances of an
irregular nature,
manifest idiosyn-
crasies of an ir-
refragable & and
even pragmatic
& latitudinarian
character, but oth-
erwise & differently
situated the reverse
is too often the case.
How does it strike *you?*
Yr Son
Sam.

ch May 27ᵗʰ 1871

Mrs. Jane Clemens | Care Mrs. P. A. Moffett | Fredonia | N. Y. [*post-marked:*] ELMIRA N.Y. JUN 12 [*on the flap:*] (OLL) [*in JLC's hand:*] Sams scrap letter | 1871

[1] Clemens wrote this letter on nine unnumbered scraps of paper, usually writing on both sides of each scrap. Three different paper stocks are represented, two from letters written to him or his publisher, with the result that someone

else's handwriting in brown (originally black) ink appears randomly beneath and around his own, which is in purple ink. One penciled calculation (on the first scrap) was even written by his wife, before he appropriated the sheet for this letter. The point of this elaborate visual joke was to tease Jane Clemens about her inveterate habit of writing letters on what Samuel C. Webster later described as "any sheet of paper that happened to be handy" (*MTBus*, 66). Clemens had complained in an April 1863 letter, written in Virginia City: "Ma, write on *whole* letter sheets—is paper scarce in St Louis?" (*L1*, 247). Webster cited this remark in 1946 when he asserted that Clemens had taken "considerable pains" to cure her of this habit by sending her from Nevada "a letter composed of papers of every size, color, and shape, including wrapping paper, the scraps all jumbled together and stuffed into an envelope. She spent several indignant hours sorting it out" (*MTBus*, 66). If Clemens did send an earlier "scraps" letter, it has not survived. It is much more probable, however, that Webster was describing the present letter at second hand, drawing on a family story and guessing, from the 1863 remark, that Clemens had sent it from the West. For a facsimile of the original letter and the procedure used to reproduce it, see Appendix F and the textual commentary.

[2] This and four other scraps evidently came from a letter to Isaac E. Sheldon asking permission to syndicate the text and eleven illustrations of "The House That Jack Built" from the *(Burlesque) Autobiography*. The letter, which Sheldon must have forwarded to Clemens, was apparently from Ansel Nash Kellogg (1832–86), editor and publisher of the New York *Railroad Gazette*, and owner of the A. N. Kellogg Newspaper Company of Chicago, a syndicate that supplied 240 country newspapers with "auxiliary sheets" or "insides"—full newspaper sheets printed weekly on one side only with features, illustrations, telegraph news, and advertising, to which a subscriber could add local matter on the blank side (Mrja, 180–82; Rowell, 205–7). No evidence has been found that Clemens agreed to the request, or that he answered the letter.

[3] See 7 June 71 to OC and MEC, n. 2.

[4] This scrap and the last one came from a letter of which little more than the dateline and part of the complimentary close and signature survive. The writer, "Vernol," has not been identified.

[5] The Fredonia *Censor* of 31 May 1871 reported that on the evening of 30 May (Decoration Day) a band of ten or fifteen "rowdies" from neighboring Dunkirk, who were "intoxicated and turbulent," caused a disturbance aboard a Fredonia horsecar, injuring the driver, who had tried to restrain them ("Riotous Doings," 3).

[6] The Dunkirk rowdies had, for the most part, escaped the police, causing the editor of the Fredonia *Censor* to remark that "if we have no material here for policemen able to cope with the Dunkirk roughs who invade the village hereafter, let some be advertised for and imported. That failing, start a Vigilance committee. Rope enough will be cheerfully donated to give each rowdy a separate noose" ("The Two Rioters . . . ," 7 June 71, 3).

[7] Possibly a scrap that originally followed here has been lost, but it is much more likely that Clemens intentionally left this sentence unfinished.

[8] See 7 June 71 to OC and MEC, n. 3.

To James Redpath
12 June 1871 • Elmira, N.Y.
(MS: MH-H)

Elmira June 12.

Dear Redpath—

Begin my tour in the West if you prefer it—it does not matter to me.[1]

What is Olive & those other dead beats charging?—or what *did* they charge last year? I don't want to be cheaper than *them*, I don't.[2]

Ys

Mark.

✉ ───

[letter docketed:] 6/*23.71*

[1] Clemens had evidently not yet received a reply to his letter of 10 June to Redpath and Fall—but he would within three days (15 June 71 to Redpath). None of Redpath's or Fall's letters to him for this period has been found; the next surviving letter from the Boston Lyceum Bureau is dated 25 November 1871 (28 Nov 71 to Fall).

[2] Figures have not been found for the 1870–71 lecture season, but in 1869–70 Olive Logan's lowest fee was $100, which she received even in small towns like Danvers, Massachusetts, where, on 17 November 1869, Clemens received $75 (*Lyceum* 1869, 3; Eubank, 134–36).

To William Bowen
12 June 1871 • Elmira, N.Y.
(Paraphrase: Hornberger, 10, and Hornberger to DeVoto, 18 Dec 1940)

One additional letter is known to be in existence, in the possession of Miss Agnes M. Bowen of Salt Lake City, Utah, a granddaughter. . . . Miss Bowen has written that it is dated at Elmira, New York, June 12. . . . She writes: "It contains some interesting data regarding a lecture tour and plans for building a new home. Reference is also made to Mrs. Clemens and my grandfather."[1]

¹ This letter, tentatively dated both 1873 and 1874 by Theodore Hornberger, was almost certainly written in 1871. On 12 June that year Clemens was in Elmira and was planning a lecture tour that might extend to the West, presumably including St. Louis, where Bowen lived. He evidently reported that possibility to Bowen, along with his intention to build a house in Hartford. Bowen's reply, not known to survive, elicited Clemens's letter of 23 July to him (9 Mar 71 to Cox; Hornberger to Bernard DeVoto, 18 Dec 1940, CU-MARK; Hornberger, 10).

To James Redpath
15 June 1871 • Elmira, N.Y.
(Horner, 172–74)

Elmira, June 15, 1871.

Dear Redpath:

1. Bully for Fall. I offer my hearty congratulations.¹

2. I use no notes in lecturing, & so I don't dare to try to use more than one lecture during a season. I shall carry the MSS. of another lecture, along, for safety, & shall discard the new one altogether if, after a few trials, it is not a success.²

3. The idea of a *woman* reading a *humorous* lecture is perhaps the ghastliest conception to which the human mind has yet given birth. It is the most depressing thought that has intruded itself upon me for many moons. Why, Redpath, the thing is wholly out of the question. I question if the woman ever lived who could read a densely humorous passage as it should be read. Tenderness, pathos, tragedy—the earnest, the beautiful, the majestic—all these they can & do succeed in, but they fail in humor, *except in the sparkling, vivacious kind*—high & brilliant comedy. They *appreciate* & enjoy my sort (you know I rely for my effects chiefly on a simulated unconsciousness & intense absurdities), but they cannot render them effectively on the platform. But I could take a *man* home with me & drill him a week (or at any rate 2 weeks), & send him out competent to deliver the lecture the way I wanted it delivered—& I wouldn't let anybody deliver a lecture written by me unless he would deliver it in my way *or else show me a better.* Now if I had a *he* comedian (I know at least 2 on the stage who certainly don't get $250 a month for slaving their lives away, & who could deliver a lecture of mine without any instruction at all), *then* we would talk. No, we couldn't talk, either,

because *he* would have that ten per cent idea, too, & I would have to get him to pay me forty. I could send such a man into the lecture field (he can't *get* there without an *excuse,* & a lecture with my name to it would furnish him that,) & he would make $2000, or $3000 in five months (& have an easy, gentlemanly time), & so would I—& you'd get your ten per cent.[3]

4. However, as I can't lay my hand on such a comedian nearer than Buffalo, I will e'en cease to lust after him, & continue in my plans about my own lecturing tour.[4]

You'll have to excuse my lengthiness—the reason I dread writing letters is because I am so apt to get to slinging wisdom & forget to let up. Thus much precious time is lost.

Yours ever,
Mark.

[1] Clemens had received Redpath's 12 June reply (now lost) to his letter of 10 June. Fall, normally in charge of scheduling and business arrangements for the Boston Lyceum Bureau, would be away from the office until late July. The occasion for Clemens's congratulations has not been identified.

[2] Redpath was preparing his promotional matter for the 1871–72 season, and had probably asked Clemens to consider offering more than one lecture. The first advertisement of the Boston Lyceum Bureau list, without lecture titles, appeared in the Boston *Evening Transcript* on 19 June ("Special Notices," 3). Redpath and Fall's *Lyceum Magazine* for 1871–72, which became available about 22 or 23 June, announced for Clemens only "An appeal in behalf of extending the Suffrage to Boys" (*Lyceum* 1871, 20; "To Lecture Committees in New England," Boston *Evening Transcript,* 24 June 71, 2).

[3] Possibly Redpath had received a proposal from Helen Potter for a tour with one of Clemens's lectures. Potter, a popular elocutionist, was preparing a new type of entertainment, "lyceum personations," which she first presented under Redpath's auspices in May 1874. These were dramatic and humorous recreations "not only of the manner, but of the rhetoric, of distinguished lecturers and elocutionists. . . . Miss Potter's personations of John B. Gough were so perfect, the wig, beard, and masculine garments so well chosen and so well arranged, and his peculiarities of voice and manner so faithfully represented, that the audience often forgot it was a personation and thought that they were listening to Gough himself" (Pond, 170–71). Her other male subjects included Edwin Booth, Henry Ward Beecher, and Robert Ingersoll (*Lyceum* 1874, 2, 11–12; Potter, vii, 1–11, 62–68, 120–24, 158–64).

[4] The Buffalo comedian is unidentified.

To Elisha Bliss, Jr.
21 June 1871 • Elmira, N.Y.
(MS: CU-MARK)

Elmira, June 71.[1]

Dear Bliss:

Here are three articles which you may have if you'll pay ~~$100 or~~ ~~$125~~ $125 for the lot., ~~according to present state of your exchequer~~—& if you don't want them I'll sell them to "Galaxy," but not for a cent less than three times the money—have just sold them a short article (shorter than either of these,) for $100.[2] If you take them, pay *one-tenth* of the ~~money a week~~ ˏ$125 in weekly instalmentsˏ to Orion till he has received it all. Don't go over the one-tenth at a time—otherwise he will do no sort of good with it. [*in margin, in pencil:* Send dozen copies of the Beecher article to T.W. Crane, Elmira.][3]

If you use the articles, print the Beecher one first, then let a whole edition go by before printing either of the others—then let the scientific articles appear one after the other in successive issues of the paper.[4]

Yes, I would like to have you mention the lecture—& you can ~~say~~ ~~that it~~ ˏadd this: "Itˏ is not a fight against Woman's rights or against any particular thing, but is only a pretentiously & ostentatiously supplicating appeal in behalf of the boys, which the *general tendency of the times* converts into a good-natured satire,—otherwise ~~it~~ ˏthe lectureˏ would ~~not deserve to be, or *seem* to be a satire at all.~~ hardly sound like a satire at all—at least to a careless listener."[5]

Have you heard anything from Routledge? Considering the large English sale he made of one of my other books (Jumping Frog,) I thought may be we might make something if I could give him a secure copyright.— There seems to be no convenient way to beat those Canadian re-publishers anyway——though I ~~could~~ can go over the line & get out a copyright if you wish it & think it would hold water.[6]

Yrs

Mark.

[1]Clemens wrote this letter just before the next one. Since he neglected to date either letter, both have been assigned the date of the postmark of the second.

[2] The enclosures were "A New Beecher Church," and "A Brace of Brief Lectures on Science," parts 1 and 2. Francis P. Church had bought "About Barbers" for the August *Galaxy* (SLC 1871m–p).

[3] "A New Beecher Church" described the radically designed church complex that Thomas K. Beecher planned for his Elmira congregation. After its publication in the July 1871 *American Publisher,* the paper claimed to have paid "in cash a large price" for it ("Editorial Notes," *American Publisher* 1 [Aug 71]: 4).

[4] Bliss followed instructions, publishing the "Brace of Brief Lectures," on paleontology, in September and October.

[5] But see 27 June 71 to OC (1st).

[6] In 1870, in a belated attempt to combat British and Canadian book pirates, Clemens consulted the New York representative of George Routledge and Sons of London—publishers of both unsanctioned and sanctioned editions of *The Celebrated Jumping Frog of Calaveras County, And other Sketches*—about British copyright on *The Innocents Abroad* (3 Mar 70 to Bliss, n. 2; 11 Mar 70 to Bliss, n. 3). Routledge and Sons had authorized Bliss to issue the American edition of one of their books, and in 1872 became the official English publishers of *Roughing It* (21? Nov 70 to OC, n. 4; SLC 1872c). The Routledge edition of that work was published a few days before the American in order to secure British copyright, but portions of it were pirated in England nevertheless, and the entire book was reprinted without authorization in London in 1880 (see *RI 1993,* 876–77, 893).

To Orion and Mary E. (Mollie) Clemens
21 June 1871 • Elmira, N.Y.
(MS: CU-MARK)

Elmira.

Dear Bro & Sister:

Am very glad, indeed, you think so well of the book.[1] I mean to make it a good one in spite of everything—then the illustrations will do the rest. When the prospectus is out I believe Bliss will sell 50,000 copies before the book need be actually issued.

Mollie, Sammy's nervous twitchings & shakings are worse than I have ever seen them before——caused by a foment for constipation. Pamela very uneasy.[2]

I am sending Bliss 3 articles at a ~~slim~~ slim price, ~~$100 or~~ $125 for the whole lot, ₓ(according to condition of his exchequer,)ₓ—⅓ their value—told him to pay the money to Orion in one-tenth instalments, weekly till the amount is exhausted. Orion can also draw small amounts from time to time as ~~he requires them~~ requirements demand.

As usual, I am running two households—one up here on the farm (Livy is here, ~~lu~~ all the time, now,) & one in Buffalo. Three servants in Buffalo & two here. One of the latter—the cook—I pay $5 a week, & the other, $2. I also pay a man $2 a week to make fires ~~on~~—for sometimes the mornings & evenings are a little chilly.[3] ˏMr & Mrs. Crane stay here with us, & we do have perfectly *royal* good times.ˏ

Yrs affly.

Sam

Orion Clemens Esq | 149 Asylum st | Hartford | Conn. [*return address:*] IF NOT DELIVERED WITHIN 10 DAYS, TO BE RETURNED TO [*postmarked:*] ELMIRA N.Y. JUN 21 [*letter docketed by OC:*] writing for me

[1] The recently delivered *Roughing It* manuscript (up through about chapter 51).

[2] Samuel Moffett's condition had recently deteriorated at the Elmira Water Cure, where the foment had evidently been prescribed for him (11 June 71 to JLC).

[3] Two of the three servants still in Buffalo were, almost certainly, a housekeeper and the coachman. Probably the Clemenses had brought Ellen White, who had served as both housekeeper and cook, to Elmira with them. The second Elmira servant, presumably there to help Olivia with the baby, may have been the Buffalo nurse, Margaret, whom Clemens had described as "staunch & true" in March (14 Mar 71 to Crane). Conceivably this was the same Margaret, described in similar complimentary terms, who was with the Clemenses in Hartford by December 1871 and remained with them until May 1872 (3 Dec 71 to OLC; 17 May 72 to Annie Moffett, NPV).

To Orion Clemens
27 June 1871 • (1st of 2) • Elmira, N.Y.
(MS: CU-MARK)

Elmira

Dˑ Bro—

    If convenient, leave out the *added remarks* to the lecture item— for ~~the~~ this reason: I ~~am writing~~ ˏwroteˏ a new lecture to-day, & don't care about having very much talk about the "Boy" one, inasmuch as I shall decide on the new one if I like it better. I somehow think I shall use the new one. You may say, if you choose that I have *two* new lectures— the Boy one & one entitled simply "~~D.——~~ "D. L. H.," & that when I have ~~dis~~ decided which one I like best I shall discard the other entirely.[1]

Ys
Sam

✉————————————————————————————

[*in ink:*] Orion Clemens Esq | 149 Asylum st | Hartford | Conn [*return address:*] IF NOT DELIVERED WITHIN 10 DAYS TO BE RETURNED TO [*postmarked:*] ELMIRA N.Y. JUN 27

[1] The July *American Publisher* printed the following:

> MARK TWAIN'S NEW LECTURE.—We have the pleasure to announce that Mark Twain will lecture in New England during the ensuing fall, and later, in the Western States. The subject is not yet decided upon. He has *two* new lectures, one an appeal in behalf of boy's rights, and one entitled simply "D. L. H." When he has decided which he likes best, he will discard the other entirely. (OC 1871e)

"D. L. H." has not been explained.

~~To George L. Fall~~
To James Redpath
27 June 1871 • (1st of 2) • Elmira, N.Y.
(MS: Axelrod)

Elmira

D[r.] ~~F~~[1] Redpath—

Don't be in any hurry about announcing the *title* of my lecture. Just say *"To be announced."*[2]

Because, I wrote a new lecture to-day, entitled simply "D. L. H." During the month of July I'll decide which I like best—& that one only will I use.

Ys
Mark.

[*letter docketed:*] BOSTON LYCEUM BUREAU. REDPATH & FALL. JUN 29 1871 [*and*]
L [*and*] *Twain* Mark | Elmira N.Y. | June 29 '71

¹ Fall, Clemens remembered, was temporarily away from the Boston Lyceum
Bureau (15 June 71 to Redpath, n. 1).
² See 15 June 71 to Redpath, n. 2, and 7–8 July 71 to Redpath.

To Orion Clemens
27 June 1871 • (2nd of 2) • Elmira, N.Y.
(MS: CU-MARK)

                                        Elmira 27
Dear Bro:
        I wrote a third lecture to-day—& tomorrow I go back on the book
again. This third lecture is the *only* one I shall deliver ~~next~~ during the
coming season,—so it isn't worth while to mention the others.¹ I call it
"Reminiscences of Some Pleasant Characters whom I have Met." (If
"whom" is bad grammar, scratch it out.[)] ˣ
        It covers my whole acquaintance—kings, humorists, lunatics, idi-
ots & all. You might add that, as coming from me.²
                                        Ys
                                        Sam

[*in ink:*] Orion Clemens Esq | 149 Asylum st | Hartford | Conn [*return
address:*] IF NOT DELIVERED WITHIN 10 DAYS, TO BE RETURNED TO [*postmarked:*]
ELMIRA N.Y. JUN 28 [*and*] N.Y. | D.P.O.

¹ See 27 June 71 to OC (1st), n. 1.
² Orion replied on 4 July:

> I do not see how you could possibly have chosen a better subject for your lecture. . . .
> "Whom" is right. I never knew you to make a grammatical error. . . .
>   I will preserve your letter concerning it (the lecture) and use it in calling attention
> to the lecture in next issue. (CU-MARK)

The new notice did not appear until the September issue of the *American
Publisher:*

MARK TWAIN'S LECTURE on his acquaintances—kings, humorists, lunatics, idiots, and all—under the title of "Reminiscences of some pleasant characters whom I have met," will be delivered during the approaching season at the prices of $100 or $110 to $250 per night. (OC 1871g)

To James Redpath
27 June 1871 • (2nd of 2) • Elmira, N.Y.
(MS: Axelrod)

Elmira 27th

Dear Redpath:

Wrote *another* lecture—a third one—to-day. *It* is the one I am going to deliver. I think I shall call it "Reminiscences of ~~Several Interesting People whom I have Met~~ Some ~~In~~ Pleasant Characters whom I have Met."

₍Or should the "whom" be out?₎

It covers my whole acquaintance—kings, lunatics, idiots & all.

Suppose you give the item a start in the Boston papers₍—& say I have written 3 lec₎[1]

If I write 50 lectures I shall only choose one & talk that one only.

No sir! Don't you put that scarecrow from the Galaxy in. I won't stand that nightmare. There isn't a cut of me in existence that I *would*. Never mind a picture—they ain't any use₍,₎ much. However, now that I think of it, "The Aldine," 23 Liberty street New York, had one in, 2 or 3 months ago that was right good. ~~Mr. E. C.~~ The editor of the Boston Gazette knows the firm well—maybe he can get a copy of that.[2]

Ys

Mark.

[*letter docketed:*] BOSTON LYCEUM BUREAU. REDPATH & FALL. JUN 30 1871 [*and*] Twain Mark | Elmira June 27 '71

[1] Clemens sent a similar request to Whitelaw Reid, who published a notice in the New York *Tribune* (see the next letter, n. 2). The *Tribune* item was picked up by newspapers in Boston and elsewhere, making intervention by Redpath un-

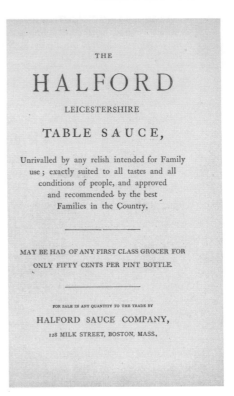

Clemens's "nightmare" portrait in the August 1870 *Galaxy*, engraved by Gaston Fay, with advertisement on facing page. See 27 June 1871 to Redpath (2nd of 2).

necessary ("Personal," Boston *Evening Transcript*, 30 June 71, 2; "In General," Boston *Advertiser*, 3 July 71, 1; "Personal," Buffalo *Courier*, 1 July 71, 1).

[2] The offending portrait, which Redpath must have proposed using for publicity, appeared as the frontispiece in the August 1870 *Galaxy*. Based on an 1870 photograph by an unidentified photographer (see Appendix F), it elicited the following comment in the Philadelphia *Evening Bulletin:*

> The number is faced by a portrait of Mark Twain, coarsely drawn by Gaston Fay. The face shows a hawking eye, and a peccant pecking beak, and looks about as "genial" as a Coshin rooster *ambitioning* a measuring worm. The latter feature is directed, however, not to "American folly," this time, but to somebody's Leicestershire table sauce, which it serves to advertise, with all Beaumarchais's "high sniffing air." ("New Periodicals," 22 July 70, 2)

The *Aldine*'s portrait, engraved by John C. Bruen from Mathew Brady's 1870 photograph of Clemens (see 8 July 70 to OLC, n. 3), was printed in April 1871 (4:52). Clemens apparently began to refer Redpath to *Aldine* editor Edson C. Chick. In referring him instead to the editor of the Boston *Saturday Evening*

SAMUEL L. CLEMENS—(MARK TWAIN).

A "right good" portrait in the April 1871 *Aldine*,
engraved by John C. Bruen from the 1870 Mathew Brady photograph. See 27 June 1871 to
Redpath (2nd of 2).

Gazette, Clemens probably meant Warren Luther Brigham. The *Gazette*'s current editor and publisher, however, was Henry G. Parker (Wilson 1871, 149; 26
or 27 Feb 71 to Chick; 1 Dec 70 to Brigham; *Boston Directory* 1871, 16, 544).

To Whitelaw Reid
27 June 1871 • Elmira, N.Y.
(MS: DLC)

Elmira 27

Dear Reid:

Thank you for kind notice of lecture[1]——would you mind saying
that after writing & throwing aside ~~two~~ ˏthat & anotherˏ new lectures, I
have built a third, which latter seems really satisfactory to me, & is the

only one I shall talk during the coming season. I call it: "Reminiscences of Some Pleasant Characters whom I have Met." (If "whom" is bad grammar, please scratch it out.)

It covers my whole acquaintance—kings, humorists, lunatics, idiots & all.[2]

Love to you.

Yrs.
Twain.

[1] "Mr. Mark Twain's lecture next season will be 'An Appeal in Behalf of Extending Suffrage to Boys.' There has been so much loose writing about suffrage, and there are so many wild speeches made about it by the ladies (God bless 'em!), and such a general fuzzification and muzzification and deconcatenation of the whole matter, that it is quite time for a fresh departure" ("Personal," New York *Tribune*, 16 June 71, 5).

[2] "Mark Twain says that after writing his lecture on the rights of children, and still another one, he has thrown both aside and built a third, entitled, 'Reminiscences of Some Pleasant Characters I Have Met.' This, he says, covers his whole acquaintances—kings, humorists, lunatics, idiots, and all—and this alone he proposes to talk to his lyceum acquaintances next Winter" ("Personal," New York *Tribune*, 29 June 71, 4).

From Olivia L. and Samuel L. Clemens
to Mary Mason Fairbanks
27 June 1871 • Elmira, N.Y.
(Paraphrase and transcript: *MTMF,* 154 n. 3)

June 27

.   .   .

[*paraphrase: Livy regrets that her husband is too busy to write, and to make the promised visit to Cleveland*] the first of next month.[1] Mr. Clemens feels that it will be a month or six weeks before his book will be finished.

.   .   .

[*in pencil:*]

P. S. I have hoped through thick [&] thin, that we would have our holiday with you, but it ain't any use—I have lost so much time that I am obliged to give it up. This book has been dragging along just 12 months, now, & I am *so* sick & tired of it.[2] If I were to chance another break or another move before I finish it I fear I never *should* get it done.

Lovingly yrs.

Saml.

[1] The trip had been planned in January (12 Jan 71 to OLC).

[2] Although Clemens had announced his decision to "do up Nevada & Cal." on 15 July 1870, he had not begun writing *Roughing It* until late August. And there had been several long interruptions since then (15 July 70 to OC; 4 Sept 70 to Bliss).

To James Redpath
28 June 1871 • Elmira, N.Y.
(MS: MH-H)

Elmira, June 28.

Dear Redpath—

1. Yes, "where a *literal* construction of instructions would cause you to make a longer trip by rail, we shall of course use a certain amount of discretion"—is right. I'll allow that latitude, of course.

2. All right. Lecture me with whom you please in Washington—I like the G. A. R. there exceedingly well.[1]

3. No *sir*, no Covenanters—no speculators—nothing but regular societies.[2] I hate speculators & charities. That reminds me that that Syracuse application looks dangerously like a private thing.

4. Trenton is nothing but private speculation—no association—I'd rather, infinitely, leave the night unoccupied than go there. I don't like that to talk for speculators at all—with them it is a monkey show one night & a lecture the next.

5. All right. Call it $100 to $150 as a general thing outside of N. E., but $100 will put me in a heap of one-horse hotels I fear. But your head is doubtless level. I could draw like the devil in Chicago, any place west of New York State, & get good prices. But whether you send me west or not I guess I will leave to your discretion & take the chances. If you *should* conclude to send me west, don't let it be further than St. Louis. I leave you without on other limit or restriction than that, west, & Washington South.

6. Leave Buffalo *out*, altogether, & make some plausible excuse. I think they hate me there, for hating their town. We are offered $20,000 for our dwelling house there, & if, in 3 months no better offer comes, we shall take it ~~&~~ and "mosey."[3] Then it wouldn't *do* to go back there & lecture.

7. Fredonia, N. Y., paid Brick Pomeroy $150, & I won't talk there for a cent less. I mention the town because my mother & sister live there & I have often been invited there to lecture & may be again. Would like to talk there very much & see the folks, but won't for less than $150. One must be allowed an hour ~~& a half~~ to get there in, from Dunkirk, & another hour to get back in—& after lecture you have to *hustle*, too, to catch the train.[4]

8. ~~I~~ Be chary of Rondout. One has to cross the river in the ice in a rubbishy ferry.

9. The N. Y. idea *is* good but not practicable, I guess. I wouldn't go into the speculation with any but the very cream of the platform—no whores & scrubs.[5]

10. My lecture will be my new one—"Reminiscences of Some un⸗ Commonplace Characters I have ~~Met.~~ ⸜chanced to meet." Put it that way.⸜ I shall deliver no lecture but that. By the time I have talked it in 12 towns, & got the hang of it, I'll engage to plug the bull's eye with it, every time. "You hear *me!*" [Were you serious in suggesting that rubbishy Sandwich Island hogwash for another campaign?]

11. Charge Elmira Anna Dickinson's price, whatever it is. She will not object to revealing it.

12. Charge Rochester & Cleveland Anna's price—& Toledo too, I should say. ⸜I am a tolerably fair card in the latter.⸝ ⸜N.B. **Sock it to Hartford!**—but **secure** Hartford, anyway.⸝[6]

I dasn't write the way you suggest. That would put *me* in a scrape, which is the next baddest thing to ~~leaving~~ ⸜having⸝ *you* in one. Hang it, why do you sleep in the day-time? Why didn't you know enough to speak up promptly & say, "*We* have engaged Mark for his first lecture, but you can have him for his *second*"? Talking in that church may make my Boston appearance a thing without eclat or importance & really damage me in New England. Therefore, you being the party that did it, must do what you unoffendingly & persuasively can to *un-*do it. Show him the enclosed—let the raped Fall shed some tears & heave some sighs—move that obdurate secretary—enlarge upon ⸜the⸝ lucrativeness of the *second* delivery, & maybe you'll fetch him.

I *dasn't* throw mud at his course, belittle his concern, & go back on my agent. Is thy servant a dog, that he should do this thing? No—perish the lecturer that would dishonor his ~~g~~ agent! ~~Let~~ Lay for that secretary— & when he looms upon your vision, *go* for him![7]

Ys Ever
Mark.

P. S. Let's not help educate any more Jamaica Plains niggers, this year! Hey?[8]

[*enclosure:*]

Elmira, June 28.

Dear Redpath:

You are making me break a promise which I made to Fall months ago. I ~~told~~ ₐengaged withₐ him that if I lectured ~~next~~ this season in Boston, I would talk *first* in the Lyceum course. When he gets home will he approve of your putting me first in the South-End course? Either way, *I* am satisfied; & if Fall objects, you can tell him what I believe is the truth—that if my new lecture draws half a house on its first delivery, it will *fill* the next one, whether it be the next week or the next month. I may be deceived in my estimate of its ability to get the advantage of pretty much *all* classes & sorts of people, but I don't really think I am. I never liked that stupid Sandwich Island lecture, but I do like this one. I won't insure it a good Boston house for the first hearing, but I will insure it a good house for the second.

Speak to Fall about this. I didn't mention the promise to you—it wasn't *my* matter, you know—but why didn't *he*̸! Aha! *You* break my promises—it isn't

Ys Truly
Mark, by
a ~~damed~~ darned sight!

Tell him *Gough* speaks twice everywhere.

✉—————————————————————————————

[*letter docketed:*] *Twain* Mark. | June 28[th.]

[1] The Grand Army of the Republic had sponsored Clemens's successful 8 December 1869 lecture in Washington (*L3*, 437, 438–39 n. 8).

[2] Presumably Redpath had been approached by a Presbyterian organization, named after the Scottish party that made several covenants in the sixteenth and seventeenth centuries to preserve the Presbyterian faith as Scotland's sole religion. But Clemens wished to speak exclusively for established lecture societies that sponsored a full season of lectures and could guarantee an audience and fee (8 Jan 70 to Redpath).

[3] The Clemenses originally hoped to recoup the full $25,000 purchase price of the house (3 Mar 71 to Riley; 10 Mar 71 to OC).

[4] Redpath charged $150 for Clemens's 8 December 1871 lecture in Fredonia. Marcus M. (Brick) Pomeroy (1833–96), journalist, author, and occasional humorist, was not represented by the Boston Lyceum Bureau. During the Civil War, Pomeroy, a Democrat who initially supported the Union cause, had become notorious for front-line correspondence highly critical of the Union command. He was nearly lynched in 1865 for publishing an editorial in his own newspaper, the La Crosse (Wis.) *Union and Democrat,* "hoping that if President Lincoln did not keep the pledges made by him in his second inaugural some daring hand would strike a poniard into his breast" ("Won Fame and Fortune," New York *Times,* 13 Apr 96, 9). The editorial was widely republished after Lincoln's assassination, and Pomeroy earned still further notoriety with his subsequent paper, the New York *Democrat,* which was subsidized by and represented the interests of the Tweed ring, although he severed that association before 1871. In December 1871, the Fredonia *Censor* reproached its Democratic rival, the Dunkirk *Advertiser and Union,* by comparing Clemens's lecture with Pomeroy's controversial performance:

> It is but fair to inform our cotemporary that Mr. Clemens never made any proposition to the Lecture Committee to lecture here in consideration of Brick Pomeroy being discarded from the course. Neither will it alleviate the disgust at Pomeroy's effort here to compare it with Twain's. The latter, though it disappointed the audience, contained nothing that could offend the most fastidious. Pomeroy's talk was much of it a downright insult to the ladies and religious portion of his listeners. They ought to have risen *en masse* and left the hall, and many regret that they didn't. ("The Advertiser on Twain," 20 Dec 71, 3)

The subject and date of Pomeroy's lecture are not known (Redpath and Fall 1871–72, 7–8; Eubank, 297–300; "The Reform Democracy," New York *Times,* 6 Oct 71, 5; "'Brick' Pomeroy Dead," New York *Tribune,* 31 May 96, 7; Rowell, 694–95).

[5] See 10 June 71 to Redpath and Fall.

[6] Redpath did not schedule lectures for Clemens in Elmira, Rochester, or Cleveland, but did engage him in both Hartford and Toledo for $150 on 8 November and 11 December, respectively. Anna Dickinson's fee in Hartford during the 1871–72 season was $200, although she spoke in many other cities for $150. Clemens had lectured successfully in Toledo on 20 January 1869 (Redpath and Fall 1871–72, 3–4, 7–8; Chester, 103; *L3,* 51–52).

[7] Redpath had evidently informed Clemens that he had booked him to lecture twice in Boston, mistakenly scheduling the first appearance in the small lecture course in the city's fashionable South End, rather than in the Boston Lyceum Bureau's own course at Music Hall. South End lecturers spoke in the Congregationalist-Unitarian Church of the Disciples, an "unpretentious, roomy edifice" at the corner of West Brookline and Warren avenues. Music Hall, on the other hand, was "the largest and finest hall" in the city, with seating for twenty-six hundred (King: 1885, 191; 1883, 303–4). Redpath's proposed solution to the problem apparently required a letter from Clemens insisting that the South End lecture be rescheduled to follow the Music Hall performance. Clemens's enclosed letter, to be shown to the secretary of the South End course, was a stratagem to achieve the same end without giving offense or attaching serious blame to anybody. The problem was not immediately resolved: see 10 July 71 to Redpath (1st and 2nd) (*Boston Directory* 1871, 896; King 1883, 434–35; Boston

Evening Transcript: "Boston Lyceum—Music Hall," 1 Nov 71, 4; "South End Lectures," 13 Nov 71, 4).

[8]Clemens had lectured on 19 November 1869 for "the benefit of a Benevolent Educational Enterprise" in Jamaica Plain, a suburb of Boston which, after the coming of the railroad and industrial development to adjacent areas, was in the 1870s an "upper middle class residential settlement" ("Unique Entertainment by Mark Twain," Boston *Evening Transcript*, 13 Nov 69, 1; Warner, 41–42).

To Orion Clemens
29 June 1871 • Elmira, N.Y.
(MS: CU-MARK)

Elmira 29th

Dear Bro:

From a remark of either yours or Mollie's in a letter to Pamela it would seem that I have sent "one of three articles" to Mr. Bliss. I sent *all 3* in one envelop—no more are to go. Haven't the 3 arrived?[1]

Ma has been making mischief, I fear—& without good grounds. I said I would not be stupid enough to offer an *opinion*, or even try to *form* an definite & conclusive one, upon a matter which a man had put all his mind & heart on for four years & I had only looked into for 2 hours. I said I wanted to see the machine working in the water first. My opinion ~~upon~~ ,of, the machine's merits would *now* ,(in the machine's incomplete stage), be worth nothing at all—my crude *conjectures* about it are certainly worth *less* than nothing.

Fools who never wrote a book are always giving me their infernal advice about how to write a book—& with this exasperation always before me I am slow to let on to know more about another man's business than he knows himself. I may have conjectured considerable to Pamela—I don't remember, now—but my main idea was that I was not competent or worthy to express an *opinion*, at all.[2] Love to Mollie

Ys affly
Sam.

P. S. Wrote 2 chapters of the book to-day—shall write chapter 53 to= morrow.[3] My ,new, lecture is the best one I ever wrote I think,—the one about characters I have met. Have ~~now one, & shall perhaps have~~ 2 Boston engagements at $250 a night. Charge the same in Phila. & N. Y. and Brooklyn[4]

—∿∿—

Orion Clemens Esq | 149 Asylum st | Hartford | Conn. [*return address:*]
IF NOT DELIVERED WITHIN 10 DAYS, TO BE RETURNED TO [*postmarked:*] ELMIRA
N.Y. JUN 30

¹See 21 June 71 to Bliss. On 4 July, Orion replied: "There is some mistake as
to somebody's meaning about the *MSS*. They have all three arrived, and I never
meant to be understood otherwise. I have read them all" (CU-MARK).
²Jane Clemens and Pamela Moffett had evidently passed along Clemens's reservations about Orion's boat invention, expressed in a letter to them (now lost).
On 4 July, Orion assured Clemens:

> The letter you refer to did no great harm. After a day's sky-colored absent-
> mindedness I considered that your opportunities for judging of the concern were not
> so good as mine, and went ahead. . . .
> I knew when I showed you the machine, it *must* produce some kind of an impres-
> sion. It might or might not be favorable. In my own view, even after all the study I have
> given the subject there are some points in relation to which I, like yourself, will not feel
> entirely satisfied till I see a little working model in the water. (CU-MARK)

Clemens had seen Orion's invention while in Hartford in early June (7 June 71
to OC and MEC).
³The two chapters, which Clemens evidently numbered 51 and 52 at this
time, probably later became chapter 54 (which Clemens had perhaps begun but
put aside earlier in the month) and chapter 55 of *Roughing It*. Clemens's chapter
53, which he hoped to complete in one day, probably became chapter 56 in the
published book (*RI 1993*, 857).
⁴Clemens received $250 in Boston on 1 November and in Philadelphia on 20
November. He received $150 for his second Boston lecture on 13 November, for
a Brooklyn appearance on 21 November, and for his New York City lecture on
24 January 1872 (Redpath and Fall 1871–72, 3–6, 13–14).

To Mary Mason Fairbanks
29 June 1871 • Elmira, N.Y.
(MS: CSmH)

Elmira, 29ᵗʰ·

Dear Mother:

It was *hard* to give up the Cleveland trip—& after the letter was
written¹ & given to Crane to mail, we so hated to give it up that we lay &
talked till midnight about it & then went & woke Crane & told him not
to mail it, but give us one more day to try to contrive the journey——so
we tried all ways, but no use—I couldn't dare make another break in my

work lest I fail entirely. So we reluctantly shipped the l/etter. Don't do anything to weaken our resolution, because it has been mighty hard to arrive at it & it would be awful to have to go through the wear & tear of it again.

I ẃ have written a lecture which I just know will "fetch" any audience I spout it before. I do hope to talk it before you in Cleveland.[2] You shall say it is tip-top. I call it "Reminiscences of some Un-Commonplace Characters I have Chanced to Meet." It tells a ˌpersonalˌ memory or so of Artemus Wardˌ; ~~Riley~~ Blucher, an eccentric, big-hearted newspaper man;[3] the King of the Sandwich Islands;[4] Dick Baker, California Miner, & his wonderful cat;[5] Dr. Jackson & the Guides;[6] the Emperor Norton, a pathetic San Franciscan lunatic;[7] Blucher & our Washington landlady, a story I told in the Galaxy;[8] ~~the~~ a grand oriental absolute monarch, the Rajah of Borneo;[9] ~~the~~ our interview with the Emperor of Russia, about as I told it before—didn't alter it ˌ(a great deal)ˌ because it always "took" on the platform in that shape;[10] & Blucher's curious adventure with a beggar. I give this man the name of Blucher merely for convenience.[11]

Of course you can't tell much about the lecture from this, but see what a splendid field it offers, & you know what a fascination there is in *personal* matters, & what a charm the *narrative* form carries with it.

Lovingly yr son

Sam'.

[1] See 27 June 71 to Fairbanks.

[2] The 1871–72 tour did not include a Cleveland appearance.

[3] Probably adapted from "Riley—Newspaper Correspondent" (8 July 70 to OLC, n. 2; 28 Nov 70 to Bliss, n. 1).

[4] Kamehameha V (1830–72), whom Clemens hoped to meet on a visit to Iolani Palace on 4 April 1866, but evidently saw only once, at a royal funeral. Clemens made both complimentary and uncomplimentary remarks about the king in his 1866 notebooks and newspaper letters, but finally held a high opinion of him (*N&J1*, 98–233 passim; *RI 1993*, 717; SLC 1866b, d–f, 1873d).

[5] See 26 Jan 70 to Gillis, n. 5.

[6] Clemens described Abraham Reeves Jackson's guide-baiting techniques in chapter 27 of *The Innocents Abroad* (*L2*, 65–66).

[7] Joshua A. Norton had proclaimed himself "Norton I, Emperor of the United States" in the late 1850s (*L1*, 324–25 n. 2; Hart 1987, 354–55). In 1880, Clemens wrote:

> O, dear, it was always a painful thing to me to see the Emperor (Norton I., of San Francisco) begging; for although nobody else believed he was an Emperor, *he* believed it. . . . Nobody has ever written him up who was able to see any but his ~~ludicrous or his~~ grotesque side; but I think that with all his dirt & unsavoriness there was a pathetic side to him. Anybody who said so in print would be laughed at in S. F., doubtless, but no

matter . . . ; I have seen him in *all* his various moods & tenses, & there was always more room for pity than laughter. (3 Sept 80 to Howells, MH-H, in *MTHL*, 1:326)

[8] Clemens first told this anecdote in an 1868 letter to the Chicago *Republican* and in 1870 retold it in "Riley—Newspaper Correspondent." The subject is the lament of an "oppressively emotional" and "morbidly sentimental" landlady for a neighbor's servant who was "'a-sitting over the red-hot stove at three o'clock in the morning and went to sleep and fell on it and was actually *roasted!* not just frizzled up a bit, but literally roasted to a crisp!'" The landlady asks Riley to suggest an appropriate epitaph: "'Put it "*Well done,* good and faithful servant!"'" said Riley, and never smiled" (SLC: 1870hhh, 727; 1868c).

[9] Joseph W. Torrey (1828–84) was an American merchant who, in 1865, acquired a ten-year concession on a large tract of land in northern Borneo. The local sultan conferred the titles of Rajah of Ambong and Marudu and Sir Maharajah of North Borneo upon Torrey. In late 1865 he established a small colony as a base for trading operations, but it was abandoned before the end of 1866. Although never formally encouraged by the United States government, Torrey continued to exploit his concession until 1881 (L. R. Wright, 49–55, 116, 142–43, 165; Tregonning, 6–12, 24–25; *MTMF*, 155–56 n. 7). Clemens had met Torrey in March of 1868 while traveling by ship from New York to San Francisco (*N&J1*, 496–97):

> We established a Jokers' Society, and fined every member who furnished an unbearably bad joke. We tried one man for his life (the Rajah of Borneo), for building a conundrum of unwarranted atrocity. Mr. Cohen disliked his trunk, and often spoke angrily of its small size. The conundrum touched upon this matter:
> "Why is one of the passengers, or his trunk, like a certain geographical, algebraical, geometrical, technical term? Answer—Because he is a truncated cone (trunk-hated Cohen)."
> We hung him. (SLC 1868c)

[10] Clemens described the encounter of the *Quaker City* passengers with Tsar Aleksandr II in his 1868–69 "American Vandal Abroad" lecture ("Mark Twain," Chicago *Republican*, 8 Jan 69, 4; "Mark Twain's Lecture," Peoria *Transcript*, 12 Jan 69, 3; Fatout 1976, 27–36). See also 30 May 70 to Bliss, n. 3.

[11] Still another anecdote about Riley, this time recalling an occasion when he treated a beggar to an elaborate meal while destitute himself. Clemens used it in chapter 59 of *Roughing It* (*RI 1993*, 407–11).

To Pierre Reynolds
July? 1871 • Elmira, N.Y.
(CU-MARK)

I only make them at funerals & places where I wish to ~~f~~ feel sad.[1]

Yrs. Truly

Sam[^l]. L. Clemens

(Mark Twain)

[1] This letter has been dated on the basis of the paper, ink, and handwriting, which are similar to those in the next letter. Accompanying it is the following explanation by H. M. Reynolds of Glendale, California, dated 18 June 1929:

> In the early seventies I had the autograph craze badly and secured many from men and women of national reputation. My cousin Pierre Reynolds was collecting at same time, and those that he secured later came to me. Pierre wrote to Mr Clemens asking that he make a pun for him. This is the reply. Along about 1910, for some reason I had taken the autograph to the store, and left it there in a desk drawer for some little time. While there a wandering rat one night located it and chewed a while on it, luckily damaging one corner only.

To Orion Clemens
2 July 1871 • Elmira, N.Y.
(MS: CU-MARK)

Elmira, July 2

Dear Bro—

My MSS? Shall bring it there myself before long. Say 2 to 4 weeks hence. Am just finishing Chapter 56.[1] Have already nearly MS enough, but am still st writing—intend to cut & cull liberally.[2]

Yrs
Sam

Orion Clemens Esq | 149 Asylum st | Hartford | Conn. [*postmarked:*] EL-MIRA N.Y. JUL 5

[1] Chapter 59 in the published book. If Clemens was still writing in sequence, he had completed four chapters in three days (29 June 71 to OC, n. 3; *RI 1993*, 860).

[2] Clemens was in fact only about three-fourths done, lacking about 450 of the 1800 pages he estimated were necessary to complete the book (*RI 1993*, 860).

To James N. Gillis
2 July 1871 • Elmira, N.Y.
(MS facsimile: CU-MARK)

Elmira, N. Y. July 2.

Dear Jim:

I am here for a months visit, from Buffalo.[1] I have only a minute to write in, but I can ask what I want to ask & say what I want to say in that time—to wit:

1. How are you?

2. How is splendid old Dick,?[2]

3. I have long ago sold out of the Express & so I suppose that worthless sheet has ceased to go to you[3]—but I am here, close to bookstores & newspapers, & you & Dick ain't; & if you will send me your address (in case you have moved & this reaches you,) I'll be proud & happy to send you any book or paper your solitude needs—for I am under large obligations to you & Dick for some pleasant old times.[4] ~~Indeed, I am under a Indeed, a suspicion comes over me that I owe you either $25 or $50. It was in this way. When I went up to your camp, I took $300 with me. We spent that for hash, & for expenses at Angels—which was correct; it about paid my board with you & old Dick. But when I went back to the Bay I was not able to pay all that I owed your Mother.~~[5]

4. Say, old philosopher, would you like to read Darwin? If you would, let me know, & I will get the books & forward them to you.[6]

How many more New Year's are going to roll round to us, in this life, & remind us of the night at Vallecito, Jim?[7]

Yr friend, just as of old,
Saml. L. Clemens

Love to old Dick!

───

——————————————————————————————

James N. Gillis Esq | Sonora | California [*postmarked:*] ELMIRA N.Y. JUL 5

[1] That is, a month *more*. Clemens had already been in Elmira for more than three months.

[2] Stoker.

[3] See 3 Mar 71 to Riley, n. 3, and 18 Apr 71 to Fairbanks, n. 1.

[4] For the best record of Clemens's December 1864–February 1865 sojourn with Jim Gillis and Dick Stoker in Jackass Hill and Angel's Camp, see his notebook for the period (*N&J1*, 63–90). He was obliged to Gillis for a number of stories and tall tales that found their way into *Roughing It* and other works (26 Jan 70 to Gillis, n. 5).

[5] Margaret Alston Gillis (1810–76) had run a boarding house in San Francisco on Brannan Street in 1864, and then at 44 Minna Street with her husband, Angus, in 1865. Although the 1864 San Francisco directory, published in October, does not show Clemens living with the Gillis family, he moved frequently during 1864 and must have moved in with them before his departure for Jackass Hill in early December. The 1865 directory shows Clemens at the Minna Street address, and Margaret Gillis was almost certainly the "generous landlady" he recalled in chapter 59 of *Roughing It*, which he had just completed (William R. Gillis to Harry A. Williams, 31 May 1924, PH in CU-MARK; Langley: 1864, 106, 174; 1865, 121, 195; *L1*, 313–14 n. 3; *RI 1993*, 404).

[6] Charles Darwin's *Descent of Man* was published in the United States in two volumes in February and March 1871 (New York: D. Appleton and Co.). Clemens, who bought his own copy of at least the first volume, had certainly read it by this time, and had probably done so by early April when he was revising chapter 19 of *Roughing It*, which alludes to Darwin's theory (*RI 1993*, 127, 606).

[7] See 26 Jan 70 to Gillis, n. 2.

To Orion Clemens
7 July 1871 • Elmira, N.Y.
(MS: NPV)

Elmira, 7th

~~The~~ Dear Bro:

Look in the library—any late work on paleontology will furnish the facts. I got mine from an article in Chamber's Edinburgh Journal (have lost it since.)[1]

It w[d] be a good idea to print such an article in the same issue with mine.

Ys

Sam

[1] On 4 July, Orion had written in regard to Clemens's "Brace of Brief Lectures on Science": "I had some notion in relation to the scientific lectures to comment editorially, taking extracts from the books to verify your statements if you will let me know where they came from. I like them, but people will think you made

the whole thing, maybe—text as well as commentary" (CU-MARK). Orion did in fact comment, drawing his information from Louis Figuier's *Primitive Man* (1870), which had been reviewed and extracted at length in *Chambers's Journal* for 13 August 1870, Clemens's source (21 June 71 to Bliss, nn. 2, 4; OC 1871f; "Our Earliest Ancestors," *Chambers's Journal of Popular Literature, Science, and Art* 47:521–24).

To James Redpath
7–8 July 1871 • Elmira, N.Y.

(MS: TxU)

Dear Redpath—

You seem to blame *me* for changing my lecture title—but if it ~~w~~ is a blamable offense it is yours, not mine. You see, I was well satisfied with my Boy Appeal, but you seemed to doubt, & suggested my *old* lectures in such a way that it scared me & I set about bettering the condition of things (thin~~g~~king I had a week or two to make up my mind in.) The result was that I wrote a second lecture. Before it was cold I grew dissatisfied with it. I wrote a third (the one about People I have ~~m~~Met,) & being *thoroughly & completely* satisfied with it, I naturally chose it & wrote you—(imagining that you w^{d} prefer that I deliver a good lecture rather than a poor one.) Now I am sure that it would be good judgment to change a lecture even after all the contracts were made, when one has such good grounds as mine in this instance. Are you still angry, now that you perceive that it was you that unsettled me about the first lecture?[1]

Yrs
Clemens

[*letter docketed:*] BOSTON LYCEUM BUREAU. REDPATH & FALL. JUL 10 1871 [*and*] *Twain* Mark | Elmira N.Y. Recd 7/10

[1] The change in lecture title had come after Redpath issued the 1871–72 *Lyceum Magazine* and began contracting for engagements (15 June 71, 27 June 71 [1st and 2nd], all to Redpath). In 1869 Clemens had made a similar late change, with annoying consequences (15 Sept 71 to Redpath, n. 5).

To Elisha Bliss, Jr.
10 July 1871 • Elmira, N.Y.
(MS: OClRC)

Elmira, July 10.

Dear Bliss:

I heard you were sick, & am glad you are getting better again.[1]

What terms did you arrive at with Routledge?[2]

Yes, I told Orion he could borrow small amounts on my account, at intervals, outside the pay for those 3 articles. So it is all right.[3]

Tomorrow I will fix up & forward as much MS as I have on hand. Some of it is tip-top.[4]

I am now waiting a day or two till I get my old Sandwich Island notes together, for I want to put in 4 or 5 chapters about the Islands for the benefit of New England—& the world.[5] When that is finished I shall come on & we will cull & cut down the MS & sock the book into the press. I think it will be a book worth reading, duly aided by the pictures. I am not scared about the result. It will sell.

I think of calling it

Ⴕ FLUSH TIMES
in the
SILVER MINES,
& other Matters.

====

A PERSONAL NARRATIVE.

====

By Mark Twain.
(Sam'. L. Clemens.)

———

How does it strike you? Offer a suggestion, if one occurs to you.

Good! We'll run the tilt with Beecher.[6]

Ys

Mark.

✉——————————————————————————————

[*letter docketed:*] √ [*and*] Twain | Elmira 1869 | Auth

[1] Clemens was replying to Bliss's letter of 7 July (CU-MARK):

Dear Clemens,

        Thanks for your contributions   I have been sick 10 days, flat on my back, most of the time—& feel hard yet.

        Will pay O. as you say $12.50 pr week. He says & shows me a letter in which you say he can draw some more on your a/c beside this, he says 5 or 10 dolls. as he wants. As you say in yours, pay him *no more* than the $12.50—"I halt between 2 opinions" of course I should let him have it, but simply felt I should mention it to you. Unless you say to the contrary, shall consider it all O. K— Have got the engravings mill driving—& shall make a merry book of it   And now, would like all the Mss. you have to be able to select subjects for *full page engravings*—want all I can of those to go in the book ,prospectus,— And now another thing we have said nothing about. What is to be the title— This is a matter of some importance you know, & necessary for the Prospectus, unless we say we dont know it yet & call it the "*Unnamed*" & wait for developments—to christen it—

        Let me have your ideas early as possible— Shall have prospectus ready early as possible to get the cuts ready, & make a sweep of the board—this fall— This & Beecher's Life of Christ—will have the field & I'll bet *we win*—

[2] Probably by this time Bliss had come to terms with George Routledge and Sons for an English edition of *Roughing It* to appear "simultaneously" with the American edition. Clemens was paid a nominal fee of £37 ($185) for the English rights (*RI 1993*, 876–77).

[3] See 21 June 71 to OC and MEC.

[4] If Clemens actually sent this batch of manuscript, his fourth, it probably consisted of what became chapters 54–57, and may have included chapters 76 and 78 if they had not already been delivered in June (*RI 1993*, 815, 861–62).

[5] Clemens evidently meant to make use of his 1866 notebooks, scrapbooks, Sacramento *Union* letters, and almost certainly the printer's copy for an unpublished book on the Sandwich Islands he had prepared from the *Union* letters in 1866–67. Instead of "4 or 5 chapters," however, he included fifteen chapters on the Sandwich Islands, all but four of them based on his *Union* letters (*RI 1993*, 862).

[6] Another subscription house, J. B. Ford and Company of New York, canvassed Henry Ward Beecher's two-volume *Life of Jesus, the Christ,* the first volume of which was published in September 1871, before and during the American Publishing Company's canvass for *Roughing It,* which began in early December (*RI 1993*, 861, 874–75).

~~To George L. Fall~~
To James Redpath
10 July 1871 • (1st of 3) • Elmira, N.Y.
(MS: ViU)

                                          Elmira, July 10.

Dear ~~F~~ Redpath:

        Excuse my delay. Your long letter about routes, engagements, &c, received. I will reply at the earliest leisure hour.

You know I never interfere with my agents after once giving them my instructions in detail, & my notions about business. But I must put down my foot on that Boston business. I expected to speak in Music Hall (Fall promised I should), & I must speak there *first* if I am to speak in Boston at all. It might seriously hurt my season to be called to open elsewhere in the chief city of New England, & I fear to run such a risk.[1]

Now you must arrange this in some way. I am cheerfully willing to speak for the South End course second, but not first. I am looking at the matter purely from a *business* point of view, & wholly without prejudice toward the South End. Mr. Dana's acquaintance with the lecture ẇ business ~~wh~~ will easily enable him to understand my position. If he will take the second delivery, I will ~~lee~~ knock $200 off my price & lecture for the South End for $50.[2]

I am sorry to interfere, but this should be fixed at once. Don't Nasby, Phillips,[3] Dickinson, & others speak more than once¿?

Yrs

Mark Twain.

[*letter docketed:*] BOSTON LYCEUM BUREAU. REDPATH & FALL. JUL 15 1871 [*and*] *Twain* Mark | Elmira July 10

[1] See 28 June to Redpath, n. 7.

[2] Thomas Dana II—of Thomas Dana and Company, wholesale grocers—was the secretary of the South End Course. He may have agreed rather easily to the rescheduling proposed here, since Clemens received $150 for the "second delivery" on 13 November (*Boston Directory* 1871, 204; Redpath and Fall 1871–72, 3–4).

[3] Wendell Phillips (1811–84), whom Clemens had met in Elmira at the Langdon house in March 1869, had first won fame in the late 1830s for his eloquent and impassioned antislavery oratory. After the Civil War he advocated a wide variety of reforms, including equal rights for women, temperance, Irish Home Rule, and the better treatment of Indians. By 1873, if not earlier, Redpath engaged some of his speakers, including Phillips, to lecture three times in Boston (*L3*, 175; Eubank, 148–50).

To James Redpath
10 July 1871 • (2nd of 3) • Elmira, N.Y.
(MS: DLC)

Elmira, July 10.

Dear Redpath:

A more careful reading of your late letter has set me thinking, & I *do* plainly see in that Southend business *calamity* for my lecture season. I *never* made a success of a lecture delivered in a church yet. People are afraid to laugh in a church. They can't be *made* to do it, in any possible way. And Lord knows it wasn't "business" to ~~pay~~ start me in my most important city in an obscure course, & that, too, in a church. What could you have been thinking about? Seems to me that an agent would feel the importance of a first-rate start for his ~~clin~~ client—is that correct?

Hang it, ~~if~~ the Southend business looks more & more fatal, the more I think of it. We *must* get rid of it, even if I have to write the proposed letter—which is a heavy pill to take, there is no question about that. Can't you fix it some way, so as to get me liberated without prejudice? I certainly haven′ nothing against that society, but to talk elsewhere than in Music Hall & in a big course may ruin me. But if ′ everything else fails, present the letter & let the heavens fall.

Read over the enclosed, & if you want it altered, return it & state the alterations.[1]

Yrs
Mark.

————————————————————————————

[*letter docketed:*] BOSTON LYCEUM BUREAU. REDPATH & FALL. JUL 15 1871 [*and*] *Twain* Mark | Elmira 7/10 '71

[1]Clemens's enclosure, a draft of a letter of withdrawal from the South End appearance to be used in case the rescheduling could not be negotiated, is not known to survive and proved unnecessary (see the previous letter, n. 2).

To James Redpath
10 July 1871 • (3rd of 3) • Elmira, N.Y.
(MS: Bentley)

10th

P. S.—

The title is: "Reminiscences of Some un-Commonplace P̌ Characters I have Chanced to Meet."

Is it too long? I fear it is, but don't know how to better it.

I have no MS sketch that is good. Shall I send you an old re-print one that is choice? If so, how long a one?[1]

Ys

Mark.

[*letter docketed:*] BOSTON LYCEUM BUREAU. REDPATH & FALL. JUL 15 1871 [*and*] *Twain* Mark | Title of Lecture | July 10

[1] Redpath was evidently planning a "Lyceum Circular" that would give the new title of Clemens's lecture and print a short literary piece as well as, presumably, reviews from his previous lecture tour (in 1869–70). The Boston Lyceum Bureau regularly issued such circulars for its clients. None has been found for Mark Twain in 1871, but a mid-season circular, dated 1 January 1872, contained reviews of the season to date, and announced still further changes in his lecture title (see Appendix D).

To James Redpath
14 July 1871 • Elmira, N.Y.
(Will M. Clemens 1900, 28)

Elmira, July 14.

Dear Redpath:

Don't lecture me at Jamestown, N. Y., unless Providence compels you. I suppose all lecturers hate that place.[1]

Shall be in Hartford 3 or 4 weeks hence & then I shall run up & bum around with you a day or two if you ain't busy.[2]

Yours,

Mark.

[1]Clemens's 21 January 1870 lecture in Jamestown had come under attack as part of a debate over which lecturers and lecture topics were appropriate, and how lecturers and lecture committees should be treated in the press (20 Feb 70 to Langdon, n. 2). Moreover, Clemens was dissatisfied with his performance, which he later characterized as "a poor lecture, & the first delivered poorly delivered; for I was fagged with railway travel" (SLC 1886). Redpath did not schedule a Jamestown lecture for 1871–72.

[2]Clemens spent most of the month of August in Hartford, but evidently did not go to Boston.

To James Redpath
19 July 1871 • Elmira, N.Y.
(MS: Axelrod)

Elmira, July 19.

Dear Redpath—

I'll speak in time. You have made no appointments for me west of Cleveland—very well, *don't.*

When I think of those awful western roads & hotel[s] I get sick—sick as death.

My season is so short that we can fill it up pretty well from Cleveland east.[1]

Have just declined a month in Kansas &c at $150 a night.[2]

Mind you charge Nasby prices—Rondout ¢ $125 wasn't, was it? *YES.*[3]

Ys

Mark

Say—am I aggravating you now, & disarranging your matters? I do hope not.

[letter docketed:] BOSTON LYCEUM BUREAU. REDPATH & FALL. AUG 3 1871 [and]
Twain Mark | Elmira N.Y. | July 19 '71

[1] Redpath's *Lyceum Magazine* announced: "Mr. Clemens has consented to lecture this season for a brief series of engagements between the middle of October and the end of January only. This, he assures us, will be positively his last season on the platform" (*Lyceum* 1871, 20). Clemens's tour lasted from 16 October 1871 to 27 February 1872, about the same length of time as his 1868–69 tour (nineteen weeks), but much longer than his 1869–70 tour (eleven weeks), which he had cut short in order to get married on 2 February. The 1871–72 tour was the most solidly booked, comprising some seventy-seven lectures compared with forty-three and about fifty, respectively, in 1868–69 and 1869–70 (Appendix C; *L3*, 481–86).

[2] This offer may have come from the Associated Western Literary Societies, which had managed the midwestern portion of Clemens's 1868–69 tour, or from O. Sackett, of Kansas City, on behalf of his Western Lyceum Bureau, which had recently represented Horace Greeley and was currently recruiting Kate Field and others for its roster. Clemens was apparently free to accept offers from regions that the Boston Lyceum Bureau did not routinely serve. But the bureau, which had opened in 1868 to handle bookings in the New England and mid-Atlantic states, was currently extending its reach. It tentatively scheduled some western, or midwestern, appearances for Clemens and by late 1871 it established a branch office in Chicago (8 Aug 71 to Redpath; *L3*, 481; Kate Field to Whitelaw Reid, 6 Nov 70, DLC; Eubank, 99, 114, 122–24).

[3] Added at the Boston Lyceum Bureau by an unknown hand. For Nasby's prices, see 10 June 71 to Redpath and Fall, n. 2.

To George L. Fall
20 July 1871 • Elmira, N.Y.
(AAA 1925, lot 28; *MTL*, 1:189–90)

Elmira, July 20.

Friend Fall:

Redpath tells me to blow you up. Here goes! I wanted you to scare Rondout off with a big price. $125 ain't big. I got $100 the first time I ever talked there, & now they've a much larger hall. It is a hard town to get to—I run a chance of getting caught by the ice & missing next engagement. Make the price $150, & let them draw out.[1]

Yours,

Mark.

[1] Rondout agreed to pay $150 for Clemens's lecture on 22 November. His previous appearances there had been on 2 December 1868 and 12 January 1870 (Redpath and Fall 1871–72, 5–6; *L2*, 423; *L3*, 486).

To William Bowen
23 July 1871 • Elmira, N.Y.
(MS: ViU)

Elmira, July 23.

Dear Will:

I have been offered ~~$5~~ $150 a night to talk 30 consecutive nights in Missouri & Kansas, but declined, partly because it was not enough & partly because I don't like so much railroad travel. I may talk in St Louis if my agents have already made a contract to that effect, but I hope they have not; for I have concluded to go no further west than Cleveland. Eastern railroading is easier & wages higher ~~in the east~~ than ˌinˌ the west. I am not particularly particular, but every man's duty is to keep up the prices of his ~~$~~ trade, & so I would not like to talk in as large a place as St Louis for less than $250. The other lecturers have never yet had to accuse me of cutting down the wages. I only want to talk 3 months & a half, & so, I think the east better suited to a short season than a long one. I mean to talk ten months on a stretch if I ever start again—which I *do* hope I never shall.[1]

The legislature that gave you a franchise permitting any such By-Law as the one you mention, was an ass.[2]

Good! Let us ~~know,~~ see you in Sept.[3]

My wife is well, but the baby is seriously ill.

Ys

Sam.

---

[1] See 12 June 71 to Bowen.

[2] " 'If the law supposes that, . . . the law is a ass' " (*Oliver Twist*, chapter 51). The "By-Law" has not been identified, but presumably affected the insurance business. Bowen was still working in St. Louis as an agent for the Phoenix Insurance Company (6 Feb 70 to Bowen, n. 1).

[3] The planned visit never took place.

To Adolph H. Sutro
24 July 1871 • Elmira, N.Y.
(MS: CLSU)

Elmira, N. Y. July 24

Dear Sutro:

Give me your address—I want to write you.[1]

Ys Truly

Saml. L. Clemens

[1] Sutro lived in San Francisco at 908 Jackson Street, but Clemens may have mailed this letter to the Sutro Tunnel Company, at 625 Montgomery Street, requesting on the envelope that it be forwarded. Sutro evidently received it in Nevada, where he remained until 15 August. His response reached Clemens on 19 August (19 Aug 71, 24 Aug 71, both to Sutro; Langley 1871, 624; Adolph Sutro, 34).

To Edward P. Ackerman
31 July 1871 • Elmira, N.Y.
(MS: NN)

Private. $\}$

Elmira, July 31.

ₐE. P. Ackerman, Esqₐ[1]

Dear Sir:

My friend Beecher has sent me your note (inquiring into the trustworthiness of my account of his proposed church) & asks me to answer it,—which I do in this wise: In ~~got~~ the first place I heard Mr. Beecher, months ago, describe ₐ(from his pulpit)ₐ the sort of church he desired to have built—& he mentioned every particular that is mentioned in my article, as nearly as I remember, baths & all. Here lately I got from an old personal friend (a member of the building committee,) the details of the projected edifice ~~stri~~ exactly as they are set forth in my article.[2] If I ₐerredₐ anywhere, it was in stating *positively* that the church would be built on that plan, when perhaps I ought not to have gone so far. As ~~close~~ ₐnearₐ as I can come ~~to~~ ₐatₐ it, I did not utter a falsity, in so speaking, but *divulged too much,* considering the fact that building committees' ‚& pastors'‚ powers are not absolute, & that their determinations are best kept to themselves till they are irrevocably compacted into brick & mortar. ‚However, the plan for the church is not likely to be altered.‚

Very Repy Yours

Sam*ᶦ*. L. Clemens.

[1] Edward P. Ackerman of Brooklyn, New York, edited the *Cherub*, a magazine published by J. Latham and Company, patent medicine manufacturers (Wilson 1871, 24; Mott 1957, 39 n. 54; "Mark Twain on the New Beecher Church," Buffalo *Courier*, 16 Sept 71, Supplement, 1).

[2] Ackerman's letter to Thomas K. Beecher has not been found. In "A New Beecher Church," in the July *American Publisher*, Clemens described Beecher's innovations, among them "six *bath-rooms!*—hot and cold water—free tickets issued to any applicant among the unclean of the congregation." The idea was "sound and sensible":

> Many members of all congregations have no good bathing facilities, and are not able to pay for them at the barber-shops without feeling the expense; and yet a luxurious bath is a thing that all civilized beings greatly enjoy and derive healthful benefit from. . . . In speaking of this bath room project, I have revealed a state secret—but I never could keep one of any kind, state or otherwise. Even the congregation were not to know of this matter; the building committee were to leave it unmentioned in their report, but I got hold of it—and from a member of that committee, too—and I had rather part with one of my hind legs than keep still about it. The bath-rooms are unquestionably to be built, and so why not tell it? (SLC 1871m)

Ackerman probably published Clemens's letter in the *Cherub*. It was published in full in the Buffalo *Courier* and in part in the Hartford *Courant*, both on 16 September 1871 ("Mark Twain on the New Beecher Church," Supplement, 1; "Odds and Ends," 2). On 6 December 1871, Beecher wrote to Olivia Clemens in appreciation of the attention Clemens's article had drawn "to the quiet devices of a country parson. . . . I might have preached & printed to no effect, but that Clemens published. Look at him gratefully, therefore & say—well done" (CU-MARK).

To James Redpath
8 August 1871 • Hartford, Conn.
(MS: IC)

Hartford, Tuesday.

Aug. 8[1]

Dear Redpath—

I am different from other women. They have their monthly period once a month, but I have mine once a week, & sometimes oftener.

That is to say, my mind changes that often. People who *have* no mind, can easily be steadfast & firm; but when a man is loaded down to the guards with it, as I am, every heavy sea of foreboding, or inclination, or mayhap indolence, shifts his cargo. See?

Therefore, if you will notice, *one* week I am likely to give rigid instructions to confine me to New England; next week, send me to Arizonia;[2] next week, withdraw my name; next week, give you untrameled swing—& the week following, *modify* it. You must try to keep the run of my mind, Redpath—it is your business, being the agent—& it always was too many for me. It appears to me to be one of the ~~most delicate~~ finest pieces of mechanism I have ever met with. Now about the West. *This* week I am willing that you should retain all the western engagements you have made, & make as many more as will *cluster* well, pay high prices & not cost too hard travel.[3]

But what I shall want *next* week, is still with God.

Let us not profane the mysteries with soiled hands & prying eyes of sin.

Yrs

Mark.

P. S. Shall be here 2 weeks—will run up there when Nasby comes.[4]

✉——————————————————————————

[*letter docketed:*] *Twain* Mark | Hartford, Conn | Aug. 8 '71 [*and*] *8/9.71*

[1] Clemens had left Elmira on 2 or 3 August. He spent at least two days in New York City, staying at the St. Nicholas Hotel while shopping for clothes and perhaps attending to other unidentified business. He arrived in Hartford on 5 or 6 August, bringing with him his fifth submission of *Roughing It* printer's copy, about 272 manuscript pages (460 equivalent pages: see 15 May 71 to Bliss, n. 3). While in Hartford he planned to give the book its final shape, cutting or adding material as needed (10 July 71 to Bliss; 10 Aug 71 to OLC; 17 Aug 71 to Greeley; *RI 1993*, 815, 863).

[2] Arizona Territory, the site of recent Indian wars, was unlikely to be included on any lecture itinerary (Appleton 1875, 723–24).

[3] Clemens had considered lecturing as far west as Davenport, Iowa. Ultimately no "western engagements" were retained (10 June 71 to Redpath and Fall; 12 June 71 to Redpath; 23 July 71 to Bowen; Appendix C).

[4] See 14 July 71 to Redpath, n. 2.

To Olivia L. Clemens
8 or 9 August 1871 • Hartford, Conn.
(MS: CU-MARK)

[*first two MS pages (about 187 words) missing*]

it isn't worth while to think about it or talk about it.

Don't fear for us darling. If you are taken away I will love the baby & have a jealous care over him. But let us hope & trust that both you & I shall tend him & watch over him till we are helped from our easy-chairs to the parlor to see his children married. Let us hope that way, sweetheart & try to trust that it will be so. In any case, you need not suffer any uneasiness about that influence you speak of. He shall never come under it. Better poison his body than his soul. Better make a corpse of him than a cur.

Livy dear, it is sad to think of your passing alone through these solemn anniversaries that are so fraught with memories of a happy time & a gracious presence; a noble heart, a beautiful spirit, a love only less than divine; a protecting arm, ~~an unselfish~~ a courage that quieted fear & brought repose, a sympathy so broad & general, & withal so strong & warm, that to possess it is to be that ~~rare that thing, crea rare creation, that~~ rare thing, that jewel of price, a Comforter.[1]

· · · ·

✉————————————————————————————

Mrs. S. L. Clemens | Care Langdon | Elmira | N. Y [*postmarked:*] HARTFORD CT. AUG 9   11 AM [*docketed by OLC:*][2] 5th

[1]Clemens probably wrote this letter soon after arriving in Hartford on 5 or 6 August. He replied to a letter in which Olivia mentioned the anniversary of her father's death on 6 August 1870. The "influence" on Langdon Clemens has not been identified.

[2]Olivia had meticulously numbered Clemens's courtship letters (see *L3*, 473–80). She had now begun a new sequence of numbers for the letters Clemens wrote since leaving Elmira on 2 or 3 August, the first four of which are lost (see the next letter). Only three letters to Olivia since their marriage and before the present letter are known to survive, all without dockets (6 July 70, 8 July 70, 12 Jan 71).

To Olivia L. Clemens
10 August 1871 • Hartford, Conn.
(MS: CU-MARK)

Hartford, 10th.

Livy darling, the dispatch came, & I answered it right away. Funny, ain't it, how the letters hang fire? I have written every day but two, I believe— one day in N. Y., & one since I arrived here. One day I wrote *two* let- ters—one of them brief. Shall do that oftener hereafter.[1]

Also the box of clothing came, & was welcome. It was thoughtful of you, my treasure. With this box came another from N. Y.,—for I bought two coats & five vests there. I am all right, now. I didn't need five vests, but sent for them in a spurt of anger when I found I had nothing with me but a lot of those hated old single breasted atrocities that I have thrown away thirteen times, given away six times, & burned up twice. Now I'll inflict them on Orion, with the understanding that the next time I find them among my traps again there shall be a permanent coolness in the Clemens family here.[2]

I wrote a splendid chapter today, for the middle of the book.[3] I ad- mire the book more & more, the more I cut & slash & lick & trim & revamp it. But you'll be getting impatient, now, & so I am going to begin tonight & work day & night both till I get through. It is a tedious, ar- duous job shaping so such a mass of MS for the press. It took me two months to do it for the Innocents. But this is another sight easier job, because it is so much better literary work—so much more acceptably written. It takes 1800 pages of MS to make this book?—& that is just what I have got—or rather, I have got 1,830. *I* thought that just a little over 1500 pages would be enough & that I could leave off all the Overland trip—& what a pity I can't.[4]

Ma bought a silk dress yesterday, for $24, & tired herself clear out, today, helping Mary & Annie make it up.[5] She looked fagged. You see, they couldn't find a sempstress, & Ma absolutely needed the dress to swell around in while she is here. Ma is a wonderfully winning woman, with her gentle simplicity & her never-failing goodness of heart & yearn- ing interest in all creatures & their smallest joys & sorrows. It is why she is such a good letter-writer—this warm personal interest of hers in every thing that others have at heart. Whatever is important to another is important to her. Her letters treat of everybody's affairs, & would make her ~~out~~ ˄seem˄ a mousing, meddling, uneasy devil of a gossip to a person who did not know her.

Annie⸢s⸥ is a very attractive & interesting girl, & your brown silk becomes her exceedingly, it is so modest & yet so dressy & handsome.

Mollie is *always* attractive & pleasant and interesting, in company.

Orion is as queer & ~~heedless~~ ˄heedless a bird˄ as ever. He met a strange young lady in the hall this evening; mistook her for the landlady's daughter (the resemblance being ~~similar~~ ˄equal˄ to that between a cameleopard & a˄ kangaroo,) & shouted: "Hello, you're back early!" She took him for a fugitive from the asylum & left without finishing her errand.

Night before last he was standing on the porch—absentminded, as usual—when a lady came out with the landlady—couldn't get the gate open—Orion said to the landlady, "Stay where you are—I'll open it for her"—which he did. Thought he knew her—which he didn't. Said: "It is getting late—I'm going to see you home." She said, "Oh, no, thank you—it isn't ⸢f⸥ very far, & I'm not afraid." Said he, gaily: "Oh, you *ain't⸢?⸥!* well if ˄you˄ ain't *I* ain't either—so come along." What could the woman do, with so cheerful an infant? Why, simply let him go home with her—which she did. She took him a route he had never traveled before—finally stopped before a house he never had seen before—said: "This is my home; I am much obliged to you, sir: Good-night"—& left him standing there wondering whether his friend had moved ˄her habitation˄ within twenty-four hours, or whether he had been making an ass of himself again. The odds were in favor of the latter—& if he had bet with himself on it he might have made some money.

But *this* won't do. Good night, my old darling & yours truly will go to work.

Sam͜ᶫ.

P. S.—I['],ll, bet Bliss is still carrying some of my letters in his pocket. That's why they don't go.   —ᴧᴧ—

———————————————————————————————

Mrs. Sam͞ᶫ. L. Clemens | Care Langdon | Elmira | N. Y. [*postmarked:*] HARTFORD CT. AUG 11 11 AM [*docketed by OLC:*][6] 8ᵗʰ

[1] Having received none of Clemens's letters, Olivia had telegraphed, perhaps on 9 August.

[2] Since early July, Orion and Mollie had been living in a second-story room at Mrs. E. M. Eaton's boarding house at 54 College Street, Hartford, "close to the Presbyterian church. The room has a fixed wash stand with hot and cold water. There is a bath room in the house. A piano dealer boards there; he owns the house and rents it to Mrs. Eaton" (OC to SLC, 4 July 71, CU-MARK). As the rest of the present letter indicates, when not working on *Roughing It*, Clemens was spending a good deal of his time at Mrs. Eaton's, and perhaps even temporarily lodged there along with his mother and niece, who were visiting Orion and Mollie. The piano dealer was W. J. Babcock, "Professor of Music. Teacher of the Piano Forte, Organ and Singing. And *sole Agent* for the sale of *Chickering & Co.'s splendid Piano Fortes*" (Geer: 1870, 44; 1871, 34; 1872, 59).

[3] Perhaps chapter 53, Jim Blaine's story of "his grandfather's old ram" (*RI 1993*, 863–64).

[4] Clemens's statement here that it "takes 1800 pages of MS" to make a six-hundred-page book is consistent with his May estimate (15 May 71 to Bliss). Even his earlier estimate (in 21? Sept 70 to Bliss) has been shown to be consistent with a total of eighteen hundred pages (*RI 1993*, 812–13, 817). It is therefore unclear when, if ever, he believed that "a little over 1500 pages would be enough." He soon discovered that even eighteen hundred thirty pages was not sufficient to make *Roughing It* six hundred pages long.

[5] Mary, otherwise unidentified, may have been a family servant from Fredonia who accompanied Jane Clemens and Annie Moffett to Hartford.

[6] A letter (now missing) of 9 August and Clemens's telegram on 9 or 10 August probably account for the two missing docket numbers, 6 and 7.

To Horace Greeley
17 August 1871 • Hartford, Conn.
(MS: NN)

                                        ₐ149 Asylum street₍ ⎫
                                        Hartford, Conn. 17th. ⎰

Horace Greeley Esq
        Dear Sir:
    I am here putting my new book on California &c., to press₍, & find that in it I have said in positive words that the famous ~~episode~~ Hank Monk anecdote ~~has no truth in it~~ refers to an episode *which never occurred*.[1]
    I got this from a newspaper editor, who said he got it from you.[2] I

never knew of his telling a lie—but to make *sure* & will you please endorse his statement if you can—or deny it if you must?ᵪ—so that I can leave my remark as it is; or change it if truth requires.ᵪ[3]

Ys Truly,

$ Mark Twain

---

[1] Clemens had probably reached chapter 20 in the *Roughing It* proofs. In that chapter he repeated the famous anecdote about the hair-raising ride that Hank Monk gave Greeley in the stagecoach between Carson City, Nevada, and Placerville, California. In a footnote at the end of the chapter Clemens reported that the incident *"never occurred"* (*RI 1993*, 131–32, 136n, 866).

[2] In 1869 Joseph Goodman had delivered to Greeley in New York a request from Monk for a railroad pass east "in memory of their celebrated mountain ride," only to have Greeley exclaim: "'Damn him! that fellow has done me more harm than any man in America! . . . there was not a damned word of truth in the whole story!'" (Joseph T. Goodman 1872; *RI 1993*, 611). Goodman had probably told this story to Clemens when he read chapter 20 in manuscript (18 Apr 71 to OC, n. 2; *RI 1993*, 866).

[3] No reply from Greeley is known to survive.

To Olivia L. Clemens
18 August 1871 • Hartford, Conn.
(MS: CU-MARK)

Friday night.

Livy darling, one of these days I propose to write an Autobiography of Old Parr, the gentleman who lived to be 153 years old & saw the reigns of 8 English kings. I must go to England to get history, materials, manners & customs of the time, &c. Will you go? It will be wonderfully fascinating work, I tell you.[1]

I am a little uneasy about you—having had no word from you for 2 days my darling wife. I only imagine that the letters are delayed, for Sue has orders to telegraph if you get sick. So I am not frightened, but a little uneasy. I guess somebody will get a dispatch if I don't hear tomorrow.

Good night, my precious, & God keep you & our child.

Sam'.

Mrs. Sam*ᶦ*. L. Clemens | Care Langdon & Co | Elmira | N. Y. [*return address:*] IF NOT DELIVERED WITHIN 10 DAYS, TO BE RETURNED TO [*postmarked:*] HARTFORD CT. AUG 19 11 AM [*docketed by OLC:*][2] 21ˢᵗ [*and*] 6.00 | 3

[1] Clemens may have been reading Henry Wilson's *Wonderful Characters; Comprising Memoirs and Anecdotes of the Most Remarkable Persons of Every Age and Nation* (1854), a copy of which he had owned since 1870. One of the book's subjects was Thomas Parr, or "Old Parr," who was reputedly born in 1483 and lived until 1635. No indication has been found that Clemens ever pursued this early plan for a work set in old England (Gribben, 2:777; Wilson and Caulfield, 364–69).

[2] Olivia had evidently received thirteen letters (twelve of which are now lost) in eight days. Among them were probably some of the delayed letters Clemens wrote in New York and during his first days in Hartford (10 Aug 71 to OLC).

To Adolph H. Sutro
19 August 1871 • Hartford, Conn.
(MS: JIm)

ˏ149 Asylum st.ˏ
Hartford, Aug. 19.

Friend Sutro—

Got your letter to-day. When do you sail? Can't you run up here for one day?[1] I'm awful busy on my new book on Nevada & California. And by the way you might tell me something about the tunnel that would make an interesting page, perhaps.[2] It was about another matter that I wanted to see you principally & very particularly,[3] but one might as well kill various birds with one stone.

Riley is in England,—London.[4]

Yrs

Sam*ᶦ*. L. Clemens

[1] Sutro's letter has not been found. He arrived in New York on 22 August, and sailed for England eight days later. He was intent on securing European investors in his proposed tunnel to the mines of the Comstock lode (2 Dec 70 to Riley, n. 3; Adolph Sutro, 33–34; "Morning Arrivals," New York *Evening Express*, 22 Aug 71, 3; "Prominent Arrivals," New York *Tribune*, 23 Aug 71, 8).

[2]Clemens may have just completed a draft of chapter 52 of *Roughing It*, which described silver mines and mining techniques, and was considering adding a description of the Sutro tunnel (*RI 1993*, 354–60, 866–67; 29 Aug 71 to Sutro).

[3]Possibly Clemens wanted advice about John Henry Riley's recommendation that a company be organized to bore wells in South Africa to facilitate diamond exploration and mining—an idea comparable in many ways to Sutro's tunnel ("Personals," Buffalo *Express*, 31 Aug 71, 2).

[4]Riley had returned from South Africa to London en route home. He had never informed Sutro of the specifics of his mission for Clemens (3 Mar 71 to Riley, n. 7).

To Adolph H. Sutro
per Telegraph Operator
24 August 1871 • Hartford, Conn.
(MS, copy received: NhD)

THE WESTERN UNION TELEGRAPH COMPANY.

6

DATED Hartford Conn   187 1

RECEIVED AT   11 15   Aug 24

TO   Adolph Sulro

Gilsey House[1]

When do you sail? how long shall you remain in NY when leave & whither

Saml L Clemens
155 Asylum St[2]

☞THIS TELEGRAM HAS JUST BEEN RECEIVED AT THE OFFICE IN

WHERE ANY REPLY SHOULD BE SENT.

15 Pdy H   DIRECT WIRES.

[*telegram docketed:*] 1871. | Sam[l] L Clemens | Hartford. | Aug 24.

[1] Sutro might have sent his New York address in the letter that reached Clemens on 19 August, or he may have wired him after his 22 August arrival at the Gilsey House, which had its own telegraph office.

[2] Three subsidiaries of the American Publishing Company—Belknap and Bliss, Richard W. Bliss, and the Columbian Book Company—were housed at this address. Clemens was probably using an office at one of them to work on *Roughing It* (Geer 1871, 226; Hill, 16).

To Adolph H. Sutro
per Telegraph Operator
25 August 1871 • Hartford, Conn.
(MS, copy received: NhD)

THE WESTERN UNION TELEGRAPH COMPANY.

6

DATED   Hartford Conn   Aug 25 187 1

RECEIVED AT   11 am

10   Adolph Sutro.

Gilsey House,

All right will see you in New York before you sail[1]

S L Clemens

☞THIS TELEGRAM HAS JUST BEEN RECEIVED AT THE OFFICE IN

Gilsey House

WHERE ANY REPLY SHOULD BE SENT.

---

10 pd y H   DIRECT WIRES.

---

[1] Sutro telegraphed that he would be in New York until 30 August, when he was scheduled to depart for Liverpool on the *Russia*. Clemens almost certainly was at the St. Nicholas Hotel between 26 and 28 August—with Olivia, Ida Langdon, and one of the Langdon cousins—and probably met with Sutro then ("Passengers Sailed," New York *Times*, 31 Aug 71, 8; "Morning Arrivals," New York *Evening Express*, 26 Aug 71, 3; *RI 1993*, 867).

To Adolph H. Sutro
per Telegraph Operator
29 August 1871 • Hartford, Conn.
(MS, copy received: NvHi)

THE WESTERN UNION TELEGRAPH COMPANY.

3

DATED ..... Hartford Conn .... 187 1 ....

RECEIVED AT .... Aug 29 ....

TO ..... Adolph Sutro. ....

Gilsey House

How long will tunnell be when finished[1] find Riley at American Minister give me your London address

Saml L Clemens

149 Asylum St

☞THIS TELEGRAM HAS JUST BEEN RECEIVED AT THE OFFICE IN

Gilsey House
....
WHERE ANY REPLY SHOULD BE SENT.

———

17 Paid   DIRECT WIRES.

[*telegram docketed:*] 1871. | Sam*l* L Clemens | Hartford | Aug 29.

[1]Sutro responded with the estimated size of the tunnel—two thousand feet deep and eight miles long—but Clemens probably did not make use of the information until December, when he read chapter 52 of *Roughing It* in proof and added a footnote about the tunnel (*RI 1993*, 360n, 867–68).

To Ella Trabue Smith
30 August 1871 • Elmira, N.Y.
(MS: Franke)

THE MᶜINTYRE COAL COMPANY   PRESIDENTS OFFICE[1]

ELMIRA, N.Y. Aug. 30 187 1

My Dear Cousin:[2]

I wish your note had arrived a day sooner, & then it would ~~haugh~~ have caught Ma, Pamela & Annie here. They left yesterday for their home in Frcdonia, N. Y. I will forward the note to them. My wife & I came down here some five months ago to visit my wife's mother, & have never been able to get home since. First my wife lay sick three months, & now our child has been ill two months. To-day its life is almost despaired of.[3]

Pamela has been here some time at the Water Cure, for her health is very bad. But Ma is hearty. She has been visiting Orion at Hartford, Conn., (where I put him last year in an editorial position under my publisher[)]. I found her in Hartford, & was surprised to see how hale & hearty she is getting.

Every time I am in New York or Boston I try to remember & get some photographs taken, but always fail. I doubt if there is a small-sized picture on hand, but think I have some large ones at the house. Will look as soon as I go up.[4]

And I will go now, inasmuch as my errand is done & I have found the doctor.[5]

With the warm regards of an unworthy but exceedingly well= meaning Cousin—

Sam⁰. L. Clemens.

Mrs. Sam⁰. E. Smith | ~~Fort Smith~~ ‚Ford | Sugar Loaf.‚[6] Ark. [*return address:*] RETURN TO MCINTYRE COAL COMPANY, ELMIRA, N. Y., IF NOT DELIVERED WITHIN 10 DAYS. [*postmarked:*] ELMIRA N.Y. SEP 1

[1]The McIntyre Coal Company, established in 1870, was a bituminous coal subsidiary of J. Langdon and Company, formed in partnership with William K. and Cornelius Vanderbilt, "who were engaged in an urgent search for fuel coal

for the steam locomotives of the New York Central Railroad which they con-
trolled." Mining operations were based in Ralston and McIntyre, in Lycoming
County, Pennsylvania, but offices were at 6 Baldwin Street in Elmira, along with
the parent company. By mid-November 1870, Charles J. Langdon, who had
been the secretary of the McIntyre company under his father, became its president, with John D. F. Slee later assuming the vice-presidency. The company's
"large scale operations" included the building of "a village with 300 small
homes, a school, a church, and several small business establishments. For 16
years, mining was carried on with an annual output of over 200,000 tons moving
by rail to destinations in New York and Canada" (Jervis Langdon, Jr., 10–11;
Boyd and Boyd, 17, 156; CJL to SLC, 15 Nov 70, CU-MARK; 15 June 74 to
Brown, NN-B).

[2]Ella Trabue (Mrs. Samuel E.) Smith was Clemens's second cousin (her
mother, Mary Paxton Trabue, was Jane Clemens's first cousin). In the late 1880s
Clemens assisted her financially on at least one occasion. The note which elicited
this response has not been found (Selby, 14, 41, 42, 143; Smith to SLC, 26 Sept
88, CU-MARK).

[3]The crisis had brought Clemens from Hartford on 29 or 30 August.

[4]If Clemens enclosed a photograph, it does not survive with the letter. He
apparently had exhausted his supply of the photographic *cartes de visite* he had
taken in Buffalo and Washington in 1870 (20? May 70 to Paige; 8 July 70 to
OLC).

[5]Presumably Clemens was waiting at the office until a J. Langdon and Com-
pany employee found the doctor. The closest doctor was Henry Sayles, the
Langdon family's friend and Jervis Langdon's former physician, at 35 Baldwin
Street (Boyd and Boyd, 188).

[6]The revision of the address is in an unidentified hand.

To Orion Clemens
31 August 1871 • Elmira, N.Y.
(MS: CU-MARK)

THE MᶜINTYRE COAL COMPANY   PRESIDENTS OFFICE

ELMIRA, N.Y. Aug. 31 187 1

My Dear Brother—

   We have scarcely any hope of the baby's recovery.

   Livy takes neither sleep nor rest.

   We have 3 old experienced nurses.[1]

   Three months of overfeeding & surreptitious poisoning with lau-
danum & other sleeping potions is what the child is dying of.[2]

                                        Yrs affl'y
                                           Sam.

◨────────────────────────────────────

O. Clemens Esq | 149 Asylum st | Hartford | *Conn* [*return address:*] RETURN
TO MCINTYRE COAL COMPANY, ELMIRA, N. Y., IF NOT DELIVERED WITHIN 10 DAYS.
[*postmarked:*] ELMIRA N.Y. AUG 31 [*rubber stamped:*] MRS. ORION CLEMENS

[1] All are unidentified, although one of them might have been the much trusted
Margaret (21 June 71 to OC and MEC, n. 3).
[2] Langdon lived until 2 June 1872.

To Olivia L. Clemens
8 September 1871 • Washington, D.C.
(MS: CU-MARK)

THE ARLINGTON.

WASHINGTON, D. C. Sept. 8 18 71

Livy darling, the invention business looked dark enough this morning
(& the clouds are not all gone yet.) By a small stretch of the law which
says "The Patent Office cannot respond to inquiries as to the novelty of
an alleged invention in advance of an application for a patent," the Patent officers have thrown open everything to me and shown me every document & drawing that bears any relationship to my invention.[1] (But that
you may keep to yourself, honey.) Therefore, I know what to claim as *my*
idea, & what to leave unclaimed as having originated with somebody
else. It makes plain sailing. Been at work at this ferreting business all
day long in the Patent Office. At first it seemed that not less than six
different people had already patented my invention (one man 33 years
ago;) but by closely scanning all the documents we found that not one of
them had got a patent for the *chief* virtues claimed in mine. So I *may*
possibly get a patent, but it will not be so broad & general in its nature
as I had hoped for. But still I may get none at all; because access cannot
be had to *European* patent records yet awhile, & so, a few weeks or
months hence it may transpire that some foreigner is ahead of me.

But I'll have to run, or I'll get no dinner. Am *so* glad to hear you &
the cubbie are improving.

Ys Lovingly
Sam*l*.

✉——————————————————————————————

Mrs. S. L. Clemens | Care Langdon & Co. | Elmira | N. Y. [*return ad-*
dress:] RETURN TO J. LANGDON & CO., ELMIRA, N. Y., IF NOT DELIVERED WITHIN
10 DAYS. [*postmarked:*] WASHINGTON D.C. SEP 8[2]

[1] "Mark Twain's Elastic Strap" (see 6 Oct 71 to Leggett). The Washington
Morning Chronicle of 8 September reported that "Mr. Samuel Clemens (Mark
Twain) arrived in the city yesterday afternoon and had an interview with General
Belknap and General Leggett. Mr. Clemens has forsaken all literary labor on
newspapers and magazines, and is concentrating all his talent on a new book he
intends soon to lay before the public" ("Personal," 8 Sept 71, 1). General Mortimer D. Leggett (1821–96), whose Civil War service included participation in
Sherman's march to the sea, had taken up his post as commissioner of patents in
the Grant administration on 16 January 1871. Clemens's business with General
William W. Belknap (1829–90), who had also served with Sherman and had
been Grant's secretary of war since 1869, has not been determined. He may have
hoped Belknap could facilitate access to the patent records.
[2] After filing his patent application on 9 September, Clemens left Washington
that day or the next, first stopping over in New York at the St. Nicholas Hotel
on 10 or 11 September, and then in Hartford for about two days before his return
to Elmira on 13 September. He returned to Washington on further patent business on 19 or 20 September ("Morning Arrivals," New York *Evening Express*,
11 Sept 71, 3; SLC 1871t; OC to MEC, 14 Sept 71, CU-MARK; *RI 1993*, 868).

To James Redpath
15 September 1871 • Elmira, N.Y.
(MS: NN-B)

J. LANGDON, MINER & DEALER IN ANTHRACITE &
BITUMINOUS COAL   OFFICE NO. 6 BALDWIN STREET

ELMIRA, N.Y. Sept 15 186 71

Dear Redpath:

(confidential.)   We don't want it mentioned, but we take up our
                       permanent residence in Hartford the last day of
this month,[1] & so I shall ~~set~~ start from there when I go lecturing. Now if
I am engaged to lecture in Buffalo, & you can very quietly get me released from it, I wish you would do your level best to accomplish it. I

mortally hate that G.A.R. there, & I don't doubt they've ~~heir~~ hired me. I once gave them a packed house, free of charge, & they never even had the common politeness to thank me.[2] They left me to shift for myself, too, a la Bret Hart at Harvard.[3] Get me rid of Buffalo. Otherwise I shall have ₐno₎ resource left ₿ but to get sick the ~~ni~~ day I am to lecture there, & remunerate them for my absence. I can get sick, easily enough, by the simple process of saying the word ₿ —— well, never mind what word. I am NOT GOING TO LECTURE THERE. But possibly I am not booked for B.—am I?[4]

Say, Redpath, I wish you would notify all my list that I have no lecture on Boy's Suffrage; & that *wherever I find myself advertised for it I shall feel myself released from my engagement & at liberty to travel on.* They can't "play me for a Chinaman" again, they way they did on that California lecture. I *will not* lecture if advertised for any but my present lecture.[5] When you make out my list of places, please send one to my publisher, E. Bliss, Jr. 149 Asylum st Hartford, for I have to read proof half the winter.

Ys
Mark

My Hartford address will be, "Nook Farm," Hartford— it is John Hooker's place. Have leased it while I build.[6]

☞Where am I on last lecture in January? *Then* I can tell you about Utica & Paterson.[7]

Ys
Mark.

Remember *home* will then be Hartford.

✉——————————————————————————

[*letter docketed:*] BOSTON LYCEUM BUREAU. REDPATH & FALL. SEP 20 1871 [*and*] *Twain* Mark. | Elmira N.Y. | Sept. 15th "71.

[1]Clemens's imminent move to Hartford had already been reported in several papers, beginning with the New York *Tribune:* "Mark Twain (Samuel L. Clemens) has purchased a house, and gone to live permanently in Hartford, Conn. That pleasant capital has long been a favorite place of residence for persons who have retired from active business" ("Personal," 31 Aug 71, 5). The Hartford *Courant,* possibly at Clemens's instigation, issued a denial: "An item is going the rounds of the newspapers that Mark Twain has purchased a house in this city for a permanent residence. He was here a month, leaving a few days ago, attending

to matters connected with the publication of his new book, 'The Innocents at Home,' which is to be brought out by the American Publishing company of this city, but he has not bought a house here as the papers state" ("Brief Mention," 2 Sept 71, 2). The actual move—to a rented house—did not take place until early October (see note 6 and 3 Oct 71 to OC, n. 1).

[2] In his only Buffalo performance to date, on 15 March 1870, Clemens had shared the platform with an English elocutionist, Henry Nichols, "under the auspices of Post Chapin No. 2" of the Grand Army of the Republic. The proceeds were intended for "disabled soldiers of the late war, and the widows and orphans of those 'boys in blue' who gave their lives for their country" ("G. A. R.—Reading Tomorrow Evening," Buffalo *Commercial Advertiser*, 14 Mar 70, 3). Clemens's reading—the Jumping Frog story and the discussion of European guides in chapter 27 of *The Innocents Abroad*—was well received by an "audience uncommonly large in size and fashionable in quality," but the behavior of his hosts had evidently so offended him that he refused an encore, and "coolly informed the assemblage that his 'contract' had been fulfilled, etc., etc." ("The Readings Last Evening," Buffalo *Express*, 16 Mar 70, 4; "G. A. R.— Readings Last Evening," Buffalo *Commercial Advertiser*, 16 Mar 70, 3).

[3] Harte had suffered neglect at Harvard University's Phi Beta Kappa society literary exercises on 29 June 1871. Scheduled to deliver a poem composed for the occasion, he arrived late and had to arrange for his own seat before disappointing his audience with a singularly inappropriate reading followed by a hasty departure. He later explained that he had originally been informed that the exercises were to take place at the end of July and had only accidentally learned of the actual date. He had not, therefore, been able to complete the poem he was preparing for the event and was forced to make do with the best of the unpublished ones he had at hand ("Bret Harte a 'Fizzle,' " Hartford *Times*, 17 July 71, 4; Munroe).

[4] Clemens did not lecture in Buffalo during his 1871–72 tour.

[5] At Clemens's request, the Boston Lyceum Bureau had originally advertised "The Curiosities of California" as " 'Mark Twain's' only lecture for the season of 1869–70." When he substituted "Our Fellow Savages of the Sandwich Islands" only a few weeks before the season began, the bureau advertised the change. Not all local lecture societies noted it, however, and on several occasions Clemens was forced to inform audiences at the last moment (*L3*, 422 n. 2).

[6] Clemens had stayed with the Hookers in January 1868 and thereafter visited the family when he was in Hartford. The Clemenses leased their large Victorian Gothic house, at the corner of Forest and Hawthorn streets, paying a quarterly rent of three hundred dollars (*L2*, 144, 146 n. 4, 166; *L3*, 147 n. 1, 404; John Hooker's receipt dated 5 Jan 72 for "quarter ending Jan. 1, 72," CU-MARK).

[7] The lecture itinerary was not yet complete (9 Oct 71 to Redpath, n. 1). Redpath had written to the Paterson lecture sponsors on 26 August, promising "Feb 1, or a date within 2 or 3 days of it[.] He may insist on closing his list in January. If so, your date w^d have to be moved back a little into January" (Redpath to SLC, 18 Jan 72, CU-MARK). By early December Clemens was at least tentatively engaged to speak in Paterson on 31 January and in Utica on 2 February 1872. He kept the Paterson engagement, but did not speak in Utica (29–30 Nov 71 to Redpath and Fall, n. 1; 7 Jan 72 to Redpath, Axelrod; Redpath and Fall 1871– 72, 13–16; Appendix C).

To Orion Clemens
16 September 1871 • Elmira, N.Y.
(MS: CU-MARK)

<table>
<tr><td>J. LANGDON,
J. D. F. SLEE,
T. W. CRANE,
C. J. LANGDON.</td><td>OFFICE OF J. LANGDON & CO. MINERS AND DEALERS IN
ANTHRACITE AND BITUMINOUS COALS. 6 BALDWIN ST.

ELMIRA, N.Y., Sept 16 187 1</td></tr>
</table>

Dear Bro—

I believe I would not bother with that knife.

Bear in mind that your wheel, to supplant others, must break ice 3 or 4 inches thick & plow through it without damage to itself.

The biggest thing is the world is to invent a *steam* railroad break that the *engineer* can apply throughout his train without needing breakmen. The N. J. RR run 105 *trains* a day, & employ say 7 *seven* breakmen on a train at about $2 a day apiece. Figure that up & you will see that that one railroad could afford to pay you $250,000 a year for the use of such an invention. Can you contrive it?

As to the button. One form of it might be a simple *hinge* without spring. The screw ˌ(button)ˌ would hold it together— passing through above the pants. But I suppose the spring is the best pattern of the two. How does it strike you?[1]

Ys

Sam.

Personal | O. Clemens Esq | 149 Asylum st | Hartford | Conn [*return address:*] RETURN TO J. LANGDON & CO., ELMIRA, N. Y., IF NOT DELIVERED WITHIN 10 DAYS. [*postmarked:*] ELMIRA N.Y. SEP 16

[1]Orion responded on 18 September. His letter contains the fullest known description of his paddle wheel invention, which he never succeeded in patenting, and answers each of Clemens's questions in turn. The hinge he described was for Clemens's garment strap invention (6 Oct 71 to Leggett, n. 7):

> My Dear Brother:—
> I was a little dubious about the knife.
> My wheel will be *below* the ice—that is, the buckets while making the stroke will be, or may as well be wholly beneath the surface of the water. While *returning*, it is

intended they shall be above water, and the wheel, both above and below the water, defended by gratings—which I see were once used on an English canal to defend the propeller, without, it seems, objection. The boat itself must be pushed through the water, and the additional resistance offered by my frame work and grating will ~~only~~ be a disadvantage only in case the added benefits fail to overbalance the added resistance.

You are right about the immense advantage of such a railroad brake—but has it not already been invented? Did you see some time ago an account of a new brake being tried on the Missouri Pacific road? It ~~was~~ stopped the train a great deal quicker and in shorter space than by brakemen, and I think it was the way you suggest—by steam under the control of the engineer. If you saw that account and it was something different from my impressions I would try to invent such a brake as you suggest.

The benefit of a hinge I think can be attained by making the part where the bend is, thin like a watch spring. My model maker says it can be filed or ground down on an emery wheel so as to be easily flexible without breaking, and he suggests that the shape be . . .

. . . making the upper edge sharp, which will make easier mark for the screw. He is to make me a german silver one and a brass and a steel one. He says the difference in cost of material is about nothing, and ~~shee~~ spring sheet brass has considerable spring, and German silver still more spring, though nothing has so much spring as steel. He has a clock hospital full of patients, and that being his regular business it is hard to get anything else out of him. He has promised to do something at ~~to~~ it to-day. I told him to do it before my other work, though as he was ˄not˄ doing any thing at my other work that injunction has only helped a shade. (CU-MARK)

Orion was correct about the train brake. George Westinghouse received his first patent for a compressed-air (not steam) brake on 13 April 1869. The brake had been previously tested in December 1868 on the Pittsburgh, Columbus, Cincinnati and St. Louis Railroad.

To Orion Clemens
17 September 1871 • Elmira, N.Y.
(MS: CU-MARK)

THE MᶜINTYRE COAL COMPANY   PRESIDENTS OFFICE

ELMIRA, N.Y. Sept. 17 187 1

My Dear Bro:

Inclose a letter from Bunker. Now as I touch him up a little in the book, I don't want to write him. So you must write him & say that as I am probably out lecturing by this time I leave all my correspondence to be answered by you & Livy for the next 5 or 6 months. That will get me out of the difficulty.[1]

The baby is doing splendidly. We go to Buffalo tonight to pack up for Hartford.

Yr Bro

Sam

[1]Benjamin B. Bunker was attorney of Nevada Territory from 1861 to 1863, when he was removed for inattention to his duties after more than a year's leave of absence. While in Nevada, Clemens sometimes wrote scornfully and irreverently of Bunker, foreshadowing the depiction of him as the gullible and pompous General Buncombe in chapter 34 of *Roughing It* (*L1*, 135 n. 6, 147–48, 170, 235 n. 4; *ET&S1*, 280–81; *RI 1993*, 221–27, 631–32). The letter from Bunker that occasioned this commission for Orion is not known to survive.

To James Redpath
22 September 1871 • Buffalo, N.Y.
(MS: Axelrod)

Buffalo 22[d].

Dear Redpath =

The YOUNG MEN'S Association here want me to lecture, & *they* are a pretty decent lot. In fact the Sec'y has almost made me feel like talking in Buffalo.[1] However, I have made such a caterwaul at you the other day on the subject that I am ashamed to discuss Buffalo with you. So I merely told him to write you & if it all fell right I would talk. I did not tell him my price is $200—you can do that yourself if you choose to open negotiations. But that GAR are not ~~no~~ nice people.

We are packing our furniture & shipping it to Hartford & we are in a mess—house upside down—my wife sick—can't leave her bed for perhaps a week yet—& yet we must take possession of our house in Hartford Oct. 1.[2]

Did I offend with my last letter? I didn't mean to, but I am such an ass that I do most things ass foremost.

Ys

Mark.

Do you ask if I know [my] mind? No, I don't. Never have had an experience of the kind.

✉———

[*letter docketed:*] BOSTON LYCEUM BUREAU. REDPATH & FALL. SEP 26 1871 [*and*]
Twain Mark. | Buffalo N. Y. | Sept. 22ⁿᵈ ''71.

¹Frederick L. Danforth, cashier at a local iron and steel works, was corresponding secretary of the Young Men's Association of Buffalo and a member of its lecture committee. Clemens had joined the association in 1869. Several of his friends were members, including Josephus N. Larned, George H. Selkirk, David Gray, and John J. McWilliams. After Clemens left Buffalo, he continued to think well of the organization. In 1885, at the request of one of its young members, James Fraser Gluck, he donated half of the manuscript of *Adventures of Huckleberry Finn* to the Young Men's Association Library, and in 1887 he sent the remaining half via Larned (*Buffalo Directory* 1871, 52, 164, 309; William H. Loos, personal communication; Loos, 1–2; 12 Nov 85 to Gluck, NBu; Gluck to SLC, 11 July 87, CU-MARK).
²Although Olivia may have been ill, she was also in her first months of pregnancy with Olivia Susan (Susy) Clemens, who was born on 19 March 1872. Two days before this letter, the Buffalo *Courier* had printed the following notice about the Clemenses' house:

> MARK TWAIN'S RESIDENCE.—For the benefit of those who are making inquiry as to the price of Mark Twain's residence, on Delaware street, just above Virginia street, we would state that the house is a new brick, of modern pattern, three stories high, Mansard roof, with bath-room, warm and cold water and gas in all the rooms—13 in number, beside the kitchen and laundry; heating furnace, dry and roomy cellar, and all the modern improvements. The wainscoting is black walnut and maple, the doors heavy black walnut, and the interior finish generally is artistic and complete.
>
> Attached to the house is a two-story brick barn, complete in all its appointments, with gas and water. The lot is 65 feet front, 130 feet deep, and is one of the most desirable locations in the city. The furniture is not for sale, and the price asked for house and barn is $20,000. This is in answer to several questions inquiring "what Mark Twain asks for his house." Hume & Sanford are the agents. (20 Sept 71, 2)

To James Redpath
26 September 1871 • Buffalo, N.Y.
(*MTL*, 1:191)

Buffalo, Sept. 26.

Dear Redpath—

We have thought it all over & decided that we can't possibly talk after Feb. 2.¹

We shall take up our residence in Hartford 6 days from now.

Yours
Mark.

[1]Clemens had originally agreed to speak only through the end of January 1872. His second wedding anniversary, 2 February 1872, was the date assigned to the Utica lecture, later canceled (*Lyceum* 1871, 20; 15 Sept 71 to Redpath, n. 7).

To John A. Lant
28 September 1871 • Buffalo, N.Y.
(MS: MoSW)

J. LANGDON,	OFFICE OF J. LANGDON & CO. MINERS AND DEALERS IN
J. D. F. SLEE,	ANTHRACITE AND BITUMINOUS COALS. 6 BALDWIN ST.
T. W. CRANE,	
C. J. LANGDON.	ELMIRA, N.Y., Sept. 28 187 1[1]

Dear Lant—[2]

Thank you kindly for the picture of the baby. But it seems to me you did not economise material to the best advantage: there is meat enough in this youngster for *twins*. You could get your family finished a good deal sooner if you would use more judgment. I wish I could send you a picture of our baby, but I cannot, for the reason that they are all gone.

With the best wishes for you & yours——

Yr friend
S. L. Clemens.

[1]Clemens, almost certainly still in Buffalo, did not bother to alter the printed dateline.

[2]Lant (b. 1840), a Missouri printer who "worked on newspapers with Mark Twain as a boy" (Chester L. Davis 1965, 3), wrote to Clemens from St. Louis in 1909:

> I have your strikingly philosophical letter to me of September 28, 1871, which remains undiminished in esteem, and indeed, in fact unpublished, which it provokingly deserved to be then and at least twice a year since.
>
> But you have forgotten this and the bunch of a printer who never ceased to adore you from that day to this. He is now in his 69th year and still at the case with unabating joy, amid the racket of monotypes, tinotypes, casting machines and the musical racket of presses on a floor below. (25 Dec 1909, CU-MARK)

To Orion Clemens
3? October 1871 • Hartford, Conn.
(Paraphrase: OC to MEC, 3 Oct 71, CU-MARK)

I had a short note from Sam this morning saying he would be over in a day or two.[1]

---

[1] The Clemenses reached Hartford on 2 or 3 October, after at least a day in New York at the St. Nicholas Hotel. (The New York *Evening Express*'s report that they were at the hotel—"Morning Arrivals," 3 Oct 71, 3—was belated.) Clemens probably had this note hand-delivered to Orion at the American Publishing Company offices.

To Mortimer D. Leggett
with an affidavit by John Hooker
6 October 1871 • Hartford, Conn.
(MS: DNA)

ˏCONCERNING "MARK TWAIN'S ELASTIC STRAP."ˏ
Hartford, Conn. Oct. 6. 1871.

Hon. M. D. Leggett
    Com'r of Patents, Washington
        In response to an official notification of interference dated Washington Sept. 30, & in compliance with the instructions accompanying the same, I make the following statement under oath—to-wit:[1]
    The *idea* of contriving an improved vest strap, is *old* with me; but the actual *accomplishment* of the idea is no older than the 13ᵗʰ of August last_ˏₐ₎ (*to the best of my memory.*)ₐ ˏThis remark is added after comparing notes with my brother.ₐ[2]
    For four or five years I turned the idea of such a contrivance over in my mind at times, without a successful conclusion;[3] but on the 13ᵗʰ of August last, as I lay in bed, I thought of it again, & then I said I would ease my mind & invent that strap before I got up—probably the only p̶h̶

prophecy I ever made that was worth its face. ~~Am~~ An *elastic* strap suggested itself & I got up satisfied. While I dressed, it occurred to me that in order to be efficient, the strap must be *adjustable* & ~~rem~~ *detachable*,, when the wearer did not wish it to be *permanent*. So I devised the plan of having two or three button-holes in each end of the strap, & *buttoning* it to the garment—whereby it could be shortened or removed at pleasure. So I sat down & drew the *first* of the accompanying diagrams (they are the *original* ones.) While washing (these details seem a little trivial, I grant, but they are *history* & therefore in some degree respect-worthy,) it occurred to me that the strap would do for pantaloons also, & I drew diagram No. 2.

After breakfast I called on my brother, ,Orion Clemens,, the editor of the "American Publisher," showed him my diagrams & explained them, & asked him to note the date & the circumstance in his note-book for future reference. [I shall get that note of his & enclose it, so that it may make a part of this sworn evidence.] While talking with him it occurred to me that this invention would apply to ladies' *stays*, & I then sketched diagram No. 3.

In succeeding days I devised the applying of the strap to shirts, drawers, &c., & when about to repair to Washington to apply for a patent, was peremptorily called home by sickness in my family. The moment I could be spared however, I went to Washington & made application—about the 10th or 12th of September, ult.,[4] I think. I believe these comprise all the facts in the case.[5]

Respectfully
Sam*ˡ*. L. Clemens

Hartford Connecticut
October 6th 1871

There personally appeared ~~bef~~ Samuel L. Clemens, whose name is subscribed to the foregoing statement, and made solemn oath that the statement so by him subscribed is true, before me

John Hooker
Commissioner at the
Superior Court for
Hartford County &
empowered to
administer oaths.[6]

[*enclosures:*]

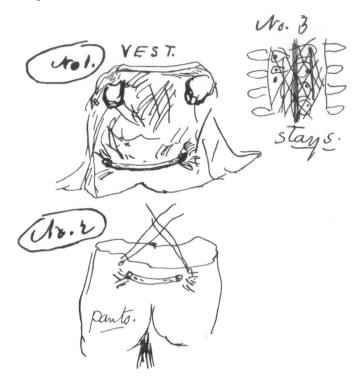

[*in pencil:*]
ₐFrom O. Clemens's Memorandum book.ₐ
[*Orion Clemens, in ink:*]

Sam's strap=Drawing shown to me and explanation made at Hartford this (Friday) 8th day of August, 1871.
NOTE.—The above date is erroneous. It should have been 11th day of August, 1871. This memorandum made Augst 14th, 1871. (Monday)
                                                                                Orion Clemens.

[*on the back, in pencil:*] A
                          B   C
[*and in ink:*]
Aug 30/71.
Wrote to Brown & Bros., ₐBrass Mfrs,ₐ Waterbury, Conn., for about 200 square inches of spring sheet brass, No. 26[7]—to be sent by express C.O.D.

✉️——

Hon. M. D. Leggett | Commissioner of Patents | Washington | D.C. [*return address:*] IF NOT DELIVERED WITHIN 10 DAYS, TO BE RETURNED TO Mark Twain, Hartford, Conn. [*postmarked:*] HARTFORD CT. OCT 6 8 PM [*docketed:*] Lockwood vs Clemens [*and*] Preliminary Statement of S.L. Clemens

[1] According to the *Journal of the Patent Office Society:*

> When the same invention is made by two or more inventors who attempt to obtain patents at about the same time, the Patent Office must find out who made the inven[t]ion first. The proceeding instituted for this purpose is called an "interference" and has the reputation of being one of the most complicated legal contests in existence. The first step is for each inventor to file a paper, called a "preliminary statement," in which he gives the essential dates and facts relating to his activities. This is to commit himself before he knows the story of the other inventor. Then each inventor presents the testimony of his witnesses, and his exhibits; and the Patent Office eventually decides which inventor was first and should receive the patent. (Federico, 225)

The present letter constitutes Clemens's "preliminary statement" in the interference case; his opponent, Henry C. Lockwood of Baltimore, whose stated occupation was "operating machinery for renovating coffee," filed a much briefer account with Leggett on 3 October 1871 (Lockwood 1871a, 1871b).

[2] But see Orion Clemens's memorandum, enclosed with his letter.

[3] Interviewed in Washington soon after applying for his patent, Clemens claimed that the idea resulted from his first meeting with Horace Greeley, in December 1870: "the extraordinary set of [Greeley's] trowsers, half in and half out of his boots, attracted his attention, and he at once set to work to see if he could not devise some plan of making them hang more gracefully" ("Mark Twain Takes Out a Patent—Why He Did It," Washington *National Republican*, 21 Sept 71, 2; *RI 1993*, 825).

[4] Clemens was called from Hartford to Elmira on 29 or 30 August, when Langdon Clemens became ill. He made his patent application on 9 September.

[5] Clemens had retained the services of patent solicitors Alexander and Mason, of Washington, D.C., when he filed his patent application, and he now sent them a copy of his preliminary statement. They replied on 9 October:

> We have this day written to [Henry C. Lockwood] with a view to settle the case by compromise & allowing your patent to issue. . . . We feel quite certain that he *goes back* of you, inasmuch as your invention is of so recent a date, hence we think it policy to get out of the matter as best as we can.—With your consent we will make the best arrangement with him in our power. If there are any States you prefer to hold *alone* name them in answer so we can be prepared for him.—He ought to give way in consideration of your nom-de-plume reputation & we shall impress this upon him. (CU-MARK)

Alexander and Mason apparently prevailed with Lockwood, who had conceived of his "elastic waist strap" in 1869 and made a model of it in July 1871, thus antedating Clemens in the invention of the device (Lockwood 1871a, 1871b). On 25 November Lockwood's attorneys signed a stipulation that his previous testimony regarding his invention "be withdrawn, cancelled or expunged from the records" and that the interference case, which had been assigned a hearing date of 29 December, be decided without "further testimony or appeal." Accordingly, on 27 November, the patent office's examiner of interferences decided the case "on the record," ruling that

Clemens filed his application for a patent September 9″ 1871. Lockwood filed his September 15″ of the same year.

In accordance with Office rule 57 priority of invention is awarded to the earlier applicant, Samuel L. Clemens. (Adams)

On 19 December Clemens was assigned patent number 121,992 for an "Improvement in Adjustable and Detachable Straps for Garments" (SLC 1871t). Lockwood was granted patent number 122,038 on the same date for a similar device, which was more specifically constructed "to provide an efficient elastic waist-strap in which the strain on the elastic pieces will be uniform at all points, so that it may wear evenly and endure as long as the pantaloons themselves." In an accompanying statement Lockwood declared: "I do not claim any right of invention to the strap for supporting pantaloons secured to Samuel L. Clemens by his patent bearing even date herewith" (Lockwood 1871c). Nevertheless, Clemens agreed to manufacture his device and allow Lockwood to share in the profits. He did not manufacture it, however, and in early 1877 Lockwood sued him in the Hartford courts for $10,000, for breach of contract, but was awarded only $300 (Hartford *Courant:* "The Courts," 10 Feb 77, 2, 17 Mar 77, 2; 23 Mar 77 to Howells, MH-H, in *MTHL*, 1:173).

[6] John Hooker, now Clemens's landlord, was an attorney, and the reporter of the Connecticut Supreme Court (Hooker, 10).

[7] For a prototype of the garment strap's flexible metallic hinge (16 Sept 71 to OC). That would have been necessary in manufacturing the device, but was not required for the patent: on 9 September Alexander and Mason had requested and received permission to dispense with a model (Alexander and Mason to the commissioner of patents, 9 Sept 71; S. S. Fahnestock, assistant patent examiner, to Alexander and Mason, 9 Sept 71, both in the records of the United States Patent Office, Department of Commerce, Washington, D.C.).

To James Redpath
9 October 1871 • Hartford, Conn.
(MS: CtHMTH)

> The "Hooker Place"
> ˄Forest street˄
> Hartford Oct 9.

Friend ~~Red~~ Redpath—

Send along the first end of my list & ₰ let me see where I am to talk.[1] Please send a copy to my publisher, *E. Bliss Jr. 149 Asylum st Hartford*— for I must read proof for the next month or so.[2]

I ~~lef~~ leave for good, next Friday.[3]

We are *settled* here.

> Ys
> Mark.

✉————————————————————————————————————

[*letter docketed:*] C̶o̶n̶n̶ *"Twain* Mark" | Hartford Conn | Oct. 9ᵗʰ "71. [*and*] *G.L.F.*⁴

¹The Boston Lyceum Bureau's chief clerk, George H. Hathaway, prepared this lecture list in a small memorandum book—6½ by 3 inches—that fit into a leather wallet, embossed in gold with Clemens's name. Presumably the bureau routinely presented similar itineraries to each of its lecturers. Ultimately Clemens's filled sixteen pages, specifying lecture dates, places, and fees, as well as rail connections, local contacts, and accommodations. Hathaway updated the book at least twice, adding entries for November and then for December through 31 January 1872, perhaps during Clemens's stops in Boston on 1 and 13 November (Pond, xxv; Redpath and Fall 1871–72; 11 Oct 71 to Redpath and Fall; 1 Nov 71 to OLC; 20 Nov 71 to Howland).

²Clemens had probably read *Roughing It* proofs through chapter 25 (less than a third of the book) while in Hartford in August. His expectation of reading the remaining proofs during the first month of his lecture tour (16 October–16 November) proved unrealistic (*RI 1993*, 864, 867–72).

³Friday, 13 October.

⁴George L. Fall.

To John Henry Riley
9 October 1871 • Hartford, Conn.
(MS: NN-B)

                                                                Hartford, Oct. 9.

Friend Riley—

It isn't *me* that is delaying the book, but sickness in my family. My present book can't get out before January I guess, I was so delayed, & as I lecture till middle of April, I can't shoulder the pen again till May.¹

My lecture being already written, I can't talk diamonds this season, but will take the field with you on that topic *next* season, if you say so.²

Don't lose your pictures—we want the book *full* of illustrations.

Let the diamond fever swell & sweat—we'll t̶i̶r̶ try to catch it at the right moment.

                                                                Ys

                                                                Mark.

Do you want to take your patent out to the fields next fall?³

¹Riley had expected to return from Africa in June 1871 and then spend July through October in Buffalo to inspire Clemens's writing of the diamond mine

book. But he did not return to London from Africa until August and probably did not reach the United States until September or early October. Clemens, busy with the move to Hartford and preparing to lecture (and with weeks of proofreading to do on *Roughing It*), was not free to begin the collaboration. His present justification for postponement was not entirely candid, however. Langdon Clemens's illness had interrupted his work on *Roughing It* in late August and early September, but so had the garment strap invention. Moreover, he had long known that his lecture tour would end in early February. His selection of May 1872 as a likely starting date apparently was influenced by a consideration he refrained from mentioning: his wife was now about three months pregnant, and he expected to be occupied with a new baby by early spring 1872. Finding Clemens unavailable, Riley went to California, returning in late November. Plans for him to come to Hartford were discussed early in 1872, then abandoned because of his deteriorating health (2 Dec 70 to Riley; 8 Sept 71 to OLC; 6 Oct 71 to Leggett; 4 Jan 72 to Riley, NN-B; 27 Mar 72 to Riley, ViU; Riley to SLC: 3 Dec 71, 27 June 72, 22 July 72, all in CU-MARK, and 16 May 72, CtY-BR).

²See 2 Dec 70 to Riley.

³Riley had conceived of a "Diamond sifting and washing machine," but by early December had "done nothing yet towards getting it patented" (Riley to SLC, 3 Dec 71, CU-MARK). He did not receive a patent before dying of cancer in September 1872 ("Death of J. H. Riley," San Francisco *Alta California*, 18 Sept 72, 1).

To James Redpath and George L. Fall
11 October 1871 • Hartford, Conn.
(MS facsimile: WU)

                                                            Hartford, Oct. 11.

Dear Boys:

The list is at hand. Thank you.

You can lecture me on Saturdays if you have the opportunity.¹ Sometimes one of those idle days is hard to put in.

                                                    Ys

                                                    Mark.

[*letter docketed:*] G.L.F.

¹Initially Clemens's lecture list included only three Saturday engagements—2 and 9 December 1871 and 6 January 1872—out of a possible seventeen be-

tween 16 October 1871 and 10 February 1872. Saturday lectures on 16 and 30 December 1871 were later added (9 Oct 71 to Redpath, n. 1; 28 Nov 71 to Fall; Appendix C; Redpath and Fall 1871–72, 7–11).

To Olivia L. Clemens
14 October 1871 • New York, N.Y.
(MS: CU-MARK)

St Nich Oct. 14.[1]

We played billiards with Ed Marsh[2] last night & then took him to see Humpty Dumpty with us—he & Charley had been there before. The thing we went to see was a cat-song, by a Swede & his wife[3]—a performance worth twice the admission fee; there is little else *t* about the show that *is* worth a great deal. The cat song is *very* pretty, notwithstanding it is *all* miawing & yowling. The air is minor & charming.

Two children rode velocipedes wonderfully well. One of the children was not larger than Lang, & yet performed finely.[4]

Charley has got the news. J. Langdon & Co lose $50,000, sure enough;[5] John Law loses $130,000—cries & wrings his hands when he talks of it.[6]

Charley left for home a few minutes ago—9 AM.

Well, I do wish I could see you, now, Livy dear, & the splendid cubbie.

Lovingly

Sam

[*in ink:*] Mrs. Sam*'*. L. Clemens | cor. Forest & Hawthorn st | Hartford | Conn [*return address:*] IF NOT DELIVERED WITHIN 10 DAYS, TO BE RETURNED TO [*postmarked:*] MAILED ST. NICHOLAS HOTEL, N.Y. OCT 14 1871 [*and*] NEW YORK OCT 14 1.30 PM

[*in OLC's hand:*]

4̶0̶0̶	600	231	600
2̶3̶1̶	231	150	381
1̶6̶9̶	369	381	219

[1]Clemens and Charles J. Langdon left Hartford on 13 October for New York City, where they registered at the St. Nicholas Hotel (OC to MEC, 13 Oct 71, CU-MARK; "Morning Arrivals," New York *Evening Express*, 14 Oct 71, 3).

[2] Edward L. Marsh, who had registered at the St. Nicholas Hotel on 12 October, was a first cousin to Charles Langdon and Olivia Clemens. After his Civil War service with the Iowa infantry, Marsh lived in New Orleans and then New York. In 1871 he lived in Cincinnati and was a partner in Marsh and Company, cement dealers. In 1877 he returned to Iowa, where his family had settled in 1857 ("Capt. E. L. Marsh," obituary from an unidentified Elmira newspaper inserted in AD, 26 Mar 1906, CU-MARK, in *MTA*, 2:250–51; *L2*, 292 n. 2; "Morning Arrivals," New York *Evening Express*, 12 Oct 71, 3; *Cincinnati Directory* 1871, 477).

[3] The popular variety show *Humpty Dumpty*, which opened in New York in 1868 and ran for over a year, was revived in August 1871 for another lucrative run at the Olympic Theatre. Among the notable new acts was the "Duo des Chats" by the Martens, husband and wife (Odell, 8:282, 433–34; 9:152–53; New York *Times:* "Amusements," 1 Sept 71, 4, 13 Oct 71, 7).

[4] According to the New York *Evening Express:* "Another very remarkable feature . . . were the performances on the bicycle of Young Adonis, aged 4½, and Little Venus, aged 2½. The boy is a bright, intelligent-looking child, and accomplishes many really astonishing feats; while his sister is a bold, fearless little imp, with great nerve and perfect self-possession" ("Pantomime at the Olympic," 1 Sept 71, 2). Langdon Clemens was only eleven months old.

[5] On 14 October 1871 the Elmira *Advertiser* observed: "The coal companies who have their headquarters in this city, it is supposed have lost very seriously by the Chicago fire" ("City and Neighborhood," 4). This was the great Chicago fire, which began on 8 October 1871 in the "lumber and coal tract, along the west bank of the [Chicago] river," soon jumped the river "into the large lumber and coal yards of the . . . South Division," and five days later was still burning. In all, eighty thousand tons of coal were consumed. The fire destroyed at least twelve thousand commercial buildings and residences, leaving over one hundred thousand homeless (New York *Times:* "A City in Ruins," 10 Oct 71, 1; "Reviving Chicago," 14 Oct 71, 1; Colbert and Chamberlin, 295).

[6] Either John S. or John H. Law of Law's Fire, Life and Marine Insurance Agency of Cincinnati, Ohio. He had arrived at the St. Nicholas Hotel at about the time the Clemenses were there in early October, and had probably been there ever since. Possibly he was related to Robert Law, Clemens's host in Chicago in December (*Cincinnati Directory* 1871, 30, 433; "Morning Arrivals," New York *Evening Express*, 4 Oct 71, 3; 3? Oct 71 to OC, n. 1; 18 Dec 71 to OLC).

To Olivia L. Clemens
15 October 1871 • Bethlehem, Pa.
(MS: CU-MARK)

Bethlehem, Sunday

Livy darling, I got here at 4 oclock yesterday afternoon. It is now nearly noon, & still I don't feel moved to begin studying my lecture[1]—so the wisdom of coming here so soon, is apparent. It is better that this feeling should be on me today than tomorrow. By tomorrow I shall be rested up & brisk.

This is an old Dutch settlement, & I hear that tongue here as often as ours.[2] All the clerks in the stores seem to talk both languages. This is one of the old original Moravian Missionary settlements;[3] & the Moravian college is still *the* feature of the place.[4]

I ~~cl~~ entered an assumed name on the hotel register (learned from Redpath that a reception was intended & ~~rooms~~ sumptuous rooms provided for me,) & so, as simple "Samuel Langhorne, New York," I occupy the shabbiest little den in the house & am left wholly & happily unnoticed.[5] It is luxury. I talk to nobody. This morning I have spent a solitary hour in the cemetery, (Theodore ought to have been there,) patiently deciphering weather-worn inscriptions[6] stating that under them lie

> JOHN GOtt/L
> IEB fm Germany,
> ~~Nat.~~ Born Feb 2, 1657.
> Died March 8, ~~1774~~ 1744.

& so on, to the number of a thousand,~~perhaps,~~ ,or so,, ancient & modern together. There are a couple of acres.

 Every grave is an exact & trim oblong square,, richly grass-sodded,, with a space of a foot between every two,—the tombstone (size of a boy's slate,) lies on *top* of the grave.

~~75~~ 100 to 150 ,years old., | | | | | | | | | | | | | | | | | | | | |
75 to 100 old | | | | | | | | | | | | | | | | | | | | |
50 to 75 old | | | | | | | | | | | | | | | | | | | | |
25 to 50 old. | | | | | | | | | | | | | | | | | | | | |
(intervening years. | | | | | | | | | | | | | | | | | | | |
| | | | | | | | | | | | | | | | | | | |
1858–9–60–1–2–3+ | | | | | | | | | | | | | | | | | | | | |
1864–5–6–7–8–9 | | | | | | | | | | | | | | | | | | | | |
1870 | | | | | | | | | | |
1871 | |

The shape, size & proportion of each grave, is that of a small mattrass covered with sod. Every grave is *alike*. Imagine acres of them! Not a monument, not a vault, not a shaft, ~~no~~ not a bush, or railing, or shrub— *nothing* but this *absolute simplicity*, this entire & complete acceptation of

Death as a great *Leveler*—a king before whose tremendous majesty ~~dif shav~~ *shades & differences in* ~~littlenesses~~ *littleness cannot be discerned,*— an Alp ~~at whose feet all ant hills are the~~ from whose summit all small things are the same size.[7]

On one decayed stone was simply:

> "Salome,
>
> wife of
>
> Nathanael.
>
> Died, Oct., ~~1871 1671.~~" 1768."

~~The month & the year~~

What a mighty thing the world was to Salome when she was in it—& what mighty matters, what *tremendous* matters, were her͜ daily needs & labors, hopes, & fears, cares & annoyances! Why, she must have ~~left~~ ͜seemed to leave͜ the world shrunken & empty behind her when she ~~left it.~~ ͜gasped out her life!͜ And yet see the result—see what it has all come to:—a hundred years of *nullity;* a hundred years of *nothingness*—a century of unconsciousness of even the drifting seasons, the idle rain, the rustling leaves. And yet these ashes of ~~for~~ Salome might smile if they only knew!—if they only knew that all those tremendous little cares were *not* lost & thrown away: for behold, after all these hundred years, here they be, upon my own shoulders, ~~just~~ intact in every item, just as they were on hers! And to-day they make the world big to *me*, & *me* the creature that would leave it shrunk & empty if I burst out of its shell. From me they will go to others, & to others still, down the long highway of the future that leads to the Last Day.

It is a handsome town, this—very substantial—set upon a hill— girdled with a deep valley—& overlooked by dominant hills beyond— & all splendid with autumn-rainbowed forests.

Well, I *would* like to see my darling & my cubbie. Love & blessings on you both—& health & good cheer—look on the bright side, sweetheart.

Saml.

[*in ink:*] Mrs. Sam*ˡ*. L. Clemens | cor Forest & Hawthorne st | Hartford | Conn [*return address:*] IF NOT DELIVERED WITHIN IO DAYS, TO BE RETURNED TO [*postmarked:*] BETHLEHEM PA. OCT 16

---

[1] "Reminiscences of Some un-Commonplace Characters I have Chanced to Meet," written in July. Clemens opened his tour with it in Bethlehem on Monday, 16 October (10 July 71 to Redpath [3rd]; McIlhaney).

²Although the earliest explorers of the area were Dutch, as evidenced by some local names, their influence all but ceased when the British took control in 1664. The large number of German immigrants who settled in Pennsylvania in the 1700s spoke a dialect known as Pennsylvania German—sometimes called Pennsylvania Dutch, from the German *Deutsch*—but it was less common in the Bethlehem area than in the surrounding counties (*Northampton County Guide*, 23, 43).

³The Moravians were members of a Christian sect founded in Bohemia in 1457 by followers of John Huss, who had been burned at the stake in 1415. By the eighteenth century, after more than two centuries of persecution, the number of adherents had dwindled to a handful. In 1727 they established the Renewed Moravian Church, also known as the United Brethren, which was active in evangelical and missionary work. In 1735 a small group emigrated to Georgia from Moravia, Bohemia, and Saxony; five years later they moved on to the Lehigh River valley region of Pennsylvania, where they founded Bethlehem, as well as nearby Nazareth.

⁴The Moravian College and Theological Seminary was founded in Nazareth in 1807 and moved to Bethlehem in 1858, where, until 1892, it was located on Church Street. Possibly Clemens was referring to an even older institution, however: the Moravian Seminary and College for Women, the first female boarding school in America, was founded in 1742 and since 1815 had also been located on Church Street (*Northampton County Guide*, 170, 189, 232, and map inside back cover; Levering, 593 n. 1).

⁵Clemens did not always seek anonymity while touring (8 Jan 70 to OLC [2nd]). He was staying at the Eagle Hotel, since 1823 located on Bethlehem's Main Street, close to both of the Moravian colleges. His host, who presumably planned the reception, was Henry T. Clauder, publisher since 1868 of the weekly Bethlehem *Moravian* and representative of the sponsoring society, the Winter Evening Entertainment Committee of the local Y.M.C.A. (Redpath and Fall 1871 72, 1 2; Levering, 634, 712; McIlhaney).

⁶The Old Moravian Burying Ground, in use since 1742, was a short walk from Clemens's hotel (*Northampton County Guide*, 146, 173–74, and map inside back cover). Theodore Crane evidently shared Clemens's interest in such historical sites (Sharlow, 2–3).

⁷"In [the Burying Ground] are laid side by side, bishops of the Moravian church, converted Indians, missionaries, Moravian soldiers of the Revolutionary and Civil Wars, and private citizens. . . . No stone is raised above the others, conforming with the sects' tradition that all men are equal in the sight of God" (*Northampton County Guide*, 173, 52 illustration).

To Olivia L. Clemens
16 October 1871 • Bethlehem, Pa.
(MS: CU-MARK)

Bethlehem of Judea, Monday.
Livy darling, this is only a line, to say I am well & comfortable—& now I will go back to the study of my lecture. In rehearsing it now, it promises to

be an hour & a half long—too long by 30 per cent. So I must trust to luck to shorten it. I shall burn the bridge behind me when I go on the plat-form—which is to say I shall not carry a shred of a note with me. If I break down I will try to scramble up again. My warm ⸍ love to you all,—my lov-ing devotion to *you*, my darling wife. Kiss mother[1] & the cubbie for me.

Saml.

Disappointed—no letter here. But don't ever write unless you are feeling well & have time to spare for it.

Burning of Michigan woods must hurt Spaulding & Sage.[2]

◪————————————————————————————

[*in ink:*] Mrs. Saml. L. Clemens | Cor. Forest & Hawthorne | Hartford | Conn. [*return address:*] IF NOT DELIVERED WITHIN 10 DAYS, TO BE RETURNED TO [*postmarked:*] BETHLEHEM PA. OCT 17

[1] Olivia Lewis Langdon had arrived in Hartford by 12 October, accompanied by her son, Charles. She remained with her pregnant daughter until 29 Decem-ber (OC to MEC, 13 Oct 71, CU-MARK; 26 Dec 71 to OLC, n. 2).

[2] Fires raging through the pine lands bordering Lake Michigan and Saginaw Bay in the second week of October had engulfed towns and left hundreds of in-habitants dead, thousands homeless, and destroyed many millions of feet of valuable timber. The first detailed newspaper reports of the disaster began ap-pearing on 13 October. Among the lumbermen potentially affected were Henry C. Spaulding and Henry W. Sage. Spaulding, father of Olivia Clemens's close friends Clara and Alice, was an Elmira dealer in lumber, coal, and building sup-plies. Sage (1814–97), was head of H. W. Sage and Company, which operated a large lumber mill on Saginaw Bay. In 1906 Clemens recalled that he had gotten Sage, "an old and warm friend and former business partner of Mr. Langdon," to provide counsel and financial assistance to J. Langdon and Company when the firm was in temporary straits after Langdon's death (AD, 23 Feb 1906, CU-MARK, in *MTA*, 2:137–38; New York *Tribune:* "Further Particulars of the For-est Fires in Michigan," 13 Oct 71, 5; "The Forest Fires," 19 Oct 71, 1; *L3*, 182 n. 6; Boyd and Boyd, 2, 197).

To Olivia L. Clemens
17 October 1871 • Allentown, Pa.
(MS: CU-MARK)

Allentown, Tues. PM

Livy darling, this lecture will *never* do. I *hate* it & won't keep it. I can't even handle these chuckle-headed Dutch with it.[1]

Have blocked ~~on~~ out a lecture on Artemus Ward, & shall write it next Saturday & deliver it next Monday in Washington.

Poor child, I am so sorry you are so lonely & forlorn—but bear up—just think, you *don't have to lecture!* ⊤ You ought to be in ecstasies. We'll come together again, & then we'll forget all our troubles.

With a world of love

Sam.

[*in ink:*] Mrs. Sam'. L. Clemens | Cor. Forrest & Hawthorne st | Hartford | Conn [*return address:*] AMERICAN HOTEL, ALLENTOWN, PA. J. F. NEWHARD,— PROPRIETOR. [*postmarked:*] ALLENTOWN PA. OCT 18

[1] Clemens delivered his "Reminiscences" lecture in Bethlehem on 16 October and in the neighboring town of Allentown on 17 October. The Bethlehem *Times* of 17 October reported that the "best and biggest part of Bethlehem's intelligent population" came away from the lecture well satisfied at having seen a celebrated author. But the paper faulted Clemens for being inaudible and for rehashing *Innocents Abroad* anecdotes, and concluded: "As a lecturer, we feel bound to say that, though not an entire failure, he is far from being instructive in his remarks or entertaining in his manner" (reprinted in McIlhaney). The second performance received an even cooler reception: "Mark Twain has the reputation of being a funny man, and the greatest joke he ever perpetrated was his 'lecture' last evening. We do not propose to make an extended notice and merely remark that we prefer *reading* to hearing him" ("Local Intelligence," Allentown *Chronicle,* 18 Oct 71, 4).

To Olivia L. Clemens
18 October 1871 • Wilkes-Barre, Pa.
(MS: CU-MARK)

Wilkesbarre, Oct. 18.

Livy darling, ~~what a thin~~ I am in a bother, & don't know whether to be irritated or amused. I was mourning over my miserable lecture this afternoon, & saying I would give Reading & Easton a lecture for *nothing* in February & do it gladly, if I could get off from those engagements now & thus gain time to write a new lecture. I was thoroughly miserable and broken-hearted. An old Californian friend[1] proposed various ways to accomplish the thing—none seemed to hit it—finally he said leave it to him

& let him telegraph those people in my name & *he* would fix it. I said *go it!* The next I saw of him he told me he had telegraphed them that I was called away immediately by sickness in my family; & that they must advertise the postponement ~~freely~~ amply at my expense, & that I would come & lecture for them for nothing between the 5th & tenth of February! Horrible—but in spite of everything I could not keep from secretly rejoicing there was such a load taken from my breast. I am beginning to get really happy & light hearted & by morning shall be absolutely jubilant, I think. Reading & Easton promptly telegraphed acceptance of the proposition.[2]

But don't let this unhappy business get into the papers—I mean *contradictions* of it. If Warner[3] speaks of it you can tell him all about it & stop the contradictions. I seem doomed to be always in the papers about private matters.

Bless your dear old heart, I shall reach Washington tomorrow night, & then for two days & nights I shall work like a beaver on my new lecture. How I ever came to get up such a mess of rubbish as this & imagine it *good*, is too many for me.[4]

But good night, my best beloved darling for I must rise & 6.30 & start.

Ever & *ever* so lovingly
Sam*l*.

Mrs. Sam*l*. L. Clemens | Cor. Forest & Hawthorne | Hartford | Conn [*postmarked:*] WILKESBARRE PA. OCT 19

[1] Unidentified.

[2] Clemens had been scheduled to lecture at Easton, Pennsylvania, on 19 October and at Reading the following evening. The Easton *Free Press*, probably of 19 October (reprinted in McIlhaney), commented on the postponement:

> We do not think the friends of Trinity church have missed much. The lecture which Mark Twain had commenced this season with is a failure. The people in Bethlehem and Allentown were greatly disappointed. It consisted of the recital of eleven jokes or stories most of which are in the "Innocents Abroad." We hope Mark will rewrite his lecture before coming to Easton.

[3] Charles Dudley Warner, associate editor of the Hartford *Courant* and a neighbor of the Clemenses'.

[4] The Wilkes-Barre *Luzerne Union* concurred with Clemens's assessment of the "Reminiscences" lecture delivered on the evening of 18 October, calling it

"stale" and remarking that "one dose of such stuff was sufficient for a genera-tion" (25 Oct 71, 3, TS in CU-MARK). The postponement of his Easton and Reading engagements gave Clemens time to prepare a new lecture for his 23 Oc-tober appearance in Washington.

To Elisha Bliss, Jr.
19 October 1871 • Wilkes-Barre, Pa.
(MS: Daley)

WYOMING VALLEY HOTEL   J. B. STARK, PROP'R.[1]

WILKES-BARRE, PA., Oct. 19 187 1

Friend Bliss—

I brought the desert chapter away with me, to write it up—but it is no use; I am driven to death, with travel, lecturing & entertaining com-mittees. It will be two weeks before I can get a chance to write up this chapter. I remember the heavy work it was to write it before, & I wish that man had the MS stuffed into his bowels that ~~wrote~~ ‚lost, it. If time presses, just leave the whole chapter out. It is all we can do.[2]

In haste

Yrs

Mark.

✉———————————————————————————————

[*letter docketed:*] √ [*and*] S L Clemens | Wilkes Barre | Pa | Oct 19/71

[1] The Wyoming Valley Hotel, "one of the best in the State, with ample accom-modation for 250 guests," was owned by Jasper Billings Stark (1823–82) and was located in a scenic valley known for its Revolutionary War associations (*Apple-tons' Hand-Book*, 167; Kulp, 2:567). Over the next few weeks, Clemens used the hotel's stationery at least three more times for letters from other places (31 Oct 71, 1 Nov 71, 9 Nov 71, all to OLC). But he was probably still in Wilkes-Barre when he hurriedly wrote the present letter before catching the train for Wash-ington, about two hundred and seventy miles south.

[2] Chapter 18 of *Roughing It* describes the crossing of an "*alkali*" desert about one hundred miles west of Salt Lake City. "It is apparent that the illustrators or the typesetters had lost part of the manuscript for this chapter, and that Bliss had asked Clemens to rewrite it, relying on what had survived. (Clemens's suggestion that Bliss leave out the 'whole chapter' if the attempt to rewrite it failed shows that not all of it had been lost.) Despite his temptation to give up, Clemens soon did rewrite the text" (*RI 1993*, 122–25, 870).

To James Redpath
24 October 1871 • Washington, D.C.
(MS: Axelrod)

ₐWashington, Tuesday.ₐ
ARLINGTON Hotel

(The only hotel in *this* town.) [WILLARD's—O, my!—seventh-rate *hash⸗ house.*][1]

Dear Red—

I have come square out, thrown "~~ɟ~~ Reminiscences" overboard & taken "*Artemus Ward, Humorist,*" for my subject. Wrote it here on Friday & Saturday, & read it from MSS[2] last night to enormous house. It suits *me*, & so I'll never deliver the nasty, nauseous "Reminiscences" any more.[3]

Please ~~give~~ make appointments for me at ~~Red~~ Reading & Easton Pa (between 5ᵗʰ & 10ᵗʰ of Feb., or sooner if it interferes with nothing,) for I am to talk for them *for nothing*—I threw them off, you know—telegram saying my folks were sick[4]—(it came just in the nick of time, I may say, for I *wanted* to go to Washington & write a new lecture—which I've done it.

MARK.

[*on the back of page 1:*][5]

I

~~Slow Railroad.~~
~~cowcatcher on wrong ₐend,ₐ~~[6]
~~heated journal.~~
~~—prisoners time expired fore they got there~~[7]

====================

~~Courting scene—56—Book 1.~~[8]
~~$10 in Jeff's pocket~~[9]
~~188–9–90. Soldier Co~~[10]
~~Besides, it improves a comic paper to put in a joke once in a while~~[11]
~~poetry—200~~[12]

[*on the back of page 2:*]

2

~~erence in his nature" (He was full of sentiment—but dared not express (voice) it lest he be thought spooney.)—61-1~~[13]

14—Source of his gift[14]

L. L.[15] great success,

—biggest he ever had.

15—Pathetic

17–16—English who "couldn't see" the fun.

17—Last hours.

(On the nip—horse attached to a wagon.[16]

Self-reliant.[17]

[*letter docketed:*] BOSTON LYCEUM BUREAU. REDPATH & FALL. OCT 27 1871 [*and*]
"Twain Mark" | Wash. D. C. | Oct. "71.[18]

[1]The Arlington Hotel on Vermont Avenue near H Street had opened in December 1869 and had been "entirely refitted and redecorated" by January 1871 ("'The Arlington,'" Washington *Globe*, 24 Jan 71, 7; Boyd 1872, 56). Clemens stayed there, perhaps for the first time, in early September (8 Sept 71 to OLC). He could also speak knowledgeably about the fare at once-fashionable Willard's Hotel, at the corner of Pennsylvania Avenue and Fourteenth Street West, because he had boarded there while rooming with Senator William M. Stewart in the winter of 1867–68 (*L2*, 116–17). Since 1869 Willard's had not been profitable; it was at present closed while its owners disputed plans for its future. Clemens's friend Hiram J. Ramsdell remarked in one of his Cincinnati *Commercial* letters that the Arlington was "the only first-class hotel in the city" and applauded the Willard's eclipse:

> Well, Willard's hotel has been dismantled, tore up, vacated. It is left to its own vile smells, its rats, its bed bugs, its intrigues, its amours, its damnation. . . .
>
> If there is any one who has ever stopped at Willard's, under the proprietorship of Sykes & Chadwick, who is not glad that the hell-hole is shut up, I shall be glad to be furnished with his name. (Ramsdell 1871b)

Willard's disappeared from the Washington directory in 1872, reappeared in 1873, and was able to advertise itself in the 1874 directory as the largest hotel in the city, "REHABILITATED and refitted throughout in the most elegant manner. . . . bedding, upholstery, furniture and equipment are entirely new, . . . costing over $200,000" (Boyd: 1873, 49; 1874, 121).

[2]Only a single page of the manuscript is known to survive:

[*in ink, canceled in pencil:*]

$90

of those quaint ferocities which poor Artemus used to put in his programmes—something like *this*, you remember—"*N. B.* Audiences declining ~negl~ to retire ~from the hall~ when the lecture is done, will be put out ~dispersed~ by the *police*." G. N.

[*on verso in pencil:*]

He left a good deal of pr money, but as far ~as~ we can learn, no good came

90.

In his will he advised his page to become a *printer*, believing that the best way to acquire a good *practical* education—& he left his library to the best boy in his native village.

He left a good deal of money, but as ∅ far as we can learn, no good came of it. He appointed too many executors, & there wasn't enough to go round, perhaps.

Thanking you very kindly for your attention, & for your presence here likewise, I will close this lecture with— —well, I'll *tell* it. (SLC 1871q†)

The eccentric will drawn up by Artemus Ward (Charles Farrar Browne) in fact

provided first that the library of books bequeathed him by his uncle, Calvin Farrar, should be given the Waterford [Maine] boy or girl who passed the best school examination between the first day of January and that of April following his decease. . . . Second, that George H. Stephens, his personal attendant, should work as a printer's apprentice for two years in the Riverside Press at Cambridge, at the end of which time, if his record was good, he was to be sent to the Academy at North Bridgton, . . . the estate to pay the cost of his education. (Seitz, 220–21)

Two trustees were appointed, as well as four literary executors, in England and America. The residue of Browne's estate, after various bequests, was to go toward the founding of "an asylum for worn-out printers in the United States," at the direction of Horace Greeley (Seitz, 220–21).

³The Artemus Ward talk attracted "the largest audience ever assembled in Lincoln Hall"—2,000 people, 150 of them crowded on stage. The Washington *Evening Star* liked the "pleasant talk," but deplored the confusion of Mark Twain's jokes with Artemus Ward's and concluded: "No lecturer has a right to trifle with his audience in that kind of style" ("Mark Ward on Artemus Twain," 24 Oct 71, 1; OC to MEC, 26 Oct 71, CU-MARK). And the Washington *Morning Chronicle*—which had heralded the coming of this "very rare and a very singular human being" who "is never tiresome; never a bore; never offers worn-out jokes; . . . he is at once charming, entertaining, and more than acceptable—the pride and the boast of our people"—was "disappointed" with the performance. It criticized Clemens's "Unfit habits of speech," called his "eccentricities of bearing" the "outward form of the inner peculiarity," and found his gestures "simply *outré* when tried by rules" ("Amusements," 23 Oct 71, 4; "Mark Twain's Lecture at Lincoln Hall," 24 Oct 71, 4). Despite these and subsequent poor reviews, however, Clemens delivered "Artemus Ward, Humorist" exclusively through 6 December. He then delivered it intermittently until the end of the month as he tinkered with and perfected yet another lecture, drawn from *Roughing It*.

⁴See 18 Oct 71 to OLC. The lectures at Easton and Reading were rescheduled for 23 and 24 November, respectively (Redpath and Fall 1871–72, 5).

⁵Clemens wrote this letter on the backs of two pages of his Artemus Ward lecture notes. As these notes indicate, and newspaper reports confirm, the lecture was a mélange of biographical information, anecdotes taken from Ward's works, and Clemens's own anecdotes (see *Inds*, 280, Fatout 1976, 41–48). *The Genial Showman: Being Reminiscences of the Life of Artemus Ward* (1870), by Ward's manager, Edward P. Hingston, seems to have been Clemens's chief biographical source.

⁶Supposedly while traveling

from Waterford to Portland on the Grand Trunk, then and now a rather deliberate railroad, Artemus was annoyed at the slow progress, and, hailing the conductor, said:

"Dear friend, it is plain from the speed of this train that it could never catch a cow if one chanced to travel on the track in front of it. Therefore, the cow-catcher is a useless protection where it is. But there is nothing to prevent a cow from catching up with us in case she should choose to follow. I beseech you, therefore, to remove the cow-catcher from the locomotive and place it on the rear car and so save us from disaster!" (Seitz, 172–73)

Clemens used the story in his lecture, but sharpened the punch line: "'You can't,' said he, 'overtake a cow, but what's to hinder one walking in the back door and biting the passengers'" ("Artemus Ward. By Mark Twain," Gold Hill [Nev.] *News*, 8 Dec 71, 2, reprinting unidentified paper; Fatout 1976, 44). In 1874 he used an abbreviated version of it—with appropriate illustrations and without attributing it to Ward—in chapter 43 of *The Gilded Age* (Pullen, 90–91).

[7] Another complaint about the "Slow Railroad" that Clemens attributed to Ward ("Artemus Ward. By Mark Twain," Gold Hill [Nev.] *News*, 8 Dec 71, 2, reprinting unidentified paper; Fatout 1976, 44).

[8] These page citations (see also notes 10 and 12) establish that Clemens was using George W. Carleton's 1867 edition of *Artemus Ward; His Book* (Charles Farrar Browne 1867a). In this case the allusion is to "The Showman's Courtship" (57–61). The 1867 edition was sold as part of a set that also included *Artemus Ward; His Travels* and *Artemus Ward in London, and Other Papers* (Charles Farrar Browne 1865 and 1867b).

[9] In his "Fourth of July Oration" Artemus Ward declares: "I tell you, feller-citizens, it would have bin ten dollars in Jeff Davis's pocket if he'd never bin born!" (Charles Farrar Browne 1867a, 182). Clemens cited Ward's "celebrated expression" in his lecture as an example of unconscious plagiarism, claiming to have come across the saying "in an English author, who wrote some fifty years ago. Pounds were substituted for dollars, and some other name appeared in the place of Jeff. Davis" ("Mark Twain on Artemus Ward," Albany *Evening Journal*, 29 Nov 71, 2).

[10] "The War Fever in Baldinsville," from *Artemus Ward; His Book* (Charles Farrar Browne 1867a, 185–90).

[11] A paraphrase of the last line of "Interview with the Prince Napoleon," from *Artemus Ward; His Book* (Charles Farrar Browne 1867a, 199). In his lecture, Clemens identified it as a comment on the demise of the comic weekly *Vanity Fair* ("The Institute Lectures," Hartford *Times*, 9 Nov 71, 2).

[12] Ward's "Some Verses Sugestid by 2 of My Uncles" (Charles Farrar Browne 1867a, 200): "Uncle Simon he / Clum up a tree / To see what he could see / When presentlee / Uncle Jim / Clum up beside of him / And squatted down by he."

[13] Unidentified.

[14] This allusion and the next five lines derive from T. W. Robertson's introduction to *Artemus Ward's Lecture* (Charles Farrar Browne 1869, 14–17).

[15] Ward's London lecture.

[16] Clemens told audiences that "Ward used to say that to be attached to anything did not argue good feeling toward it, for he knew of a horse being attached to a dray and yet being down on that dray" and cited the observation as another example of unconscious plagiarism: "A Western journalist told me that this witticism was not original with Artemus Ward, but that he himself was the author of it" ("Mark Twain on Artemus Ward," Albany *Evening Journal*, 29 Nov 71, 2).

[17] In his prefatory note to *Artemus Ward's Lecture*, Hingston remarked on Ward's "self-reliant" nature (Charles Farrar Browne 1869, 23).

[18] By the time this letter reached Redpath, Clemens had given "Artemus Ward, Humorist" in Wilmington, Delaware, on 24 October, and in Norristown,

Pennsylvania, on 25 October. Two of the Wilmington papers reacted politely, calling the lecture "exceedingly pleasant" and "interesting" ("The Lecture Last Evening," Wilmington *Every Evening,* 25 Oct 71, 4; "The Lecture Field," Wilmington *Commercial,* 25 Oct 71, 1). A third expressed its dissatisfaction, however, and concluded: "On the whole it is safe to say that there are few more unsatisfactory efforts to be chronicled in the lecture field" ("Mark Twain's Lecture," Wilmington *Delaware Gazette,* 27 Oct 71, 3). En route to Norristown, Clemens stopped in Philadelphia to see T. B. Pugh, in whose Star Course he was to lecture on 20 November. "This morning," wrote Susan Dickinson on 25 October to her sister, lecturer Anna, "I came across Mr. Pugh with an individual whom he introduced as Mr. Clemens. I can't say that I admire his personal appearance, tone, or manner" (Dickinson Papers, DLC; for Anna Dickinson's even harsher characterization of Clemens for her mother, see *L3,* 66 n. 2, which misidentifies Dickinson's correspondent as her sister). The Norristown performance was unsuccessful: reviewers called Clemens "a fraud as a lecturer" and were insulted by his departure immediately after the lecture (Norristown *Independent,* Norristown *Herald and Free Press,* excerpted in Fatout 1960, 154–55). No lecture was scheduled for 26 October, which Clemens apparently spent mostly in travel, arriving that evening in Hartford. He left early the next morning for his engagement in Great Barrington, Massachusetts (OC to MEC, 23 Oct 71, 26 Oct 71, both in CU-MARK).

To Olivia L. Clemens
28 October 1871 • Great Barrington, Mass.
(MS: Slotta)

Gt Barrington ⎱
Midnight. ⎰

Livy Darling—the lecture went off very handsomely, to a crowded house[1]—& now I'm going to bed—for I love you very very *very* much & am sleepy & stupid. Love to mother & the cubbie—

Ť Sam*ʹ*.

Mrs. Sam*ʹ*. L. Clemens | Cor Forest & Hawthorne | Hartford | Conn.
[*uncanceled, preprinted three-cent stamp*]

[1] In reviewing Clemens's 27 October performance, the Great Barrington *Berkshire Courier* of 1 November "maintained that of the crowd of four hundred, 'at

least three hundred and ninety . . . went away dissatisfied and disappointed. . . . we can only account for his plagiaristic lecture by the . . . same charge he lays upon Artemus Ward—laziness' " (Fatout 1960, 156).

To Olivia L. Clemens
31 October 1871 • Milford, Mass.
(MS: CU-MARK)

WYOMING VALLEY HOTEL   J. B. STARK, PROP'R.[1]

~~WILKES-BARRE, PA.,~~ .... 187 ....

Milford, Mass,[2] 31st

Livy darling, the same old practising on audiences still goes on—the same old feeling of pulses & altering manner & matter to suit the symptoms. The very same lecture that *convulsed* Great Barrington was received with the gentlest & most well-bred smiles & rippling comfort by Milford. Now we'll see what *Boston* is going to do. Boston must sit up & behave, & do right by me. As Boston goes, so goes New England.

I got no letters at Brattleboro. None ∤ had come. None in the post office, either. No proofs from Bliss.[3] Brattleboro is unreliable, I guess.

I didn't write last night. Felt kind of beat out. To-day I traveled the entire day in piddling trains that stopped every four or five minutes. ∤ Am lazy, but not a bit tired—hot bath fetched me around handsomely. Saw Mrs. Lee's brother tonight (we saw *her* at Gov. Hawley's.)[4]

Read Eugene Aram all day—found it tedious—skipped 4 pages out of 5. Skipped the corporal *all* the time. He don't amount to *any*thing.[5] World of love. Kiss mother & cubbie for

Sam'.

[1] See 19 Oct 71 to Bliss, n. 1.

[2] After his Great Barrington lecture of Friday, 27 October, Clemens had a free weekend. Probably he spent it in Hartford, about sixty miles away, before keeping his engagements in Brattleboro, Vermont, and Milford, on 30 and 31 October, respectively.

[3] Possibly an indication that Clemens "had received no proof at all since leaving on tour" (*RI 1993*, 870). See 9 Oct 71 to Redpath, n. 2.

[4] Possibly Mrs. William Elliott Lee, the mother of Charles Dudley Warner's wife, the former Susan Lee ("Mrs. Charles Dudley Warner," New York *Times*, 14 Jan 1921, 11). Warner's partner in the Hartford *Courant* was Joseph R. Hawley, former governor of Connecticut.

[5] Ex-corporal Jacob Bunting was a humorous character in Edward Bulwer Lytton's 1832 novel about the murderous crime of a quiet schoolmaster.

To Olivia L. Clemens
1 November 1871 • Boston, Mass.
(MS: CU-MARK)

WYOMING VALLEY HOTEL   J. B. STARK, PROP'R.

~~WILKES-BARRE, PA.,~~ .... 187 ......

Boston, Nov. 1. PM.

Livy darling, it was a bad night, but we had a packed house, & if the papers say any disparaging things, don't you believe a single *word* of it, for I never saw a lecture go off so *magnificently* before. I tell you it made me feel like my old self again. I wanted to talk a week. People say Boston audiences ain't responsive. People lie. Boston audiences get perfectly uproarious when they get started. *I* am satisfied with to-night.[1]

"Hope" & my other little Auburndale friend, Bessie, were there, in front seats.[2] They sent me a note beforehand to say so, but in the confusion after the lecture I missed seeing them. I have just written them a note urging them to visit us the first time they come to Hartford—& to let us know when they arrive, & we'll meet them at the depot & take them home & make everything jolly for them. Remember this & act accordingly in case I am away.

I am going to lunch with Ralph Keeler, Thomas Bailey Aldrich & one or two others tomorrow,[3]—& tomorrow night I talk in Exeter, N. H.

Will send you my new list tomorrow, if they've got it ready.[4]

Your Easton & Reading letters are here.

Will try & remember to send you some money for the Hookers tomorrow.[5]

I've a perfect *feast* of letters (& socks) from you tonight, darling— God bless you my dearest love, my precious wife.

Saml.

✉︎————————————————————————————————

Mrs. Sam*^l*. L. Clemens | Cor. Forest & Hawthorne | Hartford | Conn.
[*postmarked:*] BOSTON MASS. NOV. 2   2 PM

[1] Having been anxious the previous day about his Boston reception, Clemens here expressed his relief in much the same way he had after his first Boston lecture on 10 November 1869. The Boston *Evening Transcript* reported that the Artemus Ward talk was "listened to with pleasure by a very large audience" and elicited "much merriment" ("Mark Twain's Lecture on Artemus Ward," 2 Nov 71, 4). The Boston *Advertiser* published a synopsis (a practice that had irritated Clemens in 1869), nevertheless expressing disapproval of the performance ("Mark Twain in the Lyceum Course," Boston *Advertiser*, 2 Nov 71, 1; *L3*, 391–92, 394–95 n. 3).

[2] Auburndale, Massachusetts, about ten miles west of Boston, was not on Clemens's present or past lecture itineraries, but these unidentified acquaintances may have attended his 1869 Boston lecture, or one of his other lectures in the vicinity during November and December of that year (*L3*, 484–85).

[3] Clemens had known Ralph Olmstead Keeler (1840–73) since the 1860s, when they were contributors to the San Francisco *Golden Era*. Keeler had led a varied and vagrant life since the age of ten—as a performer with a minstrel troupe, an indigent student in Germany, a teacher of languages in San Francisco, and as a journalist, lecturer, and writer. He was an eastern correspondent for the San Francisco *Alta California* in 1868, then published an unsuccessful novel, *Gloverson and His Silent Partners*, in 1869 and his autobiographical *Vagabond Adventures* in 1870. While working as a special correspondent to the New York *Tribune* he was murdered at sea off the coast of Cuba in December 1873. Keeler had many good friends among the Boston literati, including Thomas Bailey Aldrich and William Dean Howells. He had only just returned from an extensive tour along the Mississippi River, which in part formed the basis of a series of articles he published in Aldrich's *Every Saturday* from 20 May through 9 December 1871. In 1898 Clemens recalled that Keeler had been a lecture tour companion, presumably during the first week or two of November 1871:

> Ralph had little or nothing to do, & he often went out with me to the small lecture-towns in the neighborhood of Boston. These lay within an hour of town, & we usually started at six or thereabouts, & returned to the city in the morning. It took about a month to do these Boston annexes, & that was the easiest & pleasantest month of the four or five which constituted the "lecture season." . . .

> Ralph Keeler was pleasant company on my lecture-excursions flights out of Boston, & we had plenty of good talks & smokes in our rooms after the committee had escorted us to the inn & made their good-night. (SLC 1898a, 5, 14)

The 2 November lunch may have been the memorable occasion attended by Clemens, Keeler, Aldrich, Howells, publisher James T. Fields, and Bret Harte, later described by Howells in three separate accounts. In a letter of 7 May 1902 to Aldrich, Howells recalled:

> That lurid lunch which the divine Keeler gave us out of his poverty at Obers, where the beefsteak with shoe-pegs (your name for the champignons) came in together with the flattened *omelette soufflé*, looms before my dim eyes, and I see Harte putting his hand on Clemens's sealskin shoulder, and sputtering out, "This is the dream of his life,"

while Fields pauses from his cursing can-of-peaches story,—O me, O my! (Howells 1928, 2:156–57)

According to Howells, the lunch was Clemens's introduction to the Boston circle, which had already warmly accepted Harte. Harte's "fleering" comment was acknowledged by a "glance from under Clemens's feathery eyebrows which betrayed his enjoyment of the fun" (Howells 1910, 6–7; see also Howells 1903, 156). If the 2 November lunch was indeed the gathering at Louis P. Ober's restaurant on Winter Place, then it may have been the first public evidence of a reconciliation between Clemens and Harte (see 26 Nov 70 to Webb and 7 June–28 Sept 71 to Harte; Walker, 138–42; Howells 1874; Howells 1900, 275–79; SLC 1898a, 1; *Boston Directory* 1871, 528, 835).

[4]Olivia received Clemens's itinerary in installments, to insure that she remained current as to his whereabouts. His own itinerary book could be most conveniently updated when he was in Boston (9 Oct 71 to Redpath, n. 1; 20 Nov 71 to Howland).

[5]Clemens did not remember to send the rent payment. See 28 Dec 71 to OLC, n. 3.

No LETTERS are known to survive between 1 and 9 November 1871. Clemens's next three lectures—at Exeter (New Hampshire), on 2 November, at Andover (Massachusetts), on 3 November, and Malden (Massachusetts), on 6 November after a weekend respite—kept him in the Boston vicinity. Critical reaction continued to be mixed: the lecture disappointed, while Clemens's manner sometimes pleased. The Exeter *News Letter* complained:

> [Mark Twain] lacks almost every element of humor, and is lamentably deficient in originality; and it passes our comprehension how any man with such a reputation as he has acquired should barter it away on the lecture platform for, comparatively, a mere pittance. . . . We further hope that the press everywhere may be so severe in its censures as to force this plagiaristic lecture off the platform; for we believe that Mark Twain is capable of better things. ("Mark Ward on Artemus Twain," 13 Nov 71, no page)

The Lawrence (Mass.) *American and Andover Advertiser* admitted that the lecturer's "quaint" locutions "often brought down the house," but concluded that a "curiosity is felt to see and hear one who is highly commended in the papers, but frequently there is more pleasure . . . in anticipation than in participation" ("The second of the course . . . ," 10 Nov 71, no page). In Malden, the *Mirror* remarked that the "so-called lecture" was "well worth $15, or even $20" of the $100 fee Clemens received ("Mark Twain's Lecture," 11 Nov 71, 4; Redpath and Fall 1871–72, 4). The Malden *Messenger* voiced the recurrent complaint that "it was difficult to tell which was Ward and which was Twain," but nevertheless judged that Clemens kept the "large audience in good humor, and whatever verdict each listener gave as to the merits or de-merits of the lecture, they were all gratified to see 'Mark Twain'" ("Mark Twain's Lecture," 11 Nov 71, no page).

On Tuesday, 7 November, with no lecture scheduled, Clemens headed home to Hartford, about one hundred and twenty-five miles away, where he lectured on 8 November at Allyn Hall. Having become a Hartford resident, he was no doubt especially anxious to equal the success of his first lecture there, on 23 November 1869 (*L3*, 407–8 n. 8). The Hartford *Courant* heralded his coming, predicting an "overflowing house" and reporting that "everybody is expecting to get a good deal of genuine fun from the lecture to-night" ("Mark Twain To-Night," 8 Nov 71, 2). The audience was not disappointed, according to the *Courant*'s review the next day: the lecturer was "infinitely droll in his manner of telling a story" and received the most "hearty welcome" of the lecture season from the "vast audience" ("Mark Twain's Lecture," 9 Nov 71, 2).

To Olivia L. Clemens
9 November 1871 • Worcester, Mass.
(MS: CU-MARK)

~~WYOMING VALLEY HOTEL~~   ~~J. B. STARK, PROP'R.~~

~~WILKES-BARRE, PA.,~~ .... ~~187~~ ......

Worcester, ——

Livy darling, am just in from the lecture—just in from talking to 1700 of the staidest, puritanical ~~g~~ people you ever saw—one of the hardest ~~g~~ gangs to ~~start that~~ move, that ever was. By George the next time I come here I mean to put some cathartic pills in my lecture. The confounded chairman sat on the stage behind me—a thing I *detest*. He is the last one that can air his good clothes & his owlish mug on *my* platform[.] I will have *no more* of this.

I'm going to bed—I'm disgusted. This chairman was in very good spirits after the lecture. Said he—"Can't *any*body rouse up our audiences, but by ɟ George *you* fetched 'em; & kept 'em at it, too." "Fetched your *grandmother!*" I said,—"a man couldn't fetch them with a hundred thousand yoke of oxen."[1]

But I love you, darling, & I'm going to scoot to bed. Kiss cubbie & mother for me. With a world of love—

Saml.

Mrs. Sam*ᶦ*. L. Clemens | Cor. Forest & Hawthorne | Hartford | Conn [*postmarked:*] WORCESTER MASS. NOV 10

[1] According to the Worcester *Spy,* the capacity audience included "a sufficient number of people with a just appreciation of wit to acknowledge the hour of fun, and laugh most heartily; but there were others who did not appreciate the treat, and went down stairs at the close, talking about the very silly lecture they had listened to" ("Mark Twain's Lecture," 10 Nov 71, 1).

To Olivia L. Clemens
11 November 1871 • Boston, Mass.
(MS: CU-MARK)

Boston (hang the date.

Livy darling, I talked in Randolph last night, to a most delightful & jolly little audience. I was happy, because I knew that as it had been fairly pouring rain for 3 hours, & was *still* pouring, nobody would be there except such as came for the love of it. House two-thirds full, & we had a royal good time.[1]

Have just arrived from Randolph & had breakfast. (11 AM.)[2] But I've been awake since 6, & I *do* feel so rusty & stupid! You see those country hotels always ring a gong at 6 & another at half-past, & between the two they would snake out Lazarus himself, let alone me, who am a light sleeper when nervous.

So with very very great love

Ys
Sam*ᶦ*.

Mrs. Sam*. L. Clemens | Cor Forest & Hawthorne | Hartford | Conn
[*postmarked:*] BOSTON MASS. NOV. 11 ◊ ◊M

¹No reviews of Clemens's 10 November lecture in Randolph, Massachusetts, have been located.
²Clemens remained in Boston to deliver "Artemus Ward, Humorist" there on Monday, 13 November, before a "large and appreciative audience" in the South End course ("South End Course of Lectures," Boston *Journal,* 14 Nov 71, 2). The Boston *Evening Transcript* and the *Advertiser,* which had reviewed his 1 November lecture, did not report this second performance (1 Nov 71 to OLC, n. 1).

To Elisha Bliss, Jr.
12 November 1871 • Boston, Mass.
(MS: CU-MARK)

Boston, Nov. 12.

Friend Bliss—.

Please send copies of "Innocents Abroad" (*marked with my compliments,*) to

{ W. D. Howells, editor "Atlantic,"
Thos. Bailey Aldrich, editor "Every Saturday"
Ralph Keeler.

Direct them all

"Care J. R. Osgood & Co. Boston."¹

I promised them. We've been having a good many dinners together.²

Yrs

Mark.

[*letter docketed:*] √ [*and*] S.L. Clemeny | Boston | Nov 12/71

¹James R. Osgood and Company at 124 Tremont Street, Boston, published both the *Atlantic Monthly* and *Every Saturday* (*Boston Directory* 1871, 539).
²See 1 Nov 71 to OLC, n. 3.

To Olivia L. Clemens
12 November 1871 • Boston, Mass.
(MS: CU-MARK)

Boston, Sunday.

Livy darling, I missed church by waking up too late, tho' I intended to go.

Went to the Press dinner last night. The responses to the *regular* toasts were tip-top; but as it was a cold-water dinner (the absurdity of it!) the flow of impromptu wit & wisdom on the *irregular* call was the flattest I *ever* heard. The thing got so melancholy that it broke up at 10.30—& with a sigh instead of a hurrah.[1] I dearly love a public dinner— but next time I'll inquire whether the inspiration is to be cold water or champagne.[2]

I "kind of" look for a letter from you to-day—it's about time. Kiss the cubbie & mother for me. With unfailing love—

Sam*l*.

Mrs. Sam*l*. L. Clemens | Cor Forest & ⅌ Hawthorne | Hartford | Conn.
[*postmarked:*] BOSTON MASS. NOV. 12   8 PM

[1] This word concluded the letter's first page. The following unexplained calculations, which Clemens evidently made before beginning the letter, appear in the upper left corner on the back of the page:

$$
\begin{array}{cc}
24 & 4 \\
\underline{9} & \underline{60} \\
216 & 240 \\
\underline{17} & \\
233 &
\end{array}
$$

Clemens completed the letter without canceling the figures.

[2] The Boston *Evening Transcript* reported that the event was "the largest and the most successful of any yet held" and clearly thought Clemens's remarks were the highlight of the evening:

Mark Twain, who came in at a late hour, was called up to respond to the toast "Woman," and said that in answer to that toast he had determined to favor the audience with his able and instructive lecture on "Artemus Ward," which would only occupy an hour and three-quarters, but which might be condensed by leaving out all the jokes, into an hour and a half; but on second thought he said he would not give it, as he already saw a look of terrible exasperation on the faces of his audience[.] He then gave some reminiscences of his reportorial career, and, strange to say, the more unfortunate his experiences were, the more uproarious was the laughter which greeted their recital; and naturally becoming discouraged at the want of sympathy exhibited, he sat down amid shouts of laughter, which made the room ring again and again. ("The Boston Press Club," 13 Nov 71, 4)

To Olivia L. Clemens
15 November 1871 • Haverhill, Mass.
(MS: CU-MARK)

Haverhill, —

Livy darling, it was a dreadfully stormy night, the train was delayed a while, & when I got to the hall it was half an hour *after* the time for the lecture to begin. But not a soul had left the house. I went right on through the audience in my overcoat & overshoes with carpet bag in hand & undressed on the stage in full view. It was no time to stand on ceremony. I told them I knew they were indignant with me, & righteously so—& that if any aggrieved gentleman would rise in his place & abuse me for 15 minutes, I would feel better, would take it as a great kindness, & would do as much for *him* some time. That broke the ice & we went through with colors flying & drums beating.[1]

You sent the "Not a stage trick" (for which I am greatly obliged to Warner—it was copied in the Boston papers,)[2] but you didn't send the Brooklyn note you speak of. What was it about?[3]

I am getting my lecture in better shape, now. I end it with the poetry, every time, & a description of Artemus's death in a foreign land.[4]

Mighty glad to hear old Twichell is back. I want to hear him howl about the for "strange, strange lands beyond the sea."[5]

Con*found* the confounded cooks. Offer *five* dollars & a week, & see if that won't fetch one. Advertise again.

I don't get a *chance* to read anything, my old darling—am patching at my lecture all the time—trying to weed Artemus out of it & work myself *in*. What *I* say, *fetches* 'em—but what *he* says, *don't*. But I'm *going* to mark Lowell for you—pity, too, to mar such dainty pages.[6]

Bless your heart, *I* appreciate the cubbie—& shall, more & more as he develops & becomes vicious & interesting. To me he is a very very dear little rip. Kiss him for me, sweetheart. I have ordered the song book[7] for him.

Since I wrote that last sentence, I have been studying the railway guide an hour, my dearie, & I think I can reach home some time Saturday afternoon or evening, & stay till after midnight, & then go on to New York, where I can rest all day Sunday & half of Monday—or possibly there may be a *daylight* train on Sunday from Hartford to New York.[8] I'll find out. I want to see my darling I do assure you.

Sleepy!

Lovingly

Sam[l].

Love[9] to M[r]. & C.[e.]

◀▶ ————————————————————————————————————

[*in ink:*] Mrs. Sam[l]. L. Clemens | Cor. Forest & Hawthorne | Hartford | Conn [*postmarked:*] HAVERHILL MASS. NOV 16

[1] "Some thought it good, others dubbed it 'Small potatoes,'" the Haverhill *Bulletin* remarked on 16 November. "Mark don't care whether he sells small or large potatoes so long as he sells them well, which he does" (excerpted in Fatout 1960, 158–59).

[2] The Hartford *Times* had reported an incident that occurred at Clemens's 8 November Hartford lecture, after his humorous introductory remarks:

> He then produced a most wretchedly torn handkerchief, which he shook out so as fully to display its state of dilapidation, and remarked, "I didn't mean to bring that here; it belongs to General Hawley." This remark was also received with laughter. ("The Institute Lectures," 9 Nov 71, 2)

Probably at Clemens's request, Hartford *Courant* associate editor Charles Dudley Warner hastened into print with "Not a Stage Trick":

> An embarrassing incident happened at the opening of Mark Twain's lecture Wednesday evening. Just as the lecturer began, he took from his pocket a dilapidated piece of linen instead of a handkerchief. The audience laughed, and Mr. Clemens, after a moment's annoyance, turned the matter off with a joke. It was only an accident, resulting from a servant's putting some old linen into the drawer where Mr. Clemens was trustingly taught to expect to find his handkerchiefs, and it might have happened to Edward Everett himself. We only refer to it because we hear that some of the audience regarded it as an arranged joke. Mr. Clemens likes a joke as well as anybody, but he is the last man to attempt a cheap trick of that sort. (10 Nov 71, 2)

Warner's correction, which has not been found in Boston papers, did not neutralize the handkerchief incident. The Boston *Journal* reported on 14 November:

> —Mark Twain, at his lecture in Hartford the other evening, took from his pocket a dilapidated piece of linen instead of a handkerchief. The audience tittered, and Mark probably curtain lectured Mrs. Clemens when he got home. ("Current Notes," 4)

Similar items appeared in the Buffalo *Courier* of 20 November ("Personal," 1), the Cleveland *Leader* of 21 November ("Gossip," 1), and the Danville (Ill.) *Commercial* of 30 November, which noted, with malicious inaccuracy: "This accident has already happened to Mark twenty-three times at his lectures" ("Mark Twain met . . . ," 1).

³ As the next letter indicates, the Brooklyn note soon arrived.

⁴ Ward died of pulmonary tuberculosis in Southampton on 6 March 1867, his delicate health having failed under the strain of a demanding London lecture schedule and the accompanying conviviality (Pullen, 157–61). As late as 8 November, Clemens had ended his talk with a humorous anecdote ("The Institute Lectures," Hartford *Times*, 9 Nov 71, 2). Over the next week he made the change to a eulogy, reciting James Rhoades's poem "Artemus Ward," originally published in the London *Spectator* on 16 March 1867 (40:295–96) and then reprinted in *Littell's Living Age* on 20 April (5:177), which was Clemens's source. His touching rendition of the verses was frequently mentioned in reviews (for example: "Artemus Ward," Portland [Maine] *Eastern Argus*, 17 Nov 71, 3; "Mark Twain on Artemus Ward," Albany *Evening Journal*, 29 Nov 71, 2; "Mark Twain," Erie [Pa.] *Observer*, 14 Dec 71, 3).

⁵ The quotation is unidentified. Twichell had arrived in New York from Liverpool aboard the *Atlantic* on 9 November, but did not return to Hartford until 14 or 15 November (New York *Evening Express:* "Express Marine List," 9 Nov 71, 3; "Passengers Arrived," 10 Nov 71, 4; Lilly G. Warner to George Warner, 13 Nov 71, CU-MARK; Hartford *Courant:* "Hartford Personals," 13 Nov 71, 2; "Brief Mention," 15 Nov 71, 2).

⁶ Probably the "Diamond Edition" of *The Poetical Works of James Russell Lowell*, published by James R. Osgood and Company, of Boston, in 1871 (Gribben, 1:426–27).

⁷ Unidentified.

⁸ This itinerary was for Friday night, 17 November, through Monday, 20 November—between Clemens's lectures on those dates in Lowell (Massachusetts), and Philadelphia. Apparently he reached Hartford as planned. He spent Sunday at home and probably took a Monday morning train to New York to make connections for Philadelphia ("Railroad Time Tables," Hartford *Courant*, 18 Nov 71, 4; 20 Nov 71 to Howland; 27 Nov 71 to OLC, n. 1).

⁹ The abbreviations stood for Mother (Olivia Lewis Langdon) and Cubbie.

To Moses S. Beach
16 November 1871 • Portland, Maine
(MS: ViU)

Portland, Me., Nov. 16.

My Dear Mr Beach—

My wife has forwarded to me from Hartford your kind note of the 10ᵗʰ inst., & I take great pleasure in accepting that part of the invitation which ~~mo of~~ offers food & shelter to *me*,[1] but I fear that Madame & the child will have to lose *their* chance. We have company at home in Hartford,[2] & Mrs Clemens will be obliged to remain there. I am sorry, for a little trip would be pleasant variety after house-moving & cook-hunting.

Please excuse the pencil—haven't any ink. With kind remembrances to the members of your family[3] & to yourself—I am

Ys Truly
Sam*l*. L. Clemens.

M. S. Beach Esq

[1] Moses Sperry Beach, the former editor and proprietor of the New York *Sun*, and his then seventeen-year-old daughter Emeline were among the "prominent Brooklynites" who made the *Quaker City* voyage of 1867, during which Emeline became part of the "charmed circle" surrounding Clemens. Clemens stayed overnight at the Beaches' Brooklyn home in January 1868 (and seems not to have won Mrs. Beach's approval), and he corresponded with Emeline until February 1868; no evidence has been found that he had since improved his acquaintance with the family. Doubtless Beach's hospitality was to follow Clemens's lecture at Plymouth Church on 21 November (*L2*, 15, 51 n. 2, 145, 172, 181–85; Hirst and Rowles, 17, 29–30).

[2] Olivia Lewis Langdon.

[3] Beach and his wife, the former Chloe Buckingham, had three daughters (including Emeline) and two sons.

To Olivia L. Clemens
17 November 1871 • Portland, Maine
(MS: CU-MARK)

Portland, Me., 16th

Livy darling—this is one of my pet places. A wretched, rainy, stormy night, but one of the most packed & crowded audiences ever seen in Portland. Lecture went off magnificently.[1] Been receiving congratulations till now—1 A.M.

Goodnight my darling.

Sam*l*.

✉️————————————————————————————————————

Send Sackett's letter to Redpath.[2]

Mrs. Sam[1]. L. Clemens

Cor Forest & Hawthorne

Hartford

Conn.

[*postmarked:*] PORTLAND ME. NOV 17

[1] The Portland *Eastern Argus* concurred:

> Mark Twain must have a wonderful hold upon the people. It was dismal, uncomfortable, and stormy last night, but nevertheless an immense audience turned out to listen to Mr. Samuel L. Clemens. Over two thousand people crowded into City Hall to see the man who wrote "The Innocents Abroad." . . .
>
> We never saw an audience enjoy itself more heartily than did Mark Twain's last evening. ("Artemus Ward," 17 Nov 71, 3)

Clemens had previously enjoyed a tremendous success in Portland, with "Our Fellow Savages of the Sandwich Islands," on 22 December 1869 ("M. L. A.": Portland *Advertiser*, 23 Dec 69, 4; Portland *Eastern Argus*, 23 Dec 69, 3; Portland *Press*, 23 Dec 69, 3; *L3*, 485).

[2] Possibly the Reverend H. A. Sackett, of Auburn, New York, had written regarding Clemens's 5 December lecture there. Sackett and his wife had been influential in the establishment of Elmira Female College, which Olivia attended as a preparatory student in 1859–60, and which Jervis Langdon served as a trustee from 1862 until 1870 (Towner, 300; Wisbey 1979, 7–8).

To Unidentified
20 November 1871 • Hartford, Conn.
(Paraphrase and transcript: Anderson Auction Company 1914, lot 101)

Hartford, Nov. 20.

. . . .

[*paraphrase: on his traveling*] from place to place lecturing, so have no time to write articles . . . Hartford is now my home

. . . .

From Olivia L. Clemens
to Robert M. Howland
20 November 1871 • Hartford, Conn.
(MS: CU-MARK)

(LLC)

Hartford Nov. 20ᵗʰ· 1871

Mr R. M. Howland
     Dear Sir
     Your letter of the 16ᵗʰ rec'd— Mr Clemens spent yesterday at home, but was too jaded out to write letters or do anything but try to get rested— He desired me to answer your letter for him—
     I do not yet know when he is to lecture in Auburn as I have only ~~his~~ a list of his engagements through Nov.[1] I shall probably have his Dec. list before very many days, if the Auburn appointment should be in that month if you will let me know where to address you, I will send you word—[2]
     I wish Mrs Howland was with you and you could come here and finish your Buffalo visit—[3] I think with great pleasure of ~~that~~ ˄the˄ day spent with us, and truly hope it is the first but far from the last visit that we may have together—
     We are all well, our baby grows fat and hearty every day—
     I wish that Mr Clemens was to be at home for two or three days while you are in New York, then perhaps you could find time to come and see us—
     You and Mrs Howland shall have pictures of the baby and myself as soon as we have any taken— We are exceedingly obliged for yours, I think them very good indeed—
     Please give my love to Mrs Howland when you write her, and express my wish to her that we may know each other better—
     With the kindest regards
                     Your Truly
                     Mrs S.L. Clemens

✉️———————————————————————————————

Mr R. M. Howland | St. Nicholas Hotel | *New York* [*on the flap:*] (LLC)
[*postmarked:*] HARTFORD CT. NOV 20 3 PM [*and*] RECEIVED ST. NICHOLAS HOTEL,
N. Y. NOV 21 1871 [*in Louise Howland's hand:*] and shall regard it a[s] a sou-
venir ~~connecting~~ ‸reminding‸ ⱡ the few brief hours enjoyed in your so-
ciety with the many ~~future~~ [*and*] Louise H——— | R | R | Robert Howland,
| R. M. H. | Louise | Mrs. Osborne | Auburn. | ssssss | //SSSss

¹There is no indication that Clemens's 5 December Auburn lecture was not
already noted in his itinerary book when he spent part of the weekend of 18–19
November with Olivia, but evidently they did not discuss his December schedule. Her own copy of his itinerary came monthly from the Boston Lyceum
Bureau.
²Howland was probably a native of Auburn: he was a volunteer fireman there
before he went to Nevada (Robert M. Gunn, personal communication). It is not
known if his visit to the town, which he was apparently planning for December,
coincided with Clemens's lecture.
³In June 1870 (1–6 or 12–21 June 70 to Howland, n. 2).

NO LETTERS are known to survive between 20 and 27 November 1871.
After his brief respite in Hartford on the weekend of 18–19 November,
Clemens traveled to Philadelphia where on 20 November he talked on
Artemus Ward at the Academy of Music, attracting the "largest audience
ever assembled within its walls to listen to a lecture" ("Mark Twain,"
Philadelphia *Inquirer,* 21 Nov 71, 3). Philadelphia paid Clemens his top
fee of $250, matching what he had received in Boston on 1 November.
But he had to share the platform, much as he had done in Washington
on 23 October: the Philadelphia *Press* reported that "benches and chairs
placed upon the stage gave accommodation to more than a hundred enthusiastic individuals" for the "peculiarly-delicious" performance
("Mark Twain," 21 Nov 71, 8).

On 21 November Clemens appeared in Brooklyn at Henry Ward
Beecher's Plymouth Church. According to the Brooklyn reviewers the
Artemus Ward lecture "heartily pleased" the large audience, evoking
"continuous fits of laughter" ("Mark Twain," Brooklyn *Times,* 22 Nov
71, no page; "Mark Twain on Artemus Ward," Brooklyn *Eagle,* 22
Nov 71, no page).

The following evening Clemens lectured in Rondout, New York, as the opening attraction of the season for "Crane's Lyceum Entertainments," managed by Henry M. Crane, who had arranged his Rondout appearances in 1868 and 1870 ("Washington Hall," Rondout *Freeman,* 10 Nov 71, 2). The Rondout *Freeman* thought the lecture

> in some degree a disappointment, though funny. Mark was by no means half as humorous as in his last lecture, but his inimitable way took with the audience and kept them in good humor. There was more of Artemas than of Mark in the lecture, but what Mark did put in was genuine humor, except the description of Ward's death, which was real pathos. It showed Mark's power of language, and how near akin to grief is genuine humor. ("Mark Twain," Supplement, 1)

On 23 and 24 November, respectively, Clemens delivered the Easton and Reading, Pennsylvania, lectures he had previously postponed. Nothing is known of his reception in Reading, but in Easton "the majority of those present appeared to greatly enjoy the lecture" ("Mark Twain," Easton *Express,* 24 Nov 71, no page). On Saturday and Sunday, 25 and 26 November, Clemens had no lectures scheduled. He seems to have spent at least part of that weekend in Elmira, before going on to Bennington, Vermont, to lecture on 27 November (24 Oct 71 to Redpath; *L2,* 246–47; *L3,* 315–16, 346–47, 353; 3 Dec 71 to OLC, n. 3).

To Olivia L. Clemens
27 November 1871 • Bennington, Vt.
(MS: CU-MARK)

(LLC)

                                                     Bennington, Monday PM
Livy darling, good house, but they laughed too much. A great fault with this lecture is, that I have no way of turning it into a serious & instructive vein at will. *Any* lecture of mine ought to be a running narrative-plank, with square holes in it, six inches apart, all the length of it; & then in my ~~head~~ mental ~~slo~~ shop I ought to have plugs (half marked "serious" & the others marked "humorous") to select from & jam into these holes according to the temper of the audience.

I am so sorry to have to leave you with all the weight of housekeeping on your shoulders—& at the same time I know that it is a blessing to you—for only wholesome care & work can make lonely people endure existence. I particularly hate to have to inflict on you the bore of answering my business letters. That is a hardship indeed.[1]

I think Bliss has gotten up the prospectus book with taste & skill.[2] The selections are good, & judiciously arranged. He had a world of good matter to select from, though. This is a better book than the Innocents, & *much* better written. If the subject were less hackneyed it would be a great success.[3] But when I come to write the Mississippi book, *then* look out! I will spend 2 months on the river & take notes, & I bet you I will make a standard work.[4]

Well, it is late bedtime—so with a loving good night kiss, I send my deep love to my mother Olivia Langdon; & to my wife Olivia Langdon; to my niece Olivia Langdon; & to my future daughter Olivia Langdon.[5]

Sam<u>ˡ</u>.

———————————————————————————————

Mrs. Sam*ˡ*. L. Clemens | Cor Forest & Hawthorne | Hartford | Conn. [*postmarked:*] BENNINGTON VT. NOV. 29

[1] On 20 November Olivia had written the following letter, which Clemens received in Rondout on 22 November (CU MARK):

(*LLC*)

Hartford Monday Eve.

My Darling

Last night you were here and how much nicer it was than it is tonight when you are away— Did n't we have a good visit together? I do hope that this will be the last season that it will be necessary for you to lecture, it is not the way for a husband and wife to live if they can possibly avoid it, is it? Seperation comes soon enough— The Pottier and Stymus bill has come, it is $128.00, I thought it would probably be 150.00, at least— Then the bill on the insurance of our goods against accident— $60.00—so it is well that you left me the additional $150.00 if you had not I should have run ashore—

I answered all your letters today except the one ˏfromˏ Meline that I could not find, if I do not find it I will get his address in some way and write him— It was a pleasure to be writing letters for you, it is a pleasure to do *any* thing for you——

As soon as I had the baby washed and dressed this forenoon I went up in the guest room and lay down and slept until two o'clock.

I am going over to "the club" now in a few minutes   I wish you were going with me   I rather dread it— I want you along to protect me.

The baby is so sweet and dear, I know as he grows older you and he will love each other like *every thing*   What a wonderful thing love is, I do trust that we shall be a *thoroughly united loving family*—it certainly is the heaven here below— Youth in certain things you must teach me a "don't care" spirit, as regards cooks and the like, and I too will endevour to teach myself— I believe there is nothing that sooner ruins the happiness of a family than a worrying woman—

Cubbie is very anxious to have you get home Sat. he hopes that you will not fail us on any account—

I hope it is a pleasant evening in Phil[a] it is rainy and unpleasant here, I have not been out today, I have slept and visited with the baby most of the day—

Mother sits near me at work on her silk quilt   I will try to add a line to this when I come home from Mr Warners

Send Annie's and Sammy's watches to me, so that I can send them with the other gifts— Am home from Mr Ws, will write about it tomorrow—too sleepy tonight

> With never ending love
> Your Livy

Pottier and Stymus, New York furniture manufacturers, had billed the Clemenses for "10 Days Labor packing furniture . . . Express, Board, &c"; the Western Insurance Company of Buffalo provided $20,000 of insurance on the furniture for its shipment to Hartford in September (receipts of 15 Nov 71, 18 Nov 71, CU-MARK). None of the business letters Olivia wrote for Clemens is known to survive. James Florant Meline (1811–73) was the author of *Two Thousand Miles on Horseback. Santa Fé and Back* (1867). His letter may have been a follow-up to one of 11 May 1871 in which he requested Clemens's help in publishing "a new, revised and enormously improved edition" of the book (CU-MARK). The club was the Hartford Monday Evening Club (founded in 1869), which met periodically at the homes of members for discussion and the reading of essays. "It was the early rule that the wife of the host invited two or three of her intimates to sit with her." On 20 November 1871, at the home of Charles Dudley Warner, Joseph R. Hawley read a paper on "Labor Reform." Clemens did not become a member of the club, or read an essay, until 1873 (*Monday Evening Club*, 3–7, 11–12, 14, 28).

[2] Bliss must have sent Clemens one of the first copies of the prospectus for *Roughing It*, which had arrived from the bindery on 22 November. A revised version with a much more complete listing of chapters and illustrations was issued on 23 January 1872 (*RI 1993*, 812, 871, 875).

[3] A proliferation of books about the West contributed to Clemens's sense that his subject was "hackneyed" (*RI 1993*, 798, 828).

[4] As early as January 1866 Clemens seems to have planned a Mississippi River book (*L1*, 329, 331 n. 8). He finally began to explore the subject in his "Old Times on the Mississippi" series, published in the *Atlantic Monthly* in 1875. A four-week tour on the river in April and May 1882 helped him expand the *Atlantic* articles into *Life on the Mississippi* (SLC 1875b; *N&J2*, 432–37).

[5] In addition to his wife and his mother-in-law, Olivia Lewis Langdon, who was still visiting Hartford, Clemens refers to his niece, Julia Olivia Langdon, born to Ida and Charles J. Langdon on 21 November 1871, and his first daughter, Olivia Susan Clemens, born on 19 March 1872. He seems to have visited Charles and Ida in Elmira on 25 or 26 November (3 Dec 71 to OLC, n. 3).

To George L. Fall
28 November 1871 • Albany, N.Y.
(MS: Karanovich)

G.H.H.[1]   Dup. to Bennington

BOSTON LYCEUM BUREAU,

NO. 36 BROMFIELD STREET.

JAMES REDPATH. - - - - GEORGE L. FALL.

OFFICE HOURS FROM 10 A.M. TO 2 P.M.

BOSTON, Nov. 25 1871.

Saml L. Clemens Esq

    Albany

      NY.

Dear Sir

WE HAVE RECORDED AN ENGAGEMENT FOR YOU AT

PLACE,   Kalamazoo Mich

DATE,   Saturday Decem. 16th '71

SUBJECT,   "Artemas Ward Humorist"

TERMS, $125

HOTEL,   will notify you[2]

CORRESPONDENT,   Delos Phillips

REMARKS,   Y. Mens Library Ass'n

ON RECEIPT HEREOF, PLEASE SIGN AND RETURN ENCLOSED
ACKNOWLEDGEMENT.

YOURS TRULY,

Redpath & Fall

H

[*in pencil across the above:*] ‸All right.‸

[*on the back:*]

Albany.

The within is noted. I particularly wanted to talk in Kalamazoo.[3]

Fall, my boy, you haven't given me a hotel, from Fredonia clear to Chicago.[4] Now *you* think I am going to roost in a tree—but I leave it to you, as a man & a brother, if a man can do that in the winter time & keep in good lecturing condition? Now *you* know he can't. Fall, this comes of your exhuberance—your inhuman gaiety of spirits. I shall come to Boston & shoot you, with no mere Colt's revolver, but with a Gatling gun.

Ys

Mark.

Did you understand the Easton telegram? I had home reasons for wanting to get rid of *Scranton* & the necessity of going out there, away from home at that time. And I thought well to get Jersey City canceled too, if possible, though it is not so very far.[5] I told Troy to-night that Feb 1 was well enough there, no doubt—it was near home.[6]

[*letter docketed:*] *Clemens* Saml L. | Hartford Cnn | Nov 25.

[1] Boston Lyceum Bureau chief clerk George H. Hathaway, who prepared this communication. The duplicate he sent to Bennington, Vermont, is not known to survive.

[2] Clemens jotted the Kalamazoo engagement in his lecture itinerary book and later added the hotel name—the Burdick (Redpath and Fall 1871–72, 7–8).

[3] Kalamazoo's attraction for Clemens has not been explained. He is not known to have lectured there previously—nor do any of his surviving letters to Redpath and Fall contain a request for an engagement there.

[4] Clemens's lecture itinerary book, as originally prepared by the Boston Lyceum Bureau, failed to specify hotel reservations for the following engagements between the Fredonia (8 December) and Chicago (18 December) lectures: Erie, Pennsylvania (9 December); Toledo, Ohio (11 December); Ann Arbor, Jackson, Lansing, and Grand Rapids, Michigan (12–15 December). Clemens himself added hotel names—presumably supplied by Fall—for Erie (the Reed) and Lansing (the Lansing) (Redpath and Fall 1871–72, 7–8).

[5] The telegram from Easton, site of Clemens's 23 November lecture, does not survive. He lectured as scheduled in Scranton, Pennsylvania, on 29 January and in Jersey City on 30 January 1872 ("Mark Twain's Lecture," Scranton *Republican*, 1 Feb 72, 6; "Roughing It," Jersey City *American Standard*, 31 Jan 72, 1).

[6] James Redpath later recalled: "You went to Albany. There the hero of Troy besieged you, & final[l]y carried you by assault. You told him that Feb 1 w^d do" (Redpath to SLC, 18 Jan 72, CU-MARK). This arrangement precipitated a difficulty between the Boston Lyceum Bureau and the Paterson, New Jersey, lecture committee, which had priority in requesting the 1 February lecture date (see the next letter, n. 1). The "hero of Troy" may have been George R. Meneely, Clemens's contact in West Troy in January 1870 (10 Jan 70 to OLL [2nd], n. 7).

To James Redpath and George L. Fall
29–30 November 1871 • ?Newark, N.J.
(Paraphrase: Redpath to SLC, 18 Jan 72, CU-MARK)

Well, Troy had telegraphed for Feb. 8. We telegraphed you. You answered with a "word with a bark to it—No"[1]

[1] Clemens probably barked from Newark, where he lectured on 29 November. Having no lecture scheduled on 30 November—which was Thanksgiving Day as well as his thirty-sixth birthday—he could have remained part of the day in Newark before making the long train trip to Oswego, New York, to lecture on 1 December. The curtness of his response may be set down to his extreme reluctance to extend his tour much into February—and to his having just committed himself to a lecture in Troy on the first of that month. Apparently in December, in a telegram now lost, he complicated matters by absent-mindedly agreeing to lecture in Paterson, New Jersey, on 1 February. (He was yielding to the importunities of a Paterson lecture committee that had been waiting since August for confirmation of an early February date.) Redpath managed to reschedule the Paterson lecture for 31 January (7 Jan 72 to Redpath, Axelrod; Redpath to SLC, 18 Jan 72, CU-MARK).

To Olivia L. Clemens
3 December 1871 • Homer, N.Y.
(MS: CU-MARK)

(LLC)

Homer, Dec 3.[1]

Livy darling, send Larned's notes to me at some town where they will have plenty of time to get there—& then the day I get there telegraph me that you have sent them—so when I get the dispatch I will ask the Secretary for the letter.[2] Maybe the notes have gone to Elmira, however—I telegraphed Bowen & Rogers to send them to me there, but they hadn't arrived when I was there.[3]

It is all right, honey,—had already sent Ma $300 on Thanksgiving Day—or rather, the day before.[4]

Tell the Brooklyn writer that the Artemas Ward poem is in Littell's Living Age for March, 1867. Artemus died January ~~187~~ 1867.[5]

Let the bill for the shirts be sent to Redpath & Fall. They'll attend to the payment. What a fool the man was to send it to Hartford. Didn't tell him to.

I am very, *very* glad you have given the nightly care of the cubbie into Margaret's hands.[6] Now darling please don't ever take charge of him again at night. I make this as a loving & special request.

Thank you most kindly for writing all those letters to people for me.

Answered Plummer's letter—told him I was glad he was safely delivered of his first child—the tape worm—but advised him in future to attend to his readings & let his new bride attend to the census.[7]

Indeed it *would* be nice to have Mother Fairbanks with us next spring—be sure & invite her—urge her—command her.[8]

Ah my darling, people *will* come in just when I am going to write you a long letter—& here they have been hour after hour till at last I *must* throw down this pencil & rush to bed—probably the only man now awake in this whole town.

With a whole world of love to you & kisses for mother & the splendid cubbie.—

Saml.

Saml.

Mrs. Saml. L. Clemens | Cor Forest & Hawthorne | Hartford | Conn [*postmarked:*] HOMER N.Y. DEC 3

[1] Clemens performed before a "large assemblage at Barber Hall" in Homer on Saturday, 2 December. According to James P. Foster, a clergyman whom he met two days later, the Artemus Ward lecture was "unexceptionably delightful; the stories were told in a masterly manner, and were chaste and delightful; the envelope of pure humor often covering a touching moral" (Foster). Clemens spent Sunday, 3 December, in Homer and then took the train to Geneva, New York, the following day.

[2] That is, the secretary of the association sponsoring Clemens's lecture.

[3] The notes were for $3,000 that Josephus N. Larned had borrowed in April 1870. The loan was to have been repaid in one year, but had evidently been extended. Dennis Bowen and Sherman S. Rogers were Clemens's Buffalo lawyers (16 and 17 Apr 70 to the Langdons). The Elmira visit probably occurred on the weekend of 25–26 November, in between lectures at Reading, Pennsylvania, and Bennington, Vermont, at which time Clemens would have seen his newborn niece, Julia Olivia Langdon, mentioned in his letter of 27 November to Olivia.

[4] This 29 November payment to Jane Clemens was the latest in the series of more or less regular, but generally smaller, payments Clemens had been making since 1868 (*L3*, 120, 121 n. 1, 425 n. 2 *bottom;* 7 Jan 70 to Fairbanks, n. 7; 17 Feb 71 to JLC and family, n. 4).

[5] Artemus Ward died on 6 March 1867. *Littell's Living Age* reprinted the poem

on 20 April 1867 (15 Nov 71 to OLC, n. 4). The "Brooklyn writer" has not been identified.

[6]This nursemaid had been with the household since early in 1871 (14 Mar 71 to Crane, n. 2).

[7]Olivia had enclosed C. B. Plummer's letter in her own of 28 November. Plummer was a minor platform performer who was a friend of Joseph T. Goodman's in Virginia City, Nevada, in 1867–68, and had admired Clemens since seeing him lecture there in April 1868. He later became a book agent in Lowell, Massachusetts. His repertoire included selections from Shakespeare, Dickens, Longfellow, Holmes, and Whittier, as well as Mark Twain. On 13 December the American Publishing Company sent Plummer a copy of *The Innocents Abroad*, at Clemens's expense. In San Francisco in January 1872, he "brought down the house" with the following passages from it, which he read in "Mark Twain's drawling twang": the discovery of the corpse by moonlight and the "skinned man" sculpture, both from chapter 18, and the tomb of Adam, from chapter 53 (SLC's account statement from the American Publishing Company for 15 Apr 72, CU-MARK; "Plummer's Entertainment," San Francisco *Evening Post*, 6 Jan 72, 3; "Amusements," San Francisco *Chronicle*, 3 Jan 72, 3; "Professor Plummer," San Francisco *Morning Call*, 6 Jan 72, 3; Plummer to SLC, 25 Mar 86, 14 Nov 90, both in CU-MARK; *L2*, 213 n. 4; Doten 1973, 2:962, 971).

[8]Olivia had written Clemens on 28 November, sending her letter to Homer, New York (CU-MARK):

Hartford Nov. 28th 1871

My Dear Heart,

It is too bad to give you the last end of my day when the life and energy are rather gone out of me—

This morning soon after breakfast I went over to Mary Burtons, had a very pleasant call, spoke to her about moving the piano which she says she will do at once, I am glad because I can make the room seem more settled—

Mary says she feels badly to think she is growing old, her last birth day was her 26th and she says she was really low spirited about it— I told her if she had a little one she would not feel so, she said she had no doubt of that— I had not hesatation about making the remark to her because she prefers not to have children is the reason that she does not have them— I never think about feeling badly to think that I am growing older— I hope that age will make me more worthy the respect of my husband and children— I do *long* (you would not allow me to say aspire I suppose) to be worthy of them, to be worthy of such a dear sweet baby as mine is, I hope that as he grows older I shall be thoroughly in sympathy with him in all ways—

Today I took him down town, he rode on the front seat in Margaret's arms, he was painfully afraid of Patrick, he would begin to cry when P. got onto the seat, then would look up to Margaret for reassurance— Oh Youth he is such a delight to me I am so thankful for him— If anything happens to me you must love him *awfully*—

Mother and I have finished The United Netherlands, and commenced Dickens' Childs History of England, it is written in the very simplest style, we read this evening only one chapter of 6 or 7 pages and it went over all the time of the rule of the Romans, the Druids and so on, I am afraid if that chapter is a fair sample that it is almost too condensed, I am fond of that time of the Druidical religion, and wanted to hear more of it— There is more in the Cyclopedia than is given there—

But I presume after the Norman Conquest that it will not be quite so condensed—

I hope that I shall get a letter from you tomorrow morning, I do like to hear from you little man, because you know—well you know all about it—

I send you a letter of C. B. Plummer, if you could tell me what to write him I would write for you— I will send him one of your photographs— He sent one photograph of himself in his natural character and fourteen of himself representing other characters.

I *love you* and want to see you, oh how I shall long to look on the dear face before I can see it again, but then in the meantime I will read new and old love letter[s], and be as content as possible—

All is going well at home, I like Ellen just as well as at first—

Mother sends love and I know the Cubbie wants to, but poor little fellow he cannot speak yet—though he certainly has a speaking face—

Do you pray for me Youth? oh we must be a prayerful family—pray for me as you used to do— I am not prayerful as of old but I believe my heart prays———

With deepest love
Your Livy—

P. S. Wouldn't it be nice to have Mother Fairbanks with me next spring?—

The postscript clearly anticipated Olivia's approaching confinement. Mrs. Fairbanks, her husband, Abel, and their daughter Mollie visited the Clemenses in Elmira in the week following the birth there of Olivia Susan Clemens on 19 March 1872 ("Morning Arrivals," New York *Evening Express*, 26 Mar 72, 3; Fairbanks to OLC, 1 Apr 72, CSmH).

To Olivia L. Clemens
4 December 1871 • Geneva, N.Y.
(MS: CU-MARK)

(LLC)

Geneva, Dec¢ 4.

Livy darling, I am thus far.[1] Coming up from Homer I got acquainted with Rev. Mr. Foster, Episcoapal City Missionary of Syracuse, a noble, splendid fellow—a Twichell. He tells yarns, smokes occasionally, has weaknesses & lovable vices, just like a good, genuine human being, instead of a half-restored theological corpse like *some* pea preachers. Sails right into the meat & marrow of a thing with a whole-hearted cordiality that makes you think what a pity it is there are so many people in the world who never know what it is to have anything more than a ˏmereˏ lukewarm, half-way interest in the pleasures & duties that fall to their lot.[2]

Foster was a Colonel, & was in 14 battles in the war—was in *active* service from the beginning of the war to the end of it. Only entered the ministry a year ago. But *I* think it requires more than *war* pluck to be a city missionary & wade into filthy Irish slums & back streets & face the insults & the hateful beastliness that offend eyes & not nose & spirit in such places. Foster looks about my age, but he has several children— the eldest a clerk in a bank, aged 17! I don't know Foster's age. I gave him "Waterloo," & told him to read it & then mail it to you, as I had marked it somewhat.³ I guess we'll have him up to Hartford, some day, & let him see Twichell.⁴

Last night when the lecture was over, two ladies came forward heartily & shook me by the hand & called me "Sam Clemens, the very same old Sam"—& when the explanations came out, by & by, they were two-little-girl friends of my early boyhood—children with me when I was half as old [as] Sammy Moffett. They both saw me once, ten years ago, but I did not see them. ⟨ One ~~had~~ has been married 13 years & the other about 20. One was Mary Bacon & the other Kitty Shoot. They seemed like waifs from some vague world I had lived in ages & ages & ~~ages~~ ago—myths—creatures of a dream.⁵

Livy dear, I didn't *see* Dʳ Taft—he wasn't in. I suppose I forgot to tell Patrick. You just send for the doctor & have a talk with him—or send Mrs Twichell to him.⁶

I suppose the watches haven't reached you yet. Livy darling, my diamonds are a daily & nightly & unceasing delight to me, they are so beautiful. I thank you with all my might, my darling.⁷

Saw Dʳ Merrill last night & treated him the best I knew how.⁸

Livy dear, my shirts are doubtless lying in the Express office, since you don't speak of their arrival.

With lots of love for you, & Mother & the cubbie.

Samˡ˙

✉ ————————————————————————————

Mrs. Samˡ. L. Clemens | Cor Forest & Hawthorne | Hartford | Conn. [*postmarked:*] GENEVA N.Y. DEC 5

¹On 4 December Clemens lectured on Artemus Ward in Geneva to "a good house—good in numbers, and appreciative in character," but the Geneva *Gazette* was unimpressed, noting that he appeared "very—*tired*, some might denominate it even less complimentarily" ("'Mark Twain' was favored . . . ," 8 Dec 71, 3).

²James P. Foster had an equally positive impression of Clemens, whom he described in a letter signed "J. P. F.," in the Syracuse *Journal* of 6 December:

> Your correspondent was on Monday [4 December] introduced to Mr. Clemens, and was his fellow passenger in a long railroad ride, and is confident . . . that he is possessed of a good generous heart. The writer has seen something of the literary "Bohemians" of the world, and Mr. Clemens is not of such. It is doubtless hard for him to dissociate the ridiculous even from the sublime,—but he has refined instincts, and his humor will do our young men, and old ones, a substantial good. (Foster)

³*Waterloo: A Sequel to The Conscript of 1813,* an English translation of a historical novel by Émile Erckmann and Alexandre Chatrian (New York: Charles

Scribner and Co., 1869). On 7 January 1872 Olivia reported that she had still not received the book from Foster (CU-MARK).

[4] Foster was three or four years older than Clemens. He had much in common with Joseph H. Twichell, a fellow clergyman, family man, and Civil War veteran. Foster had risen to the rank of lieutenant-colonel in the 128th New York Infantry. Twichell had served from 1861 to 1864 as chaplain of an infantry regiment in the 71st New York Volunteers (Heitman, 2:101; Strong, 20–37).

[5] The two women had not approached Clemens "last night," but rather on 2 December, after his lecture in Homer. Mary E. Bacon (b. 1842?) was the only daughter of Catherine Lakenan Bacon (b. 1817) and George Bacon (1809–74), Hannibal's leading wholesale grocer; her married name is unknown. Mildred Catherine (Kitty) Shoot (b. 1840?), was one of the daughters of Mary Pavey Shoot (b. 1822?) and William Shoot (1809–92), the proprietor of Hannibal's finest hotel and co-owner of a livery stable. She had married Charles P. Heywood (1833–1909), the paymaster of the Hannibal and St. Joseph Railroad and later a United States revenue collector, in 1858 (*Inds*, 347–48; Holcombe, 908, 954–55; *Portrait*, 279–80; *Hannibal Census*, 307; Mildred C. Heywood to SLC, 15 Jan 1910, CU-MARK).

[6] Here Clemens began replying to the following letter, which Olivia had sent to Geneva (CU-MARK):

Hartford Nov. 29th 1871

My darling, it is a bitter cold night, the wind blows and it seems very wintry—

I have had no letter from you yet— Don't you feel rather sorry for me? the mails must be very irregular between here and where you lectured Monday night—

I have invited Miss Lee to take dinner with me ˏus˖ tomorrow. Mr and Mrs Warner are away for Thanksgiving—

Be sure and tell me what Dr. Taftt said—

I will try to remember to enclose in this an invitation that has come from Dr Merrill for you to stop with them when you are in Geneva, if you refuse it, do it *very kindly* and make him feel satisfied and contented about your refusing, for he is a good old friend of ours, you remember he sent us plants, grape vines and so on for our wedding gift—

Youth I have been quite busy today and am somewhat tired tonight (although I had a nice nap this afternoon) so that must be my excuse for sending you such a short letter, if you have as great a dread of my letters as you have of all others, you will be rather relieved at that—

The baby has not felt quite usually well today has a little cold—and his gums hurt him—

Good night my own dear heart
Alway[s] with deepest love
Your Livy—

Clemens's attempt to consult with Dr. Cincinnatus A. Taft, doubtless about Olivia's pregnancy, occurred at the end of his 18–20 November visit to Hartford, apparently while Patrick McAleer was driving him to the railroad station (15 Nov 71 to OLC, n. 8). Miss Lee may have been Susan Lee Warner's sister.

[7] The "diamonds" must have been a gift for Clemens's thirty-sixth birthday (30 November). Several weeks later a lecture reviewer noted the "glittering diamond ring" that he wore while performing ("Mark Twain," Pittsburgh *Gazette*, 12 Jan 72, 4). For Olivia's report on the watches, see 5 Dec 71 to OLC, n. 2.

[8] George V. R. Merrill (b. 1841) had moved to Elmira as a young boy and was apparently a longtime friend of the Langdon family's. After distinguished service

as a surgeon in the Civil War, he did not resettle in Elmira until 1873; as Olivia's 29 November letter indicates, he was now living in Geneva (Towner, "Personal References," 108). It is possible that Clemens misdated his meeting with Merrill and in fact met him on 2 December, the same night he met his old Hannibal friends. In any event, he did not accept Merrill's invitation to stay at his house.

To Olivia L. Clemens
5 December 1871 • Auburn, N.Y.
(MS: CU-MARK)

Auburn, Dec. 5.[1]

Old Darling, I thank you very very much for so loving me & so missing & me & remembering my birthday & wishing for me there[2]—& I do reciprocate—I love *you* with all my heart & long to be with you again.

D[r] Merrill came again this morning[3] & we had a real good talk about all the folks—& his hearty loving gratitude to father,[4] & his ~~gener~~ genuine appreciation of father's grand character & great heart ~~quite~~ touched me deeply. Then I *wanted* to go to his house, but felt that I *must* go & see my two old playmates[5] instead, & he granted that my impulse was right. I spent a delightful hour with them. The D[r.] sent me some excellent cigars. Ever, *Ever* so lovingly,

Saml.

Mrs. Sam[l]. L. Clemens | Cor Forest & Hawthorne | Hartford | Conn [*postmarked:*] AUBURN N.Y. DEC 6

[1] After lecturing in Geneva on 4 December, Clemens probably spent the following morning there before departing for the adjacent town of Auburn. His 5 December Auburn audience numbered over a thousand, and possibly included his Nevada friend Robert M. Howland (20 Nov 71 to Howland). The Auburn *Advertiser* remarked that the Artemus Ward talk, "even had it been divested of all the embellishment of humorous anecdote, would have still been decidedly interesting" ("The Lecture," 6 Dec 71, 3).

[2] Olivia's birthday letter of 30 November—which she apparently directed to Auburn—has not been found. Her letter of 2 and 3 December, filled with love and longing for Clemens, has survived, however (CU-MARK). She directed it to Fredonia, which Clemens reached on 8 December:

(LLC)

Hartford Dec. 2nd 1871

My Dear Heart

It did me no good to wish for twenty letters, I did not get one— I have rec'd only one letter and one little note from you since you left home, they both came in the same mail— It is Saturday night, and I am homesick for you, not hearing from you makes me the feel still more homesick—

The watches have come they are all nice and just the thing, Annie's is *lovely*, as prettie as can be—you have good taste Darling— I know she will be perfectly delighted with it—

I have heard nothing from Mrs Brooks, so do not know whether she is coming or not—

It is just after dinner, I guess I will not write more until bed time, perhaps I shall then write more cheerfully   I am a little cross, beside wanting you so much and being disapointed about hearing from you— As you go further west it will take longer and longer for letters to reach me——

Bed time—

Have been drawing a plan of our house and feel better than at dinner time— This will not go until Monday morning so will finish tomorrow— Good night, sweet sleep—

Sunday Evening

I tell you I am glad that tomorrow is Monday, because I shall probably get letters—if I do not—well I do not know what I shall do, telegraph you I guess—

Mother and I went to church this morning, we found that we were the first people in the church, so went over to Mr Twichells and staid there until they were ready for church—

It is so long since I have been to church that I was mellowed by the very atmosphere I think, Mr Twichells prayer touched me and made me cry, he prayed particularly for those who had fallen away and were longing to come back to God— Youth I am ashamed to go back, because I have fallen away so many times and gone back feeling that if I ever should fall aw grow cold again, it would be useless trying, because I never could have more earnest and prayerfull and even at times heart broken determination to keep by the truth and the right, and strive for God's spirit—it would seem if I did not remain steadfast after such times, I never could— Mr Twichell is such a good earnest man and gave us a good sermon, I think we shall enjoy our church there very much— If I was just a little stronger I would go into the Sunday school, I have a great mind too as it is, but I know Mother would not be willing to have me—and I have thought that I would be as careful as I know how during these coming six months— I hope not to have as delicate a child next time as little Langdon was—

How I do want you at home Darling, I am so thankful that I do want you—you are a dear little man— I am grateful that my heart is so filled with love for you— Mrs Warner was speaking this P. M. of lukewarmness toward God, she said she used to be greatly troubled about it, but lately she thinks that is of no consequence, our moods are different we do not always feel the alike toward our husbands— I told her if I felt toward God as I did toward my husband I should never be in the least troubled— I did not tell her how almost perfectly cold I am toward God—

I think I have about decided what we shall do about building, I have *decided* so you will not have to decide you see, de Dear Heart—

We will put if it is necessary the 29000. into house, grounds, and what new furniture we may need— If we wait to know whether we can afford it we shall wait eight years, because I do not believe we shall know whether we can afford to live in this way until the end of the Copartnership— Charlie says I can perfectly well have from three to five hundred dollars a month— You may lecture *one month* in New England during the winter, that will give you 2000.00 that will give you what money you want for Ma and other incidental matters— The three hundred dollars a month with what your regular work will bring you in will be plenty— If after a time we find that the estate is not worth a living to us, we will change entirely our mode of living— That probably will not be discovered for fo three or four or perhaps the eight years—we shall involve nobody and discomfort nobody, we will not be in debt for our house— The children will then be older and I shall not need so much help in the care of them, I shall then be stronger if I keep on increasing in strength as I have done— We will either board or live in a small cottage and keep one servant, will live near the horse cars so that I can get along without a horse and carrage— I *can not* and I WILL NOT think about your being away from me this way every year, it is not half living—if in order to sustain our present mode of living you are obliged to do that, then we will change our mode of living—

We need now the comfort of a convenient home, while our babies are young and needing care— I think if we wait two years it is very likely that we shall not know any better than we do now whether we can build or not— Charlie and all talk as if there was no question about it—

I have not commenced French yet, Clara wants to study German when she comes, and I know with Baby, house and all, both would be more than it would be best for me to undertake———

Good night darling— I do love our boy better and better every day if that is possible— Richest blessings on you my Youth

Lovingly Livy—

Ever and ever so much love to Ma, Pamela, Annie, Sammy— I had forgotten that this letter was to reach you there—

Did Pamela get my letter acknowledging the rec't of her prettie bag?

[3] That is, to Geneva, before Clemens's departure.

[4] Jervis Langdon.

[5] See the previous letter, n. 5.

To James Redpath and George L. Fall
per Telegraph Operator
8 December 1871 • Buffalo, N.Y.
(MS, copy received: ODaU)

456

THE WESTERN UNION TELEGRAPH COMPANY.

39

DATED   Buffalo NY Depot 8[1]   187 1

RECEIVED AT   1.30   Dec 8

TO   Redpath & Fall

36 Bromfield

Notify all hands that ~~F~~from this date I shall talk nothing but selections from my forth-coming book Roughing it, tried it last night suits me tip top[2]

Sam[l]. L. Clemens

27 Paid

J.P.

▷◁

[*letter docketed:*] BOSTON LYCEUM BUREAU. REDPATH & FALL. DEC 8 1871 [*and*]
Clemens Sam'l L. | Hartford—.Conn | Dec. 8ᵗʰ "71.

¹Clemens sent this telegram while en route from Warsaw, New York, where he lectured on 7 December, to Fredonia, where he performed on 8 December.

²Redpath and Fall issued a "Lyceum Circular," dated 1 January 1872, which announced the "Roughing It" lecture. Among the reviews it reprinted was an enthusiastic notice of the debut performance from the Warsaw *Western New Yorker* (see Appendix D). Although Clemens had earlier deemed it unwise to lecture in Buffalo (28 June 70 to Redpath), he still managed to have the new lecture favorably noticed in the Buffalo press. His friend David Gray attended the Warsaw lecture (Warsaw was only thirty miles from Buffalo), no doubt at Clemens's invitation, and printed a complimentary review in his paper, the Buffalo *Courier* (Gray 1871b). Redpath and Fall excerpted it in their "Lyceum Circular."

To James Redpath
9? December 1871 • ?Fredonia, N.Y.
(John Anderson, Jr., 1903, lot 51, and Anderson
Auction Company, 1903b, lot 125)

· · · ·

I like this lecture first rate,—better than any I have ever had except the "Vandal"—three years ago. It is in the style of the Vandal.¹

. . . You can tell the societies they need feel no call whatever to change the advertised lecture. I simply get some fun out of changing it myself on the platform. People *won't* fill a house half so readily to hear about Artemus Ward, as they will to hear about any other subject.²

· · · ·

Mark.

¹"The American Vandal Abroad," based on *The Innocents Abroad*, was the lecture that Clemens delivered in the season of 1868–69.

²Earlier Clemens had insisted that societies be advised of changes in his advertised lecture (15 Sept 71 to Redpath). Fearing that the bad press received by the Artemus Ward lecture might discourage audiences from attending and discovering the replacement, Redpath and Fall ignored his present instruction (see the previous letter, n. 2).

To Mary Mason Fairbanks
10 December 1871 • Erie, Pa.
(MS: CSmH)

Erie, Dec. 10.

Dear Mother—

Am writing a new, tip-top lecture about California & Nevada—been at it all night—am still at it & pretty nearly ẃ dead with fatigue. Shall be studying it in the cars till midnight, & then sleep half the day in Toledo & study the rest. If I am in good condition there, I shall deliver it—but if I'm not just as bright as [a] dollar, shall talk A. Ward two or three nights longer & go on studying.[1] Have already tried the new lecture in two villages, night before last & night before that—made a tip-top success in one, but was floored by fatigue & exhaustion of body & mind & made a dismal failure in the other[2]—so now I am reconstructing & rewriting the thing & I'll *fetch* 'em next time., you

From the very *first* I was planning to spend this day with you & now you see I could not. I am as sorry & a good deal sorrier than you are.[3]

It is train time & I can only send my warm sincere love to you & yours & jump aboard.

Always lovingly
Saml.

[1] Clemens had returned to "Artemus Ward, Humorist" on Saturday, 9 December, in Erie. The Erie *Observer* called his performance a "decided failure" and a "pitiful attempt to ape the style of Artemus Ward, in which he only succeeded in reaching the standard of a negro minstrel" ("Mark Twain," 14 Dec 71, 3).

[2] For the success, see 8 Dec 71 to Redpath and Fall, n. 2. The failure came on 8 December in Fredonia, New York, where Clemens's mother and sister lived. The Fredonia *Censor* characterized the "Roughing It" lecture as "a hash of anecdotes, jokes and descriptions" that made a "rather thin diet for an evening's entertainment," and concluded that Clemens "does injustice both to himself and the societies employing him" ("Mark Twain's lecture . . . ," 13 Dec 71, 3). Probably in Fredonia Clemens received a package of *Roughing It* matter from Elisha Bliss—"all the parts of the book we have printed so far. We have set up to page 300" (Bliss to SLC, 6 Dec 71, CU-MARK; *RI 1993*, 871).

[3] Clemens had intended to stop in Cleveland, to see the Fairbankses, on his way from Erie to Toledo, Ohio.

To James Redpath
11 December 1871 • Toledo, Ohio
(MS: MH-H)

Toledo, Dec. 11.

Dear Red—

My new lecture is perfectly *bully,* now—lays over all my other$ lectures that I have ever delivered yet, *I* think. I rewrote & remodeled it entirely yesterday & last night. So *it* has never really been delivered yet—the germ of it I talked at Warsaw & made a splendid success—& at Fredonia & made a splendid failure—so tired out I came near going to sleep on the platform. I shall open up with these "Passages from 'Roughing It'" about day after tomorrow night—& shall talk without notes the first dash—or bust.[1]

Now say, with this new lecture I'm not afraid of N. Y. or London or *any* place—but I'm not going to talk in N. Y unless ₍1.₎ that is *a regular course & I am on it;* 2—& they sell *season tickets* & can give me *a season ticket audience.* Will the infallible[2] please ascertain these things at once, & if they don't fit 1 & 2 as above, just cross N Y out? Because I will not fill the appointment.[3] I *said* I would fill no private speculation appointments—& those sham courses without course tickets are a *hundred times* the meanest private speculations. I warned you, begged you, *entreated* you to look out for Syracuse=that I feared a private speculation, there— but you paid no attention, & thrust me into the meanest, lousiest, filthiest lecture course with no course tickets,[4]—& wherever I find another one on my list, so help me God I will not deliver the lecture. Lecture me for *nobody* but courses *with course tickets*—& pray don't let another nasty thieving private speculation like *Newark* creep in? Did it never suggest itself to you that a man may be ~~in~~ ₍on₎ a lecture course without being *in* the course & having the benefit of the course tickets? I would not have had Newark happen for $500.[5]

Ys

Mark

P. S. Try to overlook my huffiness. If you knew what suffering a devilish private speculation can inflict, you would excuse a little latitude of speech in the sufferer.

Mark.

✉——————————————————————————

[*letter docketed:*] BOSTON LYCEUM BUREAU. REDPATH & FALL. DEC 14 1871 [*and*] *Clemens* Sam'l. L. | Hartford—Conn | Dec 14th "71.

¹Meanwhile, on 11 December, Clemens delivered the Artemus Ward lecture in Toledo. The Toledo *Blade,* which printed a lengthy synopsis, reported that "Mr. CLEMENS' lecture at White's Hall last night was one of the most remunerative of the course, the gross receipts reaching a trifle beyond $332, leaving, after all expenses were paid, a balance of $105. . . . The lecture was frequently applauded" ("Entertainments," 12 Dec 71, 3).

²George L. Fall.

³The sponsor of Clemens's 24 January 1872 New York engagement—the Mercantile Library Association—was able to satisfy his demands. His lecture was the sixth and final of its course, which had included such speakers as Wendell Phillips and Frederick Douglass (New York *Evening Express:* "Lectures," 11 Dec, 22 Dec 71, 3; "Mark Twain," 22 Jan 72, 3).

⁴Clemens had consistently denounced "private speculations" (*L3,* 418; 8 Jan 70, 28 June 71, both to Redpath). In Syracuse on 6 December he had lectured on Artemus Ward for the Y.M.C.A. The lecture was well advertised in the Syracuse *Standard* in the preceding days and reportedly satisfied an "immense audience" that "responded unanimously" ("Mark Twain," Syracuse *Standard,* 7 Dec 71, 4).

⁵Clemens had previously held a high opinion of his regular Newark lecture sponsors, the Clayonians (10 June 71 to Redpath and Fall). The 29 November Newark lecture was advertised with an "Extra Announcement for Thanksgiving Eve," an indication that it was not part of the regular Clayonian course and did not have the "benefit of the course tickets" ("Amusements," Newark *Advertiser,* 23–25 Nov 71, 3). The Newark *Advertiser* remarked on the "many empty seats" and called the Artemus Ward talk "about the dullest entertainment ever given here" ("Mark Twain on Wednesday Night," 1 Dec 71, 2).

NO LETTERS are known to survive between 11 and 18 December 1871. After his successful Toledo lecture of 11 December, Clemens proceeded to a series of engagements in Michigan. In Ann Arbor, on 12 December, he kept the audience of college students "in a continual roar of laughter" with "Artemus Ward, Humorist," but the next evening, in Jackson, his drawling delivery of the same lecture was thought "rather monotonous and tiresome." In Lansing on 14 December he gave his revamped "Roughing It" lecture (entitled "Out West," according to the Lansing lecture committee's records), a full transcript of which was published on 21 December ("Ann Arbor—Lecture," Detroit *Post,* 15 Dec 71, 1; "Mark Twain," Jackson *Citizen,* 19 Dec 71, 7; Lansing *State Republican,*

21 Dec 71, reprinted in Lorch 1968, 305–21; Wallace, 33). Clemens was a moderate success in Grand Rapids on 15 December, probably giving "Roughing It" (Fatout 1960, 164–65). The press response to his 16 December Kalamazoo performance of "Roughing It," was sharply divided, however. According to the Kalamazoo *Telegraph*, "no lecturer . . . ever more completely disappointed his hearers":

> The substitute for a lecture which Mr. Clemens foisted upon his audience was an insult to their intelligence and capacity. . . . Capable of furnishing a good lecture, Mr. Clemens had no right to impose upon his hearers any such desultory trash as they were subjected to. They had a right to expect something worth coming out to hear, and if he is too lazy or unmindful to do justice to himself or an audience he ought not to lecture at all. He should have given the lecture he contracted to deliver, or something equally good, in its stead, and not put us off with a rambling, disconnected talk about a hackneyed subject, *sans* wit, *sans* information, *sans* sense. It is the duty of the press to expose such impositions, and if other journals remain silent, we shall not. ("Mark Twain in Kalamazoo," 18 Dec 71, no page)

The Kalamazoo *Gazette*, on the other hand, reported that Clemens alternately "enchanted" and convulsed his audience:

> No man, without it be Gough, who has ever lectured before a Kalamazoo audience, had more perfect control of his subject, himself and his listeners. A single word sometimes, said in that slow, droll, calculating way, would be like the spark in a powder magazine.
> The person who reads his writing, gets something of an idea of his humor, but to enjoy it to the fullest, requires one to see the man and hear him say the words[.] ("Mark Twain," 22 Dec 71, 3)

Leaving Kalamazoo at 4 A.M. on Sunday, 17 December, Clemens started for Chicago, 140 miles away.

To Olivia L. Clemens
18 December 1871 • Chicago, Ill.
(MS: CU-MARK)

Chicago, Dec. 16.[1]
My dear dear old darling, I went to bed considerably after midnight yesterday morning, got up again at 4 oclock & went down (breakfastless,) to the depot, & found, with unspeakable gladness that there stood a

sleeping car which I might have been occupying all night—but as usual, nobody about the hotel or among the lecture committee knew anything *certain* about *any* train. I took a berth—the train left immediately, & of course I couldn't go to sleep. We were due here ~~at~~ in two hours—we fooled along & got here in *eleven* hours—3 P. M. ~~Ha~~ Could get nothing to eat, all that time. Not a vehicle at the ~~omnibu~~ station, nor a man or a boy. Had to carry my two satchels half a mile, to Mr. Robert Law's house, & it did seem to me they weighed a couple of tons apiece before I got through. I then ate a perfectly enormous dinner (a roast turkey & 8 gallons of Oolong tea—well it was "long" something—it was the longest tea that ever went down my throat—it was hours in passing a given point.[2]

Then Mr. Law & I immediately hopped into his buggy & for 2 steady hours we capered among the solemn ruins, on both sides of the river—a crisp, bitter day, but all days are alike to my seal-skin coat[3]—I can only tell it is cold by my nose & by seeing ~~peo~~ other people's actions. There is literally no Chicago *here*. I recognize *nothing* here, that ever I saw before.

We sat up & talked till 10, & all went to bed. I worked till after midnight ~~on my~~ amending & altering my lecture, & then turned in & slept like a log—I don't mean a brisk, fresh, *green* log, but an old dead, soggy, *rotten* one, that never turns over or gives a yelp. All night long. Awoke ~~15~~ 20 minutes ago—it is now 11 A. M., & there is a gentleman up yonder at the depot with a carriage ready to receive me as I step out of the cars ~~for~~ from Kalamazoo. I telegraphed him I would be in Chicago promptly at 11 oclock this morning, & I have kept my word—here I *am*. But I can easily explain to him that the reason he missed me was that I mean 11 oclock in a *general* way, & not any particular way, & that I don't blame *him*,—particularly.[4]

~~It is~~

I shall now get ~~& g~~ up and go to Dr Jackson's house & be his guest for 2 days.[5] I feel perfectly *splendid*. One night's rest always renews me, restores me, makes my life & vigor perfect. I wish I could see my darling this morning, & rest her head on my breast & make her forget this dismal lecture business & its long separations. But time moves along, honey! Not so very many days yet!

> With a world of love
> Saml.

><

Mrs. Sam*.* L. Clemens | Cor Forest & Hawthorne | Hartford | Conn
[*postmarked:*] CHICAGO ILL. DEC 19

¹Actually Monday, 18 December.
²Robert Law was a Chicago coal dealer, undoubtedly a business acquaintance
of the Langdons'. He lived at 838 Prairie Avenue, near Lake Michigan but well
south of the area devastated by the Chicago fire in October. Although his home
was spared, Law may have suffered business losses in the fire: his coal business
was listed at three addresses in the city in 1870, but at only one location in the
1871 directory, issued after the fire (*Chicago Directory:* 1870, 484, 984; 1871, 103,
178).
³Clemens had purchased this coat in Buffalo in September 1871 (27 Dec 71 to
OLC, n. 2). In 1910 William Dean Howells still recalled the impression it had
made on him. Howells was mistaken, however, in reporting that Clemens was
wearing it at their first meeting, in November or December 1869, when he came
to the Boston offices of the *Atlantic Monthly* to express gratitude for the magazine's review of *The Innocents Abroad:*

> Clemens . . . was wearing a sealskin coat, with the fur out, in the satisfaction of a
> caprice, or the love of strong effect which he was apt to indulge through life. I do not
> know what droll comment was in [James T.] Fields's mind with respect to this garment,
> but probably he felt that here was an original who was not to be brought to any Bosto-
> nian book in the judgment of his vivid qualities. With his crest of dense red hair, and
> the wide sweep of his flaming mustache, Clemens was not discordantly clothed in that
> sealskin coat, which afterward, in spite of his own warmth in it, sent the cold chills
> through me when I once accompanied it down Broadway, and shared the immense pub-
> licity it won him. (Howells 1910, 4)

The expression of gratitude that Howells remembered, "which the mock mod-
esty of print forbids my repeating," has been shown to have been made in 1872
about *Roughing It* (Howells 1910, 3; *RI 1993,* 888 n. 270; *L3,* 382–83 n. 6).
⁴Clemens had apparently expected to spend Sunday, 17 December, in Kalamazoo. An invitation to spend Sunday night at Robert Law's home presumably
convinced him to make an early departure for Chicago.
⁵Abraham Reeves Jackson, the "doctor" of *The Innocents Abroad,* had moved
from Pennsylvania to Chicago in 1870 and had married Julia Newell, his *Quaker
City* shipmate, in February 1871. They lived at 785 Michigan Avenue. Jackson
was chief surgeon of the newly established Woman's Hospital of the State of Illinois. He was Clemens's host and companion for the balance of the Chicago visit
(*L2,* 65–66; *Chicago Directory* 1871, 94; "Personal Paragraphs," Chicago *Times,*
19 Dec 71, 8). After the first of Clemens's two Chicago lectures, on 18 December,

> a few of the journalists of the city were pleasantly entertained at the residence of Dr.
> Jackson, a gentleman whom Twain immortalized in "The Innocents Abroad." During
> this supplemental two hours, the guest of the evening was even more quaintly humor-
> ous and interesting than during his public talk, developing a strong placer of fun that
> will stand a great deal of industrious mining before it begins to be exhausted. ("Mark
> Twain Last Night," Chicago *Evening Post,* 19 Dec 71, 4)

And on 20 December, the Chicago *Times* reported that Mark Twain, swathed in a seal-skin overcoat and huge muffler, and accompanied by Dr. Jackson and Mr. Steiner, looked in upon several old and a few new acquaintances on yesterday. He leaves for the east to-day. ("Personal Paragraphs," 20 Dec 71, 2)

NO LETTERS are known to survive between 18 and 24 December 1871. Clemens's two "Roughing It" lectures in Chicago—on 18 December at the Michigan Avenue Baptist Church and on 19 December at the Union Park Congregational Church—were very successful. Reporters, some of whom Clemens had met at Dr. Jackson's, praised the lecture while refraining—at least initially—from synopsizing it. "As he repeats the lecture to-night, on the West side," explained the Chicago *Times*, "and we have been requested to restrain our desire to tell some of the good things he said, so that they will be enjoyed the more by those who have had the good fortune to secure seats, we do not give any detailed report of his lecture" ("Amusements," 19 Dec 71, 3). The Chicago *Evening Post* of 19 December extensively praised Clemens's appearance and manner, however, in a review that the Boston Lyceum Bureau extracted for its January 1872 "Lyceum Circular" (see Appendix D). Briefer reviews on 19 December in the Chicago *Mail*, and *Tribune*, and on 20 December in the *Times* were equally positive. Following Clemens's second lecture, the *Tribune* published a long, two-part synopsis that was widely reprinted ("'Mark Twain,'" 20 Dec 71, 4, 24 Dec 71, no page). And the Chicago *Republican* published a text of the Artemus Ward lecture as "What Mark Lectured About Last Night" (20 Dec 71, 2), a mistake gleefully noticed by the *Evening Post* ("Brevities," 20 Dec 71, 4).

After his Chicago triumphs, Clemens lectured in the nearby Illinois towns of Sandwich, Aurora, and Princeton, on 20, 21, and 22 December. No reports of the first two lectures have been found, but a review of his Princeton performance reveals that, because of the Chicago *Tribune* synopsis, he had returned to the Artemus Ward lecture, which the local paper found unsatisfactory ("Mark Twain's Lecture," Princeton *Bureau County Republican*, 28 Dec 71, 4; Wallace, 48). Clemens had no lecture engagements from Saturday, 23 December, through Christmas Monday, 25 December; he returned to Chicago to revise the "Roughing It" lecture yet again.

From Olivia L. and Samuel L. Clemens
to Orion and Mary E. (Mollie) Clemens
24 December 1871 • Hartford, Conn.
(MS: CU-MARK)

Hartford 1871
Christmas Eve.

Dear Orion and Mollie

I enclose our Christmas gift to you and I shall quote literally from
Mr Clemens letter to me, he says "Say something like this in your note,
'Mr Clemens instructs me to put our Christmas remembrance in this
form and says he is moved to do it for several reasons; if it were simply
a sign and token of our love we were sending we could freight *any* article
with it, and it would do its errand and do it well—but in the case of every
Christmas token we have yet projected, we have given the cold shoulder
to nonsense and tried to make the remembrance *useful* along with its loving mission—but we don't know and we can't imagine what would be
best in your case—(we know perfectly well in Orions and would go
straight and buy some wheels and pulleys for his machine[1] if we knew
the sizes needed,—but we don't know where in Mollie's pleasure may
be) so without any nonsense and foolishness (we are all too old for that)
wont you just recieve our fraternal love, and our loving wishes for your
Christmas and future happiness—and put this money with something
that you *want* and want *in dead earnest,* and with all our hearts we can
then say—"that is the very thing that I wanted to get for your Christmas
present but could not think of the name of it'"

So we send to you our love and Christmas greeting, hoping that we
may spend many happy years in Hartford together—

If Mr Clemens was here we would spend this Christmas together—

Wishing you both a merry Christmas and very Happy New Year

I am your loving sister
Livy L. Clemens

Mr and Mrs Orion Clemens | Present[2] [*on the flap:*] (LLC)

¹Presumably the paddle boat that had occupied Orion since the summer (7 June 71 to OC and MEC, n. 3).
²Olivia probably had coachman Patrick McAleer deliver this letter.

To Olivia L. Clemens
25 December 1871 • Chicago, Ill.
(MS: CU-MARK)

Chicago,

Christmas, 2 AM

Joy, & peace & the be with you & about you, & the benediction of God rest upon you this day!

It must have been about this hour, when a brooding stillness lies like a healing sleep upon all nature, & the passions are dead in tranced in human hearts & the good impulses take holiday & visit with the gentle strangers that come in dreams from some happy country beyond our ken, that ˎthatˎ marvelous vision, that diminishing milky-way of white wh wings, stretched its long course out of the firmament & from the heights of Bethlehem the angels sang Peace on Earth, good will to men!

There *is* something so beautiful about all that old hallowed Christmas legend! It mellows a body—it warms the torpid kindnesses & charities into life. And so I hail my darling with a great big, whole-hearted Christmas blessing—God be & abide with her evermore!—Amen. And God bless the boy, too—our boy.

And now to bed—for I have worked hard all day yesterday—& till late last night—& all day again & till *now*—on my lecture—& it is re-written—& is *much* more satisfactory. To-morrow I shall memorize it.¹

Get vaccinated—*right away*—no matter if you were vaccinated 6 months ago—the theory is, *keep* doing it—for if it *takes* it shows you *needed* it—& if it don't take it is *proof* that you did *not* need it—but the only safety is to apply the test, once a year. Small pox is everywhere—doctors think it will become an epidemic. Here it is $25 fine if you are not vaccinated within the next 10 days. Mine takes splendidly—arm right sore. Attend to this, my child.²

With a whole world of love & kisses.

Sam'.

[*in ink:*] Mrs. Sam*ˡ*. L. Clemens | Cor. Forest & Hawthorne | Hartford | Conn [*postmarked:*] CHICAGO ILL DEC 26

[1] Subsequent reviews do not suggest that this revised version of the "Roughing It" lecture differed much in content from the earlier one.

[2] Like many other American cities, Chicago was seeing an increase in small-pox cases, threatening an epidemic. The Chicago Board of Health responded on 21 December by announcing that "each person who has not been vaccinated or revaccinated within the last six months should have the operation performed immediately" ("Small-Pox," Chicago *Tribune*, 21 Dec 71, 2).

To Olivia L. Clemens
26 December 1871 • Champaign, Ill.
(MS: CU-MARK)

DOANE HOUSE. T. DOTY, PROPRIETOR.

CHAMPAIGN, ILL., Dec. 26 187 1

Livy Darling, it is almost lecture time, & I thought I would rattle off a line to tell you how dearly I love you, child—for I cannot abide this execrable hotel & shall leave for Tuscola after the lecture & see if I can't do better.[1] My new lecture is about licked into shape, & this afternoon; after trimming at it all day I memorized one-fourth of it. Shall commit another fourth tomorrow, maybe more—& shall begin talking it the moment I get out of the range of the cursed Chicago Tribune that printed my new lecture & so made it impossible for me to talk it with any spirit in Illinois. If these devils incarnate only appreciated what suffering they inflict with their infernal synopses, maybe they would try to have humanity enough to refrain.

I am *so* sorry you are so lonesome, honey, but keep bravely up till by & by. With ever so much love,[2]

Sam*ˡ*.

Mrs. Sam*ˡ*. L. Clemens | Cor Forest & Hawthorne | Hartford | Conn [*postmarked:*] CHAMPAIGN ILL DEC 27

[1] While still in Chicago, Clemens had noted in his lecture itinerary book, for 26 December: "Ill. Central. Leave Chicago 9.20 AM—get to Champaign 2.50 or 3 PM—128 miles" (Redpath and Fall 1871–72, 9). Like the Doane House, the Champaign lecture, presumably on Artemus Ward, was unsatisfactory. The Champaign *County Gazette* commented: "By Mark Twain's lecture the Young Men's Social Club made $159. The people who heard it are ahead 0" ("Local Chunks," 3 Jan 72, 1).

[2] Olivia replied on 30 and 31 December (CU-MARK):

(LLC)

Hartford Dec 30th 1871

My dear Darling
Your letter from Champaign has just come, I am so thankful that you love me and thankful to you for expressing it, it is always so very sweet a story, always thrills me as something new—

I am *so sorry* that you have been annoyed by those reporters again, but I don't believe people often read those long reports— I wish you would send me the paper though, as I shall not hear the lecture, and I want to know what you are talking—

Mother left me yesterday noon and Clara came last night, I did hate *dreadfully* to let Mother go, but it is perfectly delightful to have Clara here, I have wished for you incessantly, to enjoy her visit too—she is as bright and good and lovely as ever—

I am going down this morning to see about a German teacher, we are going to begin German right away— You must not think of me as lonely Dear Heart but you will let me express to you how much I love & of course miss you—you must be flattered by it—isn't it pleasant to be loved and missed so much— Oh Youth our baby is so sweet and prettie, you will love the little fellow, this morning I would say to him pet, pet-i-pet pet, the motion of my lips seemed to amuse him very much, he laughed until his little shoulders shook— Oh I do *love* the child so tenderly, if anything happens to me in the Spring you must never let him go away from you, keep him always with you, read and study and play with him, and I believe we should be reunited in the other world—

Today is the 30th it is now less than a month till you come *home*, oh am I not *thankful* with all my heart, when it comes to be this week, and then this very day I think I shall bubble over with happiness, oh it is good to love you so tenderly—

Clara and I mean to read and study and do *every thing*— As I writte write she sits the other side of the room in the daintiest bule blue morning wrapper and looks her prettiest— She brought me a very pretty tidy for a chair, and Allie sent us each an imbroydered pocket handkerchief, she imbroydered them both herself—

Sunday Evening
My Darling how can you stay away from us, Clara Sue and Theodore are here, Sue and Theodore are just now looking over Raynard the fox, Clara is looking at Fall-staff and his friends, and (Paul Konewewka's Silhouetts that I gave Mother for Christmas)— Sue is thoroughly in love with the baby, thinks him the sweetest baby she ever saw—

Clara and I have commenced "Their Wedding Journey" and I cannot help constantly wishing that you had marked it for me, I think maybe you would have said some nice sweet things in the margins that would have entitled it to a place in the green box, there are such exceedingly prettie love touches in it— I think I shall have to get you to mark it yet some time—

I *do* want you to be in these good times, all the people would enjoy having you here so very much, and you know I would tolerate it—

Mr George Warner was in here the other evening and was talking some about our house and lot—he wants you to see a house in New York, if we are going to build a kind of City house, thinks it would give us some pleasant ideas— It is on the South side of

37th St. second house from 4th Ave., if you get a chance to see it you will know where to find it— Mrs Chas Perkins, does not want us to decide on a lot over here, but wants us to build some where between Nook Farm & their place— *Youth you won't have any lecture on the 25th of next month will you?* Don't forget to answer me, I am calculating so on that time I think it would be real DREADFUL to be disapointed—they *must* NOT give you any lecture for the 25th I can't have you away any longer than the 24th. Can I Youth? Cubbie *Splendid*   Sue and Theodore are going to stay about two weeks, I wish they could stay until you come.

With deepest love
Livy—

P. S. Your patent right documents have come

In addition to Olivia Lewis Langdon and Susan and Theodore Crane, Olivia mentioned: Clara and Alice Spaulding; George H. Warner, a Forest Street neighbor and the brother of Charles Dudley Warner; and Lucy Adams Perkins, who lived on Woodland Street and whose husband, Charles, was to be the Clemenses' Hartford attorney. Clara Spaulding was looking at *Falstaff and His Companions* (1872), a collection of silhouette portraits by popular illustrator Paul Konewka (1840–71), and she and Olivia were reading Howells's *Their Wedding Journey* (1871). The edition of *Reynard the Fox* the Cranes were examining has not been identified (Geer 1871, 192, 217; "Nook Farm Genealogy," 22; *NUC*, 303:287; *Lyceum* 1872, 96).

To Olivia L. Clemens
27 December 1871 • Tuscola, Ill.
(MS: CU-MARK)

Tuscola, 27th

Livy Darling—

I made an ass of myself leaving a mean hotel at midnight to hunt up ~~another~~ a good one 20 miles away. Train was behind time & didn't get me here till 2.30 AM—& wasn't it *bitter* cold—the coldest night of the season. No one at the depot. Hunted up the hotel myself & carried my own baggage. Found *every* bed in the house occupied—so I had to sit up, in a fireless office the rest of the night.[1] My ~~spe~~ splendid overcoat earned its cost—every cent of it.[2] My *body* was not cold for a moment— but all the dirty shirts & things I could ~~pile i~~ find in my valise wouldn't keep my legs warm. I wouldn't tell who I was, or I could have fared better—I was too savage.

Got breakfast at 7.30, & then pitched into my new lecture & memorized the last half of it. So I know it all, now, & can begin to use it the moment I get away from the Chicago Tribune country.

Lectured on Ward tonight. I ~~got~~ had got through work in time to take a brief, nice nap before talking—consequently was uncommonly bright & fresh.[3]

Am in splendid condition, now to go on working till 1 o'clock—— you see they have changed the time-table, & so I have to be up the entire night to-night again. But I am in high vigor & don't mind it.

I do hope the cubbie is well again—shall be anxious to get your letter tomorrow & learn how he is.[4]

I am going to kiss you good night, my darling, & get at my work. I can do a great deal between this & train time.

Kiss mother & the baby for me, & believe that I love you with all my heart, my darling.

Saml.

Mrs. Sam*l*. L. Clemens | Cor Forest & Hawthorne | Hartford | Conn [*postmarked:*] TUSCOLA ILL. DEC 29

[1] Clemens's reservation at Tuscola's new Beach House (built in 1870), was for the night of 27 December, following his lecture (Redpath and Fall 1871–72, 9–10; Wallace, 51).

[2] Writing to Orion and Mollie Clemens from London on 12? September 1873, Clemens reported that he had "ordered a sealskin overcoat for Charley Langdon—price £50, which is just what mine cost me in Buffalo" (NPV†). He indicated that he had bought his own coat in September 1871. The price in Buffalo would have been $250.

[3] In addition to memorizing his revised "Roughing It" lecture, Clemens was reading and correcting proofs of the book (*RI 1993*, 871–72). No reviews of his Tuscola performance have been found.

[4] For more than a week, Langdon Clemens had been suffering from "lung fever" (28 Dec 71 to JLC). On 20 December Olivia had written to Clemens about the baby, but sent her letter to Mattoon, Illinois, which he did not reach until 29 December (CU-MARK):

Dec. 20th 1871

My Darling

I must not write you tonight because I should write you a homesick letter, I do so LONG to see you—

The baby has been better today, I hope he is over the worst now— Mother and Emma have gone to Miss Dickenson's lecture, I, of course, would not leave our boy—

When we say where is papa he looks right at your picture that stands on the bureau—

Good night my dearest dear heart—more than a month of seperation yet, before we even look at each other—

With deepest love
Livy—

I love you Youth—

But as the present letter shows, Olivia also reported the baby's condition in subsequent letters which Clemens had already received. Anna Dickinson lectured on "Demagogues and Workingmen" ("Anna Dickinson this Evening," Hartford *Courant*, 20 Dec 71, 2). "Emma" may have been Olivia's Elmira friend Emma Sayles.

To Olivia L. Clemens
28 December 1871 • Danville, Ill.
(MS: CU-MARK)

Danville, Dec. 28[1]

Livy Darling, I am very anxious about the baby, & still more anxious about you. I do wish Sue were there to help you—I can't & *you* can't have full confidence in anybody else. Don't overwatch yourself, my darling— don't do it. Preserve your strength—I cannot bear to think of your wearing yourself out again & throwing yourself on a sick bed. You are too dear, too precious to me. I shall telegraph you for news.[2]

I send $300—tell me if you get it. Am also sending Ma $300.[3] The debt to the firm is all paid up.[4]

Good night my own darling.

Sam*l*.

✉—————————————————————————————————

[*in ink:*] Mrs. Sam*l*. L. Clemens | Cor. Forest & Hawthorne st | Hartford | Conn [*postmarked:*] DANVILLE ILL. DEC 28

[1] "Roughing It" was "well attended" on this date, according to the Danville *Commercial*, "and like every other lecture, some appreciated it and others did not." The paper observed that Clemens might have supplemented his fee ($125) if he had posted a doorkeeper at his hotel room "and charged 25 cents admission, for all suckers wished to see him" ("Mark Twain's lecture . . . ," 4 Jan 72, 3).

[2] Clemens did indeed telegraph Olivia when he reached Mattoon, Illinois, on 29 December. Although no text of his telegram has been found, its import may be inferred from Olivia's reply by telegraph that afternoon: "Langdon about well no need of coming" (CU-MARK). And the next day she wrote that Clara Spaulding and Susan and Theodore Crane were visiting (26 Dec 71 to OLC, n. 2).

[3] The $300 that Clemens sent to Olivia was for their quarterly rent on the Hooker house in Hartford. He had promised to send it to her on 2 November. She made the payment on 5 January 1872, four days late. Clemens had previously sent $300 to his mother on 29 November (1 Nov 71, 3 Dec 71, both to OLC;

John Hooker's receipt dated 5 Jan 72 for "quarter ending Jan. 1, 72," CU-MARK).
⁴The indebtedness was for the $12,500 Jervis Langdon had contributed to Clemens's purchase of a share of the Buffalo *Express*.

To Jane Lampton Clemens
28 December 1871 • Danville, Ill.
(MS: NPV)

Danville, Ill, Dec. 28

My Dear Mother—

Enclosed I send you $300.= Just drop Livy a line acknowledging the receipt of it—so that I can know.

I am well, & hard at ~~word~~ work, but I hear bad news from home—the baby has lung fever. I am sure Livy will wear herself out again, sitting up, though she has plenty of help.

With love to all. In a great hurry—

Ys affly

Sam

To Olivia L. Clemens
31 December 1871 • Paris, Ill.
(MS: CU-MARK)

Paris, Dec. 31.¹

Livy darling, I attended church this morning in a warm drizzling rain.

It was the West & boyhood brought back again, vividly. It was as if twenty-five years had fallen away from me like a garment & I was a lad of eleven ₐagainₐ in my Missouri village church of that ancient time.²

There was the high pulpit, with the red plush pillow for the Bible; the hair sofa behind it, & the distinguished visiting minister from the great town a hundred miles away—gray hair pushed up & back in the stern, intellectual Jacksonian way—spectacles on forehead—ponderous reflection going on behind them, such as the village would expect to see indexed there; & likewise an imperfectly hidden consciousness of being the centre of public gaze & interest. There were the stiff pews; the black velvet contribution-purses attached to long poles, flanking the pulpit; the tall windows and Venetian blinds; ₐthe wonderfully ~~slender~~ scattering congregation;ₐ the gallery, with ascending seats, opposite the pulpit; six boys scattered through it, with secret spit-ball designs on the bald⸗ headed man dozing below; the wheezy melodeon in the gallery-front; ₰ the old maid behind it in severe simplicity of dress; the gay young soprano beside her in ribbons & curls & feathers; the quiet alto; the grim middle-aged bass; the smirking, ineffable tenor (tenors are always conceited.)

~~A short prayer by the local minister~~

The choir hurled its soul into a "voluntary"—one of those things where the melodeon pumps, & strains, & groans & wails a bit, & then the soprano pipes a reedy solo, the alto drops in a little after, then the bass bursts in, ₰ then the pealing tenor—then a wild chase, one trampling on the heels of the other—then a grand discordant confusion that sets one's teeth on edge—& finally a triumphant "~~Lo~~ Oh, praise the ~~Lord!~~" L - o - r - d!" in a unison of unutterable anguish,—ₐ& the crime is consummated. It was Herod's slaughter of the babes set to music.

Then there was a hymn. It was read by the local minister. He put a full stop, with strong emphasis & falling inflection, in the middle & at the end of every line—thus:

> "Come, thou *fount*. Of every *blessing*.
> Tune my *heart*. To sing thy *praise*.
> Streams of *mercy*. Never *ceasing*.
> Call for *songs*. Of endless *praise*."[3]

Presently he gave out another hymn, beginning—

> "O for a sweet, inspiring ray—"[4]

And it was old times over again, the way the choir raved & roared ~~& rent & flayed~~ around that victimɇ, & pulled & hauled it & rent & flayed it. You should have heard the tenor do the first line—

"Ow fra suh-weet insp-hiring rye."

Now I believe that such execution, honestly & sincerely done, is approved in heaven. And what large comprehension of Heaven's all=suffering charity the thought affords.

The distinguished minister took his text—he was the agent of a great missionary board—& proceeded to read his moving, argumentative, statistical appeal for money, to the thirty people in the house on this rainy, unpropitious day. That is, he did this after the local minister had read sixteen "notices" of Sunday-school & Bible class, & church, & sewing-society & other meetings; but I could not see that anybody listened to them. However, they never do. The pulpit cannot filch the newspaper's province in these progressive times.

With the first sentence of the sermon the three or four old white headed men & women bent forward to listen intently; the deaf man put his hand up to his ear; a deacon's eye-lids drooped; a young girl near me stole a furtive look at a photograph between the leaves of her hymn=book; a little wee girl gaped & stretched, & then nestled against her mother's shoulder in a way which said "He never will ₍said,₎ "We got to stay here ever so long, now;" one boy got out a peanut & contemplated it, as if he had an idea of contemplatin cracking it under cover of some consumptive's cough the first time he got a chance, another boy began to catch imaginary flies; the boys in the gallery began to edge together, with evil in their eyes; & the engaged couple in front of me began to whisper & laugh behind a hymn-book, & then straighten up & look steadily at ₵ the minister & pinch each other clandestinely. ₍You have seen this couple often.₎ She was a bright, pretty girl of nineteen, & he had his first moustache. These two did nothing but skylark all through the sermon, & I really took just as much comfort in it as if I had been ₫ young & a party to it. Only—it was such a pity to think that trouble must come to that poor child, & her face wither, & her back bend, & the gladness go out of her eyes. I harbored not a critical thought against her for her un-churchlike behavior. Lord! it was *worship!* It was the tribute of overflowing life, & youth, health, ignorance of care—it was the tribute of free, unscared, unscarred, unsmitten *nature* to the good God that gave it! I think it must have been recorded in heaven, above even the choir's "voluntary." And when these two giddy creatures stood up & bowed the head when the blessing was invoked, I made easy shift to believe that the as fair a share of the benediction descended upon their them from the

Throne as upon me, who had been decorous & reverent & had only picked flaws in the minister's logic & damned his grammar.

The ~~sermon~~ ‚missionary appeal‚ concluded, the sexton & the ~~decon~~ deacon went around, while the choir wailed, & collected seventy cents for the carrying of glad tidings of great joy to the lost souls of Further India.

Livy my darling, I am getting well rested up, to-day; & now, it being the middle of the afternoon, I am going regularly to bed, & shall rest, & read just what I please—the very first day wherein I have not worked & studied for lo, these many weeks—seven, it is, counting the week of lecture-work at home before I first started out. I tell you I never want to go ~~su~~ through such a terrific siege again, my sweetheart.

Love—oceans of it—to you; & to the cubbie & to mother;[5] & I do hope I shall hear tomorrow that the boy is doing well & that you are resting & recuperating fast after your hard troubles. Be bright & happy— accept the inevitable with a brave heart, since grieving cannot mend it but only makes it the harder to bear, for both of us. All in good time we shall be together again—& *then*—!

Sam*ˡ*.

[*unidentified hand, in ink:*] Mrs Olivia L Clemens | Hartford | Coneticut | Cor Forest & Hawthorn [*postmarked:*] PARIS ILL. JAN 1 [*and*] DUE 3 [*three-cent envelope, with two additional three-cent stamps*]

[1] No reviews have been found of Clemens's 30 December lecture in Paris, or of his lecture the preceding night in Mattoon.

[2] The First Presbyterian Church of Hannibal, Missouri. "Jane and Pamela Clemens joined the church in February 1841, at which time Samuel Clemens probably left the Methodist Sunday school and began attending the Presbyterian Sunday school instead" (*Inds*, 350). Clemens's memory of the Hannibal church had also been stirred in March 1869 (*L3*, 134–35).

[3] The first stanza of the hymn by the Reverend Robert Robinson (1735–90)— originally published in 1758—but with two changes in wording: "*praise*" for "grace" in line 2, and "endless" for "loudest" in line 4 (Wells, 321–23; Julian, 252).

[4] Composed by Anne Steele (1716–78) and first published in 1760. Olivia doubtless was familiar with this hymn and Robinson's: both were included in the widely used *Plymouth Collection of Hymns and Tunes*, which she and Clemens knew (Wells, 353; Julian, 1089; *L3*, 183–84 n. 9, 250, 384 n. 11; Henry Ward Beecher, 204, 394).

[5] Olivia Lewis Langdon had ended her Hartford visit on 29 December.

Appendixes

Appendix A

Genealogies of the Clemens and Langdon Families

THESE GENEALOGIES are documented in *Mark Twain's Letters, Volume 1: 1853–1866* (379–81) and *Volume 2: 1867–1868* (375), respectively, where they were originally published. Pamela Clemens's first name is given here as before, in accord with her preferred usage, although in fact she was named for her paternal grandmother, Pamelia Goggin, and occasionally signed herself Pamelia (*MTBus*, 4–5; quit-claim deed from Pamelia A. Moffett to Charles L. Webster, 17 Oct 81, NPV).

Clemens Family

Orion Clemens
b. 17 July 1825
d. 11 Dec 1897

m. 19 Dec 1854 ————————————————

Mary Eleanor (Mollie) Stotts
b. 4 Apr 1834
d. 15 Jan 1904

Pamela Ann Clemens
b. 13 Sept 1827
d. 31 Aug 1904

m. 20 Sept 1851 ————————————————

William Anderson Moffett
b. 13 July 1816
d. 4 Aug 1865

Pleasant Hannibal Clemens
b. 1828 or 1829
d. aged 3 months

John Marshall Clemens
b. 11 Aug 1798
d. 24 Mar 1847

m. 6 May 1823 ————————— Margaret L. Clemens
b. 31 May 1830
d. 17 Aug 1839

Jane Lampton
b. 18 June 1803
d. 27 Oct 1890

Benjamin L. Clemens
b. 8 June 1832
d. 12 May 1842

SAMUEL LANGHORNE CLEMENS
b. 30 Nov 1835
d. 21 Apr 1910

m. 2 Feb 1870 ————————————————

Olivia Louise (Livy) Langdon
b. 27 Nov 1845
d. 5 June 1904

Henry Clemens
b. 13 July 1838
d. 21 June 1858

Jennie Clemens
b. 14 Sept 1855
d. 1 Feb 1864

Annie E. Moffett
b. 1 July 1852
d. 24 Mar 1950

m. 28 Sept 1875

Charles Luther Webster
b. 24 Sept 1851
d. 26 Apr 1891

Samuel Erasmus Moffett
b. 5 Nov 1860
d. 1 Aug 1908

m. 13 Apr 1887

Mary Emily Mantz
b. 19 Aug 1863
d. 2 Oct 1940

Langdon Clemens
b. 7 Nov 1870
d. 2 June 1872

Olivia Susan (Susy) Clemens
b. 19 Mar 1872
d. 18 Aug 1896

Clara Langdon Clemens
b. 8 June 1874
d. 19 Nov 1962

m. 6 Oct 1909

1) Ossip Gabrilowitsch
b. 7 Feb 1878
d. 14 Sept 1936

m. 11 May 1944

2) Jacques Alexander Samossoud
b. 8 Sept 1894
d. 13 June 1966

Jane Lampton (Jean) Clemens
b. 26 July 1880
d. 24 Dec 1909

Alice Jane (Jean) Webster
b. 24 July 1876
d. 11 June 1916

m. 7 Sept 1915 ——————— [1 child]

Glenn Ford McKinney
b. 15 Feb 1869
d. 15 Feb 1934

William Luther Webster
b. 15 Oct 1878
d. ? Mar 1945

Samuel Charles Webster
b. 8 July 1884
d. 24 Mar 1962

m. 1920?

Doris Webb
b. ?
d. 9 July 1967

Anita Moffett
b. 4 Feb 1891
d. 26 Mar 1952

Francis Clemens Moffett
b. 1 Oct 1895
d. 4 Mar 1927

Nina Gabrilowitsch
b. 18 Aug 1910
d. 16 Jan 1966

Langdon Family

Jervis Langdon
  b. 11 Jan 1809
  d. 6 Aug 1870

  m. 23 July 1832 ——————————

Olivia Lewis
  b. 19 Aug 1810
  d. 28 Nov 1890

Susan Langdon (adopted)
  b. 18 Feb 1836
  d. 29 Aug 1924

  m. 7 Dec 1858

Theodore W. Crane
  b. 26 Sept 1831
  d. 3 July 1889

Olivia Louise (Livy) Langdon
  b. 27 Nov 1845
  d. 5 June 1904

  m. 2 Feb 1870 ——————————

SAMUEL LANGHORNE CLEMENS
  b. 30 Nov 1835
  d. 21 Apr 1910

Charles Jervis Langdon
  b. 13 Aug 1849
  d. 19 Nov 1916

  m. 12 Oct 1870 ——————————

Ida B. Clark
  b. 7 Mar 1849
  d. 17 Dec 1934

[see Clemens genealogy]

Julia Olivia (Julie) Langdon
   b. 21 Nov 1871
   d. 15 July 1948

    m. 29 Nov 1902 ———————— [2 children]

Edward Eugene Loomis
   b. 2 Apr 1864
   d. 11 July 1937

Jervis Langdon
   b. 26 Jan 1875
   d. 16 Dec 1952

    m. 2 Oct 1902 ——— ——— [2 children]

Eleanor Sayles
   b. 10 Feb 1878
   d. 15 June 1971

Ida Langdon
   b. 15 Oct 1880
   d. 9 Oct 1964

Appendix B

Enclosures with the Letters

ENCLOSURES ARE transcribed here when they are too long to be presented conveniently with the letters themselves. Textual commentaries for these enclosures appear following the commentaries for the letters.

Enclosure with 31 March 1870
To Charles F. Wingate • Buffalo, N.Y.
(Gray 1870)

NEW PUBLICATIONS.

THE INNOCENTS ABROAD, OR, THE NEW PILGRIM'S PROGRESS; Being some Account of the Steamship Quaker City's Pleasure Excursion to Europe and the Holy Land, with Descriptions of Countries, Nations, Incidents and Adventures, as they Appeared to the Author. With two hundred and thirty-four Illustrations. By Mark Twain, (Samuel L. Clemens)[.] Hartford, Conn., American Publishing Company. For sale by Agent in the City.

"The Innocents Abroad" is already a household word throughout the land. The long nights of the nearly passed winter have been shortened by it at thousands of firesides. Hundreds of thousands of readers, young and old, have feasted on its fun and have harvested the fruits of travel from its pleasant pages. There has been more of Europe and the wonderful East *stereopticonned* upon the American mind by its vivid and life-like pictures, than was ever brought from these far-off regions by a single traveler before. In short, Mark Twain's book is a success, and, at this late day, his publishers perhaps will scarcely thank a journalist for stating the fact.

But, although we were not on the ground in time to stake our critical currency on Mr. Clemens' venture as it started out, it may still be permitted us to make note of its gallant progress on the home-stretch; to speak of the qualities that make it so strong on the literary course and which ensure its bringing in to its author the most substantial results of a literary victory. Besides, one can speak with a good deal more of wisdom of a horse or a book, after the heat has been won in the one case, and the first fifty thousand copies sold in the other.

The trip of the Quaker City demanded a Mark Twain for its chronicler. It was itself a sort of a huge joke upon travel, although the grave elders and deacons who planned it were innocent of facetious intent. Its programme promised to pack the Old World's wonders into a six months['] pic-nic, with about two months of sailing time deducted. Passengers were to make an escapade at Marseilles and visit Lyons ("from the heights of which on a clear day Mont Blanc and the Alps can be distinctly seen"!),[1] Paris and the exposition, the rest of France and Switzerland, and catch the steamer again at Genoa. The foot of the Pilgrim was to enter between the straps and pass out at the toe of the Italian boot in an incredibly short space of time. The beard of the venerable East was to be pulled with a dizzy precipitance of irreverence that never had been thought of before.

Clearly, if any other of the Quaker City's cargo, than Mark Twain, had kept a diary of this trip and published it, it would have been a melancholy and calamitous work. But the occasion brought the man, and the result is a happy one, and not a line too long at 650 pages.

Let us venture to state one prime reason why the reader would rather have this book doubled in size than halved. It is because, all through its pages, he is in the company of a man who, in all situations, and upon all subjects, is thoroughly natural—unaffectedly himself. The secret of the humorist is after all the same as that of the poet, or of any of the other characters who get us in their power. There must be no visible effort in the work we are to be amused by or amazed at.

Mark Twain understands this, whether he learned it or came by it intuitively. His rhetoric fits as easily on his thoughts as the drapery on a statue; his fun is never forced; his episodes, (and the book is full of them) however wild[l]y foreign to the subject they may be, come of themselves

[1] Quoted from "the programme of the excursion" in chapter 1 of *The Innocents Abroad*.

and insist on being tagged on to the narrative; his style is of that kind which beguiles the reader to the belief that he could do the same himself if he tried. It seems to flow as water does, simply because it respects the law of gravitation. This is Mark Twain's art, and let those who think it is an easy one to acquire, write a book of six hundred pages and try to sell it!

It would have been terrible, we say, if the average Quaker City pilgrim had made us follow his tracks, partake of his stereotyped emotions and digest the amount of guide-book involved in such a tour. He was permitted to see only the very cuticle of things, but he would have felt bound to make us believe he had penetrated to their marrows and felt their hearts pulsating. Hc would have desecrated sacred things by his false pretenses, in a far worse way than some people thought Mark would do by his jokes. We would have found him out and been disgusted. Perhaps we would have been seduced into pretending we believed in his pretence, which would have been worse. But the true and born Quaker City scribe, accepts his bird's flight over the surface of many lands for what it is worth and makes the legitimate best of it. Not assuming to see more than he does, he tells us the truth about what does come within his vision. And very valuable truth it is, too. In general it is of two-fold character. The book is at once one of lively description, and of faithful, if often grotesque, *impressions de voyage*. In the illustrations which abundantly enliven the text—and which by the way are often good enough to have been "designed by Michael Angelo"[2]—this two-fold character is well set forth. One part of the picture is the foreign scene, whatever it may be; the other exhibits, in rugged comical contrast, its American observers or victims. The figure which the wandering "Innocent" presents, is as genuine a study of life, albeit done in caricature, as are the sketches of Arab donkey boy, of Mabille lorette, of greasy monk, or plain-featured lady of Italy.[3] There is something refreshingly hearty in the Innocent's refusal to be impressed according to guide-book direc-

[2] A paraphrase from chapter 27 of *Innocents*, where Clemens pokes fun at the Italian habit of attributing everything in "poetry, painting, sculpture, architecture" to Michelangelo.

[3] Arab donkey boys appear in chapters 44, 57, and 58 of *Innocents*. The *lorette*, or "lady of easy virtue" (Quackenbos, 377), is the "handsome girl" who dances the "renowned '*Can-can*'" in chapter 14, but not at Paris's "celebrated *Jardin Mabille*," which Clemens only mentions in passing. Fat friars figure in chapters 17 and 25 and "very homely" Italian women in chapter 19.

tions. Even when he shocks our sense of the venerable, in mosque or monastery, it is a healthy shock he gives. We pardon him freely for declining to appreciate "acres and acres of walls papered with the old masters,"[4] because his frank barbarity is the wholesome rebound from an opposite and morbid extreme. We imagine that the "hard pan" of incredulous honesty on which he constantly walks, would be a better basis for a true appreciation of the beautiful and noble, than oceans of frothy sentiment. Sometimes, too, the heights of the poetic are unconsciously touched while the Innocent is knocking about among venerable conventions the most recklessly. We insist that the story of Abelard and Heloise, with the poor Canon Fulbert for its hero, is a more artistic production than the poem of Pope.[5] Petrarch himself would have acknowledged that Mark beats him on his own ground, in diverting a ray of the world's sentiment from the radiant form of Laura to the unknown face of Laura's husband.[6]

When the Innocent *is* seriously impressed by aught he sees, his reader is pretty sure to be. We have such confidence in his honesty that we are not afraid to be humbugged into excess of emotion. Besides, our sentiment is made so fresh by the hearty laugh we had a page before, that we come suddenly into the presence of a noble object with feeling unjaded, and with the element of pleasant surprise added to other delight. We would rather lounge an hour about the Milan cathedral,[7] with Mark Twain, than with any architectural critic that lives. After he has had his little joke about the spectacles through which his fellow-pilgrims behold the sacred sights of Palestine, he comes out and sits at his tent door and looks with his own eyes over the moonlit Sea of Galilee.[8] His revery then is that of a poet. When he penetrates through the rubbish of the great church at Jerusalem to the top of the rock of Calvary, we do not want to hear other words than he speaks. We believe in him and with him when he says, simply: "I climbed the stairway in the church which brings one to the top of the small inclosed pinnacle of rock, and looked upon the place where the true cross once stood, with a far more absorbing interest

[4] *Innocents*, chapter 28.
[5] The history of Abelard and Héloïse and "George W." Fulbert, stripped of "nauseous sentimentality," is in *Innocents*, chapter 15. Alexander Pope's "Eloisa to Abelard" was published in 1717.
[6] A "word in behalf of poor Mr. Laura" (*Innocents*, chapter 19).
[7] Chapter 18.
[8] Chapter 48.

than I had ever felt in any thing earthly before."[9] One might suppose that the Holy Land is the last place in which a professed humorist should write a book. But the Syrian chapters[10] are really the best in Mark's volume. He is realistic and gives life-like sketches where authors have been wont to hang a religious vail, but whatever is Holy in the Land is none the worse for that, and the reader is the better. At proper times and places the man is always greater than the humorist.

Of course the book is not faultless, by any means. Some things in it might have been better said; some better left unsaid. But as a whole it merits more than the praise we have given it. What reader will refuse to say that it is the most entertaining volume of travel he has ever sat up nights with? What critic can question that it is a task of frightful literary difficulties, most satisfactorily and originally performed? We expect better books from Mark Twain, than this, *because* he has given us one, of such a kind, so good. The "kind" is not that most favorable to the display of his powers, except as these are displayed in the triumph over immense disadvantages. But that he has great powers is clearly enough shown, nevertheless. Who but Mark Twain could fire the largest reading public with enthusiasm over a six hundred page diary of European travel? It is but a reasonable inference from his success here, that no other success in essay or descriptive writing is beyond his reach. We do not now speak of him as the first of American humorists, but simply in his character as a literary man. What a delightful current is that of his thought, and through what fresh and untrodden ways it winds! His fancy is full of smiles and fair surprises. His rhetoric, as we have said, is that of a master. Language, in his hands, is an instrument upon which he plays now the best classic music of the schools, and from which, anon, he draws the quaintest lilts and cadences and turns of his own mind's melody. Add to these gifts of his, the rare and high one of humor, and the matchless art of story-telling, and we have an equipment which ought to do great things—to add something permanent to literature—to produce books which will make the world's heart genial centuries hence. Progressing toward such accomplishments, our "Modern Pilgrim" can afford to drop whatever is cheap in the material of his art. He will be more careful as to the texture of his jokes, and without ceasing to be funny will, primarily, be something more and higher. It is much to be able to make a country

[9]Chapter 53.
[10]Chapters 41–56.

laugh. The gift has good uses. But, better than to rouse men's laughter with sight of the grotesque and incongruous, is it to beguile them to smiling acceptance of that which makes them wiser, purer and happier. This latter can Mark Twain do, while certes he will not leave the other undone.

Enclosure with 1 April 1870
To Jervis and Olivia Lewis Langdon • Buffalo, N.Y.
(SLC 1870s)

"MORE WISDOM."[1]

"They that go down to the sea in ships, see the wonders of the deep;"[2] and they that buy coal mines in Pennsylvania and work them see wonders likewise.

They see the wonder of finding themselves suddenly stripped of their independence and converted into the servants of their own employés.

They learn to come and go, do and undo, bow and scrape, simper, smile, shuffle and smirk, at the behest of the "Miners' Union."[3]

They enjoy the wonder of seeing orderly men murdered and little or no notice taken of it by Pennsylvania law officers sworn to execute the statutes, but who prefer perjury to unpopularity, apparently.

[1] Evidently an allusion to Solomon's remarks in Ecclesiastes 1:16: "I communed with mine own heart, saying, Lo, I am come to great estate, and have gotten more wisdom than all they that have been before me in Jerusalem: yea, my heart had great experience of wisdom and knowledge." Clemens also used this title for a segment of a "San Francisco Letter" dated 22 December 1865 to the Virginia City *Territorial Enterprise,* where he made explicit reference to "Solomon's wisdom" (SLC 1865h; *ET&S2,* 341–42).

[2] "They that go down to the sea in ships, that do business in great waters; / These see the works of the Lord: and his wonders in the deep" (Psalms 107:23–24).

[3] The Workingmen's Benevolent Association, organized in Schuylkill, Northumberland, and Carbon counties, in the Pennsylvania anthracite coal region, in 1868. In 1869 the three locals confederated under a single governing council. The W.B.A.'s efforts in behalf of higher wages and safer working conditions were generally unsuccessful, in part because of regional, ethnic, and economic clashes among its members. It collapsed in 1875, a casualty of a disastrous strike (Aurand: 1966, 19–34; 1971, 67–95; Long, 97–110).

They enjoy also the wonder of seeing a legislature lavish all its solicitude upon the miner, without seeming to reflect that his employer has a soul to save too.[4]

They enjoy, finally, the spectacle of a legislature delivering into the hands of an irresponsible mob the actual control of property belonging wholly to their employers.

Such are some of the wonders these men see. The secret of it all lies in the fact that the members of the Miners' Union are a political power. They have votes, and therefore legislatures must not offend them nor petty officers see the small indiscretions which they commit with scalping knife and Deringer.[5]

But the latest wonder is a certain thing which has just become a law in Pennsylvania. It is, that every mine shall be under the control of three persons, whose prerogative it shall be to order alterations in the manner of opening or working it, and who shall also close up and stop work upon such mine when in their discretion it shall seem proper to do so. And who appoints these autocrats? The owners of the mine? No. *Their employees do it.*[6]

[4] In fact, the Pennsylvania legislature had long neglected the coal miners. Although anthracite production was an important industry by the early 1840s, Pennsylvania's first labor laws, enacted in 1843 and 1848, did not apply to miners. Laws passed in 1849, 1851, and in the 1860s established liens on mine owners' property in order to protect miners' wages, but the legislature failed to remedy the abusive company store system, set a uniform standard for the weighing of coal, or pass an effective eight-hour-day law. Until 1869 it ignored the miners' pleas for safety legislation, instead yielding to mine operators who were aware that "to safeguard the lives of those employed in their mines it would be necessary to make a considerable outlay for safety devices, the existence of which was known to every mine owner" (Trachtenberg, 24). Moreover, the safety act of 1869 applied only to Schuylkill County. Several months after its passage, a disaster in one of the supposedly safe mines in Luzerne County took the lives of 179 men and became the stimulus for an act of 3 March 1870, which set more rigorous safety requirements for all of the state's anthracite mines (Trachtenberg, 13–18, 23, 26–39). See also note 6.

[5] The pocket pistol invented by Philadelphia gunsmith Henry Deringer (1786–1868). The now accepted, but incorrect, spelling (derringer) reportedly originated with counterfeit weapons, on some of which "the inventor's name was misspelt, possibly to escape any legal action, although Deringer had not patented his design" (Blair, 178).

[6] The 3 March 1870 law did not provide for three "autocrats" for every mine, but rather for only six mining inspectors for the entire anthracite coal region. It stipulated that candidates for inspector be selected by court-appointed boards

Nothing need now be deemed impossible to a Pennsylvania legislature.

And who is it into whose hands the legislature has given this high appointing power? Simply an irresponsible society of men who hold meetings, pass laws, and enforce them by the agencies of terrorism and blood. When a man goes to work in a colliery tabooed by the Miners' Union, they stick a notice on his door-post suggesting that he resign his situation with all convenient dispatch—and they emphasize this suggestion by printing at its top the sign of a coffin.

That these "coffin notices," as they are called, are not inspired by empty bravado, may be gathered from the following telegram, dated Shamokin, March 5, and signed by an old and respectable resident of that locality:

> "Luke Fidler colliery was going to work without the Union. The 'Mollie McGuires' of the Union men murdered the watchman. Three superintendents in one colliery in Shamokin have been murdered since the troubles in the coal mining districts began, and nothing done about it."[7]

---

of examiners "consisting of three practical miners and two mining engineers." The boards were to report to the governor "who would appoint the inspectors, for a term of five years, from the list of men supplied. No person acting as agent or manager for the mine owners, or in any way interested in the mines, could be appointed." Inspectors were authorized to verify the implementation of safety measures, investigate all accidents, and apply to local courts to close mines if no other remedy were effective. "To make thorough investigation possible, the inspector was given the power of a coroner. He could compel people to attend hearings, and could administer oaths" (Trachtenberg, 43–45, 50).

[7] Jervis Langdon may have been Clemens's source for this telegram. Langdon's coal firm had mines in Shamokin, possibly including one or both of those mentioned by the unidentified "old and respectable resident" (16 Apr 70 to Crane, n. 1). The Molly Maguires, originally an Irish anti-landlord organization, were commonly blamed for the violence in the anthracite coal region, and reputedly flourished in Schuylkill and Northumberland counties, the latter including Shamokin (Broehl, 79–81). Their responsibility for the bloodshed is still disputed, however:

> Widespread violence and the equally widespread notion of a secret society called the Molly Maguires forced the popular equation of the two. In the resulting milieu there was an excellent outlet for pent-up frustration. It is easy to conceive of a person who, denied institutional outlets, found an outlet for his anger by evoking the Mollies. It was simple: one sent an anonymous note emblazoned with a pistol or coffin and promising vengeance on the recipient. Superintendents and foremen were the most likely targets in the anthracite regions. Men in managerial positions throughout the nation received similar warnings, but only in the Schuylkill and Lehigh anthracite regions did popular opinion make the receipt of a "coffin notice" a fearful experience. The number of "cof-

These are the sort of people who are to choose three absolute sovereigns to preside over each mine. These are the people for whose "protection" the Pennsylvania legislature is straining itself to provide. It seems an unnecessary courtesy while ammunition is so cheap.

After saying so much about it, do we suggest a remedy? A remedy for secret assassination; for blind and deaf and dumb officers of justice; for mob terrorism; for truckling legislatures? No; there is no remedy for these things. That is, no remedy that can be brought into instant use. There is one, but time is required for it. It applies itself, and is simply that remedy which comes to the relief of all disorder, viz: the teaching of reason and fair dealing to all parties concerned, through the convincing agencies of hardship, disaster and weariness of fighting each other.

However, should the Pennsylvania legislature take the only step now left it to take for the "protection" of those persecuted lambs, the miners, and make them absolute, joint and equal owners with the present nominal proprietors of the collieries, it is fair to presume that the millenium of peace and order in that Pandemonium[8] would be greatly hastened. Until then, let us continue, as is usual and proper, to wail for the poor oppressed and down-trodden miner, whose only solace, in this cold world, is putting up his little "coffin notice" on his neighbor's door and then helping to get him ready for the funeral.

---

fin notices" sent to managerial personnel was sufficient to complete a relationship in which violence equaled Molly Maguires and Molly Maguires equaled labor unions.

Calmer minds, however, could not grant the equation of the Molly Maguires and organized labor. The amount of violence actually declined during the period of the Workingmen's Benevolent Association's greatest strength. (Aurand 1971, 98–99; see also Long, 110–13)

[8]"Pandemonium, city and proud seat / Of Lucifer" (*Paradise Lost*, 10.424–25).

Enclosure with 30 January 1871
To James Redpath • Buffalo, N.Y.
(Redpath 1871)

THE LECTURE SYSTEM.

Sketches of its Humbugs.

THREE FEMALE PORTRAITS.

Confessions of a Reformed Lecturer.[1]

SKETCH THE FIRST—MISS NANCY SIKES.

[The Western press and public will find these Sketches well worthy of their study. They are literally true portraits from life; only some of the names of persons and places are changed, and every statement made in them can be confirmed by documentary evidence.—EDS. HERALD][2]

Traveling on the cars from Boston to New York I met a merry-eyed, energetic gentleman who suddenly accosted me, and gave me to understand that he had managed to survive a lecture of mine given a few weeks previously in a New England city.

"I'm the first of a long line to come," said he.

I made free inquiry which of the Original Jacobs[3] of the coming age I had now the honor to address.

"I'm a Reformed Lecturer!" he answered, as boldly as you please, with as much unction, in fact, as if he had just come from the anxious seat and there proclaimed himself a miserable sinner.

Being at that time still, as it were, in the gall of sin and bond of iniquity,[4] (my "list" had not yet been half "gone through" and it did look

[1]Clemens worried that this subtitle "pretty plainly points to me" (26 Jan 71 to Fairbanks). Both the manner and confessions of the "Reformed Lecturer" suggest that Redpath did base him, at least in part, on Clemens, but no evidence has been found that the resemblance was publicly noted.

[2]See 26 Jan 71 to Fairbanks, n. 1.

[3]Unidentified.

[4]Acts 8:23: "For I perceive that thou art in the gall of bitterness, and in the bond of iniquity."

lucrative to the mind's eye,) I asked him what special degradation there was attached in his view of it, to the modern development of the Homeric profession.

"I'm disgusted with it," he said, "it is getting into the hands of humbugs; and above all of the she-humbugs—women like—," but I will not indicate the three noted ladies whose sudden rise into newspaper notice had made their names familiar in our mouths as household words.

I remarked that they had certainly been quite successful in winning a high position and added that I presumed they were eloquent speakers.

"Eloquent!" exclaimed my nervous companion. "Eloquent! One of them makes up her lectures of froth and panier in equal parts; the second writes a smart little essay and reads it in a smart little way—without one touch of native or acquired eloquence in either; and the other couldn't compose a dozen sentences of decent English, in my opinion, to save her soul from Satan, or, what would hurt her worse, her pearls from the pawn brokers!"[5]

"And yet," I interposed, trying to quiet my excitable friend, "it seems to me you must be mistaken; the metropolitan papers speak highly of them; and, surely, (if the Arabian traditions be true, that God put down ten bushels of talk in the world and women seized nine of them)[6]— surely, we ought to have a large supply of eloquent female orators."

"That's theory," retorted—what shall I call him?—some specially distinctive name it must be—not too common nor yet wholly unfamiliar— Mr. Smith, let us christen him, and Theodosius for short—"That's *theory*," rejoined Mr. Theodosius Smith, "the fact is, that in all this broad land that has the plague of Talkists worse than old Egypt ever had the plague of lice,[7] there are only three women who would hold their present rank if they were suddenly made into men. One of them, a young woman

[5] Olive Logan, whom Redpath goes on to ridicule at length in this article; Kate Field; and, almost certainly, Lillian S. Edgarton, the "pearl of the platform," who offered two lectures during the 1870–71 season, "Woman Is Coming" and "Whither Are We Drifting?" the latter "a conservative view of the marriage question" (Odell, 9:89, 119–20; American Literary Bureau, 4). Redpath's Boston Lyceum Bureau had not represented either Field or Edgarton, and represented Logan only from 1869 until 1871 (30 Jan 71 to Redpath, nn. 2, 3; Eubank, 295–99).

[6] Redpath's source for this "tradition" has not been found. It may have been one of the many "hack versions" of the *Arabian Nights* that had long been available in English (Haddawy, xvi).

[7] Exodus 8:16–18; Psalms 105:31.

whom everybody knows, and the other two are over fifty years of age.[8] And yet the three she impostors I have named to you are mentioned ten times in the papers where these three genuine orators are mentioned once."

"How is it done?" I asked—for although I was earning money in my profession, I had never asked "favors" of the press, and my agents had never done so for me, "do you mean to say that all these notices are paid for?"

"Not all;" he replied, "I have found out the whole *modus operandi*— not all, but all in the beginning. Now what I shall tell you, isn't imaginary—I won't say how it *can* be done, I shall say how it *is* done to my own knowledge."

"Go on," I said.

"Well, one of these dear creatures,—let us be perfectly civil about it,—has an agent all to herself. I don't want to name her, but, to avoid confusion, let us give her some imaginary name. She is a virtuous and educated lady—of course. To make it impossible to detect her suppose we call her Nancy Sikes? So be it. And suppose we call her agent Bill?[9]

"Nancy's Bill makes it the one object of his life to keep Nancy's name constantly before the public. Does General Butler[10] become conspicuous for the time? Nancy's Bill immediately writes: 'Miss Nancy Sikes, the celebrated lecturer, is said to be an own cousin of General Butler.'

"Nancy's Bill has a large newspaper acquaintance. He knows the sub⸗

[8] Probably Anna E. Dickinson (1842–1932); Julia Ward Howe (1819–1910), author of the "Battle Hymn of the Republic" and one of the leaders of the American Woman Suffrage Association; and Mary A. Livermore (1820–1905), famed for her Civil War charitable work and also a leader of the American Woman Suffrage Association and the editor of its weekly *Woman's Journal*. All three were on the Boston Lyceum Bureau's lecture roster. For the 1870–71 season Redpath had offered four lectures by Dickinson: "To the Rescue!," "Joan of Arc," "A new lecture on the Woman Question," and "Out of the Depths: a lay sermon." He offered three lectures by Livermore: "The Reasons Why" (on women's suffrage), "Women in the War," and "Queen Elizabeth" (*Lyceum* 1870, 2, 3). Howe did not lecture for the bureau in 1870–71 or 1871–72, but in 1872–73 she returned to the roster with "Paris," "Representation," and "A Trip to Santo Domingo" (*Lyceum:* 1869:2; 1872:3).

[9] These sly pseudonyms for Olive Logan and her publicist, William Wirt Sikes, equated them with the murderous thief Bill Sikes and his mistress and victim, Nancy, in *Oliver Twist*. Clemens's criticisms of the Logan-Sikes partnership closely resembled Theodosius Smith's (8 Jan 70 to OLL [1st], n. 3).

[10] Benjamin F. Butler (1818–93), the controversial Union general and military governor of New Orleans, now a prominent congressman from Massachusetts (*BDUSC*, 716).

editors and reporters in New York, and he finds no difficulty in having this paragraph inserted in an evening journal. The public interest in Gen. Butler sends that item flying through the press in every Northern State.

"Out again, in a weekly paper this time, comes the indefatigable Bill once more. 'The New York Daily —— states that the popular and eloquent lecturer, Miss Nancy Sikes, is an own cousin to Gen. Butler. We cannot credit this statement, because Miss Nancy is very beautiful, and how *could* she be a relative of Gen. Butler.'

"This poisoned arrow wings its way through the Democratic press.

"The ingenious Bill hasn't exhausted his resources yet, for, in a prominent metropolitan journal a few days after, up he jumps again: 'We see a paragraph going the rounds of the country press, that the celebrated lecturer, Miss Nancy Sikes, is an own cousin to Gen. Butler. We have the best authority for stating that she is no relative whatever.'

"This is bad for Butler, but you can see how this lie, well toed, has been made to do a heap of free advertising, can't you?"

"Do you mean to say," I asked, "that this very trick has been played?"

My friend, Mr. Theodosius Smith, did not answer, but he took out a circular from his pocket and convinced me that he had not spoken a word in jest.

"Well," he resumed, "there is no end of items that Nancy's Bill starts in this way; I have no doubt from what I have seen myself and have heard from other agents, that he manages to get from twenty-five to fifty a week in different parts of the country. Anything that any paper anywhere says in praise or dispraise of his Nancy, her faithful William makes a 'point' of. And then, when this fails, Bill goes into the correspondence business. He is a good writer, and so he sends to leading papers all over the country interesting 'newsy' letters which he charges little or nothing for, just to insert ingeniously, somewhere, a puff of the celebrated Miss Nancy Sikes. The West is flooded with Bill's letters. Nancy grows famous. Committee men, seeing her name mentioned so often, think she *must* be somebody great. They send for her terms, and then they are sure she *is* great. For Bill modestly answers that if he can find a night, (which the same is doubtful) she will go for $150—the highest price you will notice, for average towns, that the most famous orators of the nation ever think of charging." [11]

[11] See 12 June 71 to Redpath, n. 2.

I looked out at the window; we had come to a depot, and the boys were calling out the New York papers.

"I'll bet you a dollar just for the fun of it," said Mr. Theodosius Smith, "that some one of these papers has an item in it about Miss Nancy Sikes!"

"Done!" said I, eagerly, for to tell the truth, I had a certain pride of profession—*un esprit du corps*—which this merciless iconoclast was wounding badly.

"Done!" he repeated. He bought half a dozen papers, and was soon lost in them. "You've lost," he said, from the depths of an evening sheet, "here are *two*, one an editorial in the ——, and the other a three line item in the ——."

I *had* lost.

"Look at this item," continued Mr. Theodosius Smith, "and see how this fellow has profited by the story of Samson, whose strength lay in his hair.

"'Miss Nancy Sikes,'" he read, "'has now entirely dispensed with her $1,500 chignon. Indeed, it is not needed, as her own luxurious hair reaches down almost to her feet when it is unloosened.'"

Here Theodosius roared.

"I wonder," he said, "how soon Bill will announce to an expectant world that Miss Nancy Sikes has cut her toe-nails! If he ever does, you may bet that three or four days afterward another paragraph will appear contradicting the first item and stating that, in consequence of the incessant demands on her time to answer the letters of lecture committees, Miss Nancy Sikes has never yet found time to cut her toe-nails, and does not hope to be able to do so until the end of the season!"

Theodosius is a very nervous gentleman, and without as much as 'by your leave,' he crumpled up the paper and threw it out of the car window.

"Just think[,]" he exclaimed, with an indignant wave of his hand, "that American journalism will so far degrade itself as to chronicle such frothing small beer! Mind you, this is the second or third little item about Nancy's hair that respectable metropolitan papers have allowed to crawl into their columns. Oh! for a conscientious small tooth comb editor! But look you[,]" continued Theodosius, "read that leader."

It was an editorial on the lecture system; it seemed honest enough, at first sight, but became a crafty puff of Miss Nancy Sikes under the light thrown on it by my traveling companion.

"That's Bill's article," he said. "Bill has brains; he is as cunning as Nancy is—complaisant. You know that Gough[12] is the most popular lecturer in the country—he stands as far ahead of all others in the public favor as the President ranks all his subordinate civil officers—and Anna Dickinson holds the same position to all the women lecturers. Now, look you, Bill has contrived to bring these three names—Gough's, Anna's and Nancy's—into this short editorial several times, as if they were acknowledged equals; read it carefully again, and you will see that without saying so in as many words, he leaves the impressions not only that they are all on a par in popularity, but that Miss Nancy is the ablest of the two. Gough amuses; Miss Dickinson instructs; *but* (ye Gods!) Miss Nancy Sikes both amuses and instructs!"

The editorial was in a respectable paper and certainly said all that, partly by inference and partly by direct statement.

Mr. Theodosius Smith relapsed into a laugh.

"Shakespeare amuses; Milton instructs; but George Francis Train both instructs and amuses.[13] By the long tresses of Miss Nancy Sikes, I swear I'll write an editorial and prove it! I'll easily get it published. I'll do as Bill does—give it to some sub-editor short of a subject and not charge the poor devil a cent for it and give him a dinner in the bargain. But then[,]" he said with a sneer, "George Francis Train could'nt pay me as Bill's bills are paid[.]"

"My dear fellow," I interposed, "all this does not account for the big pile of notices that Miss Sikes receives from the press in different parts of the country."

"It so happens," said Mr. Theodosius Smith, "that when I was in the *Journal* office in Boston, I found a lot of old papers in one corner—last summer's—and saw a far-western sheet among them. I picked it up out of curiosity. There was an editorial on Miss Nancy Sikes! Nancy had been there at the time. Read it," he said, "and compare it with the editorial in your hand."

He took out his pocket-book and handed a slip to me.

"Read it."

I opened my eyes in astonishment. There could be no doubt of it. The

---

[12] John Bartholomew Gough (22 Jan 71 to Redpath, n. 2).

[13] Train, the political agitator, self-promoter, and lecturer, was not on the Boston Lyceum Bureau's roster (Eubank, 295–99). For Clemens's opinion of him, see *L3*, 145.

same pen had written both. But here there was no inferential language. Miss Dickinson was sneered at as a scold, while Miss Nancy was extolled in the loftiest terms.

"How is this?" I asked.

"Bill was there—he and his Nancy, or Nancy and her Bill, often travel together. And Nancy talks and her William writes. And before Nancy talks William writes, and after Nancy talks Bill writes again. And so the truth is kept away from the knowledge of lecture committees until they find out by experience that although Miss Nancy is smart in her line— largely, let me say, in the clothes-line—she is no more a she Gough, nor a Miss Dickinson, than I am Hercules or Wendell Phillips a Blondin.[14]

"That's a good comparison, by the way," said Smith, pleased with his climax, "because I *have* some strength; I can 'raise a smile' sometimes, and Phillips does 'know the ropes;' but our forte would seem to lie in other directions."

When a man makes a very poor joke and thinks it tip-top, every well regulated mind expends its force on the risible muscles, as a matter of good fellowship, [so] I laughed. Besides, I had seen and heard Wendell Phillips, and to picture him dressed up in tights was not wholly a soul= calming contemplation.

"Well," went on the merciless Smith—by christen name, Theodos- ius—"when a season is over, Bill gathers up all these puffs and makes up his circulars for next year. He don't hesitate to alter them to suit. I got one of them the other day and marked it. Here it is;" and out again from his wallet he jerked, rather than drew, a circular.

"Do you see 'Bill, his mark' in these?"

He had drawn his pencil under certain phrases, which showed at once, to a practiced writer, that these notices, although published in papers as far apart as St. Paul's, Minnesota, and Orange, New Jersey, were the products of the same fertile brain.

"Does Bill always go with Nancy?" I asked.

"No; but don't you know that lecture committees are always ready to have puffs of the lecturers they engage published in advance, and that local papers have never any objection to oblige the committees, who are mostly the best men of the town? Bill sends notices; these commit the

[14]Redpath represented social reformer Phillips (1811–84), but not daredevil Charles Blondin (pseudonym of Jean François Gravelet, 1824–97), famous for crossing Niagara Falls on a tightrope (Eubank, 297–99).

paper; and even when they don't, unless the lecturer makes an awful failure, editors don't care to chronicle the true state of the case, lest they should seem to blame the committee.[15] So the truth is crushed to earth in every way—only dearly bought experience tells the committees who are and who are not humbugs."

"Well, what of it?" I said, "after all, every calling has its humbugs, and this hurts ours as little as quack advertising hurts the medical profession."

"No sir!" retorted Mr. Smith. "Not so. The Lyceum, in the hands of right-minded and clear-sighted men, might be made the college of the people, with a broader scope, and loftier purpose, than any existing college. It needs every aid that can be given to it. There is not a 'natural taste' for it. This taste needs cultivation. Every quack that is allowed to tread the platform is a small national calamity, like the plague of frogs.[16] Every friend of popular education ought to combine to suppress them. Every lyceum whose funds they obtain under these false representations, ought to expose them. Every local journal ought to give them—"

"Ten minutes for refreshments!" shouted the conductor.

We got out and suspended our conversation till the cars started again.

[TO BE CONTINUED.]

[15] One "awful" failure by Logan was long remembered in the press (31 Dec 70 to Reid, n. 4).

[16] Exodus 8:2–14; Psalms 78:45, 105:30.

Appendix C

Lecture Schedule, 1871–1872

THIS SCHEDULE, spanning volumes 4 and 5 of *Mark Twain's Letters*, lists Mark Twain's known lecture appearances during his tour of 16 October 1871–27 February 1872. This tour, like his 1869–70 tour (*L3*, 483–86), was managed by James Redpath and George L. Fall of the Boston Lyceum Bureau. It included seventy-seven engagements throughout the East and Midwest, about two dozen more than in 1869–70. The primary sources consulted in recreating this itinerary were Clemens's surviving letters and, especially, his lecture route notebook, provided by the lyceum bureau (Redpath and Fall 1871–72). Only the final two engagements, in Danbury and Amherst, are not listed in the notebook (which is cited explicitly here only when no independent confirmation of a lecture has been found). In a few instances, Clemens's letters supply the sole confirmation of a notebook listing. In most cases, however, lecture engagements have been confirmed by announcements, reviews, or reports in local newspapers (unless otherwise indicated, a cited newspaper was published in the town or city where Clemens lectured). ✽

DATE	PLACE	SOURCE
16 Oct 71	Bethlehem, Pa.	*Times* (17 Oct 71, cited in McIlhaney)
17 Oct 71	Allentown, Pa.	*Chronicle* (18 Oct 71)
18 Oct 71	Wilkes-Barre, Pa.	*Luzerne Union* (25 Oct 71)
23 Oct 71	Washington, D.C.	*Evening Star, Morning Chronicle, National Republican* (24 Oct 71), and others
24 Oct 71	Wilmington, Del.	*Every Evening* and *Commercial* (25 Oct 71), *Delaware Gazette* (27 Oct 71)
25 Oct 71	Norristown, Pa.	*Independent* and *Herald and Free Press* (cited in Fatout 1960, 154–55)
27 Oct 71	Great Barrington, Mass.	*Berkshire Courier* (1 Nov 71, cited in Fatout 1960, 156)

DATE	PLACE	SOURCE
30 Oct 71	Brattleboro, Vt.	*Vermont Phoenix* (3 Nov 71, cited in Fatout 1960, 156)
31 Oct 71	Milford, Mass.	31 Oct 71 to OLC
1 Nov 71	Boston, Mass.	*Advertiser, Evening Transcript*, and *Journal* (2 Nov 71)
2 Nov 71	Exeter, N.H.	*News Letter* (13 Nov 71)
3 Nov 71	Andover, Mass.	Lawrence *American and Andover Advertiser* (10 Nov 71)
6 Nov 71	Malden, Mass.	*Mirror* and *Messenger* (11 Nov 71)
8 Nov 71	Hartford, Conn.	*Courant* and *Times* (9 Nov 71)
9 Nov 71	Worcester, Mass.	*Spy* (10 Nov 71)
10 Nov 71	Randolph, Mass.	11 Nov 71 to OLC
13 Nov 71	Boston, Mass.	*Journal* (14 Nov 71)
14 Nov 71	Manchester, N.H.	*Union* (15 Nov 71)
15 Nov 71	Haverhill, Mass.	*Bulletin* (16 Nov 71, cited in Fatout 1960, 158–59)
16 Nov 71	Portland, Maine	*Eastern Argus* and *Advertiser* (17 Nov 71)
17 Nov 71	Lowell, Mass.	*Citizen and News* (18 Nov 71)
20 Nov 71	Philadelphia, Pa.	*Press* and *Inquirer* (21 Nov 71)
21 Nov 71	Brooklyn, N.Y.	*Eagle, Times*, and *Union* (22 Nov 71)
22 Nov 71	Rondout, N.Y.	*Freeman* (24 Nov 71)
23 Nov 71	Easton, Pa.	*Express* (24 Nov 71)
24 Nov 71	Reading, Pa.	*Times and Dispatch* (25 Nov 71, cited in Fatout 1976, 47)
27 Nov 71	Bennington, Vt.	27 Nov 71 to OLC
28 Nov 71	Albany, N.Y.	*Evening Journal* (29 Nov 71)
29 Nov 71	Newark, N.J.	*Advertiser* (1 Dec 71)
1 Dec 71	Oswego, N.Y.	*Commercial Advertiser and Times* (2 Dec 71)
2 Dec 71	Homer, N.Y.	Syracuse *Journal* (6 Dec 71)
4 Dec 71	Geneva, N.Y.	*Gazette* (8 Dec 71)
5 Dec 71	Auburn, N.Y.	*Bulletin* and *Advertiser* (6 Dec 71)
6 Dec 71	Syracuse, N.Y.	*Standard* (7 Dec 71)
7 Dec 71	Warsaw, N.Y.	*Western New Yorker* (14 Dec 71) and Buffalo *Courier* (9 Dec 71)
8 Dec 71	Fredonia, N.Y.	*Censor* (13 Dec 71)
9 Dec 71	Erie, Pa.	*Gazette* and *Observer* (14 Dec 71)
11 Dec 71	Toledo, Ohio	*Blade* and *Commercial* (12 Dec 71)
12 Dec 71	Ann Arbor, Mich.	*Chronicle* (16 Dec 71) and Detroit *Post* (15 Dec 71)

DATE	PLACE	SOURCE
13 Dec 71	Jackson, Mich.	*Citizen* (19 Dec 71)
14 Dec 71	Lansing, Mich.	*State Republican* (21 Dec 71, cited in Lorch 1966, 304–5)
15 Dec 71	Grand Rapids, Mich.	*Morning Democrat* and *Eagle* (16 Dec 71, cited in Fatout 1960, 164–65)
16 Dec 71	Kalamazoo, Mich.	*Telegraph* (18 Dec 71) and *Gazette* (22 Dec 71)
18 Dec 71	Chicago, Ill.	*Tribune* (19, 20, 24 Dec 71), *Evening Post*, *Mail*, and *Times* (19 Dec 71)
19 Dec 71	Chicago, Ill.	*Evening Post* and *Times* (20 Dec 71)
20 Dec 71	Sandwich, Ill.	Redpath and Fall 1871–72
21 Dec 71	Aurora, Ill.	*Herald* (16 Dec 71)
22 Dec 71	Princeton, Ill.	*Bureau County Republican* (28 Dec 71)
26 Dec 71	Champaign, Ill.	*County Gazette* (3 Jan 72)
27 Dec 71	Tuscola, Ill.	27 Dec 71 to OLC
28 Dec 71	Danville, Ill.	*Commercial* (4 Jan 72)
29 Dec 71	Mattoon, Ill.	Redpath and Fall 1871–72
30 Dec 71	Paris, Ill.	31 Dec 71 to OLC
1 Jan 72	Indianapolis, Ind.	*Journal* (2 Jan 72)
2 Jan 72	Logansport, Ind.	*Sun* (4 Jan 72, cited in Fatout 1960, 169)
3 Jan 72	Richmond, Ind.	Redpath and Fall 1871–72
4 Jan 72	Dayton, Ohio	*Journal* (5 Jan 72)
5 Jan 72	Columbus, Ohio	*Ohio State Journal* (6 Jan 72)
6 Jan 72	Wooster, Ohio	*Republican* (11 Jan 72)
8 Jan 72	Salem, Ohio	*Republican* (10 Jan 72)
9 Jan 72	Steubenville, Ohio	*Gazette* (12 Jan 72)
10 Jan 72	Wheeling, W.Va.	*Intelligencer* (11 Jan 72)
11 Jan 72	Pittsburgh, Pa.	*Gazette* and *Commercial* (12 Jan 72)
12 Jan 72	Kittanning, Pa.	Pittsburgh *Commercial* (12 Jan 72)
16 Jan 72	Lock Haven, Pa.	*Democrat* (11 Jan 72)
17 Jan 72	Milton, Pa.	Redpath and Fall 1871–72
18 Jan 72	Harrisburg, Pa.	*Evening Mercury*, *Patriot*, and *Telegraph* (19 Jan 72)
19 Jan 72	Lancaster, Pa.	*Intelligencer* (20 Jan 72)
22 Jan 72	Carlisle, Pa.	*Herald* (25 Jan 72)
23 Jan 72	Baltimore, Md.	*Sun* (24 Jan 72)
24 Jan 72	New York, N.Y.	*Times* and *Tribune* (25 Jan 72)
29 Jan 72	Scranton, Pa.	*Republican* (1 Feb 72)

DATE	PLACE	SOURCE
30 Jan 72	Jersey City, N.J.	*American Standard* and *Evening Journal* (31 Jan 72)
31 Jan 72	Paterson, N.J.	*Press* (1 Feb 72)
1 Feb 72	Troy, N.Y.	*Press* (2 Feb 72)
21 Feb 72	Danbury, Conn.	*News* (28 Feb 72)
27 Feb 72	Amherst, Mass.	*Record* (28 Feb 72)

Appendix D

Boston Lyceum Bureau Advertising Circular

JAMES REDPATH and George L. Fall prepared this circular in late December 1871. Clemens had made a successful debut with a "Roughing It" lecture on 7 December, in Warsaw, New York, and the following day cabled Redpath and Fall, instructing them to "Notify all hands that from this date I shall talk nothing but selections from my forth-coming book Roughing it." But after failing with the same lecture later on 8 December, in Fredonia, he set about rewriting it, temporarily falling back on "Artemus Ward, Humorist." He completed a new version of "Roughing It" on 10 December and gave it for the first time in Lansing, Michigan, on 14 December. He continued delivering and refining that lecture in preparation for Chicago performances of 18 and 19 December, both resoundingly successful, then reworked it still again over Christmas. Before the end of the month he definitively abandoned the Artemus Ward talk, and he delivered "Roughing It" exclusively during the remainder of his 1871–72 tour.

The circular (reproduced here at 88 percent of actual size) excerpts reviews from four Chicago newspapers of 19 December 1871: the *Times* ("Mark Twain's Lecture," 3); the *Evening Post* ("Mark Twain Last Night," 4); the *Mail* (title and page unidentified); and the *Tribune* ("Mark Twain," 1). It also excerpts reviews of the earliest "Roughing It" lecture from the Warsaw *Western New Yorker* (14 Dec 71, title and page unidentified) and the Buffalo *Courier* (David Gray's "A New Lecture by Mark Twain," 9 Dec 71, 2). Clemens probably provided all of these notices for the Boston Lyceum Bureau, which sent him copies of the circular in January 1872 (10 and 11 Jan 72 to OLC, CU-MARK; George H. Hathaway to SLC, envelope containing circulars, postmarked "BOSTON JAN [2]2 8 PM," CU-MARK).

Lyceum Circular.

JANUARY 1, 1872.]   BOSTON LYCEUM BUREAU.   [REDPATH & FALL.

"MARK TWAIN."

(S. L. CLEMENS.)

MARK TWAIN will not repeat his lecture on "Artemus Ward, the humorist," this season, but will deliver, instead of it, a new lecture, entitled

"ROUGHING IT,"

which he first gave in Chicago, Dec. 19.

To enable our correspondents to advertise it properly, we reprint the subjoined notices of the Chicago press.

The Chicago Times said: —

"MARK TWAIN'S LECTURE.— The brilliant and successful conclusion of the first season of the South-Side Star Lecture Course, on last evening, must have been as gratifying to the managers as it was flattering to 'Mark Twain,' whose genius drew together one of the largest as well as the most intelligent audiences, that have ever gathered in this city to hear a lecture. Over a week ago, nearly all the seats were taken ; and it became apparent, that, in order to provide for the crowd that would throng the Michigan-avenue Baptist Church, arrangements more extensive than usual would have to be made. Accordingly, on last evening, the transepts of the church, which open into the main auditorium by means of hanging-doors, were thrown open, thus adding nearly a thousand seats, — every one of which, as well as those in the body of the church, was filled. In the presence of this vast audience, at the appointed time, came strolling on the platform, in the most indifferent and careless manner, the 'hero of the hour.' As he repeats the lecture to-night on the West Side, and we have been requested to restrain our desire to tell some of the good things he said, so that they will be enjoyed the more by those who have had the good fortune to secure seats, we do not give any detailed report of his lecture.

"It consisted chiefly of reminiscences of 'roughing it' in California, with accounts of new discoveries in the animal, vegetable, and mineral kingdoms, glowing descriptions of exquisite scenery, droll yarns of life in the bush, which convulsed the audience with laughter during the entire evening. Nothing could have been more quaint than the unconscious manner in which he related his stories, and the half-surprised look he assumes when his audience laughs at some of the serious things he says."

The Chicago Evening Post said: —

"The entertainment of the season, thus far, was the curious, disjointed, delightful talk of Mark Twain (Clemens is his married name), last evening, in the Michigan-avenue Baptist Church, below Twenty-second Street.

"Every seat in the house, four hundred chairs in the aisles, and standing-room for two or three hundred, were crowded full, when the lank, lantern-jawed, and impudent Californian bestrode the stage as if it were the deck of a steamboat, and, getting to the middle of the front, rubbed his bony hands, and gazed around. A thin man of five feet ten, thirty-five, or so, eyes that penetrate like a new gimlet, nasal prow projecting and pendulous, carrotty, curly hair, and mustache, arms that are always in the way, expression dreadfully melancholy, he stares inquisitively here and there, and cranes his long neck around the house like a bereaved Vermonter who has just come from the death-bed of his mother-in-law, and is looking for a sexton. For something like a minute, he says not a word, but rubs his hands awkwardly, and continues the search. Finally, just as the spectators are about to break into giggles, he opens his capacious mouth, and begins in a slow draw, — about three words a minute by the watch.

"Mr. Twain took his auditors on a flying trip to California and the mountain mining-regions ; giving alternate glimpses of sense and nonsense, of humor, burlesque. sentiment, and satire, that kept the audience in the most sympathetic mood. He dipped into pathos, rose into eloquence, kept sledding right along in a fascinating nasal snarl, looking and speaking like an embarrassed deacon telling his experience, and punctuating his tardy fun with the most complicated awkwardness of gesture. Now he snapped his fingers ; now he rubbed his hands softly, like the catcher of the champion nine; now he caressed his left palm with his dexter fingers, like the end minstrel-man propounding a conundrum; now he put his arms akimbo, like a disgusted auctioneer; and now he churned the air in the vicinity of his imperilled head with his outspread hands, as if he was fighting mosquitoes at Rye Beach. Once he got his arms tangled so badly, that three surgeons were seen to edge their way quietly toward the stage, expecting to be summoned; but he unwound himself during the next anecdote.

"It is plain to see that Twain's success as a platformer results: first, from his being a genuine humorist with audacity and imagination; secondly, from his slow and solemn speech and his sanctimonious bearing and manner. Then the style of his delivery gives all the effect of spontaneity. The jokes are uttered as if he had just thought of them a minute before, and didn't perceive the point of them quite as soon as the audience."

The Chicago Mail says: —

"It would hardly be fair to give a full report of the lecture of Mark Twain last night, as it is to be repeated to-night at the Union-park Church, on the West Side. It is all our fancy painted it, however; and those who do not hear Twain to-night will have cause for perpetual sorrow."

The Chicago Tribune said: —

"The last lecture of the first series of the Star Course was delivered last evening in the Michigan-avenue Baptist Church, by Samuel L. Clemens, *alias* 'Mark Twain.' The audience was immense; the main auditorium, lecture-room, and Sunday-school rooms being all thronged, the aisles all filled with extra seats, and scarcely any standing-room left. After the usual organic prelude, the hero of the hour stalked into the room, and mounted the rostrum. The reminiscences consisted of exploits and discoveries in California. While truly eloquent in his glowing descriptions of California scenery, he was infinitely droll in his yarns of life on the Pacific slope. His endless stories and happy hits kept the audience convulsed with laughter, yet gave much solid information. The lecture is to be repeated this evening in the Union-park Congregational Church; and to-morrow we shall give in these columns a full synopsis of the lecture."

The Warsaw New-Yorker says of Mark Twain's first delivery of his lecture: —

"The largest audience ever assembled in Sprague's Hall was packed there on Thursday evening to listen to the author of 'The Innocents Abroad.' Every available foot of space was occupied; many persons having come from miles outside to the entertainment. 'Mark' had taken a dislike to his lecture on Artemus Ward; and his desire to repeat it was not heightened by the knowledge that a paper circulating several hundred copies here had published,

with 'enterprise' hardly fair toward one of the guild, a long report of it as delivered in Brooklyn. He had prepared a new lecture that day, drawn chiefly from his forthcoming new book, which a few hours' more time would have enabled him to deliver without notes; but, being assured that he would find a bright and quickly-responsive audience, he decided to try his new lecture here. It is entitled 'Roughing It;' and the general character of the lecture, as well as the success of the venture, are very well indicated in the extract from 'The Buffalo Courier,' published in our Localized Items to-day. It treats of various scenes and episodes in Mark's overland journey to California some ten years ago, and is interspersed and enlivened with some thoroughly Twain-ish stories, told in a manner that seemed to us the perfection of art for this style of humor. It abounded in descriptive passages of rare beauty, — really classic in their conception and expression, and delivered with all the effect of finished eloquence, holding the crowded audience in the perfect stillness of rapt attention which marks the fine periods of Curtis or Anna Dickinson. Equally well done, to our mind, were the humorous passages. The slightly-drawling and apparently seriously-unconscious manner seems to us perfectly adapted to the droll, extravagant humor of Ward and Twain. With the latter it is entirely natural, and not assumed, as some suppose. Aside from the fine descriptive passages, and the inimitable stories, his effort abounded in bits of sentiment and flashes of wit that would alone redeem many a dull lecture. The audience were 'with' him from the introduction to the close; and the hour and a half seemed robbed of half its clock-ticks."

"The Buffalo Courier," whose accomplished chief editor, Mr. David Gray, was present at Mark Twain's new lecture, thus notices his "dangerous experiment of a change of base in the face of the enemy!" "The perilous movement was brilliantly accomplished Thursday evening, before the largest audience of the season. The subject of his lecture, scarcely a day old, was, 'Roughing It, being Passages from my Forthcoming Book:' and it promises to become in his hands perhaps the most interesting of his public performance. Gracefully deprecating the possible suspicion that he is out as a book-canvasser, Mark proceeds in this lecture to cull from his unpublished volume a *mélange* of passages, — grave and gay, descriptive and humorous, — which are in his very best style, and as varied and lively in their character as can be conceived. His pictures of life in Nevada during the 'flush' period of that Territory's history, and of strange personages he there encountered, are simply inimitable. The narrative branches off occasionally into one of those extraordinary and elaborate 'yarns' for which he alone has a patent; and it encloses, also, frequent bits of word-painting which would make his fame as a serious speaker, if he were not inveterately a humorist. We predict a hearty reception for the new lecture."

REDPATH & FALL,

Boston Lyceum Bureau,

36 *Bromfield Street,*

BOSTON, MASS.

Appendix E

Book Contracts

Contract for Roughing It

IN ELMIRA on 15 July 1870, Elisha Bliss prepared a contract between Clemens and the American Publishing Company for the book eventually called *Roughing It*. Clemens's copy, signed only by Bliss and mailed later from Hartford, is in the Mark Twain Papers (CU-MARK). Bliss's copy, signed by both men, is in the Beinecke Rare Book and Manuscript Library, Yale University (CtY-BR). Clemens's copy is transcribed below. The textual commentary records the variants between the two versions.

This memorandum made this 15th day of July, A D. 1870. at Elmira state of N. York. between Saml L. Clemens of Buffalo of said N York & the American Publishing Company of Hartford state of Conn wittnesseth
The said Clemens agrees to write for said Company the manuscript for a book upon such subject as may be agreed upon between them, & to deliver the same to them as soon as practicable, but as early as 1st of January next, if said Company shall desire it— Said manuscript to contain matter sufficient for a book of about 600 pages octavo. Said Clemens is also to do the usual proofreading & give the ordinary assistance of authors in bringing out said book & render all aid he can to its sale, & is not to write or furnish manuscript for any other book unless for said company during the preparation & sale of said manuscript & book, or ~~wr~~ furnish any part of the matter of ~~this~~ ‚said‚ manuscript to other parties— The said American Publishing Company agree to publish the said Book in their best style, to commence operations at once upon receipt of manuscript, & to push it through with all the dispatch compatible

with its being well done in text & illustrations— They agree to give the book as large a sale as they possibly can do by using all means in their power, & make the utmost efforts both in preparation & sale to make it a great ~~sal~~ success. They agree to [pay] to said Clemens a copyright on every copy sold of *seven & one half* per cent of the retail or subscription price, on copies given to editors & others to advance the sale of the book, no copyright is to be paid— Statements of sales to be made to said Clemens every three months ~~from~~ ˏafterˏ time of publication, & the copyright due to be paid at same time

American Publishing Co.

E Bliss Jr Secty

The Mss for book contracted for by within contract by S. L. Clemens has been delivered to [us] entitled "Roughing It"

Am Pub Co

pr E Bliss Jr Secty[1]

[*on the back as folded:*]

Contract with Am Pub Co—July 15, 1870

[*in pencil:*]   "Roughing It'[']

7½% retail price

R. It

[*in ink:*]   Roughing It

Roughing It

Contract for Diamond Mine Book

On 6 December 1870 Elisha Bliss prepared a contract between Clemens and the American Publishing Company for a book about the South African diamond mines. He mailed it to Clemens from Hartford, probably that same day. On 20 December Clemens signed it and returned it from Buffalo, two days later requesting that Bliss send him a copy (2 Dec 70, 20 Dec 70, 22 Dec 70, all to Bliss). Clemens's copy is in the Mark Twain Papers (CU-MARK) and is transcribed below. Bliss's copy is in the Beinecke Rare Book and Manuscript Library, Yale University (CtY-BR).

---

[1] Bliss could not have added this endorsement before the early fall of 1871, when the book's title was finalized (*RI 1993*, 863, 873).

This memorandum made this Sixth day of December 1870 between Samuel L Clemens of City of Buffalo State of N. York. and American Publishing Company of city of Hartford State of Connecticut wittnesseth. The said Clemens agrees to send a proper party[1] to the Diamond Fields of Africa to prepare notes of adventure &c there, to be used by said Clemens in writing the manuscript for a book on the subject to be ready & delivered to the said Company by the 1st day of March 1872 or sooner, said manuscript to contain matter enough to fill at least 600 printed octavo pages.— Said Clemens is to do all proof reading & give all other assistance ordinarily done by authors & is to aid in the sale of the book when out, all he can. In case from any cause whatever, the said Clemens shall fail to write a book on the above mentioned subject, then he is to write one upon some other subject which shall be mutually agreed upon The manuscript for the same to be of same quantity & ready at time arranged, for above—& during the term of preparations & sale of said book, be the subject what it may, the said Clemens is not to write or furnish any one matter for another book, or throw any other obstacle in the way of the sale of this, & shall not furnish any part of the Mss. of this book to, or allow it to be used by any other party. And the said American Publishing Company agree to bring out this book in good style & to use their utmost efforts to make it a success & to effect large sales of it, & will pay said Clemens a copyright upon each copy sold of eight & one half (8½) per cent of the subscription price of the book— All copies furnished editors or others to advance the sale of the book, to be free from copyright— Statements of sales & payment of Copyright to be made every three months— As the said Clemens desires an advance on said copyright to be used in paying said person for trip to Africa, the said Company agree to furnish said advance as he the said Clemens may want to the amount of Twenty Five Hundred Dollars, the same, to amount of Fifteen hundred Dollars, to be advanced as soon as said Clemens shall call for it, the balance during the year 1871 if it shall be needed & called for by said Clemens to carry out his enterprise.[2] All such sums

[1] John Henry Riley.

[2] Clemens received advances of $1,500 on 22 December 1870 and $500 at an unknown later date (22 Dec 70 to Bliss; SLC's contract of 22 June 1872 with the American Publishing Company, CU-MARK).

advanced to be deducted from the first copyright accruing on sales of said book

E Bliss Jr. Secty

Am. Pub. Co.

[*in purple ink:*]   Saml. L. Clemens.

[*in black ink:*] ₐThis contract is hereby annulled by the substitution in its place of one dated the 22nd day of June 1872, between the parties by consent of both[3]

Am. Pub Co.

E Bliss Jr Sect

[*on the back as folded, in unidentified hands:*]

Contract with Am Pub- Co Dec 6—1870—

African ~~Diam~~ *Contract*

[*in pencil by Bliss:*]   1st Riley[4]

[3] The substitute contract stipulated that Clemens was to write the diamond mine book from Riley's South African notes "if it is possible," publishing it either as Mark Twain or, for a reduced royalty, under some other pen name. If Clemens found it "utterly impossible" to write the diamond mine book, or wrote it under an alternate pseudonym, he was to write another book as Mark Twain for the American Publishing Company (CU-MARK). He ultimately satisfied the 22 June 1872 contract with a single work, *The Adventures of Tom Sawyer* (1876).

[4] The 1872 contract was in effect a second "Riley" contract, since it provided for the writing of the diamond mine book.

Appendix F

Photographs and Manuscript Facsimiles

REPRODUCED HERE are twenty-five contemporary images, many of them never before published, of Samuel and Olivia Clemens's families, friends, associates, and places of residence during the period of these letters. Immediately following these documents is Clemens's holograph "scrap letter" of 11 June 1871 to Jane Lampton Clemens, reproduced in photofacsimile. We provide this facsimile partly for its inherent interest, and partly to afford readers a chance to see for themselves what details of the manuscript the transcription includes, as well as what it omits. Because of the difficulties in rendering into type a letter designed to be difficult to read, close comparison with the transcription may turn up apparent discrepancies between the two.

George Alfred Townsend, Clemens, and David Gray, Washington, D.C., 7 February 1871. Photographed at Mathew Brady's galleries. Mark Twain Papers, The Bancroft Library (CU-MARK).

Wedding certificate of Samuel L. Clemens and Olivia L. Langdon, signed by
ministers Thomas K. Beecher and Joseph H. Twichell and by witnesses Jervis
and Olivia Langdon, Fidele A. Brooks, Theodore W. and Susan L. Crane, Edward P. and Lottie Adams, Mary M. Fairbanks, and Talmage E. and Anna L.
(Marsh) Brown, on 2 February 1870. The stamp was initialed and dated by
Beecher. Collection of Robert T. Slotta.

House at 472 Delaware Avenue, Buffalo, New York, probably late
1870s or 1880s. Buffalo and Erie County Historical Society (NBuHi).

Samuel L. Clemens, 1870,
photographer unidentified.
Huntington Library, San Marino,
California (CSmH). A photograph
from this sitting served as the
model for the engraving in the
August 1870 *Galaxy;* see p. 416.

Langdon Clemens, 1871.
Photograph by John H. Whitley,
Elmira. Mark Twain House, Hartford,
Connecticut (CtHMTH).

Eunice Ford, 1860s. Huntington
Library, San Marino, California
(CSmH).

Langdon Clemens, 1871. Mark
Twain Archives, Center for Mark
Twain Studies at Quarry Farm,
Elmira College (NElmC).

Emma Nye, c. 1870. Mark Twain
Archives, Center for Mark Twain
Studies at Quarry Farm, Elmira
College (NElmC).

Rachel Gleason, 1870s. Mark Twain
Archives, Center for Mark Twain Studies
at Quarry Farm, Elmira College (NElmC).

Elmira Water Cure, 1860 (*Callisto* 1 [March–April 1860]: no page).

Donn Piatt, c. 1870. Photograph by
Mathew Brady or associate. Library
of Congress (DLC).

Horace Greeley, 1860s or 1870s.
Library of Congress (DLC).

Benjamin P. Shillaber, early 1860s.
Boston Athenaeum (MBAt).

John Hay, 1871. Mark Twain
Papers, The Bancroft Library
(CU-MARK).

Samuel S. Cox, 1870s? Photograph
by Mathew Brady or associate.
Library of Congress (DLC).

Thomas Nast, 1871 (*Harper's Weekly*
25 [26 August 1871]: 804).

Thomas Bailey Aldrich, 1868
(Greenslet, facing page 92).

William Bowen, 1870s. Courtesy of
Royden Burwell Bowen, Jr., and
William G. Bowen.

Olive Logan, 1870s? From a
Mathew Brady photograph.
Library of Congress (DLC).

Kate Field, 1865 (Whiting, 147).

Frank Fuller, 1860s. The James S.
Copley Library (CLjC).

Thomas Fitch, 1870. Engraved
by Charles Bryan Hall. Bosto
Athenaeum (MBAt).

James T. Fields, c. 1870 (Howells 1900, facing page 42).

Adolph Sutro, 1869, posing with "the first pick with which he struck the first blow on the Sutro Tunnel." Composite shot, London. Nevada Historical Society, Reno (NvHi).

John and Isabella Hooker's house, Nook Farm, Hartford, c. 1870. Rented by the Clemenses in October 1871. From a stereopticon photograph by Prescott and White. Harriet Beecher Stowe Center, Hartford, Connecticut (CtHSD).

Clemens to Jane Lampton Clemens, 11 June 1871, Elmira, N.Y. Mark Twain Papers, The Bancroft Library (CU-MARK). Manuscript scraps 1, 2, 3, and 4. Recto and verso. The letter, which is transcribed on pp. 403–5, is written on nine scraps, both sides of which are reproduced here at 78 percent of actual size. The apparent ink marks around the edges of some of the scraps were made not by Clemens but by Chester L. Davis, Sr., in 1978.

Manuscript scraps 5, 6, and 7, to Jane Lampton Clemens, 11 June 1871. Recto and verso.

I expect to lecture first in New England & then
& then skip to Chicago & lecture a month in the west
I may possibly take in Elmira, Buffalo, Cleve-
land & Cincinnati as I go along _____ don't you? I think it is a
subject that will take _____ don't you? I have talked

with several people about it & they say it is the best subject before the country to-day, & that if I can't do it
happy justice I can't do any subject justice.
Ma, I will help Orion with any machine
he wants help on _____ When I was there the other day, we

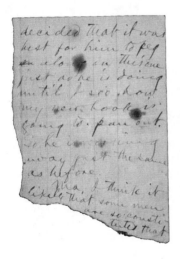

decided that it was
best for him to peg
on along in the same
just as he is doing
until I see how
my new book is
going to pan out.
So he is moving
away just the same
as before.
Ma, I think it
likely that some men
are so consti-
tuted that

they will, under cir-
cumstances of an
irregular nature
manifest idiosyn-
crasies of an ir-
refragable and
even pre-jutti-
& latitudinarian
character, but to the
revise & diffe to the
situation the reverse
is too often the case,
now as it strikes
person
him.

Manuscript scraps 8 and 9, to Jane Lampton Clemens, 11 June 1871. Recto and verso.

583

The envelope, addressed to Jane Lampton Clemens and postmarked 12 June. Jane Lampton Clemens added the year and description; the page references in the lower left corner were written by Chester L. Davis, Sr. Reproduced at 78 percent of actual size. The back flap of the envelope bears Olivia L. Langdon's monogram.

Editorial Apparatus

I<small>N</small> <small>WHAT</small> follows here we summarize information about prior publication and provenance which would otherwise have to be frequently repeated in the textual commentaries for letters in this volume. The content and purpose of the textual commentaries, as well as the special symbols and terms used in them, are described in the last part of the Guide to Editorial Practice in *L3*, 551–78. The commentaries may contain as many as six sections or parts; when there is no information to report, sections are omitted entirely.

1. Description of Texts

Individual commentaries may designate as copy-text one or both of the following publications. When the information given here is pertinent for any reason, the reader is specifically referred to it.

MTB *Mark Twain: A Biography. The Personal and Literary Life
of Samuel Langhorne Clemens by Albert Bigelow Paine,
with Letters, Comments and Incidental Writings Hitherto Unpublished; Also
New Episodes, Anecdotes, etc.* 3 vols. New York and London: Harper and
Brothers, 1912. *BAL*, p. 251. *Copy used:* copy #1, CU-MARK. Where
MTB has served as copy-text, copy #1 (publisher's code H-M on the
copyright page of volume 1, signifying the first impression, ordered in
August 1912) has been collated against copy #2 (code K-K, signifying
an impression ordered in October 1935, which is the latest impression
located). In 1935 Paine made a few corrections in the plates, but no variants in the texts of the letters collected in the present volume have been
found.

    MTB was first issued in three volumes, then in four and later in two,
all with the same pagination. Paine said that he had "obtained his data

from direct and positive sources: letters, diaries, account-books, or other immediate memoranda" (*MTB*, 1:xv). His industry in this respect was such that several letters he published have not since been found in their original form and are therefore known only from his transcriptions (or occasional facsimiles) in *MTB* and *MTL*. Although the printer's copy for *MTB* has not been found, it is known that Paine's general method of acquiring letter texts was to borrow the original whenever possible, presumably transcribe it himself, probably on a typewriter, and then return the manuscript to its owner. He presumably had full access both to the documents (now in the Mark Twain Papers) that Clemens himself defined and set aside for his official biography, and to those now in the McKinney Family Papers. He also had access to at least some of the letters in the Moffett Collection, but it is not known whether these were ever fully in his hands or transcribed for him. Although he published many of the letters now in the McKinney Family Papers, he published relatively few of those in the Moffett Collection. *MTB* is copy-text for a few letters not republished in *MTL*. But letter texts in *MTB* are generally excerpts and, judging from collation with letters that are still extant in manuscript, they were more freely edited than the corresponding passages published in *MTL*. Excerpts from *MTB* appeared in *Harper's Monthly Magazine* in thirteen installments, running from November 1911 through November 1912, hence, largely before *MTB* appeared in September 1912. Collation shows that when the book and the magazine both include text for a letter, they sometimes contain evidence of having each derived independently from a common source (very likely a typescript and its carbon copy), even though each has been separately copy-edited. Whenever persuasively authorial variants are found uniquely in both texts, the transcription is based on both. When such variants cannot be found, *MTB* is designated copy-text and the magazine, which was generally edited more heavily than the book, is treated as if it simply derived from *MTB* instead of their common source.

MTL   *Mark Twain's Letters, Arranged with Comment by Albert Bigelow Paine*. 2 vols. New York and London: Harper and Brothers Publishers, 1917. *BAL* 3525. *Copy used:* copy #1, CU-MARK. As indicated under *MTB*, the letters published in *MTL* are generally more complete as well as more reliable than those extracted or published in full in *MTB*. Because printer's copy for *MTL* has likewise not been found, it is not always clear what relation it bore to the printer's copy for *MTB*. Transcriptions are based on both *MTL* and *MTB* only when persuasively authorial variants occur uniquely in both, thus establishing their independent derivation from the lost manuscripts. Otherwise, if a letter appears both in *MTL* and *MTB*, *MTL* is chosen as copytext and *MTB* treated as if it simply derived from *MTL* instead of their common source.

Most of the letters published in *MTL* survive as original manuscripts. Collation of these documents with their transcriptions in *MTL* shows, in addition to the expected errors and omissions, that the *MTL* transcription always spelled out ampersands, and always imposed a uniform style on the dateline, greeting, complimentary closing, and signature lines. The uniformity of this house styling is established by a very large body of letter manuscript, and Clemens's consistency in using certain forms is likewise established by an even larger body of evidence. When the copy-text is *MTL*, this evidence is considered sufficient to permit the conjectural restoration of the likely forms in the original letter, at least in these uniformly styled elements. All emendations to remove this nonauthorial styling in *MTL* are, of course, published.

2. Description of Provenance

Brownell   The George H. Brownell Collection is housed in the
Collection   Rare Book Department of the Memorial Library of the
                  University of Wisconsin (WU). George H. Brownell
(1875–1950) was a midwestern newspaperman who eventually became a
full-time Mark Twain scholar, devoted especially to the task of obtaining
photocopies (or originals) of Clemens's uncollected journalism and letters. In 1935 he helped found the Mark Twain Society of Chicago and, in 1941, the Mark Twain Association of America. In January 1939 he became the first editor of the *Twainian*, a position he held until his death. In October 1936, Brownell acquired an unusual collection of Clemens material from a Mark Twain collector, Irving S. Underhill (who died in 1937, in Buffalo). According to Brownell,

> the aged, bed-ridden Irving S. Underhill had begun his preparations for death by shipping the more valuable items in his Twain collection to a New York auction concern. To me, at that time, he shipped two large cartons of miscellaneous Twainiana of no sale value, but having for me an almost inestimable bibliographical value.

> Contained in one of those cartons was a box of Mark Twain letters—not the originals, but copies of the originals made by typewriter, pen and pencil. I never learned from Mr. Underhill how he acquired this strange collection of fully 200 Twain letters. My guess is that the copies were made by some dealer, long ago, at a time when the originals were passing through his hands to the purchaser. Mr. Underhill might then have bought or traded something to the dealer for the copies. (Brownell 1943, 2)

Brownell's conjecture was correct. The copies had been made by Dana S. Ayer of Worcester, Massachusetts, a book and manuscript dealer who had been a salesman (as of the late 1890s) for the American Publishing Company (*BAL* 3521; Second Life Books, lot 764; Samuel R. Morrill to Clifton W. Barrett, 24 Apr 1957, ViU). Brownell compiled a list of Underhill's documents, which included 158 Ayer transcriptions of Clemens letters (Brownell 1941). None of these letters was written earlier than 1867, when Clemens first corresponded with Elisha Bliss of the American Publishing Company. More than half of them were addressed to Bliss or to his son, Francis E. Bliss, who were both officers of the American Publishing Company. Most of the remaining letter transcriptions were addressed to Frank Fuller, Clemens's business agent from the spring of 1867 until sometime in 1868, when Clemens presumably placed Bliss in charge of past as well as his then current business correspondence (Brownell 1941). In the fall of 1942, Brownell loaned the Ayer transcriptions to Bernard DeVoto, who in turn had the majority of them retranscribed, depositing these retranscriptions in the Mark Twain Papers (described below). Brownell ultimately bequeathed the documents to the University of Wisconsin, where they now reside.

The original manuscripts for most of the letter transcriptions in the Brownell Collection have been found and are accessible to the editors, but a few letters are known only by the copy Ayer made of the original. By assessing the overall accuracy of Ayer's transcriptions and identifying the kinds of errors he introduced into them, it is possible to emend the texts of those few letters or parts of letters for which no manuscript survives, in order to restore the likely reading of the lost original. Three letters in the present volume derive in part from Ayer transcriptions: 26 April 1870 to Frank Fuller; and 5 May 1870 and 27 June 1870, both to Elisha Bliss, Jr.

Huntington Henry E. Huntington (1850–1927), financier, railway
Library executive, and heir to Collis Potter Huntington's railroad fortune, bequeathed his San Marino, California,

estate as an endowed public museum and art gallery for his enormous collection of rare books, manuscripts, and paintings. The Clemens material at the Huntington Library includes literary manuscripts and nearly two hundred autograph letters. Over half of these letters are addressed to Mary Mason Fairbanks, and were bought by Henry Huntington from William K. Bixby in 1918 (not from the Fairbanks family, as stated in *L2*, 512, and *L3*, 583). Charles Mason Fairbanks, Mary Mason Fairbanks's son, had sold the letters in 1911 to "a collector in the West," probably Bixby (Robert H. Dodd to Charles Mason Fairbanks, 8 Mar 1911, CtHMTH). Sixteen letters in this volume to Mary Mason Fairbanks belong to the Huntington Library.

McKinney   The Jean Webster McKinney Family Papers, housed in
Family Papers   the Francis Fitz Randolph Rare Book Room, Helen D.
               Lockwood Library, Vassar College, Poughkeepsie, New York (NPV). This collection was given to Vassar in 1977 by Jean and Ralph Connor, of Tymor Farm, LaGrangeville, New York. Jean Connor inherited the papers from her mother, Jean Webster McKinney, who had in turn inherited them from her mother, Annie Moffett Webster, Clemens's niece and the wife of Charles L. Webster, his business partner from 1884 to 1888. The letters and other Clemens materials in the collection represent one of the three principal caches of family letters, which passed from Clemens to his mother, Jane Lampton Clemens (d. 1890), his brother Orion (d. 1897) and sister-in-law Mollie Clemens (d. January 1904), and ultimately to his sister, Pamela A. Moffett (d. August 1904). Some of these documents went eventually to Pamela's son, Samuel E. Moffett (see Moffett Collection, below), and some to her daughter, Annie Moffett Webster. Not surprisingly, therefore, several manuscript letters are now found partly in the McKinney Family Papers and partly in the Moffett Collection.

Mollie Clemens wrote her nephew Samuel Moffett on 31 July 1899, "We never destroyed Sams letters—*excepting* by his request, or a few no one should see" (CU-MARK). At least one partly destroyed (censored) letter survives in this collection (see *L1*, 347–49), but by far the larger toll was probably taken by accidental physical damage or loss, and by the deliberate destruction, following Mollie Clemens's death, of most of Clemens's letters to his mother. As early as 1881, Orion Clemens had assembled a number of his brother's letters written between about 1853 and 1865 as part of a sprawling manuscript for his own never-published autobiography, finding even then that not all the letters had been preserved intact. On 6 October 1899, Pamela Moffett sent an unknown number of original letters to her son, Samuel Moffett, then a journalist in California, saying in part that she "was sorry to see that parts of some of the letters were missing" (CU-MARK). He tried to publish at least a few of these letters in biographical sketches of Clemens, but was eventually told to preserve them for publication after Clemens's death. Some, if not all, of these letters must eventually have become part of the Moffett Collection.

But in 1904, according to a 1935 Associated Press story in an unidentified newspaper clipping, Mollie Clemens's executor, John R. Carpenter, burned "almost four trunks" of Clemens's letters to his mother, "as requested by the famous humorist." Carpenter confided his story, according to this report, to Dr. G. Walter Barr of Keokuk, who gave this account:

> When Mrs. Clemens died [in 1890], . . . her carefully preserved personal and family treasures went into the possession of her son, Orion. When Orion died, his wife had the succession and kept it inviolate until her own death in 1904.
>
> John R. Carpenter was administrator of Orion's wife's estate and the treasured archives of Mother Clemens were delivered to him. One item was a collection of letters from Mark Twain to his mother, running through many decades, from youth to worldwide fame.
>
> But with those three or four trunks of letters was an admonition. Mark Twain had enjoined his mother that she always burn his letters to her. She had not done so, but had passed on the mandamus to Orion and to the wife of the latter, and Carpenter was familiar with it.
>
> He had a treasure of incalculable value and an imperative order to destroy it.
>
> Carpenter realized fully the value of the material he was about to burn in his library grate. When I exclaimed that to destroy all those letters was a monstrous crime against biography, history and the record of a man who belonged to the whole world, he answered that he agreed with me—but what could be done under the circumstances?
>
> Mark Twain had written those letters to his mother in perfect candor—and about the whole sum of his candid writing was in them—intending and believing that nobody else would ever see them, and had ordered them burned.
>
> And so Carpenter burned every one. It took him several long evenings to complete the job thoroughly. ("Mark Twain Letters to Mother Burned at Direction of Author," unidentified clipping, datelined 14 Dec [1935], PH in CU-MARK; the New York *Times* also published an abbreviated version of this story on 15 Dec 1935, 2)

That this story was not a fiction is suggested by the postscript of Clemens's 14 February 1904 letter to Carpenter, the original draft of which survives in the Mark Twain Papers: "If there are any letters of mine, I beg that you will destroy them."

The McKinney Family Papers consist of Clemens documents typically left by him, at various times, with his sister. They include his earliest surviving notebook (probably written in 1855; see *N&J1*, 11–39); half a dozen literary manuscripts, incomplete and unpublished, written principally between 1859 and 1868 (see *ET&S1–3*); more than six hundred letters and telegrams from Clemens to various members of his family, and to business associates like Webster, as well as family photographs and mementoes, and letters and documents by other family members and close associates (Simpson, 6–14). Eighteen letters (or parts of letters) in this volume belong to the McKinney Family Papers: 15 January 1870, 12 June 1870, 6 August 1870, 17 or 24 August 1870?, 31 August 1870, all to Pamela A. Moffett; 26 March 1870, 27 July 1870, 17 February 1871, 15 March 1871, all to Jane Lampton Clemens and family; 25 June 1870 to Jane Lampton Clemens and Pamela A. Moffett; 9 September 1870, 5 November 1870, 21? November 1870, 4 March 1871, 30 April 1871, 7 July 1871, all to Orion Clemens; 5? January 1871 to Mary E. (Mollie) Clemens; and 28 December 1871 to Jane Lampton Clemens.

Mark Twain Papers   The Mark Twain Papers, The Bancroft Library, University of California, Berkeley (CU-MARK). The core of this collection consists of the original documents that Clemens made available to Albert Bigelow Paine for the official biography Paine was to produce, and from which (in part) Paine eventually published his selected editions of letters, notebooks, and the autobiography. Since Clemens's death in 1910, these papers were successively in the care of Paine (1910–37); Bernard DeVoto at Harvard (1938–46); Dixon Wecter at the Huntington Library, San Marino, California, and later at the University of California in Berkeley (1946–50); Henry Nash Smith (1953–63); and Frederick Anderson (1963–79), both of the latter at the University of California in Berkeley, and both successors to Paine, DeVoto, and Wecter as the official literary executor of the Clemens estate. Upon the death of Clara Clemens Samossoud in 1962, the papers were bequeathed to the University of California, and in 1971 they became part of The Bancroft Library, where they now reside.

The original collection segregated by Clemens for Paine included forty-five of the approximately fifty extant notebooks kept between 1855 and 1910; approximately seventeen thousand letters received by Clemens or his family; an estimated six hundred literary manuscripts, most of them unpublished, including the autobiographical dictations; as well as photographs, clippings, contracts, and a variety of other documents originally owned by Clemens. Twenty-five letters (or parts of letters) in this volume are definitely from this original collection: 15 July 1870, 2 September 1870, 22 February 1871, 15–18 March 1871, 4 April 1871, 18 April 1871, 27 June 1871 (1st), 27 June 1871 (2nd), 29 June 1871, 2 July 1871, 31 August 1871, 16 September 1871, 17 September 1871, all to Orion Clemens; 20 March 1871 to Elisha Bliss, Jr., and Orion Clemens; 21 June 1871, 24 December 1871, both to Orion and Mary E. (Mollie) Clemens; 26 October 1870 to Elisha Bliss, Jr.; 14 November 1870 to Charles J. Langdon; 27 or 28 November 1870, 2 December 1870, both to John Henry Riley; 27 January 1871, 6 April 1871, both to Isaac E. Sheldon; 26 or 27 February 1871 to E. C. Chick; 12 March 1871 to Susan L. Crane; and 29–30 November 1871 to James Redpath and George L. Fall. One letter may belong either to it or to the Samossoud Collection: 19–20? November 1870 to Susan L. Crane. Since Paine's tenure, primary and secondary documents have been added in various ways to the Papers—ranging from gifts of both photocopied and original manuscripts and documents, to large purchases and bequests comprising many hundreds of documents, to the systematic compilation of a secondary archive of photocopies, collected from institutions and private owners of original documents around the world, for the specific purpose of publishing a comprehensive scholarly edition of Mark Twain's Works and Papers.

Samossoud Collection (1952), The Mark Twain Papers. Among the documents in Clemens's possession at the time of his death, but not included in the Mark Twain Papers or made wholly available to Paine, were the letters written to his fiancée and wife, Olivia L. Langdon, and later to their daughters, Susie, Clara, and Jean. Dixon Wecter was permitted to transcribe most of these letters, as well as some others that were still owned and separately housed by Clara. He used these transcriptions as the basis for his selected edition, *The Love Letters of Mark Twain* (*LLMT*), published in 1949, and ultimately deposited all of them in the Mark Twain Papers. On 21 March 1952, however, the University of California purchased from Clara's husband Jacques Samossoud (d. 1966) approximately five hundred original letters written to Olivia between September 1868 and her death in 1904. Other parts of the large cache of family letters still held by Clara and her husband were sold or given at various times between 1949 and 1962 to other persons and institutions, including Chester L. Davis, Sr., and the Mark Twain Research Foundation of Perry, Missouri. This volume contains thirty-eight letters in the Samossoud Collection, all to Olivia, and one that might have been part of either it or the Mark Twain Papers: 19–20? November 1870 to Susan L. Crane.

Moffett Collection (1954), The Mark Twain Papers. This collection represents the portion of Pamela Moffett's papers which passed to her son, Samuel, instead of her daughter, Annie (see McKinney Family Papers, above). The collection became the property of Samuel Moffett's daughter Anita Moffett (d. 1952), either upon his death in 1908, or upon the death of Anita's younger brother, Francis Clemens Moffett, in 1927. The papers were discovered in 1953 by Paul P. Appel, a Mamaroneck, New York, book dealer (not in 1954 by Jacob Zeitlin, as reported in *L2*, 516), in a warehouse sale that included some of Anita Moffett's effects: sixteen hundred letters by Clemens, his family, and associates (including Pamela's letters to her son and daughter); ten scrapbooks of newspaper clippings for the period 1858–98, evidently compiled by Orion and Mollie Clemens, and containing original printings of Clemens's (and Orion's) western journalism, which had been largely unknown to Paine and all subsequent scholars (see *MTEnt*); deeds to 1860s Nevada mining claims owned by Clemens or his brother; family photographs; and a family Bible. The collection was purchased for the University of California in 1954 by a group of anonymous donors. The inventory of Clemens letters made at the time is not always specific enough to enable the editors to be certain whether some letters were part of the Moffett acquisition or were already part of the Mark Twain Papers in 1954. Seven letters (or parts of letters) in this volume belong to the Moffett Collection: 19? April 1870, 21 April 1870, 1 August 1870, 5 November 1870, 11 November 1870, 8, 9, and 10 April 1871, all to Orion Clemens; and 7 June 1871 to Orion and Mary E. (Mollie) Clemens.

Mendoza Collection (1957), The Mark Twain Papers. In January 1957 the University of California purchased a collection of one hundred sixteen Clemens letters written between 1867 and 1905 (all but one of them to Elisha Bliss or Henry H. Rogers), as well as eleven other miscellaneous items. This collection was offered for sale to the University by Aaron Mendoza of the Isaac Mendoza Book Company, New York City. The letters came from the collection of C. Warren Force (1880–1959), who had bought the letters to the Blisses in 1938 at the sale of the collection of George C. Smith, Jr. (Parke-Bernet 1938a, lot 126). In 1939 Force had given Bernard DeVoto transcripts of the letters to the Blisses. The Mark Twain Papers now contain about eighty-five letters to Rogers (or members of his family) and fifty-three original letters to Elisha Bliss or Francis E. Bliss. Of the total, all but roughly twenty-four letters were part of the Mendoza Collection, which contributes nineteen letters to this volume: 22 January 1870, 28 January 1870, 23 February 1870, 3 March 1870, 23 April 1870, 7 May 1870, 4 September 1870, 22 September 1870, 7 November 1870, 28 November 1870, 1? December 1870, 3 January 1871, 4 and 5 January 1871, 27 January 1871, 15 February 1871, 3 May 1871, 21 June 1871, 12 November 1871, all to Elisha Bliss; and 31 January 1871 to Elisha Bliss or Francis E. Bliss.

Tufts Collection (1971), The Mark Twain Papers. The James and John M. Tufts Collection was assembled chiefly by James Tufts, an acquaintance of Clemens's and, for more than forty years (1892–1935), a prominent San Francisco journalist who at various times was an editor for the *Call*, the *Chronicle*, and the *Examiner*. The collection was purchased in 1971 from Tufts's son, Dr. John M. Tufts of Kentfield, California. It includes twenty-three original letters by Clemens to various correspondents, literary manuscripts, first printings of his sketches, first editions of his books, and photographs. Three letters in this volume belong to the Tufts Collection: 8–13? October 1870 to Elisha Bliss, Jr., July? 1871 to Pierre Reynolds, and 2 July 1871 to James N. Gillis.

Appert Collection (1973 and 1977), The Mark Twain Papers. The gift of Mr. and Mrs. Kurt E. Appert of Pebble Beach, California, this collection includes more than fifty letters by Clemens to various correspondents, literary manuscripts, photographs, letters from various hands to Clemens, first editions of his works, and books from his library. One letter in this volume belongs to the Appert Collection: 11 and 13 March 1871 to Orion Clemens.

3. Textual Commentaries

■ 6 January 1870 · To Olivia L. Langdon · New York, N.Y. · *UCCL* 00402

■*Copy-text:* MS, Mark Twain Papers, The Bancroft Library, University of California, Berkeley (CU-MARK). ■*Previous publication: LLMT,* 361, brief paraphrase. ■*Provenance:* see Samossoud Collection in Description of Provenance. ■*Emendations and textual notes:*

1.13	~~expr~~ • ['r' *partly formed*]	
2.1	P.M. • P.M[◊] [*badly inked*]	

■ 7 January 1870 · To Mary Mason Fairbanks · Amenia, N.Y. · *UCCL* 00401

■*Copy-text:* MS, Huntington Library, San Marino (CSmH, call no. HM 14259). This letter, written on seven leaves torn from a pocket notebook, was the first of six surviving letters (five of them to Olivia Langdon) written on notebook pages in 1870. The notebook, larger than the one Clemens had used for letters in 1869, no longer survives (see p. 7, n. 14). ■*Previous publication: MTMF,* 112–17. ■*Provenance:* see Huntington Library in Description of Provenance. ■*Emendations and textual notes:*

3.15	boisterousness • [*possibly* 'bo~~u~~sisterousness']	
4.6	~~sa~~ season • s⟨a⟩eason	
4.11	money-making • money-|making	
4.33	store-clothes • store-|clothes	
4.35	~~fot~~ foot • fo⟨t⟩ot ['t' *partly formed*]	
4.37	& night • [*sic*]	
5.3	so • ⟨s⟩ so [*corrected miswriting*]	
5.12	would. If • ~.—|~	
5.21	~~execu~~ • ~~execu-|~~	

■ 8 January 1870 · To Olivia L. Langdon · (1st of 2) · Troy, N.Y. · *UCCL* 00403

■*Copy-text:* MS, Mark Twain Papers, The Bancroft Library, University of California, Berkeley (CU-MARK), written on two leaves of the same notebook paper as 7 Jan 70 to Fairbanks. ■*Previous publication: MTMF,* 116, excerpt. ■*Provenance:* see Samossoud Collection in Description of Provenance. ■*Emendations and textual notes:*

7.12	bedroom • bed-|room	

■ 8 January 1870 · To James Redpath · Albany, N.Y. · *UCCL* 00405

■ *Copy-text:* MS, Clifton Waller Barrett Library, University of Virginia, Charlottesville (ViU). ■ *Provenance:* deposited at ViU by Clifton Waller Barrett on 17 December 1963. ■ *Emendations and textual notes:*

10.13   enough • enough⸺

■ 8 January 1870 · To Olivia L. Langdon · (2nd of 2) · Troy, N.Y. · *UCCL* 00404

■ *Copy-text:* MS, Mark Twain Papers, The Bancroft Library, University of California, Berkeley (CU-MARK). ■ *Previous publication: LLMT,* 132–34, with omission; Chester L. Davis 1981, 1–2, with omission. ■ *Provenance:* see Samossoud Collection in Description of Provenance. ■ *Emendations and textual notes:*

12.10   of • of ~~of~~ [*canceled* 'f' *partly formed*]
12.23   ~~Ou~~ Or • Oṷr
12.24   ~~glov~~ globe • gloṿbe
12.27   ~~theology~~ • [*false ascenders/descenders*]
12.30   feeling • ∅ feeling [*doubtful, partly formed* 'p']
12.34   ~~hea~~ herds • heᵣds
13.1   ~~shot~~ shoot • ~~shoṭot~~ shoot [*revision rewritten for clarity*]
13.2   waver • ~~wav~~ waver [*miswritten; possibly* 'van']
13.7   28,000 • [*possibly* '2∅8,000'; *blotted*]
13.8   ~~an apple~~ • [*false ascenders/descenders*]
13.22   N.Y. JAN 10 • [N].Y. JAN [10] [*badly inked*]

■ 10 January 1870 · To Olivia L. Langdon · (1st of 2) · Albany, N.Y. · *UCCL* 00406

■ *Copy-text:* MS, Mark Twain Papers, The Bancroft Library, University of California, Berkeley (CU-MARK), written on three leaves of the same notebook paper as 7 Jan 70 to Fairbanks. ■ *Previous publication: LLMT,* 361, brief paraphrase. ■ *Provenance:* see Samossoud Collection in Description of Provenance. ■ *Emendations and textual notes:*

15.7   down-heartedness • down-|heartedness
15.13–14   ~~cr~~ circumstances • cᵢrcumstances
15.18   siezing • [*sic*]
15.23   ~~pal~~ • [*possibly* 'pat'; 't' *partly formed*]
15.31   Front-de-Boeuf • Front-de-~~Boeuf~~ Boeuf [*rewritten for clarity*]
16.9   sweetheart • sweet-|heart
16.12   N. Y. • N. Y[◊] [*torn*]

■ 10 January 1870 · To Olivia L. Langdon · (2nd of 2) · Albany, N.Y.
· *UCCL* 00407

■*Copy-text:* MS, Mark Twain Papers, The Bancroft Library, University of California, Berkeley (CU-MARK), written on five leaves of the same notebook paper as 7 Jan 70 to Fairbanks. ■*Previous publication: MFMT,* 209–10, excerpt; *LLMT,* 124–25, excerpt; *MTMF,* 117, excerpt. ■*Provenance:* see Samossoud Collection in Description of Provenance. ■*Emendations and textual notes:*

17.20	~~appe~~ appreciate • app¢reciate
18.17	~~Pa~~ Pegasus • P¢egasus
18.24	it₁ • [*deletion implied*]
18.32	knew • k~~hnew~~ | knew [*rewritten for clarity*]
18.33	suffice • suf-|~~fice~~ fice ['fice' *rewritten for clarity*]
18.34	sweetheart • sweet-|heart
19.21	N. Y. • N. Y[◊] [*torn*]
19.24	ALBANY N.Y. • AL[BANY] N.[Y.] [*stamped off edge; badly inked*]

■ 13 January 1870 · To Olivia L. Langdon · Cambridge, N.Y. · *UCCL* 00408

■*Copy-text:* MS, Mark Twain Papers, The Bancroft Library, University of California, Berkeley (CU-MARK), written on six leaves of the same notebook paper as 7 Jan 70 to Fairbanks. ■*Previous publication:* Wecter 1947, 71–72, with omission; *LLMT,* 134–37; *MTMF,* 112, excerpt. ■*Provenance:* see Samossoud Collection in Description of Provenance. ■*Emendations and textual notes:*

21.7	off. I • ~.—|~
21.16	theorize. Theorizing • ~.—|~
21.17	~~on~~ • ['n' *partly formed*]
21.27	argument. You • ~.—|~
21.29	~~stat~~ • [*second* 't' *partly formed*]
21.30	~~ps~~ possibly • p⌀ossibly
21.32	smoking • ~~sm~~ | smoking [*rewritten for lack of room*]
22.8	profanity • profan-|⌀ity ity [*revision rewritten for clarity*]
22.13	curtailed • curtai⌀led [*partly formed, unidentified character*]
22.16–17	that that • [*sic*]
22.24	it. Speak • ~.—|~
22.37	smoking • ~~sm~~ smoking [*miswritten;* 'm' *partly formed*]
23.16	CAMBRIDGE • [C]AMBRIDGE [*badly inked*]

■ 14 January 1870 · To Olivia L. Langdon · Troy, N.Y. · *UCCL* 00410

■*Copy-text:* MS, Mark Twain Papers, The Bancroft Library, University of California, Berkeley (CU-MARK), written on five leaves of the same notebook paper as 7 Jan 70 to Fairbanks. ∎*Previous publication: LLMT,* 137–39. ∎*Provenance:* see Samossoud Collection in Description of Provenance. ∎*Emendations and textual notes:*

24.10	~~that~~ than • tha⫽n
25.2	~~whoo~~ whole • who⫽le
25.11	Cambridge. My • ~.—|~
25.19	~~bee~~ being • be⫽ing
26.16	hand-sachel • hand-|sachel
26.18	~~or a~~ • ['a' *partly formed*]
26.21	⫽ • [*partly formed*]
26.24–25	whole-heartedness • whole-|heartedness
26.30–31	IF . . . TO • [◊◊ ◊◊◊ ◊◊◊◊◊◊◊◊◊ ◊◊◊◊◊◊ ◊◊ ◊◊◊◊◊ ◊◊ ◊◊ ◊◊◊◊◊◊R]ED TO [*torn; text of return address adopted in part from envelope of 13 Jan 70 to OLL*]
26.31	TROY N.Y. JAN 14 • [◊]ROY N.Y[◊] JAN [14] [*badly inked*]

∎ 15 January 1870 · To Olivia L. Langdon · Utica, N.Y. · *UCCL* 00411

∎*Copy-text:* MS, Mark Twain Papers, The Bancroft Library, University of California, Berkeley (CU-MARK). ∎*Previous publication: LLMT,* 361, brief paraphrase. ∎*Provenance:* see Samossoud Collection in Description of Provenance. ∎*Emendations and textual notes:*

27.14	chafings. Though • ~.—|~
28.5	in • ~~in~~ in [*corrected miswriting; possibly* 'un in']
28.9	⫽ • [*partly formed*]
28.11	bitter, bitter • bitter, bitt⫽er
28.21	~~do~~ dare • d⫽are
28.24	an • an ~~an~~ [*canceled* 'n' *partly formed*]

∎ 15 January 1870 · To Pamela A. Moffett · Utica, N.Y. · *UCCL* 00412

∎*Copy-text:* MS, Jean Webster McKinney Family Papers, Vassar College Library (NPV). ∎*Previous publication: MTBus,* 107, with omission; *MTMF,* 117, excerpt. ∎*Provenance:* see McKinney Family Papers in Description of Provenance.

∎ 20 January 1870 · To Olivia L. Langdon · Hornellsville, N.Y. · *UCCL* 00414

∎*Copy-text:* MS, Mark Twain Papers, The Bancroft Library, University of California, Berkeley (CU-MARK). ∎*Previous publication:* Wecter 1947, 72, with omission; *LLMT,* 140–41. ■*Provenance:* see Samossoud Collection in Description of Provenance. ■*Emendations and textual notes:*

32.5   them. And • ~.—|~
32.5   tomorrow • to-|morrow
32.7   box • b̶o̶ box [*corrected miswriting*]
32.20   darling. Your • ~.—|~
32.29   r̶e̶ • r̶e̶-|
32.30   s̶a̶c̶r̶e̶d̶◇ • [*partly formed character*]
32.38   HORNELLSVILLE N. Y. JAN 20 • [◇◇R]NELLS[VIL◇◇ ◇◇ ◇◇] JAN [20]
             [*badly inked*]

■ 22 January 1870 · To Elisha Bliss, Jr. · Elmira, N.Y. · *UCCL* 00415
■*Copy-text:* MS, Mark Twain Papers, The Bancroft Library, University of California, Berkeley (CU-MARK). ■*Previous publication: MTB* 1:420, excerpt; *MTMF,* 118, 144, excerpts; Hill, 39, excerpt; *MTLP,* 29–30, with omissions. ■*Provenance:* see Mendoza Collection in Description of Provenance. The MS evidently remained among the American Publishing Company's files until it was sold, and may have been at that time copied by Dana Ayer. A handwritten Ayer transcription is at CtHMTH, and a typed transcription made from it is at WU (Brownell Collection, Description of Provenance). ■*Emendations and textual notes:*

34.5   w̶i̶s̶h̶ • ['h' *partly formed*]
34.7   honorable • hor̶a̶b̶norable [*canceled* 'b' *partly formed*]
34.7   think • thi$\hat{n}$nk [*corrected miswriting*]

■ 26 January 1870 · To James N. Gillis · Elmira, N.Y. · *UCCL* 00416
■*Copy-text:* Two MS facsimiles, Mark Twain Papers, The Bancroft Library, University of California, Berkeley (CU-MARK). Copy-text for MS pages one and four (35.1–36.5 and 36.26–36, '(L) . . . they' and 'The . . . compliment?') is a photocopy of unknown origin; copy-text for MS pages two and three (36.5–25, 'filled . . . welcome.') is a photocopy of a photostat formerly at the Doheny Collection, St. John's Seminary, Camarillo, Calif. The MS facsimile of pages one and four shows that the MS, a folder, was evidently separating, or had separated, on the folds and was silked to hold it together. ■*Previous publication:* "The Insider," San Francisco *Call,* 7 Dec 1908, 6, excerpt; *MTB,* 1:393, with omissions; *MTL,* 1:170–71; West, 18; Hood, 25, excerpt; Buckbee, 336–37; "Letter from Twain," Oakland *Tribune,* 2 Oct 1949, C-1, with omissions; Chester L. Davis 1956, 2. ■*Provenance:* The present location of the MS is not known. In 1907, the letter may have belonged to James N. Gillis's brother, Stephen E. Gillis, who sent a copy to Albert Bigelow Paine. In 1924, Stephen's son James Gillis apparently owned it. By 1942, when the Willard S. Morse Collection was

given to Yale, someone—probably Morse—made a negative photostat of the letter, which in turn probably served as the source for positive photostats in several other collections, including the Doheny. ■*Emendations and textual notes:*

35.6   days. Still • ~.—|~
35.6   the • [th]e [*obscured by repair*]
36.28   Jim, • Jim[,] [*obscured by repair*]

■ 26 January 1870 · To James Redpath · Elmira, N.Y. · *UCCL* 00417
■*Copy-text:* Paraphrase, AAA 1924a, lot 530. ■*Provenance:* The present location of the MS is not known. It was in the collection of William F. Gable and after his death was sold at auction in 1924 by the American Art Association.

■ 28 January 1870 · To Elisha Bliss, Jr. · Elmira, N.Y. · *UCCL* 00418
■*Copy-text:* MS, Mark Twain Papers, The Bancroft Library, University of California, Berkeley (CU-MARK). ■*Previous publication: MTB,* 1:426, excerpt; *MTL,* 1:169, with omissions; Hill, 191, excerpt; *MTLP,* 30–32. ■*Provenance:* see Mendoza Collection in Description of Provenance. A Brownell typescript of this letter is at WU (Brownell Collection, Description of Provenance). ■*Emendations and textual notes:*

40.16   anỷ • ['y' *partly formed; possibly* 'n']
40.24   endorse,̶w̶ • [*deletion of comma implied;* 'w' *partly formed*]
41.4   p̶ • [*partly formed*]
41.5   genuine generalship • genuine genⱮeralship
41.7   s̶h̶ skirmishers • sⱮkirmishers
41.8   b̶e̶l̶ besiege • beⱮsiege

■ 28–31 January 1870 · To Joseph H. Twichell, *per* Telegraph Operator
     · Elmira, N.Y. · *UCCL* 02796
■*Copy-text: MTBus,* 108. ■*Provenance:* The present location of the telegram, the text of which was reported by Annie Moffett Webster before 1946, is not known.

■ 6 February 1870 · To William Bowen · Buffalo, N.Y. · *UCCL* 02464
■*Copy-text:* MS, Harry Ransom Humanities Research Center, University of Texas, Austin (TxU), is copy-text where extant; a photocopy of TS, a transcription typed by William Bowen and sent to his friend Albert Richardson Gunnison on 31 May 1887, is copy-text for the remainder. Even where MS survives, however, it has deteriorated, the paper is discolored, and the ink is faded in places to illegibility or near illegibility. Where the MS is extant but illegible, the Bowen TS serves as a source for emended readings. The TS was made on an all-capitals typewriter and shows a number of typographical quirks (intermittent failure to

space words after punctuation, letters typed over each other, portions of words canceled at the ends of lines when there was not enough room to complete the word). Where TS serves as copy-text, the capital letters are silently rendered as lowercase except for "I," proper names and titles, place names, and words at the beginning of sentences. In addition, the strictly typographical quirks described above are not recorded. All other emendations are listed below. ▪*Previous publication:* In 1989, before the Bowen TS was discovered, the Mark Twain Project published a text in *Inds*, 20–23, which was based in part on three transcripts: a typed transcription at CtHMTH, and two published transcriptions, SLC 1938, 8–10, and SLC 1941, 18–21. All derive directly or indirectly from the Bowen TS. ▪*Provenance:* The surviving MS was donated to TxU in the summer of 1940 by Eva Laura Bowen (Mrs. Louis Knox), daughter of William Bowen (Hornberger, 7 n. 12, 10). A photocopy of William Bowen's TS was given to the Mark Twain Papers in 1993 by Gunnison's granddaughters, Barbara Gunnison Anderson, Alberta Gunnison Stock, and Marion Gunnison Weygers. ▪*Emendations and textual notes:*

	[*MS is copy-text for* ' c ... back' *(50.1–51.26)*]
50.4	6, • 6[◊] [*ink faded and paper discolored*]
50.4	1870. (TS) • [◊◊]70[.] [*ink faded and paper discolored*]
50.6	ever! (TS) • ever[◊] [*faded*]
50.10	again; • again∅; [*doubtful canceled question mark*]
50.17	slaughter-house • slaughter-|house
50.19	Finn • F̶i̶n̶n̶ Finn [*corrected miswriting*]
50.23	publicĺ • ['*l*' *partly formed*]
51.6	array,— • [*deletion implied*]
51.7	& resumed • & ℀ resumed
51.9	school-house • school-|house
51.25	sweetheart——————— • ~———|———
	[*TS is copy-text for* 'unto . . . father-in-law' *(51.27–52.19)*]
52.9	breaks." • ~".
52.16–17	daintiest, • ~∧
52.18	won't do • wont do
	[*MS is copy-text for* 'let out . . . Clemens.' *(52.19–37)*]
52.20	himself. • himself∅. [*period over doubtful, unrecovered character*]
52.25	beforehand • before-|hand
52.27	[And • [*no closing bracket*]
52.31	it. My • ~.—|~
52.32	p̶o̶ profitable • p∅rofitable

▪ 6? February 1870 · To George E. Barnes · Buffalo, N.Y. · *UCCL* 11614

▪*Copy-text:* The envelope text is a transcript in a letter from Elizabeth D. (Mrs. Robert A.) Theobald to Cyril Clemens, 8 Dec 1956, Mark Twain House, Hartford (CtHMTH); neither of the wedding card enclosures survives with the transcript, although both are described. The two cards shown here at 86 percent of actual size are from the Mark Twain Papers (CU-MARK). ▪*Provenance:* The enclosures and envelope were in the possession of Elizabeth Theobald (George Barnes's grandniece) at least until 1956. ▪*Emendations and textual notes:*

57.4   (LC) • CL [*reported, not quoted; see p. 57, n. 1; monogram text adopted from envelope of 6? Feb 70 to Stoddard*]

▪ 6? February 1870 · To Horace E. Bixby · Buffalo, N.Y. · *UCCL* 00400

▪*Copy-text:* "Mark Twain. How the Boy Became a Pilot and the Pilot a Humorist," New Orleans *Times-Democrat,* 7 May 82, 3. ▪*Previous publication:* In addition to the copy-text, Will M. Clemens 1892, 94–95; "Pilot, 85, to Celebrate," unidentified 1911 newspaper, PH in CU-MARK; *MTMF,* 114, excerpt; Turner, 16–17. ▪*Provenance:* Bixby reported that a trunk of his effects, including the MS of this letter, was destroyed by fire in 1885 ("Pilot, 85, to Celebrate"). ▪*Emendations and textual notes:*

58.4   & • and
58.9   [*on . . .* (LC) • [*adopted from envelope of 6? Feb 70 to Stoddard*]

▪ 6? February 1870 · To Laura H. Frazer, *via* Elijah or Benjamin Hawkins · Buffalo, N.Y. · *UCCL* 09533

▪*Copy-text:* Elizabeth Davis Fielder, "Familiar Haunts of Mark Twain," *Harper's Weekly* 43 (16 Dec 99): 11. ▪*Previous publication:* In addition to the copy-text, "Mark Twain's First Sweetheart," *Sunday Magazine, New York World,* 15 June 1902, 2; "Laura Hawkins Frazer, Always Remembered as Idol of Boyhood," Hannibal *Evening Courier-Post,* 6 Mar 1935, 3C. ▪*Emendations and textual notes:*

59.7   [*on . . .* (LC) • [*adopted from envelope of 6? Feb 70 to Stoddard*]

▪ 6? February 1870 · To John McComb · Buffalo, N.Y. · *UCCL* 00420

▪*Copy-text:* Paraphrase and transcript, "'Mark Twain' Married and Settled," San Francisco *Alta California,* 14 Feb 70, 1. The author was almost certainly John McComb. ▪*Previous publication: LLMT,* 142, excerpt, addressee misidentified as William Wright. ▪*Emendations and textual notes:*

60.27   house," • ~,‸
61.2   & • and [*also at 61.5, 6, 8, 9, 11 (three times), 12, 13, 14*]
61.3   them." • ~.‸
61.6   in • [*not in*]

61.8   its • it
61.17   [*on* . . . (LC) • [*adopted from envelope of 6? Feb 70 to Stoddard*]

■ 6? February 1870 · To Charles Warren Stoddard · Buffalo, N.Y. · *UCCL* 08584

■*Copy-text:* MS, envelope only, Clem D. Johnston Collection, University of Virginia, Charlottesville (ViU). ■*Previous publication:* Goodspeed's Book Shop 1924, item 248d. ■*Provenance:* The envelope, not among the offerings in the sales of Stoddard's library in 1909 and 1910, was sold in 1924 by Goodspeed's. ■*Emendations and textual notes:*

62.1   ~~Hare~~ Harte • Har¢te

■ 6? February 1870 · To William Wright (Dan De Quille) · Buffalo, N.Y. · *UCCL* 00399

■*Copy-text:* MS, envelope only, Dan De Quille Papers, The Bancroft Library, University of California, Berkeley (CU-BANC). The envelope, which now lacks a portion of its back and all of its back flap, otherwise exactly matches the 6? Feb 70 envelope to Stoddard, with its embossed monogram on the back flap. ■*Provenance:* donated to CU-BANC in 1953 by Henry L. Day. ■*Emendations and textual notes:*

62.7   roommate • room-|mate
62.9   [*on* . . . (LC) • [*torn away; text adopted from envelope of 6? Feb 70 to Stoddard*]

■ 7? February–30? April 1870 · To John H. Bancroft · Buffalo, N.Y. · *UCCL* 02794

■*Copy-text:* AAA 1914, lot 72, which describes the letter as "CLEMENS (SAMUEL L.—American humorist). A.N.S. 1p. 12mo. Buffalo, 1870. Signed with his correct name and his pseudonym." ■*Emendations and textual notes:*

63.1   Buffalo, 1870. • [*reported, not quoted*]
63.4–5   Samuel . . . Twain • [*reported, not quoted*]

■ 8 February 1870 · To John Fuller · Buffalo, N.Y. · *UCCL* 00421

■*Copy-text:* MS, Willard S. Morse Collection, Collection of American Literature, Beinecke Rare Book and Manuscript Library, Yale University (CtY-BR). ■*Previous publication:* Dawson's Book Shop 1942, 48, excerpt; a transcription of the form letter, dated 1 Mar 70, was published in Will M. Clemens 1900, 27. ■*Provenance:* donated to CtY in 1942 by Walter F. Frear.

■ 9 February 1870 · To Francis P. Church · Buffalo, N.Y. · *UCCL* 00422

■*Copy-text:* Transcript and paraphrase, Mott 1957, 3:364. A footnote indicates that the letter was "dated February 9 [1870]." The date has been abbreviated according to Clemens's usual practice. ■*Provenance:* The MS is not known to survive. In 1938, it belonged to William Conant Church's son, Willard Church, but he was reported to have "destroyed most of his father's papers" before his death in 1944. In 1952, the remaining Church papers belonged to Willard's widow (Bigelow, 249, vii; Mott 1957, 3:361, n. 4). ■*Emendations and textual notes:*

65.1   Feb. 9. • February 9 [1870] [*reported, not quoted; the month is spelled out in the usual catalog style*]
65.5   & • and [*also at 65.7, 8 (twice)*]

■ 9 February 1870 · From Samuel L. and Olivia L. Clemens to Jervis and Olivia Lewis Langdon · Buffalo, N.Y. · *UCCL* 00423

■*Copy-text:* MS, Mark Twain House, Hartford (CtHMTH). ■*Previous publication: LLMT,* 144–46. ■*Provenance:* donated to CtHMTH in 1963 by Ida Langdon. ■*Emendations and textual notes:*

66.27   Ba Boarding • B̸oarding
67.33   us up • u̸p

■ 10 February 1870 · To Charles Cole Hine · Buffalo, N.Y. · *UCCL* 00424

■*Copy-text:* MS, Mark Twain Papers, The Bancroft Library, University of California, Berkeley (CU-MARK). ■*Provenance:* donated to CU-MARK in 1980 by Mrs. Dorothy Clark, who had inherited it from her father, an employee of Charles C. Hine. ■*Emendations and textual notes:*

69.19   FEB 11 • [F◇B 11] [*badly inked*]
69.19   MAIL • M[AI]L [*badly inked*]

■ 13 February 1870 · From Samuel L. and Olivia L. Clemens to Mary Mason Fairbanks · Buffalo, N.Y. · *UCCL* 00426

■*Copy-text:* MS, Huntington Library, San Marino (CSmH, call no. HM 14260). ■*Previous publication: MTMF,* 122–26. ■*Provenance:* see Huntington Library in Description of Provenance. ■*Emendations and textual notes:*

70.4   (which • [*no closing parenthesis*]
70.25   sieze • [*sic*]
71.8   kee keys • ke̸ys

71.11	war-whoop • war-|whoop
71.15	housekeeping • house-|keeping
71.18	C.) But • ~.)—|~
71.26	wait. I • ~.—|~
71.30	t̶h̶ with • t̶h̶ w̶i̶t̶h̶ with [*corrected miswriting*]

■ 20 February 1870 · To Joel Benton · Buffalo, N.Y. · *UCCL* 00428

■ *Copy-text:* MS, Autograph Collection, Vassar College Library (NPV). ■ *Provenance:* purchased in 1922 from Caroline B. Peters of Poughkeepsie, N.Y. ■ *Emendations and textual notes:*

73.12	Express • E̶ Express [*corrected miswriting*]
74.10	Payne's • [*sic*]

■ 20 February 1870 · From Samuel L. and Olivia L. Clemens to Olivia Lewis Langdon · Buffalo, N.Y. · *UCCL* 00430

■ *Copy-text:* MS, Mark Twain House, Hartford (CtHMTH). ■ *Previous publication:* *LLMT*, 142–43, excerpt. ■ *Provenance:* donated to CtHMTH in 1963 by Ida Langdon. ■ *Emendations and textual notes:*

74.15	A̶ • [*possibly* 'Ø']
74.18	be, • [*deletion implied*]
74.19	me. The • ~.—|~
75.4	sense. It • ~.—|~
75.10	&̶ & • &̶ | &
75.15	housekwifery • ['k' *partly formed; possibly* 'h']
75.16	a̶c̶h̶e̶v̶ achievements • achevievements
75.17	fricaseed • [*sic*]
75.23	[• ̶[̶[[*rewritten for clarity*]
76.2	l̶o̶n̶g̶ • [*possibly* 'loug']
76.9	carpet,— • [*dash over comma*]

■ 23 February 1870 · To Elisha Bliss, Jr. · Buffalo, N.Y. · *UCCL* 00431

■ *Copy-text:* MS, Mark Twain Papers, The Bancroft Library, University of California, Berkeley (CU-MARK). ■ *Previous publication: MTLP*, 32–33. ■ *Provenance:* see Mendoza Collection in Description of Provenance. ■ *Emendations and textual notes:*

77.6	at • at | at
77.8	w̶ • [*partly formed*]

■ 26 February 1870 · From Olivia L. and Samuel L. Clemens to Jervis Langdon · Buffalo, N.Y. · *UCCL* 00433

■*Copy-text:* MS, Mark Twain House, Hartford (CtHMTH). ■*Previous publication: LLMT,* 147 n. 1, excerpt. ■*Provenance:* donated to CtHMTH in 1963 by Ida Langdon. ■*Emendations and textual notes:*

79.12	c̶a̶m̶e̶ • c̶a̶m̶e̶ˌ[c◊◊◊]ₓ *[apparently corrected miswriting]*	
79.25	t̶h̶a̶t̶ that • t̶h̶a̶t̶	that	
79.27	ˌofˌ • o̶f̶ ˌofˌ *[corrected miswriting]*	
80.8	about • ['t' *over miswritten* 'u']	

■ 26 or 27 February 1870 · From Olivia L. and Samuel L. Clemens to Susan L. Crane · Buffalo, N.Y. · *UCCL* 00434

■*Copy-text: MTB,* 1:409. ■*Emendations and textual notes:*

80.23	& • and *[three times; also at 80.24]*

■ 2 and 3 March 1870 · From Samuel L. and Olivia L. Clemens to Jervis Langdon · Buffalo, N.Y. · *UCCL* 00437

■*Copy-text:* MS, Mark Twain House, Hartford (CtHMTH). ■*Previous publication: LLMT,* 147–48. ■*Provenance:* donated to CtHMTH in 1963 by Ida Langdon. ■*Emendations and textual notes:*

81.8	drawing-room • drawing-|room
81.16	gratitude • gratitu/de
81.20	afternoon • after-||noon
81.20	E̶n̶ Ellen's • E/llen's
82.8	d̶o̶ • ['o' *partly formed*]
82.11	balance. She • ~.—|~
82.17	w̶ • [*partly formed*]

■ 3 March 1870 · To Elisha Bliss, Jr. · Buffalo, N.Y. · *UCCL* 00438

■*Copy-text:* MS, Mark Twain Papers, The Bancroft Library, University of California, Berkeley (CU-MARK). ■*Previous publication: MTMF,* 126–27, excerpt. ■*Provenance:* see Mendoza Collection in Description of Provenance. ■*Emendations and textual notes:*

84.8	any • ['ny' *conflated*]
85.6	to.] We • ~.]—|~

■ 4 March 1870 · To Lewis Frank Walden · Buffalo, N.Y. · *UCCL* 00439

■*Copy-text:* Hannibal *Evening Courier-Post,* 6 Mar 1935, 9C. ■*Emendations and textual notes:*

85.13	March 4. • March 4, 1869
85.14	Friend Frank:— • [*printed out of sequence at 86.9:* 'month | Friend Frank:— | ago']
86.1	& • and [*also at 86.2, 3, 5, 9 (twice), 11, 14*]

■ 6 March 1870 · To Robert M. and Louise M. Howland with a note to James W. Nye · Buffalo, N.Y. · *UCCL* 00440

■*Copy-text:* MS, Mark Twain Papers, The Bancroft Library, University of California, Berkeley (CU-MARK). The letter was written on the same stationery as 10 Feb 70 to Hine. The monogram was excised sometime after receipt, removing portions of some characters on the back of the leaf. ■*Previous publication: LLMT,* 144, brief excerpt. ■*Provenance:* donated to CU-MARK in 1977 by Mr. and Mrs. Robert M. Gunn. Gunn was the Howlands' grandson. ■*Emendations and textual notes:*

87.1	Ⓒ • [*cut away*]
87.3	T • [*partly formed; possibly* 'F']
87.6–7	letter | [¶] I • ~.—| [¶] ~
87.8	pleasant • pleasar̸nt
87.8	as it • [a]s it [*cut*]
87.8	one's married • one['s m]arried [*cut*]

■ 7 March 1870 · To George Griswold · Buffalo, N.Y. · *UCCL* 00440

■*Copy-text:* AAA 1916, lot 157. The catalog describes the letter as "A.L.S., 2pp. 8vo, Buffalo, March 7 [1870]." ■*Emendations and textual notes:*

88.1	Buffalo, March 7. • [*reported, not quoted*]

■ 7 March 1870 · To the Public · Buffalo, N.Y. · *UCCL* 05162

■*Copy-text:* "Personal," Buffalo *Express,* 8 Mar 70, 2. ■*Previous publication:* In addition to the copy-text, "Personal," Buffalo *Commercial Advertiser,* 8 Mar 70, 3; "City and Neighborhood," Elmira *Advertiser,* 9 Mar 70, 4, excerpt; "Notes and Comments," Cleveland *Herald,* 10 Mar 70, 2, paraphrase. ■*Emendations and textual notes:*

89.3	& • and [*also at 89.5 (twice)*]
89.4	foundationless • foundationaless

■ 11 March 1870 · To Francis P. Church · Buffalo, N.Y. · *UCCL* 00442
■ *Copy-text:* Mott 1957, 364. Mott noted the letter was "dated March 11 [1870]."
■ *Provenance:* The MS, part of the Willard Church Collection in 1938, is not
known to survive (see the commentary to 9 Feb 70 to Church). ■ *Emendations
and textual notes:*

89.11   March 11. • [*reported, not quoted*]
89.13   & • and [*also at 90.1, 2*]

■ 11 March 1870 · To Elisha Bliss, Jr. · Buffalo, N.Y. · *UCCL* 00443
■ *Copy-text:* MS, Henry W. and Albert A. Berg Collection, The New York Public
Library, Astor, Lenox and Tilden Foundations (NN-B). ■ *Previous publication:*
AAA/Anderson 1934b, lot 124, excerpt; *MTMF,* 128 n. 1, excerpt; McElderry,
xii, excerpt; Hill, 41, excerpt; *MTLP,* 30, brief paraphrase. ■ *Provenance:* The
MS, in the collection of Edmund W. Evans of Oil City, Pennsylvania, was sold
in 1934; in 1935 it was offered in another sale of several collections, including
that of Mr. and Mrs. William K. Bixby of St. Louis; by 1939 it was in the collection of William T. H. Howe; in 1940, Dr. Albert A. Berg bought and donated
the Howe Collection to NN-B. ■ *Emendations and textual notes:*

90.10   f • [*partly formed*]
91.3–12   No . . . newspaper. • [*MS page renumbered from '5' to '3'*]

■ 16 March 1870 · To Unidentified · Buffalo, N.Y. · *UCCL* 09756
■ *Copy-text:* MS facsimile. The editors have not seen the MS, which is in the
collection of Wayne M. Joseph. ■ *Previous publication:* Merwin-Clayton, 1906,
lot 1018, brief quotation. ■ *Provenance:* The letter was part of the George M.
Elwood Collection when it was offered for sale in 1906.

■ 18 March 1870 · To Hattie Booth · Buffalo, N.Y. · *UCCL* 00445
■ *Copy-text:* MS, Katherine Seymour Day Collection, Harriet Beecher Stowe
Center, Hartford (CtHSD).

■ 21 March 1870 · To James T. Fields · Buffalo, N.Y. · *UCCL* 00446
■ *Copy-text:* MS, Clifton Waller Barrett Library, University of Virginia, Char-
lottesville (ViU). ■ *Provenance:* deposited at ViU by Clifton Waller Barrett on 17
December 1963. ■ *Emendations and textual notes:*

93.11   & • & | &
93.12   ~~We~~ Will • W¢ill
93.15   ~~git~~ get • g¢et

■ 22 March 1870 · To James Redpath · Buffalo, N.Y. · *UCCL* 00447

■ *Copy-text: MTL*, 1:172. The rationale for emendations to remove *MTL* styling is given in Description of Texts. ■ *Previous publication:* In addition to the copy-text, *MTB*, 1:409, with omissions. ■ *Emendations and textual notes:*

94.1	Buffalo, March 22. • BUFFALO, *March 22, 1870*.
94.2–3	Dear Red: [¶] I • [¶] DEAR RED,—I
94.5	& • and
94.8	Clemens • CLEMENS

■ 22 and 24 March 1870 · From Samuel L. and Olivia L. Clemens to Mary Mason Fairbanks · Buffalo, N.Y. · *UCCL* 00448

■ *Copy-text:* MS, Huntington Library, San Marino (CSmH, call nos. HM 14261 and 14262). ■ *Previous publication: MTMF*, 127–30; McElderry, xi, excerpt. ■ *Provenance:* see Huntington Library in Description of Provenance. ■ *Emendations and textual notes:*

95.8	bridegrooms • bride-|grooms
95.8	I • [*followed by possible uncanceled apostrophe*]
95.16	e̶n̶ • ['n' *partly formed*]
95.21	either • either̶r̶
95.21	newspaper • news-|paper
95.24	newspaper." Do • ~."—|~
96.5	Yrs Son • [*sic*]
96.24	it̶‸—̶ • [*caret with no interlineation*]

■ 26 March 1870 · To Jane Lampton Clemens and Family · Buffalo, N.Y. · *UCCL* 00449

■ *Copy-text:* MS, Jean Webster McKinney Family Papers, Vassar College Library (NPV). ■ *Previous publication: MTBus*, 112. ■ *Provenance:* see McKinney Family Papers in Description of Provenance. ■ *Emendations and textual notes:*

98.1	ẇ • [*partly formed*]
98.1	piana • [*sic*]

■ 27 March 1870 · From Samuel L. and Olivia L. Clemens to Jervis and Olivia Lewis Langdon · Buffalo, N.Y. · *UCCL* 00450

■ *Copy-text:* MS, Mark Twain House, Hartford (CtHMTH). ■ *Previous publication: LLMT*, 149–51; Chester L. Davis 1982, 4, excerpt. ■ *Provenance:* donated to CtHMTH in 1963 by Ida Langdon. ■ *Emendations and textual notes:*

99.4	*better* • be⌀tter
99.5	f • [*partly formed*]

99.20   w̶i̶t̶ wish • wi/sh ['t' *partly formed*]
99.21   letters, • [*deletion implied*]
100.10   most • [*sic*]
100.12   S̶o̶m̶ Son • Son/n
100.23   ꝏ • [*possibly* '3']

■ 31 March 1870 · To Charles F. Wingate · Buffalo, N.Y. · *UCCL* 00451

■ *Copy-text:* MS, The New York Public Library, Astor, Lenox and Tilden Foundations, New York City (NN). ■ *Provenance:* R. R. Bowker Collection. ■ *Emendations and textual notes:*

102.4   the book • the t̶h̶ b̶o̶o̶k̶ | book ['book' *rewritten for clarity*]
102.7   g̶ • [*partly formed*]
102.8   c̶r̶i̶t̶ • c̶r̶i̶t̶-|
103.7   2̶0̶0̶ 210 • 2∮10
103.7   3̶1̶ 30ᵗʰ • 3∮0ᵗʰ

■ April 1870 · To Jane L. Stanford · Buffalo, N.Y. · *UCCL* 11712

■ *Copy-text:* MS, M122 American Authors Collection, Department of Special Collections, Green Library, Stanford University (CSt).

■ 1 April 1870 · From Samuel L. and Olivia L. Clemens to Jervis and Olivia Lewis Langdon · Buffalo, N.Y. · *UCCL* 00452

■ *Copy-text:* Transcripts, Mark Twain Papers, The Bancroft Library, University of California, Berkeley (CU-MARK). A TS and its carbon transcribed from the MS and corrected and annotated by Dixon Wecter together provide the text for this letter. Wecter distinguished Olivia's and Clemens's handwriting on the TS by means of asterisks and, in part, on the carbon by means of brackets with identifying notes. The transcripts as corrected by Wecter serve as copy-text with all corrections, interlineations, and cancellations transcribed as typed and marked if they are believed to be Olivia's or Clemens's. Doubtful corrections are reported in the commentary only; changes deemed to be simple corrections of typing errors or omissions are not reported. In two cases where Wecter could not supply canceled readings the typist omitted, he wrote "[word illegible]" and his language is preserved in this text. In two instances where the TS and the carbon are marked differently, the discrepancy is reported below; the carbon is not fully marked, however, and failure to mark it is therefore not reported. ■ *Provenance:* Wecter identified his source as the "Jervis Langdon Collection." The present location of the MS is not known. ■ *Emendations and textual notes:*

104.12   England— I • ~—|~
104.14   bearable— Lovingly • ~—~
104.15   Twins • ʄTwins [*transcription corrected, probably by Wecter*]
104.16   Spauldingzes • [*marked '[sic]' by Wecter*]
105.2   Mississippi • Miss̫iss̫ippi [*transcription corrected, probably by Wecter*]
105.14   needs • need
105.18   spring • ₰spring [*transcription corrected by Wecter*]
105.23   P. S. • P.S.
105.30   um • ~~him~~ ₓum̫ [*probably corrected transcription, by Wecter*]
106.1   ~~(She~~ (TS) • ~~(she~~ (carbon) [*no closing parenthesis; transcribed by Wecter on TS and carbon*]
106.2   ~~mackerel— Still~~ (TS) • ~~mackerel—still~~ (carbon) [*transcribed by Wecter on TS and carbon*]

■ 16 April 1870 · From Olivia L. and Samuel L. Clemens to Susan L. Crane · Buffalo, N.Y. · *UCCL* 00454

■*Copy-text:* MS, Mark Twain House, Hartford (CtHMTH). ■*Provenance:* donated to CtHMTH in 1963 by Ida Langdon. ■*Emendations and textual notes:*

107.9   ones • ~~ones~~ ones [*corrected miswriting*]
107.24   m̫ • [*partly formed*]
107.24   her • ~~her~~ her [*rewritten for clarity*]
108.6   Iᵥ • ['v' *partly formed*]

■ 16 and 17 April 1870 · From Samuel L. and Olivia L. Clemens to Jervis and Olivia Lewis Langdon · Buffalo, N.Y. · *UCCL* 00455

■*Copy-text:* MS, Mark Twain House, Hartford (CtHMTH). ■*Previous publication:* Eastman, 139, excerpt. ■*Provenance:* donated to CtHMTH in 1963 by Ida Langdon. ■*Emendations and textual notes:*

109.1   ~~16~~ 17. • 1₰7. [*possibly '1₰7.'*]
109.14–15   ~~otherwise, I think, unless he is content to wait a fortnight or so~~ otherwise • other-|wise, ₓI think,ₓ ~~unless he is content to wait a fortnight or so~~ |wise
109.17   exceedingly. They • ~.—|~
110.6   sunshine • sun-|shine
110.19   ~~sem~~ sermon • ser̫rmon
110.22   Opera • Op̫era
110.24   ~~is~~ it • is̫t
110.27   us. And • ~.—|~

■ 19? April 1870 · To Orion Clemens · Buffalo, N.Y. · *UCCL* 00456 (formerly *UCCL* 00456 and 10294)

■*Copy-text:* MS, Mark Twain Papers, The Bancroft Library, University of California, Berkeley (CU-MARK). ■*Provenance:* see Moffett Collection in Description of Provenance. ■*Emendations and textual notes:*

113.7–8   BUFFALO N.Y. ◊◊◊ ◊◊ • [BUFFA]LO N[.]Y[.] [◊◊◊ ◊◊] [*badly inked*]

■ 21 April 1870 · To Orion Clemens · Buffalo, N.Y. · *UCCL* 00457

■*Copy-text:* MS, Mark Twain Papers, The Bancroft Library, University of California, Berkeley (CU-MARK). ■*Provenance:* see Moffett Collection in Description of Provenance. ■*Emendations and textual notes:*

114.4   *I* • [*partly formed*]
114.6   ~~judgment~~ • [*false ascenders/descenders*]
114.16   ~~le~~ little • l¢ittle
114.18   title • titlȩ ['tl' *crossed; malformed 'e' confused with* 'l']
115.3   tonight • to-|night
115.10   ~~would~~ was • woul̶das ['d' *partly formed*]
115.14   received • receive[d] [*torn*]
115.15   BUFFALO N.Y. • BUFF[A◊◊] N.Y[◊] [*cut away*]

■ 22 April 1870 · From Samuel L. and Olivia L. Clemens to Theodore W. Crane · Buffalo, N.Y. · *UCCL* 00458

■*Copy-text:* MS, Mark Twain House, Hartford (CtHMTH). ■*Provenance:* donated to CtHMTH in 1963 by Ida Langdon. ■*Emendations and textual notes:*

116.13   ~~infe~~ interfere • inf̶eterfere
116.14   ~~Bett~~ Between • Bet/ween
116.19   superintendent • ['ri' *conflated*]

■ 23 April 1870 · To Elisha Bliss, Jr. · Buffalo, N.Y. · *UCCL* 00459

■*Copy-text:* MS, Mark Twain Papers, The Bancroft Library, University of California, Berkeley (CU-MARK). ■*Previous publication: MTMF,* 132, brief excerpt; *MTLP,* 33–34. ■*Provenance:* see Mendoza Collection in Description of Provenance. ■*Emendations and textual notes:*

117.3   ~~tri-~~ • ~~tri-~~|
118.6   recuperate. But • ~.—|~

■ 26 April 1870 · To Frank Fuller · Buffalo, N.Y. · *UCCL* 00460

■ *Copy-text:* None. Except for the form letter text, which is taken from 8 Feb 70 to John Fuller (and identical to 16 Mar 70 and 13 Feb 71 to Unidentified), the text is based on two transcripts, each of which derived independently from the MS.

P¹	Typescript (WU)
P²	AAA 1924c, lot 64

P¹, a typescript at the Rare Book Department, Memorial Library, University of Wisconsin, Madison (WU), was probably copied by George Brownell from a handwritten transcription (now lost) of the MS by Dana Ayer (see Brownell Collection in Description of Provenance); P² was transcribed directly from the MS when it was put on sale in 1924. It describes the MS as 'Autograph Letter Signed:—"Mark," 4 pp. 8vo.' Two other typescripts, one at CtHMTH and the other made by Bernard DeVoto (CU-MARK) derive from P¹. A second auction catalog, AAA 1927a, lot 43, while it may have been transcribed from the MS, quotes only the salutation and signature and contributes no independent readings. Presumably referring to a clipping from the May *Galaxy*, P² indicates that 'Accompanying the letter is the article from the *Galaxy* to which Clemens refers.' The 1927 catalog notes that 'Accompanying the letter are the articles in question, included in the "Memoranda" for May and June.' While it is possible that Clemens enclosed a clipping from the May *Galaxy*, he could not have enclosed one from the June number, which did not issue until mid-May. Most likely the earlier clipping, like the later, was not an original enclosure but was supplied by a collector or dealer as an association item. ■ *Previous publication:* see *Copy-text;* a transcription of the form letter text was published in Will M. Clemens 1900, 27. ■ *Emendations, adopted readings, and textual notes:* Adopted readings followed by '(C)' are editorial emendations of the source readings.

119.1	Buf. Apl. 26 (P²) • Buffalo, April 26th., 1870 (P¹)
119.2–120.13	Dear . . . a (P¹) • [*not in*] (P²)
119.3	& (C) • and (P¹) [*also at 120.1, 7 (twice), 9, 11, 13, 14, 16, 25, 26*]
120.13	sneak thief (P²) • sneak-|thief (P¹)
120.13–19	in . . . name, (P¹) • [*not in*] (P²)
120.20	MSS. (P²) • ~∧ (P¹)
120.20	"A Literary (P²) • a "Literary (P¹)
120.20	Offender (P¹) • ~" (P²)
120.20–21	in Court . . . & (C) • ~ ~ . . . and (P¹); [*not in*] (P²)
120.22–34	Send . . . Ever (P¹) • [*not in*] (P²)
120.35	Mark. (P¹) • ~, (P²)
120.36–37	Frank . . . Street. (P¹) • [*not in*] (P²)
121.1–15	[*on the back:*] . . . BOSTON. • [*text of form letter taken from 8 Feb 70 to Fuller; not in P¹ or P²*]

■ 30? April 1870 · To Charles C. Converse · Buffalo, N.Y. · *UCCL* 11733

■ *Copy-text:* "Personal," Buffalo *Express*, 9 May 70, 2. ■ *Emendations and textual notes:*

123.5   & • and

■ 4 May 1870? · To Mary Janney · Elmira, N.Y. · *UCCL* 08531

■ *Copy-text:* MS, Cyril Clemens Collection, Mark Twain House, Hartford (CtHMTH). ■ *Provenance:* donated to CtHMTH in 1984 by Cyril Clemens.

■ 5 May 1870 · To Elisha Bliss, Jr. · Elmira, N.Y. · *UCCL* 00461

■ *Copy-text:* Transcript, handwritten by Dana Ayer, Rare Book Department, Memorial Library, University of Wisconsin, Madison (WU). ■ *Previous publication: MTLP*, 36 n. 1, brief excerpt. ■ *Provenance:* The MS evidently remained among the American Publishing Company's files until it was sold (and may have been at that time copied by Ayer; see Brownell Collection in Description of Provenance). Its present location is not known. The Ayer transcription was in turn copied by a typist and both the handwritten and typed transcriptions are at WU. ■ *Emendations and textual notes:*

125.7   gone. • ~$_\wedge$
125.16   [*letter docketed:*] —70 • [*The year, which Ayer transcribed as part of the dateline, was probably the American Publishing Company's docket; see, for example, the similar docket on 23 Apr 70 to Bliss.*]

■ 7 May 1870 · To Elisha Bliss, Jr. · Elmira, N.Y. · *UCCL* 00462

■ *Copy-text:* MS, Mark Twain Papers, The Bancroft Library, University of California, Berkeley (CU-MARK). ■ *Previous publication: MTLP*, 34–35. ■ *Provenance:* see Mendoza Collection in Description of Provenance. ■ *Emendations and textual notes:*

126.14   Set • [*possibly* 'Se*l*t']
127.4   t̶h̶ to • tho ['h' *partly formed*]

■ 10 May 1870 · To James Redpath · Elmira, N.Y. · *UCCL* 00463

■ *Copy-text:* None. The letter is reconstructed from five partial transcripts, each of which derived independently from the MS:

P[1]	Will M. Clemens 1900, 27
P[2]	*MTB*, 1:409–10
P[3]	*MTL*, 1:172–73
P[4]	Anderson Galleries 1919, lot 176
P[5]	Parke-Bernet 1950, lot 241

Will Clemens evidently transcribed the P[1] text from the MS before 1900. Albert Bigelow Paine must have seen and transcribed the MS before 1912 when he published the short excerpt in P[2], and he may have used the same transcription or made a second one before 1917, when he published the longer excerpts in P[3]. Both catalog texts were transcribed directly from the MS when it was advertised for sale, P[4] in 1919 and P[5] in 1950. P[4] describes it as 'A. L. S., (signed "Mark"), 2 pages, 4to, Elmira, N. Y., May 10, 1870,' and P[5] includes a similar description. ■*Previous publication:* Horner, 165–66; "Letters to James Redpath," *Mark Twain Quarterly* 5 (Winter–Spring 1942): 19, in addition to texts listed under *Copy-text.* ■*Emendations, adopted readings, and textual notes:*

128.1	Elmira, • *[reported, not quoted]* (P[4,5]); ELMIRA, (P[1,3]); [*not in*] (P[2])
128.1	N. Y., (P[1]) • *[reported, not quoted]* (P[4]); ~. ~.‸ (P[3]); [*not in*] (P[2,5])
128.1	May 10, 1870. (P[1]) • *[reported, not quoted]* (P[4,5]); *May 10, 1870.* (P[3]); [*not in*] (P[2])
128.2	[*no ¶*] Friend Redpath,— • [*no ¶*] *Friend Redpath:* (P[1]); [¶] FRIEND REDPATH,— (P[3]); [*not in*] (P[2,4,5])
128.3	[¶] I . . . permanently. (P[1,2]) • [*no ¶*] ~ . . . ~. (P[3,5]); [*not in*] (P[4])
128.3–4	I . . . them (P[1,5]) • [*not in*] (P[2,3,4])
128.4	these circulars • those circulars (P[1]); these (P[5])
128.4	all (P[1]) • [*not in*] (P[5])
128.4	applicants (P[1]) • ~, (P[5])
128.4–5	I . . . you • ~ . . . ~. (P[1]); [*not in*] (P[2,3,4,5])
128.5–6	—for . . . penmanship. (P[5]) • [*not in*] (P[1,2,3,4])
128.7–10	[¶] Have . . . platform. (P[3,4]) • [*no ¶*] ~ . . . ~? (P[2]); [*not in*] (P[1,5])
128.7	house, (P[2,3]) • ~‸ (P[4])
128.7	furnished, (P[2,4]) • ~; (P[3])
128.8	carriage, (P[2,3]) • ~‸ (P[4])
128.8	& a (P[4]) • and a (P[2,3])
128.8–9	awe-inspiring— (P[3]) • awe-|in-spiring (P[2]); awe-|inspiring (P[4])
128.9	less; (P[2]) • ~— (P[3]); ~. (P[4])
128.9	& • and (P[2,3]); And (P[4])
128.9	necessary, (P[2,4]) • ~— (P[3])
128.10	considerable, (P[2,3]) • ~— (P[4])
128.10	& (P[4]) • and (P[2,3])
128.10	therefore (P[2,3]) • ~, (P[4])
128.10	nightly (P[2,3]) • ~, (P[4])
128.11	The . . . least. (P[1,2,3]); [*not in*] (P[4,5])
128.12	[¶] Remember . . . Billings (P[1,3,5]) • [*no ¶*] ~ . . . ~ (P[4,5]); [*not in*] (P[2])
128.12	& (P[4,5]) • and (P[1,3]); [*not in*] (P[2])
128.12	Fall. (P[1,3,4]) • ~‸ (P[5]); [*not in*] (P[2])

128.12	Luck to you! (P[1,3]); • [*not in*] (P[2,4,5])
128.12–15	I . . . "hyste." (P[3]) • [*not in*] (P[1,2,4,5])
128.15–16	I . . . yet. (P[4]) • [*not in*] (P[1,2,3,5])
128.17	Yours . . . after, (P[1]) • ~ . . . ~. (P[3]); [*not in*] (P[2,4,5])
128.17	& • and (P[1,3])
128.18	Mark. • MARK. (P[1,3]); Mark (P[4,5]); [*not in*] (P[2])

■ 13 May 1870 · From Olivia L. and Samuel L. Clemens to Jervis Langdon · Buffalo, N.Y. · *UCCL* 00464

■*Copy-text:* MS, Mark Twain House, Hartford (CtHMTH). ■*Provenance:* donated to CtHMTH in 1963 by Ida Langdon. ■*Emendations and textual notes:*

129.5	check • chec*t*k
129.19	syrup • syru*t*p
130.17	~~rece~~ recipient's • rec*t*ipient's
130.22	We²ll • [*deletion of apostrophe implied*]
130.36	fanciful • fan-|ficiful

■ 20 May 1870 · To Elisha Bliss, Jr. · Buffalo, N.Y. · *UCCL* 00465

■*Copy-text:* MS, collection of Robert Daley until 1993. ■*Previous publication: MTLP*, 35. ■*Provenance:* The MS evidently remained among the American Publishing Company's files until it was sold (and may have been at that time copied by Dana Ayer; see Brownell Collection in Description of Provenance). An Ayer handwritten transcription and a typed transcription are at WU. Sold in 1993 to an unidentified purchaser (Sotheby 1993, lot 214).

■ 20? May 1870 · To Edward H. Paige · Buffalo, N.Y. · *UCCL* 11699

■ *Copy-text:* MS facsimile, on the back of a *carte de visite* photograph of Clemens. The MS, which is owned by the Detroit Public Library, Detroit (MiD), was not available for inspection.

■ 21 May 1870 · To Frank Fuller · Buffalo, N.Y. · *UCCL* 00466

■*Copy-text:* MS of letter, collection of Todd M. Axelrod; MS of envelope, collection of Victor and Irene Murr Jacobs, Roesch Library, University of Dayton (ODaU). The envelope is torn, obliterating a few words, characters, and punctuation marks. See the illustration below, editorially reconstructed. ■*Previous publication:* letter only, AAA 1924c, lot 66, excerpt; Anderson Galleries 1928, lot 55, brief paraphrase. ■*Provenance:* The letter MS was sold in 1924 by an unidentified owner, possibly a *"Prominent Pennsylvania Collector"*; in 1928 it was sold again in the liquidation sale of the George D. Smith Book Company. Probably between 1936 and 1942 George Brownell saw either the MS or a lost tran-

Letter of 21 May 1870 to Frank Fuller. The torn envelope, with missing words editorially reconstructed; reproduced at 75 percent of actual size (ODaU).

scription of it and made the typescript now at WU (see Brownell Collection in Description of Provenance). The MS was acquired by Axelrod in 1983. There is no known record of the envelope before it became part of the Jacobs Collection, where it has remained at least since 1981. ▪*Emendations and textual notes*.

133.16	*refuse!* Therefore • ~!—|~
134.3	ɟ • [*partly formed*]
134.19	stamps on the other side may • sta[m◊◊ ◊◊ ◊◊◊] other side [◊◊◊] [*torn*]
134.20	to pay • [◊◊] pay [*torn*]
134.20	remarks.} • remarks.[}] [*torn*]
134.23	Confidential • Confidentia[l] [*torn*]

▪ 21 May 1870 · To James Redpath · Buffalo, N.Y. · *UCCL* 00467

▪*Copy-text:* None. The text is based on two transcriptions, each of which derives independently from the manuscript.

P¹	Will M. Clemens 1900, 27
P²	AAA/Anderson 1935c, lot 39

P² describes and misdates the MS as a '1-p. A. L. s. "*Mark*", to Mr. Redpath, May 21 [1878].' ▪*Provenance:* The MS had been tipped into volume 1 of *The Innocents Abroad* in one of 512 sets of the American Publishing Company's Autograph Edition of the Writings of Mark Twain. The set, including the MS, was sold in 1935 as part of the library of Hannah M. Standish; its present location is not known. ▪*Emendations, adopted readings, and textual notes:* Adopted readings followed by '(C)' are editorial emendations of the source readings.

135.1   Buffalo, (C) • BUFFALO, (P^1); [*not in*] (P^2)
135.1   May 21. (C) • May 2, 1870. (P^1); May 21 [1878] [*reported, not quoted*] (P^2)
135.2   Dear Redpath: (C) • *Dear Redpath:* (P^1); To Mr. Redpath [*reported, not quoted*] (P^2)
135.3–4 I . . . papers. (P^1) • [*not in*] (P^2)
135.5   [¶] They (P^1) • [*no* ¶] ~ (P^2)
135.5   & (P^2) • and (P^1) [*also at 136.6, 8*]
135.6   P.M. (P^2) • p. m. (P^1)
135.6   house, (P^1) • ~$_\wedge$ (P^2)
135.7   though . . . too. (P^1) • [*not in*] (P^2)
135.7   & (C) • and (P^1)
135.8–9 [¶] Now . . . copies. • [*no* ¶] ~ . . . ~. (P^2); [*not in*] (P^1)
135.10   Yours, (P^1) • [*not in*] (P^2)
135.11   Mark. (C) • MARK. (P^1); Mark (P^2)

▪ 21? May 1870 · To William Bowen · Buffalo, N.Y. · *UCCL* 02136
▪*Copy-text:* MS facsimile, front and back of a *carte de visite* photograph of Clemens. The editors have not seen the MS, which is owned by William Bowen's grandson, Royden Burwell Bowen, Jr., who provided a photographic copy in 1993. ▪*Previous publication:* Hornberger, frontispiece.

▪ 22 May 1870 · To Jervis Langdon · Buffalo, N.Y. · *UCCL* 00469
▪*Copy-text:* MS, Mark Twain House, Hartford (CtHMTH). ▪*Previous publication:* *LLMT*, 151–53; Chester L. Davis 1978, 2–3, excerpt. ▪*Provenance:* donated to CtHMTH in 1963 by Ida Langdon. ▪*Emendations and textual notes:*

138.16   Land, • [*deletion implied*]
138.21   themselves. So • ~.—|~

▪ 26 May 1870 · To the Buffalo Street Commissioner · Buffalo, N.Y. · *UCCL* 11723
▪*Copy-text:* "Notes from the People," Buffalo *Express*, 27 May 70, 4. ▪*Emendations and textual notes:*

141.4   & • and [*141.5 (twice)*]

■ 28 May 1870 · To Unidentified · Buffalo, N.Y. · *UCCL* 00471

■*Copy-text:* Newark Galleries 1930, lot 40. The catalog describes the MS as 'A. N. S. "Samuel L. Clemens" *and* "Mark Twain." 1p. 16mo. Buffalo, May 28, 1870. . . . Small tear affecting last letter of signature.' ■*Provenance:* The present location of the MS, sold in 1930 as part of the collection of the late John C. Thurman, is not known. ■*Emendations and textual notes:*

142.1   Buffalo, May 28. • [*reported, not quoted*]
142.3   &c., &c., & • etc., etc., and
142.6   Mark Twain • ~ ~.

■ 28 May 1870 · To Benjamin P. Shillaber · Buffalo, N.Y. · *UCCL* 00470

■*Copy-text:* MS facsimile. The editors have not seen the MS, which is in the Rare Book Room, University of Illinois, Urbana (IU-R). ■*Provenance:* The MS, in the Franklin J. Meine Collection, was probably among the Mark Twain materials purchased from Meine's widow in 1969.

■ 29 May 1870 · From Samuel L. and Olivia L. Clemens to Mary Mason Fairbanks · Buffalo, N.Y. · *UCCL* 00472

■*Copy-text:* MS, Huntington Library, San Marino (CSmH, call no. HM 14263). ■*Previous publication:* *MTMF,* 130–33; McElderry, xiii, excerpt. ■*Provenance:* see Huntington Library in Description of Provenance. ■*Emendations and textual notes:*

144.13–14   over-ex[er]tion • over-ex-|tion
144.15   overheated • over-|heated
144.16   crowding • cro̭wding
145.7   ~~on~~ yesterday • ['yesterday' *over* 'on']
145.17   ~~under~~ under • ~~under~~ | ~~under~~ under [*first* 'under' *miswritten*]
145.19   ~~comp~~ combustible • comp̸bustible ['p' *partly formed*]

■ 30 May 1870 · To Elisha Bliss, Jr., *per* Olivia L. Clemens with revisions by Samuel L. Clemens · Buffalo, N.Y. · *UCCL* 00473

■*Copy-text:* MS, Beinecke Rare Book and Manuscript Library, Yale University (CtY-BR). The original enclosure, which does not survive, was a clipping from the Buffalo *Express* ("The Russian Minister . . . ," 23 May 70, 2). Copy-text is a microfilm edition of the newspaper in the Buffalo and Erie County Library (NBu). ■*Provenance:* The MS evidently remained among the American Publishing Company's files until it was sold (and may have been at that time copied by Dana Ayer; see Brownell Collection in Description of Provenance). An Ayer handwritten transcription and a typed transcription are at WU. ■*Emendations and textual notes:*

146.7   ~~copp~~ copy • copp̸y
146.7   soiled • ~~soiled~~ | soiled [*corrected miswriting*]
146.13–15   ~~for~~ . . . ~~book——~~ • [*canceled by SLC; deletion of dash implied*]

■ 1–6 or 12–21 June 1870 · To Robert M. Howland · Buffalo, N.Y. · *UCCL* 00476

■*Copy-text:* MS, Mark Twain Papers, The Bancroft Library, University of California, Berkeley (CU-MARK). ■*Provenance:* donated to CU-MARK in 1977 by Mr. and Mrs. Robert M. Gunn.

■ 9 June 1870 · To Elisha Bliss, Jr. · Elmira, N.Y. · *UCCL* 00478

■*Copy-text:* MS, Mark Twain House, Hartford (CtHMTH). ■*Provenance:* Jonathan Goodwin Collection, acquired by CtHMTH in 1972. ■*Emendations and textual notes:*

148.8   Bret • ~~Ber~~ Bret [*corrected miswriting*]
148.9   ~~You~~ • ['u' *partly formed*]

■ 11 June 1870 · To Ellen White · Elmira, N.Y. · *UCCL* 09890

■*Copy-text:* City Book Auction, lot 130. The auction catalog describes the MS as "Autograph Letter Signed. 1p. Sm. 4to. Elmira, June 11. . . . To Mrs. Ellen White, 472 Delaware Ave. Buffalo." ■*Provenance:* The present location of the MS (sold in 1943 by City Book Auction) is not known. ■*Emendations and textual notes:*

150.1   Elmira, June 11. • [*reported, not quoted*]
150.2   [¶] Send • [*no* ¶] ~
150.2   eleven • leven
150.3   Sam*ᴵ*. • Sam'l
150.5   Mrs. . . . Buffalo. • [*reported, not quoted*]

■ 12 June 1870 · From Samuel L. and Olivia L. Clemens to Pamela A. Moffett · Buffalo, N.Y. · *UCCL* 00479

■*Copy-text:* MS, Jean Webster McKinney Family Papers, Vassar College Library (NPV). ■*Previous publication: MTBus,* 114–15, omitting OLC's portion. ■*Provenance:* see McKinney Family Papers in Description of Provenance. ■*Emendations and textual notes:*

151.15	~~is~~ it • i$t
151.20	line. I • ~.—|~
151.29	success. We • ~.—|~
152.2	~~al~~ at • a$t
152.3	~~than~~ that • tha$t

■ 19 June 1870 · From Samuel L. and Olivia L. Clemens to Jervis and Olivia Lewis Langdon · Buffalo, N.Y. · *UCCL* 00480

■ *Copy-text:* MS, Mark Twain Papers, The Bancroft Library, University of California, Berkeley (CU-MARK). ■ *Provenance:* donated to CU-MARK in 1972 by Mrs. Eugene Lada-Mocarski, Jervis Langdon, Jr., Mrs. Robert S. Pennock, and Mrs. Bayard Schieffelin. ■ *Emendations and textual notes:*

153.2	M • [*partly formed*]
153.16	overdose • over-|dose
154.12	rosebud • roseb$ud
154.15	f • [*partly formed*]

■ 23 June 1870 · To John Munroe and Company · Elmira, N.Y. · *UCCL* 11807

■ *Copy-text:* Paraphrase in George F. Dawson, "Letter from Washington," Sacramento *Union*, 19 July 1870, 1.

■ 23–26 June 1870 · To D. Appleton and Company · Elmira, N.Y. · *UCCL* 09767

■ *Copy-text:* Anderson Auction Company 1914, lot 51. Described in the auction catalog as "A. L. S., 12mo, Elmira, n. d., to Appleton & Co., publishers." ■ *Emendations and textual notes:*

155.7	Elmira • [*reported, not quoted*]

■ 25 June 1870 · To Jane Lampton Clemens and Pamela A. Moffett · Elmira, N.Y. · *UCCL* 00481

■ *Copy-text:* MS, Jean Webster McKinney Family Papers, Vassar College Library (NPV). ■ *Provenance:* see McKinney Family Papers in Description of Provenance. ■ *Emendations and textual notes:*

156.16	at dispatch • [*sic*]
156.16	has~~sn~~ • ['n' *partly formed*]

■ 25 June 1870 · To Mary Mason Fairbanks · Elmira, N.Y. · *UCCL* 00482

■ *Copy-text:* MS, Huntington Library, San Marino (CSmH, call no. HM 14264).
■ *Previous publication: MTMF,* 133–34. ■ *Provenance:* see Huntington Library
in Description of Provenance. ■ *Emendations and textual notes:*

157.8   sieze • [*sic*]
157.8–9   ~~mul~~ must • mu/st
157.16   to-day • to-|day

■ 25 June 1870 · To Charles Scribner and Company · Elmira, N.Y. ·
UCCL 11850

■ *Copy-text:* MS facsimile, Mark Twain Papers, The Bancroft Library, University of California, Berkeley (CU-MARK). The editors have not seen the MS,
which was owned in 1992 by Mrs. T. V. Hedgpeth, who sent a photocopy to CU-MARK. ■ *Emendations and textual notes:*

158.5   Yrs • ['rs' *conflated*]

■ 27 June 1870 · To Elisha Bliss, Jr. · Elmira, N.Y. · *UCCL* 00483

■ *Copy-text:* None. The text is based on four transcriptions, each of which derives independently from the MS:

            P[1]   Ayer handwritten transcription (WU)
            P[2]   Anderson Galleries 1921, lot 151
            P[3]   Anderson Galleries 1922, lot 52A
            P[4]   Chicago 1936, lot 113

P[1] is in the Rare Book Department, Memorial Library, University of Wisconsin,
Madison (WU). P[2] and P[3] describe the MS as 'A. L. s., 1 p., 4to. Elmira, June
27, 1870. To Mr. Bliss. Signed "Mark." '; P[4] describes it as 'A. L. S. "Mark."
1p., 4to. Elmira, N. Y., June 27, 1870. To Mr. Bliss. Written on his father-in-law's business stationery. J. Langdon & Co., Elmira.' ■ *Provenance:* The MS evidently remained among the American Publishing Company's files until it was
sold (and may have been at that time copied by Ayer; see Brownell Collection in
Description of Provenance). The Ayer transcription was in turn copied by a typist and both the handwritten and typed transcriptions are at WU. The present
location of the MS, offered for sale in 1921, 1922, and 1936, is not known.
■ *Emendations, adopted readings, and textual notes:* Adopted readings followed by
'(C)' are editorial emendations of the source readings.

159.1–4   J. LANGDON . . . 1870 (C) • Elmira N.Y June 27—1870 (P[1]); Elmira, June 27, 1870. [*reported, not quoted*] (P[2,3]); Elmira, N. Y.,
               June 27, 1870. . . . Written on his father-in-law's business stationery. J. Langdon & Co., Elmira. [*reported, not quoted*] (P[4]) [*The
               text of the letterhead is in part adopted from 25 June 70 to Fairbanks.*]

159.5	Friend Bliss— (C) • Friend Bliss (P[1]); To Mr. Bliss [*reported, not quoted*] (P[2,3,4])
159.6	Yes, (P[3,4]) • ~$_\wedge$ (P[1,2])
159.6	tip-top (P[2,3,4]) • tip top (P[1])
159.6–8	We . . . away. (P[1,4]) • [*not in*] (P[2,3])
159.8	well, (P[4]) • ~$_\wedge$ (P[1])
159.9–10	This . . . Yrs (P[1]) • [*not in*] (P[2,3,4])
159.11	Mark. (P[2,3,4]) • ~$_\wedge$ (P[1])

■ 27 June 1870 · To Daniel Slote · Elmira, N.Y. · *UCCL* 00484

■*Copy-text:* MS, Mark Twain House, Hartford (CtHMTH). ■*Provenance:* donated to CtHMTH in 1962 by Ida Langdon. ■*Emendations and textual notes:*

161.4	Abyssinnia • [*sic*]
161.6	~~her~~ a • ['a' *partly formed*]
161.9	it. I • ~.—|~

■ 4 July 1870 · To Elisha Bliss, Jr. · Elmira, N.Y. · *UCCL* 00486

■*Copy-text:* MS, collection of Robert Daley until 1993. ■*Previous publication:* *LLMT*, 153, brief quotation; *MTLP*, 36. ■*Provenance:* The MS evidently remained among the American Publishing Company's files until it was sold (and may have been at that time copied by Dana Ayer; see Brownell Collection in Description of Provenance). The Ayer transcription was in turn copied by a typist and both the handwritten and typed transcriptions are at WU. Sold in 1993 to an unidentified purchaser (Sotheby 1993, lot 216). ■*Emendations and textual notes:*

162.4	spoke, • [*deletion implied*]
162.9	~~to~~ time • t∅ime
162.13	~~the~~ • ['e' *partly formed*]

■ 4 July 1870 · To Unidentified · Elmira, N.Y. · *UCCL* 02799

■*Copy-text:* MS, on a *carte de visite* photograph of Clemens, Iwaki Meisei University, Iwaki City, Japan (JIm). ■*Provenance:* The photograph was part of the collection of Theodore J. Koundakjian until 1987, when it was sold to JIm (Kodama, 94).

■ 6 July 1870 · To Olivia L. Clemens · Washington, D.C. · *UCCL* 00487

■*Copy-text:* MS, Mark Twain Papers, The Bancroft Library, University of California, Berkeley (CU-MARK). ■*Previous publication: LLMT*, 361, brief para-

phrase. ■*Provenance:* see Samossoud Collection in Description of Provenance.
■*Emendations and textual notes:*

164.14–15	father. | [¶] I • ~.—| [¶] ~
164.19	ʄ • [*partly formed*]
164.27	policy • p̶o̶l̶ | policy [*written off edge*]
164.30	l̶e̶f̶ • ['f' *partly formed*]
165.6	m̶a̶k̶ • ['k' *partly formed*]
165.13	8.30. Called on • ~.—~ | ~
165.13	Fitch's • [*sic*]
165.13	9.30. Then • ~.—|~
165.14	Mr. • ['Mr' *conflated*]
165.15	darling. Good • ~.—|~

■ 8 July 1870 · To Olivia L. Clemens · Washington, D.C. · *UCCL* 00488

■*Copy-text:* MS, Mark Twain Papers, The Bancroft Library, University of California, Berkeley (CU-MARK). ■*Previous publication: LLMT,* 154–55. ■*Provenance:* see Samossoud Collection in Description of Provenance. ■*Emendations and textual notes:*

167.3	t̶h̶ • [*partly formed*]
167.13	s̶a̶t̶i̶s̶f̶a̶c̶t̶ • [*second* 't' *partly formed*]

■ 10? July 1870 · To James Redpath · Elmira, N.Y. · *UCCL* 00485

■*Copy-text:* "Hon. Thomas Fitch, M.C.," *Lyceum* 1871, 27. Although published in July 1871, a year after Clemens wrote the letter to Fitch, the *Lyceum* provides the only complete text of the letter available. It was either transcribed directly from the MS or from an earlier transcription in a promotional brochure for Fitch issued sometime during the 1870 season by the Boston Lyceum Bureau (*BAL* 3324; no copy found for inspection). Several newspaper advertisements published in November 1870, each of which included an excerpt from the letter, were likewise probably based on a transcription prepared for advertising copy either directly or indirectly from the MS, but none provides any substantive or suggestively authorial accidental variants. They are: "Boston Lyceum—Extra Lecture," Boston *Evening Transcript,* 26 Nov 70, 4; "Boston Lyceum. Extra Lecture," Boston *Morning Journal,* 26 Nov 70, 3; "Boston Lyceum.—Extra Lecture": Boston *Advertiser,* 26 Nov 70, 2; Boston *Evening Traveller,* 29 Nov 70, 3. The first three papers repeated their advertisements on 28 and 29 November. ■*Previous publication:* "Personal," New York *Tribune,* 28 Nov 72, 2, excerpt. ■*Emendations and textual notes:*

170.1	Buffalo • Bᴜꜰꜰᴀʟᴏ
170.1	N. Y. • N.Y.

170.2	Friend Redpath • FRIEND REDPATH
170.6	& • and [*also at 170.7, 10, 13*]
170.16	Mark Twain • MARK TWAIN

■ 10? July 1870 · To Thomas Fitch · Elmira, N.Y. · *UCCL* 10553

■ *Copy-text:* Fitch 1903. ■ *Previous publication:* Fitch 1919 and Fitch 1978, 52.
■ *Emendations and textual notes:*

171.2	& • and [*twice*]

■ 15 July 1870 · To Orion Clemens · Elmira, N.Y. · *UCCL* 00489

■ *Copy-text:* MS, Mark Twain Papers, The Bancroft Library, University of California, Berkeley (CU-MARK). ■ *Previous publication: MTB,* 1:421, with omissions; *MTL,* 1:174–75. ■ *Provenance:* see Mark Twain Papers in Description of Provenance. ■ *Emendations and textual notes:*

171.8	to-day • to-|day
171.10	country₁ • [*deletion implied*]
171.18	Mollie. Mr. • ~.—|~.
172.3	N. Y., • N. [Y◇◇] [*torn*]

■ 18 July 1870 · To Elisha Bliss, Jr. · Elmira, N.Y. · *UCCL* 00490

■ *Copy-text:* MS, Albert A. and Henry W. Berg Collection, The New York Public Library, Astor, Lenox and Tilden Foundations (NN-B). ■ *Previous publication: MTLP,* 35 n. 1 *top* (misdated 18 May). ■ *Provenance:* W. T. H. Howe owned the MS until 1939; in 1940 Dr. Albert A. Berg bought the Howe Collection for NN (Cannon, 185–86). ■ *Emendations and textual notes:*

172.10	editions • edition[s] [*written off edge*]
172.18	could • [*possibly 'could'*]
173.1	No as • No a[◇] [*written off edge*]
173.1	afflably • [*sic*]

■ 18 July 1870 · To Josephus N. Larned · Elmira, N.Y. · *UCCL* 11809

■ *Copy-text:* Paraphrase, Josephus N. Larned, "Personal," Buffalo *Express,* 20 July 70, 4. ■ *Emendations and textual notes:*

173.7	sickbed • sick-|bed
173.7	Jervis • Jarvis

■ 22 July 1870 · To C. A. King · Elmira, N.Y. · *UCCL* 00491

■ *Copy-text:* MS, Special Collections, Robert Hutchings Goddard Library, Clark University, Worcester, Mass. (MWC). About five-eighths of an inch has been cut away from the bottom of the MS page below the signature and paraph. Opening and closing quotation marks and the top of a 'T' remain. The cut off portion probably read ' "Mark Twain" ' and was almost certainly not in the author's hand. ■*Emendations and textual notes:*

174.8   q̶u̶i̶e̶t̶ quit • quiett [*canceled* 't' *partly formed*]

■ 25 July 1870 · To Josephus N. Larned, *per* Telegraph Operator · Elmira, N.Y. · *UCCL* 11810

■*Copy-text:* Paraphrase, Josephus N. Larned, "Personal," Buffalo *Express*, 26 July 70, 4.

■ 27 July 1870 · To Jane Lampton Clemens and Family · Elmira, N.Y. · *UCCL* 00492

■*Copy-text:* MS, Jean Webster McKinney Family Papers, Vassar College Library (NPV). ■*Previous publication: MTBus*, 117, with omission. ■*Provenance:* see McKinney Family Papers in Description of Provenance. ■*Emendations and textual notes:*

175.4   sit up • s̶i̶t̶u̶ sit up [*false start;* 'it' *partly formed*]
175.9   me, • [*deletion implied*]
175.17   here. I • ~.—|~

■ 1 August 1870 · To Orion Clemens · Elmira, N.Y. · *UCCL* 00493

■*Copy-text:* MS, Mark Twain Papers, The Bancroft Library, University of California, Berkeley (CU-MARK). ■*Provenance:* see Moffett Collection in Description of Provenance. ■*Emendations and textual notes:*

177.13   h̶a̶s̶ have • haʃve
178.1   to. I • ~.—|~
178.4   f • [*partly formed*]
178.6   letter. I • ~.—|~
178.15   i̶n̶s̶i̶s̶t̶e̶d̶ • ['d' *partly formed*]
178.16   it), • [*deletion implied*]
178.17   wildcat • wild-|cat
178.17   OVER • [*small capitals simulated, not underscored*]
178.19   t̶h̶e̶ that • th¢at

■ 2 August 1870 · To Elisha Bliss, Jr. · Elmira, N.Y. · *UCCL* 00494

■*Copy-text:* MS, Public Library of Cincinnati and Hamilton County, Cincinnati (OCi). ■*Previous publication: MTLP*, 37. ■*Emendations and textual notes:*

179.8	I would • I would I would
179.18	⅋ • [*partly formed*]
179.23	Franks • [*sic*]

■ 5 August 1870 · To Elisha Bliss, Jr. · Elmira, N.Y. · *UCCL* 10994

■*Copy-text:* MS, James S. Copley Library, La Jolla (CLjC). ■*Previous publication:* Sotheby 1984, lot 69, excerpt. ■*Provenance:* The MS was owned by John Feldman until 1990, when it was bought by CLjC.

■ 6 August 1870 · To Pamela A. Moffett, *per* Telegraph Operator · Elmira, N.Y. · *UCCL* 00495

■*Copy-text:* MS, copy received, telegram blank filled out in the hand of a telegraph operator, Jean Webster McKinney Family Papers, Vassar College Library (NPV). ■*Provenance:* see McKinney Family Papers in Description of Provenance. ■*Emendations and textual notes:*

181.1	THE . . . COMPANY. • *Blank No. 1.*	THE WESTERN UNION TELEGRAPH COMPANY.	[¶] The rules of this Company require that all messages received for transmission, shall be written on the message blanks of the Company, under and subject to the conditions printed thereon, which conditions have been agreed to by the sender of the following message.	ANSON STAGER, Gen'l Sup't, CHICAGO, ILL. WILLIAM ORTON, Pres't, O. H. PALMER, Sec'y, NEW YORK.
181.6	S. L. • [*possibly* 'S. S.']

■ 7 August 1870 · To Josephus N. Larned · Elmira, N.Y. · *UCCL* 11729

■*Copy-text:* Josephus N. Larned, "Death of Jervis Langdon, of Elmira," Buffalo *Express*, 8 Aug 70, 4. ■*Previous publication:* Elmira *Advertiser*, 9 Aug 70, 1, in addition to the copy-text. ■*Emendations and textual notes:*

181.8	& • and [*twice; also at 181.10 (twice), 12, 14, 16; 182.1, 2, 7, 8, 9, 10 (twice), 12, 14, 17 (twice), 18 (twice), 19*]
182.1	straightened • [*sic*]

■ 11 August 1870 · To Elisha Bliss, Jr. · Elmira, N.Y. · *UCCL* 00496

■*Copy-text:* MS, Public Library of Cincinnati and Hamilton County, Cincinnati (OCi). ■*Previous publication: MTLP,* 38. ■*Provenance:* The MS evidently remained among the American Publishing Company's files until it was sold (and may have been at that time copied by Dana Ayer; see Brownell Collection in

Description of Provenance). The Ayer transcription was in turn copied by a typist and both the handwritten and typed transcriptions are at WU. ▪ *Emendations and textual notes:*

183.7   did, • [*deletion implied*]
183.11   the • the ‖ the
184.5   s̶h̶ slow • sh̷low

▪ **17 or 24 August 1870?** · To Pamela A. Moffett · Elmira or Buffalo, N.Y. · *UCCL* 00497

▪ *Copy-text:* MS, Jean Webster McKinney Family Papers, Vassar College Library (NPV). ▪ *Provenance:* see McKinney Family Papers in Description of Provenance. ▪ *Emendations and textual notes:*

185.3   James Lampton • [*underscored in pencil on MS, probably by Pamela Moffett*]

▪ **31 August 1870** · To Pamela A. Moffett · Buffalo, N.Y. · *UCCL* 00498

▪ *Copy-text:* MS, Jean Webster McKinney Family Papers, Vassar College Library (NPV). ▪ *Previous publication: MTL,* 1:176, with omissions; *MTBus,* 117, brief excerpt; Hill, 43–44, brief excerpt. ▪ *Provenance:* see McKinney Family Papers in Description of Provenance. ▪ *Emendations and textual notes:*

185.14   e̶l̶ • ['l' *partly formed*]
186.1   t̶h̶ • [*partly formed*]
186.7   style. Otherwise • ∼.—|∼

▪ **2 September 1870** · To Orion Clemens · Buffalo, N.Y. · *UCCL* 00499 (formerly 00499 and 00501)

▪ *Copy-text:* A transcript in *MTL,* 1:175, is copy-text for the letter; MS, Mark Twain Papers, The Bancroft Library, University of California, Berkeley (CU-MARK), is copy-text for the envelope. The rationale for emendations to remove *MTL* styling is given in Description of Texts. ▪ *Provenance:* The letter MS is not known to survive; for the envelope, see Mark Twain Papers in Description of Provenance. ▪ *Emendations and textual notes:*

186.17   Buf., 1870. • Buf., *1870.*
186.18   [*no* ¶] Dear Bro: • [¶] Dear Bro.,—
186.19   [¶] I • [*no* ¶] ∼
186.20   & • and [*also at 186.21*]

187.6   [¶] In • [*complimentary close position*] ~
187.8   Sam • SAM
187.11   st. • s[◇◇] [*torn*]
187.11   Mo. • [◇◇◇] [*torn*]

■ 2 September 1870 · From Samuel L. and Olivia L. Clemens to Mary
  Mason Fairbanks · Buffalo, N.Y. · *UCCL* 00500

■ *Copy-text:* MS, Huntington Library, San Marino (CSmH, call no. HM 14265).
■ *Previous publication: MTMF,* 134–37. ■ *Provenance:* see Huntington Library in
Description of Provenance. ■ *Emendations and textual notes:*

187.16   the • ʃ th the ['ʃ' *partly formed; rewritten for clarity*]
188.13   ~~him~~ his • ~~hims~~ his [*revision rewritten for clarity*]
188.14   hogwash • hog-|wash
188.18   it. ˌ~~thats~~ . . . correct—ˌ | [¶] But • ~.—|ˌ~ . . . ~—ˌ | [¶] ~
188.29   ~~yo~~ yet • yǿct
188.32   p̸ Providence • [*possibly* 'p̸ˌProvidence']

■ 4 September 1870 · To Elisha Bliss, Jr. · Buffalo, N.Y. · *UCCL*
  00502

■ *Copy-text:* MS, Mark Twain Papers, The Bancroft Library, University of California, Berkeley (CU-MARK). ■ *Previous publication: MTB,* 1:421–22, with
omissions; *MTMF,* 137 n. 3, excerpts; Hill, 44, brief excerpt; *MTLP,* 39.
■ *Provenance:* see Mendoza Collection in Description of Provenance. ■ *Emendations and textual notes:*

190.5   it. It • ~.—|~
190.5   strait • [*sic*]
190.9   Franks • [*sic*]

■ 7 September 1870 · To Ella Wolcott · Buffalo, N.Y. · *UCCL* 00503

■ *Copy-text:* MS, Mark Twain Papers, The Bancroft Library, University of California, Berkeley (CU-MARK). ■ *Provenance:* purchased June 1973. ■ *Emendations and textual notes:*

191.21   ceasing, • [*deletion implied*]
191.23   ~~tu~~ type • tǿype

■ 8?–29 September 1870 · To Pamela A. Moffett and Family, *per* Telegraph Operator · Buffalo, N.Y. · *UCCL* 11806

■ *Copy-text:* Paraphrase, *MTBus,* 49–50.

■ 9 September 1870 · To Orion Clemens · Buffalo, N.Y. · *UCCL* 00504

■*Copy-text:* MS, Jean Webster McKinney Family Papers, Vassar College Library (NPV). ■*Previous publication: MTL,* 1:176–77. ■*Provenance:* see McKinney Family Papers in Description of Provenance. ■*Emendations and textual notes:*

193.5   me. When • ~.—|~

■ 15 September 1870 · From Samuel L. and Olivia L. Clemens to Francis E. Bliss and Frances T. French · Buffalo, N.Y. · *UCCL* 00505

■*Copy-text:* MS, Mark Twain House, Hartford (CtHMTH). ■*Provenance:* donated to CtHMTH in 1965 by George H. Gilman as part of the Elisha French Bliss Collection. ■*Emendations and textual notes:*

194.8   Elmira • Elm/ira
194.14   Sam*ˡ*. • ['*ˡ*' *over miswritten* 'm']
194.16   M̶r̶s̶ Mr. • Mr.ᵢ$ ['s' *partly formed; deletion implied*]

■ 15 September 1870 · To the Postmaster of Virginia City, Mont. Terr. (Hezekiah L. Hosmer) · Buffalo, N.Y. · *UCCL* 00506

■*Copy-text:* MS facsimile. The editors have not seen the MS, which is in the Hezekiah L. Hosmer Papers, Montana Historical Society, Helena (MtHi). ■*Provenance:* donated to MtHi in 1963 by Mrs. Frank B. Austin. ■*Emendations and textual notes:*

195.4   your • [y◇◇]r [*torn*]
195.6 $ • [*partly formed character; possibly* 'n' *or* 'w']
195.10   delivered • del̶elivered [*corrected miswriting*]
195.14   N̶ • [*partly formed; possibly* 'M']
195.15   newspaper • news-|paper

■ 21? September 1870 · To Elisha Bliss, Jr. · Buffalo, N.Y. · *UCCL* 00508

■*Copy-text:* MS, on the back of J. T. Metcalf to SLC, 19 Sept 70 (*UCLC* 31687), Ella Strong Denison Library of the Claremont Colleges, Claremont (CCC). ■*Previous publication:* brief excerpts in *MTMF,* 138 n. 3; Hill, 44; *MTLP,* 41 n. 3. ■*Provenance:* The MS evidently remained among the American Publishing Company's files until it was sold (and may have been copied at that time by Dana Ayer; see Brownell Collection in Description of Provenance). The Ayer transcription was in turn copied by a typist and both the handwritten and typed transcriptions are at WU.

■ 22 September 1870 · To Elisha Bliss, Jr. · Buffalo, N.Y. · *UCCL* 00509

■*Copy-text:* MS, Mark Twain Papers, The Bancroft Library, University of California, Berkeley (CU-MARK). ■*Previous publication: MTLP,* 39–40. ■*Provenance:* see Mendoza Collection in Description of Provenance. ■*Emendations and textual notes:* Although the letter was written on a folder with the monogram ⬭*LLC*, Clemens made some effort to avoid emphasizing it by turning over the folder and beginning his letter on page 4.

198.7	& the • [*sic*]

■ 24 September 1870 · To Franklin D. Locke · Buffalo, N.Y. · *UCCL* 00432

■*Copy-text:* MS, Cyril Clemens Collection, Mark Twain House, Hartford (CtHMTH). ■*Provenance:* donated to CtHMTH in 1984 by Cyril Clemens. ■*Emendations and textual notes:*

200.1	42 472 • 4⫽72
200.6	fe favor • f⫽avor
200.7	face facing • fac⫽ing

■ 28? September 1870 · To Joseph T. Goodman · Buffalo, N.Y. · *UCCL* 11730

■*Copy-text:* Paraphrase, "Local Matters," Virginia City *Territorial Enterprise,* 7 Oct 70, 3.

■ 4 October 1870 · ~~To George M. Smith~~ To James Redpath · Fredonia, N.Y. · *UCCL* 00510

■*Copy-text:* MS, Houghton Library, Harvard University (MH-H). ■*Provenance:* bequeathed to MH in 1918 by Evert J. Wendell. ■*Emendations and textual notes:*

202.15	is it • i⫽t
202.25	it. • [*possibly* 'it.—']
202.25	ₓOVERₓ • [*capitals simulated, not underscored; deletion implied*]
202.31	OVER • [*capitals simulated, not underscored*]
202.32	it per • it per-|
202.35	this the • this⫽e
203.3	be • [*doubtful*]
203.7	⫽ • [*doubtful*]
203.8	may map • ma⫽p

■ 8–13? October 1870 · To Elisha Bliss, Jr. · Buffalo, N.Y. · *UCCL* 00543

■*Copy-text:* MS, Mark Twain Papers, The Bancroft Library, University of California, Berkeley (CU-MARK). ■*Provenance:* see Tufts Collection in Description of Provenance. ■*Emendations and textual notes:*

204.7	g̸ · [*partly formed*]
205.1	with · w̶i̶ with [*corrected miswriting*]

■ 9 October 1870 · To James Redpath · Buffalo, N.Y. · *UCCL* 10496

■*Copy-text:* MS, collection of Todd M. Axelrod. ■*Previous publication:* Bangs, lot 81, brief excerpt. ■*Provenance:* The present location of the MS, offered for sale in 1900 and owned in 1983 by Axelrod, is not known. ■*Emendations and textual notes:*

205.15	Redpath— · Red[path]— [*obscured by inkblot*]
205.17	beside— · beside—|—
206.1	t̶h̶i̶s̶ there · thisere
206.2	veto on · v[eto on] [*obscured by inkblot*]

■ 10? October 1870 · To Ainsworth R. Spofford · Buffalo, N.Y. · *UCCL* 00507

■*Copy-text:* MS note on clipping, "Fortifications of Paris," Buffalo *Express*, 17 Sept 70, 2, in Papers of Ainsworth Rand Spofford, Library of Congress (DLC). ■*Provenance:* donated to DLC between 1923 and 1982 by Mrs. Barbara Spofford Morgan.

■ 13 October 1870 · To Mary Mason Fairbanks · Buffalo, N.Y. · *UCCL* 00512

■*Copy-text:* MS, Huntington Library, San Marino (CSmH, call no. HM 14266). ■*Previous publication: MTMF,* 138–39. ■*Provenance:* see Huntington Library in Description of Provenance. ■*Emendations and textual notes:*

208.2	1̶2̶ 13 · 1⁄3
208.8	h̶a̶ · ['a' *partly formed*]
208.14	return. We'll · ~.—|~
208.27	such · suc̶h̶ch [*canceled* 'h' *partly formed;* 'ch' *over miswritten* 'u']

■ 13 October 1870 · To Elisha Bliss, Jr. · Buffalo, N.Y. · *UCCL* 00511

■*Copy-text:* MS, Boston Public Library and Eastern Massachusetts Regional Public Library System, Boston (MB). ■*Previous publication: MTB,* 1:422, brief excerpt; AAA/Anderson 1934a, lot 123, excerpts; AAA/Anderson 1936c, lot 122, excerpts; *MTMF,* 139 n. 2, brief excerpt; *MTLP,* 40–41. ■*Provenance:* The MS evidently remained among the American Publishing Company's files until it was sold (and was copied, possibly at that time, by Dana Ayer, though the present location of his transcription is not known; see Brownell Collection in Description of Provenance). The MS was sold again in 1934 and in 1936. On 11 April 1939 it was signed and dated by Josiah H. Benton. ■*Emendations and textual notes:*

209.14	What • ~~What~~ | What [*corrected miswriting*]
210.9	Ӎ • [*partly formed*]
210.11	~~pep~~ people • pe𝑝ople

■ 18 October 1870 · To Francis P. Church · Buffalo, N.Y. · *UCCL* 00513

■*Copy-text:* MS facsimile, Mott 1957, facing 255, is copy-text for the letter. The enclosed drawing (shown in partial facsimile by Mott) is reproduced here from "The Portrait" in "Memoranda," *Galaxy* 11 (Jan 71): 150–59. ■*Previous publication:* for the letter, Mott 1957, 367–68, 380, excerpts; the enclosed drawing (and the now lost MS for "The Portrait") were reproduced in several collections of sketches. ■*Provenance:* The MS, part of the Willard Church Collection in 1938, is not known to survive (see the commentary to 9 Feb 70 to Church). ■*Emendations and textual notes:*

211.1	~~work~~ • ['k' *partly formed*]
211.8	~~am~~ • [*doubtful; possibly* 'can']
211.11	I hang • I hang ~~han~~
211.14	won't • [*possibly* '𝑠 won't']

■ 26 October 1870 · To Elisha Bliss, Jr. · Buffalo, N.Y. · *UCCL* 00514

■*Copy-text:* MS of Clemens's letter, collection of Todd M. Axelrod; MS of enclosed letter from Francis Church, 22 Oct 71 (*UCLC* 31692), Mark Twain Papers, The Bancroft Library, University of California, Berkeley (CU-MARK). ■*Previous publication:* Clemens's letter only, Parke-Bernet 1940, lot 185, brief excerpt; Christie 1981, lot 54, excerpt; Neville, item 449, excerpt. ■*Provenance:* The present location of Clemens's letter, owned from at least 1983 to 1989 by Axelrod, is not known; Church's letter was probably returned to Clemens by Bliss and remained in the Mark Twain Papers. ■*Emendations and textual notes:*

212.1	~~25~~ 26 • 2𝑔6 ['5' *partly formed*]
212.6	~~th~~ • [*partly formed*]

■ 26 October 1870 · To Iretus G. Cardner · Buffalo, N.Y. · *UCCL* 00515

■ *Copy-text:* MS, collection of Victor and Irene Murr Jacobs, Roesch Library, University of Dayton (ODaU). ■ *Previous publication:* Fox, item 4, excerpts. ■ *Provenance:* Offered for sale by Alan C. Fox in 1980, the MS was in the collection of Jim Williams in 1981. ■ *Emendations and textual notes:*

214.11–12   it. Newspaper • ~.—|~
214.15   ~~Bet~~ But • Be~~t~~ut [*canceled* 't' *partly formed*]
214.15–16   ~~have~~ having • hav¢ing

■ 28 October 1870 · To Elisha Bliss, Jr. · Buffalo, N.Y. · *UCCL* 00516

■ *Copy-text:* MS, Henry W. and Albert A. Berg Collection, The New York Public Library, Astor, Lenox and Tilden Foundations (NN-B). ■ *Previous publication:* AAA 1927b, lot 99A, excerpt. ■ *Provenance:* W. T. H. Howe owned the MS until 1939; in 1940 Dr. Albert A. Berg bought the Howe Collection for NN (Cannon, 185–86). ■ *Emendations and textual notes:*

215.11   storekeeper • store-|keeper
215.18   4̶2̶ ‚45‚ • [*underscored twice*]

■ 29 October 1870 · To Elisha Bliss, Jr. · Buffalo, N.Y. · *UCCL* 00517

■ *Copy-text:* MS, collection of Robert Daley until 1993. ■ *Previous publication:* Sotheby 1993, lot 214. ■ *Provenance:* The present location of the MS is not known; sold in 1993 to an unidentified purchaser. ■ *Emendations and textual notes:*

217.8   Missippi • [*sic*]
217.9   them • ['em' *conflated*]

■ 31 October 1870 · To Elisha Bliss, Jr. · Buffalo, N.Y. · *UCCL* 00519

■ *Copy-text:* MS facsimile, Mark Twain Papers, The Bancroft Library, University of California, Berkeley (CU-MARK), courtesy of Maurice F. Neville Rare Books. The margin of one of the MS pages has been taped, partially obscuring some characters and rendering them barely visible on the facsimile. ■ *Previous publication:* Christie 1981, lot 54, excerpt; Neville, item 450, excerpt. ■ *Provenance:* The present location of the MS, sold by Christie and then by Neville in 1981, is not known. ■ *Emendations and textual notes:*

218.7   permanently. • permanen[tly.] [*taped over*]
218.7   was, • wa[s,] [*taped over*]
218.10   instance • instanc[e] [*taped over*]

218.10	about • abou[t] [*taped over*]
218.11–12	gradually • gradu[-]|ally [*taped over*]
218.12	served • serve[d] [*taped over*]
218.13	having • hav[-]|ing [*taped over*]
218.13	Lincoln— • ~—|—
218.27	Yrs • ['rs' *conflated*]

■ 2 November 1870 · To Iretus G. Cardner · Buffalo, N.Y. · *UCCL* 00521

■ *Copy-text:* MS, collection of Alan C. Fox. ■ *Previous publication:* Fox, item 5, brief paraphrase. ■ *Provenance:* The present location of the MS, owned by Alan C. Fox in 1980–81, is not known. ■ *Emendations and textual notes:*

| 219.6–7 | ~~the~~ that • th¢at |

■ 5 November 1870 · To Orion Clemens · Buffalo, N.Y. · *UCCL* 00524 (formerly 00524 and 11511) and *UCLC* 31695

■ *Copy-text:* MS, Jean Webster McKinney Family Papers, Vassar College Library (NPV), is copy-text for 'Buf. . . . And' (219.11–220.29); and MS, Mark Twain Papers, The Bancroft Library, University of California, Berkeley (CU-MARK), is copy-text for 'I am . . . Sam.' and for the enclosed letter of 2 Nov 70 from Bliss to Clemens, with Clemens's added notes to Orion (220.30–221.13 and 221.14–222.5). ■ *Previous publication:* NPV text: *MTB*, 1:425, brief excerpt; *MTBus*, 115–16; Chester L. Davis 1978, 2, brief excerpt; enclosure: *MTLP*, 42 n. 1, excerpt. ■ *Provenance:* see McKinney Family Papers and Moffett Collection in Description of Provenance. ■ *Emendations and textual notes:*

219.14	~~plent~~ • ['t' *partly formed*]
220.6–7	indispensable—ˌ • ~—ˌ—
220.14	~~sh~~ • ['h' *partly formed*]
220.28	~~this~~ thus • thisus ['i' *partly formed*]
221.3	~~dem~~ deny • derⁿny
221.36	man. Don't • ~.—|~
222.5	fifteen • fift¢een

■ 5 November 1870 · To Elisha Bliss, Jr. · Buffalo, N.Y. · *UCCL* 00523

■ *Copy-text:* MS, Henry W. and Albert A. Berg Collection, The New York Public Library, Astor, Lenox and Tilden Foundations (NN-B). ■ *Previous publication:* AAA/Anderson 1934b, lot 123, brief paraphrase; AAA/Anderson 1935b, lot 80, brief paraphrase; *MTLP*, 41–42. ■*Provenance:* The MS evidently remained among the American Publishing Company's files until it was sold (and may have been copied at that time by Dana Ayer; see Brownell Collection in Description of Provenance). The Ayer transcription was in turn copied by a typist and both the handwritten and typed transcriptions are at WU. The MS was offered for sale in 1934 and 1935. Until his death in 1939 it was owned by W. T. H. Howe; in 1940, the Howe Collection was purchased by Dr. Albert A. Berg and donated to NN (Cannon, 185–86). ■*Emendations and textual notes:*

223.3   ~~mad~~ make • ma∉ke
223.21   ~~Ys~~ Yrs • Y∉rs

■ 5 November 1870 · To Mary Mason Fairbanks · Buffalo, N.Y. · *UCCL* 00525

■*Copy-text:* MS, Huntington Library, San Marino (CSmH, call no. HM 14267). ■*Previous publication: MTMF*, 139–40. ■*Provenance:* see Huntington Library in Description of Provenance. ■*Emendations and textual notes:*

224.3   ʃ • [*partly formed*]
224.5   ∮ • [*partly formed; possibly* 'n' *or* 'r']

■ 7 November 1870 · To Olivia Lewis Langdon, *per* Telegraph Operator · Buffalo, N.Y. · *UCCL* 00526

■*Copy-text:* MS, copy received, telegram blank filled out in the hand of a telegraph operator, Mark Twain House, Hartford (CtHMTH). ■*Provenance:* donated to CtHMTH in 1965 by Mrs. Eugene Lada-Mocarski. ■*Emendations and textual notes:*

225.1   THE . . . COMPANY. • *Blank No. 1.* | THE WESTERN UNION TELEGRAPH COMPANY. | [¶] The rules of this Company require that all messages received for transmission, shall be written on the message blanks of the Company, under and subject to the conditions printed thereon, which conditions have been agreed to by the sender of the following message. | THOS. T. ECKERT, Gen'l Sup't, NEW YORK. WILLIAM ORTON, Pres't, O. H. PALMER, Sec'y, NEW YORK.

■ 7 November 1870 · To Elisha Bliss, Jr. · Buffalo, N.Y. · *UCCL* 00527

■*Copy-text:* MS, Mark Twain Papers, The Bancroft Library, University of California, Berkeley (CU-MARK). ■*Provenance:* see Mendoza Collection in Description of Provenance.

■ 8 November 1870 · To James Redpath · Buffalo, N.Y. · *UCCL* 00528

■ *Copy-text:* "Boston and Vicinity," Boston *Morning Journal*, 9 Nov 70, 2. The printings noted below all evidently derive from the copy-text. ■ *Previous publication:* "Local Intelligence," Boston *Evening Transcript*, 9 Nov 20, 2; "Local Matters," Boston *Advertiser*, 10 Nov 70, 1; "Personal," Hartford *Courant*, 11 Nov 70, 2; "Personal," New York *World*, 11 Nov 70, 5 (clipping in Olivia Clemens's Commonplace Book, Mark Twain Papers, The Bancroft Library, University of California, Berkeley [CU-MARK]); "Brief Mention," Hartford *Times*, 14 Nov 70, 1, in addition to the copy-text. ■ *Emendations and textual notes:*

227.3   & · and [*also at 227.5*]
227.7   Clemens · CLEMENS

■ 8 November 1870 · To Whitelaw Reid, *per* Telegraph Operator · (1st of 2) · Buffalo, N.Y. · *UCCL* 11734

■ *Copy-text:* Paraphrase, "Mark Twain . . . ," New York *Tribune*, 9 Nov 70, 4. ■ *Previous publication:* "Somewhat Personal," Elmira *Advertiser*, 10 Nov 70, 4; "Personal," Buffalo *Express*, 12 Nov 70, 4; "Mark Twain, Junior," San Francisco *Alta California*, 18 Nov 70, 1, in addition to the copy-text.

■ 8 November 1870 · To Whitelaw Reid · (2nd of 2) · Buffalo, N.Y. · *UCCL* 00529

■ *Copy-text:* MS, Whitelaw Reid Papers, Library of Congress (DLC). ■ *Provenance:* The Whitelaw Reid Papers (part of the Papers of the Reid Family) were donated to DLC between 1953 and 1957 by Helen Rogers Reid (Mrs. Ogden Mills Reid). ■ *Emendations and textual notes:*

228.14   Yr · [*possibly* 'Yrs']

■ 11 November 1870 · To Orion Clemens · Buffalo, N.Y. · *UCCL* 00531

■ *Copy-text:* MS, Mark Twain Papers, The Bancroft Library, University of California, Berkeley (CU-MARK). ■ *Provenance:* see Moffett Collection in Description of Provenance. ■ *Emendations and textual notes:*

229.4   beforehand · before-|hand
229.4   ~~whic~~ what · whicat

229.8   i̶s̶ itself • i̶s̶tself
229.8   price. If • ~.—|~
229.11   I̶ ̶a̶s̶ • I̶ ̶a̶s̶-|
229.19   ᶀ • [*partly formed; possibly* 'ⱡ']
230.1   worth, • [*deletion implied*]
230.6   over • ov̶ʇ̶er
230.7   t̶h̶ought • [*underscore added after* 'th' *canceled*]
230.15   carpenter's • carpen⍀ter's
230.23   m̶e̶ myself • m⍀yself

■ 11 November 1870 · To Fidele A. Brooks · Buffalo, N.Y. · *UCCL*
11745

■ *Copy-text:* "Personal," Buffalo *Courier*, 26 Dec 70, 1. ■ *Emendations and textual notes:*

231.3   & • and [*twice; also at 231.4*]

■ 11 November 1870 · To Eunice Ford · Buffalo, N.Y. · *UCCL* 00530

■ *Copy-text:* MS, Mark Twain House, Hartford (CtHMTH). ■ *Previous publication: LLMT,* 155–57. ■ *Provenance:* donated to CtHMTH in 1962 by Ida Langdon. ■ *Emendations and textual notes:*

232.1   NOTICE • [*capitals simulated with single underscore*]
232.12   h̶a̶ • ['a' *partly formed*]
232.21   I̶ˢ̶ • [*deletion implied*]
232.32   clothes. Except • ~.—|~
233.3   a̶n̶ • [*doubtful*]
233.16   medicine. *Colic* • ~.—|~
233.31   k̶e̶e̶p̶ kept • k̶e̶e̶ppt [*canceled* 'p' *partly formed*]
234.1   good-bye • good-|bye

■ 11? November 1870 · To Olivia Lewis Langdon · Buffalo, N.Y. ·
UCCL 08958

■ *Copy-text:* MS, Mark Twain House, Hartford (CtHMTH).

■ 11 or 12 November 1870 · To Edwin D. White, *per* Telegraph Operator · Buffalo, N.Y. · *UCCL* 11818

■ *Copy-text:* Paraphrase, "The Press Supper," Boston *Morning Journal*, 14 Nov 70, 2. ■ *Previous publication:* "The Boston Press Club Dinner," Boston *Evening*

Transcript, 14 Nov 70, 4; "The Boston Press Club Dinner," Boston *Advertiser,* 14 Nov 70, 1; both paraphrases.

■ 12 November 1870 · To James Redpath · Buffalo, N.Y. · *UCCL* 00532

■ *Copy-text:* MS, Houghton Library, Harvard University (MH-H). ■ *Provenance:* bequeathed to MH in 1918 by Evert J. Wendell. ■ *Emendations and textual notes:*

235.8	it • [*sic*]	
236.3	tonight • to-|night	

■ 12 November 1870 · To Joseph H. and Harmony C. Twichell · Buffalo, N.Y. · *UCCL* 00533

■ *Copy-text:* MS, Joseph H. Twichell Collection, Beinecke Rare Book and Manuscript Library, Yale University (CtY-BR). ■ *Previous publication: MTB,* 1:417, excerpts; *MTL,* 1:177–78, with omissions; *MTMF,* 140 n. 1, brief excerpt. ■ *Provenance:* It is not known when Twichell's papers were deposited at Yale, although it is likely that he bequeathed them to the university upon his death in 1918 (*L2,* 570). ■ *Emendations and textual notes:*

236.21	~~wh~~ • ['h' *partly formed*]	
236.23	standstill • stand-|still	
237.5	~~acu~~ accustomed • ac↓customed	
237.6	such • ~~such~~ such [*corrected miswriting*]	
237.9	~~18~~ 12 • 1↓2	
237.13	abed. And • ~.—|~	
237.14	it. And • ~.—|~	
237.22	night. But • ~.—|~	
237.25	to • [◇◇] [*torn*]	
237.25	uncle • [◇]ncle [*torn*]	
237.29	writte • ['t' *partly formed*]	

■ 14 November 1870 · To Jesse C. Haney · Buffalo, N.Y. · *UCCL* 00534

■ *Copy-text:* MS, Katherine Seymour Day Collection, Harriet Beecher Stowe Center, Hartford (CtHSD). ■ *Previous publication:* Goodspeed's Book Shop 1936, item 52, with omission.

■ 14 November 1870 · To Charles J. Langdon · Buffalo, N.Y. · *UCCL* 00535

■ *Copy-text:* MS, draft telegram, Mark Twain Papers, The Bancroft Library, University of California, Berkeley (CU-MARK). ■ *Provenance:* see Mark Twain Papers in Description of Provenance. ■ *Emendations and textual notes:*

239.4   *Ł* · [*partly formed; possibly* 'T']

■ 14 November 1870 · To T. B. Pugh · Buffalo, N.Y. · *UCCL* 00536

■ *Copy-text:* MS, collection of Alan C. Fox. ■ *Previous publication:* Fox, item 1, brief excerpt. ■ *Provenance:* The present location of the MS, owned by Fox in 1981, is not known. ■ *Emendations and textual notes:*

239.9   M · [*partly formed*]

■ 19 November 1870 · To Mary Mason Fairbanks · Buffalo, N.Y. · *UCCL* 00538

■ *Copy-text:* MS, Huntington Library, San Marino (CSmH, call no. HM 14270). ■ *Previous publication: MTMF,* 148–49. ■ *Provenance:* see Huntington Library in Description of Provenance. ■ *Emendations and textual notes:*

240.15   them. But · ~.—|~
240.17   liera literary · lieraterary [*canceled* 'a' *partly formed*]
241.3   Mon · ['n' *partly formed*]
241.4   headline · head-|line

■ 19 November 1870 · To Olivia Lewis Langdon · Buffalo, N.Y. · *UCCL* 00539

■ *Copy-text:* MS, Mark Twain House, Hartford (CtHMTH). ■ *Provenance:* donated to CtHMTH in 1962 by Ida Langdon. ■ *Emendations and textual notes:*

242.8   COD · [*capitals simulated, not underscored*]
242.14   most · mosty

■ 19–20? November 1870 · To Susan L. Crane · Buffalo, N.Y. · *UCCL* 08621

■ *Copy-text:* MS, Mark Twain Papers, The Bancroft Library, University of California, Berkeley (CU-MARK), reproduced at 100 percent of actual size. ■ *Prov-*

enance: either Mark Twain Papers or Samossoud Collection (see Description of Provenance). ■ *Emendations and textual notes:*

243.4–5	Two . . . asleep. • [*printed, not cursive, characters*]
243.8	~~10~~ 11 • 1∅1
244.6	~~writs~~ wrist • writsst
244.8	~~2½ 2¼~~ • 2¹/₂₄

■ 20 November 1870 · To Charles J. Langdon · Buffalo, N.Y. · *UCCL* 00541

■ *Copy-text:* MS, Mark Twain House, Hartford (CtHMTH). ■ *Provenance:* donated to CtHMTH in 1963 by Ida Langdon. ■ *Emendations and textual notes:*

244.11	~~Chal~~ Charley • Cha⌐rley
244.14	defect • defe⌐ct ['⌐' *partly formed*]
244.17	barefooted • bare-|footed
244.25	slang, • [*possibly* 'slang/,']
244.29	~~moth~~ money • mo⌐ney ['th' *partly formed*]

■ 21? November 1870 · To Orion Clemens · Buffalo, N.Y. · *UCCL* 00537

■ *Copy-text:* MS, Jean Webster McKinney Family Papers, Vassar College Library (NPV). ■ *Provenance:* see McKinney Family Papers in Description of Provenance. ■ *Emendations and textual notes:*

245.13	~~Don~~ • [*possibly* '~~Do y~~']

■ 22 November 1870 · To Elisha Bliss, Jr. · Buffalo, N.Y. · *UCCL* 00542

■ *Copy-text:* MS, Willard S. Morse Collection, Collection of American Literature, Beinecke Rare Book and Manuscript Library, Yale University (CtY-BR). ■ *Provenance:* laid in a copy of *The Innocents Abroad* (American Publishing Company, 1869) donated to CtY in 1942 by Walter F. Frear.

■ 26 November 1870 · To Charles Henry Webb · Buffalo, N.Y. · *UCCL* 00544

■ *Copy-text:* MS, Clifton Waller Barrett Library, University of Virginia, Charlottesville (ViU), is copy-text for the letter; MS, Washington University, St. Louis (MoSW), is copy-text for the envelope. ■ *Previous publication: MTLP,* 4

n. 1, brief excerpt. ■*Provenance:* letter deposited at ViU by Clifton Waller Barrett on 17 December 1963; when MoSW acquired the envelope is not known. ■*Emendations and textual notes:*

247.20   do. ~~But~~ • ~.—|~
248.6   ~~som~~ such • ~~somuch~~
248.17   Housekeeping • House-|keeping
248.20   ~~rum~~ run • ru𝑚n
248.36   publishers • [*sic*]
248.36–37 me. Mr. • ~.—|~.
249.10   N.Y. NOV 27 • [◊◊]Y. NO[V 27] [*badly inked*]

■ 27 or 28 November 1870 · To John Henry Riley · Buffalo, N.Y. · *UCCL* 11820

■*Copy-text:* Transcript, John Henry Riley to SLC, 30 Nov 71 (*UCLC* 31711), Mark Twain Papers, The Bancroft Library, University of California, Berkeley (CU-MARK). ■*Provenance:* see Mark Twain Papers in Description of Provenance. Clemens's original letter is not known to survive.

■ 28 November 1870 · To Elisha Bliss, Jr. · Buffalo, N.Y. · *UCCL* 00545

■*Copy-text:* MS, Mark Twain Papers, The Bancroft Library, University of California, Berkeley (CU-MARK). A second copy, kept by the author, is in the Mark Twain Papers, with the following notation on the back of page 1 as folded: "*No. 1* | Copy of Diamond Letter to Bliss." In it, Clemens omitted the note at 252.1–7, "Keep . . . got." ■*Previous publication: MTMF,* 141 n. 2, brief excerpt; *MTLP,* 42–44. ■*Provenance:* for the MS, copy sent, see Mendoza Collection in Description of Provenance. The MS evidently remained among the American Publishing Company's files until it was sold (and may have been copied at that time by Dana Ayer; see Brownell Collection in Description of Provenance). The Ayer transcription was in turn copied by a typist and both the handwritten and typed transcriptions are at WU. For the MS, author's copy, see Mark Twain Papers in Description of Provenance. ■*Emendations and textual notes:*

251.9   ~~jo~~ just • j∅ust
251.13   10 • [*underscored twice*]
251.13   IT ⱦ • [*deletion implied*]
251.25   ~~pro~~ • ~~pro-~~|
251.29   fortnight • fort-|night

■ 1 December 1870 · To Warren L. Brigham · Buffalo, N.Y. · *UCCL* 07285

■*Copy-text:* MS, Boston Athenaeum, Boston (MBAt). ■*Provenance:* donated to MBAt on 5 March 1982 by Dorothy Webling (Mrs. Benjamin T.) Stephenson, Brigham's granddaughter.

■ 1? December 1870 · To Elisha Bliss, Jr. · Buffalo, N.Y. · *UCCL* 00723

■*Copy-text:* MS, Mark Twain Papers, The Bancroft Library, University of California, Berkeley (CU-MARK). ■*Provenance:* see Mendoza Collection in Description of Provenance.

■ 2 December 1870 · To Elisha Bliss, Jr. · Buffalo, N.Y. · *UCCL* 00548

■*Copy-text:* MS, collection of Mrs. Robin Craven. This MS, one of two manuscript copies in Clemens's hand, each marked "[Copy.]", was the original and almost certainly the one Clemens sent to Bliss. (Although it lacks the customary American Publishing Company dockets, its provenance confirms that it must have been in the American Publishing Company's files.) Clemens may have marked it "[Copy.]" when he made the fair copy (CU-MARK), intending to send the fair copy and keep the original. Instead, he sent the original, but without deleting the word "[Copy.]". Probably after he had made the fair copy, Clemens continued to revise the original, adding two postscripts, only one of which he then transferred to the fair copy. The CU-MARK fair copy is missing the postscript at 257.23–25 ('P. S. . . . still-born.'). For his own record, he wrote on the fair copy of the letter as folded:

> Letter No. 2 to Bliss (a basis of contract, or *a contract* in its present form if he signifies willingness.)

Diamond.

Otherwise it shows only minor differences from the Craven MS. These differences, most of them stylistic, may result from haste in copying or deliberate variation in the record copy only. The more complete Craven MS has therefore been chosen as copy-text, but a full historical record of variants is provided here. ■*Previous publication:* AAA/Anderson 1934a, lot 124, excerpt; *MTLP,* 44–45. ■*Provenance:* A handwritten transcription made by Dana Ayer (probably between 1909 and 1919) clearly derives from the Craven MS as does a Brownell typescript (both are at WU; see Brownell Collection in Description of Provenance). The Craven MS was part of a collection sold in 1934, and it was later offered for sale by Brentano's (undated listing, CU-MARK). It was thereafter acquired by Mrs. Craven's father, Sidney L. Krauss. For the CU-MARK MS, see Mark Twain Papers in Description of Provenance. ■*Emendations and textual notes:*

256.2–3	ˌDon't . . . ~~P. S. S.~~ Post Scripts. | ——ˌ • ˌDon't . . . Pˌˌost, ~~S.~~ Sˌˌcripts.ˌ | ——ˌ (Craven); [*not in*] (CU-MARK)
256.4	Buf. (Craven) • Buffalo (CU-MARK)
256.7	per cent (Craven) • ~ ~. (CU-MARK)

256.7	this. You're (Craven) • ~. | [¶] ~ (CU-MARK)
256.7	*per cent* (Craven) • ~ ~. (CU-MARK)
257.3–6	book. ₄OVER. | [¶] [I . . . bye.]₄ (Craven) ['OVER' *in capitals,* *not underscored*] • book. [I . . . bye.] (CU-MARK)
257.5	than the (Craven) • than (CU-MARK)
257.5	$1500 . . . $1,000 (Craven) • $1,500 . . . $1000 (CU-MARK)
257.5–6	you, . . . *me,* (Craven) • ~₄ . . . ~₄ (CU-MARK)
257.8	600 page (Craven) • ~-~ (CU-MARK)
257.9	per cent (Craven) • ~ ~. (CU-MARK)
257.21	~~Ys Yrs~~ ₄Yrs. • ~~Y∤rs~~ ₄Yrs. (Craven); Yrs (CU-MARK)
257.22	S. L.₄ Clemens. (Craven) • S. L. Clemens. (CU-MARK)
257.23–25	P. S. . . . still-born. (Craven) • [*not in*] (CU-MARK)
257.24	tidal • tid∤al (Craven)
257.26	P. P. S. (Craven) • P. S. (CU-MARK)

■ 2 December 1870 · To John Henry Riley · Buffalo, N.Y. · *UCCL* 00547

■*Copy-text:* MS, Mark Twain Papers, The Bancroft Library, University of California, Berkeley (CU-MARK), is copy-text for '[Preserve . . . course—' (258.1–261.11) and '7. If . . . now.' (262.14–264.4). Where MS is missing—'but . . . boy.' (261.11–262.13)—copy-text is John Henry Riley's MS transcription of the letter, Henry W. and Albert A. Berg Collection, The New York Public Library, Astor, Lenox and Tilden Foundations (NN-B). Clemens's MS envelope, also at NN-B, is copy-text for '**Private.** . . . DEC 3' (264.6–12). ■*Previous publication: MTB,* 1:423, paraphrase and brief excerpt; AAA 1925, lot 108a, paraphrase and brief excerpts (from transcription and envelope); Underhill, [1]–[8] (transcription); AAA/Anderson 1936a, lot 120, paraphrase and brief excerpts (transcription and envelope); *MTLP,* 46–52. ■*Provenance:* for the letter MS, see Mark Twain Papers in Description of Provenance. The transcription and envelope were sold in 1924, 1925, and 1936 (AAA 1924a, lot 93, and 1925, lot 108a; AAA/Anderson 1936a, lot 120). Until his death in 1939 they were owned by W. T. H. Howe; in 1940, the Howe Collection was purchased by Dr. Albert A. Berg and donated to NN (Cannon, 185–86). ■*Emendations and textual notes:*

[*MS is copy-text for* '[Preserve . . . course—' *(258.1–261.11)*]

258.5	I̶ • [*partly formed*]
258.7	boundless • bound~~ees~~less
259.2	*insure* • *insu~~ss~~re* [*underscore added after revision*]
259.2	~~Africa offers~~ • [*false ascenders/descenders*]
259.5	i̶n̶ • ['i' *partly formed*]
259.9	re-elect • re-|elect
259.20	earnest • ear-|∤nest

259.26	~~prof~~ prospect • pro∫spect [*canceled* 'f' *partly formed*]
260.7	Į • [*partly formed*]
260.9	print. [I • ~.—I[~
260.30	ɱ • [*partly formed; possibly* 'ŋ' *or* 'w']
260.31	~~plam~~ plan • plaɱn
260.32	y̶ • [*partly formed*]
261.4	~~cou~~ • ['u' *partly formed*]
261.8	returned • retur¢ned
261.8–9	night & after • [*sic*]
261.10	~~ex~~ • ['x' *partly formed*]

[*Transcript is copy-text for* 'but . . . boy.' *(261.11–262.13)*]

261.12	& • and [*also at* 261.13 *(twice)*, 16, 21, 23, 24, 25 *(twice)*, 28, 29 *(three times)*; 262.3, 6, 9, 10, 12]
261.17	"I . . . etc." • '~ . . . ~.' "
261.21	so • ⱥ so

[*MS is copy-text for* '7. If . . . DEC 3' *(262.14–264.4)*]

262.15	~~$0~~ $5,000 • $∅5,000
262.32–33	~~have~~ had • ha~~ve~~d
262.35	~~ure~~ *urge* • ur¢ge
262.38	ho◊ • [*possibly* 'ha◊']
263.1	ravenousness. *Now* • ~.—I~
263.2	Years:–⊢ • [*deletion implied*]
263.23	*will* ^ • [*possibly* 'WILL']
263.28	ties. Run • ~.—I~
263.35	~~ha~~ heart • h⁄eart
264.12	BUFFALO N.Y. • [B]UFFALO [◊◊Y◊] [*badly inked*]

■ 3 December 1870 · To James Redpath · Buffalo, N.Y. · *UCCL* 00549

■ *Copy-text:* MS, Norman D. Bassett Collection, Rare Book Department, Memorial Library, University of Wisconsin, Madison (WU). ■ *Previous publication:* Merwin-Clayton 1905, lot 108, excerpt. ■ *Provenance:* The Bassett Collection was donated to WU on 9 July 1955. ■ *Emendations and textual notes:*

266.5	~~talk~~ take • ta~~lk~~ke [*canceled* 'k' *partly formed*]
266.6	~~ap~~ as • ap̸s ['p' *partly formed*]
266.8	~~he~~ his • h¢is
266.9–10	~~trut~~ true • tru⁄e
267.2	~~thee~~ *three* • the̶ree
267.8	~~wh~~ • ['h' *partly formed*]
267.8–9	wasting • ~~wasting~~ wasting [*corrected miswriting*]
267.11	~~th~~ • ['h' *partly formed*]

267.13–14   ~~str~~ stirred • st/irred
267.18   ~~50~~ • [*deletion of hyphen implied*]
267.18–19   ~~wall~~ walk • wal/k

■ 11 December 1870 · To the Editor of the New York *Tribune* · New
York, N.Y. · *UCCL* 11731

■ *Copy-text:* "The Famous Sanitary Flour Sack," New York *Tribune*, 13 Dec 70,
5. ■ *Emendations and textual notes:*

270.4   & • and [*also at 270.6, 7; 271.2, 5, 6, 7 (three times), 8 (twice), 9,
             10, 11, 12 (three times), 13, 14, 15, 16, 18*]
271.19   S. L. C. • s. l. c.

■ 13 December 1870 · To Elisha Bliss, Jr. · Buffalo, N.Y. · *UCCL*
11732

■ *Copy-text:* Paraphrase, Bromer, item 10.

■ 17 December 1870 · To Elisha Bliss, Jr., *per* Telegraph Operator ·
Buffalo, N.Y. · *UCCL* 00550

■ *Copy-text:* MS, copy received, telegram blank filled out in the hand of a telegraph operator, Henry W. and Albert A. Berg Collection, The New York Public
Library, Astor, Lenox and Tilden Foundations (NN-B). ■ *Previous publication:*
AAA/Anderson 1934a, lot 125, excerpt; AAA/Anderson 1935a, lot 101, excerpt. ■ *Provenance:* The telegram, apparently part of the William K. Bixby Collection, was sold in 1934 and again in 1935. It is not known when the MS became
part of the Berg Collection, given by Dr. Albert A. Berg to NN in 1940 but continuously enlarged since then. ■ *Emendations and textual notes:*

272.5   THE . . . COMPANY. • [*words on telegram blank identical to those
             reported in the commentary for 7 Nov 70 to Langdon*]

■ 17 December 1870 · From Samuel L. and Olivia L. Clemens to Mary
Mason Fairbanks · Buffalo, N.Y. · *UCCL* 00551

■ *Copy-text:* MS, Huntington Library, San Marino (CSmH, call no. HM 14268).
■ *Previous publication: MTMF,* 142–44. ■ *Provenance:* see Huntington Library
in Description of Provenance. ■ *Emendations and textual notes:*

273.6   you. As • ~.—|~
273.14–15   ~~thou~~ thoroughly • thou/roughly

273.21	~~cubs~~ • [*canceled by OLC*]
273.22	~~cubs~~ • [*canceled by OLC*]
274.6	copyright • copy-|right
274.11–12	future. For • ~.—‖~

■ 19 December 1870 · To Joseph H. Twichell · Buffalo, N.Y. · *UCCL* 02783

■ *Copy-text:* MS, Joseph H. Twichell Collection, Beinecke Rare Book and Manuscript Library, Yale University (CtY-BR). ■ *Previous publication: MTB*, 1:417–18, excerpts; *MTL*, 179–80, with omission; *LLMT*, 139, brief excerpt; *MTMF*, 143 n. 1, brief excerpt. ■ *Provenance:* It is not known when Twichell's papers were deposited at CtY, although it is likely that he bequeathed them to the university upon his death in 1918 (*I.2*, 570). ■ *Emendations and textual notes:*

275.4–5	has was • ℏwas
275.5	~~cond~~ consider • con∮sider
275.6	~~be~~ brother • b∮rother
275.15	ℏ • [*partly formed*]
275.19	night. But • ~.—‖ [B]ut [*obscured by glue*]
275.19	when Livy • w[he]n [Li]vy [*obscured by glue*]
275.26	pity • [◊]ity [*torn*]
275.27	didn't • [◊]idn't [*torn*]
275.27	rightly • [r◊]ightly [*torn*]
275.27	back • [b]ack [*torn*]
275.31	it. Why • ~.—|~
276.9	& • ∮ & [*rewritten for clarity*]
276.10	weeks.⌋ • [*deletion of period implied*]
276.12	~~Warren~~ Warner • Warrenrner

■ 20 December 1870 · To Elisha Bliss, Jr. · Buffalo, N.Y. · *UCCL* 11725

■ *Copy-text:* MS, Christie's. ■ *Previous publication:* Christie 1991, lot 201, with omission. ■ *Provenance:* The present location of the MS (formerly property of "A Lady"), sold at auction in 1991, is not known. ■ *Emendations and textual notes:*

277.3	~~it~~ • [*deletion implied*]
277.15	~~teel~~ tel[e]graphed • teellgraphed
277.17	on • [*sic*]

■ 20 December 1870 · ~~To Edward T. Howard~~ To A. Francis Judd · Buffalo, N.Y. · *UCCL* 02784

■*Copy-text:* MS facsimile, Beinecke Rare Book and Manuscript Library, Yale University (CtY-BR). The five-page MS consists of four pages of a folder of the same monogrammed stationery as 21 Apr 70 to OC (off-white laid paper, approximately 4^{15}⁄$_{16}$ by 7^{15}⁄$_{16}$ inches), and a fifth page written on another leaf torn from a similar folder. About one-half of MS page 5 is missing, which evidently contained further text, at least the complimentary close and signature. Only the tops of two ascenders remain, however, which do not provide enough evidence even to identify the missing letters. ■*Previous publication: MTH*, 467–68. ■*Provenance:* The present location of the MS is not known; the MS facsimile was donated to CtY in January 1936 by Albert F. Judd, eldest son of A. Francis Judd. ■*Emendations and textual notes:*

278.6	name.) I • ~.)—|~
278.7	~~oc~~ of • o¢f
278.10	did. I • ~.—|~
278.12	~~icl~~ icicle • icʃicle
278.17	again. I • ~.—|~
279.17	Return to Mark • [◊◊◊◊]rn [t]o [M]ark [*torn*]
279.18	BUFFALO N.Y. DEC 21 • [BUF◊]ALO [N.Y.]. [◊E◊ 21] [*badly inked*]
279.18	SAN FRANCISCO • [S◊◊ ◊RA◊]CISCO [*badly inked*]

■ 22 December 1870 · To Elisha Bliss, Jr. · Buffalo, N.Y. · *UCCL* 02785

■*Copy-text:* MS, Willard S. Morse Collection, Beinecke Rare Book and Manuscript Library, Yale University (CtY-BR), is copy-text for '(*c*) . . . Albemarle' and '√' (281.1–12 and 281.31); MS, Clifton Waller Barrett Library, University of Virginia, Charlottesville (ViU), is copy-text for 'Hotel . . . known.' and 'Write . . . Hotel' (281.12–21 and 281.30–31); and MS, collection of Todd M. Axelrod, is copy-text for 'I . . . Mark' and 'Mark . . . Author' (281.22–28 and 281.31–32). The left margin of MS page 2 (CtY-BR) is torn, obliterating some characters or portions of characters. ■*Previous publication: MTLP*, 52–53 (CtY-BR text only). ■*Provenance:* MS donated to CtY by Walter F. Frear in 1942; MS deposited at ViU by Clifton Waller Barrett on 17 December 1963; present location of the MS owned by Noël J. Cortés in 1975 and by Axelrod in 1983 is not known. ■*Emendations and textual notes:*

281.9	the man • [◊h]e man [*torn*]
281.10	the pictures • [th]e pictures [*torn*]
281.10	Sisters • [Si]sters [*torn*]
281.10	he • [h]e [*torn*]
281.11	money • [m]oney [*torn*]

281.12   ⱳ • [*partly formed*]
281.22   Webb, • [*deletion implied*]
281.24   ~~fresh~~ • ['h' *partly formed*]

■ 23 December 1870 · To Francis P. Church · Buffalo, N.Y. · *UCCL*
02786

■*Copy-text:* Mott 1957, 366–67. A footnote indicates that the letter was "dated
December 23 [1870]." The date has been abbreviated according to Clemens's
usual practice. ■*Provenance:* The MS, part of the Willard Church Collection in
1938, is not known to survive (see the commentary to 9 Feb 70 to Church).
■*Emendations and textual notes:*

283.1   Dec. 23. • [*reported, not quoted*]
283.4   Sheldons • Sheldon's
283.7   & • and [*also at 283.10, 15*]

■ 25? December 1870 · To Eunice Ford · Buffalo, N.Y. · *UCCL* 02787

■*Copy-text:* MS, Mark Twain House, Hartford (CtHMTH). ■*Provenance:* donated to CtHMTH in 1962 by Ida Langdon. ■*Emendations and textual notes:*

285.5   ~~it~~ at • ⱡat
285.11   ve virtues • v⊄irtues

■ 26 December 1870 · To Alfred B. Crandell and Other Members of the
Farmers' Club · Buffalo, N.Y. · *UCCL* 02788

■*Copy-text:* MS, collection of Nick Karanovich. ■*Previous publication: MTL,*
1:180–81; Karanovich, item 21. ■*Provenance:* apparently acquired by Karanovich after 1986. ■*Emendations and textual notes:*

286.10   ~~ot out~~ • o⊄ut [*first canceled* 't' *partly formed*]

■ 26 December 1870 · To John R. Drake · Buffalo, N.Y. · *UCCL*
02789

■*Copy-text:* MS, Beinecke Rare Book and Manuscript Library, Yale University
(CtY-BR). ■*Provenance:* laid in a copy of *The Adventures of Tom Sawyer* (American Publishing Company, 1876), donated to CtY by Owen F. Aldis. ■*Emendations and textual notes:*

287.4   the • the͜e ['e' *over miswritten* 'h']

■ 26 December 1870 · To Francis S. Drake · Buffalo, N.Y. · *UCCL* 02790

■ *Copy-text:* MS, Henry W. and Albert A. Berg Collection, The New York Public Library, Astor, Lenox and Tilden Foundations (NN-B). ■ *Previous publication:* Anderson Galleries 1924, lot 208, excerpt. ■ *Provenance:* Owen D. Young Collection, acquired by NN-B in 1941 (Bruccoli, 218). ■ *Emendations and textual notes:*

287.11–12   within. There • ~.—|~
287.17 $ • [*partly formed*]
288.3   chei chief • cheiief [*canceled* 'i' *partly formed*]

■ 26 December 1870 · To Whitelaw Reid · Buffalo, N.Y. · *UCCL* 02791

■ *Copy-text:* Transcript, "Personal," New York *Tribune,* 29 Dec 70, 4, is copy-text for 'Mark . . . Co.' (288.7–8), and MS, Whitelaw Reid Papers, Library of Congress (DLC), is copy-text for the remainder. The top half of MS page 1 is missing, presumably having been cut away by Reid and sent to the *Tribune's* compositor. ■ *Provenance:* The MS for the *Tribune* squib is not known to survive. The Whitelaw Reid Papers (part of the Papers of the Reid Family) were donated to DLC between 1953 and 1957 by Helen Rogers Reid (Mrs. Ogden Mills Reid). ■ *Emendations and textual notes:*

               [*Tribune is copy-text for* 'Mark . . . Co.' *(288.7–8)*]
288.7   [¶] Mark • [*no* ¶] ~
               [*MS is copy-text for* 'Buffalo . . . Mark.' *(288.9–289.4)*]
288.12   little • [*possibly* 'ƀ little']
289.4   Mark • ['ar' *conflated;* 'k' *partly formed*]

■ 31 December 1870 · To Whitelaw Reid · Buffalo, N.Y. · *UCCL* 02793 (formerly 02793 and 02792)

■ *Copy-text:* MS, Whitelaw Reid Papers, Library of Congress (DLC), is copy-text for the letter; transcript, "John H. Surratt," New York *Tribune,* 4 Jan 71, 5, is copy-text for the enclosure. ■ *Provenance:* The Whitelaw Reid Papers (part of the Papers of the Reid Family) were donated to DLC between 1953 and 1957 by Helen Rogers Reid (Mrs. Ogden Mills Reid). ■ *Emendations and textual notes:*

               [*MS is copy-text for* 'Buf . . . Clemens.' *(290.1–20)*]
290.1   3̶0̶ 31ˢᵗ· • 3ɸ1ˢᵗ·
               [*Tribune is copy-text for* 'To . . . 1870.' *(290.22–292.10)*]
290.24   & • and [*also at 290.27 (twice), 28, 32; 291.1, 6, 10, 13, 17, 22, 23, 24, 25, 28, 31 (twice), 32, 35, 36 (twice), 37, 38; 292.4, 5 (twice), 6 (twice), 7*]

291.1   the land • t[he] land [*badly inked*]
292.8   stench. • stench[.] [*badly inked*]

■ 3 January 1871 · To Joseph H. Twichell · Buffalo, N.Y. · *UCCL* 00554

■ *Copy-text:* MS, collection of Mrs. Robin Craven. ■ *Previous publication:* Parke-Bernet 1945, lot 90, excerpt. ■ *Provenance:* In or after 1945, the MS was acquired by Mrs. Craven's father, Sidney L. Krauss. ■ *Emendations and textual notes:*

294.3   ~~perfectly~~ • [*false ascenders/descenders*]
294.6   fancy—Warner's • ~—|—~
294.7   splendid. But • ~.—|~

■ 3 January 1871 · To Elisha Bliss, Jr. · Buffalo, N.Y. · *UCCL* 00553

■ *Copy-text:* MS, Mark Twain Papers, The Bancroft Library, University of California, Berkeley (CU-MARK). ■ *Previous publication: MTMF,* 144 n. 1, brief excerpt; *MTLP,* 53. ■ *Provenance:* see Mendoza Collection in Description of Provenance. A handwritten transcription by Dana Ayer and a Brownell typescript are at WU (see Brownell Collection in Description of Provenance). ■ *Emendations and textual notes:*

295.11   *I* • [*partly formed*]

■ 4 and 5 January 1871 · To Elisha Bliss, Jr. · Buffalo, N.Y. · *UCCL* 00555

■ *Copy-text:* Transcript and paraphrase, AAA 1927a, lot 244, is copy-text for 295.14–296.2; MS, Mark Twain Papers, The Bancroft Library, University of California, Berkeley (CU-MARK), is copy-text for the remainder. The auction catalog describes (and misdates) the transcribed and paraphrased MS as 'Autograph Letter Signed by "Mark Twain" to Mr. Bliss of the American Publishing Co., one page, 8vo, Jan. 4 [1875].' The quotation marks around the pseudonym are catalog style and almost certainly not indicative of how Clemens signed his name. ■ *Previous publication: MTMF,* 118 n. 2, excerpt, in addition to the copy-text. ■ *Provenance:* The present location of the MS for 295.14–296.2 is not known; for the CU-MARK MS see Mendoza Collection in Description of Provenance. ■ *Emendations and textual notes:*

[*AAA 1927a is copy-text for 295.14 –296.2*]
295.14   Jan. 4. • [*reported, not quoted*]
295.16   *writing* • writes
         [*MS is copy-text for* 'P. S. . . . . Mark.' *(296.3 –11)*]

296.6   Pre-duluge • [sic]
296.8   man, • [deletion implied]

■ 5 January 1871 · To Elisha Bliss, Jr. · Buffalo, N.Y. · UCCL 04138
■ Copy-text: MS, Cape Ann Historical Association, Gloucester (MGlHi).
■ Emendations and textual notes:

297.3   brother • broth∤er
297.4   return. ‸He's • ∼.—|‸∼
297.5   spirits • spir~~t~~sits [partly formed 't' reused as 'i']

■ 5? January 1871 · From Samuel L. and Olivia L. Clemens to Mary E.
   (Mollie) Clemens · Buffalo, N.Y. · UCCL 02795
■ Copy-text: MS, Jean Webster McKinney Family Papers, Vassar College Library (NPV). ■ Previous publication: MTBus, 118, excerpt. ■ Provenance: see
McKinney Family Papers in Description of Provenance. ■ Emendations and textual notes:

298.6   T • [partly formed]
298.8   wife—‸& • ∼—‸—&
298.12   business • busin~~i~~ess
298.17–18   comeliness • com∤liness
298.18   proportion • pro-|~~pro~~portion
298.18   ~~fed~~ feel • fe~~d~~el feel [rewritten for clarity]
298.19   ~~humping~~ • [canceled by OLC]
298.24   2‸ • ‸⫮ 2‸ [rewritten for clarity]

■ 6? January 1871 · To John M. Hay · Buffalo, N.Y. · UCCL 11849
■ Copy-text: None. The text of this paraphrase, in a letter from Hay to Joseph
Bucklin Bishop, 11 Jan 89, is based on two published transcriptions of it.

         P1   Joseph Bucklin Bishop, 777
         P2   Thayer, 1:375

P1 was probably transcribed directly from the MS of Hay's letter, which Bishop
owned in 1906; and P2 either from the MS or from a carbon copy in Hay's letterbook (Thayer, 1:vii–viii). ■ Emendations, adopted readings, and textual notes:

299.1   "J. B.," (P1) • ∧∼. ∼.,∧ (P2)
299.1   me, (P2) • ∼∧ (P1)
299.2   engineer, (P2) • ∼∧ (P1)

■ 6 or 7 January 1871 · To Earl D. Berry · Buffalo, N.Y. · *UCCL* 00556

■ *Copy-text:* MS, Clifton Waller Barrett Library, University of Virginia, Charlottesville (ViU). ■ *Provenance:* deposited at ViU by Clifton Waller Barrett on 17 December 1963.

■ 12 January 1871 · To Olivia L. Clemens · Cleveland, Ohio · *UCCL* 00557

■ *Copy-text:* MS, Mark Twain Papers, The Bancroft Library, University of California, Berkeley (CU-MARK). ■ *Previous publication: LLMT*, 361, brief paraphrase; *MTMF*, 143 n. 1, 145, 147 n. 2, brief excerpts. ■ *Provenance:* see Samossoud Collection in Description of Provenance. ■ *Emendations and textual notes:*

301.1	~~Wednes~~Thursday • ~~Wednes~~Thurs-day
301.6	*I* • [*partly formed*]
301.11	tomorrow • to-|morrow
301.12	presents. *I* • ~.—|~
301.19	~~was~~ wants • wa$ɡ$nts
302.7	N. Y. • N. [Y◇] [*torn*]
302.8	CLEVELAND • CL[EVE]LAND [*badly inked*]

■ 14 January 1871 · To Charles Henry Webb · Buffalo, N.Y. · *UCCL* 00558

■ *Copy-text:* MS, George N. Meissner Collection, Washington University, St. Louis (MoSW). ■ *Previous publication:* AAA/Anderson 1936a, lot 122, excerpts. ■ *Provenance:* donated to MoSW about 1960 by the estate of George N. Meissner. ■ *Emendations and textual notes:*

303.9–10	grindstone • grind-|stone

■ 15 January 1871 · To the Editor of *Every Saturday* (Thomas Bailey Aldrich) · Buffalo, N.Y. · *UCCL* 00559

■ *Copy-text:* MS, George N. Meissner Collection, Washington University, St. Louis (MoSW). ■ *Previous publication:* "Mark Twain Says He Did n't Do It," *Every Saturday* 2 (4 Feb 71): 118; Greenslet, 95; AAA/Anderson 1937, lot 75, excerpts. ■ *Provenance:* in the collection of Albert Bigelow Paine when he died in 1937; donated to MoSW about 1960 by the estate of George N. Meissner.

■ 22 January 1871 · To Thomas Bailey Aldrich · Buffalo, N.Y. ·
UCCL 00560

■*Copy-text:* MS, Houghton Library, Harvard University (MH-H). ■*Previous publication:* Greenslet, 95–96; *MTL*, 1:181–82, without the postscript. ■*Provenance:* deposited at MH-H in 1942 and donated in 1949 by Talbot Aldrich. ■*Emendations and textual notes:*

305.16   ~~own good~~ own good • [*wavy underscore over straight*]

■ 22 January 1871 · To James Redpath · Buffalo, N.Y. · *UCCL* 00561

■*Copy-text:* MS, Henry W. and Albert A. Berg Collection, The New York Public Library, Astor, Lenox and Tilden Foundations (NN-B). ■*Previous publication:* Will M. Clemens 1900, 27, with omissions; *MTMF*, 145 n. 2, brief excerpt. ■*Provenance:* Until his death in 1939 the MS was owned by W. T. H. Howe; in 1940, the Howe Collection was purchased by Dr. Albert A. Berg and donated to NN (Cannon, 185–86). ■*Emendations and textual notes:*

306.5   days. It • ~.—|~
306.5   se • se-|
306.7   ǥ • [*partly formed*]
306.9   distinct • distincɇt
306.11   Sacramento₎ • [*deletion implied*]
306.12   ᵱ • [*partly formed*]

■ 24 January 1871 · To Elisha Bliss, Jr. · Buffalo, N.Y. · *UCCL* 00562

■*Copy-text:* MS, collection of Todd M. Axelrod. ■*Previous publication:* Henkels 1920, lot 297, excerpt; Henkels 1925, lot 57, paraphrase; Hill, 44, excerpt; *MTLP*, 54. ■*Provenance:* sold by Henkels in 1920 and 1925; an Ayer transcription and a Brownell typescript are both at WU (see Brownell Collection in Description of Provenance); the present location of the MS, owned by Axelrod in 1983, is not known. ■*Emendations and textual notes:*

309.1   good, • [*possibly* 'good₎,']
309.7   many • ['a' *over miswritten* 'm']

■ 24 January 1871 · To C. F. Sterling · Buffalo, N.Y. · *UCCL* 00563

■*Copy-text:* MS, Clifton Waller Barrett Library, University of Virginia, Charlottesville (ViU). ■*Provenance:* deposited at ViU by Clifton Waller Barrett on 17 December 1963.

■ 25 January 1871 · From Olivia L. and Samuel L. Clemens to Alice Hooker Day · Buffalo, N.Y. · *UCCL* 00564

■ *Copy-text:* MS, Katherine Seymour Day Collection, Harriet Beecher Stowe Center, Hartford (CtHSD). ■ *Emendations and textual notes:*

311.13	babies • ~~babies~~ babies [*corrected miswriting*]
311.20	~~pris~~ prize • priϕze
311.29	we • ~~we~~ we [*corrected miswriting*]
312.7	$\int$ • [*partly formed; possibly* 'ϕ']
312.24	~~car~~ charming • carharming
312.24	fairy • [*possibly* 'faiery']
312.34	Clemens • ['s' *over miswritten* 'ns']

■ 26 January 1871 · To Mary Mason Fairbanks · Buffalo, N.Y. · *UCCL* 00566

■ *Copy-text:* MS, Huntington Library, San Marino (CSmH, call nos. HM 14269 and 14271). ■ *Previous publication: MTMF*, 145–47. ■ *Provenance:* see Huntington Library in Description of Provenance. ■ *Emendations and textual notes:*

314.9	~~is~~ it • iϕt
314.11	way. ~~And~~ • ~.—|~
315.4	now. We • ~.—|~

■ 27 January 1871 · To Thomas Bailey Aldrich · Buffalo, N.Y. · *UCCL* 00567

■ *Copy-text:* MS, Houghton Library, Harvard University (MH-H). ■ *Previous publication:* Aldrich 1872; Greenslet, 97–99; *MTL*, 1:182–84. ■ *Provenance:* deposited at MH-H in 1942 and donated in 1949 by Talbot Aldrich. ■ *Emendations and textual notes:*

316.12	~~keep~~ kept • keeppt [*canceled* 'p' *partly formed*]
317.1	every_wҺere_ • every|where_
317.19	bear. But • ~.—|~
317.25	Harte • Harte | ~~Harte~~
317.27	~~save~~ savagery • savϕagery

■ 27 January 1871 · To Elisha Bliss, Jr. · Buffalo, N.Y. · *UCCL* 00568

■ *Copy-text:* MS, Mark Twain Papers, The Bancroft Library, University of California, Berkeley (CU-MARK). ■ *Previous publication:* Hill, 44, excerpt; *MTLP,*

54–55. ■*Provenance:* see Mendoza Collection in Description of Provenance.
■*Emendations and textual notes:*

319.4   ~~well~~ week • wel/k ['l' *reused as* 'e']

■ 27 January 1871 · To Isaac E. Sheldon · Buffalo, N.Y. · *UCCL* 11799

■*Copy-text:* MS paraphrase on envelope of OC to SLC, 25 Jan 71 (*UCLC*
47023), Mark Twain Papers, The Bancroft Library, University of California,
Berkeley (CU-MARK). ■*Provenance:* see Mark Twain Papers in Description of
Provenance.

■ 28 January 1871 · To Willard McKinstry · Buffalo, N.Y. · *UCCL*
00569

■*Copy-text:* MS, Clifton Waller Barrett Library, University of Virginia, Charlottesville (ViU). ■*Previous publication:* "From Mark Twain," Fredonia *Censor,*
8 Feb 71, 1. ■*Provenance:* deposited at ViU by Clifton Waller Barrett on 17 December 1963. ■*Emendations and textual notes:*

321.7   ~~fifth~~ fiftieth • ~~fiftieth~~ fiftieth
                                  ^   ^

■ 30 January 1871 · To James Redpath · Buffalo, N.Y. · *UCCL* 00570

■*Copy-text:* MS, Houghton Library, Harvard University (MH-H). ■*Provenance:* bequeathed to MH in 1918 by Evert J. Wendell. ■*Emendations and textual
notes:*

322.6   editors. Do • ~.—|~
322.11   f • [*partly formed*]
322.12   ~~or~~ on • o/n
322.13   & • & /

■ 31 January 1871 · To Elisha Bliss, Jr., or Francis E. Bliss, *per* Telegraph Operator · Buffalo, N.Y. · *UCCL* 00571

■*Copy-text:* MS, copy received, telegram blank filled out in the hand of a telegraph operator, Mark Twain Papers, The Bancroft Library, University of California, Berkeley (CU-MARK). ■*Provenance:* see Mendoza Collection in Description of Provenance. ■*Emendations and textual notes:*

324.1   THE . . . COMPANY. • [*words on telegram blank identical to those
               reported in the commentary for 7 Nov 70 to Langdon*]
324.2   1257 • [*possibly* '1259']

■ 9 February 1871 · To Louis Prang and Company · Buffalo, N.Y. · *UCCL* 00573

■ *Copy-text:* MS facsimile. The editors have not seen the MS, which is in the collection of Hallmark Cards, Kansas City (MoKHC). ■ *Emendations and textual notes:*

329.13   Sa • [*possibly* 'Sam'; 'm' *partly formed*]

■ 13 February 1871 · To Unidentified · Buffalo, N.Y. · *UCCL* 00574

■ *Copy-text:* MS facsimile. The editors have not seen the MS, which is at the University of Chicago Library (ICU).

■ 15 February 1871 · To Elisha Bliss, Jr. · Buffalo, N.Y. · *UCCL* 00576

■ *Copy-text:* MS, Mark Twain Papers, The Bancroft Library, University of California, Berkeley (CU-MARK). ■ *Previous publication: MTLP,* 55–56. ■ *Provenance:* see Mendoza Collection in Description of Provenance. ■ *Emendations and textual notes:*

331.7   T • [*partly formed*]

■ 17 February 1871 · To Jane Lampton Clemens and Family · Buffalo, N.Y. · *UCCL* 00577

■ *Copy-text:* MS, Jean Webster McKinney Family Papers, Vassar College Library (NPV). ■ *Provenance:* see McKinney Family Papers in Description of Provenance. ■ *Emendations and textual notes:*

332.8   be. She • ~.—|~
332.12   made. But • ~.—|~
332.14   tak • ['t' *and* 'k' *partly formed*]

■ 17 February 1871 · To Fannie Dennis · Buffalo, N.Y. · *UCCL* 00578

■ *Copy-text:* MS, collection of Todd M. Axelrod. ■ *Provenance:* The current location of the MS, owned in 1980 by James Pepper and in 1983 by Axelrod, is not known. ■ *Emendations and textual notes:*

334.10   It Isn't • I/sn't
334.12   Truly • [*possibly* 'Y Truly'; 'Y' *partly formed*]

■ 22 February 1871 · To Orion Clemens · Buffalo, N.Y. · *UCCL* 00579

■*Copy-text:* MS, Mark Twain Papers, The Bancroft Library, University of California, Berkeley (CU-MARK). ■*Provenance:* see Mark Twain Papers in Description of Provenance. ■*Emendations and textual notes:*

335.1   non-resident · non-|resident

■ 22 February 1871 · To James Redpath · Buffalo, N.Y. · *UCCL* 00580

■*Copy-text:* MS, Houghton Library, Harvard University (MH-H). ■*Provenance:* bequeathed to MH in 1918 by Evert J. Wendell. ■*Emendations and textual notes:*

336.8   BOSTON · [◇◇◇TON] [*badly inked*]
336.8   REDPATH · [◇◇D]PATH [*badly inked*]

■ 22 February 1871 · To Whitelaw Reid · Buffalo, N.Y. · *UCCL* 00581

■*Copy-text:* MS, Whitelaw Reid Papers, Library of Congress (DLC). ■*Provenance:* The Whitelaw Reid Papers (part of the Papers of the Reid Family) were donated to DLC between 1953 and 1957 by Helen Rogers Reid (Mrs. Ogden Mills Reid). ■*Emendations and textual notes:*

336.12   ~~offense~~ · [*false ascenders/descenders*]

■ 26 or 27 February 1871 · To E. C. Chick · Buffalo, N.Y. · *UCCL* 11797

■*Copy-text:* Paraphrase in MS, James Sutton to SLC, 2 Mar 71 (*UCLC* 31762), Mark Twain Papers, The Bancroft Library, University of California, Berkeley (CU-MARK). ■*Provenance:* see Mark Twain Papers in Description of Provenance.

■ 3 March 1871 · To John Henry Riley · Buffalo, N.Y. · *UCCL* 00582

■*Copy-text:* MS, Henry W. and Albert A. Berg Collection, The New York Public Library, Astor, Lenox and Tilden Foundations (NN-B). ■*Previous publication:* *MTMF,* 149 n. 1, brief excerpt. ■*Provenance:* Owen D. Young Collection, acquired by NN-B in 1941 (Bruccoli, 218).

■ 4 March 1871 · To Orion Clemens · Buffalo, N.Y. · *UCCL* 00583

■*Copy-text:* MS, Jean Webster McKinney Family Papers, Vassar College Library (NPV). ■*Previous publication: MTL,* 1:185–86, with omission; Mc-

Elderry, xiv, brief excerpt; Hill, 47, 50, brief excerpts; *MTMF,* 149, brief excerpt. ■*Provenance:* see McKinney Family Papers in Description of Provenance. ■*Emendations and textual notes:*

341.12	leave •	[*possibly* 'lea$ve'; '$' *partly formed*]
341.29–30	it. Hold •	~.—|~
342.1	~~the~~ this •	th¢is
342.3–4	~~writing~~ . . . ~~book~~ •	[*The canceled passage is at the top of an MS page numbered 5. Clemens replaced the page with a new page 5, and then reused the canceled page as page 6, where the canceled passage appears out of place.*]
342.7	~~st~~ •	['t' *partly formed*]
342.8–9	~~it~~ is •	i∤s
342.14	4½ •	[*underscored twice*]

■ 9 March 1871 · To Orion Clemens · Buffalo, N.Y. · *UCCL* 00584

■*Copy-text:* MS, Robert B. Honeyman Collection, Linderman Library, Lehigh University, Bethlehem, Pa. (PBL). ■*Provenance:* deposited at PBL in March 1957. ■*Emendations and textual notes:*

346.6	security •	['ty' *over miswritten* 'it']
346.9	Yrs •	['Y' *miswritten*]

■ 9 March 1871 · To Samuel S. Cox · Buffalo, N.Y. · *UCCL* 11006

■*Copy-text:* MS, Cyril Clemens Collection, Mark Twain House, Hartford (CtHMTH). ■*Provenance:* donated to CtHMTH in 1984 by Cyril Clemens. ■*Emendations and textual notes:*

347.2	Piatt∤ •	[*deletion implied*]
347.4	~~this~~ that •	th~~is~~at

■ 10 March 1871 · To Orion Clemens · Buffalo, N.Y. · *UCCL* 02453

■*Copy-text:* MS, Henry W. and Albert A. Berg Collection, The New York Public Library, Astor, Lenox and Tilden Foundations (NN-B). ■*Previous publication:* Hill 44–45, brief excerpt; *MTLP,* 61 n. 1, brief excerpt. ■*Provenance:* It is not known when the MS became part of the Berg Collection, given by Dr. Albert A. Berg to NN in 1940 but continuously enlarged since then. A Brownell typescript is at WU (see Brownell Collection in Description of Provenance). ■*Emendations and textual notes:*

348.12	indeed •	in[◊]|deed [*obscured by glued edge*]
348.16	detail •	['t' *uncrossed*]

348.16   exploit • ['t' *over miswritten* 'it']
348.19   ~~in~~ it • i̶n̶t

■ 11 and 13 March 1871 · To Orion Clemens · Buffalo, N.Y. · *UCCL* 00587

■ *Copy-text:* MS, Mark Twain Papers, The Bancroft Library, University of California, Berkeley (CU-MARK). ■ *Previous publication:* Hill, 50–51, excerpts; *MTLP,* 56–60; McElderry, xiv, brief excerpts; Chester L. Davis 1985a, 4 (first half), and 1985b, 1 (second half). ■ *Provenance:* see Appert Collection in Description of Provenance. A handwritten Ayer transcription is at CtHMTH, and a Brownell typescript is at WU (see Brownell Collection in Description of Provenance). ■ *Emendations and textual notes:*

349.9–10   too. [¶] You • ~.—| [¶] ~
349.15   ~~au~~ other • a̶u̶ther ['a' *reused as* 'o']
350.2   reputation • reput̸ation
350.7   *weight.* Haven't • ~.—|~
350.8   sufficiently • sufficeii̸ently
350.11   it̸, • [*deletion implied*]
350.19   ~~her~~ hear • he̸ar
351.1   f̸ • [*partly formed; possibly* 'f']
351.14   ~~Taking~~ • ['g' *partly formed*]
351.19   next̸, • [*deletion implied*]
351.19   Wednesday; • [*possibly* '~,.' *or* '~,;'; *deletion implied*]
351.35–36   *lower.* [¶] I • ~.|— [¶] ~
351.37–352.1 *me.* [¶] I • ~.—| [¶] ~
352.11   nothing • nothiṅ̸hng

■ 12 March 1871 · To Susan L. Crane · Buffalo, N.Y. · *UCCL* 00588

■ *Copy-text:* MS, Mark Twain Papers, The Bancroft Library, University of California, Berkeley (CU-MARK). ■ *Provenance:* see Mark Twain Papers in Description of Provenance.

■ 14 March 1871 · To Susan L. Crane · Buffalo, N.Y. · *UCCL* 00589

■ *Copy-text:* MS, Mark Twain Papers, The Bancroft Library, University of California, Berkeley (CU-MARK). ■ *Provenance:* This letter remained in the Langdon family until 1972, when it was donated to CU-MARK by Mrs. Eugene Lada-Mocarski, Jervis Langdon, Jr., Mrs. Robert S. Pennock, and Mrs. Bayard Schieffelin. ■ *Emendations and textual notes:*

358.8	first. She • ~.—|~
358.11	loggerheads • logger-|heads
358.11	~~she ref refused~~ • [*possibly* 'she ref refused']
358.21	thermometer. It • ~.—|~
358.30	~~Eur~~ Euchre • Eur̯chre
359.2	*farrago* • *farr̶a̶arrago* [*corrected miswriting*]
359.3	fool— • ~—|—
359.3	(Livy's • [*redundant opening parenthesis*]
359.5	~~dro~~ • ['o' *partly formed*]
359.21	~~see~~ self • sé̶lf

■ 14 March 1871 · To Mary Mason Fairbanks · Buffalo, N.Y. · *UCCL* 00590

■ *Copy-text:* MS, Huntington Library, San Marino (CSmH, call no. HM 14272). ■ *Previous publication: MTMF,* 150–51. ■ *Provenance:* see Huntington Library in Description of Provenance. ■ *Emendations and textual notes:*

360.7	lately, • [*deletion implied*]
360.19	affairs • affa̶irs
360.22	~~& y~~ • ['y' *partly formed*]
360.23	deeds • dee̶ds
360.23–24	~~appe~~ appreciated • app̶reciated
361.1	ń • [*possibly* 'ẅ']

■ 15 March 1871 · To Jane Lampton Clemens and Family · Buffalo, N.Y. · *UCCL* 00591

■ *Copy-text:* MS, Jean Webster McKinney Family Papers, Vassar College Library (NPV). ■ *Previous publication: MTMF,* 150 n. 2, brief excerpt. ■ *Provenance:* see McKinney Family Papers in Description of Provenance. ■ *Emendations and textual notes:*

361.11	live, • [*deletion implied*]

■ 15 March 1871 · To James Redpath · Buffalo, N.Y. · *UCCL* 10175

■ *Copy-text:* Transcript and paraphrase, National Book Auctions, lot 157. The auction catalog describes the letter as 'Original Autograph Letter, Signed. 8 vo, about 150 words, both sides, ink. To "Dear Redpath", SIGNED "MARK", (Weak in the folds).' ■ *Emendations and textual notes:*

362.1	Buf., 15. • Buf., 15 (1871).
362.2	Dear Redpath— • To "Dear Redpath"

362.4–5	not less than $250.00 in Boston. • "NOT LESS THAN 250.00 IN BOSTON.. [*no closing quotation marks*]
362.7	*because . . . contemplated* • becouse . . . contemploted
362.9	Mark. • SIGNED "MARK"

■ 15–18 March 1871 · To Orion Clemens · Buffalo, N.Y. · *UCCL* 00592 (formerly *UCCL* 00592 and 10080)

■ *Copy-text:* MS, Mark Twain Papers, The Bancroft Library, University of California, Berkeley (CU-MARK). ■ *Provenance:* see Mark Twain Papers in Description of Provenance. ■ *Emendations and textual notes:*

363.9	sympathize • ['p' *over miswritten* 'm']
363.9	with. Your • ~.—|~
363.9	₦ • [*possibly* 'ℱ']
363.9	article. Then • ~.—|~
363.12	~~valu~~ • [*possibly* '~~natu~~']
363.14–15	literature. Therefore • ~.—|~
363.31	molehills • mole-|hills
363.31	individual's • indiviᶠdual's ['ℱ' *partly formed*]
363.34	₦a • ₦|a
364.1	truth. • ~..
364.6–7	rest. [¶] If • ~.—| [¶] ~
364.11	~~the~~ these • ~~the~~hese
364.16	it. Meantime • ~.—|~
364.17	of, or • of oᶠf, or

■ 17 March 1871 · To Elisha Bliss, Jr. · Buffalo, N.Y. · *UCCL* 02455

■ *Copy-text:* MS, Henry W. and Albert A. Berg Collection, The New York Public Library, Astor, Lenox and Tilden Foundations (NN-B). ■ *Previous publication:* Hill, 47, brief excerpt; *MTLP*, 60–61, excerpt. ■ *Provenance:* Until his death in 1939 the MS was owned by W. T. H. Howe; in 1940, the Howe Collection was purchased by Dr. Albert A. Berg and donated to NN (Cannon, 185–86). ■ *Emendations and textual notes:*

365.7	~~jun~~ • [*possibly* '~~jan~~']
365.16–17	God. [¶] Take • ~.—| [¶] ~
366.3	~~we~~ • ['e' *partly formed*]
366.6	bottled • bot-|~~teletled~~
366.7	emptied. By • ~.—|~
366.16	~~if~~ it • iᶠt

■ 20 March 1871 · To Elisha Bliss, Jr., and Orion Clemens · Elmira, N.Y. · *UCCL* 00595

■ *Copy-text:* MS, Mark Twain Papers, The Bancroft Library, University of California, Berkeley (CU-MARK). ■ *Previous publication:* Hill, 52, brief excerpts; *MTLP*, 61–62. ■ *Provenance:* see Mark Twain Papers in Description of Provenance. ■ *Emendations and textual notes:*

367.10   ~~hear~~ here • he<u>a</u>rre

■ 27 March 1871 · To Donn Piatt · Elmira, N.Y. · *UCCL* 00596

■ *Copy-text:* Transcript and paraphrase, Benjamin 1947, item A 1438. The catalog describes the MS as 'A.L.S., 4pp., large 4to, "Office of J. Langdon & Co . . . Elmira, N. Y." (letterhead of his father-in-law), Mar. 27, 1871.' ■ *Previous publication:* McElderry, xiv, excerpt, in addition to the copy-text. ■ *Emendations and textual notes:*

369.1–4   J. LANGDON . . . Mar. 27 187 1. • [*text of letterhead adopted in part from 28 Sept 71 to Lant; date reported, not quoted*]
369.10   *Clemens's* • his

■ 27 March 1871 · To John Henry Riley · Elmira, N.Y. · *UCCL* 00597

■ *Copy-text:* MS, Beinecke Rare Book and Manuscript Library, Yale University (CtY-BR). ■ *Previous publication:* Boesen, item 67, with omission. ■ *Provenance:* The MS, formerly in the collection of Dr. Samuel W. Bandler, was bought in 1947 and donated to CtY by the class of 1884. ■ *Emendations and textual notes:*

371.14   T • [*partly formed*]

■ 4 April 1871 · To Orion Clemens · Elmira, N.Y. · *UCCL* 00598

■ *Copy-text:* MS, Mark Twain Papers, The Bancroft Library, University of California, Berkeley (CU-MARK). ■ *Previous publication:* Hill, 52, excerpt; *MTLP*, 62–63. ■ *Provenance:* see Mark Twain Papers in Description of Provenance. ■ *Emendations and textual notes:*

372.15   ~~by~~ but • b<u>y</u>ut

■ 4 April 1871 · To Thomas Nast · Elmira, N.Y. · *UCCL* 00599

■ *Copy-text:* MS, Clifton Waller Barrett Library, University of Virginia, Charlottesville (ViU). ■ *Provenance:* deposited at ViU by Clifton Waller Barrett on 17 December 1963. ■ *Emendations and textual notes:*

373.9   ~~word~~ world • wor<u>d</u>ld

■ 6 April 1871 · To Robert M. and Louise M. Howland · Elmira, N.Y.
· *UCCL* 00600

■*Copy-text:* MS, Mark Twain Papers, The Bancroft Library, University of California, Berkeley (CU-MARK). ■*Provenance:* donated to CU-MARK in 1977 by Mr. and Mrs. Robert M. Gunn.

■ 6 April 1871 · To Isaac E. Sheldon · Elmira, N.Y. · *UCCL* 00601

■*Copy-text:* MS, Mark Twain Papers, The Bancroft Library, University of California, Berkeley (CU-MARK). ■*Provenance:* see Mark Twain Papers in Description of Provenance. ■*Emendations and textual notes:*

375.4   mean · ~~mean~~ | mean [*corrected miswriting*]

■ 8, 9, and 10 April 1871 · To Orion Clemens · Elmira, N.Y. · *UCCL*
00602

■*Copy-text:* MS, Mark Twain Papers, The Bancroft Library, University of California, Berkeley (CU-MARK). ■*Previous publication:* Hill, 53, excerpts; *MTLP,* 63–64. ■*Provenance:* see Moffett Collection in Description of Provenance. ■*Emendations and textual notes:*

376.7   ȼ 570th · [*possibly* 'ȼ570th']
376.7   page · [*possibly* 'pages'; 's' *partly formed*]
377.14   P. S. · [*capitals underscored three times*]
377.22   OVER · [*capitals simulated, not underscored*]
377.25   to-night, · [*deletion implied*]

■ 18 April 1871 · To Orion Clemens · Elmira, N.Y. · *UCCL* 00603

■*Copy-text:* MS, Mark Twain Papers, The Bancroft Library, University of California, Berkeley (CU-MARK). ■*Previous publication: MTMF,* 153, brief excerpt; *MTLP,* 64–65. ■*Provenance:* see Mark Twain Papers in Description of Provenance.

■ 18 April 1871 · To Mary Mason Fairbanks · Elmira, N.Y. · *UCCL*
00604

■*Copy-text:* MS, Huntington Library, San Marino (CSmH, call no. HM 14273). ■*Previous publication: MTMF,* 151. ■*Provenance:* see Huntington Library in Description of Provenance.

■ 18 April 1871 · To Unidentified · Elmira, N.Y. · *UCCL* 11014

■*Copy-text:* MS, Cyril Clemens Collection, Mark Twain House, Hartford (CtHMTH). ■*Provenance:* donated to CtHMTH in 1984 by Cyril Clemens.

■ 26 April 1871 · To Mary Mason Fairbanks · Elmira, N.Y. · *UCCL* 00606

■*Copy-text:* MS, Huntington Library, San Marino (CSmH, call no. HM 14274). ■*Previous publication: MTMF,* 153. ■*Provenance:* see Huntington Library in Description of Provenance. ■*Emendations and textual notes:*

381.7	aɳ́ •	['ɳ́' *partly formed*]
381.12	ɳ́ •	[*possibly* 'ɰ́']

■ 27? April 1871 · To Thomas Nast · Elmira, N.Y. · *UCCL* 00605

■*Copy-text:* Merwin-Clayton 1907a, lot 60. The catalog describes the MS as "A. L. S. *Twain.* 1 page, 8vo, Elmira, n. d., to Nast." ■*Emendations and textual notes:*

382.1	Elmira •	[*reported, not quoted*]
382.3	[*no* ¶] Take •	[¶] "∼
382.3	& •	and
382.4	best •	∼," etc.

■ 29 April 1871 · To Whitelaw Reid · Elmira, N.Y. · *UCCL* 00607

■*Copy-text:* Copy-text for the letter is MS, Whitelaw Reid Papers, Library of Congress (DLC); copy-text for the enclosure is "A Substitu[t]e for Rulloff," New York *Tribune,* 3 May 71, 2. ■*Previous publication:* none known for the letter; *MTB,* 3:1628–29, for the enclosure, which, according to Albert Bigelow Paine, was widely copied although its author was never explicitly identified (*MTB,* 1:437). ■*Provenance:* The Whitelaw Reid Papers (part of the Papers of the Reid Family) were donated to DLC between 1953 and 1957 by Helen Rogers Reid (Mrs. Ogden Mills Reid). The MS of the enclosure is not known to survive. ■*Emendations and textual notes:*

	[*MS is copy-text for* 'Elmira . . . Clemens.' *(382.6–383.13)*]	
383.6	bully. Silly •	∼.—|∼
	[*Tribune is copy-text for* 'To . . . LANGHORNE.' *(383.15–384.29)*]	
383.18	& •	and [*also at 383.21, 22, 28, 31, 33, 36; 384.3 (twice), 7, 8, 10, 11, 13, 14, 16, 17, 19, 21, 23, 25, 26 (twice), 27 (twice)*]
384.25	& •	*and*

■ 30 April 1871 · To Orion Clemens · Elmira, N.Y. · *UCCL* 00609

■ *Copy-text:* MS, Jean Webster McKinney Family Papers, Vassar College Library (NPV). ■ *Previous publication: MTBus,* 118–19; Chester L. Davis 1954, 4. ■ *Provenance:* see McKinney Family Papers in Description of Provenance. ■ *Emendations and textual notes:*

386.3   more. Leave • ~.—|~
386.7   letters. Yours • ~.—|~
386.21   re • [*doubtful*]

■ 3 May 1871 · To Elisha Bliss, Jr. · Elmira, N.Y. · *UCCL* 00610

■ *Copy-text:* MS, Mark Twain Papers, The Bancroft Library, University of California, Berkeley (CU-MARK). ■ *Previous publication: MTLP,* 65–66. ■ *Provenance:* see Mendoza Collection in Description of Provenance.

■ 5 May 1871 · To Henri Gerard · Elmira, N.Y. · *UCCL* 02456

■ *Copy-text:* MS, Henry W. and Albert A. Berg Collection, The New York Public Library, Astor, Lenox and Tilden Foundations (NN-B). ■ *Previous publication:* Bibliophile Society, 125–26. ■ *Provenance:* A handwritten transcription made by Dana Ayer between 1910 and 1919 and a Brownell typescript are at WU (see Brownell Collection in Description of Provenance). At some time the MS was acquired by W. T. H. Howe, who died in 1939; in 1940, the Howe Collection was purchased by Dr. Albert A. Berg and donated to NN (Cannon, 185–86). ■ *Emendations and textual notes:*

390.4   lacks • [*sic*]
390.6   lu let • lʉet

■ 15 May 1871 · To Elisha Bliss, Jr. · Elmira, N.Y. · *UCCL* 00612

■ *Copy-text:* MS, Clifton Waller Barrett Library, University of Virginia, Charlottesville (ViU). ■ *Previous publication: MTB,* 1:438, 440, excerpt; *MTL,* 1:187–88, with omissions; *MTMF,* 154 n. 1, brief excerpt; AAA/Anderson 1934a, lot 126, excerpt (includes facsimile of MS page 3); McElderry, xiv, excerpt. ■ *Provenance:* A Brownell typescript is at WU (see Brownell Collection in Description of Provenance). The MS, part of the collection of Edmund W. Evans until its sale in 1934, was deposited at ViU by Clifton Waller Barrett on 17 December 1963. ■ *Emendations and textual notes:*

390.20   book • blook book
391.14   boo but • boout
391.14–15 am an • arʌn

391.18   ~~ov~~ of • o⟨y⟩f
391.27   65⟨,⟩—~~part~~ • [*deletion of dash implied*]

■ 15 May–10 June 1871 · To Donn Piatt · Elmira, N.Y. · *UCCL* 11833
■ *Copy-text:* Paraphrase, "Answers to Correspondents," probably written by Francis P. Church, in "The Galaxy Club-Room," *Galaxy* 12 (Oct 71): 588.

■ 7 June 1871 · To Orion and Mary E. (Mollie) Clemens · Elmira, N.Y. · *UCCL* 00613
■ *Copy-text:* MS, Mark Twain Papers, The Bancroft Library, University of California, Berkeley (CU-MARK). ■ *Provenance:* see Moffett Collection in Description of Provenance. ■ *Emendations and textual notes:*

396.5   health. However • ∼.—|∼
396.5   It • [It] ⟨It⟩ [*torn*]
396.12   once. Mind • ∼.—|∼
396.13   ~~that~~ than • tha⟨t⟩n

■ 7 June–28 September 1871 · To Bret Harte · Elmira, N.Y. · *UCCL* 11811
■ *Copy-text:* MS on *carte de visite* photograph in the collection of Mrs. Robin Craven. ■ *Previous publication:* Winterich, 20. ■ *Provenance:* The photograph, on exhibition in 1936 at the bookshop of G. A. Baker and Co., was at an unspecified date acquired by Mrs. Craven's father, Sidney L. Krauss.

■ 10 June 1871 · To James Redpath and George L. Fall · Elmira, N.Y. · *UCCL* 00614
■ *Copy-text:* MS, New York Historical Society, New York (NHi). ■ *Emendations and textual notes:*

399.5   OVER • [*simulated small capitals underscored twice*]
399.9   good sized • [*possibly* 'good-sized'; *blotted*]
399.22   hotels • hotel⟨l⟩s
399.28   extremes • extreme⟨s⟩s
399.35   eastern & • easte[rn ◊] [*pasted over*]
399.37   ~~so suit~~ • s⟨o⟩uit
400.26   expenses⟨,⟩ • [*deletion implied*]

■ 10 June 1871 · To David Gray · Elmira, N.Y. · *UCCL* 11746

■ *Copy-text:* Paraphrase, David Gray, "Mark Twain in the Lecture Field," Buffalo *Courier,* 12 June 71, 2. ■ *Previous publication:* reprinted in the Buffalo *Courier,* 13 June 71, 2. ■ *Emendations and textual notes:*

402.1   FIELD.— • FIELD.[◊] [*badly inked*]

■ 11 June 1871 · To Jane Lampton Clemens · Elmira, N.Y. · *UCCL* 00615

■ *Copy-text:* MS, Mark Twain Papers, The Bancroft Library, University of California, Berkeley (CU-MARK). For a photofacsimile of this letter, see Appendix F. Clemens seems to have deliberately varied the shapes of these nine scraps, which were torn (not cut) from at least three different sources. Seven of the nine came from two letters he received, one of which Olivia Clemens used first, as evidenced by her penciled calculations on the scrap he tore from it. Clemens's text cannot be read by fitting the scraps together, as in a jigsaw puzzle. Instead he wrote on both sides of each scrap, successively, except in two cases. In these instances one of the two sides shows only the original inscription of his source. The text has been transcribed with the usual conventions, except that some alterations are presented more literally than they otherwise might be ('un~~ci~~der cir-' rather than '~~unci~~ under cir-'), and the type is also line for line with the original, chiefly because that was the least arbitrary way to render the text in discrete but intelligible fragments. The actual shapes of the scraps are only approximated by the type and by an editorial outline—again, as the least arbitrary way of representing some shape. Each outline appears twice, representing each side of the scrap in the intended order. The transcription also includes the words or parts of words left over from the source letter, even though these were not intended in the ordinary sense to be read, and their placement relative to Clemens's inscription can only be approximated. ■ *Previous publication:* Chester L. Davis 1978, 2–3; Christie 1993, lot 23. ■ *Provenance:* The letter was returned to Clemens, presumably after the death of his mother or sister. It was among those letters which, in the 1950s, Clara Clemens Samossoud gave or sold to Chester L. Davis, Sr. After his death in 1987, it became part of the collection of Chester L. Davis, Jr. Purchased for CU-MARK in 1993 through the Joseph Z. and Hatherly B. Todd Fund. ■ *Emendations and textual notes:*

404.33   N̸ • [*partly formed*]
405.1   months • month[◊] [*obscured by foxing*]
405.6–7   sub-|ject • sub-|[je]ct [*obscured by foxing*]

■ 12 June 1871 · To James Redpath · Elmira, N.Y. · *UCCL* 00616

■ *Copy-text:* MS, Houghton Library, Harvard University (MH-H). ■ *Provenance:* bequeathed to MH in 1918 by Evert J. Wendell.

■ 12 June 1871 · To William Bowen · Elmira, N.Y. · *UCCL* 11808

■ *Copy-text:* None. The text derives from a paraphrase of the MS made by Agnes M. Bowen, William Bowen's granddaughter, in a letter she wrote in 1940 to Theodore Hornberger of the University of Texas at Austin. As her letter has not been found, the text is based upon Hornberger's two accounts of her paraphrase: (P¹) Hornberger to Bernard DeVoto, 18 Dec 1940, Mark Twain Papers, The Bancroft Library, University of California, Berkeley (CU-MARK), and (P²) Hornberger, 10. In P¹, Hornberger conjectured that Clemens's letter was written "probably about 1873," and in P², he reported that Agnes Bowen thought it was written "probably in 1874." Contextual evidence strongly suggests, however, that 1871 was more likely (see p. 408, n. 1). ■ *Provenance:* Agnes Bowen may have sold the letter during or after 1941 (Hornberger to DeVoto, 28 Mar 1941, CU-MARK). ■ *Emendations, adopted readings, and textual notes:* Adopted readings followed by '(C)' are editorial emendations of the source readings.

407.11	One . . . possession (P²) • A fourteenth letter, written probably about 1873, is in the hands (P¹)
407.12	Bowen . . . Salt (P²) • Bowen, 434 South Edgehill, Salt (P¹)
407.12	Utah, a granddaughter. (P²) • Utah. (P¹)
407.13	Miss (C) • It has proved impossible to make arrangements to print this with the others, but Miss (P²); [*not in*] (P¹)
407.13	Bowen . . . June (P²) • [*not in*] (P¹)
407.14	12. (C) • 12, probably in 1874. (P²); [*not in*] (P¹)
407.14	She writes: "It contains (P¹) • It "contains (P²)
407.15–16	Reference . . . grandfather. (P¹) • [*not in*] (P²)

■ 15 June 1871 · To James Redpath · Elmira, N.Y. · *UCCL* 00617

■ *Copy-text:* Horner, 172–74. ■ *Previous publication:* "Letters to James Redpath," *Mark Twain Quarterly* 5 (Winter–Spring 1942): 21 (derives from Horner). ■ *Emendations and textual notes:*

408.4	& • and [*also at 408.6, 14, 15, 16, 17, 19 (twice), 20, 24; 409.1, 3, 4 (twice), 5 (twice), 8, 11*]
409.14	Mark • MARK

■ 21 June 1871 · To Elisha Bliss, Jr. · Elmira, N.Y. · *UCCL* 00618

■ *Copy-text:* MS, Mark Twain Papers, The Bancroft Library, University of California, Berkeley (CU-MARK). ■ *Previous publication:* *MTB*, 1:440–41, excerpt; *MTLP*, 66–67. ■ *Provenance:* see Mendoza Collection in Description of Provenance. ■ *Emendations and textual notes:*

410.2	Dear • ['ar' *conflated*]
410.15–16	~~say that it~~ ,add this: "It, • ~~say that~~ ,add this: ",It
410.24–25	copyright.— • [*possibly* 'copyright.+'; *deletion implied*]

■ 21 June 1871 · To Orion and Mary E. (Mollie) Clemens · Elmira, N.Y. · *UCCL* 00619

■ *Copy-text:* MS, Mark Twain Papers, The Bancroft Library, University of California, Berkeley (CU-MARK). ■ *Provenance:* see Mark Twain Papers in Description of Provenance.

■ 27 June 1871 · To Orion Clemens · (1st of 2) · Elmira, N.Y. · *UCCL* 00620

■ *Copy-text:* MS, Mark Twain Papers, The Bancroft Library, University of California, Berkeley (CU-MARK). ■ *Provenance:* see Mark Twain Papers in Description of Provenance. ■ *Emendations and textual notes:*

412.17   ~~the~~ this · th∉is
413.5   ~~dis~~ decided · di~~s~~ecided

■ 27 June 1871 · ~~To George L. Fall~~ To James Redpath · (1st of 2) · Elmira, N.Y. · *UCCL* 00621

■ *Copy-text:* MS, collection of Todd M. Axelrod. ■ *Previous publication:* Will M. Clemens 1900, 28; Horner, 166–67, with omission; "Letters to James Redpath," *Mark Twain Quarterly* 5 (Winter–Spring 1942): 20. ■ *Provenance:* The present location of the MS, owned by Axelrod in 1983, is not known.

■ 27 June 1871 · To Orion Clemens · (2nd of 2) · Elmira, N.Y. · *UCCL* 00622

■ *Copy-text:* MS, Mark Twain Papers, The Bancroft Library, University of California, Berkeley (CU-MARK). ■ *Previous publication: MTMF,* 154 n. 2, brief excerpt. ■ *Provenance:* see Mark Twain Papers in Description of Provenance. ■ *Emendations and textual notes:*

414.7   ~~next~~ · ['t' *partly formed*]
414.10   *∤* · [*deletion implied*]

■ 27 June 1871 · To James Redpath · (2nd of 2) · Elmira, N.Y. · *UCCL* 00623

■ *Copy-text:* MS, collection of Todd M. Axelrod. ■ *Previous publication:* excerpts in *MTL,* 1:189; Will M. Clemens 1900, 28; Horner, 166; AAA 1928, lot 77; "Letters to James Redpath," *Mark Twain Quarterly* 5 (Winter–Spring 1942): 19–20; *MTMF,* 154; Chester L. Davis 1978, 3; The Rendells, undated notice of sale.

■*Provenance:* The MS was sold in 1928 by AAA to an unknown purchaser, and before 1983 by The Rendells to Todd M. Axelrod. Its present location is not known.

■ 27 June 1871 · To Whitelaw Reid · Elmira, N.Y. · *UCCL* 00624

■*Copy-text:* MS, Whitelaw Reid Papers, Library of Congress (DLC). ■*Provenance:* The Whitelaw Reid Papers (part of the Papers of the Reid Family) were donated to DLC between 1953 and 1957 by Helen Rogers Reid (Mrs. Ogden Mills Reid).

■ 27 June 1871 · From Olivia L. and Samuel L. Clemens to Mary Mason Fairbanks · Elmira, N.Y. · *UCCL* 00625

■*Copy-text:* Paraphrase and transcript, *MTMF,* 154 n. 3. ■*Previous publication:* Hill, 54, brief excerpt. ■*Provenance:* In 1949, Wecter wrote in *MTMF* that the letter "dated June 27, is found in the T. N. Fairbanks Collection"; its present location is not known. ■*Emendations and textual notes:*

418.9	June 27 •	[*reported, not quoted*]
418.15	[*in pencil:*] •	Clemens himself adds in pencil:
418.16	thick [&] thin •	thick thin [*sic*]

■ 28 June 1871 · To James Redpath · Elmira, N.Y. · *UCCL* 00627 (formerly *UCCL* 00626 and 00627)

■*Copy-text:* MS, Houghton Library, Harvard University (MH-H). ■*Provenance:* bequeathed to MH in 1918 by Evert J. Wendell. ■*Emendations and textual notes:*

419.25	~~on~~ other •	on̸ther
420.9	$150. One •	~.—|~
420.18–19	un-Commonplace •	un-Common-|place
420.30	~~leaving~~ ˌhavingˌ •	leaᵥhaving
420.36	*un*-do •	[*possibly 'undo'*]
421.1	back •	back ~~back~~
421.29	~~damed~~ darned •	damerned

■ 29 June 1871 · To Orion Clemens · Elmira, N.Y. · *UCCL* 00628

■*Copy-text:* MS, Mark Twain Papers, The Bancroft Library, University of California, Berkeley (CU-MARK). ■*Previous publication: MTLP,* 68 n. 1 *top,* brief

excerpt. ■*Provenance:* see Mark Twain Papers in Description of Provenance.
■*Emendations and textual notes:*

423.23　　　ₓnewₓ • [*written off edge*]
423.23　　　think₍ • [*deletion implied*]

■ 29 June 1871 · To Mary Mason Fairbanks · Elmira, N.Y. · *UCCL* 00629
■*Copy-text:* MS, Huntington Library, San Marino (CSmH, call no. HM 14275).
■*Previous publication: MTMF,* 154–56. ■*Provenance:* see Huntington Library in Description of Provenance. ■*Emendations and textual notes:*

425.5　　　w̸ • [*partly formed*]

■ July? 1871 · To Pierre Reynolds · Elmira, N.Y. · *UCCL* 10651
■*Copy-text:* MS, Mark Twain Papers, The Bancroft Library, University of California, Berkeley (CU-MARK). The lower right corner of the MS page, probably cut from a larger sheet, is missing, reportedly having been eaten by a rat (see p. 427, n. 1 *top*). ■*Provenance:* see Tufts Collection in Description of Provenance. ■*Emendations and textual notes:*

426.1　　　ß • [*partly formed; possibly* 'g̸']
426.4　　　Twain) • Twa[◊◊◊] [*nibbled away*]

■ 2 July 1871 · To Orion Clemens · Elmira, N.Y. · *UCCL* 00630
■*Copy-text:* MS, Mark Twain Papers, The Bancroft Library, University of California, Berkeley (CU-MARK). ■*Previous publication: MTLP,* 67–68. ■*Provenance:* see Mark Twain Papers in Description of Provenance. ■*Emendations and textual notes:*

427.5　　　am still • amȿ still [*false start*]
427.9　　　Conn. • Conn[◊] [*torn*]

■ 2 July 1871 · To James N. Gillis · Elmira, N.Y. · *UCCL* 00631
■*Copy-text:* MS facsimile, Mark Twain Papers, The Bancroft Library, University of California, Berkeley (CU-MARK). ■*Provenance:* see Tufts Collection in Description of Provenance. Although the present location of the MS is not known, two other facsimiles are known to exist—one at CtY-BR, and one sold at auction in 1989, formerly in the Estelle Doheny Collection at St. John's Seminary in Camarillo, California (Christie 1989, lot 1752). ■*Emendations and textual notes:*

428.18–19   ~~Mother.~~ ‖ [¶] 4. • [*MS page 2 ends here and page 3 begins. The canceled passage may have continued onto another MS page 3 which Clemens discarded when he wrote the present one.*]

428.28   ELMIRA N.Y. JUL • [E◊◊◊◊A] N.Y. [JUL] [*badly inked*]

■ 7 July 1871 · To Orion Clemens · Elmira, N.Y. · *UCCL* 00633

■ *Copy-text:* MS, Jean Webster McKinney Family Papers, Vassar College Library (NPV). ■ *Provenance:* see McKinney Family Papers in Description of Provenance.

■ 7–8 July 1871 · To James Redpath · Elmira, N.Y. · *UCCL* 00632

■ *Copy-text:* MS, Harry Ransom Humanities Research Center, University of Texas, Austin (TxU). ■ *Provenance:* The MS, owned until his death by James Gordon Bennett, Jr. (1841–1918), editor of the New York *Herald*, was included in a sale of his estate in 1926 (Anderson Galleries 1926, lot 149). ■ *Emendations and textual notes:*

430.2   ẇ • [*partly formed*]
430.6   thin~~g~~king • ['g' *partly formed*]

■ 10 July 1871 · To Elisha Bliss, Jr. · Elmira, N.Y. · *UCCL* 11312

■ *Copy-text:* MS, Rowfant Club, Cleveland (OClRC). ■ *Provenance:* The MS, presumably kept in the American Publishing Company files after receipt, was in 1899 tipped into volume 1 of *The Innocents Abroad*, the first volume of set 272 of the "Autograph Edition" of *The Writings of Mark Twain*. The book and manuscript were owned by Adrian G. Newcomb, later by Dr. and Mrs. Charles Herndon, and finally by the Rowfant Club. ■ *Emendations and textual notes:*

431.16   T̶ • [*partly formed*]
431.16   FLUSH TIMES • [*capitals simulated, not underscored*]
431.18–21   SILVER MINES . . . A PERSONAL NARRATIVE [*small capitals simulated, not underscored*]

■ 10 July 1871 · ~~To George L. Fall~~ To James Redpath · (1st of 3) · Elmira, N.Y. · *UCCL* 00634

■ *Copy-text:* MS, Clifton Waller Barrett Library, University of Virginia, Charlottesville (ViU). ■ *Provenance:* deposited at ViU by Clifton Waller Barrett on 17 December 1963. ■ *Emendations and textual notes:*

432.3   letter • l~~l~~etter
433.9   prejudice • preju~~j~~dice

433.10   ẇ • [*partly formed*]
433.14   once. Don't • ~.—|~

■ 10 July 1871 · To James Redpath · (2nd of 3) · Elmira, N.Y. · *UCCL* 00634

■ *Copy-text:* MS facsimile. The editors have not seen the MS, which was owned in 1981 by Mr. and Mrs. Roy J. Friedman, who provided a photocopy. The MS is now at the Library of Congress (DLC). ■ *Previous publication:* excerpts in Will M. Clemens 1900, 28; *MTL,* 1:189; Horner, 167; "Letters to James Redpath," *Mark Twain Quarterly* 5 (Winter–Spring 1942): 20; Chester L. Davis 1978, 3. All excerpts include a last line which does not appear in the MS and which is evidently taken from a letter of 13 February 1872 to Redpath: "Success to Fall's carbuncle and many happy returns." ■ *Provenance:* deposited in DLC by Roy J. Friedman in 1993. ■ *Emendations and textual notes:*

434.4   Southend • South-|end
434.7   pav • [*possibly* 'pay'; 'y' *partly formed*]
434.10   clin client • clińent

■ 10 July 1871 · To James Redpath · (3rd of 3) · Elmira, N.Y. · *UCCL* 00634

■ *Copy-text:* MS facsimile. The editors have not seen the MS, which is in the collection of Fred D. Bentley, who provided a photocopy in 1983. ■ *Previous publication:* Swann Auction Galleries, lot 61. ■ *Provenance:* Sold by Swann in 1942, the MS was eventually acquired by Bentley. ■ *Emendations and textual notes:*

435.3   un-Commonplace • un-Commonçplace
435.12   Lecture • Lectur[◊] [*written off edge*]

■ 14 July 1871 · To James Redpath · Elmira, N.Y. · *UCCL* 00637

■ *Copy-text:* Will M. Clemens 1900, 28. ■ *Previous publication:* Horner, 167–68; "Letters to James Redpath," *Mark Twain Quarterly* 5 (Winter–Spring 1942): 20. ■ *Emendations and textual notes:*

435.13   Elmira, July 14. • ELMIRA, July 14, 1871. [*dateline emended to Clemens's usual form; see 10 July 71 to Redpath (1st) and (2nd)*]
435.14   Dear Redpath: • *Dear Redpath:*
436.1   & • and [*twice*]
436.4   Mark • MARK

■ 19 July 1871 · To James Redpath · Elmira, N.Y. · *UCCL* 10497

■ *Copy-text:* MS, collection of Todd M. Axelrod. ■ *Previous publication:* Bangs, lot 81, brief excerpt. ■ *Provenance:* The present location of the MS, sold to an unidentified purchaser in 1900 and owned by Axelrod in 1983, is not known.

■ 20 July 1871 · To George L. Fall · Elmira, N.Y. · *UCCL* 00638

■ *Copy-text:* None. The text is based on two transcripts, each of which derives independently from the MS:

P¹	*MTL*, 1:189–90
P²	AAA 1925, lot 28

The rationale for emendations to remove *MTL* styling is given in Description of Texts. P² introduces the letter as "Elmira, July 20, To Friend Fall, reading in part." ■ *Emendations, adopted readings, and textual notes:* Adopted readings followed by '(C)' are editorial emendations of the source readings.

437.1	Elmira, July 20. (C) • ELMIRA, *N. Y. July 20, 1871.* (P¹); Elmira, July 20, (P²) [*reported, not quoted*]
437.2–3	Friend Fall: | [¶] Redpath (C) • FRIEND FALL,—Redpath (P¹); To Friend Fall, reading in part,—"Redpath (P²)
437.3	blow you (P²) • blow (P¹)
437.3	goes! (P¹) • ~. (P²)
437.3	wanted you (P¹) • wanted (P²)
437.4	ain't (P¹) • aint (P²)
437.5	there, & now (C) • there and now (P¹); there, now (P²)
437.5	they've (P²) • they have (P¹)
437.5	a hard town to (P¹) • as hard to (P²)
437.6–7	—I . . . engagement. (P¹) • [*not in*] (P²)
437.6	& (C) • and (P¹)
437.7	$150, (P²) • ~∧ (P¹)
437.7	& (P²) • and (P¹)
437.8–9	Yours, | Mark. (C) • Yours, | MARK. (P¹); Mark. (P²)

■ 23 July 1871 · To William Bowen · Elmira, N.Y. · *UCCL* 00639

■ *Copy-text:* MS, Clifton Waller Barrett Library, University of Virginia, Charlottesville (ViU). ■ *Provenance:* The MS was evidently owned at least until 1921 by Dora C. Bowen, William Bowen's second wife (signed statement dated 16 Oct 1921, ViU). It was deposited at ViU by Clifton Waller Barrett on 17 December 1963. ■ *Emendations and textual notes:*

438.3	$5 $150 • $$150 ['$' *partly formed*]

■ 24 July 1871 · To Adolph H. Sutro · Elmira, N.Y. · *UCCL* 00640

■ *Copy-text:* MS, Hamlin Garland Collection, the University Library, University of Southern California, Los Angeles (CLSU). ■ *Provenance:* The Garland Collection was acquired by CLSU in 1940 and shortly thereafter.

■ 31 July 1871 · To Edward P. Ackerman · Elmira, N.Y. · *UCCL* 00641

■ *Copy-text:* MS, in Edward P. Ackerman's autograph album, The New York Public Library, Astor, Lenox and Tilden Foundations (NN). ■ *Previous publication:* "Mark Twain on the New Beecher Church," Buffalo *Courier,* 16 Sept 71, Supplement, 1, with omissions; "Odds and Ends," Hartford *Courant,* 16 Sept 71, 2, excerpt.

■ 8 August 1871 · To James Redpath · Hartford, Conn. · *UCCL* 00642

■ *Copy-text:* MS, Chicago Public Library (IC). ■ *Previous publication:* Will M. Clemens 1900, 28; *MTL,* 1:190; Horner, 168–69; "Letters to James Redpath," *Mark Twain Quarterly* 5 (Winter–Spring 1942): 20; all with omissions. ■ *Provenance:* donated to IC in 1976 by Mrs. Leon Mandel. ■ *Emendations and textual notes:*

441.8   it. You · ~.—|~

■ 8 or 9 August 1871 · To Olivia L. Clemens · Hartford, Conn. · *UCCL* 00643

■ *Copy-text:* MS, Mark Twain Papers, The Bancroft Library, University of California, Berkeley (CU-MARK). ■ *Previous publication: LLMT,* 158. ■ *Provenance:* see Samossoud Collection in Description of Provenance. ■ *Emendations and textual notes:*

442.4   him. But · ~.—|~
442.21   CT. · [CT◊] [*badly inked*]

■ 10 August 1871 · To Olivia L. Clemens · Hartford, Conn. · *UCCL* 00644

■ *Copy-text:* MS, Mark Twain Papers, The Bancroft Library, University of California, Berkeley (CU-MARK). ■ *Previous publication:* Hill, 48, 54, brief excerpts; *LLMT,* 159–60. ■ *Provenance:* see Samossoud Collection in Description of Provenance. ■ *Emendations and textual notes:*

443.19   s̶o̶ such · s◊uch
444.8   h̶e̶e̶d̶l̶e̶s̶s̶ · [*false ascenders/descenders*]

444.15	landlady • land-|lady
444.24	Good-night • Good-|night
444.29	do. Good • ~.—|~
444.37	CT. • [CT]. [*badly inked*]

■ 17 August 1871 · To Horace Greeley · Hartford, Conn. · *UCCL* 00645

■ *Copy-text:* MS, The New York Public Library, Astor, Lenox and Tilden Foundations (NN). ■ *Provenance:* Before the MS was acquired by NN, it was in the collection of businessman and patron of the arts Gordon Lester Ford (1823–91). ■ *Emendations and textual notes:*

446.5	$ • [*partly formed*]

■ 18 August 1871 · To Olivia L. Clemens · Hartford, Conn. · *UCCL* 00646

■ *Copy-text:* MS, Mark Twain Papers, The Bancroft Library, University of California, Berkeley (CU-MARK). ■ *Previous publication: LLMT*, 361, brief paraphrase. ■ *Provenance:* see Samossoud Collection in Description of Provenance. ■ *Emendations and textual notes:*

446.8	reigns • reighns ['h' *partly formed*]
447.4	CT. • [CT]. [*badly inked*]

■ 19 August 1871 · To Adolph H. Sutro · Hartford, Conn. · *UCCL* 00647

■ *Copy-text:* MS, Iwaki Meisei University, Iwaki City, Japan (JIm). ■ *Previous publication:* Chester L. Davis 1949, 8. ■ *Provenance:* The letter was sold by the Holmes Book Company, Oakland, probably in 1949; again in 1969 (and perhaps in 1972) by the Scriptorium, Los Angeles; and by 1976 it had been bought by Theodore H. Koundakjian, who sold it to JIm in 1987. ■ *Emendations and textual notes:*

447.8	to-day • to-|day
447.14	England, • [*deletion implied*]

■ 24 August 1871 · To Adolph H. Sutro, *per* Telegraph Operator · Hartford, Conn. · *UCCL* 03649

■ *Copy-text:* MS facsimile. The editors have not seen the MS, copy received, telegram blank filled out in the hand of a telegraph operator, Dartmouth College

LIST OF OFFICES IN NEW YORK AND BROOKLYN.			
NAME OF OFFICE.	LOCATION.	NAME OF OFFICE.	LOCATION.
* † GENERAL OFFICE......	145 Broadway, cor. Liberty.	GRAND HOTEL.........	Cor. Broadway and 31st St.
ASTOR HOUSE.........	Broadway, cor. Vesey.	HOFFMAN HOUSE......	Broadway, bet. 24th and 25th Sts.
ASTORIA, L. I.........	Cor. Fulton and Main.	HUNTER'S POINT, L. I..	Long Island Railroad Depot.
ALLERTON'S, WEST....	Drove Yards, W. 40th St., cor. 11th Ave.	HARLEM..............	Harlem R. R., 4th Ave., b. 124th & 125th Sts.
APPLETON'S, N. Y......	D. Appleton & Co.'s, 549 & 551 B'way.	METROPOLITAN HOTEL	Cor. Broadway and Prince.
APPLETON'S, L. I......	D. Appleton & Co.'s Factory, W'msburgh.	MADISON SQUARE.....	945 Broadway.
BROAD STREET........	No. 22, near Exchange Place.	MANHATTANVILLE....	Hudson River R. R., 125th St., N. R.
† BROOKLYN, L. I......	333 Washington St., near Post Office.	NEW YORK HOTEL....	Broadway, cor. Washington & Waverley Place.
" "	338 Fulton St. (Erie R. R. Office).	NEWS ROOM..........	Merchants' Exchange, 50 and 52 Pine.
" "	Hamilton Ave., cor. Union St.	NAT'N'L DROVE YARDS	100th St., bet. 3d and 4th Aves.
" "	67 North 4th St., E. D.	PIER 30, N. R........	
BROADWAY...........	Junction, 6th Ave., near 35th St.	PIER 40, N. R.	
BEAVER & WILLIAM ST.	S. E. corner.	PARK HOTEL.........	Cor. Beekman and Nassau.
BARGE OFFICE........	Marine News Depot, near South Ferry.	PEARL STREET........	No. 134, near Beaver.
BOARD OF BROKERS..	Stock Exchange, 12 Broad.	PARK PLACE.........	Wescott's Express, No. 7 Park Place.
COSMOPOLITAN HOTEL.	129 Chambers, cor. West Broadway.	ST. JOHN'S PARK.....	H.R.R.R Freight Depot, cor. Laight & Varick.
CHAMBERS STREET....	S. W. cor. Broadway.	ST. JAMES HOTEL....	Cor. Broadway and 26th St.
CANAL STREET........	S. E. cor. Broadway.	ST. NICHOLAS HOTEL.	515 Broadway, cor. Spring.
CLAFLIN'S............	H. B. Claflin & Co.'s store, 140 Church.	SPRING ST...........	N. W. cor. Broadway.
CORN EXCHANGE......	Cor. Pearl and Moore.	SIXTH AVENUE.......	C. A. Kittle's, 765 Sixth Ave., near 43d St.
COLEMAN HOUSE......	Cor. Broadway and 27th St.	STEWART'S...........	A. T. Stewart & Co.'s, cor. B'way & Cham's.
CASTLE GARDEN......	The Battery.	STATION "H"........	P. O. Station "H," 978 3d Ave.
COOPER UNION........	7th St., cor. 3d and 4th Aves.	TWO FORTY-ONE B'W'Y	241 Broadway, near Park Place.
DRY DOCK...........	Greenpoint Ferry House, foot E. 10th St.	TWENTY-THIRD ST....	N. W. cor. Broadway.
DUANE STREET........	S. W. cor. Broadway.	TRINITY BUILDINGS...	Room No. 9.
EARLE'S HOTEL.......	Cor. Canal and Centre.	TWENTY-SIXTH STREET	Cor. 4th Ave., Harlem R. R. Depot.
EVERETT HOUSE......	Union Square, cor. 4th Ave. & E. 17th St.	TWENTY-SEVENTH ST.	Cor. 4th Ave., New Haven R. R. Depot.
EIGHTH AVENUE......	No. 95, bet. 14th and 15th Sts.	THIRTIETH STREET....	Cor. 10th Ave., Hudson River R. R. Depot.
* † FIFTH AVE. HOTEL.	5th Ave., cor. 23d St.	UNION LEAGUE CLUB.	Cor. 26th St. and Madison Ave.
FRANKLIN STREET....	Comm'l Agent's Exchange, cor. B'dway.	WALL STREET........	No. 21, cor. Broad.
FULTON MARKET......	83 Fish Market.	WASHINGTON MARKET	100 Vesey St.
FORT HAMILTON, L. I...	Church's Store.	WILLIAMSBURGH, L. I.	67 North 4th St.
GILSEY HOUSE........	Cor. Broadway.	WESTCHESTER HOUSE.	Cor. Bowery and Broome.
GR'ND CENTRAL HOTEL	Broadway, opp. Bond St.	YORKVILLE...........	P. O. Station "K," 171 E. 86th St., n. 3d Ave.
GOLD ROOM...........	18 New St.		

Offices marked * are always open.   Offices marked † are open on Sundays.

The verso of the telegraph form for 24 August 1871 to Sutro, on which New York City and Brooklyn telegraph offices were listed. Dartmouth College Library, Hanover (NhD). The docket in the upper right hand corner is transcribed on p. 448. The telegrams of 25 and 29 August 1871 to Sutro were transmitted on identical forms.

Library, Hanover (NhD). The printed verso of the telegraph form has not been transcribed as part of the text. It is reproduced in facsimile above at 61 percent of actual size. ■*Provenance:* donated to NhD in 1981 by Dr. Joseph H. Placak. ■*Emendations and textual notes:*

448.1   THE . . . COMPANY. • [*words on telegram blank identical to those reported in the commentary for 7 Nov 70 to Langdon*]

448.5   Sulro • [*sic*]

■ 25 August 1871 · To Adolph H. Sutro, *per* Telegraph Operator · Hartford, Conn. · *UCCL* 02815

■*Copy-text:* MS facsimile. The editors have not seen the MS, copy received, telegram blank filled out in the hand of a telegraph operator, Dartmouth College Library, Hanover (NhD). The printed verso of the telegraph form, identical to the form reproduced in facsimile above, has not been transcribed as part of the text. ■*Provenance:* donated to NhD in 1981 by Dr. Joseph H. Placak. ■*Emendations and textual notes:*

| 449.1 | THE . . . COMPANY. • [*words on telegram blank identical to those reported in the commentary for 7 Nov 70 to Langdon*] |
| 449.5 | Sulro • [*sic*] |

■ 29 August 1871 · To Adolph H. Sutro, *per* Telegraph Operator · Hartford, Conn. · *UCCL* 10728

■*Copy-text:* MS facsimile. The editors have not seen the MS, copy received, telegram blank filled out in the hand of a telegraph operator, Nevada State Historical Society, Reno (NvHi). The printed verso of the telegraph form, identical to the form reproduced in facsimile on p. 680, has not been transcribed as part of the text. ■*Emendations and textual notes:*

| 450.1 | THE . . . COMPANY. • [*words on telegram blank identical to those reported in the commentary for 7 Nov 70 to Langdon*] |

■ 30 August 1871 · To Ella Trabue Smith · Elmira, N.Y. · *UCCL* 00648

■*Copy-text:* MS facsimile. The editors have not seen the MS, which was owned by Mrs. Paul W. Franke in 1982. ■*Provenance:* Until 1972, the MS was owned by Mrs. Franke's mother, who provided a photocopy to CU-MARK in 1967, courtesy of Claude S. Brinegar. ■*Emendations and textual notes:*

| 451.4 | ~~haugh~~ • [*second 'h' partly formed*] |

■ 31 August 1871 · To Orion Clemens · Elmira, N.Y. · *UCCL* 00649

■*Copy-text:* MS, Mark Twain Papers, The Bancroft Library, University of California, Berkeley (CU-MARK). ■*Provenance:* see Mark Twain Papers in Description of Provenance. ■*Emendations and textual notes:*

| 452.7 | overfeeding • over-|feeding |

■ 8 September 1871 · To Olivia L. Clemens · Washington, D.C. · *UCCL* 00650

■*Copy-text:* MS, Mark Twain Papers, The Bancroft Library, University of California, Berkeley (CU-MARK). ■*Previous publication: LLMT,* 361, brief paraphrase. ■*Provenance:* see Samossoud Collection in Description of Provenance. ■*Emendations and textual notes:*

453.9	novelty • nov⁄elty
454.4	WASHINGTON • WASH[I◇G]TON [*badly inked*]

■ 15 September 1871 · To James Redpath · Elmira, N.Y. · *UCCL* 02457

■ *Copy-text:* MS, Henry W. and Albert A. Berg Collection, The New York Public Library, Astor, Lenox and Tilden Foundations (NN-B). ■ *Previous publication:* excerpts in *MTL*, 1:190–91; Horner, 169; Will M. Clemens 1900, 28; American Autograph Shop, Merion Station, Pa., undated catalog, item 70, with omissions; "Letters to James Redpath," *Mark Twain Quarterly* 5 (Winter–Spring 1942): 20. ■ *Provenance:* Until his death in 1939 the MS was owned by W. T. H. Howe; in 1940, the Howe Collection was purchased by Dr. Albert A. Berg and donated to NN (Cannon, 185–86). ■ *Emendations and textual notes:*

455.4	Bret Hart • [*sic*]
455.5	₿ • [*partly formed*]
455.7	₿ • [*partly formed*]
455.7	word. I • ~.—|~

■ 16 September 1871 · To Orion Clemens · Elmira, N.Y. · *UCCL* 00652

■ *Copy-text:* MS, Mark Twain Papers, The Bancroft Library, University of California, Berkeley (CU-MARK). ■ *Provenance:* see Mark Twain Papers in Description of Provenance. ■ *Emendations and textual notes:*

457.9	thing is • [*sic*]
457.9	railroad • rail-|road

■ 17 September 1871 · To Orion Clemens · Elmira, N.Y. · *UCCL* 00653

■ *Copy-text:* MS, Mark Twain Papers, The Bancroft Library, University of California, Berkeley (CU-MARK). ■ *Provenance:* see Mark Twain Papers in Description of Provenance. ■ *Emendations and textual notes:*

458.5	must write • must w̶r̶ write [*corrected miswriting; canceled 'r' partly formed*]

■ 22 September 1871 · To James Redpath · Buffalo, N.Y. · *UCCL* 10498

■ *Copy-text:* MS, collection of Todd M. Axelrod. ■ *Previous publication:* Bangs, lot 81, brief excerpt. ■ *Provenance:* The present location of the MS, sold to an

unidentified purchaser in 1900 and owned by Axelrod in 1983, is not known.
■ *Emendations and textual notes:*

459.13   ~~no~~ nice • nǿice

■ 26 September 1871 · To James Redpath · Buffalo, N.Y. · *UCCL*
00654

■ *Copy-text: MTL*, 1:191. The rationale for emendations to remove *MTL* styling
is given in Description of Texts. ■ *Emendations and textual notes:*

460.4   Buffalo, Sept. 26. • BUFFALO, *Sept. 26, 1871.*
460.5–6   Dear Redpath— | [¶] We • [¶] DEAR REDPATH,—We
460.6   & • and
461.1   now. • ∼∧
461.3   Mark. • MARK.

■ 28 September 1871 · To John A. Lant · Buffalo, N.Y. · *UCCL* 00655

■ *Copy-text:* MS, William K. Bixby Collection, Washington University, St. Louis
(MoSW).

■ 3? October 1871 · To Orion Clemens · Hartford, Conn. · *UCCL*
11800

■ *Copy-text:* Paraphrase in MS, Orion Clemens to Mary E. (Mollie) Clemens, 3
Oct 71 (*UCLC* 47049), Mark Twain Papers, The Bancroft Library, University
of California, Berkeley (CU-MARK).

■ 6 October 1871 · To Mortimer D. Leggett with an affidavit by John
Hooker · Hartford, Conn. · *UCCL* 00656

■ *Copy-text:* MS, United States National Archives and Records Service, National
Archives Library, Washington, D.C. (DNA). ■ *Previous publication:* Federico,
226–29; "Patent Files Hold Mark Twain Story," New York *Times*, 12 Mar 1939,
sec. 3:4; Brownell 1944, 2–3; and "Twain, the Patent Poet," *American Heritage*
29 (June–July 1978): 36, excerpts. ■ *Emendations and textual notes:*

462.18–463.1 ~~ph~~ prophecy • p/hrophecy [*canceled* 'h' *partly formed*]
463.1   ~~Am~~ An • A/mn
463.29   ~~bef~~ • ['f' *partly formed*]
465.4   HARTFORD CT. • [◊A]RTFORD [◊T.] [*badly inked*]

■ 9 October 1871 · To James Redpath · Hartford, Conn. · *UCCL* 00657

■*Copy-text:* MS, Cyril Clemens Collection, Mark Twain House, Hartford (CtHMTH). ■*Previous publication:* Anderson Auction Company 1903a, lot 123, brief paraphrase. ■*Provenance:* donated to CtHMTH in 1984 by Cyril Clemens. ■*Emendations and textual notes:*

466.4   Red—Redpath • Red⊥path

■ 9 October 1871 · To John Henry Riley · Hartford, Conn. · *UCCL* 02458

■*Copy-text:* MS, Henry W. and Albert A. Berg Collection, The New York Public Library, Astor, Lenox and Tilden Foundations (NN-B). ■*Provenance:* Until his death in 1939 the MS was owned by W. T. H. Howe; in 1940, the Howe Collection was purchased by Dr. Albert A. Berg and donated to NN (Cannon, 185–86). ■*Emendations and textual notes:*

467.12   tir try • tirry ['i' *partly formed*]

■ 11 October 1871 · To James Redpath and George L. Fall · Hartford, Conn. · *UCCL* 00659

■*Copy-text:* MS facsimile, University of Wisconsin, Madison (WU). ■*Provenance:* The present location of the MS is not known; the MS facsimile was donated to WU in March 1943 by E. E. Moore.

■ 14 October 1871 · To Olivia L. Clemens · New York, N.Y. · *UCCL* 00660

■*Copy-text:* MS, Mark Twain Papers, The Bancroft Library, University of California, Berkeley (CU-MARK). ■*Previous publication: LLMT*, 361, brief paraphrase. ■*Provenance:* see Samossoud Collection in Description of Provenance. ■*Emendations and textual notes:*

469.5   little else • little⊄ else [*false start; deletion implied*]
469.23   400 600 • ⱥ600
469.25   169 369 • ⱦ369

■ 15 October 1871 · To Olivia L. Clemens · Bethlehem, Pa. · *UCCL* 00661

■*Copy-text:* MS, Mark Twain Papers, The Bancroft Library, University of California, Berkeley (CU-MARK). ■*Previous publication: MFMT*, 50, excerpt;

LLMT, 361, brief paraphrase. ▪*Provenance:* see Samossoud Collection in Description of Provenance. ▪*Emendations and textual notes:*

471.7	~~cl~~ • [*possibly* 'sl']
471.14–15	JOHN GOttⱢL	IEB • [*capitals simulated, not underscored*]
471.17	~~1774~~ 1744 • 17⫽44
471.28	(intervening • [*no closing parenthesis*]
471.36	vault • vaulⱢt
472.2	~~shav~~ shades • sha⫽des
472.9	~~1871 1671~~ • 1⫽671
472.20	away • [a]away [*torn*]
472.22	to-day • to-|day

▪ 16 October 1871 · To Olivia L. Clemens · Bethlehem, Pa. · *UCCL* 00662

▪*Copy-text:* MS, Mark Twain Papers, The Bancroft Library, University of California, Berkeley (CU-MARK). ▪*Previous publication: LLMT,* 361, brief paraphrase. ▪*Provenance:* see Samossoud Collection in Description of Provenance. ▪*Emendations and textual notes:*

474.4	Ɫ • [*partly formed*]
474.13	oct • o[ct] [*badly inked*]

▪ 17 October 1871 · To Olivia L. Clemens · Allentown, Pa. · *UCCL* 00663

▪*Copy-text:* MS, Mark Twain Papers, The Bancroft Library, University of California, Berkeley (CU-MARK). ▪*Previous publication: LLMT,* 161–62. ▪*Provenance:* see Samossoud Collection in Description of Provenance. ▪*Emendations and textual notes:*

474.16	chuckle-headed • chuckle-|headed
475.1	~~on~~ out • o⫽ut ['n' *reused as* 'u']

▪ 18 October 1871 · To Olivia L. Clemens · Wilkes-Barre, Pa. · *UCCL* 00664

▪*Copy-text:* MS, Mark Twain Papers, The Bancroft Library, University of California, Berkeley (CU-MARK). ▪*Previous publication: LLMT,* 362, brief paraphrase. ▪*Provenance:* see Samossoud Collection in Description of Provenance. ▪*Emendations and textual notes:*

476.19   rise & • [*sic*]
476.25   WILKESBARRE PA. • [WIL◇E◇B]ARR[◇ ◇◇]. [*badly inked*]

■ 19 October 1871 · To Elisha Bliss, Jr. · Wilkes-Barre, Pa. · *UCCL* 00665

■*Copy-text:* MS, collection of Robert Daley until 1993. ■*Previous publication:* Hill, 54, brief excerpt; *MTLP,* 68; Sotheby 1993, lot 214, excerpt. ■*Provenance:* The MS evidently remained among the American Publishing Company's files until it was sold (and may have been at that time copied by Dana Ayer; see Brownell Collection in Description of Provenance). An Ayer handwritten transcription and a typed transcription are at WU. Robert Daley acquired the MS by 1974; Sotheby's sold it in 1993 to an unidentified purchaser.

■ 24 October 1871 · To James Redpath · Washington, D.C. · *UCCL* 00666

■*Copy-text:* MS, collection of Todd M. Axelrod. ■*Previous publication:* excerpts in Bangs, lot 81; Will M. Clemens 1900, 28; *MTL,* 1:193; Horner, 169–70; "Letters to James Redpath," *Mark Twain Quarterly* 5 (Winter–Spring 1942): 20; and Chester L. Davis 1978, 3. ■*Emendations and textual notes:*

478.3–4   *hash*-house • *hash*-h̶a̶s̶house
478.16   MARK. • [*capitals simulated, not underscored*]
478.18   I • [*possibly '7'*]

■ 28 October 1871 · To Olivia L. Clemens · Great Barrington, Mass. · *UCCL* 00667

■*Copy-text:* MS, collection of Roberт T. Slotta. ■*Previous publication:* Chester L. Davis 1977, 1–2; Christie 1991, lot 200, excerpt. ■*Provenance:* The MS, part of the Samossoud Collection in the late 1940s when it was transcribed by Dixon Wecter, was acquired before 1952 by Chester L. Davis, Sr., from Clara Clemens Samossoud (see Samossoud Collection in Description of Provenance). After Davis's death in 1987, the MS was owned by Chester L. Davis, Jr. In 1991, it was bought by the present owner. ■*Emendations and textual notes:*

482.6   T̶ • [*partly formed*]

■ 31 October 1871 · To Olivia L. Clemens · Milford, Mass. · *UCCL* 00668

■*Copy-text:* MS, Mark Twain Papers, The Bancroft Library, University of California, Berkeley (CU-MARK). ■*Previous publication: LLMT,* 162–63; Chester

L. Davis 1977, 1, excerpt. ■*Provenance:* see Samossoud Collection in Description of Provenance. ■*Emendations and textual notes:*

483.13	trains • ['in' *conflated*]
483.15	brother • broetther [*canceled* 't' *partly formed*]
483.15	tonight • to-|night

■ 1 November 1871 · To Olivia L. Clemens · Boston, Mass. · *UCCL* 00669

■*Copy-text:* MS, Mark Twain Papers, The Bancroft Library, University of California, Berkeley (CU-MARK). ■*Previous publication: LLMT,* 362, brief paraphrase. ■*Provenance:* see Samossoud Collection in Description of Provenance. ■*Emendations and textual notes:*

484.23	letters • ll letters
485.3	BOSTON • [BO◊◊◊N] [*badly inked*]

■ 9 November 1871 · To Olivia L. Clemens · Worcester, Mass. · *UCCL* 00670

■*Copy-text:* MS, Mark Twain Papers, The Bancroft Library, University of California, Berkeley (CU-MARK). ■*Previous publication. MFMT,* 45, with omissions. ■*Provenance:* see Samossoud Collection in Description of Provenance. ■*Emendations and textual notes:*

487.8	chairman • chair-|man [*also at 487.11*]
488.10	NOV • N[o◊] [*badly inked*]

■ 11 November 1871 · To Olivia L. Clemens · Boston, Mass. · *UCCL* 00671

■*Copy-text:* MS, Mark Twain Papers, The Bancroft Library, University of California, Berkeley (CU-MARK). ■*Previous publication: LLMT,* 362, brief paraphrase. ■*Provenance:* see Samossoud Collection in Description of Provenance. ■*Emendations and textual notes:*

488.11	(hang • [*no closing parenthesis*]
488.15	it. House • ~.—|~
488.19	hotels • hotelɇs
489.3	BOSTON MASS. NOV. 11 ◊ ◊M • [◊◊◊◊◊O]N [◊◊SS]. NOV. 11 [◊ ◊M] [*badly inked*]

■ 12 November 1871 · To Elisha Bliss, Jr. · Boston, Mass. · *UCCL* 00672

■*Copy-text:* MS, Mark Twain Papers, The Bancroft Library, University of California, Berkeley (CU-MARK). ■*Provenance:* see Mendoza Collection in Description of Provenance. ■*Emendations and textual notes:*

489.18   Clemeny · [*sic*]

■ 12 November 1871 · To Olivia L. Clemens · Boston, Mass. · *UCCL* 00673

■*Copy-text:* MS, Mark Twain Papers, The Bancroft Library, University of California, Berkeley (CU-MARK). ■*Previous publication:* Wecter 1948, 84. ■*Provenance:* see Samossoud Collection in Description of Provenance. ■*Emendations and textual notes:*

490.15   ₣ · [*partly formed*]
490.15   Hawthorne · Hawthorn[e] [*torn*]
490.16   BOSTON MASS. · [BOSTON MAS◇◇] [*badly inked*]
490.16   8 PM · [8 P]M [*badly inked*]

■ 15 November 1871 · To Olivia L. Clemens · Haverhill, Mass. · *UCCL* 00674

■*Copy-text:* MS, Mark Twain Papers, The Bancroft Library, University of California, Berkeley (CU-MARK). ■*Previous publication:* Wecter 1948, 84, with omission; *LLMT,* 163–64. ■*Provenance:* see Samossoud Collection in Description of Provenance.

■ 16 November 1871 · To Moses S. Beach · Portland, Maine · *UCCL* 00675

■*Copy-text:* MS, Clifton Waller Barrett Library, University of Virginia, Charlottesville (ViU). ■*Provenance:* deposited at ViU by Clifton Waller Barrett on 17 December 1963. ■*Emendations and textual notes:*

494.1   m̶o̶ · [*doubtful*]

■ 17 November 1871 · To Olivia L. Clemens · Portland, Maine · *UCCL* 00676

■*Copy-text:* MS, Mark Twain Papers, The Bancroft Library, University of California, Berkeley (CU-MARK). ■*Previous publication:* *LLMT,* 362, brief para-

phrase. ■*Provenance:* see Samossoud Collection in Description of Provenance.
■*Emendations and textual notes:*

495.4   Hawthorne • Hawthorn[◊] [*torn*]
495.7   PORTLAND ME. • P[ORT]L[AND ◊E◊] [*badly inked*]

■ 20 November 1871 · To Unidentified · Hartford, Conn. · *UCCL* 09850

■*Copy-text:* Paraphrase and transcript, Anderson Auction Company 1914, lot 101. The catalog describes the MS as 'CLEMENS (S. L.—"Mark Twain"). A. L. S., 8vo, Hartford, Nov. 20, 1871, on a full letter-sheet with his monogram.' The quotation marks around Clemens's pseudonym reflect catalog style and do not indicate how he signed his letter. He and Olivia were both using only her monogramed stationery at this time (see OLC to Howland, 20 Nov 71, and SLC to OLC, 27 Nov 71). ■*Emendations and textual notes:*

495.8   (LLC) • [*reported, not quoted*]
495.9   Hartford, Nov. 20. • [*reported, not quoted*]

■ 20 November 1871 · From Olivia L. Clemens to Robert M. Howland · Hartford, Conn. · *UCCL* 00677

■*Copy-text:* MS, Mark Twain Papers, The Bancroft Library, University of California, Berkeley (CU-MARK). ■*Provenance:* donated to CU-MARK in 1977 by Mr. and Mrs. Robert M. Gunn. ■*Emendations and textual notes:*

497.3   HARTFORD CT. • HAR[TFO]RD [C◊◊] [*badly inked*]
497.3–4   ST. NICHOLAS HOTEL, N. Y. • [◊T.] NICHOLAS H[OT◊]L[,] N. [Y]. [*badly inked*]

■ 27 November 1871 · To Olivia L. Clemens · Bennington, Vt. · *UCCL* 00680

■*Copy-text:* MS, Mark Twain Papers, The Bancroft Library, University of California, Berkeley (CU-MARK). ■*Previous publication: LLMT,* 165–66. ■*Provenance:* see Samossoud Collection in Description of Provenance. ■*Emendations and textual notes:*

498.2   Monday • M Monday [*corrected miswriting*]
498.3   much. A • ~.—|~
499.13   bedtime • bed-|time
499.19   BENNINGTON • B[EN◊◊N◊]TON [*badly inked*]
499.19   NOV. • [◊◊◊◊] [*badly inked*]

■ 28 November 1871 · To George L. Fall · Albany, N.Y. · *UCCL* 11412

■ *Copy-text:* MS, collection of Nick Karanovich. ■ *Previous publication:* Heritage Book Shop, item 31, excerpt. ■ *Emendations and textual notes:*

501.19–20	~~ON~~ . . . ~~ACKNOWLEDGMENT.~~ •	[*canceled by George Hathaway*]
502.3	exhuberance •	[*sic*]

■ 29–30 November 1871 · To James Redpath and George L. Fall · ?Newark, N.J. · *UCCL* 11823

■ *Copy-text:* Paraphrase in MS, James Redpath to SLC, 18 Jan 72 (*UCLC* 31791), Mark Twain Papers, The Bancroft Library, University of California, Berkeley (CU-MARK).

■ 3 December 1871 · To Olivia L. Clemens · Homer, N.Y. · *UCCL* 00684

■ *Copy-text:* MS, Mark Twain Papers, The Bancroft Library, University of California, Berkeley (CU-MARK). ■ *Previous publication:* LLMT, 362, brief paraphrase. ■ *Provenance:* see Samossoud Collection in Description of Provenance. ■ *Emendations and textual notes:*

503.14	~~187~~ 1867 •	18⫽67
504.22	HOMER N.Y. DEC 3 •	[HOM]ER [N.]Y[◊] DEC [3] [*badly inked*]

■ 4 December 1871 · To Olivia L. Clemens · Geneva, N.Y. · *UCCL* 00685

■ *Copy-text:* MS, Mark Twain Papers, The Bancroft Library, University of California, Berkeley (CU-MARK). ■ *Previous publication:* LLMT, 362, brief paraphrase. ■ *Provenance:* see Samossoud Collection in Description of Provenance. ■ *Emendations and textual notes:*

506.7	~~pea~~ preachers •	peareachers
506.8	whole-hearted •	whole-|hearted
506.16	~~not~~ •	['t' *partly formed*]
507.9	them⸲ ⫽ One •	~⸲— ⫽ | ~
507.9	~~had~~ has •	ha⫽s
507.26	GENEVA •	[GENE]VA [*badly inked*]

■ 5 December 1871 · To Olivia L. Clemens · Auburn, N.Y. · *UCCL* 00686

■ *Copy-text:* MS, Mark Twain Papers, The Bancroft Library, University of California, Berkeley (CU-MARK). ■ *Previous publication: LLMT,* 362, brief paraphrase. ■ *Provenance:* see Samossoud Collection in Description of Provenance. ■ *Emendations and textual notes:*

509.3	& me · [*sic*]
509.6–7	~~gener~~ genuine · gene*ruine*
509.10	some · so¢me

■ 8 December 1871 · To James Redpath and George L. Fall, *per* Telegraph Operator · Buffalo, N.Y. · *UCCL* 00687

■ *Copy-text:* MS, copy received, telegram blank filled out in the hand of a telegraph operator, collection of Victor and Irene Murr Jacobs, Roesch Library, University of Dayton (ODaU). ■ *Previous publication:* Will M. Clemens 1900, 28; John Anderson, Jr., 1903a, lot 49, excerpt; Anderson Auction Company 1910, lot 180; *MTL,* 1:193; AAA 1925, lot 108, excerpt; Horner, 170; "Letters to James Redpath," *Mark Twain Quarterly* 5 (Winter–Spring 1942): 20, excerpt. ■ *Emendations and textual notes:*

511.2	THE . . . COMPANY. · [*words on telegram blank identical to those reported in the commentary for 7 Nov 70 to Langdon*]

■ 9? December 1871 · To James Redpath · ?Fredonia, N.Y. · *UCCL* 09706

■ *Copy-text:* None. The text is based on two partial transcripts, each of which derives directly from the MS.

P¹	John Anderson, Jr., 1903, lot 51
P²	Anderson Auction Company 1903b, lot 125

P¹ describes the MS as "A. L. S. 2pp. 8vo. 1871"; P² repeats the description, but misdates the letter 1877. Neither catalog identifies the addressee. ■ *Emendations, adopted readings, and textual notes:* Adopted readings followed by '(C)' are editorial emendations of the source readings.

512.4–5	. . . .	[¶] I (C) · [¶] "* * * ~ (P¹); [*not in*] (P²)
512.5–6	like . . . Vandal. (P¹) · [*not in*] (P²)
512.6	"Vandal" (C) · 'Vandal' (P¹)
512.7	. . . You (P²) · [*not in*] (P¹)
512.7–9	can . . . platform. (P²) · [*not in*] (P¹)
512.9	*won't* (P²) · won't (P¹)
512.9	so (P²) · as (P¹)

512.10　　　Ward, (P²) • ∼∧ (P¹)
512.10　　　subject. (C) • ∼." Etc. (P¹); ∼," etc. (P²)
512.12　　　Mark. (P²) • [*not in*] (P¹)

■ 10 December 1871 · To Mary Mason Fairbanks · Erie, Pa. · *UCCL* 00688

■ *Copy-text:* MS, Huntington Library, San Marino (CSmH, call no. HM 14256). ■ *Previous publication: MTMF,* 157. ■ *Provenance:* see Huntington Library in Description of Provenance. ■ *Emendations and textual notes:*

513.4　　　ẇ • [*partly formed*]
513.12　　　rewriting • re-|writing

■ 11 December 1871 · To James Redpath · Toledo, Ohio · *UCCL* 00689

■ *Copy-text:* MS, Houghton Library, Harvard University (MH-H). ■ *Provenance:* bequeathed to MH in 1918 by Evert J. Wendell. ■ *Emendations and textual notes:* The top left/right corners of every leaf were pasted together in the MS covering some portions of words; the top leaf has been torn away, leaving fragments of the corner pasted to the next leaf. All characters transcribed can be seen either in the fragments or through the pasted paper.

514.21　　　tickets/ • [*deletion implied*]

■ 18 December 1871 · To Olivia L. Clemens · Chicago, Ill. · *UCCL* 00690

■ *Copy-text:* MS, Mark Twain Papers, The Bancroft Library, University of California, Berkeley (CU-MARK). ■ *Previous publication:* Wecter 1948, 84–85; *LLMT,* 169–70. ■ *Provenance:* see Samossoud Collection in Description of Provenance. ■ *Emendations and textual notes:*

517.3　　　train. I • ∼.—|∼
517.4　　　hours—we • hours—ẇ‖ —we
517.16　　　p̶e̶o̶ • ['o' *partly formed*]
517.20　　　o̶n̶ ̶m̶y̶ • ['my' *conflated*]
517.31　　　&̶ ̶g̶ • ['g' *partly formed*]
518.3　　　CHICAGO ILL. • [CHICA◊O ILL.] [*badly inked*]

■ 24 December 1871 · From Olivia L. and Samuel L. Clemens to Orion and Mary E. (Mollie) Clemens · Hartford, Conn. · *UCCL* 00692

■ *Copy-text:* MS, Mark Twain Papers, The Bancroft Library, University of California, Berkeley (CU-MARK). ■ *Provenance:* see Mark Twain Papers in Description of Provenance.

■ 25 December 1871 · To Olivia L. Clemens · Chicago, Ill. · *UCCL* 00693

■*Copy-text:* MS, Mark Twain Papers, The Bancroft Library, University of California, Berkeley (CU-MARK). ■*Previous publication: MFMT,* 53, excerpt (includes as part of text an excerpt from 21 Nov 73 to OLC). ■*Provenance:* see Samossoud Collection in Description of Provenance. ■*Emendations and textual notes:*

521.24	epidemic. Here • ~.—|~
522.3	ILL • [ILL] [*badly inked*]

■ 26 December 1871 · To Olivia L. Clemens · Champaign, Ill. · *UCCL* 00694

■*Copy-text:* MS, Mark Twain Papers, The Bancroft Library, University of California, Berkeley (CU-MARK). ■*Previous publication: LLMT,* 171; *MTMF,* 159 n. 2, brief excerpt. ■*Provenance:* see Samossoud Collection in Description of Provenance. ■*Emendations and textual notes:*

522.9	afternoon • after-|noon
522.21	Hawthorne • Hawthorn[◊] [*torn*]
522.22	ILL • [◊◊◊] [*badly inked*]

■ 27 December 1871 · To Olivia L. Clemens · Tuscola, Ill. · *UCCL* 00695

■*Copy-text:* MS, Mark Twain Papers, The Bancroft Library, University of California, Berkeley (CU-MARK). ■*Previous publication: MFMT,* 48–49, excerpt. ■*Provenance:* see Samossoud Collection in Description of Provenance. ■*Emendations and textual notes:*

524.4	behind • be⌀hind
524.7	baggage. Found • ~.—|~
524.8	~~spe~~ splendid • sp⌀lendid
524.10	~~pile~~ i • [*second 'i' partly formed*]
525.1	tonight • to-|night
525.1	~~got~~ • ['t' *partly formed*]
525.5	time-table • time-ti~~m~~able
525.16	TUSCOLA ILL. DEC 29 • [T◊◊COL]A [I]LL. DEC 2[9] [*badly inked*]

■ 28 December 1871 · To Olivia L. Clemens · Danville, Ill. · *UCCL* 00696

■*Copy-text:* MS, Mark Twain Papers, The Bancroft Library, University of California, Berkeley (CU-MARK). ■*Previous publication: LLMT,* 362, brief para-

phrase. ∎*Provenance:* see Samossoud Collection in Description of Provenance.
∎*Emendations and textual notes:*

526.13   st • s[◊] [*torn*]
526.14   DEC 28 • D[EC 28] [*badly inked*]

∎ 28 December 1871 · To Jane Lampton Clemens · Danville, Ill. ·
  UCCL 00697

∎*Copy-text:* MS, Jean Webster McKinney Family Papers, Vassar College Library (NPV). ∎*Provenance:* see McKinney Family Papers in Description of
Provenance. ∎*Emendations and textual notes:*

527.5   ~~word~~ work • wor◊k

∎ 31 December 1871 · To Olivia L. Clemens · Paris, Ill. · *UCCL* 00700

∎*Copy-text:* MS, Mark Twain Papers, The Bancroft Library, University of California, Berkeley (CU-MARK). ∎*Previous publication: MFMT,* 9–12, with
omissions. ∎*Provenance:* see Samossoud Collection in Description of Provenance. ∎*Emendations and textual notes:*

528.12–13   gallery-front; ◊ • [*possibly* 'gallery-front; &']
528.13   severe • ~~sev~~ | severe [*corrected miswriting*]
529.19   peanut • pea-|nut
529.27   skylark • sky-|lark
529.28–29   ◊ young • ['y' *over* 'a']
529.32   un-churchlike • un-church-|like
530.12   ~~su~~ • ['u' *partly formed*]
530.12   sweetheart • sweet-|heart
530.15   troubles. Be • ~.—|~
530.21   Coneticut • Conetic[◊◊] [*torn*]
530.22   PARIS • [PARIS] [*badly inked*]

∎ Appendix B: Enclosure with 31 March 1870 · To Charles F. Wingate
  · Buffalo, N.Y.

∎*Copy-text:* Copy-text is the typesetting of David Gray, "New Publications,"
Buffalo *Courier,* 19 Mar 70, which appeared unaltered in both the "Saturday
Morning" edition, 2, and the "Saturday Evening" edition, no page. The more
legible reading is chosen from either of two copies in CU-MARK: a PH of the
"Morning Edition," faint in places, or a clipping of the "Evening Edition,"
partly torn; the original clipping Clemens enclosed is not known to survive.

■ Appendix B: Enclosure with 1 April 1870 · To Jervis and Olivia Lewis Langdon · Buffalo, N.Y.

■ *Copy-text:* "More Wisdom," Buffalo *Express,* 9 Mar 70, 2 (SLC 1870s). Copy-text is a microfilm edition of the newspaper in the Buffalo and Erie County Public Library, Buffalo, N.Y. (NBu). The original clipping Clemens enclosed, a reprint of the Buffalo *Express* from an unidentified Pottsville, Pennsylvania, newspaper, is not known to survive. ■ *Emendations and textual notes:*

546.16   Shamokin · Skamokin
547.19   down-trodden · ~-|~

■ Appendix B: Enclosure with 30 January 1871 · To James Redpath · Buffalo, N.Y.

■ *Copy-text:* James Redpath, "The Lecture System," Cleveland *Herald,* 28 Jan 71, no page. Copy-text is a photograph of the article from the newspaper in the Ohio Historical Society, Columbus; the original clipping Clemens enclosed is not known to survive. ■ *Emendations and textual notes:*

550.9   the whole · the | the whole
552.7   *un esprit du corps* · [*sic*]
553.21   could'nt · [*sic*]

■ Appendix E: Contract for *Roughing It* · 15 July 1870 · Elmira, N.Y.

■ *Copy-text:* MS of Clemens's copy, drafted by Elisha Bliss, Jr., Mark Twain Papers, The Bancroft Library, University of California, Berkeley (CU-MARK). ■ *Provenance:* see Mark Twain Papers in Description of Provenance. ■ *Emendations and textual notes:*

565.3   wittnesseth · [*sic*]
566.15   Sccty · ['cty' *conflated*]

■ *Collation:* Variant readings from the photofacsimile of Elisha Bliss's copy of the contract, Mark Twain House, Hartford (CtHMTH), are recorded below (entries on the right of the bullet). The original is at CtY-BR.

565.1   A D. · ~ ~∧
565.2   said N York · said state
565.2–3   the American · American
565.7   next, · ~∧
565.7   if said Company · if they ∧the sd company∧
565.7   it— · ~.—
565.9   proofreading · proof reading
565.9–10 authors · Authors

565.10   sale, • ~ₐ

565.12   company • ~,

565.12   preparation . . . book, • term said manuscript & book are being prepared & sold or throw any other obstacle in the way of sale of said book

565.12–14   or w̶r̶ furnish . . . parties— • ₐor w̶r̶ ₐfurnishₐ . . . parties—ₐ

565.14   [*no* ¶] The • [¶] ~

565.15   Book • book

565.15   style, • ~—

565.16   manuscript, • Manuscript

566.2   do • ~,

566.4   s̶a̶l̶ • [*not in*]

566.4   to [pay] • also to pay

566.5   the retail • the s̶e̶l̶l̶i̶n̶g̶ ̶p̶r̶i̶c̶e̶ ̶a̶t̶ ₓtheₓ retail

566.6   book, • work

566.7   said • sd

566.9   time • ~—

566.10–11   American Publishing Co. | E Bliss Jr Secty • Sam' L. Clemens. | E Bliss Jr Secty | American Pub. Co

566.12–22   The . . . Roughing It • [*on the back as folded:*] S L Clemens | contract No 2 | July 15ᵗʰ 1870 | for Roughing It | ₐEndorsed on the Duplicate—that the book Mss has been deliveredₐ

■ Appendix E: Contract for Diamond Mine Book · 6 December 1870 · Hartford, Conn.

■*Copy-text:* MS of Clemens's copy, drafted by Elisha Bliss, Jr., Mark Twain Papers, The Bancroft Library, University of California, Berkeley (CU-MARK). ■*Provenance:* see Mark Twain Papers in Description of Provenance. ■*Emendations and textual notes:*

567.3–4   wittnesseth • [*sic*]

568.12   6— • [*badly written dash retraced for clarity in pencil by Bliss*]

References

THIS LIST defines the abbreviations used in this book and provides full bibliographic information for works cited by the author's name and publication date, or by a short title. Alphabetization is letter-by-letter: i.e., "Anderson Galleries" precedes "Anderson, John."

AAA.
   1914. *Catalogue of Autograph Letters and Documents . . . the Private Collection of George P. Upton, Esquire.* Sale of 23 April. New York: American Art Association.
   1916. *Catalogue of Autograph Letters and Documents of Royalty, Statesmen, Authors and Other Celebrities.* Sale of 11 and 12 May. New York: American Art Association.
   1924a. *The Renowned Collection of the Late William F. Gable of Altoona, Pennsylvania.* Part 4. Sale of 10 and 11 March. New York: American Art Association.
   1924b. *The Renowned Collection of the Late William F. Gable of Altoona, Pennsylvania.* Part 5. Sale of 24 and 25 November. New York: American Art Association.
   1924c. *Fine Books and Manuscripts of the Greatest Rarity and Interest. Including the Further Property of a Prominent Pennsylvania Collector.* Sale of 1 and 2 December. New York: American Art Association.
   1925. *The Renowned Collection of the Late William F. Gable of Altoona, Pennsylvania.* Part 6. Sale of 8 and 9 January. New York: American Art Association.
   1927a. *Autograph Letters by Celebrated Authors . . . the Estate of John Quinn, Deceased, with Additions as Indicated.* Sale of 8 and 9 February. New York: American Art Association.
   1927b. *The Notable Library of Major W. Van R. Whitall of Pelham, New York.* Sale of 14, 15, and 16 February. New York: American Art Association.
   1927c. *First Editions of XIXth Century Authors.* Sale of 31 March and 1 April. New York: American Art Association.
AAA/Anderson.
   1934a. *First Editions and Manuscripts Collected by the Late Mr. and Mrs. William*

K. Bixby, Sold by Order of the Heirs. Sale no. 4098 (4 and 5 April). New York: American Art Association, Anderson Galleries.

1934b. *The Fine Library of the Late Mrs. Benjamin Stern, Together with Autograph Letters from the Collection of William L. Clements and E. W. Evans, Jr., and Other Properties.* Sale no. 4111 (9, 10, and 11 May). New York: American Art Association, Anderson Galleries.

1935a. *Books, Autographs and Drawings.* Sale no. 4143 (9 and 10 January). New York: American Art Associaton, Anderson Galleries.

1935b. *First Editions and Manuscripts of Modern Authors, Early English Literature. . . . The Balance of the Eugene Field Collection of the Late Mr. and Mrs. William K. Bixby, St. Louis, Missouri; and Other Properties.* Sale no. 4160 (13 and 14 March). New York: American Art Associaton, Anderson Galleries.

1935c. *Handsomely Bound Set of Esteemed Authors . . . the Library of the Late Richard P. H. Durkee, New York . . . the Remaining Portion of the Library of the Late Hannah M. Standish, Pittsburgh, Pennsylvania, and Other Properties.* Sale no. 4215 (14 December). New York: American Art Association, Anderson Galleries.

1936a. *The Library of the Late Elbridge L. Adams, New York City, . . . First Editions and Manuscripts of Works by Samuel L. Clemens, Mainly the Collection of Irving S. Underhill, Buffalo, N.Y.* Sale no. 4228 (29 and 30 January). New York: American Art Association, Anderson Galleries.

1936b. *First Editions, Autograph Letters and Manuscripts, Original Drawings and Standard Sets.* Sale no. 4238 (3 and 4 March). New York: American Art Association, Anderson Galleries.

1936c. *First Editions and Autograph Letters and Manuscripts. The Library of Abel Cary Thomas, New York City.* Sale no. 4242 (18 and 19 March). New York: American Art Association, Anderson Galleries.

1937. *First Editions, Autograph Letters, Manuscripts and Standard Sets Including . . . Manuscripts and Letters by Samuel L. Clemens, the Collection of the Late Albert Bigelow Paine.* Sale no. 4346 (11 and 12 November). New York: American Art Association, Anderson Galleries.

AD. Autobiographical Dictation.

Adams, Joseph H. 1871. Decision dated 27 November, in the interference proceeding between Henry C. Lockwood and Samuel L. Clemens, in the records of the United States Patent Office, Department of Commerce, Washington, D.C.

Affleck, J. O. 1888–90. "Typhus, Typhoid, and Relapsing Fevers." *The Encyclopaedia Britannica: A Dictionary of Arts, Sciences, and General Literature.* 9th ed. Vol. 23. New York: Henry G. Allen and Co.

Albany Directory.
1868. *The Albany Directory, for the Year 1868: Containing a General Directory of the Citizens, a Business Directory, a Record of the City Government, Its Institutions, &c., &c.* Albany: Sampson, Davenport and Co.

1869. *The Albany Directory, for the Year 1869: Containing a General Directory of the Citizens, a Business Directory, a Record of the City Government, Its Institutions, &c., &c.* Albany: Sampson, Davenport and Co.

1870. *The Albany Directory, for the Year 1870: Containing a General Directory of the Citizens, a Business Directory, a Record of the City Government, Its Institutions, &c., &c.* Albany: Sampson, Davenport and Co.

Aldrich, Thomas Bailey.
1859. *The Ballad of Babie Bell, and Other Poems.* New York: Rudd and Carleton.

1869. *The Story of a Bad Boy.* Boston: Fields, Osgood and Co.

1871. "Mark Twain Says He Did n't Do It." *Every Saturday,* n.s. 2 (4 February): 118.

1872. "Concerning a Bear." *The Pellet,* 18 April, no page. Reprinted in the *Howells Sentinel,* 1 November 1962, 8.

Allibone, S. Austin. 1874. *A Critical Dictionary of English Literature and British and American Authors Living and Deceased, from the Earliest Accounts to the Latter Half of the Nineteenth Century.* 3 vols. Philadelphia: J. B. Lippincott and Co.

American Literary Bureau. 1870. *The Lecture Season.* Vol. 1 (June). New York: American Literary Bureau.

AMT. 1959. *The Autobiography of Mark Twain.* Edited by Charles Neider. New York: Harper and Brothers.

Anderson Auction Company.
1903a. *Catalogue of a Remarkably Interesting Collection of Books and Autograph Letters, Mainly from Private Collections.* Sale no. 235 (17 and 18 November). New York: Anderson Auction Company.

1903b. *Catalogue of Rare and Choice Books from Private Sources, Including a Fine Sporting Library, Together with Some Interesting Autograph Letters.* Sale no. 245 (14 and 15 December). New York: Anderson Auction Company.

1904. *A Catalogue of Choice Books and Autograph Letters.* Sale no. 347 (15 December). New York: Anderson Auction Company.

1910. *Library and Art Collection of George Bentham of New York City.* Part 1. Sale no. 867 (28 and 29 November). New York: Anderson Auction Company.

1912. *The Library of the Late Captain J. F. Hinckley of St. Louis.* Sale no. 941 (27, 28, and 29 February). New York: Anderson Auction Company.

1914. *Literary and Historical Letters and Documents Collected by the Late Rev. Edwin F. Hatfield.* Sale no. 1032 (3 June). New York: Anderson Auction Company.

Anderson, Frederick, and Kenneth M. Sanderson, eds. 1971. *Mark Twain: The Critical Heritage.* New York: Barnes and Noble.

Anderson Galleries.
1919. *Autograph Letters and Original Manuscripts Formerly in the Collection of the Late James Carleton Young.* Sale no. 1414 (31 March, 1 and 2 April). New York: Anderson Galleries.

1921. *The Sporting Library of William Brewster of New York City.* Sale no. 1583 (9, 10, and 11 May). New York: Anderson Galleries.

1922. *Rare Autographs and Manuscripts of Famous Authors, Composers, Artists,*

Rulers, Admirals, Marshals, Etc. Sale no. 1624 (9 January). New York: Anderson Galleries.

1924. *Catalogue of the William Harris Arnold Collection of Manuscripts, Books and Autograph Letters.* Sale no. 1873 (10 and 11 November). New York: Anderson Galleries.

1926. *Important Letters and Documents from the Estate of the Late James Gordon Bennett.* Sale no. 2107 (23 November). New York: Anderson Galleries.

1928. *Autographs Sold by Order of the George D. Smith Book Company, Inc., in Liquidation.* Part 3. Sale no. 2275 (18 May). New York: Anderson Galleries.

Anderson, John, Jr. 1903. *Catalogue of a Fine Collection of American Historical Autograph Letters.* Sale no. 168 (15 April). New York: John Anderson, Jr.

Angel, Myron, ed. 1881. *History of Nevada.* Oakland, Calif.: Thompson and West. See Poulton's *Index to History of Nevada.*

APC (American Publishing Company).
1866–79. "Books received from the Binderies, Dec 1st *1866* to Dec 31. *1879*," the company's stock ledger, NN-B.

Appleton.
1873. *The American Annual Cyclopædia and Register of Important Events of the Year 1870.* New York: D. Appleton and Co.

1875. *The American Annual Cyclopædia and Register of Important Events of the Year 1871.* New York: D. Appleton and Co.

Appletons' Hand-Book. 1867. *Appletons' Hand-Book of American Travel.* New York: D. Appleton and Co.

Armstrong, Robert D. 1994. "'The Matter of Printing': Public Printing in the Western Territories of the United States." *Journal of Government Information* 21:34–47.

Aurand, Harold W.
1966. "The Workingmen's Benevolent Association." *Labor History* 7 (Winter): 19–34.

1971. *From the Molly Maguires to the United Mine Workers.* Philadelphia: Temple University Press.

Austin, Franklin H. 1926. "Mark Twain Incognito—A Reminiscence." *Friend* 96 (September, October, November): 201–4, 224–29, 248–54. Partly reprinted in *MTH*, 75–79.

Axelrod. Collection of Todd M. Axelrod.

BAL. 1957. *Bibliography of American Literature.* Compiled by Jacob Blanck. Vol. 2. New Haven: Yale University Press.

Bangs. 1900. *Catalogue of Books.* Sale of 22 and 23 January. New York: Bangs and Co.

BDUSC. 1989. *Biographical Directory of the United States Congress, 1774–1989.* Bicentennial Edition. Washington, D.C.: Government Printing Office.

Beecher, Henry Ward. 1864. *Plymouth Collection of Hymns and Tunes; for the Use of Christian Congregations.* New York: Barnes and Burr.

Beecher, Thomas Kinnicut. 1870. *Jervis Langdon. 1809. 1870.* Elmira: Privately printed.

Benjamin, Walter R. 1947. *The Collector.* No. 60 (September). New York: Walter R. Benjamin Company.

Benton, Joel. 1898. "Reminiscences of Eminent Lecturers." *Harper's New Monthly Magazine* 96 (March): 603–14.

Berkove, Lawrence I. 1988. "Jim Gillis: 'The Thoreau of the Sierras.'" *Mark Twain Circular* 2 (March–April): 1–2.

Berlin, Ellin. 1957. *Silver Platter.* Garden City, N.Y.: Doubleday and Co.

Bibliophile Society. 1919. *The Eighteenth Yearbook: 1919.* Boston: Bibliophile Society.

Bierce, Ambrose. 1870. "The Town Crier." *San Francisco News Letter and California Advertiser* 20 (20 August): 9.

Bigelow, Donald Nevius. 1952. *William Conant Church and "The Army and Navy Journal."* Studies in History, Economics and Public Law, no. 576. New York: Columbia University Press.

Bishop, Coleman E.
1870a. "Review of Mark Twain's Lecture.—Respectfully Dedicated to Those People Who Admire Gough and Can't Bear Independent Criticism." Jamestown (N.Y.) *Journal,* 22 January, no page. Reprinted in the Jamestown *Weekly Journal,* 28 January, 8, and in Parker 1990a, 4.
1870b. "Criticism on 'Mark Twain's' Lecture for Adult Readers—Not to Be Read by People with Weak Stomachs." Jamestown (N.Y.) *Journal,* 22 January, no page. Reprinted in the Jamestown *Weekly Journal,* 28 January, 8, and in Parker 1990a, 4.

Bishop, Joseph Bucklin. 1906. "A Friendship with John Hay." *Century Magazine* 71 (March): 773–80.

Blair, Claude, ed. 1983. *Pollard's History of Firearms.* New York: Macmillan Publishing Company.

Boesen, Charles S. 1947. *American and English Literature: First Editions, Manuscripts, Autograph Letters.* Part 2. New York: Charles S. Boesen.

Book of Common Prayer. 1857. *The Book of Common Prayer, and Administration of the Sacraments; and Other Rites and Ceremonies of the Church, According to the Use of the Protestant Episcopal Church in the United States of America: Together with the Psalter, or Psalms of David.* New York: D. Appleton and Co.

Boston Directory.
1869. *The Boston Directory, Embracing the City Record, a General Directory of the Citizens, and a Business Directory . . . for the Year Commencing July 1, 1869.* Boston: Sampson, Davenport, and Co.
1870. *The Boston Directory, Embracing the City Record, a General Directory of the Citizens, and a Business Directory . . . for the Year Commencing July 1, 1870.* Boston: Sampson, Davenport, and Co.
1871. *The Boston Directory, Embracing the City Record, a General Directory of*

the Citizens, and a Business Directory . . . for the Year Commencing July 1, 1871. Boston: Sampson, Davenport, and Co.

Bowen. Collection of R. B. Bowen.

Boyd, Andrew, and W. Harry Boyd, comps. 1872. *Boyds' Elmira and Corning Directory: Containing the Names of the Citizens, a Compendium of the Government, and Public and Private Institutions . . . 1872–3.* Elmira: Andrew and W. Harry Boyd.

Boyd, William H., comp.
1870. *Boyd's Directory of Washington, Georgetown, and Alexandria, Together with a Compendium of their Governments, Institutions and Trades.* Washington, D.C.: William H. Boyd.

1871. *Boyd's Directory of Washington, Georgetown, and Alexandria, Together with a Compendium of their Governments, Institutions and Trades.* Washington, D.C.: William H. Boyd.

1872. *Boyd's Directory of the District of Columbia, Together with a Compendium of Its Governments, Institutions, and Trades.* Washington, D.C.: William H. Boyd.

1873. *Boyd's Directory of the District of Columbia, Together with a Compendium of Its Governments, Institutions and Trades.* Washington, D.C.: William H. Boyd.

1874. *Boyd's Directory of the District of Columbia, Together with a Compendium of Its Governments, Institutions and Trades.* Washington, D.C.: William H. Boyd.

Branch, Edgar Marquess. 1983. "Mark Twain: Newspaper Reading and the Writer's Creativity." *Nineteenth-Century Fiction* 37 (March): 576–603.

Broehl, Wayne G., Jr. 1964. *The Molly Maguires.* Cambridge: Harvard University Press.

Bromer. 1992. *Selections from Our Stock to Be Featured . . . February 14, 15, 16, 1992 at the Los Angeles Airport Hilton.* Boston: Bromer Booksellers.

Browne, Charles Farrar [Artemus Ward, pseud.].
1865. *Artemus Ward; His Travels.* New York: Carleton.

1867a. *Artemus Ward; His Book.* New York: Carleton.

1867b. *Artemus Ward in London, and Other Papers.* New York: G. W. Carleton and Co.

1869. *Artemus Ward's Lecture.* Edited by his executors, T. W. Robertson and E. P. Hingston. London: John Camden Hotten; New York: G. W. Carleton and Co.

Browne, Junius Henri. 1872. *Sights and Sensations in Europe.* Hartford: American Publishing Company.

Brownell, George H.
1941. "Letters of Mark Twain, 1867–1909, Chiefly to Bliss of the American Publishing Company. Copies Made by Dana Ayer, Worcester, Massachusetts." PH in CU-MARK.

1943. "From 'Hospital Days.'" *Twainian* 2 (March): 1–5.

1944. "Mark Twain's Inventions." *Twainian* 3 (January): 1–5.

Bruccoli, Matthew J. 1986. *The Fortunes of Mitchell Kennerley, Bookman*. San Diego: Harcourt Brace Jovanovich.

Bryan, George B., comp. 1991. *Stage Deaths: A Biographical Guide to International Theatrical Obituaries, 1850 to 1900*. 2 vols. Westport, Conn.: Greenwood Press.

Buckbee, Edna Bryan. 1935. *The Saga of Old Tuolumne*. New York: Press of the Pioneers.

Buffalo Directory.

1866. *Thomas' Buffalo City Directory for 1866. To Which Is Prefixed "Buffalo: Its Manufacturing, Commercial and Business Position." By Guy H. Salisbury. Also a Sketch Relative to the Early Residents of Buffalo. To Which Is Added a Business Directory of Buffalo*. Buffalo: C. F. S. Thomas.

1869. *Buffalo City Directory. Embracing a General Directory of Residents, a Street and Avenue Directory, Climatology of Buffalo, City and County Officers, Societies and Incorporated Companies, Banks, Telegraph and Railroad Companies, Table of Stamp Duties, Rates of Postage, Etc*. Buffalo: Warren, Johnson and Co.

1870. *Buffalo City Directory. Embracing Trade and Commerce of Buffalo, History of the Buffalo Board of Trade, a General Directory of Residents, a Street and Avenue Directory, Climatology of Buffalo, City and County Officers, Societies and Incorporated Companies, Banks, Telegraph and Railroad Companies, Churches, Public Buildings, Ward Boundaries, Table of Stamp Duties, Rates of Postage, Etc. To Which Is Added a Business Directory of Buffalo. With a New City Map Showing the Boundaries of the Proposed Central Park*. Buffalo: Warren, Johnson and Co.

1871. *Buffalo City Directory for the Year 1871. Embracing a Brief Historical Sketch of Buffalo, a General Directory of Residents, a Street and Avenue Directory, Climatology of Buffalo, City and County Officers, Societies and Incorporated Companies, Banks, Telegraph and Railroad Companies, Churches, Public Buildings, Ward Boundaries, Table of Stamp Duties, Rates of Postage, Etc. To Which Is Added a Business Directory of Buffalo*. Buffalo: Warren, Johnson and Co.

Byng, Carl [pseud.?].

1870a. "Agricultural Twaddle at the Institute Farmer's Club." Buffalo *Express*, 12 November, 2.

1870b. "Jenkins at Wilhelmshohe." Buffalo *Express*, 19 November, 2.

1870c. "Three Aces: Jim Todd's Episode in Social Euchre." Buffalo *Express*, 3 December, 2.

1870d. "Some Unpublished Literature of Patent Medicine." Buffalo *Express*, 17 December, 2.

1870e. "Review of Holiday Literature." Buffalo *Express*, 24 December, 2.

1870f. "Advice to Parents." Buffalo *Express*, 31 December, 2.

1871a. "That Book Agent." Buffalo *Express*, 7 January, 2.

1871b. " 'Train Up a Child, and Away He Goes.['] " Buffalo *Express*, 28 January, 2.

Cannon, Carl L. 1941. *American Book Collectors and Collecting from Colonial Times to the Present*. New York: H. W. Wilson Company.

Carson, Gerald. 1961. *One for a Man, Two for a Horse*. New York: Bramhall House.

Casual [pseud.]. 1871. "From Washington. Buffalo Matters at the Capitol." Buffalo *Courier*, 6 February, 1.

CCC. Ella Strong Denison Library of the Claremont Colleges, Claremont, California.

Chamlee, Roy Z., Jr. 1990. *Lincoln's Assassins: A Complete Account of Their Capture, Trial, and Punishment*. Jefferson, N.C., and London: McFarland and Co.

Chautauqua County. 1904. *The Centennial History of Chautauqua County.* 2 vols. Jamestown, N.Y.: Chautauqua History Company.

Chester, Giraud. 1951. *Embattled Maiden: The Life of Anna Dickinson*. New York: G. P. Putnam's Sons.

Chicago. 1936. *Library of the Hanna Homestead, Fort Wayne, Ind., with Selections from Libraries of Chicago's First Families: Burley, Tyrrel, et al.* Sale no. 58 (25 and 26 February). Chicago: Chicago Book and Art Auctions.

Chicago Directory.
1870. *Edwards' Thirteenth Annual Directory of the Inhabitants, Institutions, Incorporated Companies, and Manufacturing Establishments of the City of Chicago, Embracing a Complete Business Directory for 1870*. Chicago: Richard Edwards.
1871. *Fire Edition. Edwards' Chicago Directory*. Chicago: Richard Edwards.

Christie.
1981. *The Prescott Collection: Printed Books and Manuscripts . . . The Property of the Estate of Marjorie Wiggin Prescott*. Sale of 6 February. New York: Christie, Manson and Woods International.
1989. *The Estelle Doheny Collection from the Edward Laurence Doheny Memorial Library, Camarillo, California*. Sale of 21 and 22 February (Doheny V). New York: Christie, Manson and Woods International.
1991. *Printed Books and Manuscripts . . . The Estates of Chester Davis, Augustus Maxwell, and from Various Sources*. Sale no. 7378 (5 December). New York: Christie's.
1993. *Printed Books and Manuscripts . . . The Estate of Chester L. Davis and from Various Sources*. Sale no. 7700 (9 June). New York: Christie's.

Christie's. Christie, Manson and Woods International, New York City.

Cincinnati [pseud.]. 1871. "Washington Letters." Letter dated 6 February. Cincinnati *Commercial*, 9 February, 2.

Cincinnati Directory.
1870. *Williams' Cincinnati Directory, Embracing a Full Alphabetical Record of the Names of the Inhabitants of Cincinnati, a Business Directory, United States Post Office Directory, Municipal Record, City Map, &c., &c*. Cincinnati: Williams and Co.
1871. *Williams' Cincinnati Directory, Embracing a Full Alphabetical Record of*

the *Names of the Inhabitants of Cincinnati, a Business Directory, United States Post Office Directory, Municipal Record, Etc. Etc.* Cincinnati: Williams and Co.

City Book Auction. 1943. *Books on Many Subjects*. Sale no. 222 (9 January). New York: City Book Auction.

CJL. Charles Jervis Langdon.

Clark, Charles Heber [John Quill, Max Adeler, pseuds.].
1869a. "How Wm. McGinley Suffered." Philadelphia *Evening Bulletin*, 26 November, 6.
1869b. "That Horse of Mine." Philadelphia *Evening Bulletin*, 4 December, 1.
1869c. "The Fate of Joe M'Ginnis: A Warning to Mothers." Philadelphia *Evening Bulletin*, 22 December, 1. Reprinted in the San Francisco *Golden City* 5 (23 January 1870): 2.
1881. *An Old Fogey and Other Stories*. London: Ward, Lock and Bowden. Includes "Professor Baffin's Adventures."
1882. *The Fortunate Island and Other Stories*. Boston: Lee and Shepard.

Clemens, Cyril, ed. 1965. *Mark Twain's Jest Book*. 3d ed. Kirkwood, Mo.: Mark Twain Journal.

Clemens, Orion. See OC.

Clemens, Samuel L. See SLC.

Clemens, Will M.
1892. *Mark Twain: His Life and Work; A Biographical Sketch*. San Francisco: Clemens Publishing Company.
1900. "Mark Twain on the Lecture Platform." *Ainslee's Magazine* 6 (August): 25–32.

Cleveland Census. [1850] 1964. "Free Inhabitants in . . . Cleveland." *Population Schedules of the Seventh Census of the United States, 1850*. Roll 672. Ohio: Cuyahoga County (pt.). National Archives Microfilm Publications, Microcopy no. 432. Washington, D.C.: General Services Administration.

Cleveland Directory.
1870. *Directory of the City of Cleveland and Adjoining Towns, for 1870–71*. Cleveland: Wiggins and Weaver.
1871. *Cleveland Directory, 1871–72. Comprising an Alphabetical List of All Business Firms and Private Citizens; A Classified Business Directory; and a Directory of the Public Institutions of the City*. Compiled by A. Bailey. Cleveland: W. S. Robison and Co.

CLSU. University of Southern California, Los Angeles.

CLU-S/C. Department of Special Collections, University of California, Los Angeles.

Colbert, Elias, and Everett Chamberlin. 1871. *Chicago and the Great Conflagration*. Cincinnati and New York: C. F. Vent.

Congressional Globe.
1870. *The Congressional Globe: Containing the Debates and Proceedings of the Second Session Forty-First Congress; Together with an Appendix, Embracing the*

Laws Passed at That Session. 7 vols. Washington, D.C.: Office of the Congressional Globe.

1871. *The Congressional Globe: Containing the Debates and Proceedings of the Third Session Forty-First Congress; Together with an Appendix, Embracing the Laws Passed at That Session.* 3 vols. Washington, D.C.: Office of the Congressional Globe.

Cotton, Michelle L. 1985. *Mark Twain's Elmira, 1870–1910.* Elmira: Chemung County Historical Society.

Cox, Samuel Sullivan.
1852. *A Buckeye Abroad; or, Wanderings in Europe, and in the Orient.* New York: G. P. Putnam.

1865. *Eight Years in Congress, from 1857 to 1865.* New York: D. Appleton and Co.

1869. *Search for Winter Sunbeams in the Riviera, Corsica, Algiers, and Spain.* London: Sampson, Low, Son, and Marston.

Coyle, William, ed. 1962. *Ohio Authors and Their Books.* Cleveland and New York: World Publishing Company.

Craven. Collection of Mrs. Robin Craven.

CSmH. Henry E. Huntington Library, San Marino, California.

CSt. Department of Special Collections, Green Library, Stanford University, Stanford, California.

CtHMTH. Mark Twain House, Hartford, Connecticut.

CtHSD. Harriet Beecher Stowe Center, Hartford, Connecticut.

CtY. Yale University Library, New Haven, Connecticut.

CtY-BR. Beinecke Rare Book and Manuscript Library, Yale University, New Haven, Connecticut.

CU-BANC. The Bancroft Library, University of California, Berkeley.

CU-MARK. Mark Twain Papers, CU-BANC.

Cummings, Sherwood. 1988. *Mark Twain and Science: Adventures of a Mind.* Baton Rouge and London: Louisiana State University Press.

DAB. 1928–36. *Dictionary of American Biography.* Edited by Allen Johnson and Dumas Malone. 20 vols. New York: Charles Scribner's Sons.

Daley. Collection of Robert Daley.

Davis. Collection of Chester L. Davis, Sr., Mark Twain Research Foundation, Perry, Missouri.

Davis, Chester L., Sr.
1949. "Adolph Sutro." *Twainian* 8 (March–April): 8.

1954. "Orion Clemens and the American Publisher." *Twainian* 13 (September–October): 3–4.

1956. "Letters from Steve Gillis." *Twainian* 15 (March–April): 1–4.

1965. "Mahan Correspondence with Albert Bigelow Paine." *Twainian* 24 (September–October): 1–3.

1970. "Letters from Twichell to Paine." *Twainian* 29 (November–December): 3–4.

1977. "Family Letters of the 1870's." *Twainian* 36 (July–August): 1–4.

1978. "Mark's Playful Letters (Mixed Scraps)." *Twainian* 37 (November–December): 1–3.

1981. "Mark Twain Reading 'Side-Lights on Astronomy.'" *Twainian* 40 (September–October): 1–3.

1982. "Rare Paper-back 'Sketches, No. 1' (Continuation)." *Twainian* 41 (September–October): 1–4.

1985a. *"Mark Twain's Letters to His Publishers." Twainian* 44 (March–April): 4.

1985b. *"Mark Twain's Letters to His Publishers* (Conclusion of Reprinting)." *Twainian* 44 (May–June): 1.

Davis, Samuel Post. 1893. "The 'Enterprise's' Poets." In "The Passing of a Pioneer." San Francisco *Examiner,* 22 January, 15. Reprinted as "The *Enterprise* Poets" in Lewis, 17–22.

Dawson, George F. 1870. "Letter from Washington." Sacramento *Union,* 19 July, 1.

Dawson's Book Shop.
1925. *A Catalogue of Rare Books.* No. 37 (February). Los Angeles: Dawson's Book Shop.

1942. *A Check List of the Mark Twain Collection Assembled by the Late Willard S. Morse . . . Prepared by Ellen K. Shaffer and Lucille S.J. Hall.* June. Los Angeles: Dawson's Book Shop.

De Ferrari, Carlo M.
1964. "Mark Twain Was Here." *The Quarterly of the Tuolumne County Historical Society* 4 (October–December): 107–9. Reprinted in De Ferrari et al., 133–40.

1984a. "About the Chaparral Quails." *Chispa: The Quarterly of the Tuolumne County Historical Society* 23 (January–March): 780.

1984b. "Mark Twain's Letter." *Chispa: The Quarterly of the Tuolumne County Historical Society* 23 (January–March): 783.

De Ferrari, Carlo M., and Richard L. Dyer, Joan C. Gorsuch, Sharon Marovich, Jean McClish, Lyle Scott, Dolores Yescas Nicolini, Mary Grace Paquette, Mary Etta Segerstrom, Tillie Sheatsley, comps. 1987. *Mark Twain's Sojourn in Tuolumne County, California: Genesis of a Literary Giant.* Sonora, Calif.: Tuolumne County Historical Society.

Des Moines Directory.
1869. *Des Moines City Directory and Business Guide for the Year 1869.* Des Moines: Mills and Co.

1871. *Bushnell's Resident and Business Directory of Des Moines, Iowa. Containing an Epitome of the Early History of the State, County, and City; a List of State, County, and City Officers; a Street, Resident, and Business Directory; Map of the State, Views of Public Buildings, and Post-Office Directory of the State.* Compiled by Joseph P. Bushnell. Des Moines: Joseph P. Bushnell.

1873. *Bushnell's Des Moines Residence and Business City Directory. Containing an Epitome of the Early History of the City and County; an Important Railroad Centre. The Natural Advantages of Des Moines as a Commercial and Manufacturing City. A Resident, Business and Street Directory; a Church, School and Society Directory; State, County and City Officers; a Census of the City, and a Post Office Directory of the State.* Compiled by Joseph P. Bushnell. Des Moines: Capital City Publishing Company.

1874. *Bushnell's Des Moines Residence and Business City Directory. Containing an Epitome of the Early History of the City and County; the Natural Advantages of Des Moines as a Commercial and Manufacturing City. A Resident, Business and Street Directory; a Church, School and Society Directory; State, County, and City Officers.* Compiled by Joseph P. Bushnell. Des Moines: J. P. Bushnell and Co.

DLC. United States Library of Congress, Washington, D.C.

DNA. United States National Archives and Record Service, National Archives Library, Washington, D.C.

Doten, Alfred.
    1866. "Mark Twain's Lecture—An Immense Success." Virginia City *Territorial Enterprise*, 1 November, 3.
    1973. *The Journals of Alfred Doten, 1849–1903.* Edited by Walter Van Tilburg Clark. 3 vols. Reno: University of Nevada Press.

Drake, Francis Samuel. 1872. *Dictionary of American Biography, Including Men of the Time.* Boston: James R. Osgood and Co.

Drake, Samuel Gardner. 1867. *Drake of Hampton, New Hampshire.* Boston.

Dussere, David Philip. 1974. "A Critical Biography of Charles Heber Clark ('Max Adeler'): American Journalist and Humorist." Ph.D. diss., University of Arkansas.

Eastman, Max. 1938. "Mark Twain's Elmira." *Harper's Magazine* 177 (May): 620–32. Reprinted in Max Eastman, *Heroes I Have Known* (New York: Simon and Schuster, 1942), and in Jerome and Wisbey 1977, 129–47.

Edwards, Richard.
    1868. *Edwards' Tenth Annual Director to the Inhabitants, Institutions, Incorporated Companies, Manufacturing Establishments, Business, Business Firms, etc., etc., in the City of St. Louis, for 1868.* St. Louis: Richard Edwards.
    1869. *Edwards' Eleventh Annual Directory to the Inhabitants, Institutions, Incorporated Companies, Manufacturing Establishments, Business, Business Firms, etc., etc., in the City of St. Louis, for 1869.* St. Louis: Charless Publishing and Manufacturing Company.
    1870. [*Edwards' Twelfth Annual Director to the . . . City of St. Louis, for 1870*]. St. Louis: Southern Publishing Company.
    1871. *Edwards' Thirteenth Annual Director to the Inhabitants, Institutions, Incorporated Companies, Business, Business Firms, Manufacturing Establishments, etc., in the City of Saint Louis, for 1871.* St. Louis: Southern Publishing Company.

Elmira Female College. 1862. *The Seventh Annual Catalogue and Circular of the Elmira Female College, 1861–1862.* Elmira: Elmira Female College.

Estavan, Lawrence, ed. 1938–42. *San Francisco Theatre Research.* 18 vols. San Francisco: Works Projects Administration.

ET&S1. 1979. *Early Tales & Sketches, Volume 1 (1851–1864).* Edited by Edgar Marquess Branch and Robert H. Hirst, with the assistance of Harriet Elinor Smith. The Works of Mark Twain. Berkeley, Los Angeles, London: University of California Press.

ET&S2. 1981. *Early Tales & Sketches, Volume 2 (1864–1865).* Edited by Edgar Marquess Branch and Robert H. Hirst, with the assistance of Harriet Elinor Smith. The Works of Mark Twain. Berkeley, Los Angeles, London: University of California Press.

Eubank, Marjorie Harrell. 1969. *The Redpath Lyceum Bureau from 1868 to 1901.* Ph.D. diss., University of Michigan, Ann Arbor.

Evans, Albert S. [Amigo, pseud.].
1866a. "Our San Francisco Correspondence." Letter dated 2 February. Gold Hill (Nev.) *Evening News,* 5 February, 2.
1866b. "Our San Francisco Correspondence." Letter dated 9 February. Gold Hill (Nev.) *Evening News,* 12 February, 2.
1866c. "Our San Francisco Correspondence." Letter dated 14 February. Gold Hill (Nev.) *Evening News,* 19 February, 2.
1870. *Our Sister Republic: A Gala Trip through Tropical Mexico in 1869–70.* Hartford: Columbian Book Company.

Evans, Peter A., William R. Gillis, and Henry Alston Williams.
1970. Gillis family genealogy. Unpublished manuscript documents. PH in CU-MARK.

Fairbanks, Lorenzo Sayles. 1897. *Genealogy of the Fairbanks Family in America, 1633–1897.* Boston: American Printing and Engraving Company.

Fairbanks, Mary Mason, ed. 1898. *Emma Willard and Her Pupils; or, Fifty Years of Troy Female Seminary, 1822–1872.* New York: Mrs. Russell Sage.

Fatout, Paul.
1960. *Mark Twain on the Lecture Circuit.* Bloomington: Indiana University Press.
1976. *Mark Twain Speaking.* Iowa City: University of Iowa Press.

Fawkes, Richard. 1979. *Dion Boucicault: A Biography.* London, Melbourne, New York: Quartet Books.

Federico, P. J. 1939. "The Facts in the Case of Mark Twain's Vest Strap." *Journal of the Patent Office Society* 21 (March): 223–32. Reprinted in *Twainian* 16 (November–December 1957): 1–4.

Fielder, Elizabeth Davis. 1899. "Familiar Haunts of Mark Twain." *Harper's Weekly* 43 (16 December): 10–11.

Feinstein, Herbert Charles Verschleisser. 1968. "Mark Twain's Lawsuits." Ph.D. diss., University of California, Berkeley.

Finley, Ruth E. 1929. *Old Patchwork Quilts and the Women Who Made Them.* Philadelphia and London: J. B. Lippincott Company.

Fitch, Thomas.
1903. "Some Old Friends." San Francisco *Call*, 4 October, 14.

1919. "Fitch Recalls Mark Twain Bonanza Times." San Francisco *Chronicle*, 30 March, 6F.

1978. *Western Carpetbagger: The Extraordinary Memoirs of "Senator" Thomas Fitch.* Edited and with a foreword by Eric N. Moody. Reno: University of Nevada Press.

Ford, Darius R.
1870a. "Around the World. Letter Number IX." Letter dated 19 November 1869. Buffalo *Express*, 12 February, 2.

1870b. "Around the World. Letter Number X." Letter dated 17 and 24 January. Buffalo *Express*, 5 March, 2.

Foster, James P. 1871. "Mark Twain." Undated letter to the editor. Syracuse (N.Y.) *Journal*, 6 December, no page.

Fox. Collection of Alan C. Fox.

Fox, Alan C. 1980. *Catalogue One.* Sherman Oaks, Calif.: Alan C. Fox.

Freeman. 1936. *Valuable Library of Rare Books and Autographs of the Late Charles T. Jeffery of Merion, Pa.* Part 1. Sale of 23 March. Philadelphia: Samuel T. Freeman and Co.

French, Bryant Morey. 1965. *Mark Twain and "The Gilded Age": The Book That Named an Era.* Dallas: Southern Methodist University Press.

French, John Homer. 1860. *Gazetteer of the State of New York.* Syracuse, N.Y.: R. Pearsall Smith. Citations are to the 1980 reprint edition, Interlaken, N.Y.: Heart of the Lakes Publishing.

Fulton, Robert. 1914. "Glimpses of the Mother Lode." *Bookman* 39 (March): 49–57.

Geer, Elihu, comp.
1869. *Geer's Hartford City Directory; For 1869–70: Containing Every Kind of Desirable Information for Citizens and Strangers; Together with a Classified Business Directory, and a Newly Engraved Map of the City.* Hartford: Elihu Geer.

1870. *Geer's Hartford City Directory; For 1870–71: Containing Every Kind of Desirable Information for Citizens and Strangers; Together with a Classified Business Directory, and a Newly Engraved Map of the City.* Hartford: Elihu Geer.

1871. *Geer's Hartford City Directory, for 1871–72: Containing Every Kind of Desirable Information for Citizens and Strangers; Together with a Classified Business Directory, and Engravings of Church and Other Edifices, Which Have Been Drawn and Engraved Expressly for This Directory; and a Newly Engraved Map of the City; Also, a Full Re-print of the Contents of Our 1841 Directory.* Hartford: Elihu Geer.

1872. *Geer's Hartford City Directory, for 1872–73: Containing Every Kind of Desirable Information for Citizens and Strangers; Together with a Classified Business Directory, and Engravings of Church and Other Edifices, Which Have Been*

Drawn and Engraved Expressly for This Directory; and a Newly Surveyed and Engraved Map of the City. Hartford: Elihu Geer.

Gillette, Jay. 1984. "I Am Not in the Imitation Business": Mark Twain, the Carl Byng Controversy, and a Computer-Assisted Solution." Unpublished TS, CU-MARK.

Gillis, William R. 1930. *Gold Rush Days with Mark Twain.* New York: Albert and Charles Boni.

Goodman, Caleb. 1946. Record of relocation of Goodman family remains to vault 1023, Cypress Lawn Cemetery, Colma, California. Record dated 16 September. PH in CU-MARK, courtesy of Jay N. Miller.

Goodman, Joseph T.
1872. "Greeley and Hank Monk." Virginia City *Territorial Enterprise*, 24 July, 2.

1910. "Jos. Goodman's Memories of Humorist's Early Days." San Francisco *Examiner*, 22 April, 3.

Goodspeed's Book Shop.
1924. *Rare First Editions, Colonial Ex-libris, Autographs.* Catalog no. 156 (April). Boston: Goodspeed's Book Shop.

1936. *Autographs.* Catalog no. 271 (November). Boston: Goodspeed's Book Shop.

Gray, David.
1870. "New Publications." Buffalo *Courier*, 19 March, "Morning Edition," 2. Reprinted in "Evening Edition," no page.

1871a. "Mark Twain in the Lecture Field." Buffalo *Courier*, 12 June, 2.

1871b. "A New Lecture by Mark Twain." Buffalo *Courier*, 9 December, 2.

Greenslet, Ferris. 1908. *The Life of Thomas Bailey Aldrich.* Boston: Houghton Mifflin Company.

Gregory, Winifred, ed. 1937. *American Newspapers, 1821–1936: A Union List of Files Available in the United States and Canada.* New York: H. W. Wilson Company. Citations are to the 1967 reprint edition, New York: Kraus Reprint Corporation.

Gribben, Alan. 1980. *Mark Twain's Library: A Reconstruction.* 2 vols. Boston: G. K. Hall and Co.

Gunn. Collection of Mr. and Mrs. Robert M. Gunn.

Haddawy, Husain, trans. 1990. *The Arabian Nights.* New York and London: W. W. Norton and Co.

Hall, Edward H. 1867. *Appletons' Hand-Book of American Travel.* New York: D. Appleton and Co.

Hamilton, Sinclair. 1958. *Early American Book Illustrators and Wood Engravers, 1670–1870.* Princeton, N.J.: Princeton University Library.

Hannibal Census. [1850] 1963. "Free Inhabitants in . . . Hannibal." *Population Schedules of the Seventh Census of the United States, 1850. Roll 406. Missouri: Marion, Mercer, Miller, and Mississippi Counties.* National Archives Microfilm

Publications, Microcopy no. 432. Washington, D.C.: General Services Administration.

Harrison, John M. 1969. *The Man Who Made Nasby, David Ross Locke.* Chapel Hill: University of North Carolina Press.

Hart, James D.
1950. *The Popular Book: A History of America's Literary Taste.* New York: Oxford University Press.

1987. *A Companion to California.* Rev. ed. Berkeley, Los Angeles, London: University of California Press.

Harte, Bret.
1870a. "Current Literature." *Overland Monthly* 4 (January): 100–104. Reprinted in Anderson and Sanderson, 32–35.

1870b. "Plain Language from Truthful James." *Overland Monthly* 5 (September): 287–88.

"Hartford Residents." 1974. Unpublished TS by anonymous compiler, CtHSD.

Hay, Clara Louise, ed. 1908. *Letters of John Hay and Extracts from Diary.* 3 vols. Washington, D.C.: Privately printed.

Hay, John M.
1870. "Little-Breeches." New York *Tribune*, 19 November, 5. Reprinted in the Buffalo *Express*, 22 November, 2.

1871. "Jim Bludso, (of the Prairie Belle.)" New York *Tribune*, 5 January, 5.

Hebb, Ray M. 1990. Langdon family ancestor chart of twelve pages, PH in CU-MARK. Courtesy of Jervis Langdon, Jr.

Heitman, Francis B. 1903. *Historical Register and Dictionary of the United States Army, from Its Organization, September 29, 1789, to March 2, 1903.* 2 vols. Washington, D.C.: Government Printing Office.

Henkels.
1920. *Valuable Autograph Letters and Historical Documents and Literary Manuscripts.* Sale no. 1249 (16 January). Philadelphia: Stan. V. Henkels.

1925. *Important Autograph Letters and Historical Documents, Literary Manuscripts.* Sale no. 1368 (28 January). Philadelphia: Stan. V. Henkels.

Heritage Book Shop. 1987. *Autograph Letters Catalogue.* Los Angeles: Heritage Book Shop.

HF. 1988. *Adventures of Huckleberry Finn.* Edited by Walter Blair and Victor Fischer, with the assistance of Dahlia Armon and Harriet Elinor Smith. The Works of Mark Twain. Berkeley, Los Angeles, London: University of California Press.

Hill, Hamlin. 1964. *Mark Twain and Elisha Bliss.* Columbia: University of Missouri Press.

Hingston, Edward P. 1871. *The Genial Showman: Being Reminiscences of the Life of Artemus Ward and Pictures of a Showman's Career in the Western World.* London: John Camden Hotten. First published in 1870 in two volumes.

Hirst, Robert H.
1975. "The Making of *The Innocents Abroad:* 1867–1872." Ph.D. diss., University of California, Berkeley.

1978. " 'He Trimmed & Trained & Schooled Me': How Bret Harte Edited *The Innocents Abroad.*" Unpublished TS, CU-MARK.

Hirst, Robert H., and Brandt Rowles. 1984. "William E. James's Stereoscopic Views of the *Quaker City* Excursion." *Mark Twain Journal* 22 (Spring): 15–33.

Holcombe, Return I. 1884. *History of Marion County, Missouri.* St. Louis: E. F. Perkins. Citations are to the 1979 reprint edition, Hannibal and Marceline: Marion County Historical Society and Walsworth Publishing Company.

Holstein, Jonathan. 1982. *The Pieced Quilt: An American Design Tradition.* A New York Graphic Society Book. Boston: Little, Brown and Co.

Hood, Juliette Mouron. 1931. "Reminiscences of Twain's 'Chaparral Quails,' Belles of Old Tuolumne." Stockton (Calif.) *Record,* 26 September, 23, 25. Reprinted in *Chispa: The Quarterly of the Tuolumne County Historical Society* 23 (January–March 1984): 781–83, and in De Ferrari et al., 122–33.

Hooker, John. 1899. *Some Reminiscences of a Long Life.* Hartford: Belknap and Warfield.

Horan, James D. 1955. *Mathew Brady: Historian with a Camera.* New York: Crown Publishers.

Hornberger, Theodore, ed. 1941. *Mark Twain's Letters to Will Bowen.* Austin: University of Texas.

Horner, Charles F. 1926. *The Life of James Redpath and the Development of the Modern Lyceum.* New York and Newark: Barse and Hopkins.

House, Edward H.
1875a. *The Japanese Expedition to Formosa.* Tokyo.

1875b. *The Kagosima Affair: A Chapter of Japanese History.* Tokyo.

1875c. *The Shimonoseki Affair: A Chapter of Japanese History.* [Tokyo].

1881. *Japanese Episodes.* Boston: James R. Osgood and Co.

1888. *Yone Santo: A Child of Japan.* Chicago: Belford, Clarke and Co.

Howard, Peter B. 1992. *Mark Twain.* Undated catalog of two pages. Berkeley: Serendipity Books. With letter of 11 February 1992 from Peter Howard to Anthony Bliss and Stephen Black.

Howe, M. A. DeWolfe. 1922. *Memories of a Hostess: A Chronicle of Eminent Friendships Drawn Chiefly from the Diaries of Mrs. James T. Fields.* Boston: Atlantic Monthly Press.

Howells, William Dean.
1874. "Ralph Keeler." *Atlantic Monthly* 33 (March): 366–67.

1900. *Literary Friends and Acquaintance: A Personal Retrospect of American Authorship.* New York and London: Harper and Brothers.

1903. "Editor's Easy Chair." *Harper's Monthly* 108 (December): 153–59. Reprinted as "A Belated Guest" in 1910 edition of Howells's *Literary Friends and Acquaintance.*

1910. *My Mark Twain: Reminiscences and Criticisms*. New York and London: Harper and Brothers.

1928. *Life in Letters of William Dean Howells*. Edited by Mildred Howells. 2 vols. Garden City, N.Y.: Doubleday, Doran and Co.

Howland, Louise. 1933. Recollections of Robert M. Howland and Samuel L. Clemens. MS of five pages, rough draft of account prepared for Clara Clemens Gabrilowitsch. Gunn, PH in CU-MARK.

Hudson, Frederic. 1873. *Journalism in the United States, from 1690 to 1872*. New York: Harper and Brothers.

IC. Chicago Public Library, Chicago, Illinois.

ICU. University of Chicago, Chicago, Illinois.

Inds. 1989. *Huck Finn and Tom Sawyer among the Indians, and Other Unfinished Stories*. Foreword and notes by Dahlia Armon and Walter Blair. Texts established by Dahlia Armon, Paul Baender, Walter Blair, William M. Gibson, and Franklin R. Rogers. The Mark Twain Library. Berkeley, Los Angeles, London: University of California Press.

InU-Li. Lilly Library, Indiana University, Bloomington.

IU-R. Rare Book Room, University of Illinois, Urbana.

James, U. P. 1857. *River Guide: Containing Descriptions of All the Cities, Towns, and Principal Objects of Interest, on the Navigable Waters of the Mississippi Valley*. Cincinnati: U. P. James.

Jerome, Robert D., and Herbert A. Wisbey, Jr.
1977. *Mark Twain in Elmira*. Elmira: Mark Twain Society.

1981. "Editors' Note" in "Letters to the Editors." *Mark Twain Society Bulletin* 4 (June): 2.

1983. "Girlhood Stories of Livy Langdon Clemens." *Mark Twain Society Bulletin* 6 (July): 1–3.

1990. "Details of Langdon-Clemens Wedding Described in Diary." *Mark Twain Society Bulletin* 13 (January): 4–5.

1991a. "Munson Diary, 1870." *Mark Twain Society Bulletin* 14 (January): 3–5.

1991b. "Livy's College Texts." *Mark Twain Society Bulletin* 14 (July): 6.

JIm. The Library, Iwaki Meisei University, Iwaki City, Japan.

JLC (Jane Lampton Clemens).
1861–70. Financial record kept in SLC's Notebook 3, CU-MARK. Page references are to a sixteen-page TS in CU-MARK.

Jones, Alexander E. 1954. "Mark Twain and the 'Many Citizens' Letter." *American Literature* 26 (November): 421–25.

Joseph. Collection of Wayne M. Joseph.

Joseph, Bea, Charlotte Warren Squires, and Rita Volmer Louis, eds. 1953. *Biography Index: A Cumulative Index to Biographical Material in Books and Magazines*. Vol. 2 (August 1949–August 1952). New York: H. W. Wilson Company.

Julian, John, ed. 1907. *A Dictionary of Hymnology.* 2d rev. ed. London: John Murray.

Karanovich. Collection of Nick Karanovich.

Karanovich, Nick, William Cagle, and Joel Silver. 1991. *Mark Twain: Selections from the Collection of Nick Karanovich.* Bloomington: The Lilly Library, Indiana University.

Kelly, J. Wells, comp.
1862. *First Directory of Nevada Territory.* San Francisco: Valentine and Co.
1863. *Second Directory of Nevada Territory.* San Francisco: Valentine and Co.

Kesterson, David B. 1973. *Josh Billings (Henry Wheeler Shaw).* Twayne's United States Authors Series, edited by Sylvia E. Bowman, no. 229. New York: Twayne Publishers.

Ketterer, David. 1986. " 'Professor Baffin's Adventures' by Max Adeler: The Inspiration for *A Connecticut Yankee in King Arthur's Court?" Mark Twain Journal* 24 (Spring): 24–34.

Keyes, J. J. 1870. "Letter from Virginia." Letter dated 8 July. Elmira *Advertiser,* 15 July, 2.

King, Moses.
1883. *King's Dictionary of Boston.* Edited by Edwin M. Bacon. Cambridge: Moses King.
1885. *King's Hand-Book of Boston.* 7th ed. Cambridge: Moses King.

Kirk, John Foster. 1892. *A Supplement to Allibone's Critical Dictionary of English Literature and British and American Authors.* 2 vols. Philadelphia: J. B. Lippincott Company.

Knight, William H., ed. 1864. *Hand-Book Almanac for the Pacific States: An Official Register and Business Directory of the States and Territories of California, Nevada, Oregon, Idaho, and Arizona; and the Colonies of British Columbia and Vancouver Island, for the Year 1864.* San Francisco: H. H. Bancroft and Co.

Kodama, Mitsuo. 1987. *Catalogue of Mark Twain Collection in the Library of Iwaki Meisei University.* Tokyo.

Krause, David, ed. 1964. *The Dolmen Boucicault.* Dublin: Dolmen Press.

Krohe, James, Jr., ed. 1976. *A Springfield Reader: Historical Views of the Illinois Capital, 1818–1976.* Bicentennial Studies in Sangamon History, edited by Richard E. Hart. Springfield, Ill.: Sangamon County Historical Society.

Kruse, Horst H.
1990. "Mark Twain's *A Connecticut Yankee:* Reconsiderations and Revisions." *American Literature* 62 (September): 464–83.
1991. "Literary Old Offenders: Mark Twain, John Quill, Max Adeler and Their Plagiarism Duels." *Mark Twain Journal* 29 (Fall): 10–27.

Kulp, George B. 1885–90. *Families of the Wyoming Valley: Biographical, Genealogical, and Historical.* 3 vols. Wilkes-Barre, Pa.: E. B. Yordy, Printer.

L1. 1988. *Mark Twain's Letters, Volume 1: 1853–1866.* Edited by Edgar Marquess Branch, Michael B. Frank, Kenneth M. Sanderson, Harriet Elinor Smith,

Lin Salamo, and Richard Bucci. The Mark Twain Papers. Berkeley, Los Angeles, London: University of California Press.

L2. 1990. *Mark Twain's Letters, Volume 2: 1867–1868*. Edited by Harriet Elinor Smith, Richard Bucci, and Lin Salamo. The Mark Twain Papers. Berkeley, Los Angeles, London: University of California Press.

L3. 1992. *Mark Twain's Letters, Volume 3: 1869*. Edited by Victor Fischer, Michael B. Frank, and Dahlia Armon. The Mark Twain Papers. Berkeley, Los Angeles, London: University of California Press.

Lampton, Lucius Marion.
1989. "Hero in a Fool's Paradise: Twain's Cousin James J. Lampton and Colonel Sellers." *Mark Twain Journal* 27 (Fall): 1–56.

1990. *The Genealogy of Mark Twain*. Jackson, Miss.: Diamond L Publishing.

Lane, Sally. 1984. "Then and Now." Trenton (N.J.) *Sunday Times Magazine*, 8 April, 18.

Langdon, Ida. 1955. "Elmira's Langdon Family." *Chemung Historical Journal* 1:51–58.

Langdon, Jervis. 1870. "Last Will and Testament of Jervis Langdon, deceased." Dated 25 June, probated 12 August, Surrogate's Court, Chemung County, New York. NElmC.

Langdon, Jervis, Jr. 1993. "Jervis Langdon, Mark Twain's Father-in-Law." Unpublished TS, CU-MARK.

Langley, Henry G., comp.
1863. *The San Francisco Directory for the Year Commencing October, 1863*. San Francisco: Towne and Bacon.

1864. *The San Francisco Directory for the Year Commencing October, 1864*. San Francisco: Towne and Bacon.

1865. *The San Francisco Directory for the Year Commencing December, 1865*. San Francisco: Towne and Bacon.

1871. *The San Francisco Directory for the Year Commencing April, 1871*. San Francisco: Henry G. Langley.

Larned, Josephus Nelson.
1870a. "Personal." Buffalo *Express*, 20 July, 4.

1870b. "Personal." Buffalo *Express*, 26 July, 4.

1870c. "Death of Jervis Langdon, of Elmira." Buffalo *Express*, 8 August, 4.

1870d. "The Election." Buffalo *Express*, 9 November, 1.

1870e. "The General Result." Buffalo *Express*, 11 November, 2.

1870f. "Is Heat a Mode of Motion?" Buffalo *Express*, 3 December, 2.

1888. *Letters, Poems and Selected Prose Writings of David Gray*. 2 vols. Buffalo: Courier Company.

1910. "Mark Twain." Buffalo *Express*, 26 April, 5. Reprinted in part in *MTB*, 1:399.

Lehr, Eugene R. 1982. List of Samuel L. Clemens's Copyrights, 1867–1910. Prepared by Eugene R. Lehr, Biblographer, Reference and Bibliography Section, Copyright Office, Library of Congress (DLC). Unpublished TS, CU-MARK.

Levering, Joseph Mortimer. 1903. *A History of Bethlehem, Pennsylvania, 1741–1892, with Some Account of Its Founders and Their Early Activity in America.* Bethlehem, Pa.: Times Publishing Company.

Lewis, Oscar, ed. 1971. *The Life and Times of the Virginia City "Territorial Enterprise": Being Reminiscences of Five Distinguished Comstock Journalists.* Ashland, Oreg.: Lewis Osborne.

Libbie. 1918. *Autographs. Letters and Manuscripts Left by the Late Frank B. Sanborn, Concord, Mass. . . . The Collection of James Terry, of Hartford, Conn.* Sale of 23 April. Boston: C. F. Libbie and Co.

LLMT. 1949. *The Love Letters of Mark Twain.* Edited by Dixon Wecter. New York: Harper and Brothers.

Lockwood, Henry C.
1871a. Statement dated 3 October, forming part of the interference proceeding between Lockwood and Samuel L. Clemens, in the records of the United States Patent Office, Department of Commerce, Washington, D.C.

1871b. Statement dated 8 November, forming part of the interference proceeding between Lockwood and Samuel L. Clemens, in the records of the United States Patent Office, Department of Commerce, Washington, D.C.

1871c. Statement dated 19 December, forming part of Letters Patent No. 122,038, "Henry C. Lockwood, of Baltimore, Maryland. Improvement in Adjustable and Detachable Straps for Garments," in the records of the United States Patent Office, Department of Commerce, Washington, D.C.

Long, Priscilla. 1989. *Where the Sun Never Shines: A History of America's Bloody Coal Industry.* New York: Paragon House.

Loos, William H. 1991. "Mark Twain, James Fraser Gluck and the Manuscript of *Adventures of Huckleberry Finn:* A Chronology." Unpublished TS, compiled 23 April, PH in CU-MARK.

Lorch, Fred W.
1949. "'Doesticks' and *Innocents Abroad.*" *American Literature* 20 (January): 446–49.

1953. "Mark Twain's 'Sandwich Islands' Lecture and the Failure at Jamestown, New York, in 1869." *American Literature* 25 (November): 314–25.

1954. "Reply to Mr. Alexander E. Jones." *American Literature* 26 (November): 426–27.

1968. *The Trouble Begins at Eight: Mark Twain's Lecture Tours.* Ames: Iowa State University Press.

Lossing, Benson J. 1884. *History of New York City, Embracing an Outline Sketch of Events from 1609 to 1830, and a Full Account of Its Development from 1830 to 1884.* New York and Chicago: A. S. Barnes and Co.

Lounsbury, Thomas R. 1904. "Biographical Sketch." In *The Complete Writings of Charles Dudley Warner,* vol. 15. Hartford: American Publishing Company.

Love, Robertus. 1902. "Mark Twain Dines with His Sweetheart of Old Time Days." St. Louis *Dispatch,* 31 May, 1–2.

Lyceum.

1869. *The Lyceum.* Boston: [Redpath and Fall].

1870. *The Lyceum: Containing a Complete List of Lecturers, Readers, and Musicians for the Season of 1870–71.* Boston: Redpath and Fall.

1871. *The Lyceum Magazine: Edited by the Boston Lyceum Bureau, and Containing Its Third Annual List. For the Season of 1871–1872.* Boston: Redpath and Fall.

1872. *The Lyceum Magazine: Edited by the Boston Lyceum Bureau, and Containing Its Fourth Annual List. Season of 1872–1873.* Boston: Redpath and Fall.

1873. *The Lyceum Magazine: Edited by the Boston Lyceum Bureau, and Containing Its Fifth Annual List. Season of 1873–1874.* Boston: Redpath's Lyceum Bureau.

1874. *Redpath's Lyceum: Organ of Redpath's Lyceum Bureau.* [Season of 1874–75.] Boston: [Redpath's Lyceum Bureau].

1875. *Redpath's Lyceum: Organ of the Redpath Lyceum Bureau.* [Season of 1875–76.] Boston: [Redpath's Lyceum Bureau].

1876. *The Redpath Lyceum: Circular of the Redpath Lyceum Bureau.* [Season of 1876–77.] Boston and Chicago: [Redpath's Lyceum Bureau].

1883. *The Redpath Lyceum Magazine. An Annual Publication Issued by the Redpath Lyceum Bureau, Sole Agents for the Principal Lecturers, Readers and Musical Celebrities of the Country. Season of 1883–84. Fifteenth Year.* Boston and Chicago: [Redpath Lyceum Bureau].

McCullough, Joseph B.

1969. "A Complete Edition of the Contributions of Hy Slocum and Carl Byng to the Buffalo *Express,* 1868–1871, with a Discussion of Samuel L. Clemens' Authorship." Ph.D. diss., Ohio University, Athens.

1971. "Mark Twain and the Hy Slocum–Carl Byng Controversy." *American Literature* 43 (March): 42–59.

1972. "A Listing of Mark Twain's Contributions to the Buffalo *Express,* 1869–1871." *American Literary Realism* 5 (Winter): 61–70.

McElderry, Bruce R., Jr. 1961. *Contributions to "The Galaxy," 1868–1871, by Mark Twain (Samuel Langhorne Clemens).* Gainesville, Fla.: Scholars' Facsimiles and Reprints.

McIlhaney, Asa K. 1935. "Mark Twain in the Lehigh Valley." PH of unidentified clipping at Northampton County (Pa.) Historical Society, in CU-MARK.

Mansfield, Lillian M. 1965. *The History of Asylum Hill Congregational Church.* Hartford: Connecticut Printers.

Many Citizens [pseud.]. 1870. "Mark Twain Criticized—An Indignant Spectator." Jamestown (N.Y.) *Journal,* 24 January, no page. Reprinted in the *Weekly Journal,* 28 January, 8, and in Parker 1990a, 5.

MB. Boston Public Library and Eastern Massachusetts Regional Public Library, Boston, Massachusetts.

MBAt. Boston Athenaeum, Boston, Massachusetts.

MEC. Mary E. (Mollie) Clemens.

Merwin, Henry Childs. 1911. *The Life of Bret Harte.* Boston and New York: Houghton Mifflin Company.

Merwin-Clayton.
1905. *Catalogue of Elegant and Rare Books from the Library of Mr. John Kendrick Bangs . . . and Autograph Letters of Famous Authors.* Sale of 8, 9, and 10 February. New York: Merwin-Clayton Sales Company.

1906. *Collection of the Late Mr. George M. Elwood of Rochester, N. Y.* Sale of 12–16 November. New York: Merwin-Clayton Sales Company.

1907a. *Catalogue of Autograph Letters, Manuscripts and Documents.* Sale of 6 February. New York: Merwin-Clayton Sales Company.

1907b. *Catalogue of the Autograph Collection of the Late Dr. Ottocar E. Kopetschny of Jersey City, N. J., with Some Additions from Other Private Sources.* Sale of 1 April. New York: Merwin-Clayton Sales Company.

Meyer, Henry A., Frederic R. Harris, William J. Davey, John K. Bash, et al. 1948. *Hawaii: Its Stamps and Postal History.* New York: Philatelic Foundation.

MFMT. 1931. *My Father, Mark Twain.* By Clara Clemens. New York and London: Harper and Brothers.

MGlHi. Cape Ann Historical Association, Gloucester, Massachusetts.

MH. Harvard University, Cambridge, Massachusetts.

MH-H. Houghton Library, MH.

MiD. Detroit Public Library, Detroit, Michigan.

Miller, James, comp. 1866. *Miller's New York as It Is.* New York: J. Miller. Citations are to the 1975 reprint edition, *The 1866 Guide to New York City,* New York: Schocken Books.

MoKHC. Hallmark Cards, Kansas City, Missouri.

Monday Evening Club. 1954. *The List of Members of the Monday Evening Club, Together with the Record of Papers Read at Their Meetings, 1869–1954.* Edited by Howell Cheney. Hartford: Privately printed.

Morgan, Speer. 1989. "Mark Twain's 'Unmailed Answer' to a Critic." *Missouri Review* 12:93–98.

MoSW. Washington University, St. Louis, Missouri.

Mott, Frank Luther.
1938. *A History of American Magazines, 1850–1865.* Cambridge: Harvard University Press.

1950. *American Journalism: A History of Newspapers in the United States through 260 Years, 1690 to 1950.* Rev. ed. New York: Macmillan Company.

1957. *A History of American Magazines, 1865–1885.* 2d printing [1st printing, 1938]. Cambridge: Belknap Press of Harvard University Press.

Mrja, Ellen M.
1983. "Ansel Nash Kellogg." In *American Newspaper Journalists, 1873–1900,* edited by Perry J. Ashley. Vol. 23 of *Dictionary of Literary Biography.* Detroit: Gale Research Company.

MTA. 1924. *Mark Twain's Autobiography*. Edited by Albert Bigelow Paine. 2 vols. New York: Harper and Brothers.

MTB. 1912. *Mark Twain: A Biography*. By Albert Bigelow Paine. 3 vols. New York: Harper and Brothers. [*Volume numbers in citations are to this edition; page numbers are the same in all editions.*]

MTBus. 1946. *Mark Twain, Business Man*. Edited by Samuel Charles Webster. Boston: Little, Brown and Co.

MTE. 1940. *Mark Twain in Eruption*. Edited by Bernard DeVoto. New York: Harper and Brothers.

MTEnt. 1957. *Mark Twain of the "Enterprise."* Edited by Henry Nash Smith, with the assistance of Frederick Anderson. Berkeley and Los Angeles: University of California Press.

MTH. 1947. *Mark Twain and Hawaii*. By Walter Francis Frear. Chicago: Lakeside Press.

MtHi. Montana Historical Society, Helena.

MTHL. 1960. *Mark Twain–Howells Letters*. Edited by Henry Nash Smith and William M. Gibson, with the assistance of Frederick Anderson. 2 vols. Cambridge: Belknap Press of Harvard University Press.

MTL. 1917. *Mark Twain's Letters*. Edited by Albert Bigelow Paine. 2 vols. New York: Harper and Brothers.

MTLP. 1967. *Mark Twain's Letters to His Publishers, 1867–1894*. Edited by Hamlin Hill. The Mark Twain Papers. Berkeley and Los Angeles: University of California Press.

MTMF. 1949. *Mark Twain to Mrs. Fairbanks*. Edited by Dixon Wecter. San Marino, Calif.: Huntington Library.

MTTB. 1940. *Mark Twain's Travels with Mr. Brown*. Edited by Franklin Walker and G. Ezra Dane. New York: Alfred A. Knopf.

Munroe. 1871. "Gossip from Massachusetts." Letter dated 4 July. New York *Times*, 6 July, 6.

MWC. Special Collections, Robert Hutchings Goddard Library, Clark University, Worcester, Massachusetts.

N&J1. 1975. *Mark Twain's Notebooks & Journals, Volume I (1855–1873)*. Edited by Frederick Anderson, Michael B. Frank, and Kenneth M. Sanderson. The Mark Twain Papers. Berkeley, Los Angeles, London: University of California Press.

N&J2. 1975. *Mark Twain's Notebooks & Journals, Volume II (1877–1883)*. Edited by Frederick Anderson, Lin Salamo, and Bernard L. Stein. The Mark Twain Papers. Berkeley, Los Angeles, London: University of California Press.

N&J3. 1979. *Mark Twain's Notebooks & Journals, Volume III (1883–1891)*. Edited by Robert Pack Browning, Michael B. Frank, and Lin Salamo. The Mark Twain Papers. Berkeley, Los Angeles, London: University of California Press.

Nast, Thomas. 1871. *Th. Nast's Illustrated Almanac for 1872*. New York: Harper and Brothers.

National Book Auctions. 1946. *Important Books from Several Choice Libraries*. Sale no. 1 (15 April). New York: National Book Auctions.

NAW. 1971. *Notable American Women 1607–1950: A Biographical Dictionary*. Edited by Edward T. James, Janet Wilson James, and Paul S. Boyer. 3 vols. Cambridge: Belknap Press of Harvard University Press.

NBu. Buffalo and Erie County Public Library, Buffalo, New York.

NCAB. 1898–1984. *The National Cyclopedia of American Biography*. Volumes 1–62 and A–M plus index. New York: James T. White and Co.

NElmC. Mark Twain Archives and Center for Mark Twain Studies at Quarry Farm, Elmira College, Elmira, New York.

Neville. 1981. Catalog no. 6 (April). Santa Barbara, Calif.: Maurice F. Neville, Rare Books.

Newark Galleries. 1930. *Important Autographs: the Collection of the Late John C. Thurman of Green Bay, Wis., with Additions*. Sale no. 128 (5 December). Newark, N.J.: Newark Galleries.

Newman, Mary Richardson (May Wentworth), ed. 1867. *Poetry of the Pacific: Selections and Original Poems from the Poets of the Pacific States*. San Francisco: Pacific Publishing Company.

New York Directory. 1915. *R. L. Polk & Co.'s 1915 Trow General Directory of New York City, Embracing the Boroughs of Manhattan and the Bronx*. New York: R. L. Polk and Co.

NHi. New York Historical Society, New York City.

NN. The New York Public Library, Astor, Lenox and Tilden Foundations, New York City.

NN-B. Henry W. and Albert A. Berg Collection, NN.

"Nook Farm Genealogy." 1974. Unpublished TS by anonymous compiler, CtHSD.

Northampton County Guide. 1939. Written and compiled by the Federal Writers' Project, Work Projects Administration. Bethlehem, Pa.: Times Publishing Company.

Norwood, William Frederick. 1971. *Medical Education in the United States Before the Civil War*. New York: Arno Press and the New York Times.

NPV. Vassar College Library, Poughkeepsie, New York.

NUC. 1968–81. *The National Union Catalog Pre-1956 Imprints*. With supplements. 754 vols. London: Mansell Publishing.

NvU. University of Nevada Reno.

OC (Orion Clemens).
1871a. "The American Publisher's Proclamation." *American Publisher* 1 (April): 4.
1871b. "Editorial Notes." *American Publisher* 1 (April): 4.

1871c. "North, East, South, West . . ." *American Publisher* 1 (April): 4.

1871d. "Number One." *American Publisher* 1 (April): 4.

1871e. "Editorial Notes." *American Publisher* 1 (July): 4.

1871f. "Antiquity of Man." *American Publisher* 1 (September): 4.

1871g. "Editorial Notes." *American Publisher* 1 (September): 4.

OCi. Public Library of Cincinnati and Hamilton County, Cincinnati, Ohio.

OClRC. Rowfant Club, Cleveland, Ohio.

ODaU. Collection of Victor and Irene Murr Jacobs, Roesch Library, University of Dayton, Dayton, Ohio.

Odell, George C. D. 1927–1949. *Annals of the New York Stage*. 15 vols. New York: Columbia University Press.

OHi. Ohio Historical Society, Columbus.

OLC. Olivia Langdon Clemens.

OLL. Olivia Louise Langdon.

Paff, Harriet Lewis. 1897. "What I Know about Mark Twain." MS of twelve pages, CtY-BR.

Palmer, Barbara Heslan. 1980. "Lace Bonnets and Academic Gowns: Faculty Development in Four Women's Colleges, 1875–1915." Ph.D. diss., Boston College.

PAM. Pamela Ann Moffett.

Park Church. 1896. *The Park Church. 1846–1896*. Elmira: Park Church.

Park, Edwin J. 1886. "A Day with Mark Twain." Chicago *Tribune*, 19 September, 12. Reprinted in *Mark Twain Society Bulletin* 2 (June 1979): 3–5.

Parke-Bernet.
1938. *William Blake . . . Samuel L. Clemens Manuscripts, Autographs, First Editions Including the Manuscript of "Tom Sawyer" from Which the London Edition Was Printed . . . Collected by the Late George C. Smith, Jr., New York, N.Y.* Sale no. 59 (2–3 November). New York: Parke-Bernet Galleries.

1940. *Autograph Letters, Manuscripts and Rare Books: The Entire Collection of the Late John Gribbel, Philadelphia*. Part 1. Sale no. 223 (30 and 31 October, 1 November). New York: Parke-Bernet Galleries.

1942. *The Work of the Great English Illustrators and Authors of the XVII–XIX Centuries . . . Collected by the Late William H. Woodin, New York*. Part 2. Sale of 6, 7, and 8 January. New York: Parke-Bernet Galleries.

1945. *Autograph Letters, Manuscripts and Rare Books. The Entire Collection of the Late John Gribbel, Philadelphia*. Part 3. Sale no. 662 (16 and 17 April). New York: Parke-Bernet Galleries.

1950. *Autograph Letters, Manuscripts and Documents of Three Centuries . . . Comprising Selections from the Collection of the Late Oliver R. Barrett, Kenilworth, Ill.* Sale no. 1190 (30 and 31 October, 1 and 2 November). New York: Parke-Bernet Galleries.

1953. *Rare Books, Manuscripts, Broadsides Including . . . Property of the Estates of the Late Paul L. Feiss, Cleveland, Ohio, . . . Samuel Katz, Port Chester, New York, . . . and Other Owners.* Sale no. 1478 (15 and 16 December). New York: Parke-Bernet Galleries.

Parker, Patricia Appleyard.
1990a. "Did Mark Twain Flop When He Spoke Here in 1870?" Jamestown (N.Y.) *Post-Journal*, 24 November, *Tempo Magazine*, 4–5.

1990b. "The Jamestown Editor and the Letter Mark Twain Didn't Mail." Jamestown (N.Y.) *Post-Journal*, 24 November, *Tempo Magazine*, 16.

PBL. Robert B. Honeyman Collection, Linderman Library, Lehigh University, Bethlehem, Pennsylvania.

PH. Photocopy.

Phisterer, Frederick. 1912. *New York in the War of the Rebellion, 1861 to 1865.* 3d ed. 6 vols. Albany: J. B. Lyon Company, State Printers.

Piatt, Donn.
1871a. "Washington Letter." Letter dated 8 February. Cincinnati *Commercial*, 11 February, 2.

1871b. "Introductory." In "The Galaxy Club-Room." *Galaxy* 11 (May): 751–52.

Pond, James B. 1900. *Eccentricities of Genius.* New York: G. W. Dillingham Company.

Poore, Benjamin Perley, comp.
1870. *Congressional Directory for the Second Session of the Forty-First Congress of the United States of America.* 2d ed. Washington: Government Printing Office.

1871. *Congressional Directory for the Third Session of the Forty-First Congress of the United States of America.* 2d ed. Washington: Government Printing Office.

Portrait. 1895. *Portrait and Biographical Record of Marion, Ralls and Pike Counties, with a Few from Macon, Adair, and Lewis Counties, Missouri.* Chicago: C. O. Owens and Co. Citations are to the 1982 revised reprint edition, New London and Marceline: Ralls County Book Company and Walsworth Publishing Company.

Potter, Helen. 1891. *Helen Potter's Impersonations.* New York: Edgar S. Werner.

Prang, Louis.
1870a. *Prang's European War Map, Showing All the R.R.'s and Other Means of Communication.* No. 1–3. Boston: Louis Prang and Co.

1870b. *Prang's Plan of Paris & Its Surroundings, Showing All Fortifications.* Boston: Louis Prang and Co.

Price, Kenneth M. 1988. "Thomas Bailey Aldrich." In *American Literary Critics and Scholars, 1880–1900,* edited by John W. Rathbun and Monica M. Grecu. Vol. 71 of *Dictionary of Literary Biography.* Detroit: Gale Research Company.

Pullen, John J.
1983. *Comic Relief: The Life and Laughter of Artemus Ward, 1834–1867.* Hamden, Conn.: Archon Books.

Quackenbos, G. P., ed. 1867. *Spiers and Surenne's French and English Pronouncing Dictionary.* New York: D. Appleton and Co.

Quill, John. See Charles Heber Clark.

Ramsdell, Hiram J. (H. J. R.).
    1871a. "Santo Domingo." Letters dated 23 January–3 February. New York *Tribune,* 21 February, 1, 8.
    1871b. "Washington Letter." Letter dated 19 July. Cincinnati *Commercial,* 24 July, 5.

Rapidan [pseud.]. 1870. "From New York." Letter dated 14 December. Buffalo *Courier,* 17 December, 1.

Reade, A. Arthur, ed. 1883. *Study and Stimulants; or, The Use of Intoxicants and Narcotics in Relation to Intellectual Life.* Philadelphia: J. B. Lippincott and Co.; Manchester: Abel Heywood and Son.

Redpath, James.
    1860. *The Public Life of Capt. John Brown.* Boston: Thayer and Eldridge.
    1871. "The Lecture System." Cleveland *Herald,* 28 January, Supplement.
    1875. "George L. Fall." In *Lyceum* 1875, unnumbered prefatory page.
    1876. "To Our Patrons." In *Lyceum* 1876, unnumbered prefatory page.
    1968 [1859]. *The Roving Editor: or, Talks with Slaves in the Southern States.* New York: Negro Universities Press.

Redpath, James, and George L. Fall.
    1871–72. Notebook containing Clemens's lecture itinerary for 1871–72 in the hand of George H. Hathaway of the Boston Lyceum Bureau. MS of sixteen pages entitled "Lecture-route, winter of 1871" and annotated by Clemens. Accompanied by its own black leather wallet, which is engraved in gold on an interior flap "Sam'l L. Clemens," CU-MARK.
    1872. "Mark Twain." *Lyceum Circular,* 1 January. Boston: Redpath and Fall.

Redpath, James, and Richard J. Hinton. 1859. *Hand-book to Kansas Territory and the Rocky Mountains' Gold Region, Accompanied by Reliable Maps and a Preliminary Treatise on the Pre-emption Laws of the United States.* New York: J. H. Colton.

Reigstad, Tom.
    1989. "Twain's Langdon-Appointed Guardian Angels in Buffalo: 'Mac,' 'Fletch,' and 'Dombrowski.'" *Mark Twain Society Bulletin* 12 (July): 1, 3–6, 8.
    1990. "Twain's Buffalo Clergyman and the Beecher Preacher Exchange." *Mark Twain Society Bulletin* 13 (July): 1–3.

Rendells. [1983?]. *Autograph Letters, Manuscripts and Documents from Ancient & Medieval Times to the Present.* Newton, Mass.: The Rendells.

RI 1993. 1993. *Roughing It.* Edited by Harriet Elinor Smith, Edgar Marquess Branch, Lin Salamo, and Robert Pack Browning. The Works of Mark Twain. Berkeley, Los Angeles, London: University of California Press.

Riley, John Henry. 1871. "Memoranda." Carbon MS of sixteen pages from a manifold journal, numbered [1]–5 and 9–19, written periodically between early January and 23 March 1871, CU-MARK.

Rochester Directory. 1870. *The Rochester Directory, . . . No. XXI. For the Year Commencing July 1, 1870.* Rochester, N.Y.: C. C. Drew.

Rodecape, Lois Foster. 1942. "Tom Maguire, Napoleon of the Stage." Chapters 6–9. *California Historical Society Quarterly* 21 (June): 141–82.

Roper, Gordon. 1966. "Mark Twain and His Canadian Publishers: A Second Look." *Papers of the Bibliographical Society of Canada* 5:30–89.

Rose, William Ganson. 1950. *Cleveland: The Making of a City.* Cleveland and New York: World Publishing Company.

Rowell, George P. 1870. *The Men Who Advertise; American Newspaper Rate-Book; Geo. P. Rowell & Co.'s American Newspaper Directory.* New York: Nelson Chesman and George P. Rowell and Co.

RPB-JH. John Hay Library of Rare Books and Special Collections, Brown University, Providence, Rhode Island.

Russkii Biograficheskii Slovar. 1896–1913. *Russkii Biograficheskii Slovar.* 25 vols. St. Petersburg: Tipografiya Glavnogo Upravleniya.

Samuels, Peggy, and Harold Samuels. 1976. *The Illustrated Biographical Encyclopedia of Artists of the American West.* Garden City, N.Y.: Doubleday and Co.

Scharf, J. Thomas. 1883. *History of Saint Louis City and County, from the Earliest Periods to the Present Day.* 2 vols. Philadelphia: Louis H. Everts and Co.

Second Life Books. 1983. *Samuel L. Clemens (Mark Twain), 1835–1910: A Collection of His Works, 1852–1983, Gathered by Samuel N. Freedman.* Catalog printed in March. Lanesborough, Mass.: Second Life Books (Russell and Martha Freedman, proprietors).

Seitz, Don C. 1919. *Artemus Ward (Charles Farrar Browne): A Biography and Bibliography.* New York: Harper and Brothers.

Selby, P. O., comp. 1973. *Mark Twain's Kinfolks.* Kirksville, Mo.: Missouriana Library, Northeast Missouri State University.

Seventy-five Years. 1927. *Seventy-five Years; or, The Joys and Sorrows of Publishing and Selling Books at Dutton's from 1852 to 1927.* New York: E. P. Dutton and Co.

Severance, Frank H., comp. 1912. *The Picture Book of Earlier Buffalo.* Publications of the Buffalo Historical Society, vol. 16. Buffalo: Buffalo Historical Society.

Sharlow, Gretchen E. 1990. "Theodore Crane: A New Perspective." *Mark Twain Society Bulletin* 13 (January): 1–4, 6.

Sikes, William Wirt. 1871. Marginalia dated "Columbus, O. March 13, 1871. | 75ᶜ" in a copy of *Mark Twain's (Burlesque) Autobiography and First Romance* (SLC 1871a). Roberton F. Williams Collection, CU-MARK.

Simpson, Alan. 1977. *Mark Twain Goes Back to Vassar: An Introduction to the Jean Webster McKinney Family Papers.* Poughkeepsie, N.Y.: Vassar College.

SLC (Samuel Langhorne Clemens).
1863. "'Mark Twain's' Letter." Letter dated 5 July. San Francisco *Morning Call*, 9 July, 1. Reprinted in *ET&S1*, 254–58.

1864a. "Letter from Mark Twain." Letter dated 14 January. Virginia City *Territorial Enterprise*, [15] January, clipping in Scrapbook 4:4, CU-MARK. Reprinted in *MTEnt*, 134–38.

1864b. "Whereas." *Californian* 1 (22 October): 1. Reprinted in *ET&S2*, 88–93, and in part as "Aurelia's Unfortunate Young Man" in SLC 1867a, 20–25.

1865a. "Answers to Correspondents." *Californian* 3 (3 June): 4. Reprinted in *ET&S2*, 177–80.

1865b. "Answers to Correspondents." *Californian* 3 (10 June): 9. Reprinted in *ET&S2*, 182–86.

1865c. "Answers to Correspondents." *Californian* 3 (17 June): 4. Reprinted in *ET&S2*, 189–96.

1865d. "Answers to Correspondents." *Californian* 3 (24 June): 4. Reprinted in *ET&S2*, 200–207.

1865e. "Answers to Correspondents." *Californian* 3 (1 July): 4–5. Reprinted in *ET&S2*, 211–18.

1865f. "Answers to Correspondents." *Californian* 3 (8 July): 4–5. Reprinted in *ET&S2*, 221–32.

1865g. "Jim Smiley and His Jumping Frog." New York *Saturday Press* 4 (18 November): 248–49. Reprinted in *ET&S2*, 282–88.

1865h. "San Francisco Letter." Letter dated 22 December. Virginia City *Territorial Enterprise*, 24 or 26 December, no page. Reprinted in *ET&S2*, 337–42.

1866a. "The Steed 'Oahu,'" in "Scenes in Honolulu—No. 6." Letter dated March. Sacramento *Union*, 21 April, 3. Reprinted in SLC 1867a, 179–81, and *MTH*, 284–90.

1866b. "Scenes in Honolulu—No. 12." Letter dated 23 May. Sacramento *Union*, 20 June, 1, clipping in Scrapbook 6:116–17, CU-MARK. Reprinted in *MTH*, 318–22.

1866c. "Scenes in Honolulu—No. 13." Letter dated 23 May. Sacramento *Union*, 21 June, 3, clipping in Scrapbook 6:117–18, CU-MARK. Reprinted in *MTH*, 323–27.

1866d. "Scenes in Honolulu—No. 13." Letter dated 22 June, number 14 in the sequence. Sacramento *Union*, 16 July, 3, clipping in Scrapbook 6:118–19, CU-MARK. Reprinted in *MTH*, 328–34.

1866e. "Scenes in Honolulu—No. 14." Letter dated 30 June, number 16 in the sequence. Sacramento *Union*, 30 July, 1, clipping in Scrapbook 6:121–22, CU-MARK. Reprinted in *MTH*, 348–55.

1866f. "Scenes in Honolulu—No. 15." Letter dated 1 July, number 17 in the sequence. Sacramento *Union*, 1 August, 1, clipping in Scrapbook 6:122–23, CU-MARK. Reprinted in *MTH*, 356–64.

1866g. "How, For Instance?" New York *Weekly Review* 17 (29 September): 1.

1867a. *The Celebrated Jumping Frog of Calaveras County, And other Sketches.* Edited by John Paul. New York: C. H. Webb.

1867b. *The Celebrated Jumping Frog of Calaveras County, And other Sketches.* Edited by John Paul. London: George Routledge and Sons.

1867c. "Letter from 'Mark Twain.' Number VII." Letter dated 6 January. San Francisco *Alta California*, 23 March, 1. Reprinted in *MTTB*, 69–81.

1867d. "Americans on a Visit to the Emperor of Russia." Letter dated 26 August. New York *Tribune*, 19 September, 1. Reprinted in *TIA*, 142–50.

1867e. "The Holy Land Excursion. Letter from 'Mark Twain.' [Number Twenty-two.]" Letter dated 27 August at "Yalta." San Francisco *Alta California*, 6 November, 1. Reprinted in *TIA*, 150–57.

1867f. "The Holy Land Excursion. Letter from 'Mark Twain.' [Number Twenty-three.]" Letter dated 27 August at "Yalta, Russia." San Francisco *Alta California*, 10 November, 1. Reprinted in *TIA*, 157–63.

1868a. "Mark Twain's Letters from Washington. Number II." Letter dated 16 December 1867. Virginia City *Territorial Enterprise*, 7 January, [2].

1868b. Untitled speech in response to the toast to "Woman," delivered 11 January, as reported in "Annual Banquet of the Corres[pon]dents' Club." Washington *Evening Star*, 13 January, 2.

1868c. "Letter from Mark Twain." Letter dated 1 May. Chicago *Republican*, 19 May, 2.

1868d. "Eulogy on Woman." *Excelsior Monthly Magazine*, August, 99–100. Reprinted in *L2*, 415–16.

1868e. "Cannibalism in the Cars." *Broadway: A London Magazine*, n.s. 1 (November): 189–94.

1869a. *The Innocents Abroad; or, The New Pilgrims' Progress*. Hartford: American Publishing Company.

1869b. "Letter from Mark Twain." Letter dated July. San Francisco *Alta California*, 1 August, 1.

1869c. "The 'Monopoly' Speaks." Buffalo *Express*, 20 August, 2.

1869d. "A Day at Niagara." Buffalo *Express*, 21 August, 1.

1869e. "English Festivities. And Minor Matters." Buffalo *Express*, 28 August, 1.

1869f. "Journalism in Tennessee." Buffalo *Express*, 4 September, 1.

1869g. "The Last Words of Great Men." Buffalo *Express*, 11 September, 1.

1869h. "The 'Wild Man.' 'Interviewed.'" Buffalo *Express*, 18 September, 1.

1869i. "Rev. H. W. Beecher. His Private Habits." Buffalo *Express*, 25 September, 1.

1869j. "The Latest Novelty. Mental Photographs." Buffalo *Express*, 2 October, 1.

1869k. "Around the World. Letter No. One." Letter dated 10 October. Buffalo *Express*, 16 October, 1.

1869*l*. "The Legend of the Capitoline Venus." Buffalo *Express*, 23 October, 1.

1869m. "Around the World. Letter No. 2." Letter dated 5 October. Buffalo *Express*, 30 October, 1.

1869n. "Around the World. Letter No. 3." Undated letter. Buffalo *Express*, 13 November, 1.

1869o. "Browsing Around." Letter dated November. Buffalo *Express*, 27 November, 2.

1869p. "Browsing Around." Letter dated November. Buffalo *Express*, 4 December, 2.

1869q. "Around the World. Letter Number 4." Undated letter. Buffalo *Express*, 11 December, 2.

1869r. "Around the World. Letter Number 5." Undated letter. Buffalo *Express*, 18 December, 2.

1869s. "Ye Cuban Patriot." Buffalo *Express*, 25 December, 2.

1870a. *The Celebrated Jumping Frog of Calaveras County, and Other Sketches.* Toronto: A. S. Irving.

1870b. *The Innocents Abroad; or, The New Pilgrims' Progress.* Clifton (Ont.) and Detroit: W. E. Tunis. Also issued in Canada under other imprints, including Montreal: Dawson Brothers; Hamilton (Ont.): Joseph Lyght; Toronto: A. S. Irving; and Montreal and Toronto: C. K. Chisholm and Co.

1870c. *The Innocents Abroad. . . . The Voyage Out.* London: John Camden Hotten.

1870d. *The Jumping Frog and Other Humourous Sketches.* London: John Camden Hotten.

1870e. *Mark Twain's Celebrated Jumping Frog of Calaveras County, and Other Sketches.* London: George Routledge and Sons.

1870f. *The New Pilgrim's Progress. . . . The Journey Home.* London: John Camden Hotten.

1870g. "An Awful—Terrible Medieval Romance." Buffalo *Express*, 1 January, 2.

1870h. "Mrs. Stowe's Vindication." Buffalo *Express*, 6 January, 2.

1870i. "Around the World. Letter Number 6." Undated letter. Buffalo *Express*, 8 January, 2–3.

1870j. "A Ghost Story." Buffalo *Express*, 15 January, 2.

1870k. "Around the World. Letter Number 7." Undated letter. Buffalo *Express*, 22 January, 2.

1870*l*. "Around the World. Letter Number 8." Letter dated 20 November 1869. Buffalo *Express*, 29 January, 2.

1870m. Untitled MS of two pages, written in early February, CU-MARK. Later titled "Housekeeping" by Albert Bigelow Paine.

1870n. Untitled MS of two pages on housekeeping, written in early February, CU-MARK.

1870o. "Nasby's Lecture." Buffalo *Express*, 19 February, 4.

1870p. "Anson Burlingame." Buffalo *Express*, 25 February, 2. Reprinted in SLC 1923, 17–23.

1870q. "The Blondes." Buffalo *Express*, 28 February, 2.

1870r. "To the Public." Notice dated 7 March. Buffalo *Express*, 8 March, 2.

1870s. "More Wisdom." Buffalo *Express*, 9 March, 2.

1870t. "A Big Thing." Buffalo *Express*, 12 March, 2.

1870u. "The Crime of Captain Eyre." Buffalo *Express*, 14 March, 2.

1870v. "Literary." Buffalo *Express*, 19 March, 2.

1870w. "A Mysterious Visit." Buffalo *Express*, 19 March, 2.

1870x. "The Facts in the Great Land Slide Case." Buffalo *Express*, 2 April, 2.

1870y. "A New Department in Agriculture." Elmira *Advertiser*, 11 April, 4.

1870z. "Mark Twain on Agriculture." Buffalo *Express*, 12 April, 2.

1870aa. "The New Crime." Buffalo *Express*, 16 April, 2.

1870bb. "The Story of the Good Little Boy Who Did Not Prosper." Buffalo *Express*, 23 April, 3. Reprinted from SLC 1870dd, 724–26.

1870cc. "Curious Dream." Buffalo *Express*, 30 April, 2.

1870dd. "Memoranda." *Galaxy* 9 (May): 717–26. Includes: "Introductory," "The Facts in the Case of the Great Beef Contract," "George Wakeman," "About Smells," "Disgraceful Persecution of a Boy," "The Story of the Good Little Boy Who Did Not Prosper," and four untitled items.

1870ee. "Curious Dream." Buffalo *Express*, 7 May, 2.

1870ff. "Murder and Insanity." Buffalo *Express*, 7 May, 2.

1870gg. "Personal." Buffalo *Express*, 9 May, 2.

1870hh. "Our Precious Lunatic." Buffalo *Express*, 14 May, 2.

1870ii. "Street Sprinkling." Notice written on 26 May. Buffalo *Express*, 27 May, 4.

1870jj. "Thanks to the thoughtful . . ." Buffalo *Express*, 31 May, 4.

1870kk. "Memoranda." *Galaxy* 9 (June): 858–67. Includes: "A Couple of Sad Experiences," "The Petrified Man," "My Famous 'Bloody Massacre,' " "The Judge's 'Spirited Woman,' " " 'Hogwash,' " "A Literary 'Old Offender' in Court with Suspicious Property in His Possession," "Post-Mortem Poetry," "Wit-Inspirations of the 'Two-Year-Olds,' " and four untitled items.

1870ll. "How Higgins Gently Broke the News." Buffalo *Express*, 4 June, 3. Reprinted from untitled item in SLC 1870kk, 862.

1870mm. "More Distinction." Buffalo *Express*, 4 June, 2.

1870nn. Report on "committee upon composition" in "Buffalo Female Academy." Buffalo *Express*, 24 June, 4.

1870oo. "The Editorial Office Bore." Buffalo *Express*, 25 June, 2. Reprinted from SLC 1870pp, 140–41.

1870pp. "Memoranda." *Galaxy* 10 (July): 133–41. Includes: "How I Edited an Agricultural Paper Once," "The 'Tournament' in A. D. 1870," "Enigma," "Unburlesquable Things," "The Late Benjamin Franklin," "The Editorial Office Bore," "A Daring Attempt at a Solution of It," "To Correspondents," and one untitled item.

1870qq. "How I Edited an Agricultural Paper." Buffalo *Express*, 2 July, 3. Reprinted from SLC 1870pp, 133–35.

1870rr. "The European War!!!" Buffalo *Express*, 25 July, 2.

1870ss. "Memoranda." *Galaxy* 10 (August): 286–87. Includes: "A Memory," "Personal Explanation."

1870tt. Tribute to Jervis Langdon. MS (now lost) enclosed in letter of 7 August to Josephus N. Larned. In Larned 1870c.

1870uu. "Domestic Missionaries Wanted." Buffalo *Express*, 25 August, 2.

1870vv. "Memoranda." *Galaxy* 10 (September): 424–32. Includes: "Political Economy," "John Chinaman in New York," "The Noble Red Man," "A Royal Compliment," "The Approaching Epidemic," "Favors from Correspondents."

1870ww. "Fortifications of Paris." Buffalo *Express*, 17 September, 2. Reprinted in SLC 1870xx and SLC 1870ggg.

1870xx. "Fortifications of Paris." Buffalo *Express*, 21 September, no page. *BAL* 3320; no copy found for inspection.

1870yy. "Memoranda." *Galaxy* 10 (October): 567–76. Includes: "The Reception at the President's," "Goldsmith's Friend Abroad Again," "Curious Relic For Sale," "Science vs. Luck," "Favors from Correspondents" (including "Johnny Skae's Item").

1870zz. "At the President's Reception." Buffalo *Express*, 1 October, 2. Reprinted from SLC 1870yy, 567–69.

1870aaa. "Johnny Skae's Item." Buffalo *Express*, 1 October, 2–3. Reprinted from SLC 1870yy, 575–76.

1870bbb. "Curious Relic for Sale." Buffalo *Express*, 8 October, 2–3. Reprinted from SLC 1870yy, 571–74.

1870ccc. "It is said . . ."; "And with the . . ." Buffalo *Express*, 15 October, 2. Untitled items reprinted from SLC 1870hhh, 735.

1870ddd. "Mark Twain. His Map of the Fortifications of Paris." Buffalo *Express*, 15 October, 2. Reprinted from SLC 1870ggg, 723.

1870eee. "The Libel Suit." Buffalo *Express*, 21 October, 2.

1870fff. "On Riley—Newspaper Correspondent." Buffalo *Express*, 29 October, 2. Reprinted from "Riley—Newspaper Correspondent," SLC 1870hhh, 726–27.

1870ggg. "Mark Twain's Map of Paris." *Galaxy* 10 (November): 724–25.

1870hhh. "Memoranda." *Galaxy* 10 (November): 726–35. Includes: "Riley—Newspaper Correspondent," "Goldsmith's Friend Abroad Again," "A Reminiscence of the Back Settlements," "A General Reply," "Favors from Correspondents," and two untitled items.

1870iii. "A Reminiscence of the Back Settlements." Buffalo *Express*, 5 November, 2. Reprinted from SLC 1870hhh, 731–32.

1870jjj. "A General Reply." Buffalo *Express*, 12 November, 2. Reprinted from SLC 1870hhh, 732–34.

1870kkk. "The 'Present' Nuisance." Buffalo *Express*, 19 November, 2. Reprinted from SLC 1870nnn, 880–81.

1870*lll*. "Running for Governor." Buffalo *Express*, 19 November, 2. Reprinted from SLC 1870nnn, 878–80.

1870mmm. "My Watch—An Instructive Little Tale." Buffalo *Express*, 26 November, 2. Reprinted from SLC 1870nnn, 882–83.

1870nnn. "Memoranda." *Galaxy* 10 (December): 876–85. Includes: "An Entertaining Article," "'History Repeats Itself,'" "Running for Governor," "The 'Present' Nuisance," "Dogberry in Washington," "My Watch—An Instructive Little Tale," "Favors from Correspondents," and two untitled items.

1870ooo. "An Entertaining Article." Buffalo *Express*, 3 December, 2–3. Reprinted from SLC 1870nnn, 876–78.

1870ppp. "Dogberry in Washington." Buffalo *Express*, 10 December, 2. Reprinted from SLC 1870nnn, 881–83.

1870qqq. "The Famous Sanitary Flour Sack." Letter to the editor dated 11 December. New York *Tribune*, 13 December, 5.

1870rrr. "War and 'Wittles.' " Buffalo *Express*, 16 December, 2.

1870sss. "The Facts in the Case of George Fisher, Deceased." Buffalo *Express*, 17 December, 2. Reprinted from SLC 1871b, 152–55.

1870ttt. " 'Waiting for the Verdict.' " Buffalo *Express*, 19 December, 2.

1870uuu. "A Sad, Sad Business." Buffalo *Express*, 24 December, 2. Reprinted from SLC 1871b, 158–59.

1871a. *Mark Twain's (Burlesque) Autobiography and First Romance*. New York: Sheldon and Co.

1871b. "Memoranda." *Galaxy* 11 (January): 150–59. Includes: "The Portrait," "The Facts in the Case of George Fisher, Deceased," "A 'Forty-Niner' . . . ," " 'Doggerel,' " "Goldsmith's Friend Abroad Again," "Mean People," "A Sad, Sad Business," "Concerning a Rumor," "Answer to an Inquiry from the Coming Man."

1871c. "John H. Surratt." Letter to the editor dated 29 December 1870. New York *Tribune*, 4 January, 5.

1871d. "New Books." Buffalo *Express*, 14 January, 2.

1871e. "The Danger of Lying in Bed." Buffalo *Express*, 28 January, 2. Reprinted from SLC 1871f, 317–18.

1871f. "Memoranda." *Galaxy* 11 (February): 312–21. Includes: "The Coming Man," "A Book Review," "The Tone-Imparting Committee," "The Danger of Lying in Bed," "One of Mankind's Bores," "A Falsehood," "The Indignity Put Upon the Remains of George Holland by the Rev. Mr. Sabine."

1871g. "An Autobiography." *Aldine* 4 (April): 52.

1871h. "Memoranda." *Galaxy* 11 (April): 615–18. Includes: "Valedictory," "My First Literary Venture," "About a Remarkable Stranger."

1871i. "A Question Answered." *American Publisher* 1 (April): 4. Extract reprinted from SLC 1867a, 45–48.

1871j. "Answers to Correspondents." MS of one page, probably written in May 1871, Historic Hudson Valley Library, Tarrytown, N.Y. An edited version was published anonymously under the title "To a Correspondent," *Galaxy* 12 (July): 141.

1871k. "The Old-Time Pony Express of the Great Plains." *American Publisher* 1 (May): 4. Extract from SLC 1872b, chapter 8.

1871*l*. "A Substitu[t]e for Rulloff. Have We a Sydney Carton among Us?" Letter to the editor dated 29 April. New York *Tribune*, 3 May, 2.

1871m. "A New Beecher Church." *American Publisher* 1 (July): 4.

1871n. "About Barbers." *Galaxy* 12 (August): 283–85.

1871o. "A Brace of Brief Lectures on Science." Part 1. *American Publisher* 1 (September): 4.

1871p. "A Brace of Brief Lectures on Science." Part 2. *American Publisher* 1 (October): 4.

1871q. "Artemus Ward, Humorist." MS of one page, from lecture written on 20 and 21 October, CU-MARK.

1871r. "A Big Scare." *American Publisher* 1 (November): 8. Reprinted from SLC 1867c.

1871s. "My First Lecture." *American Publisher* 1 (December): 4. Reprinted from SLC 1872b, chapter 78.

1871t. Statement dated 19 December, forming part of Letters Patent No. 121,992, "Samuel L. Clemens, of Hartford, Connecticut. Improvement in Adjustable and Detachable Straps for Garments," in the records of the United States Patent Office, Department of Commerce, Washington, D.C.

1872a. *Mark Twain's Sketches*. Selected and Revised by the Author. Copyright Edition. London: George Routledge and Sons.

1872b. *Roughing It*. Hartford: American Publishing Company.

1872c. *"Roughing It"* and *The Innocents at Home*. 2 vols. London: George Routledge and Sons.

1872d. "A Nabob's Visit to New York." *American Publisher* 1 (January): 4. Reprinted from SLC 1872b, chapter 46.

1872e. "Dollinger the Aged Pilot Man." *American Publisher* 1 (February): 8. Reprinted from SLC 1872b, chapter 51.

1872f. Untitled extract. *American Publisher* 1 (February): 8. Reprinted from SLC 1872b, chapter 15.

1872g. "'Roughing It.'" *American Publisher* 1 (March): 8. Reprinted from SLC 1872b, chapter 57.

1872h. "Horace Greeley's Ride." *American Publisher* 2 (April): 8. Reprinted from SLC 1872b, chapter 20.

1872i. "Mark Twain on the Mormons." *American Publisher* 2 (June): 8. Reprinted from SLC 1872b, chapter 15.

1872j. "Mark Twain at the Grave of Adam." *American Publisher* 2 (July): 8. Reprinted from SLC 1869a, chapter 53.

1873a. *The Choice Humorous Works of Mark Twain*. Now First Collected. With Extra Passages to the "Innocents Abroad," Now First Reprinted, and a Life of the Author. Illustrations by Mark Twain and other Artists; also Portrait of the Author. London: John Camden Hotten.

1873b. A set of sheets from the unauthorized *Choice Humorous Works* (SLC 1873a) revised and annotated by Mark Twain for an authorized edition (SLC 1874a), NN.

1873c. "The Sandwich Islands." Letter dated 3 January. New York *Tribune*, 6 January, 4–5. Reprinted in *MTH*, 489–94.

1873d. "The Sandwich Islands." Letter dated 6 January. New York *Tribune*, 9 January, 4–5. Reprinted in *MTH*, 494–500.

1874a. *The Choice Humorous Works of Mark Twain*. Revised and Corrected by the Author. With Life and Portrait of the Author, and Numerous Illustrations. London: Chatto and Windus.

1874b. *The Gilded Age: A Tale of Today*. Charles Dudley Warner, coauthor. Hartford: American Publishing Company.

1874c. *Mark Twain's Sketches. Number One*. New York: American News Company.

1875a. *Mark Twain's Sketches, New and Old*. Hartford: American Publishing Company.

1875b. "Old Times on the Mississippi." Articles 1–7. *Atlantic Monthly* 35 (January–June): 69–73, 217–24, 283–89, 446–52, 567–74, 721–30; *Atlantic Monthly* 36 (August): 190–96.

1876. *The Adventures of Tom Sawyer*. Hartford: American Publishing Company.

1878. *Punch, Brothers, Punch! and Other Sketches*. New York: Slote, Woodman and Co.

1880. *A Tramp Abroad*. Hartford: American Publishing Company.

1883. *Life on the Mississippi*. Boston: James R. Osgood and Co.

1885. "The Chicago G. A. R. Festival." TS of seven pages, CU-MARK. Published in *MTA*, 1:13–19, and *AMT*, 241–45.

1886. "Unmailed Answer." MS of four pages. An undated letter to "Many Citizens," an unidentified critic in the Jamestown (N.Y.) *Journal* of 24 January 1870. The current location of the MS (formerly in the Estelle Doheny Collection at St. John's Seminary in Camarillo, California) is not known. Published in Lorch 1953, 315, and in facsimile in Morgan, 95–98.

1890. "Concerning the Scoundrel Edward H. House." MS of fifty-two pages, CU-MARK.

1891. "The Innocents Adrift." MS of 174 pages, CU-MARK. Published in part as "Down the Rhone" in SLC 1923, 129–68.

1897–?1902. "Tom Sawyer's Conspiracy." MS of 241 pages, CU-MARK. Published in *HH&T*, 163–242, and *Inds*, 134–213.

1898a. "Ralph Keeler." MS of twenty-four pages, CU-MARK. Published in *MTA*, 1:154–64.

1898b. Untitled autobiographical reminiscence. MS of sixteen pages, CU-MARK. Published in part as "Old Lecture Days in Boston" in *MTA*, 1:147–53, and, untitled, in *AMT*, 166–69.

1905. "John Hay and the Ballads." MS of six pages, RPB-JH. Published in *Harper's Weekly* 49 (21 October): 1530.

1923. *Europe and Elsewhere*. New York: Harper and Brothers.

1938. *Mark Twain's Letter To William Bowen*. Prefatory note by Clara Clemens Gabrilowitsch. Foreword by Albert W. Gunnison. San Francisco: Book Club of California.

Slocum, Hy.

1868a. "Hy Slocum's Views." Buffalo *Express*, 31 March, no page. Reprinted in McCullough 1969, 55–60.

1868b. "Hy Slocum Again." Buffalo *Express*, 15 April, no page. Reprinted in McCullough 1969, 64–71.

1868c. "Hy Slocum's Letter." Buffalo *Express*, 25 April, no page. Reprinted in McCullough 1969, 74–79.

1868d. "The Last Speech and Dying Confession of the Confidence Man." Buffalo *Express*, 18 August, no page. Reprinted in McCullough 1969, 80–83.

1869a. "Another View of the Great Jubilee." Buffalo *Express*, 19 June, 2.

1869b. "Benjamin Franklin." Buffalo *Express*, 26 June, 2.

1869c. "Hy Slocum on Female Suffrage." Buffalo *Express*, 5 July, 2.

1869d. "Andy on Grant." Buffalo *Express*, 9 July, 2.

1869e. "The Eclipse: How It Appeared to Hy Slocum at Balcom's Corners." Buffalo *Express*, 11 August, 2.

1869f. "The Philosophy of Heat." Buffalo *Express*, 19 August, 4.

1869g. "A New Theory of Gravitation." Buffalo *Express*, 2 September, 2.

1869h. "Electricity: With the Modern Improvements." Buffalo *Express*, 25 September, 2.

1869i. "Concerning Dreams." Buffalo *Express*, 23 October, 2.

1869j. "Another Fossil." Buffalo *Express*, 30 October, 4.

1869k. "Appendix Concerning Dreams." Buffalo *Express*, 6 November, 2.

1869*l*. "Yaller Dogs: An Allusion to Them." Buffalo *Express*, 15 November, 2.

1869m. "Yaller Dogs: Final Allusions." Buffalo *Express*, 20 November, 2.

1869n. "Hash: Concocted by Hy Slocum." Buffalo *Express*, 4 December, 2.

1869o. "Answers to Correspondents." Buffalo *Express*, 18 December, 2.

1869p. "Aladdin: or, The Wonderful Scamp." Buffalo *Express*, 25 December, 2.

1870a. "The Trail of the Serpent: Eve in Full Dress." Buffalo *Express*, 8 January, 2.

1870b. "What I Don't Know of Farming." Buffalo *Express*, 15 January, 3.

1870c. "What I Don't Know of Farming." Buffalo *Express*, 22 January, 2.

1870d. "What I Don't Know of Farming." Buffalo *Express*, 29 January, 3.

1870e. "The Coming Woman: A Romance of the XVIth Amendment." Buffalo *Express*, 19 February, 2.

1870f. "Stoicism: Incoherent Observations." Buffalo *Express*, 5 March, 3.

1870g. "The Feminine Grand Jury." Buffalo *Express*, 12 March, 2.

1870h. "Another Big Thing: A Safe and Re-lie-able Investment." Buffalo *Express*, 19 March, 2.

1870i. "Orthographic Retrenchment." Buffalo *Express*, 2 April, 2.

1870j. "Some Life Insurance." Buffalo *Express*, 16 April, 2.

1870k. "Self Made Men: Biography A La Mode—Robert Kidd, Pirate." Buffalo *Express*, 14 May, 2.

1870*l*. "Fearful Domestic Tragedy!: Shocking Result of Miscegenation and Jealousy—Two Attempted Assassinations—Three Horrible Murders, and One Suicide!!" Buffalo *Express*, 21 May, 2.

1870m. "One of the 'Polite Circles': The Prize Ring." Buffalo *Express*, 4 June, 2.

1870n. " 'Lo' at the Capitol." Buffalo *Express*, 18 June, 2.

1870o. "The Trotting Season." Buffalo *Express*, 16 July, 2.

1870p. "The John Question." Buffalo *Express*, 23 July, 2.

1870q. "Napoleon After Hagenau" and "Chassepot vs. Needle Gun." Buffalo *Express*, 12 August, 2.

1870r. "Jim Todd: A Sketch in Crude Oil." Buffalo *Express*, 3 September, 2.

1870s. "Tom Smith: His Official Thrift and Prosperous Remorse." Buffalo *Express*, 10 September, 2.

1870t. "De Coy's Moral Tonic." Buffalo *Express*, 8 October, 2.

Slotta. Collection of Robert T. Slotta.

Smith, Henry Nash, and Frederick Anderson, eds. 1957. *Mark Twain: San Francisco Correspondent*. San Francisco: Book Club of California.

Smith, H. Perry, ed. 1884. *History of the City of Buffalo and Erie County*. Vol. 2. Syracuse, N.Y.: D. Mason and Co.

Sobel, Robert, and John Raimo, eds. 1978. *Biographical Directory of the Governors of the United States, 1789–1978*. 4 vols. Westport, Conn.: Meckler Books.

Sotheby.
1984. *English Literature and English History, Comprising Printed Books, Autograph Letters and Manuscripts*. Sale of 16 and 17 July. London: Sotheby Parke Bernet and Co.

1993. *Fine Books and Manuscripts*. Sale no. 6515 (10 and 11 December). New York: Sotheby's.

Southern, Eileen. 1971. *The Music of Black Americans: A History*. New York: W. W. Norton and Co.

Stanley, Henry M. 1867. "Mark Twain at the Mercantile Library Hall Tuesday Night." St. Louis *Missouri Democrat*, 28 March, 4.

Stevens, Walter B. 1911. *St. Louis: The Fourth City, 1764–1911*. 2 vols. St. Louis: S. J. Clarke Publishing Company.

Stewart, George R., Jr.
1931. *Bret Harte: Argonaut and Exile*. Boston and New York: Houghton Mifflin Company; Cambridge: Riverside Press.

1936. "Webb, Charles Henry." In *DAB*, 19:572–73.

Stewart, Robert Ernest, Jr. 1958. "Adolph Sutro: A Study of His Early Career." Ph.D. diss., University of California, Berkeley.

Storey. 1871. *Storey, Ormsby, Washoe and Lyon Counties Directory, . . . For 1871–72*. Sacramento: H. S. Crocker and Co.

Strong, Leah A. 1966. *Joseph Hopkins Twichell: Mark Twain's Friend and Pastor*. Athens: University of Georgia Press.

Sutro, Adolph. 1872. *Closing Argument of Adolph Sutro on the Bill Before Congress to Aid the Sutro Tunnel, Delivered Before the Committee on Mines and Mining of the House of Representatives of the United States of America, Monday, April 22, 1872*. Washington, D.C.: M'Gill and Witherow.

Swann. 1942. *Autographs and Manuscripts*. Sale no. 24 (16 October). New York: Swann Auction Galleries.

"Territorial Letters Received." 1870. Letters received from Secretary Orion Clemens in "Letters Received from Territorial Officials." Office of the First Comptroller of the Treasury Department, RG217, Records of the General Accounting Office, DNA.

Thayer, William Roscoe. 1915. *The Life and Letters of John Hay.* 2 vols. Boston and New York: Houghton Mifflin Company.

Thomas, Jeffrey F. 1975. "The World of Bret Harte's Fiction." 2 vols. Ph.D. diss., University of California, Berkeley.

TIA. 1958. *Traveling with the Innocents Abroad: Mark Twain's Original Reports from Europe and the Holy Land.* Edited by Daniel Morley McKeithan. Norman: University of Oklahoma Press.

Towner, Ausburn [Ishmael, pseud.]. 1892. *Our County and Its People: A History of the Valley and County of Chemung from the Closing Years of the Eighteenth Century.* Syracuse, N.Y.: D. Mason and Co.

Townsend, George Alfred [G. A. T., Gath, and Gate, pseuds.].
1871a. "Washington." Chicago *Tribune,* 14 February, 2.
1871b. "Washington." Chicago *Tribune,* 6 March, 2.

Trachtenberg, Alexander. 1942. *The History of Legislation for the Protection of Coal Miners in Pennsylvania 1824–1915.* New York: International Publishers.

Tregonning, K. G. 1965. *A History of Modern Sabah (North Borneo 1881–1963).* 2d ed. Singapore: University of Malaya Press.

TS. Typescript.

TS. 1980. *The Adventures of Tom Sawyer; Tom Sawyer Abroad; Tom Sawyer, Detective.* Edited by John C. Gerber, Paul Baender, and Terry Firkins. The Works of Mark Twain. Berkeley, Los Angeles, London: University of California Press.

Turner, Arlin. 1954. "Notes on Mark Twain in New Orleans." *McNeese Review* 6 (Spring): 10–22.

TxU. Harry Ransom Humanities Research Center, University of Texas, Austin.

UCCL. 1986. *Union Catalog of Clemens Letters.* Edited by Paul Machlis. Berkeley, Los Angeles, London: University of California Press. [*In a few cases,* UCCL *catalog numbers cited in this volume supersede those assigned in 1986 and reflect corrections or additions to the catalog since publication.*]

UCLC. 1992. *Union Catalog of Letters to Clemens.* Edited by Paul Machlis with the assistance of Deborah Ann Turner. Berkeley, Los Angeles, Oxford: University of California Press.

Underhill, Irving S. 1930. "Diamonds in the Rough." *Colophon* 13 (Spring): [1]–[8].

U.S. Congress, Senate. 1870. *A Bill to Divide the State of Tennessee into Two Judicial Districts.* 41st Cong., 2d sess. S. 1025.

U.S. Department of State. 1870. *Register of the Department of State.* Washington, D.C.: Government Printing Office.

ViU. University of Virginia, Charlottesville.

Wakeman, George.
   1866a. "Tormenting the Alphabet." *Galaxy* 1 (1 July): 437–45.
   1866b. "Sound and Sense." *Galaxy* 1 (1 August): 634–44.
   1866c. "Verbal Anomalies." *Galaxy* 2 (1 September): 29–39.
   1866d. "Live Metaphors." *Galaxy* 2 (1 October): 272–80.
   1866e. "The Confusion of Tongues." *Galaxy* 2 (1 November): 443–52.
   1866f. "Macaronics." *Galaxy* 2 (1 December): 757–64.
   1867a. "Advertising." *Galaxy* 3 (1 January): 202–11.
   1867b. "Conundrums." *Galaxy* 3 (15 February): 416–25.
   1867c. "Grotesque Songs." *Galaxy* 4 (November): 789–96.
   1868a. "Popular Songs." *Galaxy* 5 (February): 157–64.
   1868b. "Literary Transfer Work." *Galaxy* 6 (August): 205–16.
   1868c. "A Literal Turn of Mind." *Galaxy* 6 (September): 403–6.
   1869a. "Don't Get Excited." *Galaxy* 7 (February): 279–82.
   1869b. "Acuteness." *Galaxy* 7 (May): 752–55.
   1869c. "Paradoxical Words." *Galaxy* 8 (September): 416–20.
   1869d. "Wrecks of Words." *Galaxy* 8 (December): 848–50.
   1870a. "Keep Your Equilibrium." *Galaxy* 9 (January): 120–23.
   1870b. "Idioms." *Galaxy* 9 (February): 271–74.
   1870c. "Metaphors of the People." *Galaxy* 9 (May): 695–700.

Walker, Franklin. 1969. *San Francisco's Literary Frontier.* Rev. ed. Seattle: University of Washington Press.

Wallace, Robert D. 1960? "A Gentleman of Some Notoriety: Mark Twain Speaks in Illinois." Unpublished TS, CU-MARK.

Warner, Sam Bass, Jr. 1978. *Streetcar Suburbs: The Process of Growth in Boston, 1870–1900.* 2d ed. Cambridge: Harvard University Press.

Watson, Margaret G. 1964. *Silver Theatre: Amusements of the Mining Frontier in Early Nevada, 1850 to 1864.* Glendale, Calif.: Arthur H. Clark Company.

Webb, Charles Henry [John Paul, pseud.]. 1871. "To the Editor of Every Saturday." *Every Saturday,* n.s. 2 (28 January): 91.

Weber, Carl J. 1959. *The Rise and Fall of James Ripley Osgood.* Waterville, Me.: Colby College Press.

Wecter, Dixon.
   1947. "The Love Letters of Mark Twain." *Atlantic Monthly* 180 (December): 66–72.
   1948. "The Love Letters of Mark Twain." *Atlantic Monthly* 181 (January): 83–88.

Wells, Amos R. 1945. *A Treasure of Hymns.* Boston: W. A. Wilde Company.

West, George P. 1924. "Bret Harte's 'Roaring Camp' Still Producing: Mother Lode Country Rich in Reminiscences of Mark Twain's Youth." San Francisco *Call and Post,* 24 May, sec. 2:13, 18.

Whiting, Lilian. 1900. *Kate Field: A Record.* Boston: Little, Brown, and Co.

Whitney, William Dwight, and Benjamin E. Smith, eds. 1913. *The Century Dictionary: An Encyclopedic Lexicon of the English Language.* Rev. and enl. 12 vols. New York: Century Company.

Willard, Frances E. and Mary A. Livermore, eds. 1893. *A Woman of the Century: Fourteen Hundred-Seventy Biographical Sketches Accompanied by Portraits of Leading American Women in All Walks of Life.* Buffalo, Chicago, New York: Charles Wells Moulton.

Wilson, Colin, and Patricia Pitman. 1962. *Encyclopedia of Murder.* New York: G. P. Putnam's Sons.

Wilson, H., comp.

1866. *Trow's New York City Directory, . . . Vol. LXXX. For the Year Ending May 1, 1867.* New York: John F. Trow.

1867. *Trow's New York City Directory, . . . Vol. LXXXI. For the Year Ending May 1, 1868.* New York: John F. Trow.

1868. *Trow's New York City Directory, . . . Vol. LXXXII. For the Year Ending May 1, 1869.* New York: John F. Trow.

1869. *Trow's New York City Directory, . . . Vol. LXXXIII. For the Year Ending May 1, 1870.* New York: John F. Trow.

1870. *Trow's New York City Directory, . . . Vol. LXXXIV. For the Year Ending May 1, 1871.* New York: John F. Trow.

1871. *Trow's New York City Directory, . . . Vol. LXXXV. For the Year Ending May 1, 1872.* New York: John F. Trow.

Wilson, Henry, and James Caulfield. 1869. *The Book of Wonderful Characters: Memoirs and Anecdotes of Remarkable and Eccentric Persons in all Ages and Countries.* London: John Camden Hotten. Clemens owned an American edition by Henry Wilson, published in 1854: *Wonderful Characters; Comprising Memoirs and Anecdotes of the Most Remarkable Persons of Every Age and Nation. Collected from the Most Authentic Sources,* Louisville: Morton and Griswold.

Winterich, John T. 1936. "The Compleat Collector." *Saturday Review of Literature* 14 (3 October): 20.

Wisbey, Herbert A., Jr.

1979. "Olivia Clemens Studied at Elmira College." *Mark Twain Society Bulletin* 2 (June): 7–8.

1985. "Mark Twain's Elmira." In Cotton, 4–5.

1990. Biographical information on Elmira residents. Unpublished TS, CU-MARK.

1991. "The Tragic Story of Emma Nye." *Mark Twain Society Bulletin* 14 (July): 1–4.

1993. Biographical information on Elmira residents. Unpublished TS, CU-MARK.

Wolcott, Samuel. 1881. *Memorial of Henry Wolcott, One of the First Settlers of Windsor, Connecticut, and of Some of His Descendants.* New York: Anson D. F. Randolph and Co.

Wolf, Virginia L. 1985. "Thomas Bailey Aldrich." In *American Writers for Children Before 1900,* edited by Glenn E. Estes. Vol. 42 of *Dictionary of Literary Biography.* Detroit: Gale Research Company.

Wright, L. R. 1970. *The Origins of British Borneo*. Hong Kong: Hong Kong University Press.

Wright, William [Dan De Quille, pseud.].
1863. "No Head nor Tail." San Francisco *Golden Era* 11 (6 December): 5.

1891. "Natural or Supernatural: Our Mundane Sphere and Some of Its Inhabitants." Letter dated 16 July. Salt Lake City *Tribune*, 19 July, 11. Excerpt entitled "The Thoreau of the Sierras" reprinted in Berkove, 2.

1893. "Salad Days of Mark Twain." San Francisco *Examiner*, 19 March, 13–14. Reprinted in Lewis, 37–52.

WU. Memorial Library, University of Wisconsin, Madison.

Ziporyn, Terra.
1988. *Disease in the Popular American Press: The Case of Diphtheria, Typhoid Fever, and Syphilis, 1870–1920*. New York, Westport, Conn., and London: Greenwood Press.

Index

THE FOLLOWING have not been indexed: fictional characters, Editorial Signs, Description of Texts, Description of Provenance, and Textual Commentaries. Place names are included when they refer to locations that Clemens lived in, visited, or commented upon, but are excluded when mentioned only in passing.

Alphabetizing is *word-by-word*, except for the following. (1) When persons, places, and things share the same name, they are indexed in that order: thus "Washington, George," "Washington, D.C.," "Washington book (planned)." (2) Formal titles (Mr., Mrs., Dr., and so forth) may be included with a name, but are ignored when alphabetizing. (3) The subheadings "letters to," "notes to," "letters by," and "letters from" *precede* all other subheadings.

Recipients of Clemens's letters are listed in **boldface type**; boldface numbers (**304n1**) designate principal identifications. Numbers linked by an ampersand (98 & 100n1) indicate that the allusion in the letter text is not explicit, and can best be located by reading the note first. Works written by Mark Twain are indexed separately by title *and* under "Clemens, Samuel Langhorne: works," as well as, when appropriate, under the publishing journal. Works written by others are indexed both by title and by author's name. Newspapers are indexed by their location (city or town), other periodicals by title.

A. N. Kellogg Newspaper Company, 406n2
Abelard, Peter, 542, 542n5
Abyssinia, 161, 161n1
Academy of Design, New York, 373n1
Academy of Music, Philadelphia, 2n4, 240n1, 497
Ackerman, Edward P., 440n1
 letter to, 439–40
 letter by, 439, 440n2
Ackley Concert Hall, Cambridge, N.Y., 25 & 27n2
Adams, Charlotte Stanley (Lottie; Mrs. Edward Payson), 43, 44, 572
Adams, Edward Payson, 43, 44, 572
Adelaide Ristori, 323n3
Adeler, Max (Charles Heber Clark), 122n4
Adirondack Mountains
 proposed trip by SLC and OLC, 125, 127, 138, 142, 144, 145, 149, 151, 152n2, 162, 167, 169n7
Adventures of Huckleberry Finn, 37–38n5, 53n1, 53n4, 59n2, 460n1
The Adventures of Tom Sawyer, 35n7, 53n1, 53n3, 59n2, 568n3
"Advice for Good Little Girls," 374n2, 382n1*bottom*
Agassiz, Louis, 339n6
Albany, N.Y., 502n6
 letters from, 10–11, 15–20, 501–2
 lectures by SLC, 10n4, 11n1, 15, 16n2, 17, 19n1, 558
Albany *Argus*
 review of SLC's lecture, 19n1
Albany *Evening Journal*
 reviews of SLC's lectures, 19n1, 481n9, 481n16, 493n4
Albemarle Hotel, New York, 269, 271, 281, 282n1, 289n2, 296
Alderman Library, 174n1
Aldine, 299n1
 contribution by SLC, 337n1
 portrait of SLC, 337n1, 415, 416n2, 417*illus*
Aldrich, Lilian Woodman (Mrs. Thomas Bailey), 304n1
Aldrich, Thomas Bailey, 303n4, 398n1, 484, 485n3, 489, 577*illus*
 letters to, 304–6, 316–19
 letters by, 305–6n1, 318–19n7
 meets SLC, **304n1**
 writings, 304n1, 317 & 318n4
Aleksandr Nikolaevich (Aleksandr II), 147, 147n3, 172, 425, 426n10
Alexander and Mason, 465n5, 466n7
 letter by, 465n5
Allegheny College, 385n4
Allen, Elizabeth Anne Chase Akers (Florence Percy), **235n1**
Allentown, Pa.
 letter from, 474–75
 lecture by SLC, 475n1, 476n2, 557
Allentown *Chronicle*
 review of SLC's lecture, 475n1
Allyn Hall, Hartford, 297n2, 487
Amenia, N.Y., 2n1
 letter from, 3–7
 lecture by SLC, 1, 8–9n2
 visit of SLC. 7–8 & 8n2, 23n6
Amenia *Times*, 8n2, 74, 74n2
Ament, Joseph P., 86n1
American Hotel, Allentown, Pa.
 envelope, 475
American Institute of the City of New York, 286n1
American Literary Bureau, 307n2
American Publisher, 219n3, 220, 222n6
 contributions by SLC: xxviii, 218, 220, 221, 222n3, 222n7, 320n1*top*, 341, 345n3, 346, 348, 349–52, 352–54n1, 354n2, 354n12, 354–57n13, 365–66, 367nn4–6, 367, 377, 378, 379, 379n3, 386, 387n1; "A Brace of Brief Lectures on Science," 354n2, 410, 411n2, 411n4, 411, 423, 424n1, 429; "A New Beecher Church," 354n2, 410, 411nn2–3, 411, 423, 424n1, 431, 439–40, 440n2; "The Old-Time Pony Express of the Great Plains," 368, 368–69n3, 369n4
 editorship of Orion Clemens: xxviii, 219–21, 223, 229–30, 245–46, 275, 277, 282n5, 297, 297n3, 298, 298–99n2, 341, 342, 345n3, 345–46n7, 346, 348, 349–52, 352–53n1, 354–56n13, 362–64, 364nn1–2, 365n5, 368, 369n3, 377, 378, 379, 379n3, 386, 396n3, 412–13, 413n1, 414, 414–

The text of this book is set in Mergenthaler Linotype Plantin. Headings are in Plantin Light. Plantin was originally designed for the Monotype Company by F. H. Pierpont in 1913. The paper is Glatfelter Offset, Eggshell Cream, acid-free. The book was composed by Wilsted & Taylor Publishing Services of Oakland, California, using Data General Nova 4c and Nova 4x computers, Penta software, and a Linotron 202 typesetter. It was printed and bound by Maple-Vail Book Manufacturing Group in Binghamton, New York.